T0331630

Extending Mechanics to Minds

This book deploys the mathematical axioms of modern rational mechanics to help the reader understand minds as mechanical systems that exhibit actual, not metaphorical, forces, inertia, and motion. Using precise mental models developed in artificial intelligence, the author analyzes motivation, attention, reasoning, learning, and communication in mechanical terms.

These analyses provide psychology and economics with new characterizations of bounded rationality, provide mechanics with new types of materials exhibiting the constitutive kinematic and dynamic properties characteristic of different kinds of minds, and provide philosophy with a rigorous theory of hybrid systems combining discrete and continuous mechanical quantities. The resulting mechanical reintegration of the physical sciences that characterize human bodies and the mental sciences that characterize human minds opens traditional philosophical and modern computational questions to new paths of technical analysis.

JON DOYLE is SAS Institute Distinguished Professor of Computer Science at North Carolina State University in Raleigh, North Carolina. His formative contributions helped generate widespread studies of reason (or truth) maintenance and nonmonotonic logic; self-governing reflective agents; rational and economic foundations for reasoning, representation, and learning; and qualitative decision theory. Dr. Doyle is a Fellow of the American Association for Artificial Intelligence (AAAI). He has served as a member of the AAAI Executive Council, as chairman of ACM SIGART, and as a member of several editorial boards, including those of the *Journal of Artificial Intelligence Research*, *Computational Intelligence*, *ACM Computing Surveys*, the *Journal of Logic, Language and Information*, and *AI Communications*.

Extending Mechanics to Minds

The Mechanical Foundations of Psychology and Economics

JON DOYLE

North Carolina State University

CAMBRIDGE
UNIVERSITY PRESS

Shaftesbury Road, Cambridge CB2 8EA, United Kingdom

One Liberty Plaza, 20th Floor, New York, NY 10006, USA

477 Williamstown Road, Port Melbourne, VIC 3207, Australia

314–321, 3rd Floor, Plot 3, Splendor Forum, Jasola District Centre, New Delhi – 110025, India

103 Penang Road, #05–06/07, Visioncrest Commercial, Singapore 238467

Cambridge University Press is part of Cambridge University Press & Assessment,
a department of the University of Cambridge.

We share the University's mission to contribute to society through the pursuit of
education, learning and research at the highest international levels of excellence.

www.cambridge.org
Information on this title: www.cambridge.org/9780521861977

First published 2006

A catalogue record for this publication is available from the British Library

Library of Congress Cataloging-in-Publication data
Doyle, Jon.
Extending mechanics to minds : the mechanical foundations of psychology
and economics / Jon Doyle.
p. cm.
Includes bibliographical references and index.
ISBN 0-521-86197-7 (hardcover)
1. Mechanics, Applied – Mathematics. 2. Artificial intelligence. I. Title.
TA350.D69 2006
006.3 – dc22 2006002823

ISBN 978-0-521-86197-7 Hardback

For Carol

Wife of noble character,
Clothed with strength and dignity,
Worth far more than rubies,
Gift of God.

O unaussprechlich süßes Glück!   O unspeakably sweet fortune!
Wer ein holdes Weib errungen,   Let him who has won a fair wife
Stimm in unsern Jubel ein!   join in our rejoicing!
Nie wird es zu hoch besungen,   Our song can never praise too much
Retterin des Gatten sein.   the savior of her husband.

Beethoven, Bouilly, & Sonnleithner, *Fidelio*, Act II Finale

Contents

Preface

This book uses concepts from mechanics to help the reader understand and formalize theories of mind, with special concentration on understanding and formalizing notions of rationality and bounded rationality that underlie many parts of psychology and economics. The book provides evidence that mechanical notions including force and inertia play roles as important in understanding psychology and economics as they play in physics. Using this evidence, it attempts to clarify the nature of the concepts of motivation, effort, and habit in psychology and the ideas of rigidity, adaptation, and bounded rationality in economics. The investigation takes a mathematical approach. The mechanical interpretations developed to characterize mechanical reasoning and rationality also speak to other questions about mind, notably questions of dualism and materialism.

More generally, the exposition sketches the development of psychology and economics as subfields of mechanics by showing how one might formalize representative psychological and economic systems in such a way that these formalized systems satisfy modern axiomatic treatments of mechanics. This formalization explicates psychological and economic concepts under study by identifying corresponding properties of certain mechanical systems. Not all concepts of psychology and economics correspond to mechanical notions, and among those that do, not all concepts currently popular in psychology and economics correspond to natural mechanical ones. The concepts studied nevertheless permit natural identifications of familiar psychological or economical notions as natural mechanical notions, formalizing the memory of an agent as its mass and internal configuration, and the agent's motivations as forces that produce changes in the agent's momentum by means of changes in its mass and velocity.

Psychology and economics have endured many attempts at physical analogy, most perhaps deserving the apparent failure they reaped as a result of inadequate formal basis, lack of ties to concrete problems, or sheer wrong-headedness about the phenomena and concepts of physics, psychology, or economics. The present effort avoids a similar fate by combining modern mathematical axiomatizations of mechanics developed by Walter Noll (1958, 1963, 1972, 1973) with concrete examples of proven interest from computation and artificial intelligence. The result shows that at least some minds constitute actual mechanical systems, not merely participants in occasional mechanical analogies.

Program

There is no philosophy that is not founded upon knowledge of the phenomena, but to get any profit from this knowledge it is absolutely necessary to be a mathematician.
 Daniel Bernoulli, 1763 letter to John Bernoulli III (Truesdell 1984b, pp. 19–20)

I approach the foundations of psychology and economics dissatisfied with the analytical and mathematical concepts typically employed to describe these fields, concepts that, especially in psychology, frequently vex the student, fail the scholar, and leave the subject needlessly disconnected from the rest of science. At the same time, I rejoice in the panoply of concepts and methods current mathematics offers for ordering the world, to borrow Jaffe's (1984) apt phrase, concepts that have been applied relentlessly to understanding physics and more recently computation and economics but less so to psychology. The past century of mathematics has provided astounding progress in understanding logic, computation, meaning, and ideal rationality, but one need not assume that in coming to a mathematical understanding of mind these contributions will continue to play the roles current sensibilities might assign them.

The search for better ways of formulating problems and possible solutions forms the most fundamental activity of any field, and indeed of much of thinking and computing. Hamming (1962) wrote that "The purpose of computing is insight, not numbers," and Minsky (1974, pp. 78, 56) wrote that "thinking begins first with suggestive but defective plans and images, that are slowly (if ever) refined and replaced by better ones," and that "[t]he primary purpose in problem solving should be better to understand the problem space, to find representations within which the problems are easier to solve."

In searching for better and more appropriate formulations, each field of thought seizes upon successive sets of fundamental concepts and uses these conceptual "atoms" as the basis for its views of the problems and theories of the field. Each set of atoms has its day, with intensive exploration revealing how well it illuminates the problems and how well it eases their solution. As its limits become clearer, theorists introduce some new atom or set of atoms to provide an even better point of view. The aim of the search is to find the most appropriate conceptual atoms, those that cleanly divide the phenomena and problems in powerful ways. As Miller (1986) points out, most conceptualizations of psychology in the past have focused on sets of atoms inadequate to the task, "dismembering cognition," in his vivid phrase, with a set of concepts that "leaves its object shattered in lumps" rather than a set that "carves a topic at its joints." Mathematicians use the terms *beauty* and *depth* as terms of approbation for good theories, expressing something of the same theoretical esthetic as Miller, reviling the logger and applauding the wright. One can observe the search process especially clearly in mathematics. In the large, one finds alternative foundations for all of mathematics, foundations based on logic, set theory, category theory, and intuitionism. In the small, specific mathematical theories are decomposed into parts (matrix theory into noncommutative algebra and representations over specific rings) and recast by exchanging conclusions and axioms (exchanging natural numbers and arithmetic for zero, a successor function, and an exclusion or comprehension principle).

I use the term *rational psychology* to name the branch of mathematics aiming to investigate psychology by means of the most fit mathematical concepts, that is, the mathematical concepts that yield the simplest, most elegant, most powerful, and most insightful formulation of psychological theories (Doyle 1983f). *Rational* here refers to conceptual, mathematical analysis, not to any putative rationality or irrationality of the systems under study. Historically the term referred to the philosophical study of psychology. My use of the term follows the model of rational mechanics, which has named the study of the foundations of mechanics since the time of Newton.

Rational psychology studies mathematically possible organizations for agents. I call these possible organizations "psychologies" (Doyle 1982a, 1990a). One can thus view rational psychology as seeking to classify all possible psychologies in the same way that group theory seeks to classify all possible groups. The special laws of mechanics represent such classificatory devices. Identifying special psychological materials or structures characteristic of interesting classes of agents represents a central method of the field.

The present effort draws directly on the model of rational mechanics by eschewing theories formulated in terms of representations in favor of theories cast in terms of the behaviors themselves, and by treating the problem of understanding different types of mental organization and behavior as formalization of distinct types of psychological materials, rather than as a search for the "true" theory of psychology or economics. Each type of psychological material obeys not only the general mechanical laws applicable to every material but also special laws characteristic of the specific material.

Prerequisites

The ideas presented in this book draw on a broad range of fields, including mathematics, physics, philosophy, psychology, economics, politics, logic, and computation. The ideal reader of this book would bring to the reading a solid grasp of the foundations and development of mathematics, classical and relativistic rational mechanics, quantum theory, logic, probability, the theory of computation, psychology, artificial intelligence, and mathematical, psychological, and political economics. Undoubtedly a keen appreciation of Aeschylus and Aristophanes would also help, but even the former list probably rules out everyone, including the author. Cognizant of the demands of the material, the book has been written with hopes that readers possessing common college acquaintance with mathematical physics, computation, and artificial intelligence will find something intelligible and interesting in the book. Familiarity with (not necessarily mastery of) the mathematical way of thinking, the broad spectrum of mathematical ideas, and their basic mechanical applications would be very valuable; Mac Lane's (1986) useful survey represents a good model of this knowledge. The interior survey chapters of Penrose's (1989) book and Gurtin's (1981) introduction to continuum mechanics might offer useful supplements. Truesdell's (1968b; 1984c) essays and Benvenuto's (1991) history of mechanics provide valuable perspective on the recency and impermanence of current interpretations of mechanical concepts. Russell and Norvig's (2002) textbook of artificial intelligence employs economic rationality to convey a unified perspective of that field in a manner reasonably consonant with the approach taken here.

Plea

The player who stakes his whole fortune on a single play is a fool, [but the science of mathematics] merely shows that other players are greater fools.
(Julian Lowell Coolidge 1909, p. 189)

I am fortunate that virtually every element of the development presented here is known, even well known, in at least one field of scholarly thought. While I know much about some of these fields, *la vida breve* frustrates gaining thorough expertise in each. Accordingly, much as I love books that present what for a generation or two seem the most elegant, general, or final forms of ideas, completing this book required continuous battle against the urge to perfect. My aim in writing instead was to develop each component enough to show its place in the theory and to make the basic ideas formal enough to enable interested parties to find their proper mathematical form. To reapply another sentiment earlier expressed by Julian Lowell Coolidge (1940, p. xii), while my own inadequacy for such a task has been abundantly evident to me, it did not seem sufficient reason for not making the attempt.

Although many research monographs provide a chapter outlining future work, such a chapter would seem a joke here, for one may view the entire book as outlining a program of future work. I am told that Paul Halmos once ended a talk by saying words to the effect that "If I stopped now, I'd be stopping before the most important point, but I don't have anything more to say" and then walking away. I am sure this book stops before the most important point, and I hope the reader will press on regardless.

Because of the diversity of the subject matter and background, a careful reading is likely to require substantial effort, even for a reader familiar with the technical developments of a relevant field. I know of no short-term remedy for this difficulty, but I try to provide some repetition of explanation and motivation appropriate to points at which readers of different interests might take up the text.

Completing this exposition proved difficult because numerous possible alternative treatments presented themselves at every point of the development, and at times I despaired of pulling together sensible selections from the great and bewildering variety of alternative views. At such times, the best hope for completing any exposition seemed to be to write a collection of interrelated and potentially competing vignettes of each alternative view of each topic, in the style of Minsky's (1986) *Society of Mind*. Although that approach has something to recommend it, not least that it may offer the only feasible possibility for describing systems as complicated as the mind with instruments as simple as the mind, I rebelled against the approach because mechanics, unlike psychology, possesses an extended and ordered conceptual development. Surely, I thought, a mechanical understanding of mind must admit at least some of this logical development.

Even if one finds the development presented here compelling or convincing, one should not assume the main interpretations presented here to be the best ones, no matter how many interesting and intuitive properties they exhibit. Although I believe many interpretations presented here lie on the right path, there might be more than one reasonable mechanical interpretation of some psychological or economic systems. Sufficiently abstract systems might admit alternative possible mechanical interpretations. Common computational models, such as Turing machines (Turing 1936), finite automata (Rabin & Scott 1959), and the random-access stored program machine, or RASP (Elgot & Robinson 1964), might fall in this class. One can blame some of the difficulty I experienced in completing this exposition on the interpretational ambiguities I encountered in analyzing the more structured equilibrium-transition model of the Reason Maintenance System, or RMS (Doyle 1983e, 1994), which served as the primary focus of my formalization efforts for many years.

Dana Scott (1989, p. 5) once wrote that "[y]ou cannot have a clear conscience in Mathematics if you do not follow up the possibilities," and in this respect my conscience is not clear, for I regard the theory presented here merely as a down payment on a true mechanics of mind. In some ways, the theory that follows hews much too closely to traditional mechanical formalism, and thus raises the suspicion that it simplifies too much to capture the true complexities of the mind. I would love to learn that one loses nothing by these simplifications and that this traditional mechanical form suffices to characterize even the most subtle mental phenomena and properties, but I do not expect to live long enough to see such good news or its refutation. The present volume gives some indications of developments in the direction of these mental subtleties. I hope to write another examining even more in further detail.

I thus expect that further examination of these topics will find ways to justify and perfect the interpretation given here, to identify and justify other interpretations, or both. My own limitations—in knowledge, in competence, in vision, and in time—require me to leave most such investigations to others.

Past

This book represents part of a larger effort aiming to come to a mathematical understanding of rationality and, more generally, all of thinking. My work on mathematical and computational analysis of thinking began in about 1973, yielding the early works *A Truth Maintenance System* (Doyle 1979), *Explicit Control of Reasoning* (de Kleer *et al.* 1977), *Non-Monotonic Logic I* (McDermott & Doyle 1980), and *A Model for Deliberation, Action, and Introspection* (Doyle 1980). Those works bear few traces of the mechanical perspective explored here, apart from a concern with the kinematical, mechanistic approach that underlies most machine computation and modern artificial intelligence, but they provided the central concrete example of the nonmonotonic RMS and the insight used to construct the mechanical interpretation of thinking presented here.

The present investigation of mechanical treatments of mind began in about 1981 as I sought to understand RMS conservatism in terms of least action principles and Lagrangian formalism. The first outlines and partial drafts of this book date from 1982–1983, during which time the importance of inertia for psychology and economics became clear. In 1984 I completed the first extended draft, numerous portions of which survive in the present version. A variety of interruptions delayed completion, so that the present exposition took form in 1998–1999 and underwent gradual expansion before coming into nearly final form in 2003, with brief synopses circulated along the way (Doyle 2001, 2002a).

The prolonged period of completion is misleading, however. Mechanical investigations provided the direct inspiration for and some technical elements of numerous ideas presented in earlier monographs, including *The Foundations of Psychology* (Doyle 1982a, 1990a), *What Is Church's Thesis?* (Doyle 1982b, 2002b), *Some Theories of Reasoned Assumptions* (Doyle 1983e), *Artificial Intelligence and Rational Self-Government* (Doyle 1988a), *Rationality and Its Roles in Reasoning* (Doyle 1992a), and *Reasoned Assumptions and Rational Psychology* (Doyle 1994). The present book provides numerous references to these writings, wherein the interested reader might find additional details.

Acknowledgments

The first debt of the present work accrues to the writings of Clifford Truesdell and Walter Noll. As a first approximation, one might regard the contributions of the present work as constituting a footnote to Noll's achievements.

I owe great debts to the Laboratory for Computer Science of the Massachusetts Institute of Technology (1988–2001), to the Computer Science Department of Carnegie Mellon University (1981–1988), and to the Computer Science Department of Stanford University (1980–1981) for supporting me materially and intellectually during the development of these ideas, as well as to the Fannie and John Hertz Foundation for supporting my graduate work at the Massachusetts Institute of Technology Artificial Intelligence Laboratory (1975–1980). Since 2001, a SAS Institute Professorship in the Computer Science Department of North Carolina State University has provided me the freedom to complete this work.

I owe much to stimulation afforded by conversations over the years about mechanics, physics, and related ideas with Harold Abelson, John Baez, Jaime Carbonell, Randall Davis, Johan de Kleer, Merrick Furst, Clark Glymour, Robert Hartwig, Robert Hermann, David Israel, Norman Margolus, Matthew Mason, John McCarthy, Marvin Minsky, Joel Moses, Allen Newell, Walter Noll, Ramesh Patil, Michael Rabin, Larry Rudolph, Elisha Sacks, Dana Scott, Herbert Simon, Richard Statman, Guy Steele, Ernest Stitzinger, Richmond Thomason, Tommaso Toffoli, Robert Hugh Walker, Michael Wellman, and Jack Wisdom. I owe much to the instruction of my late teachers David Bourgin, John Mac Nerney, and Jürgen Schmidt. I also thank Matthias Stallman for help with translations from the German.

I especially thank Joseph A. Schatz, Gerald Sussman, and Peter Szolovits for boundless insight and encouragement. Joe started me thinking about many of these problems and taught me the perspective needed to persevere. Many

were the times the words of the Teacher rang in my ears as I wondered if all
this were foolishness and vanity. Joe helped remind me that even if all this
proved foolishness, which he doubted, I would find it greater foolishness not
to, as Rilke says, try the last. In earlier years Gerry provided encouragement
sufficient for seven and taught me how to think about physics, computation,
and intelligence. In later years he organized informal seminars on mechanics
and quantum theory with Jack Wisdom that helped keep truth, beauty, and key
questions in view. Pete provided me a home constantly filled with life, ideas,
and friendship.

My greatest debts accrue to my parents, Leo and Marilyn Doyle, for suste-
nance and shaping in ways I continue to learn to appreciate; to my bride Carol,
son Alan, and daughter Emily for their patient love, encouragement, and help
in retaining what vestiges of humanity I bear; and to God for giving me life,
time, joy, and inspiration. If there be goodness here, *soli Deo gloria.*

Raleigh, North Carolina   Jon Doyle
July 2005

Outline of the book

This book motivates the mechanical study of intelligence and rationality, reviews modern mechanics and its historical relations to psychology, adapts mechanical axioms to cover hybrid and discrete systems, presents illustrative formalizations of representative rational systems in psychology and economics, and reflects on the character of mechanical laws and theories. My exposition of these ideas divides the development into several parts.

Part I: Reconciling Natural and Mental Philosophy

Part I introduces the problem, the aims of the project, and some of its background.

- Chapter 1 introduces the subject and ideas of the book in the context of understanding the mind and constructing mechanical persons.
- Chapter 2 discusses the benefits of the mechanical approach, especially in shedding new light on questions of materialism and new methods for characterizing limits to rationality.
- Chapter 3 explores in greater detail the mechanical viewpoint and its history, briefly relating the project to past efforts on mechanical interpretations of psychological and economic phenomena as an aid to understanding better the subsequent development.

Part II: Reconstructing Rational Mechanics

Part II explains the structure of modern rational mechanics and reformulates the axiomatic development in a manner appropriate to hybrids of continuous, discrete, physical, and mental mechanical subsystems.

- Chapter 4 summarizes the theoretical structure of modern rational mechanics, including the modern conception of physical law and the division of mechanical laws into general and special laws.

- Chapter 5 develops the kinematic axioms of mechanics, generalizing the usual axioms to accommodate discrete aspects of space, hybrid mechanical systems, and indeterministic worlds.

- Chapter 6 develops the dynamical axioms, which parallel the usual developments in most respects, evidencing the modesty of the reformation of mechanics needed to cover psychology and economics.

- Chapter 7 reconsiders several characteristics of mechanical systems in light of the reconstruction of kinematical and dynamical axioms, including determinism, continuity, conservation principles, least action principles, reversibility, and locality.

Part III: Mechanical Minds

Part III presents mechanical formalizations of key psychological and economical notions.

- Chapter 8 notes the wide variety of mental organizations presumed or postulated by theorists in many fields, identifies one special class involving plural, discrete, affective cognition for special examination, and summarizes the structure of the Reason Maintenance System, or RMS, that illustrates this class of psychologies.

- Chapter 9 uses the mechanical formalism to examine mind–body duality and the plurality inherent in mental organization and faculties.

- Chapter 10 sets out the basic framework of discrete mechanical motion, mass, and force underlying the analyses of the following chapters.

- Chapter 11 takes a detailed look at simple reasoning patterns as exemplifying mechanical forces and then offers speculative relations between these simple forces and more complex mathematical concepts and mechanical phenomena.

- Chapter 12 analyzes the mechanical nature of rationality and limits on rationality, including effort, volition, inherent intelligence, and the forces generated by desire, intention, habit, refraction, and other rational motives.

- Chapter 13 characterizes learning in terms of mechanical concepts of mass, persistent configuration, plastic deformation, and relaxation responses to applied forces.

- Chapter 14 studies mental uncertainty as a mechanical phenomenon, constructing a straightforward theory of measurement that yields structures akin to subjective probabilities and weakness of will, and then presenting a speculative subjective measurement structure with connections to concepts of quantum theory.

Part IV: The Metaphysics of Mechanics

Part IV discusses a number of mainly philosophical characteristics of physical theories in relation to mechanics.

- Chapter 15 discusses implications of the mechanical axioms for traditional philosophical questions of materialism, especially similarities between the numerous past broadenings of concepts of materialistic theories and the present further broadening to the materials of psychology and economics.
- Chapter 16 addresses the reducibility of physical law to behaviors of elementary particles and considers related topics including the possibility of discovering additional physical laws, the uniformity of physical laws, and other topics connected with the completeness of physics.
- Chapter 17 relates mental mechanics to notions of effective computation, both to understand computation in mental terms and to understand the relation of effectiveness to mechanical theory.
- Chapter 18 examines issues pertaining to the finiteness or infiniteness of the universe, especially as these relate to discrete models of mechanics as developed here.

Part V: Conclusion of the Matter

- Chapter 19 summarizes and assesses the work, identifies some additional issues for future exploration, and reflects on the history of some of the ideas.

Part I

Reconciling Natural and Mental Philosophy

1

Mechanical intelligence

What do you think when someone claims that people are mechanical?

Some people find this claim offensive, as likening their own thoughtful behavior to the unthinking behavior of the machine, as in Skinner's famous aphorism "The real question is not whether machines think but whether men do" (Skinner 1969, p. 288). Even though passing time has changed the prototypical machine from the pulley in the well to the steam locomotive to the automobile to the home computer, a comparison to machines represents one common form of insult ("Dali, pfui. He paints like a machine."). In this view, depicted in Figure 1.1, claiming people to be mechanical brings people down to a lower level.

Students of artificial intelligence seeking to construct intelligent machines often share the underlying revulsion against comparing people to washing machines and other "dumb" appliances, but usually take a broader view of machines that includes ones not yet constructed, and paint a picture in which one

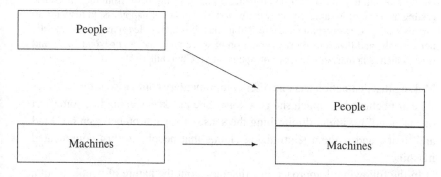

Fig. 1.1. Bringing people down to the level of machines.

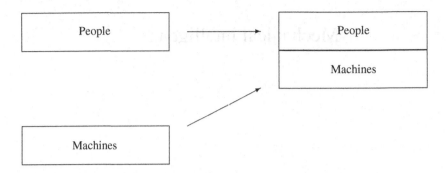

Fig. 1.2. Bringing machines up to the level of people.

endeavors to raise machines up to the level of humans, in stages of approximation if not all at once, as depicted in Figure 1.2. For example, throughout history clothes have been washed by people, and it is not demeaning to
compare a person with a person who washes clothes. If only we could make
washing machines as smart and capable and, well, as personable as people, say
students of artificial intelligence, surely comparison to such machines need not
be offensive.

This response does not placate those who view the hypothetical assumption
as an offensive impossibility, or who think people have a character that no
machine, no matter how intelligent, could possess. For example, many think
that people have a spiritual character that sets them apart from merely material
devices like machines, which only contain what their human designers put into
them. Churchill famously advanced such a concern in his own inimitable way:

The destiny of man is not decided by material computation. When great causes are
on the move in the world, stirring all mens' souls, drawing them from their firesides,
casting aside comfort, amusement, wealth, and the pursuit of happiness, in response to
impulses at once awe-striking and irresistible, then it is that we learn that we are spirits,
not animals, and that something is going on in space and time, and beyond space and
time, which, whether we like it or not, spells duty. (Churchill 1941)

Making this distinction lets one offer complimentary comparisons to machines
("I can't believe how much she gets done. She just keeps going like some sort
of machine!") without diminishing the sense of separation between our kind
and theirs, and without legitimizing claims that people are just complicated
machines.

In the following, I approach this dispute about the nature of people from a
different direction.

1.1 Mechanical philosophy

Behold the man!
    John 19:5 (KJV)

Thoughtful ancients saw mysteries everywhere, in space, in time, in matter, and in themselves. Some of the greatest puzzles turned on the multiple natures of things; a beach might look as smooth as the water shaping it, but close inspection reveals an array of grains of sand as seemingly numerous as the more obviously discrete stars in the heavens. The ancients recognized themselves as providing the greatest of such puzzles: once dead, composed of matter suitable for the worms of the soil; in life, manifesting both the smooth motions of the gymnasium and distinct decisions of judge and marketplace, in body bound to a location changing only a few kilometers a day, in mind free to range unbounded through worlds real and fanciful, past, present, and future, all within minutes, and for many, contemplating a life for the soul unhindered by the death of the body.

The new sciences developing across the centuries explored evidence that man's body exists subject to various regularities or laws of physics, chemistry, biology, and physiology, with some of these laws explaining much more than the human body. The array of scientific theories yielded by these explanations have greatly increased understanding of the world, and have supported powerful technologies affecting almost all areas of life: labor, transportation, communication, agriculture, medicine, manufacturing, trade, and war. We share species with the ancients, but increase in knowledge has transformed the environment of life in fundamental ways.

The advance of transformative science proceeded slowly before a dramatic acceleration in the seventeenth and eighteenth centuries, when discoveries in mathematics and rational mechanics altered the character of natural philosophy in fundamental ways.

The term *rational mechanics* has fallen out of general use, but it remains the traditional name given to the conceptual or mathematical investigation of mechanical concepts (Truesdell 1958). The term has persisted from the time of Newton to the revival of rational mechanics by Truesdell and others in the past century. Although today the scientific term *rational* is closely tied to the concept of rational decision and action in much of the literature, the term *rational mechanics* itself in no way refers to rational action as studied in psychology and economics.

Rational mechanics, as developed by Newton, Euler, and others, reworked natural philosophy into the modern sciences we know today. Earlier natural philosophy was dominated by informal, largely philosophical debate and observation. Rational mechanics, and the mathematical viewpoint more generally, focused on technical investigation, on explicit models of the evolution of physical systems in accordance with specific mathematical equations, and on explicit calculation from specific hypothesized initial conditions to observable and unobservable properties of physical systems. These mathematical models enabled scientists to refine physical theories, and enabled engineers to construct complicated physical systems to meet precise specifications. The advance in understanding changed perspectives so much that Leibniz claimed sufficiently great calculating abilities and a full description of conditions at some initial time would permit determination of the entire future of the world subsequent to the initial time.

1.2 The great divorce

The optimism expressed by the natural philosophers did not bear out in the contemporaneous early stages of the human sciences of psychology and economics. In contrast to the progress seen in understanding the physical world, understanding the mind has proven very difficult. We understand much today compared with past centuries, but in honest appraisal this represents comparison of infinitesimals.

Why did the advance of science scant mental philosophy even while enriching natural philosophy? Part of the explanation might lie in the limited applicability of the new conceptual tools.

Recall that the seventeenth century also saw Descartes' promulgation of a dualistic theory of mind, in which a mental substance of the mind accompanied the physical substance of the body. Discourse at the time also spoke of forces on minds and bodies, just as it does today. In spite of such conceptions in which mind and body consisted of substances acted upon by forces, the mathematical tools of the new mechanics did not apply to Cartesian minds, for their mental substances lacked physical position, meaning that mental actions lacked description in terms of the physical motion treated by mechanics. The new mechanics thus offered no way to apply its developing formal concepts to understanding the relation of the mind to the body or the nature of forces acting on minds.

The study of the mind did not stagnate, however, and mathematical theories of psychology and economics emerged later from nonmechanical theories of logic, probability, and utility. These theories gave central place to the notion of rational action, eventually understood as action chosen so as to maximize the expected utility of action. The principle of rational action provided the study of the mind with a formal framework for investigation and analysis comparable with the formal framework that the central mechanical notions of force, mass, and motion provided for physics. This difference with respect to mathematical formalism produced an increasingly wide separation of the mental and the physical sciences, between those based on the concept of rationality and those based on the concept of force.

The scientific import of this divorce of mental and physical sciences became clearer later as psychology began to explore computational characterizations of reasoning and behavior, and as economics began to cast about for theories that match human capabilities better than its foundational theory of ideal rational choice. Computational formalizations of psychological theories involved motion in "spaces" of mental states that, though very different than physical space, at least proved susceptible to mathematical formalization. Realistic economists grew appreciative of the hard work involved in making choices and of the slowness of the mind to change when subjected to new information or other influences. Popular discourse still spoke of mental forces, work, and inertia to reflect these concerns ("I had to force myself to concentrate"), much as in the days of Descartes and Newton. People also came to use mechanical concepts of inertia, force, energy, and pressure informally in describing economic markets and behavior ("Market forces are putting increasing pressure on oil prices"). In spite of the continuing application of seemingly similar concepts, the divorce of the mental and physical sciences impoverished the mental sciences when compared with the physical sciences by abandoning to the purely physical realm mechanical concepts of force and inertia that proved fruitful in analyzing physical behaviors. Study a physical problem, and one has recourse to physics, chemistry, and biology, as well as differential equations and mathematical theorems that aid in analysis and prediction. Study a mental system, and one lacks almost all of this intellectual heritage, for the traditional conceptual tools do not apply.

1.3 The awaiting reconciliation

The scientific separation of mental and physical need not stand. In the following, I bridge the gap between matter and mind with mechanics, and explore the possibility that people are indeed mechanical, in both mind and body, but are not necessarily machines or material machines. I do this, as depicted in Figure 1.3, by understanding "mechanical" in the sense of the science of mechanics, and show how one can rework the traditional mechanics one learns in high school or college physics classes to cover reasoning and other mental phenomena in a natural way.

Specifically, I show that the mathematical concepts of modern axiomatic rational mechanics apply more broadly than generally recognized. The quiet progress of mechanics in recent years provides formal concepts of force, mass,

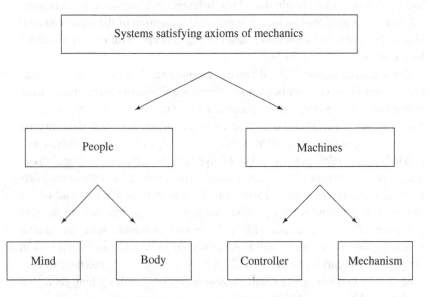

Fig. 1.3. Understanding people and machines as mechanical systems. Not all machines have nontrivial controllers.

momentum, and work that enable one to transform some heretofore metaphorical uses of these terms into meaningful, true or false, nonmetaphorical statements about psychological and economic systems within the axiomatic framework of modern rational mechanics.

In psychology, applying the mechanical perspective to mental inertia and mental forces helps one understand and formalize the difficulty of changing one's mind, of learning, of maintaining a focus of attention in the presence of distractions, and of overcoming habitual behaviors. Mechanics helps one understand the different characters of people and types of people.

In economics, nonphysical applications of mechanical axioms provide new means for characterizing more realistic notions of economic rationality and limits on reasoning abilities, and translate studies of different types of psychological and economic agents into studies of new types of mechanical materials.

In artificial intelligence, mechanics provides new concepts for analyzing the structure of artificial agents, new terms with which to specify desired characteristics of agents, and new paths for implementing agents efficiently.

The mechanical perspective provides these benefits without requiring one to give up nonmechanical perspectives. It instead provides an additional perspective offering clearer paths to some familiar apprehensions than those offered by traditional perspectives.

The mechanical perspective does not demote people to the level of machines. One might think of the human body as a machine of magnificent design, or one might not, for even traditional mechanics appears to transcend standard conceptions of "machine," especially the notion crystallized by Turing and popularized in today's digital computers. In a similar way, one might think of the human mind as a machine, or as something more, because mechanics itself does not say what sorts of forces exist in the world, nor from whence they issue.

2

Why mechanics?

The mechanical understanding of mind bridges both the gap between the mental and the physical and the gap between the rational and the dynamical. In addition to seeking a better understanding of the relation of mind to body, one specific motivation in pursuing this understanding stems from an interest in finding new means with which to characterize and analyze limits to rationality, a central interest common to psychology, economics, and artificial intelligence. Pursuing this motivation requires facing philosophical problems that have puzzled people for millennia.

Although science has answered some of these philosophical questions about nature and mind, it has left others unanswered. For example, one ancient question concerns determinism, or more generally, lawfulness. Many views hold the mind to exhibit essential freedoms not enjoyed by matter; other views hold the mind subject to various laws of psychology, economics, sociology, and anthropology, and argue about the precedence of these competing regulations. Though scientific progress has inspired some of the competing variants and the development of quantum theories has complicated the stark alternatives contemplated by earlier generations, scientific evidence has done less than one might expect to support or weaken the cases for the fundamental alternatives. The liberty or lawfulness of the mind remains controversial.

Unresolved questions do not represent failures of science. They represent the human condition. Given the long lifetime of fundamental questions, one measures the contribution of science not so much in terms of how many questions it has answered, but in terms of how many problems it made amenable to technical and experimental investigation. Truesdell, as usual, states the issue beautifully:

Now a mathematician has a matchless advantage over general scientists, historians, politicians, and exponents of other professions: He can be wrong. *A fortiori*, he can also be right. (Truesdell 1968b, p. 140)

The quickest way to tire the lay observer is with what appears to be philosophical debate, for philosophical debate has the reputation, perhaps deserved, of never resolving anything. The mathematical and theoretical advances of modern natural science have left some fundamental questions unanswered, but they have shown how to remove others from the domain of opinion into the domain of knowledge.

The continuing lack of consensus on fundamental characteristics of mind illustrates the paucity of progress in converting the questions of mental philosophy into subjects for technical and experimental investigation. Accordingly, I believe the primary immediate benefit provided by the reconciliation of the mental and the physical comes not in providing immediate answers to longstanding questions but in opening some long-standing philosophical problems to serious mathematical investigation. The more one removes technical limitations that handicap the human sciences relative to the physical sciences, the more one improves prospects for rich and effective mental sciences.

We cannot yet see all the ramifications of the mechanical perspective. Nevertheless, it seems likely that augmentation of the existing technical conceptions of logic, economics, and computational intelligence with the formal concepts of mechanics will permit construction of mechanical theories of the interaction of mind and body and of limits on ideal economic rationality. These mechanical theories in turn seem likely to offer improvements in techniques used in engineering artificial agents. The remainder of this chapter sketches elements of such potential benefits. Later chapters return to the ideas to provide more details.

2.1 Rethinking materialism

The ancient question of materialism, as regards psychology, asks whether people have minds or spirits distinct from their body, or whether these are mere by-products of brain and body. Philosophers have speculated for centuries about possible relations between mind and body, with theories ranging from nonexistence of mind to nonexistence of body, and from complete disconnection of mind from body to complete correspondence of mind and body.

Although Descartes viewed mind and body as somewhat separate entities acting on each other, dualistic theories fell into disrepute for at least two reasons. First, proponents of dualistic theories could not supply any formal model for or rules governing either mental motions or the proposed interactions between mind and body. Science was just beginning to understand physical forces in mathematical terms, but not in a way that applied to understanding interactions of mind and body. Second, even setting aside the lack of a formal

model for mind–body forces, proponents could not identify measurable forces
of this type. Everyone knew that lifting one's arm caused one's arm to rise, but
this apparently causal relation did not seem to fit the mechanical mold because
the mental effort required to lift the arm did not clearly vary with the weight of
things held by the arm.

The demise of dualism and the everyday incredibility of idealism have fa-
cilitated the dominance of the scientific viewpoint by materialism (or more
precisely, physicalism), which today we interpret as the view that everything
in the world consists of the material particles and fields of physics. Materialism even dominates thinking in psychology, where a tradition of behav-
iorism, computational mechanism, and neurophysiological primacy sidelines
the rather obvious disconnection between the experience of mental life and
the specific circumstances of embodiment. Though many have observed the
tenuous and inessential grounding of commonsense psychological concepts
in the physical, chemical, and neurophysiological bodily base, better understanding of the dramatic effects of certain chemicals and bodily trauma on
mental behavior has led others to dismiss ordinary psychological talk about
beliefs, desires, emotions, volition, and the like as hopelessly flawed, even as
an approximation to some supposed neurophysiological truth. This philosophical attitude has developed along with a shift in emphasis in artificial intelligence away from symbolic models of thought toward models in which numerical pseudoneurological quantities overlay varying kinds of nonnumerical
pseudosynaptic structure.

Economics, in contrast, represents perhaps the last holdout of amaterialist
thinking, even though it epitomizes "materialistic thinking" in an irrelevant
popular sense. Theoretical economics deals mainly with a theory of ideal rationality based solely on belief, preference, and choice independent of any
materialist grounding. The preferences economists attribute to humans may
derive from complex balances among underlying motivations, emotions, and
sentiments, but these underlying origins do not concern the economist as long
as these origins yield preferences fitting the form demanded by ideal
rationality.

The present work provides both formal means to rehabilitate dualistic psychologies and motivations for doing so. I use the modern axioms of mechanics to characterize the structure of forces exerted by mind on body, by body
on mind, and by mind on mind in exactly the same way that these axioms
characterize forces among physical bodies. Though the early formulations
of mechanics did not cover the Cartesian conception of mental substances,
the mathematically refined axioms developed in the twentieth century provide
the necessary breadth. The resulting mechanical characterization of mental

substances calls into question the conventional conception of materialism, much as discoveries in physics have extended the ancient concept of materialism to include the invisible fields of electromagnetism and various quantum particle fields unobservable in everyday life, and to include a theory of gravitation in which energy itself has mass.

2.1.1 Interacting minds and bodies

The formal framework developed later in this book offers the following simple straightforward technical application to addressing psychological theories of the interaction of mind and body. The illustration given here uses only two elements of modern mechanical formalism: the notion of *material universes*, which consist of lattices of simple and complex bodies, that is, sets of bodies ordered by the "part-of" relation, and the notion of *systems of forces*, which consist of assignments of force values to pairs of bodies, assigned in a way that satisfies mechanical principles including the vectoral force-addition (or parallelogram) law.

The mechanics developed in the following allows us to formalize persons as mechanical systems composed of hybrids of two component mechanical systems, one physical, one mental. Let us consider here the body and mind of a person I call René. Figure 2.1 depicts a division of René into mental and physical bodies. For the physical part of René we presume a standard mechanical model, and identify the body of René as a body $\mathcal{B}_p$ existing within a universe $\mathcal{B}_p$ of physical bodies. Similarly, for the mental part of René we identify the mind of René as a body $\mathcal{B}_m$ existing within a distinct universe $\mathcal{B}_m$ of mental bodies. We denote the lattice join of bodies $\mathcal{B}$ and $\mathcal{B}'$ by $\mathcal{B} + \mathcal{B}'$, and denote the largest, most inclusive, or "universal" body in a material universe by $\mathcal{U}$. Our simple illustration then uses the hybrid body $\mathcal{B}_R = \mathcal{B}_p + \mathcal{B}_m$ to model the person René, and the hybrid body $\mathcal{U} = \mathcal{U}_p + \mathcal{U}_m$ to model the universal body.

Let us now consider the total force acting on René at some instant. In the hybrid mechanical formalism, we write this force as $f(\mathcal{B}_R, \mathcal{U})$, that is, the force exerted on $\mathcal{B}_R$ by the universal body $\mathcal{U}$. The separation of the mental and physical bodies and the axioms for forces then let us rewrite this force as

$$f(\mathcal{B}_R, \mathcal{U}) = f(\mathcal{B}_p, \mathcal{U}) + f(\mathcal{B}_m, \mathcal{U}). \tag{2.1}$$

Let us look first at $f(\mathcal{B}_p, \mathcal{U})$, which represents the force on the physical body. We decompose $\mathcal{U}$ into separate components

$$\mathcal{U} = \mathcal{B}_R + \mathcal{B}_R^e = \mathcal{B}_p + \mathcal{B}_m + \mathcal{B}_p^{pe} + \mathcal{B}_m^{me}, \tag{2.2}$$

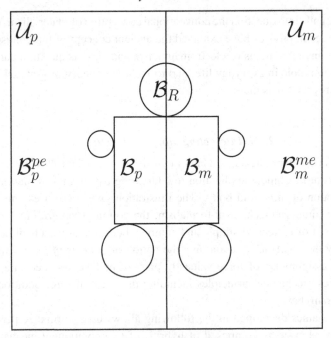

Fig. 2.1. Schematic division of a world containing a person $\mathcal{B}_R$ into mental and physical bodies ($\mathcal{B}_p$ and $\mathcal{B}_m$), plus mental and physical exteriors ($\mathcal{B}_m^{me}$ and $\mathcal{B}_p^{pe}$), all comprising universal mental and physical bodies ($\mathcal{U}_m$ and $\mathcal{U}_p$).

where $\mathcal{B}_R^e$ denotes the environment of $\mathcal{B}_R$, obtained as the relative complement of $\mathcal{B}_R$ with respect to the hybrid universal body $\mathcal{U}$; where $\mathcal{B}_p^{pe}$ denotes the physical environment of the physical body, obtained as the relative complement of $\mathcal{B}_p$ with respect to the greatest physical body $\mathcal{U}_p$; and where $\mathcal{B}_m^{me}$ denotes the mental environment of the mind, obtained as the relative complement of $\mathcal{B}_m$ with respect to the greatest mental body $\mathcal{U}_m$. With this partition of the hybrid universal body, we apply the axioms for forces to rewrite the force on the physical body as

$$ f(\mathcal{B}_p, \mathcal{U}) = f(\mathcal{B}_p, \mathcal{B}_p) + f(\mathcal{B}_p, \mathcal{B}_m) + f(\mathcal{B}_p, \mathcal{B}_p^{pe}) + f(\mathcal{B}_p, \mathcal{B}_m^{me}). \quad (2.3) $$

This just says the total force on the physical body consists of the sum of the forces exerted on the body by the body itself, by the mind, by the physical environment, and by the mental environment. From a similar decomposition, we obtain the force on the mind as

$$ f(\mathcal{B}_m, \mathcal{U}) = f(\mathcal{B}_m, \mathcal{B}_m) + f(\mathcal{B}_m, \mathcal{B}_p) + f(\mathcal{B}_m, \mathcal{B}_m^{me}) + f(\mathcal{B}_m, \mathcal{B}_p^{pe}). \quad (2.4) $$

The forces $f(\mathcal{B}_p, \mathcal{U})$ and $f(\mathcal{B}_m, \mathcal{U})$ constitute hybrid forces, containing components in both the physical and mental worlds. We can thus decompose them into components, for example, writing

$$f(\mathcal{B}_p, \mathcal{U}) = f_p(\mathcal{B}_p, \mathcal{U}) + f_m(\mathcal{B}_p, \mathcal{U}), \tag{2.5}$$

where $f_p(\mathcal{B}_p, \mathcal{U})$ denotes the component of $f(\mathcal{B}_p, \mathcal{U})$ that lies in physical space, and $f_m(\mathcal{B}_p, \mathcal{U})$ denotes the component of $f(\mathcal{B}_p, \mathcal{U})$ that lies in mental space. Either or both of these components might be zero. Deformations or motion of the physical body and the mind depend only on these respective components in the hybrid mechanics, so motion of the physical body depends only on

$$f_p(\mathcal{B}_p, \mathcal{U}) = f_p(\mathcal{B}_p, \mathcal{B}_p) + f_p(\mathcal{B}_p, \mathcal{B}_m) + f_p(\mathcal{B}_p, \mathcal{B}_p^{pe}) + f_p(\mathcal{B}_p, \mathcal{B}_m^{me}). \tag{2.6}$$

Thus the physical motion stems from physical forces, but the origin of these forces might include mental bodies. Similarly, motion of the mind depends only on

$$f_m(\mathcal{B}_m, \mathcal{U}) = \\ f_m(\mathcal{B}_m, \mathcal{B}_p) + f_m(\mathcal{B}_m, \mathcal{B}_m) + f_m(\mathcal{B}_m, \mathcal{B}_p^{pe}) + f_m(\mathcal{B}_m, \mathcal{B}_m^{me}). \tag{2.7}$$

By providing a rigorous conception of forces between mind and body, the present work provides new avenues for exploring questions about the existence, nature, and origin of such forces. For example, Truesdell once posed a brief query seeking evidence of measurable nonphysical forces on material objects. The query in its entirety reads:

Can any reader supply examples of magic whose effect is measured? E.g., a magician whose spells could lift a ten-pound weight, but none heavier. (Truesdell 1956, p. 59)

The query does not spell out whether Truesdell had in mind psychokinetic or supernatural forces. Possibly he offered the query in jest or ridicule, for Truesdell usually mentioned psychology, and artificial intelligence for that matter, as in the conclusion to (Truesdell 1984a), only to disparage the intellectual shoddiness of that field in comparison with the rigor attained in mechanics and other sciences. But publishing in *Isis* does not bespeak jest, and it seems reasonable to interpret the query as indicating that Truesdell considered mechanics as a broad subject, covering potential interactions between the physical and the mental as well as interactions among the purely physical. In the current setting, one can read the query as asking whether the cross-terms in (2.6) always vanish, that is, whether we have in fact

$$f_p(\mathcal{B}_p, \mathcal{U}) = f_p(\mathcal{B}_p, \mathcal{B}_p) + f_p(\mathcal{B}_p, \mathcal{B}_p^{pe}). \tag{2.8}$$

The formal framework of forces provided by mechanics covers many possibilities with no presumption that any or all of these exist in our world. It provides a formalization of interaction in which the mind raises the arm by forcing communication of information that initiates a physical action, with the distinction between informational force and physical force resolving the lack of proportionality between will and lift that puzzled earlier mental philosophers. The formal framework provided here makes sense of the possibility of telekinesis in the same way that traditional mechanics makes room for all sorts of possible forces not known to the ancients. The formal framework offered here also retains the traditional modest aspirations of mechanics. Just as Newton's mechanics did not presume to identify all types of physical forces, we make no suppositions regarding telekinesis or other undemonstrated forces and leave questions about the existence additional forces beyond those commonly recognized to future physical and psychological investigation. What we do show is that such questions have an empirical character, and that mechanics alone does not restrict the types of conceivable forces.

2.1.2 Correlation

Few have ever thought of mind and body as operating completely independently of one another. Someone hit will hurt, and may choose to react by moving and speaking. Mental and physical events enjoy some degree of correlation. The debate in philosophy over the centuries has concerned the degree and nature of such correlation. The constitutive assumptions that traditional mechanics uses to characterize special materials provide models for phrasing assumptions about the correlation of mental and physical events.

Traditional mechanics characterizes rigid bodies by a constitutive kinematic assumption, namely the assumption that the relative positions of all body parts remain constant throughout all motions. One might use similar "kinematic" assumptions to require that certain physical events always co-occur with certain mental events in some or all circumstances, as is the content of some identity theories of mind, and of some idealistic theories that posit unexceptional co-occurrence of mental and physical events. For example, one might assume that certain stimulations of the visual cortex always correlate with certain perceptions about surroundings. Such correlations amount to a path of communication between physical and mental bodies, and open the possibility that mental events can generate physical forces even without the explicit cross-terms of (2.6).

At the same time, one might not assume that decisions based on these percepts correlate in any regular way with activity in other portions of the brain.

Indeed, with a bit of stretching, one might interpret Penrose's (1989) speculations on the role of quantum gravity in consciousness as suggesting that mental events might influence certain delicate physical events but otherwise stem directly from the major flow of physical bodily events. The large range of possibility between no regular co-occurrence and completely regular co-occurrence offers room for many different theories of mind.

When one does not assume complete correlation between mental and physical events, one expects divergence between mental and physical states to occur. We see such divergence in the experience of the disoriented and the insane. The ordinary sort of disorientation represented by discrepancies between what the agent thinks about the world and the way it really is poses no philosophical difficulties. Most people lose this correlation a few times each day, and in rare cases lose it seriously and permanently, but ordinarily this sort of disorientation requires only minor, even unconscious or automatic, effort by the sufferer to correct the discrepancy, by changing mental or physical state to match the other. People who build robots go to some trouble to prevent such disorientation from crippling their robots by reducing thinking as much as possible to direct perception or reaction to overt physical states (Rosenschein & Kaelbling 1986; Brooks 1991). Such designs sometimes employ feedback control systems to imitate mechanical elasticity, in which perturbation from certain states generates restorative forces to bring the configuration back to the equilibrium one. The more thinking abstracts from these lower levels to construct plans and formulate long-term desires, the greater the openings provided for introducing discrepancies and disorientation.

2.1.3 Mechanical reasoning

As noted in the preceding discussion, Cartesian dualism failed to endow mental substances with familiar properties of location and mass. The absence of these notions posed far bigger problems for the theory than a mere lack of ways of making formal reference to forces involving minds. The present development addresses this gap in Cartesian theory by using modern mechanics to identify locations and masses in some of the simple but relatively detailed models of reasoning agents developed in artificial intelligence.

To illustrate the ideas briefly, I now sketch a mechanical interpretation of a simple but concrete formal model of reasoning, in which reasoning occurs through selection, interpretation, and application of explicit rules of reasoning. The mechanical restatement first identifies the underlying mathematical spaces characterizing mental motion and mass in the reasoner, and then identifies the forces generated by reasoning rules.

2.1.3.1 States of reasoning

In this illustration, let us regard each mental state of the reasoner as reflecting
a set of beliefs, desires, intentions, or other mental attitudes drawn from a
finite or infinite set $\mathcal{D}$ (Doyle 1983e, 1994). More generally, we regard $\mathcal{D}$ as
comprising all identifiable elements of mental states in the model, including
explicit rules of reasoning.

We regard the possible sets of attitudes and rules in the power set $\mathcal{P}(\mathcal{D})$ as
elements of the binary vector space $\mathbb{D} = (\mathbb{Z}_2)^{\mathcal{D}}$ over the field $\mathbb{Z}_2$, so that each
vector in $\mathbb{D}$ represents the characteristic function of a set of attitudes and rules.
We use set and vector notation interchangeably in the following as convenient,
writing $\mathbf{0}$ to denote the vector of zeros corresponding to $\emptyset \in \mathcal{P}(\mathcal{D})$, and $\mathbf{1}$
to denote the vector of ones corresponding to $\mathcal{D} \in \mathcal{P}(\mathcal{D})$. We write $\bar{x} =
\mathbf{1} - x$ to indicate the vector or set $\mathcal{D} \setminus x$ complementary to x. Because $\mathbb{Z}_2$ has
characteristic 2, we have $x = -x$ for every $x \in \mathbb{D}$. $\mathbb{D}$ also forms a ring under
pointwise binary multiplication.

2.1.3.2 Structure of reasoning

The term *reason* reflects the appearance of such rules in the Reason Maintenance System, or RMS, also called the *Truth Maintenance System*, or TMS
(Doyle 1979), in which the growth and change of the set of reasons highlights
the cumulative action of reasoning rules on memory and states of reasoning.

Section 8.4 describes reason maintenance in more detail, but I summarize
the ideas briefly as follows. The RMS and similar reasoning systems record
dependencies or argument or proof steps in long-term memory in service of
a reasoning system external to the RMS. These recorded dependencies represent propositional nonmonotonic default rules, which here I call *reasons*. The
RMS uses these reasons to maintain a set of conclusions in working memory.
The RMS constructs the conclusions so as to represent a set that is closed with
respect to consequences of reasons and grounded with respect to the recorded
reasons and starting assumptions. The nonmonotonicity of reasons supports
a form of reasoning in which all changes to conclusions can, if desired, be
effected by means of adding new reasons, which can either generate new conclusions or defeat earlier ones. When current conclusions are defeated by new
information, the RMS traces through the reasons supporting consequences of
the defeated conclusion and removes any that do not have some other means
of support. This process becomes complicated when, as commonly happens,
reasons form circular arguments in which different conclusions support each
other. When consequences are changed, the RMS notes the changes and in-
forms the external reasoner.

Let us divide mental states into two parts. One part reflects mental positions or points of view that we regard as a space $\mathcal{S}$ of locations of the agent. The other part reflects habits of thought or rules that we regard as the mass of the agent, with values in a set $\mathcal{M}$. Forces acting on the agent can cause spatial motion, change of mass, or both, with momenta and forces taking values in a set $\mathcal{P}$. As in traditional mechanics, $\mathcal{S}$ and $\mathcal{P}$ form vector spaces, and $\mathcal{M}$ forms a ring of scalars acting on $\mathcal{P}$, but in the setting of discrete mental attitudes these vector spaces and ring are discrete.

In the simplest conception, reasoning constitutes change of view or position, and learning constitutes change of habits or mass. This fits with common conceptions in which habits and knowledge persist across episodes of reasoning, and in which not all conclusions reached in reasoning lead to long-term changes.

We use $\mathbb{D}$ to represent instantaneous spatial and mass values, with $\mathcal{S} = \mathbb{D} = \mathcal{M}$, and use $\mathbb{D}$ to represent the translation spaces (sets of difference vectors) of these sets as well, thus permitting us to use $\mathcal{P} = \mathcal{M} \times \mathcal{S} = \mathbb{D}^2$ to represent momentum and force values. For each instant t in an interval of discrete times, we write x_t to denote the position, $\dot{x}_t$ the velocity, $\ddot{x}_t$ the acceleration, m_t the mass, $\dot{m}_t$ the mass flux, and p_t the momentum of the reasoner at t. We assume the set of discrete instants to be enumerated, so that $t + 1$ denotes the instant succeeding instant t. For present purposes we regard instantaneous position, mass, and velocity as constituting an instantaneous mechanical state, denoted by $(x_t, m_t, \dot{x}_t)$ or (x_t, p_t), the latter form using momentum values $p_t = (m_t, \dot{x}_t)$ to pair mass and velocity values. We regard histories or trajectories of the reasoner as functions mapping instants in a temporal interval to the mechanical states occurring at those instants. We write f_t to denote the applied force acting on the reasoner at t, and call a history a mechanical process just in case it satisfies Euler's equation

$$f = \dot{p} \qquad (2.9)$$

at each instant.

In the discrete setting, we interpret $\dot{x}_t$, $\dot{m}_t$, and $\dot{p}_t$ in terms of discrete differences. We identify $\dot{x}_t$ as the trailing velocity $\dot{x}_t = x_t - x_{t-1}$, but identify acceleration $\ddot{x}_t = \dot{x}_{t+1} - \dot{x}_t$, mass flux $\dot{m}_t = m_{t+1} - m_t$, and change of momentum $\dot{p}_t = p_{t+1} - p_t = (\dot{m}_t, \ddot{x}_t)$ as leading differences. The difference in formal treatment reflects a common design for reasoning systems. In this design, changes in attitudes trigger application of reasoning rules. Mechanically, this means the reasoner generates self-forces that depend on current position, mass, and trailing velocity. Such a reasoner also suffers changes imposed by users or other portions of their environments on its attitudes and rules. Mechanically, we regard such imposed changes as forces applied to the reasoner. These external changes affect or produce future mental states and so represent leading changes.

2.1.3.3 Reasoned motion

Explicit rules of logical, probabilistic, and heuristic reasoning appear in many forms in artificial intelligence systems, including production systems, logic programming languages, semantic networks, conceptual inheritance systems, Bayesian networks, Boolean computation circuits, and Minsky's (1980) K-lines (see Russell & Norvig 2002 for more on most of these). Although each of these forms exhibits a mechanical character, we focus on reasoning generated by simple types of nonmonotonic rules, or reasons (Doyle 1983e, 1994), such as the rule

> "Conclude (c) 'Sasha can fly' whenever
>> it is believed that (a) 'Sasha is a bird,' and
>>> it is not believed that (b) 'Sasha cannot fly.'"   (2.10)

Each reason involves four sets of beliefs, desires, intentions, rules, or other elements of $\mathcal{D}$, any or all of which might be empty. We denote a reason r with the notation

$$r = A_r \setminus\!\setminus B_r \Vdash C_r \setminus\!\setminus D_r,$$ (2.11)

which we read as "A_r without B_r gives C_r without D_r," where $A_r, B_r, C_r, D_r \subseteq \mathcal{D}$. We thus might write (2.10) as the reason

$$\{a\} \setminus\!\setminus \{b\} \Vdash \{c\} \setminus\!\setminus \emptyset.$$ (2.12)

We interpret each reason r as stating that each element of C_r should be held and each element of D_r should not be held if each element of A_r is held and each element of B_r is not held.

One can interpret reasons of the form of (2.11) synchronously, as applying to instantaneous states of the reasoner, or diachronically, as relating successive instantaneous states of the reasoner. In a synchronous interpretation, reason (2.11) expresses the rule that the reasoner's conclusions contain each element of C and no element of D if it contains each element of A and no element of B. In a diachronic interpretation, reason (2.11) concerns presence or absence of state characteristics at different times, saying that if $A \setminus\!\setminus B$ applies to the state prior to a change, then $C \setminus\!\setminus D$ should apply to the state after.

In our simple illustration, we assume the reasoner's environment initiates episodes of reasoning by changing the reasoner's memory to include a new reason, whereupon the reasoner applies reasons that change position until either no reasons remain unapplied or the environment imposes further changes on memory. This assumption is compatible with simple perception and communication or imposition of new attitudes because reasons of the form $\emptyset \ \backslash\backslash$ $\emptyset \Vdash C \ \backslash\backslash \ \emptyset$ produce conclusions without requiring antecedent or ancillary conditions. We regard such motion as reflecting the combination of an external force $(\dot{m}, \mathbf{0})$ with a self-generated force $(\mathbf{0}, \ddot{x})$ to produce a total force $f = (\dot{m}, \ddot{x})$.

In considering a mechanical state $(x_t, m_t, \dot{x}_t)$ at instant t, we regard application of a single reason $r = A_r \ \backslash\backslash \ B_r \Vdash C_r \ \backslash\backslash \ D_r$ as generating the acceleration

$$\ddot{x}_t = \begin{cases} C_r \overline{x}_t + D_r x_t - \dot{x}_t & \text{if } A_r \overline{x}_t + B_r x_t = 0 \\ \dot{x}_t & \text{otherwise,} \end{cases} \tag{2.13}$$

which yields the new velocity

$$\dot{x}_{t+1} = \begin{cases} C_r \overline{x}_t + D_r x_t & \text{if } A_r \overline{x}_t + B_r x_t = 0 \\ \mathbf{0} & \text{otherwise,} \end{cases} \tag{2.14}$$

and hence the expected new position

$$x_{t+1} = \begin{cases} x_t + C_r \overline{x}_t + D_r x_t & \text{if } A_r \overline{x}_t + B_r x_t = 0 \\ x_t & \text{otherwise.} \end{cases} \tag{2.15}$$

2.1.3.4 Reason forces

Define the function $U : \mathcal{D} \rightarrow (\mathbb{D} \rightarrow \mathbb{D})$ by

$$U(r)(x) = \begin{cases} C_r \overline{x}_t + D_r x_t & \text{if } A_r \overline{x}_t + B_r x_t = 0 \\ \mathbf{0} & \text{otherwise.} \end{cases} \tag{2.16}$$

This value for $U(r)(x)$ is thus the same product from a reason and position as was identified in expression (2.14) for the velocity produced in single-reason motion, so that $\ddot{x}_t = U(r)(x_t) - \dot{x}_t$. As we are assuming that application of rules changes only position and not mass, appearance of reasoned motion (2.15) in a mechanical process satisfying (2.9) requires us to identify

$$f_r(x_t, m_t, \dot{x}_t) = (\mathbf{0}, U(r)(x_t) - \dot{x}_t), \tag{2.17}$$

as the force generated by the reason r in the state $(x_t, m_t, \dot{x}_t)$.

To obtain the force $f_R(x_t, m_t, \dot{x}_t)$ due to applying a set of reasons R in a mechanical state $(x_t, m_t, \dot{x}_t)$, we lift U to a function $U : \mathcal{P}(\mathcal{D}) \rightarrow (\mathbb{D} \rightarrow \mathbb{D})$

by additive superposition

$$U(R)(x) = \sum_{r \in R} U(r)(x), \qquad (2.18)$$

following the convention that an empty sum equals 0. Thus if R_t denotes the set of reasons acting at time t, we obtain the acceleration

$$\ddot{x}_t = U(R_t)(x_t) - \dot{x}_t, \qquad (2.19)$$

and so define the force generated by R_t by

$$f_{R_t}(x_t, m_t, \dot{x}_t) = (0, U(R_t)(x_t) - \dot{x}_t). \qquad (2.20)$$

One easily verifies that $f_{\{r\}}(x_t, m_t, \dot{x}_t) = f_r(x_t, m_t, \dot{x}_t)$.

2.2 Characterizing rationality

Even if mechanics helps provide a better understanding of the interaction of mind and body in terms of forces and masses, it provides no guidance about how to understand the specific forces involved. Although one can view human minds as suffering and generating a variety of forces, as does Shand (1920), the present effort focuses on using mechanics to understand the forces characteristic of rational thought and action. Used in this way, mechanics provides a "new" formal language for characterizing limits to rationality, a language in which mental effort relates to mechanical work, in which attention relates to directions of resultant forces, and in which dimensionality of communication channels places bounds on the magnitude of possible forces.

2.2.1 What is rationality?

People use the term *rational* in many senses. In the terms *rational mechanics* and *rational psychology*, the word means conceptual or mathematical, as opposed to speculative or experimental. In everyday life, however, the three main senses consist of the psychological, logical, and economic, corresponding to whether the agent reasons according to rules, draws sound and consistent conclusions, and makes the best choices possible given the available knowledge.

Of these three everyday senses, the logical and economic have received the most attention as formal subjects, developing from philosophical roots two millennia ago and flowering in the development of mathematics in the past few centuries.

Today, the theory of economic rationality reigns supreme in the social sciences. In the modern formulations of von Neumann and Morgenstern (1953) and Savage (1972), which formally characterize rational beliefs and preferences and how the agent's beliefs change with the acquisition of new information, the economic ideal of rational choice supports a deep mathematical development unrivaled by any science outside the physical sciences save for mathematical logic and the mathematical theory of computation. The conceptual coherence and power of the theory of economic rationality permit it to serve as the basis for quite elaborate theoretical developments in the theory of markets and other topics. As an organizing principle, the theory and its underlying assumptions also undergird much thinking in modern politics, management, and, increasingly, artificial intelligence, psychology, the theory of computation, and even biology. Policy analysis now involves explicit decision-theoretic and game-theoretic analyses; computational agents explicitly represent and reason with probabilistic and utilitarian information; psychologists study the probabilistic and preferential reasoning of ordinary people; computation theorists and algorithm engineers augment notions of worst-case and average-case complexity with expected utility models; and biologists employ economic choice models at many levels, ranging from the resource economics of ecosystems to the more controversial genetic levels.

Despite its preeminence in our current views of sciences and humanities, however, the theory of economic rationality suffers from many problems. These are most clearly seen in the broader context of human rationality. To understand these problems and to see how mechanics provides a path to remedying at least some of them, we examine the several notions of rationality and irrationality in turn.

2.2.1.1 Psychological rationality

The psychological sense of rationality means basing beliefs, decisions, and actions on explicit reasoning and argument about what must true (as in logical rationality) and about what must be good or what must be done (as in economic rationality), given one's assumptions and goals. The picture underlying this sense depicts thought and action guided by rules and procedures in a way that permits one to explain the reasons underlying specific actions and attitudes by articulating the rules and attitudes that constitute the reasons. One can regard psychological rationality as related to the practical reasoning reflected in Aristotle's (1962) practical syllogism "I desire D; action A will achieve D; therefore I do A," and to Newell's (1982) modern restatement in his principle of rationality.

Many common uses of the psychological sense of rationality contrast "rational" with "emotional," often presupposing that action based on emotion cannot also be based on reasoning, but as understood here, psychological rationality refers only to actions having reasons, not to the emotional or epistemic content of those reasons. Psychological rationality thus says nothing about the emotional or nonemotional basis of thought and behavior. One can exhibit psychological rationality and still have major elements of behavior under nonrational control.

The psychological sense of rationality makes far weaker assumptions about the nature of the rules involved in reasoning than do the logical and economic senses. In contrast to the stronger notions, one cannot characterize psychological rationality exactly because it denotes an indefinite range of mental characters rather than the singular crisp ideal characters of logical and economic rationality (see Doyle 1983e, 1994 for an elaboration of some of the varieties). Instead, one must look to formal frameworks that cover a variety of psychological organizations, each interpretable as involving some sort of rule-guided reasoning or action.

Mathematical studies of some varieties in which explicit reasons of the form shown in (2.11) mediate reasoning states and reasoned state-changes have been elaborated in some detail in theories of reasoned assumptions (Doyle 1983e, 1994) and nonmonotonic logics (Marek & Truszczyński 1993), as well as examined philosophically in Doyle (1982a, 1990a, 1988a). Though simple in structure, analysis of such reasons reveals a fairly deep structure, with many connections to philosophy, logic, and economics. Indeed, the logical and economic senses of rationality refine this picture by understanding reasoning rules as rules of logical inference and understanding RMS interpretation of nonmonotonic reasons as choosing sets of conclusions that maximize expected utility.

2.2.1.2 Logical rationality

The logical sense of rationality specializes the psychological sense of action based on reasoning by viewing thought as concerning logical propositions and logical relations among them, and by requiring that one's beliefs and intentions remain free of contradiction and include only their deductive consequences.

The first requirement of logical rationality is that thoughts be interpretable as statements or propositions in a logical language, or more accurately, as attitudes toward such statements, such as a belief that p, desire that p, or intention that p. Such interpretations let one then judge logical relations among the propositions involved in thinking. Formally, logical rationality views a belief state, for example, as a set (a "proposition") p of possible ways the world might be, or alternatively, as a set S of statements expressing the proposition p.

The second requirement of logical rationality is that beliefs, preferences, and intentions are consistent, regarding these relations as semantic ones holding between the meanings of thoughts. Thus the logically rational agent cannot believe simultaneously, as did Carroll's Red Queen, eight impossible things, whether before, during, or after breakfast. Formally, and with respect to beliefs, this amounts to the requirement that the proposition p characterizing beliefs is nonempty, $p \neq \emptyset$, and in particular, that any set of statements S expressing p does not contain an explicit contradiction; that is, there is no statement q such that S contains both q and $\neg q$.

The third requirement of logical rationality is that beliefs, preferences, and intentions are closed under entailment. This means that the agent must believe every consequence of its beliefs, prefer every consequence of its preferences, and intend every consequence of its intentions. Formally, and again with respect to belief, this means that if the proposition p characterizes the agent's beliefs and p is contained in q, then the agent also believes q, or alternatively, that if S expresses p, then S is its own deductive closure, $S = Th(S)$.

The fourth requirement of logical rationality is that reasoning only adds deductive consequences of current beliefs, and that only perception and action make other additions or subtractions. This means that each new conclusion reached by thinking or reasoning must follow by deductive inference from current conclusions, so that beliefs change only by means of perception and action. Thus the third requirement of deductive closure captures all consequences of reasoning.

Logical rationality requires only a propositional character of beliefs, as this semantic character suffices to identify notions of consistency and closure. In mental organizations that employ sentential or other syntactic representations of semantic propositions, logical rationality carries over to deductive consistency and closure requirements.

Although the pure notion of logical rationality involves only propositional character, consistency, and deductive closure and character, some regard the notion as also requiring that reasoning reflect deduction and that revision maintains information content as the agent accommodates new information and takes action (Gärdenfors 1988). In particular, when new information conflicts with existing beliefs, this strengthened notion of logical rationality requires that any accommodation of the new information retain as many of the existing beliefs as possible, for example, by moving to a maximal consistent subset of the union of existing beliefs with the new information. I regard such strengthenings as extralogical, embodying value information in addition to mere logic; in particular, such strengthenings imply that all information is intrinsically valuable, and that information is more valuable than lack of information (Doyle 1991).

2.2.1.3 Economic rationality

The economic sense of rationality means acting optimally with coherent beliefs and preferences or utility judgments. The notion of coherence employed in the economic sense of rationality includes the logical notions of consistency and deductive closure, so it is fair to say that the economic sense of rationality subsumes the pure notion of logical rationality. More importantly, the economic notion has received extensive axiomatic and mathematical study as a theory of ideal agents, in contrast to the notions of argument and logic, which though studied extensively, have not been understood as theories of agents until recently.

More specifically, ideal economic rationality means acting to maximize expected utility. The theory views agents as facing a set of alternatives or actions, each of which has many different possible consequences or outcomes. The theory assumes the agent assigns probabilities to these outcomes given the actions, and that the agent has some way of ordering all outcomes by degree of desirability, such that degrees of desirability can be represented by a numerical utility function over outcomes. The theory then defines the expected utility of an alternative as the average utility of its outcomes, with the utility of each individual outcome weighted by its probability. The theory calls the agent rational if the agent always acts to choose alternatives of maximal expected utility.

The axioms for rational economic agents start by characterizing a notion of preference-based choice among alternative actions (von Neumann & Morgenstern 1953). The theory begins with a set $\mathcal{A} = \{A_1, A_2, \ldots\}$ of alternatives and a binary choice relation $\precsim_{\mathcal{A}} = \precsim$ of *weak preference* over $\mathcal{A}$, where $A \precsim B$ means that the agent weakly prefers B to A in that it finds B at least as desirable as A. The theory defines two additional relations in terms of weak preference. The theory defines *indifference* among alternatives, written $A \sim B$, so that $A \precsim B$ and $B \precsim A$, meaning that the agent finds that whatever differences exist between the alternatives leave them equally desirable. The theory defines *strict preference*, written $A \prec B$, so that $A \precsim B$ but $A \not\succsim B$, meaning the agent finds B more desirable than A.

Three axioms characterize the notion of ideal preference by requiring that weak preference constitute a complete preorder, that is, a complete reflexive and transitive relation. These requirements entail that strict preference is transitive and asymmetric, and that indifference is an equivalence relation. A fourth axiom then requires that the agent choose alternatives maximal with respect to the ordering of weak preference. The axioms on preferences ensure that every finite set of alternatives offers at least one rational choice. Infinite sets of alternatives can lack any rational choice without constraints on the nature of the preferences and the structure of alternatives.

The subjective Bayesian theory of rational decision adds the notion of a set Ω of decision outcomes, meaning states or futures that can result from actions and in which the agent takes action. It posits another preference order $\precsim_\Omega$ over these outcomes that compares desirability of outcomes rather than actions. It posits a belief function $pr_A : \Omega \to \mathbb{R}$ for each action $A \in \mathcal{A}$ that assigns to each outcome the agent's degree of belief that the outcome results from A.

Three axioms require $\precsim_\Omega$ to constitute a complete preorder, just as with $\precsim_\mathcal{A}$. These axioms imply the existence of numerical utility functions $u : \Omega \to \mathbb{R}$ that represent $\precsim_\Omega$ in the sense that $A \precsim_\Omega B$ iff $u(A) \le u(B)$. Another axiom requires that the belief functions representing beliefs about the consequences of choices constitute probability measures over outcomes. One can develop this probabilistic axiom in turn from further axioms about belief comparisons (Savage 1972).

The theory combines the numerical utility and probability functions into an expected utility function $\hat{u} : \mathcal{A} \to \mathbb{R}$ such that $\hat{u}(A) = \int_\Omega pr_A(\omega)u(\omega)$. A fourth axiom then makes preferences among actions correspond to comparisons of expected utility by requiring that $A \precsim_\mathcal{A} B$ iff $\hat{u}(A) \le \hat{u}(B)$.

The theory of multiattribute decision making extends the concepts of subjective Bayesian decision theory by decomposing utility functions over outcomes into functions over properties or characteristics of those outcomes. The set of properties of interest induces a multidimensional representation of the set of outcomes. The theory then studies utility functions over the multidimensional representation that can take the form of functional compositions of "subutility" functions over lesser-dimensional subspaces of the multiattribute representation.

Recent approaches to machine computation of rational decisions augment multidimensional decompositions of preference and utility information with multidimensional decompositions of probability measures, for example, using Bayesian networks to express probability distributions relatively succinctly in terms of causal relations among propositions holding true in different outcomes (Pearl 1988; Boutilier, Dean, & Hanks 1999).

Finally, the theory of rational group decisions extends the theory of rational individual decisions just summarized by setting requirements on choices made by a group of rational individuals (Arrow 1963). The theory of rational group decisions consists of three axioms characterizing the group preference order $\precsim_\mathcal{G}$ in terms of member preference orders $\precsim_i$ for each member i of the group $\mathcal{G}$. The first axiom of collective rationality requires that the group preferences derive from a function over all possible rational preference relations of the

individuals. The second axiom, of Pareto optimality or unanimity, insists that
the group preferences agree with the individual preferences for alternatives on
which the individuals agree. The third axiom, of "independence of irrelevant
alternatives," requires that the ranking of two alternatives in the global order
depends only on how the individual orders rank those two alternatives, independent of how they rank other alternatives relative to the given two.

Social fairness concerns in human decision making suggest adding a fourth
axiom of nondictatorship that ensures none of the group members acts as a
"dictator" whose preferences automatically determine the group's, independent of the other individual orderings. Arrow (1963) proved this requirement
conflicts with the first three. Some theories of group rationality abandon or
modify some of the first three in order to adopt this fourth restriction.

Markets represent a familiar context for group decisions. The competing
individual preferences determine demand functions. Markets provide auctions
in which these group demand functions combine with supply levels to produce
equilibrium prices or exchange ratios for sets of goods.

2.2.2 Human rationality

People sometimes seem to reason and can give explanations of how they arrived at conclusions or came to decisions. People sometimes change their beliefs to avoid contradiction, and sometimes seek to determine consequences of
their beliefs. People sometimes make decisions by assessing utility and probability and comparing the expected utility of different alternatives. This lets
one say people are sometimes rational, but much evidence exists to show that
people do not fully meet the standards of the logical and economic ideals.

2.2.2.1 Humane logical rationality

First consider rationality in the logical sense. The sad law of unexpected consequences testifies to the difficulty people have of seeing consequences, even
in cases in which explanations after the fact involve no facts not already known
before the event. Grand masters of chess might see that the capture $KP \times QB$
will lead unavoidably to losing the game, but the rest of us remain blind to that
consequence. Indeed, the $P = NP?$ problem in the theory of computation
reflects this asymmetry between the difficulty of finding an argument and the
difficulty of following an argument.

Logical consistency also is problematic, for everyone knows the ease with
which one can detect inconsistencies in the beliefs of one's opponents compared with the difficulty one has in detecting inconsistencies in one's own
beliefs. In some cases, these inconsistencies reflect the incompleteness or lack

of deductive closure of beliefs, as real people remain ignorant of many of the consequences of their own beliefs, including consequences that would highlight inconsistencies. In other cases, people hold inconsistent beliefs due to strong motivations or principles. In the most benign case, someone holds two conflicting beliefs indefinitely while seeking out or awaiting ways of reconciling the two.

It is also easy to observe that much commonsense reasoning is not deductive, but presumptive, as people make defeasible assumptions left and right that stand until overridden by new information or until the consequences of prior knowledge become clear.

2.2.2.2 *Humane economic rationality*

People are notorious for making poor choices that indicate a degree of economic irrationality. The serious study of the human form of economic rationality came to prominence in the work of Simon (1955, 1956), who presented one of the first critiques of the ideal conception of economic rationality in his theory of bounded rationality, in which he sought to take into account the limits on ratiocination, information, and consistency common to people.

Simon pointed out that although people enjoy seemingly endless possibilities for action at every instant, they can comprehend only a few samples or dimensions of variation in these possibilities. Embodying the ideal theory in a world as complex as ours apparently requires fairly complete probabilistic and preferential information about truly vast or even infinite numbers of possible circumstances and events. Economic rationality encompasses large action spaces without difficulty, but one simply does not see this sort of synoptic awareness in people, who routinely find themselves or others ignorant of the consequences of their actions, and find making decisions overwhelming when faced with the myriad possibilities and ramifications of even simple decisions. For instance, medical practice these days tends to distress people in part because clinics routinely ask patients to sign consent forms that list death as a possible outcome, even for such minor procedures as removing an ingrown toenail. Few people think of dying when contemplating toenail removal, though making rational decisions about the procedure must take that possibility into account, even if only to dismiss it because of its improbability. Death, however, is only the most easily foreseen unlikely possibility, and people pass over infinitely many other possibilities without ever thinking about them.

Similarly, an person unable to comprehend sufficient quantities of information will experience difficulty observing the inconsistency of separate pieces of information, even if the person can easily see the inconsistency when the pieces are presented together. Decision making based on inconsistent preference information can result in failure to find any rational choice when inconsistent preferences rule each alternative strictly worse than others.

Economics shows how with special effort one can hide some of the complexity of real circumstances of choice by circumscribing the scope of each decision to a carefully constructed "small world" (Savage 1972). In spite of such practices, the issue of the quantity of information required by rational agents becomes inescapable in subjective Bayesian decision theory, which requires agents to employ Bayesian conditionalization to update beliefs to reflect new information. Conditionalization implies that the beliefs of the agent at any instant suffice to determine the appropriate updates for every possible sequence of future information updates. In a world with an unbounded continuum of future times, this leads quickly to the need for belief states that represent infinite quantities of information.

Although economics posits beliefs and preferences that exhibit unbounded degrees of accuracy, completeness, and consistency at each instant of acting, humans find thinking difficult. As noted earlier, they have trouble seeing the consequences of their beliefs and preferences for the decisions that economics supposes they rationally make. But beyond these failures of awareness, people also suffer failures of agility, for when confronted with new information, they often fail to adjust their expectations in the comprehensive way prescribed by economics, or can take a long time to do so. This slowness to update does not fit the economic ideal, which is a theory of specified results and behavior, not of incremental and accumulating change. When an agent receives a new piece of information, the ideal theory says it changes its beliefs by conditionalizing the old on the basis of the truth of the new. While the ideal theory does not specify how long this process takes, it does formulate sequential action by presuming that the updates take place prior to decisions about the next action, so as a practical matter one must view the ideal theory as requiring the updates to take place arbitrarily quickly. Worse still, the new information may change the belief state completely, so there need be no proportionality between the new information and change of state. The ideal conception of rationality thus involves changing beliefs arbitrarily much arbitrarily quickly.

Rational economic agents do not exhibit weakness of will because they have no goals or intentions against which to measure success, but instead only have instantaneous choices that can change with their beliefs and preferences. Yet people do not seem to have the ability to assess expected utilities in the coherent way demanded by economic rationality, for even when people come to rational decisions, impulsive desires or persistent habits can interfere and cause them to act against their own rational judgments.

2.2.2.3 Humane psychological rationality

Finally, it is also clear that although psychological rationality does not constitute a rationalistic ideal in the way that logical and economic rationality do, many aspects of human behavior have little to do with overt ratiocination, but instead have much to do with the functioning of the human body. Most people have personal experience with how pure physiological responses to medications, intoxicants, and illnesses can produce or undercut beliefs and desires without any involvement of recognizable reasoning processes. More generally, people do numerous things seemingly without reason that they cannot explain.

Although it is true that we have no strong evidence to say that all of these stem from the operation of unidentified rules of reasoning, failures of introspection do not in themselves count as evidence against psychological rationality. Neurophysiology has revealed portions of the brain that not only play large but subconscious roles in perception and motor control, but also appear to provide related functions in the course of thinking. Such structure-sharing suggests that a person might be conscious of some reasoning in some settings and unconscious of the same reasoning in other settings. In addition, we can construct reason-based interpretations of a wide range of behaviors (Doyle 1994). Although we might thus regard organs of perceptual and motor activity as effecting a very complicated sort of reasoning, we might instead regard it as more straightforward to view these mental changes as nonrational elements of thought, more akin to the trained muscular reflexes of an athlete than to the trained inference of a physician.

2.2.2.4 Do the differences matter?

One might excuse departures from logical and economic rationality to some extent by noting that these senses of rationality represent ideals, not practical observations, and that individuals can achieve greater rationality by expending greater effort toward that end. Indeed, economists tend to think that large numbers of people acting in markets generally do produce rational decisions, with the flaws of one person canceling out the flaws of another and with the correct judgments of each reinforcing each other. Of course, no one expects reality to fit the ideal perfectly, but even granting such claims, observed individual behavior approximates the ideal conception of rationality only poorly. Some consider the departures from the ideal severe enough and common enough to call into question the suitability of the ideal as the standard by which to judge rationality.

In practical terms, the perfection and strength of the economic concept of rationality means that only agents of extreme simplicity, such as thermostats and toasters, can satisfy its strict requirements under suitable imputations of beliefs and preferences. Realistic agents of even moderate complexity, to say nothing of the great complexity of the human mind, suffer various physical, computational, and informational limitations that generally prevent action in accord with the ideal.

Yet one should not abandon the economic ideals too hastily, nor in all applications. Acting rationally means taking into account one's limitations, including limitations on one's own rationality. In particular, mitigating the effects of limitations on rationality requires recognizing and exploiting the limitations. Recognizing limitations allows the agent to allocate its scarce resources to obtain better results than those resulting from haphazard or uniform allocation to all deliberative tasks. Exploiting limitations allows conservation of resources by removing some possibilities from consideration in the first place, lessening the complexity of the deliberative task to be faced at future times to more manageable levels. I use the terms *rational self-government* (Doyle 1988a) or *rational self-management* (Doyle 1980) to describe methods for recognizing and exploiting one's own limitations.

2.2.3 Mechanical rationality

Recognizing the mismatch between the strong theoretical ideal of economic rationality and the sometimes appalling reality of decision making by humans of limited mental capacity and rationality, thoughtful economists have sought theories of more realistic conceptions of rationality for some time. They have explored a fair number of ways of trying to weaken the ideal theory, with some conceptual successes in theories of consumer and organizational behavior. Unfortunately, none of the weakenings explored to date serve well the standing needs of economics. As Truesdell and Noll (1992, p. 4) remark, "[t]he task of the theorist is to bring order into the chaos of the phenomena of nature, to invent a language by which a class of these phenomena can be described efficiently and simply," but the weakenings explored to date all seem too weak or too complex to serve as starting points for a realistic reconstruction of the theory of markets and other economic subtheories.

The search for a realistic theory of rationality has met with only modest success because developing a characterization of realistic rationality implies development of a serviceable mathematical model of human or human-like thinking. Economics should find such a model in psychology, but psychology has no such model to provide. Neurophysiological models exist in mathematical form, but the mathematical concepts they involve say nothing about the properties of interest to the economist.

In the following chapters, I interpret aspects of psychological limitations in terms of mechanical characteristics of mass, force, and effort in hopes of transferring at least some of the theoretical conclusions available in traditional mechanics to psychology and economics as part of an analytical and predictive theory of mechanical rationality. To wit, some psychological limitations involving update reflect the role of mental mass; some limitations involving habit and character reflect constitutional properties of the psychological material in question; some limitations of attention reflect the additivity of forces and energetic properties; and some limitations of consistency reflect multiple bodies as well as the additivity of forces. Roughly speaking, one can find masses in memory, intention, habits, skills, and other forms of human capital; forces in motivations, desires, sensation, and attention; energy in effort; and constitution in character. The hope in seeking such a transfer of mechanical concepts to psychology is that a mathematical basis of mechanics may provide more realistic foundations for economics, foundations that help reconstruct the standard theoretical economic superstructures in more useful ways.

We find evidence of the possibility of such transfer in psychological truisms. Numerous truisms attest to the limits of economic formalism and point to a solution. Everybody knows from self-help books that one has to force oneself to change, and the bigger the desired change, the more one has to work at it. Everybody knows that the more one knows about some question the harder it is to change one's position. Everybody knows that getting going on tackling a task is often the hardest problem faced in carrying out the task, and that once one overcomes this initial inertia, progress generates its own momentum that keeps one going. Everybody knows that maintaining direction or focus requires forcing oneself to ignore distractions. We can speculate that people express and use such truisms because people have well-developed abilities for predicting the motions of physical objects in such terms and because everyone gains some understanding by applying the same terms and abilities to mental behavior, even after acknowledging the unpredictable ways minds can act compared to inanimate objects.

Science, when confronted by things "everybody knows," can seek to confirm, disprove, refine, or correct the claims experimentally or theoretically. Doing any of these requires making the claims precise, preferably in measurable ways. This was done in natural philosophy at the time of Newton. "Everyone knew" many things about the behavior of ordinary objects. Newton captured some of these in his three laws of mechanics—and arguably his law of inertia was something almost everyone thought false. Finding sensible mathematical formalizations of Newton's laws posed major difficulties in the century following their statement.

In the same way, finding appropriate formalizations of psychological truisms in mechanical form poses a major difficulty for developing a theory of
realistic rationality, whether the appropriate formalism involves mechanics or
not. If scientists judge they can never make the claims precise, they may dismiss them as nonsense or misunderstandings. Scientists have regarded many
psychological truisms as nonsense for centuries because the mathematical formalism developed in physics has not applied in clear ways to mental forces or
inertia, even though truisms about these make sense in everyday life and seem
consonant with physical intuition. This creates an uncomfortable conflict for
the humble and reflective scientist, since everyday living involves applying
terms one disbelieves intellectually.

The mechanics developed in subsequent chapters points a way to reducing
these conflicts. The formalizations that follow identify notions of psychological and economic force, mass, and momentum as precise as the familiar physical ones and obeying essentially the same laws and interrelations. This lets
us transform some truisms and common beliefs about psychology into sensible formal statements of mechanics, statements that we might then endeavor to
show true or false. We certainly do not yet know how to make all such truisms
and beliefs sensible, and some might remain formally uninterpretable forever,
but some truisms do appear to correspond to true formal statements, justifying
their persistence despite centuries of scientific censure.

2.2.3.1 Mental inertia

From the mechanical point of view, motion corresponding to ideal rationality,
in which new information produces arbitrarily high velocities, requires either
infinite forces or massless bodies, neither of which characterizes human bodies
or minds. Instead, as noted previously, people take time to adjust their beliefs
and expectations after acquiring new information. One fits this delay into the
ideal of economic rationality only by distinguishing receipt from acquisition
of information, and saying that one has "acquired" new information only once
one has assimilated all the implications of the new information. This termi-
nological dodge does not really solve the problem, of course, especially as it
means that people never acquire new information, because they never fully
comprehend all the consequences.

In contrast to the economic ideal, the mechanical view of learning and reasoning explicitly recognizes that effecting change takes time, and that the concept of inertia represents a key element of describing the resistance to or slowness of change, with forces producing changes in momentum. The sketch of
mechanical reasoning in Section 2.1.3 illustrated this in part by characterizing reasoning states in terms of both position—the current conclusions—and

momentum—reason memory and current changes or velocity. As illustrated in the reason forces identified earlier, reasoning rules change the conclusions a few at a time, with each reason adding or subtracting some set of conclusions, and so change the velocity of the reasoner.

In the case of RMS and similar reasoning systems, some learning consists of corresponding changes to the set of reasoning rules used to conduct reasoning. In reasoners employing memory structures other than sets of reasoning rules, one finds related mechanical interpretations. For example, in kernel-based learning methods (Müller *et al.* 2001), such as support-vector machines (Burges 1998), learning corresponds to the notion of deformation that underlies much of continuum mechanics. To separate two disjoint subsets X and Y of a set Z of data points expressed using a space A of data-attribute tuples, kernel-based methods aim to construct a nonlinear mapping $\Phi : A \rightarrow A'$ from the given space A of data-attribute tuples to a space A' of higher dimensionality such that X and Y are separable by hyperplanes in the enlarged space. The nonlinear mapping is defined in terms of a kernel function. A kernel function k is a positive-definite symmetric function of pairs of points in the original data space; that is, $k(x, y) \geq 0$ and $k(x, y) = k(y, x)$ for each $x, y \in A$. Such kernels can be viewed as representing inner products in the transformed space. The Gram matrix of the full data set $Z = \{z_1, \ldots, z_n\}$ consists of the square matrix with entries $k(z_i, z_j)$. The Gram matrix has a natural interpretation in mechanics as the spatial configuration of the data points, that is, as the matrix of distances between points in Z. The process of constructing a set of distances that separates the two classes corresponds to identification of a deformation of the original configuration of the data that exhibits the desired separation of the body part inhabiting the points X from the body part inhabiting Y.

2.2.3.2 *Mental effort*

Identifying mechanical forces and masses in psychology and economics provides a new formal vocabulary for characterizing limits on rationality. In traditional settings, mechanics expresses some limitations on behavior in terms of summary measures of mass, distance, speed, and energy that characterize gross characteristics of bodies and motions without reference to the fine details. Many limitations on mechanical systems translate into limitations on these summary characteristics, providing the basis for familiar back-of-the-envelope calculations. Limitations on speed, whether maximum stable speeds of an aircraft or relativistic restrictions to the speed of light, provide lower bounds on the times needed to traverse specific distances. Mass itself limits the average speed of travel, assuming bounded forces. Limits on forces arise in turn in considering the actions of finite bodies on each other and in considering transmission of forces through limited linkages between bodies. Knowledge of the magnitudes of possible forces, or relative size of masses, thus allows one to rule out some conceivable motions as mechanically impossible.

Mechanical expressions of limits offer a similar promise in the psychological setting, with mechanical concepts of mass and force used to express limits on the speed with which agents can change mental state and direction in accommodating new information and in reasoning and deliberation. The mechanical notions of force, momentum, and work also play roles in constructing measures of psychological effort or ratiocinative complexity.

Physics textbooks use calculations of work performed or energy expended to answer a variety of questions. We find reflections of the physical notion in self-help truisms like "bigger changes require more work" that apparently concern not physical work but instead a common reckoning of effort of reasoning or will. In fact, the mechanical interpretation of reasoning provides some justification to such truisms.

For example, we can calculate the mechanical work performed in reasoning by building on the mechanical reasoning interpretation of Section 2.1.3. In the case examined earlier of pure reasoning without any learning, the formalization obtained a force $f_t = (\mathbf{0}, \ddot{x}_t)$ resulting from applying the reasons R_t according to (2.20). Applying the elementary rule that work equals force applied times distance moved, we obtain the work expended in the motion as

$$w_t = (\mathbf{0}, \ddot{x}_t \dot{x}_{t+1}). \tag{2.21}$$

This product combines acceleration at t with velocity at $t+1$ because we have defined the velocity $\dot{x}_{t+1}$ as a trailing difference in the formalization, so that acceleration at one instant acts across the same temporal interval as the velocity at the next instant. The contribution to work of the mass component of reasoning is zero. Because $\ddot{x}_t = \dot{x}_{t+1} - \dot{x}_t$, we can write the contribution to work from the spatial component of force and distance as

$$(\dot{x}_{t+1} - \dot{x}_t) \cdot \dot{x}_{t+1} = \dot{x}_{t+1} \cdot \dot{x}_{t+1} - \dot{x}_t \cdot \dot{x}_{t+1}. \tag{2.22}$$

If we now recall the meaning of the forces identified in (2.20), we see that the first term $\dot{x}_{t+1} \cdot \dot{x}_{t+1}$ represents a count of the number of changes made by the reasons operating at instant t, which is certainly one natural measure of work performed in reasoning. If we consider only motion in which the reasoner does not immediately reverse conclusions made or removals performed at the preceding step, the second term of this expression vanishes. If we do not restrict attention in this way, the measure assigns no effort to immediate changes of mind. Indeed, we shall see later that repetitive reversals correspond to inertial motion, which, as expected, does no work.

This same calculation extends to multistep reasoning episodes by summing the work performed at each instant, with the total work representing the number of changes made to spatial attributes throughout the episode.

We obtain one simple overestimate of this measure of reasoning by multiplying the number of temporal steps by the total number of spatial attributes changed across the reasoning episode. This overestimate has some similarity to time–space products sometimes used as measures of computational effort. One of the founding students of computational complexity, Juris Hartmanis, started his career as a physicist, and reports that physical analogy played an important role in his identification and study of computational measures (Hartmanis 1973). More fundamentally, bounded changes of memory in computational systems capture an essential ingredient of Turing's concept of mechanical computation.

I note in passing that the analysis of mental effort in mechanical terms takes place at a much finer level of detail than that typical in the standard theory of computational complexity, in which most of the focus rests on complexity classes defined by functional properties of fixed sets of inference rules, such as whether the time or space they require for convergence on a closed set of conclusions grows polynomially or exponentially with the number of the initial hypotheses. The focus in mechanical measures of mental work rests not on placement of some problem in the complexity hierarchy but on comparison of the fruits of particular resource allocations. Cobham's (1966) celebrated analysis of time–space trade-offs in recognizing palindromes provides an early model here. Roughly stated, Cobham proved that the lower bounds for recognizing palindromes of length n satisfies $Time(n) \cdot Space(n) = \mathcal{O}(n^2)$. Standard separation theorems of complexity theory then imply one can split the factors pretty much any way one wants, from time n and space n, with each reduction in space increasing the time needed. More prosaic forms of such trade-offs play a role in the economics of computational resource allocation in the work of Horvitz (1987) and others.

Bounded forces play a key role in artificial intelligence. Many approaches to automatic reasoning seek to exhibit psychological rationality and use explicit rules as the basis for conscious reasoning. Even though one can conceive of individual rules conditional on enormous numbers of beliefs and producing enormous numbers of changes, conscious human reasoning appears to involve only finite steps conditioned on and changing only fairly small numbers of mental attitudes. This limitation arises in part because practical reasoning rules act as a form of communication, either in the reasoner telling itself some consequences of what it knows in order to get it to change its state, or of the reasoner explaining to others how it arrived at some conclusion. This role in communication means that useful reasons must be individually intelligible. If some large change is needed, the inference must be broken down into smaller steps. This means that practical psychology places upper bounds on the size of reasons, and because reasons serve as the generators of forces in reasoning systems, practical psychology involves bounded forces operating on bodies of nonzero mass.

We also find bounded forces in other aspects of the structure of reasoners, as the dimensionality of communication channels within agents imposes limits on contact forces in ways related to the limits on communication rates developed in Shannon's (1948) information theory. Indeed, we might regard the limits on reason sizes as having a similar origin as bounds on the amount of information the reasoner can pass through its own consciousness. For example, if consciousness depends on having representations in short-term or working memory, then the size of this memory imposes the indicated limits.

2.2.3.3 Self-control

The preceding discussion of mental inertia and mental effort touched on predictions of limitations based on comparing the magnitude of force available with the magnitude of forces needed. But force has both magnitude and direction, and similar limitations can be predicted by comparing the directions of available and needed forces. In psychology, these directional questions come to the fore in analyzing the maintenance of focus of attention in the presence of competing motivations.

Section 2.1.3 identified reason forces that can combine the contributions of several reasons by additive superposition, as made explicit in (2.18). Additive superposition of forces forms the standard combination seen in physics, and is reflected in the mechanical axioms for forces. When one looks at common designs for reasoners, however, one does not usually see obvious superpositions, but instead sees a variety of methods for resolving conflicts among reasoning rules. The additive combinations of rule conclusions used here presumes that any "conflict resolution" method used by the reasoner comes into play in determining the set R_t of reasons applicable at instant t, prior to combining the conclusions of these reasons. Reasoners employing different conflict-resolution methods constitute different mental materials exhibiting different responses to stress.

Put another way, the mechanical centrality of additive superposition of forces gives rise to the common psychological notion of focus of attention. As in everyday mechanics, if one wants to move a body from here to there, one must apply forces that not only push the body in the desired direction, but that also counteract gravity or any other forces that might act during the motion to push the body so as to miss the target location. The same considerations apply in human reasoning and action, in which reasoning unrelated to achieving the goal can distract one into irrelevancies, and in which habits can cause failure through weakness of will when action is based merely on easily changed position rather than on enforced intentions. In general, work on one goal requires application of forces to counteract distractions of all sorts, whether from irrelevant reasoning rules or other habits.

To plan effective reasoning strategies, the reasoner must have some judgment about the possibility of distractions and the availability of forces able to boost itself into the right position. If there are forces that can push in directions other than the desired one, the reasoner must look to apply opposing forces in those directions. In the simple context of the reasoner formalized in Section 2.1.3, one can regard reasons as the only generator of forces, and so look to the conclusions of reasons to find those that can directly influence the desired path of reasoning. In practice, the problem is more complicated because chaining of reasoning rules requires one to consider more than the immediate influences.

One can use mechanical notions akin to elasticity to analyze habitual and refractory behavior, in which movement away from ordinary positions or pathways produces forces directed so as to restore motion to the usual pattern. Mechanical notions of force can also be used to view some equilibrium notions of economics in terms of static balance of forces and relaxed or equilibrium states of materials.

2.2.3.4 Self-consciousness

The first step in counteracting distracting events and habits is to recognize or perceive them. More generally, exercising the self-control needed to succeed in the face of limitations on available mental effort requires knowledge of one's own limitations.

As noted earlier, however, realistic agents cannot exhibit the consequential omniscience characteristic of logical rationality, so the question shifts to what knowledge about the reasoner's limitations can be available to the reasoner.

A first step toward a more realistic conception of the self-awareness underlying economic rationality is to use measures of mental effort to separate conscious self-perception from potential but unconscious self-perception. The obvious candidate is to characterize limits of rationality in terms of resource volumes, namely the sets of conclusions or degrees of rationality in action that can be achieved without exceeding specified limits on reasoning effort. For example, treatments of "feasible inference" or "obvious" inference (Davis 1981) have studied concepts such as conclusions derivable by means of a fixed or expected number of applications of inference rules, such as "all conclusions

within 40 applications of Modus Ponens to the axioms," or by means of closure with respect to a fixed set of finite inference rules that are guaranteed to
reach a definite conclusion quickly. These notions all aim to capture the automatic or habitual inference that people perform with no apparent effort or
intention.

Unfortunately, circumscribing self-awareness in terms of resource limits
does not yield very clear characterizations of the extent of a reasoner's knowledge. Instead of some simply checked criterion for feasible implications, one
instead has a complicated volume in a space of irregular topology. For illustration, consider the motion of Simon's (1981) ant on the beach or the shape of a
chess search tree as developed by a modern search algorithm. In both examples, the shape of the conclusions—the positions reached—in a fixed number
of steps may exhibit a very complex structure, depending on the environment
represented by the beach detrius or the initial chess board position.

One might seek to obtain more intelligible characterizations of the accessi-
ble volumes resulting from resource allocations by approximating the surfaces,
smoothing over the bumps and holes to achieve larger and simpler surfaces,
since the volumes themselves represent the superficial descriptions of greatest detail. If done in a principled way, for example using an appropriate machine learning method (Russell & Norvig 2002), one might regard the resulting
smoothing as an approximately correct characterization of the reasoner's conscious mental state. Unfortunately, even if one can smooth such volumetric
characterizations of limits to rationality, such characterizations do not necessarily address one other source of complexity, namely the starting set from
which conclusions proceed. Even if one finds a simple resource measure according to which the conclusions inhabit a bubble-like, easily characterizable
volume about each starting point (such as 40 applications of Modus Ponens), a
complex set of initial hypotheses or axioms that form the centers of the bubbles
can appear in a complex overall pattern. Aggregating all these bubbles into one
large volume might yield a hopelessly inaccurate approximation to the actual
volume, including many more things not in the volume than conclusions actually in the volume. One can certainly group together various shadings of
"yes" as the bubble of positive responses, and the various shadings of "no" as
the negative responses, but trying to smooth the description of these two together may yield a volume including everything, including all the shadings of
"maybe."

However, nothing guarantees that ordinary intelligence is easily intelligible. In particular, nothing guarantees the existence of approximations smooth
enough to aid understanding yet accurate enough to avoid gross misrepresentations. Though people generally seem capable of identifying and predicting
many elements of someone else's thinking, decisions and other behavior that

rely on balancing many factors against each other often prove difficult to predict with confidence, since the outcome depends on details elided by smooth approximations. Indeed, artificial intelligence experience with formalizing knowledge of practical matters has shown repeatedly the pervasiveness of special cases and exceptions, all of which prevent the capture of many subjects in a few easily comprehended and delimited axioms. Important parts of artificial intelligence treat the problem of how to capture these irregularities in regular ways, notably by using nonmonotonic logics and by following practical guidelines for their use that provide a form of approximation by exception. Some view the irregularity of knowledge as indicating the futility of some conceptions of artificial intelligence, but this fear seems as baseless as a fear that our inability to predict the weather more than a few days hence renders planning of long-term activities impossible or useless.

Even if resource-bound characterizations of inferential limitations do not serve to provide the desired self-understanding, one need not be discouraged, for other paths might lead to this goal. In particular, one can use sets of reasons both to describe the limits to reasoning and to compare degrees of rationality (Doyle 1988a, Chapter 5). Reasons serve these purposes because reasons admit natural logical and economic interpretations. The sets of conclusions derived from sets of reasons exhibit a natural equilibrium structure akin to rational equilibrium notions from market theory, and constitute direct means for characterizing the limits to rationality inherent in reasoned self-government (Doyle 1983e, 1994). In particular, reasons themselves bear a natural interpretation as expressions of preferences over agent states, such that the states derived from reasons correspond to Pareto optimal choices (Doyle 1985b), that is, selections which satisfy maximal sets of these preferences. This sort of distributed self-construction raises standard social-choice issues (Doyle & Wellman 1991) and offers possibilities for addressing reasoned state construction using the analytical tools of general equilibrium theory. In addition to expressing preferences themselves, reasons embody decisions or policies, and oftentimes may be interpreted directly as reasoning policies adopted rationally in response to economic decisions about the value of different habits of reasoning (see Doyle 1980, 1983e). Because of these close connections between reasons and rational decision making, one may view reasoned self-government as a computationally tractable (or hopefully tractable) approximation to or mechanism for rational self-government. In particular, the economic interpretation of reasons permits one to use reasoned states themselves as an accurate characterization of limits to rational reasoning.

As with attempts to characterize limits to reasoning in terms of resource-bounded inference, characterizations of degrees of rationality in terms of sets of reasons also need not always be very intelligible, again necessitating some sort of summary characterizations. But some such summaries take the form of reasons themselves, as in approaches to learning based on chunking (Laird, Newell, & Rosenbloom 1987), derivational analogy (Carbonell 1986), and explanation-based learning (Mitchell, Keller, & Kedar-Cabelli 1986).

2.3 Designing minds

Progress toward achieving the scientific aims of psychology and economics promises to aid in furthering the engineering aims of artificial intelligence and economics. Scientific progress aids most noticeably in providing methods for specifying the desired characteristics of objects or systems, methods for predicting whether specific designs will achieve the stated specifications, and knowledge that points the way to improvements to known solutions or compromises.

2.3.1 Design specifications

Rationality constitutes just one notable characteristic of humans. The economic conception of rationality abstracts from the many sources of belief and preference in the underlying psychology. Some of these underlying sources vary from person to person and from time to time, but others characterize different personalities or psychological types. The mechanical perspective offers additional insight in understanding such classifications of minds through the notion of distinct mechanical materials.

The problem at issue is that psychological engineering at present has relatively few formal concepts for specifying designs of minds. Some come from various areas of the theory of computation, such as liveness, fairness, and availability; some come from control theory, such as controllability and reachability; some come from psychology and philosophy, such as knowledge, belief, desire, intention, plan, reasoning, and memory; and some come from economics and philosophy, such as rationality and justice.

The mechanical concepts of mass, force, and the like provide an additional "new" theoretical language of terms with which to specify desired behaviors, initial conditions, and the material laws embodied in designs. One might expect conformance of system behavior with human predictions based on informal mechanical truisms to represent one of the more important uses of these concepts. Such uses aim not to facilitate predictions by the design engineer, but to improve the accuracy of predictions made by the users of the designed system.

The language of mechanical specification includes the variety of ideal materials as well as general terms like *mass* and *force*. One can expect a similar role for ideal materials in psychology and economics. Some of these might correspond to ideal types familiar in traditional mechanics. For example, one way of looking at reasons makes reasoning agents have the character of elastic materials. Other ideal types in psychology and economics will reflect instead the standard types of minds and markets studied in those fields.

People differ with respect to several underlying native mental competences, motivations, and proclivities that do not correspond to any known properties of neurons or even assemblages of neurons, but do correspond in fairly direct ways to material characterizations familiar in mechanics. Some important components of native competence find reflection in kinematic assumptions that restrict mental states to ones exhibiting certain degrees of local consistency and completeness in the same way that rigidity assumptions restrict material states to ones exhibiting certain relationships among distances between portions of bodies. Similarly, important characterizations of inherent motivations and reasoning processes, such as common human drives and variations in the deliberativeness, wantonness, and conservatism exhibited in different personality types, in turn find reflection in assumptions about the forces generated by and acting in different types of persons and their behaviors. The mechanical interpretation developed here treats personality types and more refined classifications of human character on a par with mechanical identifications of elastic, electromagnetic, and gravitational materials.

2.3.2 Predicting performance

Truesdell and Noll (1992, pp. 2–3) observe that "the aim of theoretical physics is to construct mathematical models such as to enable us, from the use of knowledge gathered in a few observations, to predict by logical processes the outcomes in many other circumstances." Although mechanics seeks to enable people to make predictions in this way, nothing in the character of mechanics ensures that making predictions must be easy. The same holds true in psychology, economics, and artificial intelligence. In each of these areas, the specific aim of theory is to substitute logic for simulation in obtaining predictions.

Traditional applications of mechanics use mechanical laws to make predictions by two means: by applying theorems that yield conclusions about future behavior from specific facts about past and present behavior, and by detailed numerical calculation or simulation of behavior. In practice, scientists and engineers address most problems of prediction with numerical calculation, sometimes because of ignorance of or impatience with theoretical conclusions, but more commonly because theoretical methods do not seem to provide a solution. In fact, people often turn to simulation because not all predictions prove amenable to analytic solution, even in traditional mechanical applications. If one cannot predict the behavior or underlying structure of a system analytically from its axioms, at least one can try to simulate the temporal evolution and look to see what happens.

In most of science and engineering this simulation consists of solving differential equations numerically. Such simulation suffers from two main problems: numerical inaccuracy engendered by floating-point numerical computation and computational difficulty that increases with the temporal distance of the prediction from the present. The field of numerical analysis seeks to minimize the numerical inaccuracies, but even when minimized, such errors call for hesitation in believing numeric results (Truesdell 1984a). As Hamming (1962) put it, "the purpose of computing is insight, not numbers." The "arithmetic mechanics" of Donald Greenspan (Greenspan 1972; LaBudde & Greenspan 1974) represents an attempt to avoid these inaccuracies in mechanical computations, not by proving theorems, but instead by reformulating standard mechanical computations in terms of exact rational-number formulas that can be performed using roundoff-free integer operations. More recent work along these lines recasts variational techniques in discrete terms to produce accurate integration methods for dynamical systems (e.g., Wendlandt & Marsden 1997; Guo & Wu 2003).

The discrete character of much of the structure of psychological and economic behavior removes many prediction problems from the realm of applicability of traditional differential equations and numerical calculation. This does not make the notion of simulation less important. In the discrete realm of psychology, simulation amounts to application of discrete rules or transition systems, such as application of argument steps to obtain conclusions or reasoned changes of mental state. This sort of simulation is exactly that practiced in artificial intelligence and cognitive simulation, in which one writes a program to describe (rather than compute) the desired behavior and then runs the program to observe the resulting behavior (Doyle 1985a). Though different in the operations performed, symbolic or reasoned calculation corresponds directly to ordinary numerical integration, which one may view as a method for discrete simulation of continuous flows.

Mathematical development of the mechanical perspective on psychology presented in the following may lead eventually to a practice of artificial intelligence less reliant on simulation. As one illustration, the cornerstone of understanding rigid body motion is that for many purposes the shape and mass distribution of the body, however complex, are irrelevant except insofar as they determine three directions called the Euler axes and their associated principal moments of inertia. Knowledge of the conservation of these moments of inertia permits straightforward calculation of many behaviors, even if the bodily shape and mass distribution resist simple or even finite characterization. In a similar way, we may view reasons of the form considered in Section 2.1.3 as representing "invariant" properties of or integrity conditions on bodies: simple properties that must be satisfied by the body no matter how complex the rest of the configuration becomes. Knowledge of the reasons shaping the motion of a reasoner thus might permit straightforward calculation of some properties of mental states, even for infinite and incompletely understood models.

We can view reasons as invariants mainly because we regard the reasoner as satisfying constitutive kinematic conditions concerned with the stability or closure and grounding of conclusions in reasons. In a similar way, kinematic assumptions about limited logical consistency and closure might provide additional bases for efficient prediction. Such conditions have the same character as familiar mechanical assumptions about kinematic structure, such as rigidity of certain bodies or incompressibility of certain fluids.

In the short term, however, the primitive state of mathematics appropriate to psychology and economics promises to slow progress, because the ability to make powerful theoretical predictions that short circuit or simplify simulations depends critically on the power of the available mathematics to formalize and analyze the central structures under study.

Even if simulation remains the rule, one can expect mental mechanics to provide an increase in the degree of clarity and intelligibility of the designs proposed and examined by artificial intelligence. Natural sciences seeking to understand some phenomenon must work with the situation they find, but engineers of artificial systems can choose designs to facilitate prediction and analysis as well as to minimize cost or to facilitate manufacture. This ability to choose the target can render the limitations of theoretical prediction less onerous in engineering than in science.

2.3.3 Achieving efficiency

Many common conceptions of reasoning, like some clockworks and the theory of computation more generally, focus on reasoners that act in limited steps, do not proceed further without instruction, and thus exhibit velocity-dependent forces of the kind represented by (2.20) that traditional mechanics would regard as frictional. The mechanical view of reasoning need not stop with characterization of these familiar reasoning forces, but instead might continue on and look for ways of implementing reasoning that achieve greater efficiency by avoiding the frictional component $-\dot{x}_t$ in reason forces. In particular, one might investigate the design of artificial agents that, like other familiar mechanical systems, exhibit free inertial motion between application of impulsive forces. The primary investigation to date examines the notion of conservative or reversible logic systems (Fredkin & Toffoli 1982).

3

Why mechanics now?

Mechanics has enjoyed some four centuries of sustained development without producing results in psychology or economics. The mental sciences have enjoyed a couple centuries of sustained development without requiring mechanical intervention. To use the standard economic argument, if there was a connection worth pursuing, would not one have already been made?

In fact, people have made numerous attempts at connecting mechanics and mind. Although those attempts at establishing such connections have failed, there are identifiable changes in scientific circumstances that explain why a mechanical approach to psychology and economics should prove more fruitful now.

To see the reasons for the lack of successful connections in the past, this chapter examines some of the difficulties prevailing at earlier times and how they have undercut historical attempts at connecting physics and psychology. Readers wishing to proceed to mechanics proper can skip ahead to Chapter 4 or Chapter 5 without loss of understanding.

3.1 Impediments to understanding

Why have the mental sciences lagged the physical so markedly? The answer could involve social factors, such as the stimulus to physical discovery made by war and trade, but one might expect that discoveries about the mind might benefit these activities to some extent as well, as was assumed by Joseph Göbbels and is known by advertising agencies today. The answer could involve philosophical considerations, such as those regarding free will that led Herbart (1891) to deny the possibility of psychological experimentation, but these apparently seemed as unconvincing to his contemporaries as they do to many today. For deeper answers, we must look elsewhere.

3.1.1 Phenomenal complexity

Even if one deems the mind subject to laws just like those governing matter, as have many in the past century, the sheer complexity of mental phenomena poses a barrier to understanding.

It is worth recognizing that the mind, even in routine operation and behavior, seems quite exotic and complex compared to the simple mechanical systems on which traditional mechanics cut its teeth, such as flying cannon balls, falling objects, pendulums, and planets moving in space. Ballistics, for example, advanced its development by discovery that many characteristics of ballistic motion depend little on the composition of the projectile, with the motion determined to a reasonable approximation by three quantities: the weight of the projectile, and its speed and direction upon exit from the hand, sling, bow, or barrel. Though these observable properties did not suffice to determine the motion, it was not hard to identify the most common additional influences, such as gusts of wind or accidental or intended collisions with men, wildlife, or other objects, and the most obvious exceptions, such as throwing feathers or substituting balloons for the archer's arrows.

In contrast, the inscrutability of human motivations has provided the material for legend, epic, story, and novel. Even when one knows something of the motivations of a person, even when one has observed the person acting in a regular, habitual manner in the past, one cannot rule out unknown and perhaps unobservable factors influencing the person's actions that might divert him or her from what one expects on the basis of the known motivations. The best one can hope to achieve is to find explanations of the actions actually taken when these differ from the expected ones.

To find psychological or computational systems of apparent complexity similar to the simple systems of textbook physics, one must diminish aspirations to simple operations such as computing the factorial function, as does Hermann (1990), following the example of Abelson and Sussman (1985). Even the RMS (Doyle 1979), a simple device for tracking the grounded conclusions of a nonmonotonic reasoner, proves vastly more complicated than the factorial computation, even though it represents one of the simplest systems that both exhibits characteristics akin to those of the mind and admits concrete and unambiguous formalization. The unadorned RMS is in turn a pale reflection of the complexity of the human mind. One should thus expect psychological laws to be looser, behavior wilder, and discovery harder. If chaotic physics had been the rule of observable nature instead of the periphery, with most of experience more like the turbulence of rapids than the flow of smooth streams, or more like the flight of leaves in a thunderstorm than the flight of an arrow in calm weather, one can expect that physics would have been much slower to develop as well.

3.1.2 Inadequate mathematics

A lack of mathematical tools appropriate to analyzing mental phenomena has aggravated the difficulty of understanding the mind.

Recall that natural philosophy grew and flourished in concert with mathematical analysis, with the concepts of calculus invented to formalize mechanics, and with physical problems posing ever more demanding challenges to mathematical invention. Most of the mathematics that give physics its current power—differential calculus, integration techniques, power series, matrix algebra, Fourier expansions, partial differential equations, manifolds—was developed long after Newton (1687) propounded his "laws," which were informal statements that resisted mathematical formalization of any generality for many decades after their informal statement in the *Principia*. Even the familiar equation $f = ma$ was not available as a general equation of mechanics until its identification as such by Euler in 1750.

The mathematical analysis developed to understand physical systems concentrated on continuous processes, with characterizations exemplified by differential equations and continuous algebraic transformations. This wonderful body of continuous mathematics offered little help in understanding discrete processes, such as the discrete transitions between discrete states characteristic of sequential reasoning, deliberation, and modern-day digital computers. Enjoying a scientific understanding of the mind comparable with the present scientific understanding of the physical world calls for development of a body of mathematics of comparable power.

One need look no further than mechanics itself to see the direct dependence of scientific progress on mathematical progress. For long stretches, mechanics endured relative stagnation awaiting development of mathematical concepts and techniques adequate to formulating and solving the problems mechanics posed. It is not hard to see the reason why, for if one lacks mathematics adequate to make competing alternatives precise enough to distinguish them, one likely cannot test them either and so determine the appropriate course of investigation. In this way, limits on mathematical understanding have limited progress in physical thought.

To date, mathematical progress has come only because individual people have worked to gain better understandings of problems and then to communicate these understandings to others. Reliance on this developmental pathway has meant that progress in mathematics is slow and difficult. No individual can comprehend more than a small fraction of the field, so progress relies on some individual's seeking out and comprehending the right fraction needed to see the next step. No one has yet found a way of speeding up this process other than by producing more mathematicians.

If it takes Euler and the Bernoullis decades to move from Newton's informal laws to the equation $f = ma$, slow progress on developing the mathematics needed to support mental mechanics should not surprise anyone.

3.1.3 Piecemeal models

The additional initial complexity of mental phenomena noted in the preceding paragraphs compounds the inadequacy of mathematics for psychology in comparison with physics.

The mental sciences struggled first to find ways of applying existing mathematics to psychological problems, and then to invent appropriate mathematics where the existing concepts failed. These efforts toward what we can now view as a mathematical psychology produced probability theory first, followed by mathematical logics, utility theory, game theory, information theory, automata theory, denotational semantics, and various special logics including modal, dynamic, and nonmonotonic logics. The growth of mathematical tools and understanding has permitted continuing attempts to reapply concepts from other parts of mathematics, especially several classes of variational methods (see, e.g., Ackley, Hinton, & Sejnowski 1985; Hermann 1990, 1991).

Although physics has no lack of variety in theoretical concepts ranging from mechanics, to electrodynamics, to gravitation, to quantum theory and beyond, the variety seen in the history of physics is much greater than that seen today. Euler's law $f = ma$, for example, served to unify a large number of more special analyses, as did Cauchy's theory of stress. As these examples illustrate, physicists have continually sought out more comprehensive formulations of physical law, and in so doing, increase the comprehensibility of the whole field.

Mathematical psychology today continues to produce a large number of analyses of specific systems and problems, just as in the history of mathematical physics. Some of these yield mathematical formalizations of large ideas, such as ideal economic rationality. Others formalize individual ideas, such as theories of measurement (Krantz *et al.* 1971; Roberts 1979). Still others identify parametric statistical models to which one can seek to fit a set of experimental data. The pattern of these contributions to a mathematical psychology departs from the pattern seen in the history of mathematical physics mainly in a lack of connection between many of the essentially isolated analyses.

Although the theory of rational decisions provides some glue to hold together some studies involving decision making, many of the more statistical models have little to connect them to anything else besides the underlying statistical methodology. In mechanical terms, many such studies provide at best a kinematical or behavioral description of mental processes, and lack the conceptual connections provided by mechanical characterizations that relate underlying forces to behavior.

3.1.4 Simplistic models

The complexity of everyday mental phenomena has also promoted an unintended concentration in the mental sciences on systems even more idealized than those of textbook physics.

In the mental sciences, as in any field, people tend to study problems for which technical formulations already exist, rather than problems, however important, that lack adequate formalizations. For example, recurrent complaints accuse mathematical economics of adopting many assumptions about the nature of economic systems, not because these assumptions capture an obvious reality, but because the idealizations and extreme simplifications represented by the assumptions seem necessary in order to reduce the behavioral equations to mathematical forms one can solve using standard mathematical tools.

Now economics hardly stands alone in receiving such accusations. All scientific fields use idealizations and simplifications to get traction on difficult problems. The issue is how conscientiously people in the field recall that these formulations are idealizations and simplifications, and how vigorously they work to move formalizations closer to reality. Economics argues that these idealizations still yield correct predictions in many important cases, and these arguments have substantial merit, at least in some cases. The arguments nevertheless rub some observers the wrong way because economics sometimes seems to take the arguments as a license to stick with its idealizations and simplifications even when the assumptions strike most outsiders as obviously suspect.

If economics were not the queen of the mathematical mental sciences, such devotion to idealizations and simplifications might not matter much. But as the primary exemplar of the use of advanced mathematics in support of a unifying theory of behavior, this devotion might strike many observers as reason to suspect all unifying mathematical concepts as means for the mathematically sophisticated to hold reality at arm's length. Yet who but noneconomists would be prone to insist on discussing the phenomena rather than the simplification? By concentrating analysis on these tractable special cases while waiting for someone else to address the problem of developing conceptual tools for the unidealized problems, mathematical economics risks stranding itself in psychological backwaters.

3.1.5 Repugnant formalisms

Formal mathematical exploration of psychology may suffer guilt by association, for if a sound mathematical psychology must resemble mathematical economics, some might expect the wicked to stay and the righteous to flee.

Numerous sciences meet and battle on the field of psychology, which grounds the theory of personal interactions in the theory of personal action. The battles arise because not all social theories employ the same conception of psychology and human nature. Economics, of course, thinks of people as rational agents; sociology views people as nonrational rule followers; anthropology takes either view as convenient; and history tends to describe people in rational, moral, or Freudian terms.

Most of these sciences come lightly armed in mathematical terms, and fear the giant of mathematical economics, which wields strong, strange, and to some, sinister mathematics. In earlier centuries, economics bore the burden of association with human greed and utilitarianism, long despised in much of western thought; in recent times, it gained popularity by shedding this burden for a more neutral amorality, though observers differ on whether the popularity stems from an appreciation for its analytical utility or from a degradation of popular morals to the moral vacuity of modern economics. To many, no doubt, economics still represents reduction of human, social, moral, and theological values to the currency of the hustler. To many, no doubt, mathematics—especially apparently aggressively esoteric mathematics—recalls schoolroom perplexities and schoolyard bullies. One can expect such associations to foster a resistance to exploring psychology using the conceptual tools of mathematical economics. Since rapid scientific progress requires making conceptual issues formal enough to pose well-defined experiments and to perform mathematical analysis, an avoidance of mathematical studies of psychological theories may well impede the advance of thc science.

3.2 Vital analogy

Students of mind have applied one analogy after another in seeking, as people do, to make sense of their observations, attempting to use human success at reasoning in other areas as a way of understanding or reproducing human success—such as it is—at reasoning about human behavior and thinking. The years have seen attempts to understand the mind by making analogies to biology, anthropology, theology, and physics. Let us examine these in turn.

3.2.1 Biological analogy

Biological analogies have a long history. Life abounds around us, and the marvelous complexity of organisms remains unmatched by anything made by humans. People, as self-aware living beings, naturally developed biological analogies to understand the mind.

Many organisms exhibit obvious structural decomposition into distinct organs and organ systems. Organic or physiological structure thus provides a basis for several biological views of mind. Such include the now discredited cardiovascular and pulmonary pictures of mind, in which the mind pumps around thoughts or vital spirits as a sort of heart, as well as the informal organic or systemic functional theories, including various philosophical theories of mental organs (reason, perception, etc.).

Organic structure also offers support to popular neurological views of mind, in which the structure of thinking is closely identified with the structure of neurophysiological systems. Although direct correspondences between neurons and thoughts have not held up under philosophical scrutiny, modern neurophysiology has revealed areas of correspondence between identifiable structures in the brain and some common patterns of commonsense thought and action (Lakoff & Núñez 2000). Such correspondences shed some light on innate patterns of thought, but offer little help in understanding the structure of thinking shaped by experience and education. Environmental and deliberate influences on how one thinks can develop modes of cognition bearing little resemblance to the innate structures. For example, mathematicians who study complex analysis reportedly learn ways of visualizing such functions, even the simplest of which involves four ordinary dimensions.

Artificial neural networks and related formalisms provide further evidence of the essential independence of patterns of thought from neural structure. Although human brains develop common structures, standard approaches to artificial neural networks employ an essentially formless starting point unlike the innate structures of the brain. With enough patience, these artificial neural networks can be trained well enough to serve as useful solutions to some practical decision problems. Supplying "innate" structure can help speed the training process in some cases, and one can sometimes trim the resulting network to leave a more structured subnetwork providing about the same performance. But in the end, the relative independence of network performance from network structure argues that theories of neural organs have limited prospects for explaining the richness and power of educated thought.

Beyond such direct analogies to biological structure, theorists have also attempted to view the mind in terms of biological processes. Such approaches also offer some attractions, but have proven very limited in scope because, apart from an essentially economic theory of ecology, biology provides little in the way of a theory other than idealized theories of genetics and evolution.

Pursuing a genetic analogy, the field of artificial intelligence has worked out moderately successful formal computer programs describing the evolution of some types of thought in an individual agent. Methods of genetic algorithms appealing directly to theories of genetic combination provide means for generating new candidates during search, with random genetic mutation and recombination introducing a stochastic element into the search. However, most of the appeal of genetic algorithms to date stems more from the genetic analogy than to any technical contribution. Other search techniques introduce stochastic elements in more controlled and comprehensible ways than do many genetic algorithms. Many of the original genetic algorithms also relied heavily on bit-level representations of genotypes that shed little light on the structure or representation of information, despite the strong and well-known influence that representation has on the efficacy of thinking and learning. More generally, the silence of genetic analogies on the organization of thoughts and of thinking has provided little evidence of efficacy except when these systems are set to work in carefully constructed situations, as in genetic engineering and market innovation.

Numerous authors make an evolutionary analogy, viewing the operation of the mind in terms of interdependent selection processes filtering a stream of small changes in the available information. The economist Marshall (1949) used biological as well as mechanical terminology in his treatise, and viewed the notion of gradual adaptive evolution as central to economics. His successors have made serious, attractive attempts at working out the evolutionary theories of economics in formal detail. Schumpeter (1934) shared this perspective, and it has been pursued vigorously in recent years by Elster (1979) and Nelson and Winter (1982). Nelson's and Winter's approach also has something in common with that of Simon (1982), for whom learning and reasoning are best viewed as gradual adaptive search processes generally lacking long-term controls, and Minsky (1963, 1965, 1967, 1986), for whom the point of reasoning is to increase the applicability of ideas to the problems at hand.

3.2.2 *Anthropological analogy*

People socialize and accomplish many things in groups, and theories based on anthropological analogies relate mental structure and function to the organization and behavior of human groups. The most direct of these theories posits social structures in the mind, in many ways close kin to the organic structures of some biological analogies. Minsky's (1986) society of mind theory provides an example, as do earlier theories of mental functional differentiation and division of labor, especially common artificial intelligence views of the mind in terms of large software systems organized along bureaucratic lines. Earlier still, Le Bon (1895) and later theorists of "collective" minds claimed similarities between the behavior of mobs and other unorganized assemblies and the behavior of certain kinds of minds.

All aspects of human group behavior have found a role in such theories, including politics, especially the theory of conflict and group choice in society of mind theories (Doyle & Wellman 1991); economics, viewing the mind as a market in ideas and tasks; law, the common rule-guided view of much of thinking (Loui 1998); and culture, with many theories of common sense (Geertz 1983) and some tribal aspects of society of mind theories. The difficulty for some of these views has been tying them down to concrete formal interpretations adequate to making or computing predictions. Formal theories are sparse in most of the social sciences save economics, and without a precise target, most theories based on anthropological analogy depend on *ad hoc* application to specific situations.

3.2.3 *Theological analogy*

Theological analogies for understanding the mind have been proposed as well, though here some resulting theories have been even more informal than in the analogies derived from social sciences. The least distinguished theological analogies view thinking in terms of a war between good and evil, or between competing deities attempting to work their way in a person's behavior. Little distinguishes most of such portrayals from political battles between mental homunculi in a society of mind. The most fruitful theological studies have attempted to understand the characteristics of human minds by understanding and then degrading divine characteristics. The best known of these studies stem from the western monotheisms, and especially from the Judaic tradition in which God creates man as *imago Dei*, the "image" of God. Most of the early works in modal and philosophical logics began as theological studies of concepts of divine goodness, omniscience, law, and license, though these theological origins play little or no role in the modern technical sequelae. More generally, one can view any ideal theory, even one infeasible or impossible to implement in this world, as a theory of divine thought, as in Bram's (1980, 1983) game-theoretic analyses of theological issues and biblical events.

*   *   *

While biological, anthropological, and theological analogies have offered some insight, search techniques, and important modal logics, they mainly served to provide evidence for common abstractions used in understanding experience across many fields, and mainly failed to produce a science of mind exhibiting the rigor and formality of the physical sciences. The identification of common abstractions aids current work on formalizing human knowledge but must certainly count as a disappointment to the grander aspirations of scientific psychology.

3.3 Physical analogy

Some of the most technically successful analogies for understanding the mind have drawn on physics and chemistry, representing hopes that the success of those fields would rub off on the application to psychology. Other physical analogies, however, evoke the poignancy of a child's imitation of a more mature brother or sister.

3.3.1 Chemical analogy

Chemistry provides notions of atomic structures and of specific rules governing the combination of atomic structures. Thinking about the nature of thought has drawn on analogies reflecting both of these aspects of chemical theory.

Syllogisms and other logical rules have been known from ancient times, and so have interest that is independent of any chemical analogy. Nevertheless, the numerous specific qualitative and quantitative rules expressing chemical reactions have engendered additional efforts at viewing thinking in chemical terms, comparing the way in which logical rules produce specific conclusions from specific antecedents with the way in which chemical rules produce specific molecules from other molecules exhibiting specific valences. Such molecular comparisons entered into some thinking about associations, a mainstay of Enlightenment philosophers of mind and one that, in the hands of Wundt, developed into the first quantitative theories of psychophysical measurements.

The notion of chemical atoms or molecular primitives has had immense influence as an exemplar in conceptual theories. The notion of conceptual or theoretical atoms underlies many ideas in empiricism and philosophy of science, notably the ideas of Ernst Mach and the logical positivists, and more recently formed the basis of theories of conceptual primitives proposed by Schank (1982) and others.

Despite the analogical attractions of the atomic concept, none of the theories of conceptual atoms have intimated any specific connection between the chemical properties of matter and the structure of thinking. Indeed, the most interesting connection was made by Turing (1952), who originated one of the first chemical theories seeking to bridge the chemical and biological or informational levels. Turing's theory of morphogenesis has remained of fundamental importance in biochemistry, though it still leaves the chemical level itself having little implication for the mental levels.

3.3.2 Dynamical analogy

Physical analogy has included mechanical analogies to forces, energetics, and thermodynamics.

As noted earlier, dynamical analogies occur routinely in ordinary speech to describe the behavior of minds and economies, as in "It will take a lot of pressure to force him to change his position," "She felt the weight of his argument holding her back," "Falling oil prices exerted downward pressure on refinery shares today," or "Economic forces tilted the election in favor of the challenger." Tolstoy even used theoretical mechanical analogies explicitly in *War and Peace*:

At Borodino the armies meet. Neither army is destroyed, but the Russian army, immediately after the conflict, retreats as inevitably as a ball rebounds after contact with another ball flying with greater impetus to meet it. And just as inevitably (though parting with its force in the contact) the ball of the invading army is carried for a space further by the energy, not yet fully spent, within it. (Tolstoy 1869, Pt. 11, Ch. 2)

An innumerable collection of freely acting forces (and nowhere is a man freer than on the field of battle, where it is a question of life and death) influence the direction taken by a battle, and that can never be known beforehand and never corresponds with the direction of any one force.

If many forces are acting simultaneously in different directions on any body, the direction of its motion will not correspond with any one of the forces, but will always follow a middle course, the summary of them, what is expressed in mechanics by the diagonal of the parallelogram of forces. (Tolstoy 1869, Pt. 13, Ch. 7)

Secondly, it was impossible [to cut off the retreat of Napoleon's army], because to paralyze the force of inertia with which Napoleon's army was rebounding back along its track, incomparably greater forces were needed than those the Russians had at their command. (Tolstoy 1869, Pt. 14, Ch. 19)

What is the force that moves nations? (Tolstoy 1869, Epilogue, Pt. 2, Ch. 2)

Herbart (1891) made much of the forces conflicting concepts exert on each other, and devised a numerical scheme for calculating the magnitudes of these forces. He gave no formal mechanical basis within which to interpret these quantities—no bodies, no space, no motions—so the entire scheme moved only slightly away from mere suggestive analogy toward a quantitative theory of strength of belief. Subsequent psychologists dropped the mechanical conceptualization but modified the numerical schemes into theories of psychophysical measurement that formed the basis for the emerging experimental psychology: an outcome of no little irony, seeing how Herbart explicitly denied the very possibility of psychological experimentation.

A century later, Shand also used an explicit mechanical terminology of forces and characteristic properties in discussing motivation, emotion, and character.

The processes of perception and thought, of feeling and will, have been detached from the forces of character at their base. We have what purports to be a science of these processes; while that which alone directs and organises them is left out of account as if it had no importance. Yet we find in the text-books a small and subordinate place allotted to the emotions which, rightly conceived, are among these forces; but too often, as William James complained in his time, they are treated in such a way as to deprive them of the living interest which they have in the drama and the novel.

If we are to have a complete science of the mind, this will include a science of character as the most important part of it; and if we are to make any approach to such a science, it would seem that we must begin by a study of the fundamental emotions and of the instincts connected with them. But we have to conceive of the problem as essentially dynamical. The emotions are forces, and we have to study them as such. (Shand 1920, p. 1)

We have then first to investigate the forces at the base of character, and the part they play in the general economy of mind.

The solution of this problem presupposes that we can profitably study the emotions dynamically, and that for this purpose we can sufficiently isolate them from one another and from the character as a whole. . . . In a strict sense we can never isolate the emotions. Each is bound up with others. Each subsists and works in a mental environment in which it is liable to be interfered with by the rest. Nor do these forces keep themselves, like human beings in the social environment, always distinct. On the contrary, they frequently become blended together, and often what we feel is a confused emotion which we cannot identify. (Shand 1920, p. 2)

Shand provided no formalism comparable to standard mechanics or to Herbart's quantification of forces, but presented detailed discussions of the roles different emotions and sentiments play in generating forces. Each of these emotions generated characteristic dynamics, in his view, acting to increase the order exhibited in mental states.

We also find dynamical analogies provided in more recent works. For example, Burges and Schölkopf sketch the following mechanical interpretation of the Lagrangian optimization methods used in support-vector machine methods to construct the separating Gram matrix in terms of a set of "support vectors" drawn from the data set.

The structure of the optimization problem closely resembles those that typically arise in Lagrange's formulation of mechanics. (Schölkopf 2000, p. 8)

If we assume that each support vector $\bar{s}_j$ exerts a perpendicular force of size α_i and sign y_i on a solid plane sheet lying across the hyperplane $\bar{\Psi} \cdot \bar{x} + b = (k_0 + k_1)/2$, then the solution satisfies the requirements of mechanical stability. At the solution, the α_j can be shown to satisfy $\sum_{j=1}^{N_S} \alpha_j y_j = 0$, which translates into the forces on the sheet summing to zero; and Equation (4) implies that the torques also sum to zero. (Burges & Schölkopf 1997, p. 377)

As we shall see, similarity to Lagrangian formulations of mechanics has less import than one might think. Nevertheless, the suggestion illustrates that opportunities for mechanical analysis of mental phenomena are not hard to find.

I digress briefly before proceeding to point out some potentially misleading mathematical terminology. The word *dynamics* comes from δύναμη, the Greek word for force, and the discussion in this book attempts to use it primarily in connection with the notion of force. In mathematics, however, the term *dynamical system* today refers to a conceptual method for describing differential equations. Dynamical systems in mathematics have no connection with force or other physical content, any more than general differential equations do. Dynamical systems serve only as a useful framework for describing any sort of mathematical function, whether it be the orbit of the Moon, the multiplication of bacteria in vitro, or the growth of the number of prime factors of integers. Indeed, as Rubel's (1981) universal differential equation suggests, even a single differential equation might satisfy almost every purpose. The recent claim of van Gelder (1998) that the mind is a dynamical system thus means little more than the mind changes.

The primary concern of a mathematical scientific theory of mind is not the mathematical method or form used in describing the mind, but rather the content of the description. My interest in this book is to indicate the value of concepts of force and mass in analyzing the mind. Dynamical analogy thus refers to analogies to the notion of force, not to description based solely on the fact of change.

3.3.3 Energetical analogy

Psychology has produced numerous theories based on analogies to mechanical energy and to motion determined by fields of potential energy. Freud (1895) proposed an early theory involving energy flows between id, ego, and super-ego, but this theory was always purely informal and suggestive, never respectable. Similar insubstantiality appears in Zipf's (1949) work in linguistics, metaphorically connecting the structure of language to least action principles in physics. Though this work proved premature as an application of physics to language, "Zipf's Law" relating word length and word frequency in language use represents an anticipation of important notions in information theory and statistics. Lewin's (1951) topological theory of psychology cast mental dynamics in terms of potential field theory. Unfortunately, there was never any real substance to his theory: like Freud's, it relied mainly on purely suggestive terminology, but unlike Freud's, in a presentation laced with a few unsupported mathematical symbols to lend an air of mathematical rigor and meaning. The well-publicized catastrophe theory of Thom (1975) and Zeeman (1977) drew on respectable mathematical structures and represented talk by mathematicians who knew whereof they spoke mathematically, but conveyed only suggestive psychological concepts. With the mathematical structures providing no guidance to the applier, other than to choose the application so as to obtain the desired answer, catastrophe theory provided no more specifically psychological conclusions than did number theory (cf. Truesdell 1984d).

In economics, which stands on a much more extensive and fruitful mathematical basis than psychology, people have proposed both mechanical analogies and formal theories regularly for many years, to the point where Samuelson (1971) complained of the flow of such "crank" papers onto his desk. Without having seen Samuelson's crank papers, one might suspect many rely on vacuous energetic analogies. Some nonphysicists see physicists using Hamiltonian equations throughout classical and quantum mechanics, note how physicists explain these equations in terms of energy functions, infer that the notion of energy suffices to construct a physical theory, and conclude that the notion of energy therefore suffices to construct a physical theory of minds, of economies, or of what have you.

What nonphysicists (and perhaps even some physicists) do not see as clearly is that physicists' use of Hamiltonian and other energetic equations assumes one already has a detailed physical theory of how mechanics, electrodynamics, gravitation, and the like play out in the system under analysis. Physicists use these overtly physical concepts to construct Hamiltonian functions representing real or abstract notions of energy that encode all the underlying physical laws. Outsiders say "Assume a Hamiltonian" and think the rest follows for free, when in fact nothing in science comes for free; without an underlying theory justifying the construction of specific Hamiltonians, the outsiders get only an unspecified Hamiltonian to which they attribute talismanic powers.

Energetic analogies that rely only on an abstract notion of energy and variational or Hamiltonian formalisms exhibit a theoretical vacuity reflecting the physical vacuity of the underlying variational theories. One can fit almost any theory of anything into a variational theory over abstract potential functions, whether the theory is correct or not. Indeed, Feynman motivated variational theories in terms of an "unworldliness" function U, defined essentially to be the square of the difference between a conceivable system behavior and the "legal" behaviors of interest. Vacuous energetic theories lack even the suggestion of properly mechanical notions like mass and force. One encounters only potential fields and dynamical systems, general mathematical structures for describing almost any changing system as long as one can encode all the laws of the system, physical or otherwise, into the Lagrangian function (cf. Sussman & Wisdom 2001). This psychological and mechanical vacuity reduces these theories, when formal, to merely another way of writing systems of differential or difference equations. Although rewriting equations characterizing economic dynamics in terms of conjugate pairs of variables (symplectic structures) can offer computational advantages (Cass & Shell 1976), Hamiltonian methods cannot create laws where none existed. "Physical" theories of mind relying only on conceptually impoverished imitations of variational mechanical methods do little to illuminate relations between mechanics and economics, and bring disrepute upon the enterprise (Mirowski 1989).

In fact, the mechanical perspective on mind developed in the following might offer some insight into Samuelson's crank papers. It may well be that all of those papers were hopelessly flawed, justifying Samuelson's judgments of them. The ideal rational agent studied by economists lacks the important mechanical property of inertia. Inertia, as resistance to change, entails limitations on abilities that constitute some of the most obvious differences between the imaginary species *homo economicus* and the actual species *homo sapiens sapiens*. Thus looking back at discussions of mechanics by economists, one can say that Marshall (1949) was justified in his mildly apologetic use of mechanical analogies, for he talked of people. Knight (1956) was also justified in his criticism of Marshall's analogies, for Knight talked of an ideal. In both cases, the focus was properly not on purely mathematical variational methods but on the underlying properties and characteristic laws of economic systems.

3.3.4 Thermodynamical analogy

Thermal theories and theories based on statistical mechanics may have not inspired any overall psychological theories, though they regularly figure in macroeconomic reporting, as in "economic competition heats up as the economy contracts and cools as it expands." The primary formal application of these concepts has appeared in application of methods of statistical mechanics to search and learning problems in which statistical techniques serve to introduce a measure of randomizing noise into the search, noise introduced to avoid the local minima that capture and stall standard gradient-following search methods. Search algorithms, however, say little about mental organization and the structure of thinking. The behaviors of the algorithms instead derive their most important properties from those nonsearch characteristics of mind concerned with how one poses and designs the search problem.

3.4 Machine analogy

The preceding analogies to chemistry, mechanical forces, energetics, and thermodynamics represent the failures, not the successes, of physical analogy. From the perspective of the mechanical understanding of psychology and economics developed in the following chapters, one can say that failures occurred for three main reasons.

First, many of these physically inspired analogies were presented to illustrate imprecise and informal psychological theories. The analogies thus bore the complete burden of providing a formalization. Without any independent verification of the psychological plausibility of the formalizations so produced, the analogies failed to provide the desired understanding and prediction. Putting vague ideas into otherwise meaningless symbols benefits neither the vague ideas nor the pathetic symbols.

Second, some physically inspired theories lacked much in the way of psychological theories altogether. The theorist using the analogy was supposed to provide the missing laws prior to making the analogy. This constitutes science by appropriation rather than science by investigation.

Third, some attempts at physical analogy required no small suspension of belief, as they required ignoring the mismatch between the continuous models of physical behavior and the partially continuous but undeniably discrete nature of thought. No one disputes the importance of chemical dynamics and thermomechanics in baking a cake, but expressing the baker's recipe in differential equations—or even expecting such expression to convey understanding—is ludicrous.

However, if the preceding chemical, dynamic, energetic, and thermodynamic analogies represent failures of physical analogy, then computational analogy to machines, based on purely kinematical concepts akin to clockwork gears, has delivered the major success of mechanical analogy to date.

The idea of creating artificial intelligences or persons has a long history, tracing backward through the stories of Dr. Frankenstein's monster and the Golem to early Greek and Chinese automata and perhaps even the god-creation implicit in the construction of Mesopotamian idols.

The philosophers of the Enlightenment believed animals to be automata, merely complicated biological machines, but believed humans to have free souls controlling their bodies that, were the soul to depart, would exhibit only innate automatic behavior. The development of the Church–Turing theses of mechanizability of a wide range of procedures began to push back the boundary between mechanism and mind, to the point where Turing's (1950) speculations on the mechanization of thought, capping two decades of cascading conceptual and technical advances by Turing, von Neumann, Wiener, McCulloch, and others, gave rise to the modern field of artificial intelligence, typically viewed as dating from the famed Dartmouth meeting of 1956.

The decades of investigation subsequent to the Dartmouth meeting have not proven Turing's conjecture that one can reduce all intelligence to computation. Much experience suggests that many of the formal tasks one learns to do through formal education admit approximate mechanizations, with no apparent limit on how far one can improve the approximations through refining the underlying formalized knowledge and methods. Capturing all this knowledge requires much human work, even with the development of some techniques for automation of learning. In the most advanced investigations to date, the complexity of the body of mechanized knowledge makes it difficult to distinguish an automaton basing its conclusions and actions on that knowledge from a human performer, at least as long as one restricts the attempts to distinguish the two to viewing task performance in isolation, forbidding free-ranging questioning of the sort envisaged by Turing (1950) in his imitation game. No technical advance has yet resolved the fundamental questions posed by Turing's conjecture. Some argue we will replicate human intelligence by formalizing commonsense knowledge and reasoning and adding in vast stores of specific expertise; others object that common sense and consciousness require something beyond Turing's notion of mechanical computation, be it some form of hypercomputation (Copeland 2002) or even esoteric physical notions like quantum gravity (Penrose 1989).

3.4.1 Examples and exceptions

Whether or not one can automate thinking, and regardless of the technological value of artificial intelligence systems, modern automata theory has provided mathematical tools for analyzing and understanding far more complex kinematic mechanisms than ever before conceived. Work on artificial intelligence has exploited this capability to produce precise formal models of thinking far more concrete and complex than any prior psychological system. These models capture at least some aspects of human thought. Sometimes the models capture only superficial aspects, and sometimes not. In either case, the models do something to aid psychological analysis by providing a serviceable toehold for the mathematical analysis of thinking. In particular, many of the computational models embody structural hypotheses that serve as complements and alternatives to statistical models developed in mathematical psychology.

Development of such models changes the landscape of psychological investigation. Making precise mathematical models of vagueness and nonsense hardly seems worth the effort, but without a sound theory of mental structure and behavior suitable for formalization, earlier attempts to make mathematical or mechanical theories of psychology were bound to founder. Artificial intelligence and computational cognitive simulations altered this situation by providing the large yet precise models of a number of complex psychological phenomena so conspicuously lacking in earlier efforts. It matters little whether these particular models prove correct. Their value for psychological investigation derives not from their correctness but instead from their visible structure, formal character, and amenability to experimentation. These qualities offer far easier material for technical investigation and analysis than human minds. As long as these models exhibit some plausibly mental behavior, their easier access and testability may outweigh concerns about some differences from humans.

Despite technological advances flowing from the machine analogy, one might judge the conceptual perspective of current artificial intelligence a failure. Artificial intelligence, at base, instructs one to understand thinking by viewing mental behavior as computation, whether the steps be digital or neural. On its face, this is preposterous. People demonstrate reasonable powers of understanding of human behavior, including moderate abilities to predict what they themselves and others will do. People also have little difficulty understanding plans consisting of a sequence of simple steps. These abilities notwithstanding, any introductory programming instructor can testify how students struggle to comprehend the nature of even simple computations. Even when the flow of control involves only simple sequences and loops, compositions of compositions and nontrivial mappings between intuitive concepts and the machine states identified in test steps move programs beyond easily understood levels of complexity.

Although a focus on computation certainly aids construction of useful cognitive processes in artificial intelligence, this focus does little to exploit the power of concepts that have proven useful in understanding behavior in other realms of worldly events. People use many concepts transcending the computational in understanding human behavior, viewing individuals and groups through the prism of multiple analogies and metaphors, including but not limited to the biological, anthropological, theological, and machine analogies discussed earlier. To gain added powers of understanding in psychology, we cannot rest content with only the concepts of machines. The present investigation thus seeks to move beyond the machine metaphor toward understanding thinking in mechanical terms at the level of intentional or rational agents, or, in Newell's (1982) phrase, at the *knowledge level*.

3.4.2 Machines without mechanics

Artificial intelligence seeks to use computational ideas to help explain and understand the structures of realistic psychologies and the nature of limited rationality, but the pallid kinematic picture provided by automata theory provides little help in this effort. Pursuing a richer conception of the mechanical analogy requires facing up to two central problems: developing a mechanics appropriate to both continuous and discrete motion, and transferring mechanical concepts of force and mass to the mental realm.

As noted earlier, some attempts to bring the mind under the analysis of physical law have foundered on the apparent discreteness exhibited by reasoning and deliberation. Most of the success of physical theory relies on mathematics developed for the analysis of smooth motions, mathematics inapplicable, at least in direct approaches, to analysis of discrete thought. The superficial discreteness of mind might, of course, prove illusory, with physiological theories of neural function providing smooth mechanisms for mental operation. Even supposing such a theory to hold, however, neurophysiological smoothness seems to miss the point, as the existence of discontinuous phenomena, in both ordinary physics and in the mental realm, requires a theory at the discrete level. Some of the apparent constraints on behavior relate to constraints between the discrete states of reasoning, not on any constraints visible in microscopic smooth motion between the discrete states. Little compares with the change one observes as one makes a decision and then finds the need to defend it, fixing the decision in an essentially discrete operation. Indeed, the need for a discrete theory arises in many mechanical situations. Consider the pendulum clock. Its pendulum provides a literal textbook example of smooth motion, while its discrete gear motions provide prime examples of discrete motion. No wonder some automata derived from the clockmakers.

Recent work on hybrid system models has provided mathematical tools for describing systems exhibiting both discrete and continuous behaviors (Alur *et al.* 1993; Branicky 1995; Davoren 1998). The simplest such models characterize the system motion in terms of the product of a finite automaton and a space of smooth motions. Each state of the automaton corresponds to a different regime of smooth motion, a regime with its own acceptable operating region in the continuous portion of the state space. Smooth motions that move outside the acceptable region trigger transitions between the discrete states and corresponding transitions between operating regimes of smooth motion. The nature of the triggering conditions and the automaton structure guide the actual discrete state transitions. The smooth motion continues under the regime imposed by the new discrete state.

The pendulum clock, for example, corresponds to a fairly trivial system in which the smooth dynamics remain the same in all discrete states, but in which movement of the pendulum to certain angles triggers transitions from one gear state to the next, with groups of these gear states representing the times displayed by the clock through its second, minute, and hour hand positions.

These hybrid models, though useful in providing conceptual tools for analyzing complex systems, do not in themselves restrict system structure or behavior in any way. The hybrid models themselves can involve any possible discrete and continuous structures, whether or not these structures appear in physical law. In particular, extant hybrid models by themselves provide no means for reconciling rather than merely juxtaposing rational psychological and economic behavior with physical law.

To date, most works in philosophy and artificial intelligence that consider hybrid models have been content to adopt the restrictions on smooth dynamics identified in standard physical theories, viewing the body as a massy electro-chemical-neural system subject to the usual laws. Indeed, many such works regard the physical system as the determining element, viewing the behavior of the mind as something akin to the behavior of the gears in the pendulum clock: mediated by the body but shaped by the arrangement of the discrete computer instructions.

3.4.3 The costs of division

Artificial intelligence has benefited greatly from the separation or isolation of the discrete level of mental behavior from the continuous level of physical behavior because this separation provides freedom to ignore the underlying physics and concentrate on studying the organization of knowledge and thought. Just as the written word permits one to understand thoughts across space and time regardless of details of lingual motions and communication media, a focus on the structure of reasoning, independent of the physical origin, representation, or maintenance of thoughts, has supported much progress in understanding how to organize thoughts into conceptual representations, how to reason about situations, decisions, and plans, and how to interpret and learn from experience.

Separating mental and physical behavior provides benefits familiar in all traditional methods of analysis, which aim to divide problems into parts that can be solved separately for later reconstitution into solutions to the original problem. Separation of the mental from the physical has not been without costs, however. Much has been written about the danger of taking the separation of levels as license to view thinkers as divorced from their bodies, which can lead to loss of correlation between what the agent thinks about the world and the way the world really is. Proper agent design seems to avoid the worst problems.

The most serious cost, however, has not been practical, but intellectual. By separating the mental from the physical, we have abandoned to the purely physical realm concepts that have proven fruitful in analyzing physical behaviors. The result has been to impoverish the mental sciences when compared with the physical sciences. Study a physical problem, and one has recourse to physics, chemistry, and biology, as well as differential equations and mathematical theorems that greatly aid in analysis and prediction. Study a mental system, and one lacks almost all of this intellectual heritage, with or without a hybrid modeling method, for the traditional conceptual tools do not apply. This puts the analysis of mental phenomena at a great disadvantage.

Reasoning about physical motions provides a case in point. People seem pretty good at predicting the motions of physical objects, at least in qualitative terms, yet we have had no way to apply this same reasoning formally to predicting or analyzing mental behaviors. Of course, mental behavior can be unpredictable in ways not commonly seen in inanimate objects, but current formal tools do not permit use of the same concepts to make predictions of the least surprising mental behaviors.

Some aspects of the modern theory of computation stem in part from a reaction against this intellectual decoupling of psychology and physics. Juris Hartmanis, one of the founders of the field, recounts his motivations in the following terms (see also Hartmanis 1973):

I loved physics for its beautifully precise laws that govern and explain the behavior of the physical world. In Shannon's work, for the first time, I saw precise quantitative laws that governed the behavior of the abstract entity of information. For an ex-physicist the idea that there could be quantitative laws governing such abstract entities as information and its transmission was surprising and immensely fascinating. Shannon had given a beautiful example of quantitative laws for information which by its nature is not directly constrained by physical laws. This raised the question whether there could be precise

quantitative laws that govern the abstract process of computing, which again was not
directly constrained by physical laws. Could there be quantitative laws that determine
for each problem how much computing effort (work) is required for its solution and
how to measure and determine it? (Hartmanis 1994, p. 38)

3.5 Appraisal

There is nothing so absurd but some philosopher has said it.
    M. T. Cicero, *De Divinatione*

Attempts to understand psychology and economics in terms of physical science have exploited many different mechanical analogies, including analogies
to forces, energetics, thermodynamics, and machines. None of these attempts
succeeded. One should not, however, tar the mechanical approach to understanding minds presented in the following chapters with the failures of these
precursors, for the present understanding rests not on analogy but on reality.

   In particular, I use mathematics to forfend the target of Cicero's pessimistic
observation. As Truesdell remarks,

There is nothing that can be said by mathematical symbols and relations which cannot
also be said by words. The converse, however, is false. Much that can be and is said
by words cannot successfully be put into equations, because it is nonsense. (Truesdell
1966, p. 35)

Turning around Truesdell's implication, I subsequently work to rehabilitate
some of the earlier physical analogies by combining mathematical concepts
of mechanics with models from artificial intelligence to show that some psychological and economic systems satisfy an appropriate reformulation of mechanical axioms. Because such psychological and economic systems satisfy
the axioms of mechanics, they *are* mechanical systems that actually have mass
and exhibit forces. One may thus apply theorems of mechanics to make predictions and to characterize behavior. Systematic application of existing theorems
requires additional progress in mathematics to provide the analytical concepts
and techniques necessary to understand the complex systems of psychology
and economics.

Part II

Reconstructing Rational Mechanics

4

What is mechanics?

The common picture of mechanics embodies many unfortunate misconceptions about the nature, scope, and structure of mechanics, with many people having the idea that mechanics consists of applying to physical systems the three axioms stated by Newton. Applying mechanics to psychology and economics requires a firmer theoretical basis than that provided by popular misconceptions. To proceed, we thus must confront and set aside mechanical misconceptions, lest the misconceptions prevent proper appreciation of the contribution mechanics makes to understanding the world. Accordingly, the present chapter examines the nature of mechanics at a high level, reconsidering the content and form of mechanical theories in light of the history of mechanical concepts and mathematical formalisms. This examination highlights the common misconceptions and how they divert one from the proper understanding needed for the following development.

Readers wishing to skip this somewhat philosophical discussion in favor of the development of the mechanical axioms themselves might proceed directly to Chapters 5 and 6, which review the structure and content of the axioms of modern rational mechanics. The modern axioms have enjoyed widespread use for decades among mathematicians studying mechanics and among mechanical engineers, although not in beginning physics textbooks. In contrast to the postulates of popular legend, the modern axioms provide a formal characterization of the notion of force, and reveal the true generality of mechanics in ways that usual textbook presentations do not.

4.1 The nature of mechanics

It might sound odd to say that some psychological and economical notions are mechanical as well, for we have been taught that physics makes the only precise uses of terms like *mass* and *force*, and that all other uses merely corrupt

71

the physical. This seeming oddity reflects an anachronism of current scientific pedagogy. Prior to Newton and Euler, speakers applied mechanical terms as widely as they do today, to both physical and nonphysical situations.

Much of the effort of the early natural philosophers went to arguing over the nature of mechanical concepts in physical situations. To some, what we call *mass* today was a *force*; to some, *force* was *energy*; and on and on. Eventually the natural philosophers discovered and propagated the fruitful identifications of the meanings of these terms that we use today. We forget that these interpretations, now so standard and taken on faith, required effort to discover, and we easily believe early-seventeenth-century physics to have originated the mechanical terms.

Newton and his contemporaries translated what they understood of the mechanical structure of nature into mathematical terms in the natural and limited mathematical languages of the day. One need not regard that translation as any more accurate or authoritative than the roughly contemporaneous translation commissioned by King James of England of Biblical Hebrew and Greek into the refined English of the day.

4.1.1 Mechanical laws

Many people have been taught a concept of mechanics based on popular legends about "the" axioms of mechanics. Many have heard that Newton propounded three axioms, and many might even remember paraphrased translations from the Latin. Readers of introductory physics texts might recall the equation $f = ma$ (force equals mass times acceleration) as the formal embodiment of mechanics, and Newton's law of universal gravitation $f = gm_1m_2/r^2$ and Maxwell's laws of electromagnetism as the primary laws of nature. Physics textbooks show how to use these equations to treat simple machines (levers, pendulums, inclines), ballistics, planetary motion, and rigid bodies (spinning tops, tumbling satellites). If one presses on, advanced textbooks show how to reexpress these basic concepts and laws in Lagrangian and Hamiltonian formalisms, and how to reformulate and revise the underlying laws themselves to fit in theories of relativistic mechanics or quantum mechanics.

Popular legends aside, Newton's axioms arguably do not deserve coronation as the proper axioms of mechanics, even though their introduction revolutionized how natural philosophers approached their subject. Newton's postulates lack any precise formal meaning, and have little to do with what modern physics reads into them. In particular, they do not state the equation $f = ma$, which was developed as a general mechanical equation by Euler and published half a century after Newton's book. Nor does this equation provide an axiomatic basis for mechanics, though it appears as an expression within one axiom among many in some modern formulations. In the present treatment, it appears in Axiom F19.

Quibbling about which axioms state the laws of mechanics, however, misses the most important question about just what it means to be a law. Though people hear about the "laws" of mechanics, the axioms of mechanics form a purely mathematical, not physical, theory. The axioms do not represent laws of anything by themselves. This may not have been Newton's view, who imitated the example of Euclid in providing axioms of mechanics extending those of geometry. At the time, prior to the discovery of non-Euclidean geometries, natural philosophers viewed geometry as a fixed subject, and viewed mechanics the same way. Today, however, we recognize that the formal theory of mechanics merely presents a mathematical theory, one neither right nor wrong on its own in the absence of specific interpretations of its concepts. Like group theory, and indeed, like the theory of ideal rationality in psychology and economics, the formal theory of mechanics is only applicable or inapplicable to systems of interest, satisfied or unsatisfied by them under specific interpretations.

If we believe that mechanics provides a useful framework for thinking about the world, then we should seek to apply it to systems of interest, and look for objects and relationships with which to interpret its terms. Mechanics relates forces, masses, motions, and energies, but leaves them abstract. To apply mechanics we must determine or decide what sorts of masses exist and where forces come from: that is, we must determine what these terms mean in the systems of interest. In this way the utility of mechanical laws in physics derives from conventional interpretations of their objects as things in the real world—physical bodies, masses, forces, and so on.

Schools today teach students physical identifications of mechanical concepts as an inseparable part of the theory, and there seems to be little confusion; masses are masses, forces are forces, and the axioms are laws. In some cases, teachers use the theory to help correct misapprehensions, explaining (as with the logician's notion of Ramsey sentences) that mass is not weight but instead the quantity that satisfies the properties of mass. Teachers might explain that most ordinary uses of these terms in language (*force of will, inertia of habit, mental energy*) are uninterpreted metaphor, legacies of license granted to poets and self-help authors. Such explanations, though true, require qualification. Although many ordinary uses of mechanical terms do exhibit the same squishy vagueness characteristic of pre-Newtonian mechanics, one can find important and sizable classes of uses that do fall under the mathematical concepts. In the following chapters I indicate how to provide formal mechanical interpretations for concepts pervasive in everyday discourse about psychology and economics. It should not be surprising if someday psychological masses, forces, and energies may become as familiar and conventional as those of physics. Students might then be taught mechanics as part of the laws of psychology, and this will be as misleading as in the case of physics.

4.1.2 Defining mechanics

Any logically sound theory [enabling logical prediction of outcomes from partial observations] is a good theory, whether or not it be derived from "ultimate" or "fundamental" truth. It is as ridiculous to deride continuum physics because it is not obtained from nuclear physics as it would be to reproach it with lack of foundation in the Bible. (Truesdell & Noll 1992, pp. 2–3)

Once we discount misrepresentations of the nature of mechanics, we appreciate more clearly the implications for psychology and economics of a point made by David Hilbert a century ago.

Standing on the post-Newtonian discoveries of non-Euclidean geometries, Hilbert emphasized that mathematical notions have no definite meaning apart from the axioms that characterize the relations of these notions to one another. In the sixth problem he gave in his famous address of 1900, he called for the axiomatization of the physical sciences, especially mechanics, probability, and statistical physics, so as to provide a clearer foundation for scientific analysis.

6. MATHEMATICAL TREATMENT OF THE AXIOMS OF PHYSICS. The investigations on the foundations of geometry suggest the problem: *To treat in the same manner, by means of axioms, those physical sciences in which mathematics plays an important part; in the first rank are the theory of probabilities and mechanics.* (Hilbert 1902, p. 418)

We recognize that we get axioms for a subject by abstracting from specific examples of known interest, and by refining the axioms after looking to see what satisfies them that should not. Once formalization of disparate examples forces the axioms to exhibit some level of abstraction or generality, we ordinarily regard additional satisfiers as new examples of that concept, not as uninvited guests.

The mechanical axioms devised by Noll (1958) to solve Hilbert's sixth problem really do seem to capture the general intuitions underlying the subject of mechanics. They identify the basic structure and interrelations of the concepts of bodies, masses, motions, and forces. The level of generality they exhibit stems directly from the variety of acknowledged mechanical systems Noll intends them to characterize. We can rejoice in discovering that these axioms also characterize important psychological and economic systems with only minor and inessential changes, changes mainly aimed at removing assumptions of continuity rather than at changing any of the directly mechanical characteristics.

Mechanics in its essence involves no notion of continuity. People informally understood motion long before mathematicians developed any formal notion of continuity. To see this, recall the difficulties Zeno revealed in trying to gain a precise understanding of continuous motion prior to the development of adequate intellectual tools, and recall that Galileo explicitly treated mechanical motion as concatenation of many small discrete changes. Indeed, much of what we call mechanical today, such as gears and clockworks, involves discrete kinematic motions intelligible quite apart from the continuous mathematics needed to understand smooth motions. Extending mechanics to discrete systems thus seems a natural enterprise, not like abandonment of some tenet essential to the identity of the subject. Force and motion constitute the central notions of mechanics. Neither of these notions necessarily involves continuity.

4.1.3 Distinguishing mechanics from mathematics

The mathematical tools used to formalize and analyze mechanics also magnify the apparent distance between traditional mechanical subjects and those of psychology and economics. Mechanics makes heavy use of vector calculus, smooth functions, linear operators, and the partial differential equations of the Lagrangian and Hamiltonian formalisms. One finds bits and pieces of such mathematics in psychology, and more in economics, in which the theory of general market equilibrium has been formulated in terms of calculus on manifolds and in Hamiltonian terms. Nevertheless, the mechanical tools that pervade traditional mechanics seem absent from most treatments of psychology and economics. This dissimilarity in the level of mathematical analysis does not provide a reliable indicator of whether a subject has mechanical nature, however.

Close examination of the content of mechanics reveals that many of the most prominent features of mathematical formulations of mechanics actually have very limited connections with the conceptual content of mechanics. Most people recognize that the calculus, for example, has no mechanical content in itself, and that it provides means for formalizing mechanical and nonmechanical subjects alike. As noted in the preceding discussion of energetical analogies, fewer people recognize that the same holds true for Euler–Lagrange equations and Hamilton's equations that supposedly represent the acme of mechanics, and of variational theories generally. The Lagrangian and Hamiltonian mathematical forms for equations were initially developed for aiding the solution of equations describing specific mechanical systems, but the equational forms themselves possess no mechanical content whatsoever. Indeed, to apply the Euler–Lagrange or Hamiltonian equations, one must first concoct (no other word fits the process so well) a function that, all by itself, encodes all the laws governing the system of interest. Even basic mechanical principles like $f = ma$ must be encoded in the Lagrangian or Hamiltonian functions or the resulting equations will not yield mechanical behaviors. In this regard, Lagrangian and Hamiltonian theories resemble the universal computational machines invented by Turing; they take as input a description of the motion or computation of interest, and then use that description to determine or carry out the motion or computation so described. Rather than representing the quintessence of mechanical law, Lagrangian and Hamiltonian formalisms represent the abandonment of all mechanical content.

4.2 The structure of modern mechanics

Mechanical laws divide into general laws governing all bodies and special laws characterizing special classes of materials or systems.

4.2.1 General laws

The general laws set forth mechanical principles applying to all types of bodies, motions, and forces. Some general laws characterize the basic notions of bodies, forces, and motions in their own right; other general laws characterize their relation to one another.

In broad terms, the axioms for bodies say that bodies exhibit a part–whole relationship with familiar properties, and that continuous bodies exhibit the structure of a manifold.

The axioms for forces say that forces may be added together, that systems of forces identify the force each body exerts on each other body, and that the sum of all forces on each body is zero. This last condition may seem strange, but really just generalizes the familiar $f = ma$ by treating an inertial force $-ma$ as just one special sort of force canceling out the sum of all the other forces on the body ($f - ma = 0$). The force laws are more general than might appear, since they apply to all bodies and parts of bodies, not merely the body points addressed in textbook mechanics.

Further general laws instead place restrictions on the relationship between forces and their possible sources. These laws state conditions on legitimate force-determination prescriptions rather than on the values taken by functions at particular points. The most common such restrictions are those of locality, determinism, and realism or frame indifference.

The locality axiom specifies that at any instant the forces acting in some localities in time and space depend only on the bodies and events in that locality. This rules out what is called *action at a distance* in the sense that distant bodies and events must cause a change in the local bodies and events in order to change the forces acting in a locality.

The determinism axiom states that the dependence of forces on histories is unique, that the history of the system leading up to some instant determines the forces acting at that instant.

The frame-indifference axiom states that forces acting at some instant do not depend on the frame of reference of any observer, although the appearance of those forces may vary with such frames of reference. This requirement is also familiar, but it is rarely stated explicitly in elementary mechanics and often goes by different names. Most people learn mechanics from books that introduce mechanical concepts and laws in particular coordinate systems—the familiar xyz coordinates of the Euclidean space $\mathbb{R}^3$, for example. Most things, however, do not come with names or numbers written on them. Except when one is describing hopes, dreams, and plans, there usually is little point in working hard to carefully describe something that does not exist. One thus expects characterizations of mechanical objects to reflect that namelessness and focus instead on the actual structural relations present among the objects. Rational mechanics does just this by introducing the concepts and laws as independent of particular coordinate systems, employing a geometric language that refers directly to the mechanical components of a system, such as points on surfaces and mass values, rather than to their representations as vectors or scalars in some system of coordinates or units. The fundamental methodological principle underlying the coordinate-free approach is called realism by Gärdenfors (1988), meaning that the theory should speak of the reality under study, not of descriptions of that reality imposed by observers. Physicists also sometimes use the term *covariance* for some ideas related to frame indifference.

The "realistic" approach also has the practical virtue of emphasizing the invariance of reality under changes of representation, giving the analyst the freedom to choose representations so as to make descriptions simple and computations easy. In theoretical reasoning, the simpler a description the easier it is to understand. Many mechanical concepts and their interrelations can be stated quite simply in coordinate-free terms, so avoiding the unnecessary complexity of description entailed by phrasing everything in terms of a particular coordinate system, and free of the need to complicate matters further by

supplying additional rules for changes of coordinates. In practical calculations, starting with the invariant structure allows us to rerepresent the structure
as desired, for each calculation choosing the coordinate system that makes that
calculation easiest. In fact, because of the relative simplicity of the invariant
descriptions, some calculations may be avoidable, with the desired results following directly from qualitative reasoning over the essential structures, without descent to computation in coordinates. Rational mechanics is replete with
powerful theorems about qualitative behavior that are independent of particular
coordinate systems (Truesdell 1958).

4.2.2 Special laws

In themselves, the general laws provide a weak basis for mechanical prediction and analysis because they make no assumptions about the properties of
specific materials. The builder's choice of reinforcing steel over bamboo, the
auto mechanic's choice of lubricating motor oil over sand, and the magician's
choice of levitating magnetic steel over wooden containers all exploit the different characteristics of different materials. Mechanics thus incorporates many
different specialized axioms characterizing the properties of special materials.
These constitutive assumptions may characterize broad classes and abstract
properties, or narrow and specific ones.

In particular, none of the most general laws say anything about *which* forces
exist, or even that *any* particular forces exist. Similarly, the most general laws
do nothing to distinguish different types of bodies, shapes, or substances. Such
statements instead come in special laws of mechanics that characterize the
behavior of special types of materials. The vast variety of materials observed
in the world all share the underlying general mechanical laws, but the casual
observer might have difficulty noticing that small patch of concord amidst the
overwhelming overall differences.

Some special laws take the form of kinematical constraints on bodies. For
example, rigid body mechanics comes from adding kinematical constraints to
the general theory, namely constraints that fix the relative distances of body
parts. Other kinematical constraints characterize the structure of solids, linkages, crystals, liquid crystals, isotropic materials, incompressible fluids, and
other mechanical materials and systems.

Special laws of *dynamogenesis*, on the other hand, characterize the origin of
forces. For example, the theory of rubber comes from augmenting mechanics
with the configuration-dependent forces characteristic of rubber, and the theory of charged particles characterizes the electromagnetic forces generated by
electromagnetic charges. More generally, Euler's laws stating the balances of

momentum and rotational momentum represent the most widely applicable of the special laws. These laws provide a place for inertial forces, special forces generated by masses that play an important role in many, but not all mechanical problems. Noll (1995) cites the motion of toothpaste out of a squeezed tube as an example showing the occasional effective irrelevance of mass to motion. Einstein's (1916) theory of general relativity extends Euler's laws to relate the spatial distribution of masses to the structure of space itself.

Other special laws constrain the form of forces without necessarily stipulating their values. Examples here include laws characterizing elastic materials and materials with fading memory.

Mechanics uses the term *constitutive assumption* to refer to the laws characterizing special materials, choosing this term because the laws reflect assumptions about the constitution of the material. Mechanical practice depends critically on these special laws. Rather than restrict attention to the basic mechanical axioms and use them to draw conclusions for each system in isolation, we create and study extensions of mechanics, each describing a class of systems of interest, each a powerful theory of a special, idealized material or of a special, separable aspect of general materials. These narrow theories not only yield qualitative understanding, but also more efficient computational methods that take advantage of the restricted nature of the materials.

For some years the most visible work in physics has been construction of theories and particle accelerators aimed at uncovering so-called fundamental laws, laws of the very small and very fast from which all other physical law is supposed to flow. Although this work has led to advances in understanding, these fundamental laws stand largely irrelevant to the special laws of mechanics because rigorous derivation of most special laws from fundamental properties of elementary particles or strings remains well beyond present theoretical capabilities (Truesdell & Toupin 1960).

4.3 A path to a general mechanics

Presenting a more general mechanics that accommodates and illuminates the mathematical structure of psychology and economics requires some reformation of the assumptions embodied in traditional mechanical formalism. Although an ultratraditionalist might view this reformation as undercutting the use of the term *mechanics* to name the result, that view makes sense only if one holds that the nature of physics was somehow set in stone at the time of Newton. A more realistic view of the history of the subject recognizes that mechanics is a living subject, not a petrified specimen or one preserved for perpetual reference. Different areas of mechanics make do with different assumptions, and our reformations, though themselves nontraditional, maintain this familiar catholicism of tradition.

The remainder of this section examines the alternative formalisms available for use as starting points in developing a more general mechanics, and it sketches the types of changes needed in carrying out the broadening of mechanical theory.

4.3.1 Formal bases for mechanics

Formalisms adequate for many mechanical calculations have existed since the time of Euler, Cauchy, and the Bernoullis, who created much of what we today call mechanics, including the familiar mechanics of elementary physics textbooks, in which $f = ma$ is complemented with Newtonian gravitation and Hooke's law of springs to solve textbook problems. Although the mathematical and physical discoveries underlying this calculational picture represent great triumphs, this approach cannot serve here, as it provides no formal characterizations of anything, only semiformal examples and solutions.

One cannot properly start the task of reforming traditional mechanics to cover the mind with the picture of mechanics propagated in freshman physics textbooks, or even most graduate physics textbooks, though to paraphrase Truesdell (1991, p. xviii), even this degraded encounter with mechanical formalism can represent a first step useful in obtaining a better understanding of the subject. Instead one must start the task by considering the axiomatic structure of mechanics. As noted earlier, we do not count Newton's postulates as comprising such an axiomatic basis, though those surely win the most votes in any determination of the popular conception of the "axioms of mechanics." It should surprise no one that most people have never seen a proper set of axioms for mechanics. It should surprise more that even most physicists have never seen a plausible set of axioms for mechanics; and surprise more still that many mechanical engineers have.

Hilbert's call to find good axiomatic bases for mechanics and other physical sciences was taken up soon thereafter by Hamel (1908), who made progress but lacked a full axiomatization of the key notion of force. The axiomatic project regarding mechanics then languished for several decades before being revived in the work of McKinsey, Suppes, and Sugar (1953a, 1953b), who took the standard physics notations and set them in a logical axiomatic form that hews closely to the numerical textbook formulations of particle mechanics. Although one can regard any consistent axiomatic foundation as better than none, this numerically framed axiomatization does not address the present needs. Adapting mechanics to psychological and economic systems requires a conceptual basis that separates central mechanical concepts as much as possible from particular numerical representations. Formulating mechanical notions directly in terms of continuous number systems, as do Suppes and his collaborators, makes adaptation of mechanics to psychology much harder by hiding mechanical essence within a sheathing of numerical accident. Truesdell (1984f) criticized this axiomatization on a variety of other grounds as well, but one need not take a stand on those criticisms to appreciate the unsuitability of the McKinsey, Suppes, and Sugar axioms to the present purposes. One might read the "synthetic mechanics" project of Burgess (1984) as an additional critique of axiomatizations like that of McKinsey, Suppes, and Sugar, although in fairness Burgess's synthetic mechanics has no mechanical content. It instead uses the language of philosophical nominalism to express the standard practice of rational mechanics as conceived by Hilbert, Truesdell, and Noll.

The first axiomatic basis suitable for both modern continuum and particle mechanics was developed in 1958 by Walter Noll and extended by Noll and others in subsequent decades (Noll 1958, 1963, 1973, 1972, 1974; Noll & Virga 1988). Through clear formulation in terms of modern mathematical concepts, these axioms distinguish many central properties of mechanical concepts from special characteristics of physical space and time, and so reduce the revisions needed to adapt the axioms to cover discrete psychological systems.

Noll focuses his axiomatic effort on obtaining the most mathematically elegant representations for standard continuum mechanics. Although this focus increases the beauty and simplicity of the development, it also incorporates more of the continuum structure than I desire. To develop axioms suitable to a general mechanics covering both physical and mental systems, I thus base my development on both Noll's works and on the exposition given by Truesdell in his introductory textbook on continuum mechanics (Truesdell 1991), and his longer survey article with Toupin (Truesdell & Toupin 1960), which provide more detail on the historical, conceptual, and axiomatic interrelations of mechanical notions.

4.3.2 Broadening the general laws

Noll's axioms characterize the nature of space-time events, the variety and interrelationships of mechanical bodies, mechanical quantities of mass, inertia, energy, and most centrally, the notion of force and the laws relating force to motion. In fact, his axioms already exhibit much of the structure needed to facilitate adaptation to psychology and economics. Abstracting away the special characteristics of the many types of physical materials, and introducing natural mathematical separations among distinct formal concepts, leaves Noll's axioms with a very general structure.

4.3.2.1 Discrete mechanics

As with all traditional treatments of mechanics, Noll's axioms embed mechanical ideas in a setting of continuous motions of continuous bodies in smooth spaces. Broadening mechanics to cover minds and markets as well as flesh and bone requires recasting the mathematical axioms of mechanics in a way that separates out assumptions about smoothness of the space in which motion takes place.

To do this, I separate Noll's axioms into those parts that rely on smoothness or continuity assumptions (or more properly, involve continua) and those parts that do not. Removing smoothness assumptions changes the formalism less than one might think, for in seeking to abstract away from the highly varied properties of physical materials and to separate notions in the most mathematically natural way, Noll's axioms already characterize many concepts in ways independent of the nature of the underlying space. For example, his theory of bodies stays away from any requirements on geometry, and assumes geometric structure only when considering specific universes of bodies. His axioms for force systems likewise characterize an algebraic structure independent of geometry, and only at the end add assumptions about how force values relate to spatial entities.

In view of this existing partial separation of continuity assumptions, I carry over all axioms independent of continuous space and time directly. The axioms that depend on the usual continuum structure of space and time I decompose into subaxioms that characterize the essential structure and sub-axioms that require continuity. I then retain all the structural axioms. My reconstruction then makes assumptions about smoothness only for the special case of ordinary physical materials and systems.

Noll (1972, p. 48) himself made first steps in this direction by indicating a generalization of his most abstract mechanical theory away from familiar physical space to the level of the abstract state spaces of general systems theory (Kalman, Falb, & Arbib 1969). Unfortunately, that generalization abandons all traces of mechanical concepts, and so provides few insights into psychology beyond those already familiar from pure dynamical systems theory and automata theory.

Mathematically, the upshot of the extension of mechanics to discrete systems comes primarily in changes in assumptions made about the algebraic structure of space, time, and motion. Traditional mechanics formalizes these structures in terms of real vector spaces, that is, continuous vector spaces over scalars in $\mathbb{R}$. Discrete mechanics first pulls back from real vector spaces to discrete vector spaces over discrete fields, such as the binary vector spaces $\mathbb{Z}_2^n$ over $\mathbb{Z}_2$. These constitute discrete algebraic structures that serve well in almost all standard mechanical roles. The requirements of hybrid mechanics call for additional changes to geometric and algebraic properties of space, described shortly.

Scientists have much familiarity in working with discrete time representations of continuous behaviors, and such prove useful here too in the form of tools for analyzing difference equations and the like. On the whole, however, the new discrete setting calls for development of additional mathematical ideas that extend traditional techniques of continuous analysis to treat the discrete correspondents.

4.3.2.2 Hybrid mechanics

The other step in broadening Noll's axioms consists of extending each of his formal theories to cover hybrid structures that combine notions of ordinary physical space and mass with additional dimensions of space and mass in much the same way that traditional control theory and the more recent hybrid system theories (Alur *et al.* 1993) extend notions of physical state with additional dimensions of abstract and possibly discrete state. Making hybrid composites of ordinary mechanical systems involves few significant changes to the mathematical form of mechanics, so the constructions stay close to traditional mechanical concepts. Indeed, we might view one of Noll's constructions, in which he takes a full Euclidean vector space to represent the exterior of a body, as a very simple instance of a hybrid mechanics (Noll 1973, p. 77).

Roughly speaking, a hybrid mechanical system exhibits a geometry obtained as the product of the geometries of the factor mechanical systems, and a space of forces obtained as the product of the force spaces of the factor systems, a hybrid time that linearizes the factor timelines, and involves hybrid bodies that act in each of the factor systems.

The product structure of space in hybrid mechanical systems requires adjustment to the mechanical characterization of space in terms of vector spaces. Although products of vector spaces over the same field of scalars are also vector spaces, hybrid mechanics in which the factor spaces are vector spaces over different fields require a different treatment. The natural scalars for such products consist of the products of the corresponding scalar fields, but fields do not retain their character under hybridization. Thus to obtain a discrete mechanics that works properly within a hybrid mechanics, we pull back a bit more from vector spaces to free modules over commutative rings of scalars, and require these modules to possess scalar-valued symmetric bilinear forms that serve the

Table 4.1. *Disposition of the axiomatic elements of traditional mechanics in the mechanics modified to cover the mind.*

Axiom Subject	Disposition
Bodies	retained
Time	retained
Space	modified
Masses	modified
Forces	modified
Energy	modified
Frame indifference	retained
Locality	specialized
Determinism	specialized

roles of inner products. Every field is a commutative ring, and every vector space is a free module. Some rings differ from fields in not possessing a notion of division. Accordingly, some free modules differ from vector spaces in not supporting some of the standard algorithms of vector algebra. This mild algebraic weakening of the geometric assumptions does not affect the underlying description of motion, but it can limit the applicability of some traditional analytic techniques.

The factor systems interact through the forces characteristic of the hybrid material, or more specifically, through the way the the product states give rise to the product forces. This formulation permits, but does not require, each factor system to contribute to the forces acting in other factor systems. Artificial intelligence provides examples in which these hybrid forces play crucial roles within the nonphysical factor spaces.

4.3.2.3 The bottom line

Table 4.1 summarizes the extent to which we carry over the standard axiomatic structure to the mechanics of mental bodies. Several of the basic axiomatic elements carry over essentially unchanged, while most others appear in forms modified to regard traditional unidimensional continuous quantities as multidimensional discrete quantities. I abandon the general requirement of determinism, but do not require indeterminism, and say little about locality in the present treatment. Even in terms of physical experience, determinism and locality rest on much shakier ground than do the deeper mechanical underpinnings. I retain them as types of special laws rather than as general laws, applicable to special systems or parts of systems rather than as necessary regulators of all bodies.

Quantum mechanics, of course, denies determinism, or perhaps more accurately, transforms it to determinism in a more abstract space. The psychological systems of interest seem at least as indeterministic as quantum theory, which perhaps lies behind Penrose's curious interest in finding explanations of consciousness in quantum gravity.

Quantum theory and general relativity both dispute locality in various ways. I see numerous reasons for doubting the necessity of locality, at least when one defines locality in terms of physical space. As with the issue of quantum determinism, one might salvage mechanical locality by redefining it in terms of more abstract spaces, but this possibility seems peripheral to most of the topics considered here.

4.3.3 Adding new special laws

Special laws play a very natural role in psychology and economics, though we expect the important special laws in those fields to differ greatly from those important in physics. A theory of a specific psychological material, such as the typical human, if such there be, or the ideal rational agent of economics need not look much like the theory of rigid bodies or the theory of ideal fluids. On the other hand, the theories of acknowledged mechanical materials do not look much like each other either. One should thus not regard similarity of superficial appearance to traditional mechanical theories as a necessary criterion of mechanical nature. Newton sought to see beyond superficial dissimilarities of everyday materials to their common underlying mechanical properties. We need not regard that effort as finished.

Mathematical economists have familiarity with the concept of special laws, having developed theories of special economic types including n-person games, deterministic games, markets with a continuum of agents, and agents with convex preferences.

Psychologists may find special laws less familiar, partly because of the lack of mathematical formulations of theories, and partly because of an excessive focus on finding "the" theory of human psychology. We do not assume humans exhibit any unexceptional psychological uniformity, but even if they did, the complexity of human nature makes it worthwhile to develop special theories of special aspects of human mental structure and behavior, in order to speed the discovery of the actual combination characterizing people. Without the assumption of uniformity of people, we expect benefits from studying theories of special classes of people.

Artificial intelligence provides examples of such an approach, wherein a variety of different organizations or architectures for agents and for representing knowledge have been proposed and studied. Each of these organizations may have provable qualitative behaviors and efficiencies. To choose an organization, the designer would compare the results of such specialized analyses.

The monograph (Doyle 1983e) illustrates this approach, analyzing the structure of agents constructed from a number of sorts of special reason-based psychological materials. Here also, special theories of special aspects allow the designer to combine different decisions about the different aspects and have some understanding of the properties of the resulting system. In this instance, the special theories of agent and representation types describe the toolkit of materials available to the psychological engineer, just as the variety of special theories of physical materials describe the factors available to the mechanical engineer. As with all engineering disciplines, psychological engineering requires a keen sense of the limits of the possibilities and an ample helping of designer's wisdom.

I offer laws concerning the genesis of forces mainly for the special sort of materials I called reasons in Section 2.1.3, and say little about the sources of forces more generally. Chapter 11 presents details of the main interpretation, in which the reasoner or agent constitutes a body, the conclusions of reasoning constitute the position or shape of the body, the base set of reasons constitutes the mass of the agent, and changes to these base reasons represent components of forces, the other components consisting of changes to the signals or reports of changes that represent velocities. The difficulty of changing mental states is then reflected in limits on forces and the accumulation in momentum, principally through the accumulation of mass.

I believe it is significant that Noll classifies Euler's laws as special rather than general laws, since this makes it clear that physical mass need not always play a role in mental motion, and that mental mass need not always play a role in physical motion. Nothing in the treatment given here forbids forces from being determined by nonphysical laws, whether psychological law, the economic law of acting to maximize expected utility, or for that matter, some sort of theological law.

Psychologists have sought to classify fundamental human motivations (Bolles 1975). If such classes of motivations have any reality, they should make possible definitions of classes of special psychological materials and the psychological forces associated with these materials.

4.4 Organization of the exposition

In each part of Chapters 5 and 6, I first repeat axioms that characterize traditional mechanical foundations, and then develop modified axioms covering hybrid mechanical systems that couple traditional physical systems with discrete mental systems.

Not everyone likes axiomatics. Many just want to see the results, and the same person can seek to consider axioms at some times and to avoid axioms at other times. Thus even though articulation and examination of axioms characterizing mechanics forms a part of our investigation, a part necessary to appreciate the similarities and differences of mechanical concepts in traditional physics and psychology and economics, I attempt to satisfy everyone by prefacing each bit of axiomatic development with a summary of the development and of its upshot.

Overall, and in many details, the organization of my presentation borrows heavily from those of Noll (1972) and Truesdell (1991), which one should regard both as a testimony to their insight and a tribute to how close rigorous development of traditional mechanical concepts brings one to the broader mechanics we seek.

The modified axioms developed here need not represent the best possible formulation. I explain reasons why the particular form of my modifications seem attractive, but further investigations might well reveal better means to the same end.

5

Kinematics

Mechanics traditionally divides into kinematics, which studies bodies and their motions across space and time, and dynamics, which studies mass, force, energy, and the shaping of motions by forces. I treat kinematics in this chapter, and dynamics in the next.

Traditional kinematics axiomatizes a hierarchy of continuous and discrete bodies, a continuum of temporal instants, and a three-dimensional affine space of locations. It states general axioms that assume little about the specific structure of the world.

The part of the subsequent formalization that concerns hybrid mechanics assumes a set of mechanical systems indexed by indices i in an index set $\mathcal{I}$, with each factor mechanical system characterized by factor material universes $\mathcal{B}_i$, times $\mathcal{T}_i$, places $\mathcal{S}_i$, and so on for each factor mechanics. Applications of the formalization will typically take a standard mechanics as one of the factor systems, but the general axioms do not require that any factor system consists of traditional physical mechanics.

5.1 Bodies

Bodies form the objects or parts from which a world is constructed. A particular universe may contain many sorts of bodies. Mechanics treats both discrete bodies, such as the sets of point bodies familiar in analytical mechanics, and continuous bodies, such as solid rigid bodies, rods, and shells, among others (all ordinarily conceived as consisting of sets of body points).

For the time being I follow continuum mechanics in assuming that all materials persist without creation or destruction, just reshuffling into different forms. Ultimately, however, the theory should address creation, destruction, and nonrealization of bodies, and determine whether this is best formulated in terms of realized forms rather than changing materials.

Even though the subject in this chapter is mainly traditional physical systems, I look to the following development and add agents, organizations, subagents, suborganizations, and others to this list. These classes of bodies may overlap. I use either of the terms *body* and *agent* as convenient. At first, *body* will be most appropriate. Once I assume enough psychological structure, *agent* can replace it as the usual term.

To summarize this section, I recapitulate Noll's (1972) axioms for bodies. These axioms characterize *material universes* of bodies and their parts. A material universe consists of a set $\mathcal{B}$ of *bodies* together with a *subbody* or part-of relation $\precsim$ on $\mathcal{B} \times \mathcal{B}$. We read $\mathcal{B} \precsim \mathcal{C}$ as saying that $\mathcal{B}$ is a (possibly improper) subbody or part of $\mathcal{C}$. Six axioms—stating antisymmetry and transitivity of the subbody relation, the existence of greatest and least bodies, the existence of a unique exterior $\mathcal{B}^e$ of each body $\mathcal{B} \in \mathcal{B}$, the separateness of body parts from the body exterior, and the existence of meets—characterize the material universe, and together imply that the material universe forms a Boolean lattice. I will follow almost all treatments of mechanics and assume for simplicity that each body consists of a set of *body points*. Bodies consisting of single points can represent the point masses of analytical mechanics. Bodies consisting of continua of points of different dimensions represent the bodies studied in continuum mechanics. The assumption that bodies consist of sets implies the material universe forms a Boolean lattice or field of sets.

The notion of body changes least when moving from traditional to discrete and hybrid mechanical systems. Indeed, the only changes noted here involve speculations about the possible desirability of new structures for bodies that reflect self-referential or self-inclusive representations in psychology.

5.1.1 Universes

In each world, all bodies fit together in a mathematical structure called a *Boolean lattice*. The set $\mathcal{B}$ of all bodies constitutes the *universe*, also known as the material universe in rational mechanics. In each branch of mechanics, computation, psychology, or economics, one begins the specification of a system by specifying a universe.

For example, the most familiar classical mechanics typically assumes a universe of bodies in which each body consists of a set of independent point bodies or extended rigid bodies. Continuum mechanics considers richer universes in which individual bodies form rods, shells, solids, fluids, and other extended structures. One can regard economics as considering bodies much like those of classical mechanics, in which individual economic agents form the point bodies and organizations or economies form larger bodies constructed by aggregating the point bodies. Psychology makes room for richer structures in which minds form bodies that themselves include substructures corresponding to different types of memory or even mental subagencies, as in Minsky's (1986) society of mind model.

5.1.1.1 Ordering

The *part* relation forms the fundamental relation (other than identity) between bodies. I write $B \overset{B}{\precsim} C$ to mean that a body B is a part of body C. I ordinarily omit the superscript and write just $\precsim$, reverting to the more explicit notation only when necessary.

To characterize the body-part relation, let us adopt three axioms jointly stating that $\precsim$ partially orders the set $\mathcal{B}$, that is, for all bodies $B, C, D \in \mathcal{B}$,

Axiom B1 $B \precsim B$.

Axiom B2 *If* $B \precsim C$ *and* $C \precsim B$, *then* $B = C$.

Axiom B3 *If* $B \precsim C$ *and* $C \precsim D$, *then* $B \precsim D$.

That is, B is a part of itself; it is the largest of its subparts; and parts of parts are themselves parts.

5.1.1.2 Bounding bodies

A body $\mathcal{O} \in \mathcal{B}$ is called the *null body* iff it is a part of every body in $\mathcal{B}$, that is, if $\mathcal{O} \precsim B$ for each $B \in \mathcal{B}$. $\mathcal{B}$ need not contain such an element, but if it does, it is unique by Axiom B2.

A body $\mathcal{U} \in \mathcal{B}$ is called the *universal body* iff every body in $\mathcal{B}$ is part of it, that is, if $B \precsim \mathcal{U}$ for each $B \in \mathcal{B}$. Again, $\mathcal{B}$ need not contain such an element, but if it does, it is unique, again by Axiom B2.

If $\mathcal{B}$ does not contain a null or universal body, we may adjoin such to form

$$\overline{\mathcal{B}} = \mathcal{B} \cup \{\mathcal{O}, \mathcal{U}\}, \tag{5.1}$$

the *closed universe* corresponding to $\mathcal{B}$. We extend the partial order $\precsim$ on $\mathcal{B}$ to a partial order on $\overline{\mathcal{B}}$ in the obvious way.

Axiom B4 *For all* $B \in \overline{\mathcal{B}}$, $\mathcal{O} \precsim B \precsim \mathcal{U}$.

Thus if $B \precsim \mathcal{O}$, then $B = \mathcal{O}$, and if $\mathcal{U} \precsim B$, then $B = \mathcal{U}$. Clearly, $\overline{\mathcal{B}}$ is thus partially ordered by $\precsim$, with null body $\mathcal{O}$ and universal body $\mathcal{U}$, and for each

$\mathcal{B} \in \overline{\mathcal{B}}$,

$$\mathcal{B} \sqcap \mathcal{O} = \mathcal{O} \qquad (5.2)$$

$$\mathcal{B} \sqcup \mathcal{O} = \mathcal{B} \qquad (5.3)$$

$$\mathcal{B} \sqcap \mathcal{U} = \mathcal{B} \qquad (5.4)$$

$$\mathcal{B} \sqcup \mathcal{U} = \mathcal{U}. \qquad (5.5)$$

Thus each two bodies $\mathcal{B}$ and $\mathcal{C}$ in $\overline{\mathcal{B}}$ have at least one common part, namely $\mathcal{O}$.

5.1.1.3 Separation

If the null body is the only common part of $\mathcal{B}$ and $\mathcal{C}$, we say these bodies are *separate*. Thus $\mathcal{B}$ and $\mathcal{C}$ are separate iff

$$\mathcal{B} \sqcap \mathcal{C} = \mathcal{O}. \qquad (5.6)$$

We say that a body $\mathcal{B}$ is *atomic* if it has no proper parts, that is, if $\mathcal{A} \precsim \mathcal{B}$ implies $\mathcal{A} = \mathcal{O}$ or $\mathcal{A} = \mathcal{B}$.

We wish to speak not only of a body in a universe, but of everything else as well, that is, of the body's *environment* or *exterior*. We assume that each body has an environment, and that all environments are themselves bodies.

Axiom B5 *For each $\mathcal{B} \in \overline{\mathcal{B}}$, there exists a unique body $\mathcal{B}^e$, called the* exterior *of $\mathcal{B}$, such that $\mathcal{B} \sqcap \mathcal{B}^e = \mathcal{O}$, $\mathcal{B} \sqcup \mathcal{B}^e = \mathcal{U}$, and if $\mathcal{C} \sqcap \mathcal{B}^e = \mathcal{O}$, then $\mathcal{C} \precsim \mathcal{B}$.*

Thus $\mathcal{B}^e$ is separate from $\mathcal{B}$, only $\mathcal{U}$ contains them both, and the only bodies separate from $\mathcal{B}^e$ are the parts of $\mathcal{B}$. It is easy to see that

$$\mathcal{O}^e = \mathcal{U} \qquad (5.7)$$

$$\mathcal{U}^e = \mathcal{O} \qquad (5.8)$$

$$(\mathcal{B}^e)^e = \mathcal{B}. \qquad (5.9)$$

5.1.1.4 Overlap

A body $\mathcal{D}$ containing both bodies $\mathcal{B}$ and $\mathcal{C}$ is called an *envelope* of $\mathcal{B}$ and $\mathcal{C}$. If some envelope $\mathcal{A}$ is part of every envelope of $\mathcal{B}$ and $\mathcal{C}$, then it is called the *join* of $\mathcal{B}$ and $\mathcal{C}$, written

$$\mathcal{A} = \mathcal{B} \sqcup \mathcal{C}. \qquad (5.10)$$

That is, $\mathcal{A} = \mathcal{B} \sqcup \mathcal{C}$ if $\mathcal{A} \precsim \mathcal{D}$ whenever $\mathcal{B} \precsim \mathcal{A}, \mathcal{C} \precsim \mathcal{A}, \mathcal{B} \precsim \mathcal{D}$, and $\mathcal{C} \precsim \mathcal{D}$. Dually, the greatest common part of $\mathcal{B}$ and $\mathcal{C}$, if one exists, is called the *meet* of $\mathcal{B}$ and $\mathcal{C}$, and written

$$\mathcal{A} = \mathcal{B} \sqcap \mathcal{C}. \qquad (5.11)$$

That is, $\mathcal{A} = \mathcal{B} \sqcap \mathcal{C}$ if $\mathcal{D} \precsim \mathcal{A}$ whenever $\mathcal{A} \precsim \mathcal{B}, \mathcal{A} \precsim \mathcal{C}, \mathcal{D} \precsim \mathcal{B}$, and $\mathcal{D} \precsim \mathcal{C}$.

The next axiom asserts that the pairwise lower bounds represented by meets always exist.

Axiom B6 *For each* $\mathcal{B}, \mathcal{C} \in \overline{\mathcal{B}}$, $\mathcal{B} \sqcap \mathcal{C} \in \overline{\mathcal{B}}$.

It follows that all joins exist as well because $\mathcal{B} \sqcup \mathcal{C} = (\mathcal{B}^e \sqcap \mathcal{C}^e)^e$.

Though by induction Axiom B6 implies that meets and joins exist for any finite collection of bodies, it does not imply that infinite collections of bodies also have lower and upper bounds.

5.1.1.5 Subuniverses

When a subset of a universe and a restriction of the part relation to this subset satisfies the axioms for universes, we call it a *subuniverse*. For example, if $\mathcal{B} \in \overline{\mathcal{B}}$, the set

$$\overline{\mathcal{B}} \upharpoonright \mathcal{B} = \{\mathcal{A} \in \overline{\mathcal{B}} \mid \mathcal{A} \precsim \mathcal{B}\} \tag{5.12}$$

of all parts of $\mathcal{B}$ forms a subuniverse with universal body $\mathcal{B}$; more generally, if $\mathcal{A} \precsim \mathcal{B}$, then the set

$$\overline{\mathcal{B}} \upharpoonright [\mathcal{A}, \mathcal{B}] = \{\mathcal{C} \in \overline{\mathcal{B}} \mid \mathcal{A} \precsim \mathcal{C} \precsim \mathcal{B}\} \tag{5.13}$$

of all bodies $\mathcal{C}$ such that $\mathcal{A} \precsim \mathcal{C} \precsim \mathcal{B}$ forms a subuniverse with null body $\mathcal{A}$ and universal body $\mathcal{B}$.

5.1.1.6 Substructure

With the structure for universes given by these axioms, bodies may always be represented as sets of *body points*, indeed, as subsets of a set $\mathcal{U}$ of points chosen to represent the universal body $\mathcal{U}$. In finite universes, one can choose the set of body points so that the material universe is isomorphic the powerset of the set of body points, but nothing forces this interpretation. Let us simplify the problems of formalizing mechanics in the following development by always taking bodies to be sets of body points.

Assumption B7 *Each* $\mathcal{B} \in \overline{\mathcal{B}}$ *is a set, so that* $\mathcal{U} = \mathcal{U}$, *and for each* $\mathcal{B}, \mathcal{C} \in \overline{\mathcal{B}}$, $\mathcal{C} \precsim \mathcal{B}$ *iff* $\mathcal{C} \subseteq \mathcal{B}$.

Given this assumption, the closed universe $\overline{\mathcal{B}} \subset \mathcal{P}(\mathcal{U})$ is a Boolean sublattice of $\mathcal{P}(\mathcal{U})$. It is common to represent the null body $\mathcal{O}$ by the empty set of points $\emptyset$, but mechanics admits inclusion in every body of some fixed subset of points, with this subset representing the points comprising the null body.

In fact, let us assume further that body points support a topological structure giving bodies a natural topological structure. A topology $(\mathcal{U}, \Theta)$ consists of a set Θ of all open sets of $\mathcal{U}$. For each set $\mathcal{B} \subseteq \mathcal{U}$, we write $\overline{\mathcal{B}}$ to denote the topological closure of $\mathcal{B}$, and write int $\mathcal{B}$ to denote the interior of $\mathcal{B}$, that is, the largest open set contained in $\mathcal{B}$.

The *regularly open* sets in a topology are the sets of points $\mathcal{B} = \mathrm{int}\, \overline{\mathcal{B}}$ equal to the interior of their closures. Regularly open sets are ones that do not have any obvious omissions. In the ordinary topology of the Euclidean plane, for example, an open disk with one interior point removed is not regularly open, because the interior of its closure would contain the missing interior point. In the discrete topology over a finite set of body points, every set is regularly open because the discrete topology makes every set its own interior and its own closure.

In the following, let us assume that $\overline{\mathcal{B}}$ consists of regularly open sets.

Assumption B8 *There exists a topology $(\mathcal{U}, \Theta)$ on the universal set $\mathcal{U}$ of body points such that each body in $\overline{\mathcal{B}}$ consists of a regularly open set in Θ.*

In this setting, exteriors are interiors of complements, that is, $\mathcal{B}^e = \mathrm{int}\, (\mathcal{U} \setminus \mathcal{B})$, and finite meets are just intersections. Meets of larger collections $\mathcal{B}_k$ are interiors of closures of intersections, that is,

$$\sqcap_k \mathcal{B}_k = \mathrm{int} \, \overline{\bigcap_k \mathcal{B}_k}. \tag{5.14}$$

The join of any collection $\mathcal{B}_k$ of bodies is the regularization of the union, that is

$$\sqcup_k \mathcal{B}_k = \mathrm{int} \, \overline{\bigcup_k \mathcal{B}_k}. \tag{5.15}$$

5.1.1.7 Examples

The first class of examples employs the set conception of bodies most thoroughly. Let $\overline{\mathcal{B}} = \mathcal{P}(\mathcal{U})$, and let $\mathcal{A} \precsim \mathcal{B}$ mean $\mathcal{A} \subseteq \mathcal{B}$. As is well known, this universe is a Boolean lattice with

$$\mathcal{A} \sqcap \mathcal{B} \;=\; \mathcal{A} \cap \mathcal{B} \tag{5.16}$$

$$\mathcal{A} \sqcup \mathcal{B} \;=\; \mathcal{A} \cup \mathcal{B} \tag{5.17}$$

$$\mathcal{A}^e \;=\; \mathcal{U} - \mathcal{A} \tag{5.18}$$

$$\mathcal{O} \;=\; \emptyset. \tag{5.19}$$

When $\mathcal{U}$ carries the discrete topology, every set is regularly open.

When $\mathcal{U}$ is a finite set

$$\mathcal{U} = \{X_1, \ldots, X_n\}, \tag{5.20}$$

this provides the universe for classical analytical dynamics, where the bodies $\{X_i\}$ are called *particles* or *mass-points*. However, $\mathcal{B}$ contains other bodies as well, for example, $\{X_i, X_j\}$ and $\{X_i, X_j, X_k\}$.

The single-agent or point universe forms the simplest nonvacuous example. Here

$$\mathcal{U} \;=\; \{X\} \tag{5.21}$$
$$\overline{\mathcal{B}} \;=\; \{\emptyset, \{X\}\} \tag{5.22}$$
$$\{X\}^e \;=\; \emptyset. \tag{5.23}$$

In this universe there is only one particle, $\{X\}$, and only one nonnull body, $\mathcal{U} = \{X\}$.

The two-point universe forms the simplest universe useful for analyzing actual systems, as it includes a body to represent the system of interest plus a body to represent the environment of the system of interest. We employ this type of universe later to analyze embodied minds in mechanical terms. In the universe based on two points X_1 and X_2, we have

$$\mathcal{U} \;=\; \{X_1, X_2\} \tag{5.24}$$
$$\overline{\mathcal{B}} \;=\; \{\emptyset, \{X_1\}, \{X_2\}, \{X_1, X_2\}\} \tag{5.25}$$
$$\{X_1\}^e \;=\; \{X_2\} \tag{5.26}$$
$$\{X_2\}^e \;=\; \{X_1\}. \tag{5.27}$$

The second class of examples steps back from using all subsets of a universal set as bodies, and instead bases the notion of body more specifically on topological concepts. One universe $\overline{\mathcal{B}}$ that satisfies all the axioms, but not Assumption B8, consists of the set of all closures of open sets in a topological space. Here exteriors are closures of complements, that is, $\mathcal{B}^e = \overline{\mathcal{U} \setminus \mathcal{B}}$, and meets are closures of intersections of interiors, that is,

$$\mathcal{A} \sqcap \mathcal{B} = \overline{\text{int}\,\mathcal{A} \cap \text{int}\,\mathcal{B}}. \tag{5.28}$$

Finite joins are merely unions, but for any collection of bodies $\mathcal{B}_k$, the join is

$$\sqcap_k \mathcal{B}_k = \overline{\bigcup_k \text{int}\,\mathcal{B}_k}. \tag{5.29}$$

Universes based on topological assumptions provide the common universes of continuum mechanics. Several restricted forms of the closed-body universe just described are also natural in continuum mechanics. For example, one may restrict attention to finite unions of closed polyhedra and closed exteriors of polyhedra in Euclidean space, to closed regular regions (those with piecewise smooth boundaries), and to sets of finite perimeter (Truesdell 1991). Closed regular regions, however, do not constitute a proper universe as they do not satisfy Axiom B6 on the existence of meets. Noll and Virga (1988) identified a suitable universe of topological sets called the *fit regions*, which are regularly open, bounded, of finite perimeter, and with negligible boundary; these do form a Boolean lattice.

These topological universes also appear in continuum economics, which studies markets over an uncountable measure space of consumers and producers (Aumann 1964; Arrow & Hahn 1971). Such universes aim to capture markets in which no single agent has any influence on prices, but in which market shares do.

5.1.2 Extensions

Neither discrete mechanics nor hybrid mechanics requires any immediate change to the axioms for bodies already presented.

Traditional mechanics already considers discrete bodies forming discrete material universes, such as the first material universes discussed in the preceding section.

Traditional mechanics also already contains within it the structure for hybrid bodies and hybrid material universes by simple reinterpretation of the notion of subuniverses discussed in Section 5.1.1.5. We obtain the bodies of a hybrid mechanics by simple combination of the bodies of the component mechanics. Each component universe of bodies $\mathcal{B}_i$ comprises a Boolean lattice, and we form the hybrid universe $\mathcal{B} = \bigoplus_i \mathcal{B}_i$ by taking the direct sum of these lattices. A standard theorem of lattice theory says that the direct sum of Boolean lattices also forms a Boolean lattice, so the hybrid universe satisfies Axioms B1, B2, B3, B4, B5, and B6.

For Boolean lattices the direct sum and direct product have the same structure, with the hybrid body $\mathcal{B}_i$ for $\mathcal{B}_i \in \mathcal{B}_i$ represented in the product by an element $\mathcal{B}'$ such that $\mathcal{B}'_i = \mathcal{B}_i$ and $\mathcal{B}'_j = \mathcal{U}_j$ for each $j \in \mathcal{I} \setminus \{i\}$, where $\mathcal{U}_j$ stands for the maximum element in $\mathcal{B}_j$. This equivalence frees us to use either notation as convenient. I typically use the sum notation in preference to the product notation for hybrid bodies because it usually makes it easier to discuss forces among bodies of different type.

The assumption that each component universe consists of a Boolean lattice of sets of point bodies permits us to view each body in the hybrid universe as a set of point bodies as well.

Although mechanics has provided both the notions of discrete and continuous bodies for centuries, and so does not require discrete mechanics to call for a new type of body, some of the structures explored in logic and computation in recent decades might point the way to interesting new categories of bodies.

The assumption that bodies consist of sets of points constitutes the most obvious candidate for revision or replacement in the standard theory. Philosophers and logicians have long studied models of self-referential statements and conscious agents that seem to call for models that contain elements referring to themselves, and so pose difficult problems for models built on standard sets. One approach to treating such problems involves using a set theory lacking the axiom of foundation (Aczel 1988). Sets in such theories need not be reducible to constructions over atomic elements alone, and so rule out Assumption B7. More significantly, bodies forming such structures could exhibit a cyclic subbody relation, and so require weakening or abandonment of Axiom B2.

Axiom B5 requiring that bodies have unique exterior bodies also constitutes a candidate for reconsideration. Prior to the identification of fit regions, continuum mechanics had to choose between working either with material universes that did not include all bodies of interest, or with material universes that included the bodies of interest even though not all such bodies had exteriors in the designated universe.

Scott's (1973, 1976) theory of functions and domains forms the basis for major elements of the theory of computation and data structures. It interprets data structures in terms of sets of pointlike information elements and partial functions over these sets, and focuses on a notion of continuity based on a domain-based approximation relation between elements and partial functions. This approximation relation gives the domain the structure of a T_0 topology. One might naturally consider this approximation relation to provide the body-part relation for bodies taking the structure of elements in such a domain. These topologies do not always support a notion of unique complements, so if motivation exists for considering bodies with such structure, one would have to abandon Axiom B5, or perhaps weaken it to only require relative complements, in which case the universe of bodies would form a *generalized Boolean lattice*.

One might also want to modify Axiom B5 for other reasons. As noted earlier, Noll's axioms for bodies build into their very structure an assumption that the set of bodies persists independently of time and motion of the bodies. This views bodies in terms of component materials rather than human-identified objects, so that destruction of a book in a shredder only destroys the form of the body, not the body itself. A more general mechanics might hew closer to human thought and permit the set of bodies to grow or shrink over time. One way of doing this might be to distinguish the set of all possible bodies from the bodies realized at a given time. The axioms above continue to serve as characterization of the set of all possible bodies, but treating the notion of realized bodies requires modification of Axiom B5 to permit the realized exterior of a realized body to change over time as bodies separate from the realized body appear and disappear.

5.2 Events

We analyze the world under inspection into a set $\mathcal{W}$ of *events*, called the *event world*. These events make up the spatiotemporal activities of classical and relativistic mechanics. Each deterministic history consists of a linearly ordered set of events involving a system of bodies. Each nondeterministic history consists of a set of contemporaneous deterministic ones.

Events may have many properties. Every event has the two properties of *place* and *time*, where and when. Other properties of events, which I treat later, include occupation by bodies and fields, and indirectly, the qualities of the occupying bodies and fields. As each event enjoys a unique combination of place and time, we may think of all other properties as fields over the space-time projection of the event world. In the following, I abuse the terminology in the standard way and identify the event world with its space-time portion, and speak separately about the other properties of events.

I develop the structure of space and time in stages. I start with geometric structures that individuate places and times and measure duration and distance. I add algebraic structure that characterizes the translational structure of space. I finish with differential structure that combines topological notions of limits with algebraic conceptions of vectors to characterize motions locally in terms of derivatives and paths on manifolds.

5.2.1 Framings

Abstractly, we regard the event world $\mathcal{W}$ as a topological space homeomorphic (at least locally) to a product $\mathcal{S} \times \mathcal{T}$ of two topological spaces, space $\mathcal{S}$ and time $\mathcal{T}$, representing places and instants. We call a homeomorphism

$$\phi : \mathcal{W} \to \mathcal{S} \times \mathcal{T} \tag{5.30}$$

a *framing* of $\mathcal{W}$, and the inverse homeomorphism

$$\phi^{-1} : \mathcal{S} \times \mathcal{T} \to \mathcal{W} \tag{5.31}$$

a *slicing* of $\mathcal{W}$ (by $\mathcal{S}$). We write $\Phi(\mathcal{W}, \mathcal{S}, \mathcal{T})$ to mean the set of all framings of $\mathcal{W}$ with $\mathcal{S}$ and $\mathcal{T}$.

Framings amount to labelings of events with names for their places and times. As these names are just names and not reality, we aim to make all statements about events themselves independent in meaning, if not in statement, of which labeling we choose. We describe this property of such statements by calling them realistic, or frame indifferent.

We also can think of each framing as corresponding to a possible observer of events. The variety of framings corresponds to the variety of possible observers.

General mechanics assumes a variety of structures for time and space, in that particular mechanical theories place restrictions on the sorts of framings with which one can interpret the event world. Continuum mechanics and relativity are the showcases for the manifold modeling of space-times. In classical continuum mechanics, for example, $\mathcal{T}$ is the Euclidean space $\mathbb{R}$ and $\mathcal{S}$ is the Euclidean space $\mathbb{R}^3$ or the spatial manifold of a constrained system. In special relativity, for example, worlds are pseudo-Riemannian manifolds with a Minkowski metric that determines whether the difference between events is spacelike, timelike, or null (lightlike). In special relativity, framings are restricted to those in which each slice of the world is spacelike, that is, in which no two distinct events in the same slice have lightlike or timelike separation (see Bressan 1978; Misner, Thorne, & Wheeler 1973; Noll 1964, 1973). In such cases, the relevant set of framings forms a proper subclass of $\Phi(\mathcal{W}, \mathcal{S}, \mathcal{T})$. Relativistic metrics and framings have been deployed in analyses of distributed computation as well (Lamport 1978).

5.2.2 Neoclassical event worlds

To simplify the introduction of discrete and hybrid mechanics, I restrict attention in the following development to *neoclassical event worlds* that involve only products of flat (Euclidean) spaces with time. One can vary the development that follows to obtain axioms for event worlds bearing the structure of curved manifolds, but I avoid that complication here. Curved space-times appear to have application to describing some geometries of reasoning in psychology, but impose unnecessary distractions when setting out the notions of psychological mechanics in the first place.

In summary, discrete mechanics makes no changes to the notions of event worlds already developed in traditional and hybrid mechanics apart from changes in the notions of time and space. In discrete mechanics time and space can form discrete sets rather than continua. Moreover, space can have more than three dimensions without necessarily being considered a hybrid space, although the algebraic structures involved can be identical. Hybrid mechanics in turn broadens the notion of place to include the possibility of additional dimensions beyond the familiar three, but still supposes that each event happens at some place, at some instant. This change in character appears in the formalism mainly in a change of the algebraic composition and character of event worlds.

I develop the structures for time and space separately before considering the detailed space-time structure of the event world. Discrete time has much familiarity from automata theory, discrete event systems, and discrete dynamics, and difference equations. Discrete space has less familiarity in mechanics, being mainly a concern of automata and coding theory.

5.3 Time

The notion of time enters modern physics as one component of the more general notion of space-time. In the traditional conception, time consists of a linearly ordered continuum $\mathcal{T}$ of *times* or *instants* along with a temporal metric or measure of duration.

I begin this section by summarizing Noll's formalization of the traditional conception, but then progress to consider modified formalizations that permit discrete and hybrid conceptions of time.

5.3.1 Continuous metric time

Noll's (1973) standard axiomatization of time adds to the event world a *time-lapse* function $\hat{t} : \mathcal{W} \times \mathcal{W} \to \mathbb{R}$ giving the duration of the temporal interval between events, where $\hat{t}(e, e') > 0$ means e occurs before e'. Three axioms characterize this function as antisymmetric under time reversal, additive for intervals sharing a common event endpoint, and reflecting a continuum of events and times. We state these formally as follows.

Axiom T1 $\hat{t}(e, e') = -\hat{t}(e', e)$ *for each* $e, e' \in \mathcal{W}$.

The second metric axiom characterizes time lapse as additive for intervals sharing a common endpoint, or formally

Axiom T2 $\hat{t}(e, e') + \hat{t}(e', e'') = \hat{t}(e, e'')$ *for each* $e, e', e'' \in \mathcal{W}$.

Axiom T3 *For each* $e \in \mathcal{W}$ *and every* $t \in \mathbb{R}$, *there exists an event* $e'' \in \mathcal{W}$ *such that* $\hat{t}(e, e') = t$.

Axiom T3 implies that time forms a continuum with the usual topology representing the standard notion of an unbroken progression of instants. Axioms T1 and T2 imply that the absolute value $|\hat{t}|$ of the time-lapse function forms a Euclidean metric on $\mathcal{W}$.

The time-lapse function $\hat{t}$ induces on $\mathcal{W}$ an equivalence relation $\approx_{\mathcal{W},\hat{t}}$ of *simultaneity* on $\mathcal{W}$. When the context permits, we drop the subscripts and write $e \approx e'$ to mean that events e and e' are simultaneous. The simultaneity relation in turn induces a partition $\Gamma[\approx]$, normally abbreviated Γ, of $\mathcal{W}$ into sets of simultaneous events, or instants. Intuitively, each instant consists of events corresponding to all the locations in space at that instant. Mechanics typically assumes each instant looks just like the others.

We write $\tau(e)$ to mean the equivalence class containing e, that is, $\tau(e) = \{e' \in \mathcal{W} \mid e \approx e'\}$. Thus $\tau(e)$ is the instant containing e, so that $\tau(e) = \tau \in \Gamma$ iff $e \in \tau$.

One obtains a time-lapse function $\bar{t} : \Gamma \times \Gamma \to \mathbb{R}$ over instants from $\hat{t}$ and Γ in the obvious way, defining $\bar{t}$ so that $\bar{t}(\tau(e), \tau(e')) = \hat{t}(e, e')$ for all events $e, e' \in \mathcal{W}$, and hence for all instants. Combining this definition with Axiom T1 and Axiom T2, we see that $\bar{t}(\tau, \tau') = -\bar{t}(\tau', \tau)$ and $\bar{t}(\tau, \tau') + \bar{t}(\tau', \tau'') = \bar{t}(\tau, \tau'')$ for each $\tau, \tau', \tau'' \in \Gamma$, and that $\bar{t}(\tau, \tau') = 0$ iff $\tau = \tau'$. The absolute value of $\bar{t}$ thus constitutes a Euclidean metric on Γ.

Although I usually represent time in terms of a linear numerical space like $\mathbb{Z}$ or $\mathbb{R}$, this representation does not convey the essence of the role of time in space-time, but instead confuses times with measurements of durations. In axiomatizing the properties of time, I employ a more realistic identification of time in terms of the event world, in which each instant consists of a set of events that I interpret as simultaneous events.

5.3.2 Discrete time

The notion of discrete time is familiar from automata theory and other subjects in which one instant follows another without intervening instants, yielding a notion of the "next" instant and a progression of discrete times. One need not change the axioms for continuous metric time by much to permit discrete sequences of instants; dropping Axiom T3, which requires instants to form a continuum, suffices. This allows instants to take forms including discrete points, isolated continua, or mixtures of the two. Naturally, this change has no impact on the notions of simultaneity or on the identification of instants.

However, I go further than merely dropping the continuity axiom and dissect the metric axioms into a more detailed picture of time. I do this because some discrete systems of interest, such as automata theory, carry no natural notion of or role for temporal metrics. One can introduce temporal metrics in such systems, but for most purposes any metric will do as long as it is compatible with a specified temporal order. Other systems, such as the mechanics of Minkowskian relativity, involve incomplete metrics, as discussed by Noll (1964). Looking ahead to discrete-continuous hybrids, I find it makes more sense to think of formalizations of discrete systems as adopting temporal metrics used in the continuous systems rather than as starting out with their own. I thus begin by formulating more detailed temporal axioms characterizing temporal ordering relationships among events and instants, and then proceed to augment these essentially topological ordering assumptions with metric assumptions.

5.3.2.1 *Ordering and intervals*

Let us relate events in W to each other by a binary relation $\lesssim^{\mathcal{T}}$. I ordinarily omit the superscript on the order relation to write $\lesssim$ when this introduces no ambiguity. We read $e \lesssim e'$ as "e occurs no later than e'." The fundamental properties of this relation are given by three axioms stating reflexivity, transitivity, and completeness properties. First, no event occurs before itself, or formally,

Axiom T4 *For each $e \in W$, $e \lesssim e$.*

Second, times occurring after times that occur after others occur after the others as well, or formally

Axiom T5 *For each $e, e', e'' \in W$, if $e \lesssim e'$ and $e' \lesssim e''$, then $e \lesssim e''$.*

Finally, distinct instants occur either before or after each other, or formally

Axiom T6 *For each $e, e' \in W$, either $e \lesssim e'$ or $e' \lesssim e$.*

Together these three axioms give $\lesssim$ the structure of a complete preordering of W.

The simultaneity equivalence relation $\approx$ between events identified earlier corresponds, in the temporal ordering, to events occurring as late as each other, so that $e \approx e'$ iff $e \lesssim e'$ and $e' \lesssim e$.

As before, the simultaneity relation $\approx$ partitions W into instants Γ, and the order on events induces a similar lifted order $\lesssim$ on Γ, such that for $\tau, \tau' \in \Gamma$, we have $\tau \lesssim \tau'$ just in case $e \lesssim e'$ for some $e \in \tau$ and some $e' \in \tau'$. Because simultaneity forms an equivalence relation, the induced ordering relation on instants is antisymmetric, that is, $\tau \approx \tau'$ implies $\tau = \tau'$. The completeness of the event order also implies the completeness of the ordering of instants, making the ordering of instants a complete linear order.

The linear order generates the usual order topology on Γ. This topology in turn yields the familiar notion of temporal intervals as the set of times occurring between two instants. Let us call intervals open, closed, or half-open, respectively, depending on whether the interval contains neither, both, or one of the bounding instants.

5.3.2.2 Temporal indices

I often identify the set $\mathcal{T}$ of times as a set indexing the set of instants Γ by means of a one-to-one function $t : \Gamma \to \mathcal{T}$, with $\mathcal{T}$ possessing a linear order $\lesssim$ compatible with the order over Γ, that is, $t(\tau) \lesssim t(\tau')$ whenever $\tau \lesssim \tau'$. While one can simply use the set Γ as its own index by taking $\Gamma = \mathcal{T}$, common practice takes $\mathcal{T}$ to consist of numerical or seminumerical sets, such as

   (i) A finite set, such as $\{-, 0, +\}$ representing "past", "present", and "future", or the numbers $0, \ldots, n$, representing the history of some computation;

  (ii) A calendar, such as $Years \times Months \times Days$, where $Years = \mathbb{Z} \setminus \{0\}$, $Months = \{January, \ldots, December\}$, and $Days = \{1, \ldots, 31\}$;

 (iii) A countable set, such as the integers $\mathbb{Z}$ under the usual order and discrete topology, representing an infinite succession of clock ticks;

 (iv) A continuum, such as $\mathbb{R}$ under the usual ordering and topology, representing the standard notion of an unbroken progression of instants; or

  (v) A mixture of these, such as $\{-\} \cup [0, 100] \cup \{+\}$, representing a bounded unbroken progression augmented by "earlier and "later.""

Naturally, numerical temporal index sets suggest temporal metrics on events and instants. Mixed index sets, however, need not have the homogeneity needed to support trivial metric constructions.

5.3.2.3 Duration

In addition to recognizing temporal order and topological structure, physics seeks to *measure* time. Zeno's paradox and the impatience of infants do not make sense without measures that assign durations to intervals or the separation of events.

Familiar notions of duration correspond to different temporal metrics. For example, one might identify the discrete metric that maps all trivial intervals to 0 and all nontrivial intervals to 1 as the temporal metric employed by the impatient infant, for whom everything is too late if it is not done now. Index-based metrics can identify temporal distances with differences in temporal indices of instants, taking the duration of the interval between τ and τ' as given by $|t(\tau) - t(\tau')|$.

Physics typically regards temporal metrics as measuring durations by real numbers $\mathbb{R}$, and I follow this tradition here by employing the time-lapse functions $\hat{t} : \mathcal{W} \times \mathcal{W} \to \mathbb{R}$ and $\bar{t} : \Gamma \times \Gamma \to \mathbb{R}$ introduced earlier.

The first axiom of temporal duration constrains the time-lapse functions to agree with the temporal ordering of events.

Axiom T7 *For each $e, e', e'' \in \mathcal{W}$, $\hat{t}(e, e') \geq 0$ iff $e \lesssim e'$.*

With this relation between time lapse and order, we have $\bar{t}(\tau, \tau') > 0$ just in case τ occurs before τ', and $\bar{t}(\tau, \tau') = 0$ just in case $\tau = \tau'$.

Axiom T7 requires only that the time-lapse function provides a numerical representation of temporal ordering, not that its values constitute meaningful measures of temporal duration. We obtain the structure of a measure or metric on events and instants by reaffirming for discrete time the earlier Axioms T1 and T2.

Coupled with Axiom T7 and the standard properties of numbers, the original axioms, T1 and T2, imply the three ordering axioms, T4, T5, and T6.

5.3.3 Hybrid time

Although the event world as portrayed in the preceding section may seem a uniform stage on which processes unfold, we can interpret the same event world as encompassing the progress of different processes unfolding at different scales and rates, so that what constitutes an instant from the point of view of one subprocess can constitute an interval from the point of view of another subprocess. For example, a yearbook chronology might divide history into years, each of which would consist of hundreds of days in a more refined chronology. In addition, different processes might exhibit more complex relationships than mere subdivision; consider, for example, chronologies in which days start at midnight and chronologies in which days start at sunset. We can, in fact, make such complicated identifications of temporal substructures using the notions of temporal ordering already introduced by considering temporal orderings consistent with a specified one, and so obtain a notion of hybrid time that models time at multiple granularities.

5.3.3.1 Hybrid instants

We now consider an indexed set $\{\hat{t}_i \mid i \in \mathcal{I}\}$ of temporal metrics on $\mathcal{W}$, such that each metric $\hat{t}_i$ satisfies Axioms T4–T6. As before, each factor metric $\hat{t}_i$

gives rise to a set of instants Γ_i. For each $e \in \mathcal{W}$ we define $\vec{\tau}(e)$ to be the vector or function from indices $\mathcal{I}$ to instants defined so that $[\vec{\tau}(e)]_i = \tau_i(e)$.

We define $\tau(e)$, the hybrid instant containing e, by $\tau(e) = \cap_i \tau_i(e)$. By definition, $e \in \tau_i(e)$, so we know that $e \in \tau(e)$. We define the set of hybrid instants Γ to consist of all such intersection equivalence classes; that is, $\Gamma = \{\tau(e) \mid e \in \mathcal{W}\}$. Because each of the intersected sets constitutes an equivalence class or partition element, so do the intersections. Hybrid instants thus partition the set of events.

5.3.3.2 Hybrid order and duration

We order instants in Γ by projection of the product order over the factor instants, so that $e \lesssim e'$ just in case $e \lesssim_i e'$ for each $i \in \mathcal{I}$ and $e < e'$ just in case $e \lesssim e'$ and $e <_i e'$ for some $i \in \mathcal{I}$. A time-lapse function $\hat{t}$ on the hybrid event world $\mathcal{W}$ must match up with the hybrid event ordering $\lesssim$.

A hybrid temporal metric, however, need not bear any relation in scale to its component temporal metrics. Even when two of the factor systems each employ continuous time, nothing in mechanics forces us to assume the systems measure duration the same way. Certainly as human observers we know people who live in the same world but seem to experience duration at different rates, whether by occupying different stages of life, or because, though seated in the same grand hall, one loves the opera while one's companion does not.

When traditional physical mechanics forms one of the factor mechanics, we can expect that the usual notion of continuous time also forms the hybrid notion of time. We see this sort of hybrid time in the theory of discrete event systems, in which discrete events exist for some nontrivial interval of continuous time.

5.3.4 Extensions

Traditional continuous time need not absorb the times of all factor mechanics. For example, some approaches (Iwasaki *et al.* 1995) in hybrid systems theory consider temporal orderings isomorphic to subsets of the nonstandard real numbers $^*\mathbb{R}$. The nonstandard reals augment ordinary numbers with infinitesimal numbers. One can use first-order infinitesimals to model an infinite sequence of discrete computational steps occurring between any distinct real numbers, no matter how close, by considering a series of numbers $t, t + \alpha, \ldots, t + n\alpha, \ldots$ for some infinitesimal number α. From the point of view of ordinary continuous time, one can regard this series of nonstandard reals as all occurring within the single instant t. Indeed, one can even consider higher-order infinitesimals, and consider such infinite sequences occurring within infinitesimals themselves. In this way the nonstandard reals $^*\mathbb{R}$ under the usual ordering and topology embed the infinite product $\mathbb{R}^\omega$ into a continuum.

One might wish to weaken the temporal axioms somewhat for certain applications. For example, some ways of describing nondeterministic event worlds might call for using partially ordered times, forgoing T6. Some cosmologies might conceive of time as a cyclical chain of distinct instants, a possibility incompatible with the present axiomatization, because it would collapse all events in such a cycle to a single instant. Standard Minkowskian relativity, in particular, abandons the completeness of the event preordering, which turns the ordering of instants into a partial ordering. Noll (1964) develops axioms for Minkowskian time related to those given here for discrete time.

5.4 Space

The temporal ordering divides the event world into instants. We intend each instant to correspond to a set of locations, but the mere grouping of events into instants says nothing about the structure of these instants. The portion of kinematics concerned with space develops axioms that characterize the structure of these instants in spatial terms.

We ordinarily regard our bodies and other objects as occupying a three-dimensional space $\mathcal{S}$, which, perspective aside, appears Euclidean to the unaided senses. Nonrelativistic mechanics thus models space as Euclidean 3-space, using $\mathbb{R}^3$ as the typical representation, and models restricted subspaces of interest with real differentiable manifolds of dimension 1, 2, or 3, that is, topological spaces locally diffeomorphic to one-, two-, or three-dimensional Euclidean space, possibly with a boundary locally homeomorphic to the one-, two-, or three-dimensional Euclidean half-space.

Relativistic mechanics models space as only locally Euclidean. Space is locally Euclidean and globally Minkowskian in special relativity, a three-dimensional spatial manifold slicing a four-dimensional event world manifold. Space in general relativity is locally Minkowskian. I treat only neoclassical space here, which is globally Euclidean.

5.4.1 Continuous Euclidean space

A Euclidean vector space, or *inner product* space, is a vector space $\mathcal{V}$ over $\mathbb{R}$ that has an inner product. An inner product, of course, is a symmetric bilinear form $\langle, \rangle : \mathcal{V} \times \mathcal{V} \to \mathbb{R}$ for which the associated quadratic form is positive definite, meaning that $\langle v, v \rangle$ is always nonnegative, and is zero only when v is the zero vector. The inner product determines a *quadratic form* $q : \mathcal{V} \to \mathcal{V}$ defined so that $q(v) = \langle v, v \rangle$ for each $v \in \mathcal{V}$. The inner product provides a metric d on $\mathcal{V}$ by applying the quadratic form to differences of points and defining

$$d(v, w) = \sqrt{q(v - w)} = \sqrt{\langle v - w, v - w \rangle}. \tag{5.32}$$

Although we want to assume that mechanical space has a Euclidean character, mechanical space consists of a set of locations, not a vector space. Following Noll (1964; 1973), let us thus define the notion of a *Euclidean space* as a set endowed with a *Euclidean metric*, meaning a metric representable by a quadratic form on the *translation space* of the set. I explain these terms as follows.

Consider a metric $d : \Lambda \times \Lambda \to \mathbb{R}^+$ on the set of locations Λ. We say that a function $\phi : \Lambda \to \Lambda$ is an *isometry* just in case ϕ is a bijection that preserves distances; that is, $d(\lambda, \lambda') = d(\phi(\lambda), \phi(\lambda'))$ for each $\lambda, \lambda' \in \Lambda$. Because inverses and compositions of isometries are isometries, and because the identity function is an isometry, the isometries of Λ with respect to d form a group $\overline{\mathcal{V}}_d$, abbreviated $\overline{\mathcal{V}}$, by taking composition of isometries as the group operation.

The familiar notion of translation consists of mappings of a space onto itself that preserve distances and compose in a commutative and reversible way. We thus look for the set of translations $\mathcal{V}$ to form a subgroup of the full isometric group $\overline{\mathcal{V}}$, almost always a proper subgroup because the set of isometries of Λ can include plenty of mappings, such as rigid rotations, beyond the desired translations. We express the desired properties of translations in terms of commutativity, transitivity, and free action.

Commutativity, of course, means that one can combine translations in any order and get the same result, as seen in the standard parallelogram law of vector addition. We say that a subgroup $\mathcal{V}$ of $\overline{\mathcal{V}}$ is commutative just in case $v \circ v' = v' \circ v$ for each $v, v' \in \mathcal{V}$. The full group of isometries is not generally commutative. For example, taking two steps forward and then facing right leaves one with a different view of the world than does facing right and then taking two steps forward.

To better reflect the usual notation for vectors, we write translations and other isometries in additive terms, even though isometries in general lack the usual commutativity of addition. For $\lambda \in \Lambda$ and $v \in \overline{\mathcal{V}}$, we write $\lambda + v$ to denote the application $v(\lambda)$ of the isometry v to the location λ, and for $v' \in \overline{\mathcal{V}}$

we write $v + v'$ to denote $v \circ v'$. In the additive notation, the commutativity requirement is that $v + v' = v' + v$.

Transitivity means one can always form translations that carry one location into another. In vector terms, this means we can form vectors denoted as $\lambda' - \lambda$, and can connect any two locations through such translations. We say a subgroup $\mathcal{V}$ acts *transitively* just in case for each $\lambda, \lambda' \in \Lambda$ there exists a translation $v \in \mathcal{V}$ such that $v(\lambda) = \lambda'$, or $\lambda + v = \lambda'$ in additive notation.

Free action, in turn, means that translations affect the whole space uniformly, so that a translation that leaves one location fixed must leave all locations fixed. We say a subgroup $\mathcal{V}$ acts *freely* just in case v consists of the identity mapping $0_\mathcal{V}$ whenever $v(\lambda) = \lambda$ for some λ, or in additive notation, whenever $\lambda + v = \lambda$.

We combine these notions to define a *translation group* of isometries as a commutative, transitive, and free-acting subgroup of isometries.

A translation space of Λ then consists of an inner product space over the underlying translation group. Thus $\mathcal{V}$ constitutes a translation space of Λ only if it admits a scalar multiplication $(\alpha, v) \mapsto \alpha v \in \mathcal{V}$ making $\mathcal{V}$ into a vector space, along with an inner product $\langle \cdot, \cdot \rangle : \mathcal{V} \times \mathcal{V} \to \mathbb{R}$ such that

$$d(v, w) = \sqrt{\langle v - w, v - w \rangle}. \tag{5.33}$$

Noll proves that for each metric space of locations there is at most one translation group admitting the structure of an inner product space, and that the inner product space is unique if it exists. In such a case we say that the metric is a Euclidean metric.

Some axiomatizations of space simply assume the typical representation at the start by postulating that each instant is a copy of $\mathbb{R}^3$, as in McKinsey, Sugar, and Suppes (1953a). At a more appropriate level of generality, one can state axioms characterizing the specific properties wanted of space, rather than tying the theory to the specific space $\mathbb{R}^3$. Noll (1973) takes this approach by assuming that space consists of a Euclidean metric space of dimension 3.

Noll's axiomatization starts by assuming that each instant $\tau \in \Gamma$ admits a *distance* function $\hat{d}_\tau : \tau \times \tau \to \mathbb{R}^+$ taking pairs of simultaneous events to nonnegative numbers. We ordinarily abbreviate $\hat{d}_\tau$ to $\hat{d}$ when the instant in question is understood. If we call each event in an instant a *location*, we can say that the distance function takes each pair of locations to nonnegative distance separating the two locations.

Noll's first axiom states that the space of locations is Euclidean.

Axiom S1 *For each instant* $\tau \in \Gamma$, *the distance function* $\hat{d}_\tau : \tau \times \tau \to \mathbb{R}^+$
is a Euclidean metric, and hence endows τ *with the structure of a Euclidean
space.*

Noll's second axiom specifies that the dimensionality of space is uniform across
all instants, with the familiar value.

Axiom S2 *For each instant* $\tau \in \Gamma$, *the dimension of the translation space* $\mathcal{V}_\tau$
is three.

Because each instant consists of a three-dimensional Euclidean space, each
instant is isomorphic to every other, and to any other three-dimensional Euclidean space. We can thus pick a three-dimensional Euclidean space $\mathcal{S}$ to serve as
a standard representative of the instants of the event world.

5.4.2 Frame indifference

A frame of reference corresponds to the perspective of some possible observer.
Each observer sees exactly the same space, but from a perspective that can
change from instant to instant. A change of frame at some instant represents
an isomorphism

$$\phi : \mathcal{S} \to \mathcal{S} \tag{5.34}$$

of the space of positions with itself. Such changes of representation play a key
role in solving practical problems by allowing one to choose the frame to simplify the statement and solution of the problem. Some of the fundamental laws
or principles of mechanics concern invariance of basic mechanical notions under changes of frame.

In the mechanics considered here, we consider only rigid changes of perspective that do not change distances, so that each change of reference frame
reflects an isometry of the space of locations.

Axiom S1 states that the space of locations is a Euclidean space. Euclidean spaces have the characteristic that one can decompose each isometry into
the composition of a translation and an *orthogonal* transformation or gener-
alized rotation. We call an isomorphism $Q : \mathcal{V} \to \mathcal{V}$ orthogonal if $\langle v, w \rangle =$
$\langle Q(v), Q(w) \rangle$ for every $v, w \in \mathcal{V}$. We can think of orthogonal transformations
as preserving angles and distances. The stated property of Euclidean spaces is
thus that if ϕ is an isometry of Λ, then there exists a $\lambda_0 \in \mathcal{V}$ and an orthogonal
transformation Q such that

$$\phi(\lambda) = \phi(\lambda_0) + Q(\lambda - \lambda_0) \tag{5.35}$$

for every $\lambda \in \Lambda$.

The requirement of frame indifference placed on mechanical laws states that true properties of the world do not depend on how we name or label them, and thus do not depend on the choice of reference frame.

Indifference to changes of frame does not mean strict invariance. It means that the quantity in question changes in a manner consonant with the change in frame.

A frame-indifferent scalar quantity is a scalar quantity that is the same independent of choice of reference frame. If we write s_ϕ to denote the value of the scalar quantity s in the frame ϕ, frame indifference of s means just that $s_\phi = s_{\phi'}$ for all isometries ϕ and ϕ'.

A frame-indifferent vector quantity is a vector quantity that rotates with the rotation of the change in frame. If we write v_ϕ to denote the value of the vector quantity v in the frame ϕ, where $\phi(\lambda) = \phi(\lambda_0) + Q(\lambda - \lambda_0)$, frame indifference of v means just that $v_\phi = Qv$ for each ϕ. One defines frame-indifferent tensor quantities in an analogous manner.

Mechanical position or location is frame indifferent but not invariant, as it changes directly with the frame. Velocity, however, is not in general frame indifferent since it tracks only the rotational component of the change of frame, and not the translational component, which can generate the familiar effect of relative velocity.

In the presentation that follows, I imitate Truesdell (1991) and simplify most discussions of changes of frame by means of notation in which I omit explicit denotation of a framing function and use a superscript $\star$ to indicate a quantity after a change of frame. Thus if we write v to denote a vector given a frame ϕ, we can write $v^\star$ to denote the corresponding vector given the frame $\phi^\star$.

5.4.3 Discrete space

Moving from traditional mechanical space to discrete mechanical spaces requires identifying the characteristics of space that prove crucial to the practice of mechanics. We of course need an algebraic character like that of vector spaces, allowing calculation of translations, velocities, and accelerations. We also need an algebraic character like that of Euclidean spaces, allowing expression of rigid changes of frame as translations and rotations. We do not need, however, the involvement of the continuum $\mathbb{R}$ in discrete spatial structures.

The quickest path to discrete spatial structures simply moves from Euclidean spaces over $\mathbb{R}$ to Euclidean spaces over finite fields, such as the binary vector space $\mathbb{Z}_2^n$ over the field $\mathbb{Z}_2$. We follow this path, and go a bit further, relaxing the vector-space requirement to the slightly weaker algebraic notion of free modules over commutative rings.

5.4.3.1 Algebraic structures

Ordinary vector spaces consist of additive groups augmented with multiplication by elements of a scalar field. *Fields*, of course, are algebraic structures permitting addition, subtraction, multiplication, and division (except by zero). Vector spaces admit bases, sets of vectors that generate the rest of the vectors in the space through suitable addition and scalar multiplication.

Modules over rings are much like vector spaces; the difference is that division of scalars by each other need not be possible.

A *ring* is an algebraic structure in which one can add, subtract, and multiply, but not necessarily divide, and in which multiplication distributes over addition. Commutative rings are rings in which addition and multiplication commute. A field is a ring in which one can always divide by nonzero elements.

A *module* over a ring is just like a vector space, except that the scalars need only form a ring, and need not form a field. Modules thus have the usual "vector" addition and scalar multiplication, with multiplication distributing over addition. A module over a ring that is not also a field need not allow one to normalize vectors, since one cannot always find a multiplicative inverse to scalar multipliers. A module over a ring that is not also a field need not possess a well-defined dimension, in that the module might be generated by linearly independent sets of different sizes.

A *free module* is a module that has a basis, that is, a linearly independent set of generators such that each module element has a unique representation (up to commutativity) in terms of the generators. When the ring of scalars is commutative or is a field, all bases of a free module have the same size, and thus one can speak sensibly of the dimension of the module. In this book, all free modules we consider are free modules over commutative rings, so all have well-defined dimensions.

A ring (or field) has *characteristic* n if adding 1 to itself n times yields zero. The rings $\mathbb{Z}_k$ for integer k have characteristic k.

A *linear* form over a module $\mathcal{V}$ is a function $f : \mathcal{V} \to \mathcal{R}$ such that $f(\alpha v + \beta w) = \alpha f(v) + \beta f(w)$. A *bilinear* form is a function $f : \mathcal{V}^2 \to \mathcal{R}$ such that both $f(v, \cdot)$ and $f(\cdot, v)$ are linear forms for each choice of $v \in \mathcal{V}$. A *symmetric* bilinear form is a bilinear form f such that $f(v, w) = f(w, v)$ for each $v, w \in \mathcal{V}$. A bilinear form f is *nondegenerate* if $f(v, \cdot)$ and $f(\cdot, v)$ are never the constant zero mappings for any nonzero v. A *quadratic* form is a function $q : \mathcal{V} \to \mathcal{R}$ such that there exists a nondegenerate symmetric bilinear form f such that $q(v) = f(v, v)$ for each $v \in \mathcal{V}$.

We call a nondegenerate symmetric bilinear form a *generalized inner product*. We say that an isomorphism $Q : \mathcal{V} \to \mathcal{V}$ of a module $\mathcal{V}$ with itself is *orthogonal* with respect to a generalized inner product $\langle , \rangle$ just in case Q preserves the generalized inner product, that is, if $\langle v, w \rangle = \langle Qv, Qw \rangle$ for all $v, w \in \mathcal{V}$.

5.4.3.2 Pseudo-Euclidean space

Axiom S1 requires that the distance notion characterizing space give rise to a Euclidean translation space over the set of locations. The metric strongly shapes the form of the translation space in two ways. First, the metric and inner product conditions force the uniqueness of the translation space, if one exists, and guarantee the decomposability of isometries into translations and rotations. Second, the resulting translation space necessarily exhibits a continuum character, because scalar multiplication by numbers in $\mathbb{R}$ forces each dimension to resemble a continuum in any space of positive dimension.

Discrete mechanics only needs to consider abandoning the second of these two consequences of Axiom S1. Indeed, mechanics demands retaining all or most of the first consequence.

Fortunately, we can abandon the continuum aspects of Axiom S1 with little difficulty, as shown by Noll (1964, pp. 134–136, esp. Remark 1). Although the usual development of Euclidean translation space assumes a real-valued distance metric on locations and $\mathbb{R}$ as the field of scalars, in almost all cases the same algebraic constructions and theorems hold when one replaces the field $\mathbb{R}$ with a commutative ring $\mathcal{R}$.

The more general construction of translations spaces starts with a *separation* function $\sigma : \Lambda \times \Lambda \to \mathcal{R}$ taking pairs of locations to values in a commutative ring $\mathcal{R}$. To recover the continuous case, we just take $\sigma = \hat{d}^2$. The modified axioms to come will give σ the structure of a quadratic form. One then considers separation-preserving isomorphisms of the set of locations in place of isometries. We define the set $\overline{\mathcal{V}}_\sigma$ of σ-preserving isomorphisms of Λ with itself to contain exactly those bijections $\phi : \Lambda \to \Lambda$ in which $\sigma(\lambda, \lambda') = \sigma(\phi(\lambda), \phi(\lambda'))$ for each $\lambda, \lambda' \in \Lambda$. As with ordinary isometries, the separation-preserving bijections form a group by taking composition of functions as the group operation.

The more general construction also foregoes the requirement that the translation space forms a real vector space, and instead requires that the translation group admits the structure of a module over $\mathcal{R}$ on which a generalized $\mathcal{R}$-valued inner product $\langle , \rangle$ induces the given separation function through its associated quadratic form, in the sense that $\sigma(\lambda, \lambda') = \langle \lambda - \lambda', \lambda - \lambda' \rangle$ for each $\lambda, \lambda' \in \Lambda$.

Noll proves that for rings of characteristic other than 2 there is at most one such module structure, and that this module structure provides for unique representations of all isometries in the form given in (5.36). With this more general setting of Noll's axioms available, we obtain axioms for discrete mechanics by assuming a suitable separation function and then modifying Axioms S1 and S2 appropriately.

I augment the assumption of a metric on the space of locations with a separation function $\sigma : \Lambda \times \Lambda \to \mathcal{R}$ taking pairs of locations to values in a commutative ring $\mathcal{R}$. I require compatibility between the metric and separation function in the following axiom.

Axiom S3 *The separation function σ is such that*

  (i) $\sigma(\lambda, \lambda') = 0$ *(in $\mathcal{R}$) whenever $d(\lambda, \lambda') = 0$, and*

  (ii) *Each bijection $\phi : \Lambda \to \Lambda$ preserves distance only if it also preserves separation; that is, if $d(\lambda, \lambda') = d(\phi(\lambda), \phi(\lambda'))$ for every $\lambda, \lambda' \in \Lambda$, then $\sigma(\lambda, \lambda') = \sigma(\phi(\lambda), \phi(\lambda'))$ for every $\lambda, \lambda' \in \Lambda$.*

Thus the separation function preserves locations, and the separation-preserving maps $\overline{\mathcal{V}}_\sigma$ include the isometries $\overline{\mathcal{V}}_d$; that is $\overline{\mathcal{V}}_d \subseteq \overline{\mathcal{V}}_\sigma$.

I next split Axiom S1 into parts. The first part states that a translation group exists with respect to the metric function.

Axiom S1a *The isometric group $\overline{\mathcal{V}}_d$ includes a translation subgroup $\mathcal{V}$.*

By Axiom S3, this means that $\mathcal{V}$ also forms a subgroup of the separation-preserving maps $\overline{\mathcal{V}}_\sigma$.

The second part requires the existence of a free inner product module over the translation group.

Axiom S1b *There exist a scalar multiplication operation $\cdot : \mathcal{R} \times \mathcal{V} \to \mathcal{V}$ giving $\mathcal{V}$ the structure of a free module over the commutative ring $\mathcal{R}$, and a generalized inner product $\langle \cdot, \cdot \rangle : \mathcal{V} \times \mathcal{V} \to \mathcal{R}$ over $\mathcal{V}$ such that $\sigma(\lambda, \lambda') = \langle \lambda - \lambda', \lambda - \lambda' \rangle$ for every $\lambda, \lambda' \in \Lambda$.*

It could be that some other structure would serve the purpose better than free modules over commutative rings, but I do not address that possibility here.

The third part ensures the decomposability of separation-preserving maps into translations and rotations.

Axiom S1c *For every every isometry $v \in \overline{\mathcal{V}}_d$, there exists a location $\lambda_0 \in \Lambda$ and transformation Q orthogonal with respect to $\langle \cdot, \cdot \rangle$ on $\mathcal{V}$ such that*

$$v(\lambda) = v(\lambda_0) + Q(\lambda - \lambda_0) \qquad (5.36)$$

for each $\lambda \in \Lambda$.

Noll's theorem ensures that Axiom S1c follows from Axioms S1a and S1b when $\mathcal{R}$ has characteristic other than 2. However, Chapter 10 shows that the case of characteristic 2, in which $x + x = 0$, has significant interest. We thus adopt Axiom S1c to ensure the needed character of mechanical space pending a proof that isometries decompose properly even in the case of rings of characteristic 2. Note that Dieudonné (1963) shows how one can define quadratic forms for inner product modules over rings of characteristic 2, such as $\langle v, w \rangle = vw + v + w$, and Milnor and Husemoller (1973) provide related results.

Discrete mechanics also weakens Axiom S2 to ensure only uniformity of dimension, omitting the specific dimensionality of ordinary physical space.

Axiom S2a *For each $\tau, \tau' \in \Gamma$, the dimension of the translation space $\mathcal{V}_\tau$ equals that of $\mathcal{V}_{\tau'}$.*

These axioms imply the isomorphism of all instants to each other, so we can still pick a representative set $\mathcal{S}$ isomorphic to each instant.

Continuous Euclidean space carries a natural topology defined by the metric. The following axiom ensures even discrete pseudo-Euclidean space carries a uniform topology compatible with the metric or separation function.

Axiom S4 *The locations in each instant $\tau \in \Gamma$ form a topological space $(\Lambda_\tau, \Theta(\Lambda_\tau))$ such that*

    (i) *The ϵ-balls (interiors of "spheres" of radius ϵ for each ϵ) of Λ_τ with respect to $\hat{d}_\tau$ form open sets in $\Theta(\Lambda_\tau)$, and*

    (ii) *The spaces $(\Lambda_\tau, \Theta(\Lambda_\tau))$ and $(\Lambda_{\tau'}, \Theta(\Lambda_{\tau'}))$ are homeomorphic for each $\tau, \tau' \in \Gamma$.*

Because all instants are homeomorphic, we can represent the topology on each with a topology $(\mathcal{S}, \Theta_\mathcal{S})$ on the index space $\mathcal{S}$ that makes $\mathcal{S}$ homeomorphic to each of the instants.

5.4.3.3 Examples

Discrete mechanical spaces include many discrete vector spaces, such as $\mathbb{Z}_p^n$ over $\mathbb{Z}_p$ for prime p, and thus include the binary vector spaces $\mathbb{Z}_2^n$ over $\mathbb{Z}_2$

familiar in computing. The standard L-norms provide natural metrics, defined by

$$d^l(x, y) = \left(\sum_{i=1}^{n} (x_i - y_i)^l \right)^{-l}. \tag{5.37}$$

When $l = 2$, we have the standard Euclidean (L_2) metric. When considering vectors in $\mathbb{Z}_2^n$ and taking $l = 1$, we have the Hamming (L_1) metric. We obtain natural generalized inner products by employing the same forms as in (5.37), but taking sums in the scalar field (denoted by $\sum(p)$) rather than in $\mathbb{R}$, that is,

$$d^l(x, y) = \left(\sum_{i=1}^{n} (p) \, (x_i - y_i)^l \right)^{-l}. \tag{5.38}$$

Working in $\mathbb{Z}_2$ when $l = 1$, this yields the parity of the binary sum of vectors. The same constructions work as well for mechanical spaces based on the modules $\mathbb{Z}_k^n$ over the finite rings $\mathbb{Z}_k$.

In fact, one can construct such spaces using an arbitrary finite set of cardinality k by identifying the elements of the set with the elements of the finite ring $\mathbb{Z}_k$. One obtains translations by arranging the elements of the set in a circle, as on a roulette wheel. Translations in this finite set then correspond to rotations of the circle bringing one element to the place formerly held by another. We need not assume anything additional just to get a linear module structure for translations. Every commutative group, and in particular the translation group, supports a linear space structure in the form of a module over the ring of integers $\mathbb{Z}$. The natural $\mathbb{Z}$-module structure need not be the module structure of importance in mechanics, however. For example, the ordinary three-dimensional space of traditional mechanics forms a $\mathbb{Z}$-module, but the module structure of interest is the very different $\mathbb{R}$-module (the real vector space) structure.

Alternatively, one can derive finite algebraic structures from stipulated metrics. Each metric on a set of k locations determines between 1 and $k(k-1)/2$ distances between the locations. Each separation function satisfying the preceding axioms determines between 1 and $k(k-1)/2$ separation values for the locations. The compatibility requirement ensures that there are no more distinct separation values than metric values, and that partitioning pairs of locations into the equivalence classes according to the metric refines the corresponding partition into equivalence classes according to separation values. One can thus enumerate the equivalence classes of separation values in order of increasing metric value. If there are n such equivalence classes according to separation value, one can consider modules over $\mathbb{Z}_n$. Alternatively, one can represent locations as vectors in the vector space $\mathbb{Z}^k$ over the binary field $\mathbb{Z}_2$.

It would be good to understand better the implications of basing mechanics on free modules over commutative rings rather than on vector spaces. Do the mathematical differences between these notions really matter to mechanics or its development?

Several trains of work do follow paths that diverge from the usual vector-space setting in different ways. Noll's construction of translation spaces exhibits the methods used in synthetic differential geometry (Kock 1981). Lawvere (2002) presents constructions from a similar viewpoint. Baez and Gilliam (1994, 1996) exploit ideas of synthetic differential geometry and commutative algebra to develop the discrete translation spaces comparable with the ones here for vector spaces over $\mathbb{Z}_2$. One might view these constructions as following on Kalman's (1969) use of modules over polynomial rings, which he views as the most natural structural assumption about state spaces in system theory.

5.4.3.4 Extensions

Axiom S1b requires that the translation space of locations forms a free module. The requirement that the module have a basis certainly reflects the familiar case of physical space, but might not always be appropriate for some discrete systems. We have yet to understand the consequences of dropping the basis requirement in favor of requiring only a module with a generalized inner product.

5.4.4 Hybrid space

While the different notions of time in hybrid mechanical systems merge into a common refinement, the different notions of space do not combine into a common structure, but retain their independent characters, something like the different notions of bodies in hybrid systems.

In the setting of hybrid mechanics, we consider distance metrics $\hat{d}_\tau : \tau \times \tau \to \mathbb{R}^+$ for each $\tau \in \Gamma_i$ and $i \in \mathcal{I}$. Each distance metric takes pairs of simultaneous events to nonnegative reals that represent distance or metric values in one-factor mechanics, and that satisfy the axioms given earlier for space. Each factor metric thus yields a set of locations $\Lambda_i(\tau)$. Each event contained in $\lambda \in \Lambda_i(\tau)$ has the same position in the ith mechanical factor space $\Lambda_i(\tau)$, but different events contained in the same factor location will have different locations in some other factor mechanics. Thus if $e, e' \in \lambda \in \Lambda_i(\tau)$ and $e \neq e'$, there should be some other factor instant $\tau' \in \Gamma_j$ and location $\lambda' \in \Lambda_j(\tau')$ such that $e, e' \in \tau'$ and $e \in \lambda'$ but $e' \notin \lambda'$.

Just as each event determines a hybrid instant $\tau(e)$ defined as the intersection of the vector $\vec{\tau}(e)$ of factor instants, each event also determines a vector of factor locations and hybrid location. We define $\lambda_i(e)$ to denote the location of e in the ith factor mechanics, that is, the location $\lambda \in \Lambda_i(\tau_i(e))$ such that $e \in \lambda$. We define the hybrid location $\lambda(e)$ of e to consist of the tuple or function taking indices in $\mathcal{I}$ to factor locations, such that $[\lambda(e)]_i = \lambda_i(e)$.

One can lift the metrics $\hat{d}_\tau : \tau \times \tau \to \mathbb{R}^+$ over simultaneous events to a metric $\hat{d}_i : \Lambda_i \times \Lambda_i \to \mathbb{R}^+$ over locations in the natural way by defining $\hat{d}_i(e, e') = \hat{d}_{\tau(e)_i}(\lambda(e)_i, \lambda(e')_i)$.

By definition, we know $e \in [\lambda(e)]_i$, so we know that $e \in \bigcap_i [\lambda(e)]_i$. We also know that $\lambda_i(e) \subseteq \tau_i(e)$, so that $\bigcap_i \lambda_i(e) \subseteq \bigcap_i \tau_i(e) = \tau(e)$, so that the events common to all the factor locations containing e exist within the same hybrid instant.

The prime axiom characterizing hybrid space ensures that the combination of hybrid instant and hybrid location allows no ambiguity about events.

Axiom S5 *For each $\tau \in \Gamma$ and $e \in \tau$, $\bigcap_{i \in \mathcal{I}} [\lambda(e)]_i = \{e\}$.*

That is, the set of factor locations containing an event identifies the event uniquely. The second axiom characterizing hybrid space ensures uniformity of hybrid structure by requiring each hybrid instant to reflect all combinations of factor locations.

Axiom S6 *For each $\tau \in \Gamma$ and selection $\vec{\lambda} \in \prod_i \Lambda_i$, there exists some event e such that $e \in \tau$ and $e \in \bigcap_i [\vec{\lambda}]_i$.*

Together Axioms S5 and S6 imply the existence of a bijection between each hybrid instant and the space of product locations $\Lambda = \prod_i \Lambda_i$. If we choose $\mathcal{S}_i$ to represent the locations Λ_i, then $\mathcal{S} = \prod_i \mathcal{S}_i$ represents hybrid locations, so that the axioms yield an isomorphism between $\mathcal{W}$ and $\mathcal{T} \times \mathcal{S}$.

Many times we will want to consider mechanical systems augmenting traditional physical space with additional spatial dimensions. If we write $\mathcal{S}_p$ and $\mathcal{S}_{\bar{p}}$ to indicate a distinguished decomposition of the factor spaces into the factor $\mathcal{S}_p$ representing a traditional physical space of dimension at most 3 and $\mathcal{S}_{\bar{p}}$ to represent the product of all other factor spaces, we can reexpress hybrid space $\mathcal{S} = \prod_i \mathcal{S}_i$ as the product $\mathcal{S} = \mathcal{S}_p \times \mathcal{S}_{\bar{p}}$.

5.4.4.1 Hybrid translation space

To verify the pseudo-Euclidean nature of hybrid space, we start with the factor translation spaces $\mathcal{V}_i$ on Λ_i induced by the factor metrics $\hat{d}_i$. Axiom S1b requires each $\mathcal{V}_i$ to be a free module over a commutative ring $\mathcal{R}_i$. If we define the hybrid separation function σ to be the product function $\prod_i \sigma_i$, so that $[\sigma(\lambda, \lambda')]_i = \sigma_i(\lambda_i, \lambda'_i)$, it is easy to obtain the hybrid translation space $\mathcal{V}$ as the product module $\mathcal{V} = \Pi_i \mathcal{V}_i$ over the product ring $\mathcal{R} = \Pi_i \mathcal{R}_i$. The product of commutative rings is again a commutative ring, and the product of free modules is again a free module, so hybrid translation space fits the mold required of the factor translation spaces.

This construction indicates why we cannot in general expect a hybrid translation space to be a vector space. The product of vector spaces over the same field is indeed a vector space, but the product of vector spaces, considered as free modules, over nonisomorphic fields requires taking as scalars the product of the scalar fields, considered as rings. The ring product of nonisomorphic fields is only a ring, not a field.

Consider, for example, a simple model of a human employing $\mathbb{Z}_2^n$ to represent mental locations and $\mathbb{R}^3$ to represent physical locations. Though both $\mathbb{Z}_2^n$ and $\mathbb{R}^3$ form vector spaces, these vector spaces employ different fields of scalars, respectively $\mathbb{Z}_2$ and $\mathbb{R}$. Forming the product space $\mathbb{Z}_2^n \times \mathbb{R}^3$ thus leads to scalars in $\mathbb{Z}_2 \times \mathbb{R}$. This space of scalars does not form a field since some nonzero elements have zero product, as in $(a, 0)(0, b) = (a0, 0b) = (0, 0)$, where $(0, 0)$ serves as the zero element of the product space. The product of the scalar fields thus only forms a ring, making the product of the factor spaces form only a module rather than a vector space.

For hybrid distance, one can take the natural Euclidean metric over the factor metrics, defining the hybrid metric $\hat{d}$ on hybrid locations Λ by

$$\hat{d}(\lambda, \lambda') = \sqrt{\sum_i \hat{d}_i^2(\lambda_i, \lambda'_i)}. \tag{5.39}$$

This hybrid metric agrees with the factor metrics on the factor spaces, but otherwise has little import.

5.4.4.2 Hybrid frames

The requirement that isometries of hybrid space also be hybrid separation-preserving maps restricts the relevant isometries of hybrid space to the *hybrid isometries*. A hybrid isometry of an instant $\tau \in \Gamma$ is a bijection $\phi : \tau \to \tau$ that preserves the integrity of factor spaces in the sense that $e, e' \in \tau_i$ iff

$[\phi(e)]_i = [\phi(e')]_i$ for each $e, e' \in \mathcal{W}$ and $i \in \mathcal{I}$. We call ϕ a hybrid isometry just in case each $\phi_i : \Lambda_i \rightarrow \Lambda_i$ is an isometry of Λ_i with respect to $\hat{d}_i$.

The requirement of compatibility between separation and metric thus means that hybrid isometries factor into hybrid translations plus hybrid rotations. That is, in the hybrid setting, we view observers as observing individual factor spaces separately, so that observers of the hybrid space do not confuse events in one factor mechanics with events in others. We thus obtain a set of representations

$$\phi_{i,t}(x) = \phi_{it}(x_{i,o}) + Q_{i,t}(x - x_{i,o}), \tag{5.40}$$

making the hybrid frame a hybrid translation composed with a hybrid rotation along each of the factor spaces.

All the important mechanical structure of the hybrid space comes from the factor spaces. The true hybrid metric values outside the factor spaces play no role in the resulting hybrid mechanical structure. One can take this to indicate that hybrid space need not sustain any common measure of overall distance, but need only make sense of the notion of distance within each type of component space. When psychology is formalized, this lack of comprehensive notions of distance reflects the Cartesian intuitions of incommensurability of mental and physical distances.

5.4.4.3 Hybrid substructure

It might prove feasible and desirable to follow traditional mechanics a bit further and assume that each factor translation space forms a vector space.

Assumption S7 *For each $i \in \mathcal{I}$, the scalars $\mathcal{R}_i$ of the translation space $\mathcal{V}_i$ form a field, so that $\mathcal{V}_i$ forms a vector space.*

In particular, going back to earlier remarks on the typical decomposition $\mathcal{S} = \mathcal{S}_p \times \mathcal{S}_{\bar{p}}$, the traditional physical vector space factor $\mathcal{S}_p$ satisfies Assumption S7. The assumption just requires that each of the other factor systems possess a similarly strong algebraic character.

However, this strengthening of assumptions about factor mechanics still does not make the hybrid translation space into a vector space for the reasons just explained. If all factor spaces can be viewed as modules over a common field, then the hybrid space will have the structure of a vector space. If two factor spaces lack translation spaces over a common field, then the hybrid translation space will only have the structure of a free module, not the structure of a vector space.

One can partition the factor spaces by grouping together factor spaces having translation spaces over the same fields and form the vector spaces corresponding to the products of the factor spaces in each partition element. The full hybrid translation space thus consists of the product of these "super-factor" vector spaces. For example, if all the factor spaces making up $S_{\bar{p}}$ are binary vector spaces, one can combine them so that $S_{\bar{p}}$ is also a binary vector space. Similarly, if some such factors are vector spaces over $\mathbb{R}$ and the rest are binary, one can combine the factor spaces over $\mathbb{R}$ with the S_p factor and group all the remainder together as a vector space over $\mathbb{Z}_2$.

The reasonability of Assumption S7 would be strengthened if it were true that every free module over a commutative ring can be viewed as the product of vector spaces over a product ring.

5.4.5 Extensions

Translation space fits sets conceived of as flat or affine spaces, that is, spaces with no curvature. One treats the more general case of curved spaces in terms of manifolds and local translation spaces called *tangent spaces*. Manifolds provide a means for studying globally complicated but locally Euclidean spaces. General relativity provides the most famous examples of space modeled as a curved manifold, but special systems of classical mechanics provide others, such as the submanifold of space through which a pendulum moves. I forego repetition of the usual examples (see Abraham & Marsden 1978; Marsden & Hughes 1983; Misner, Thorne, & Wheeler 1973).

5.4.5.1 Manifolds

An n-dimensional *topological manifold* is a topological space locally home-omorphic to $\mathbb{R}^n$, possibly with a boundary locally homeomorphic to the n-dimensional real half-space. A *differentiable manifold* is a topological manifold with interior and boundary diffeomorphic to real spaces and half-spaces. I review the definition of these concepts, consider their relation to discrete and hybrid spaces, and examine a notion of *premanifold* generalizing the standard continuum notions.

Formally, an n-dimensional topological manifold is a topological space M together with a set of the local homeomorphisms, called *local charts*, that consist of homeomorphisms $\phi : U \rightarrow \mathbb{R}^n$ between subsets U of M and open subsets of $\mathbb{R}^n$. A compatible covering collection of charts is called an *atlas*. Formally, writing a local chart ϕ on U as (U, ϕ), we see that an atlas on M is a family

$$\mathcal{A} = \{(U_i, \phi_i) : i \in I\} \tag{5.41}$$

of charts. We require that the charts of the atlas cover the manifold

$$M = \bigcup_i U_i. \tag{5.42}$$

For every two charts (U_i, ϕ_i) and (U_j, ϕ_j) with overlapping domains $U_i \cap U_j \neq \emptyset$, we form the *overlap maps*

$$\phi_{ji} = \phi_j \circ \phi_i^{-1} \upharpoonright \phi_i(U_i \cap U_j). \tag{5.43}$$

Compatibility requires that each overlap map $\phi_{ji}(U_i \cap U_j)$ is open in $\mathbb{R}^n$ and that ϕ_{ji} is a homeomorphism.

Two atlases $\mathcal{A}_1$ and $\mathcal{A}_2$ are *equivalent* iff $\mathcal{A}_1 \cup \mathcal{A}_2$ is an atlas. An *atlas structure* $\mathcal{A}^*$ on M consists of an equivalence class of atlases. The union of atlases in $\mathcal{A}^*$,

$$\mathcal{A}_{\mathcal{A}^*} = \bigcup \mathcal{A}^* = \bigcup \{\mathcal{A} \mid \mathcal{A} \in \mathcal{A}^*\}, \tag{5.44}$$

is the *maximal atlas* of $\mathcal{A}^*$, and a chart $(U, \phi) \in \mathcal{A}_{\mathcal{A}^*}$ is an *admissible local chart*. If $\mathcal{A}$ is an atlas on M, the set of all atlases equivalent to $\mathcal{A}$ is called the atlas structure *generated* by $\mathcal{A}$.

Differentiable manifolds are topological manifolds for which the charts and their inverses (as well as all translation maps between overlapping charts) are C^∞ diffeomorphisms, not just homeomorphisms. One builds up tangent spaces over differentiable manifolds as follows. At each point p of a manifold M, one defines *tangents* to curves on M through p, using any of several equivalent methods. One method characterizes tangents as equivalence classes of curves, calling two curves through p equivalent if their images in a local chart at p have the same derivative (that is, are mutually tangent). Curves equivalent in one local chart at p must be equivalent in all local charts at p, so this is a good definition. The set of all tangents to M at p is a vector space T_pM, which is the tangent space to M at p, isomorphic to $\mathbb{R}^n$. The set TM of all tangent spaces to M,

$$TM = \bigcup_{p \in M} T_pM, \tag{5.45}$$

is called the *tangent bundle* of M. It is also a manifold, a $\mathbb{R}^{2n}$ manifold if M is an $\mathbb{R}^n$ manifold. I will not dwell on the details of the construction of tangent spaces to manifolds since so many good expositions exist.

The notion of manifold fits naturally into hybrid mechanics, because the product of topological manifolds is again a topological manifold, and the product of differentiable manifolds is again a differentiable manifold.

5.4.5.2 Discrete manifolds

Consideration of mechanics in the setting of discrete space and motion opens the question of whether discrete spaces admit characterization in terms of something like the notion of manifold.

A step in this direction forms the basis of hybrid systems theory (Alur *et al.* 1993; Branicky 1995; Davoren 1998), which, building on the theory of discrete event systems (Ramadge & Wonham 1982, 1987), provides a model for such multifactor spaces by employing products of automata and differentiable manifolds. Discrete event systems in turn have significant similarities to Noll's (1972, p. 48) abstract version of his theory of simple materials and to Willems (1972a, 1972b) similar approach in systems theoretic terms. Although the result is a differentiable manifold as long as at least one of the factors is, the models of hybrid systems theory do not in themselves exhibit all the properties one might desire. Discrete sets may be modeled as topological manifolds using the discrete topology on the set, which makes each discrete point homeomorphic to the zero-dimensional topological manifold $\mathbb{R}^0$. We cannot directly extend this to the differentiable case, however, because $\mathbb{R}^0$ is not a differentiable manifold, although the product of a point with a differential manifold is of course a differentiable manifold when the product points are given a topology mirroring that of the differentiable manifold. More to the point, however, the hybrid systems model leaves the automaton states outside the algebraic framework imposed on the continuum physical states. It makes no distinctly spatial interpretation of the automata state space, and does not distinguish or require any portion of the manifold to represent any part of physical space. For the purposes of mechanics, we seek theories of space that treat all factors in comparable algebraic, geometric, and topological terms.

As considered in later chapters, the representational systems studied in psychology and artificial intelligence often decompose into hybrids and sums of several types of representations. The concepts underlying the notion of manifolds might prove useful in studying these discrete representational systems as well, for example, as a way of studying local representations or encodings of logical, computational, or psychological information. In particular, one thinks of the structure of a network of markets incorporating both simple local structures consisting of sets of participants in an auction for a specific good, and complicated global structure in terms of the topological relations between markets in different goods.

I turn to this question briefly and introduce a variant of the notion of atlas appropriate to discrete spaces in a frankly speculative notion, which is the premanifold. I introduce this concept not because it seems right—indeed, it seems to miss the mark in several important ways—but because it might help in finding the right way of formulating an invariant notion of representational structure. In particular, this completely straightforward way of adapting the standard chart and atlas notions yields a construction that collapses in the end, and permits global representations of the discrete spaces as subsets of discrete vector spaces. Perhaps the synthetic structures proposed by Lawvere (2002) would serve these purposes better.

Formally, we get the structure of premanifolds by essentially the same construction as that for topological manifolds after changing the notion of local charts from functions that represent open subsets of the underlying set as open sets in $\mathbb{R}^n$ to functions that represent these open subsets as open sets in some other topological module. Real vector spaces with the usual topology constitute the topological modules of interest in ordinary manifolds. In the discrete setting, we consider finite vector spaces under the discrete and other topologies as well.

Formally, we take a local chart on M to be a bijection ϕ from a subset U of M to an open subset of a free topological module $\mathcal{M}_\phi$ over a commutative ring $\mathcal{R}_{\mathcal{M}_\phi}$. We go beyond the generality common in the usual notion of topological manifold to permit the coordinate module $\mathcal{M}_\phi$ to vary with the subset U under consideration, but it is not clear that treating the discrete systems of interest requires this added generality. The primary focus here falls on premanifolds in which all local charts map to the same topological module.

We define atlases of charts in the same was as for topological manifolds, requiring that the overlap domains $\phi_{ji}(U_i \cap U_j)$ be open in $\mathcal{M}_i$, and that the overlap maps ϕ_{ji} be homeomorphisms. When all charts in $\mathcal{A}$ map to the same module $\mathcal{M}$, we call $\mathcal{A}$ an atlas modeled on $\mathcal{M}$ or $\mathcal{M}$-atlas. The notions of atlas equivalence, structure, and maximal atlases carry over directly. We then define a premanifold M as a pair $(M, \mathcal{A}^*)$, where M is a set and $\mathcal{A}^*$ is an atlas structure on M.

A premanifold is an $\mathcal{M}$-premanifold iff for each point $a \in M$ there exists an admissible local chart (U, ϕ) with $a \in U$ and $\phi(U) \subset \mathcal{M}$. A premanifold is an n-premanifold iff it is an $\mathcal{M}$-premanifold and $\mathcal{M}$ has dimension n, such as $\mathcal{M} = \mathbb{R}^n$ or $\mathcal{M} = \mathbb{Z}_2^n$.

Note that all differentiable n-manifolds are n-premanifolds, the only extra conditions being that the charts map M to $\mathbb{R}^n$, and that the overlap maps are C^∞ diffeomorphisms.

Premanifolds become topological spaces by defining the open sets of M to be those $A \subset M$ such that for each $a \in A$ there is an admissible local chart (U, ϕ) such that $a \in U$ and $U \subset A$.

We note that if M is a $\mathbb{Z}_2^n$-premanifold, then the derived topology for M is discrete, and there is a global chart (M, ϕ) representing each point of M as a vector in $\mathbb{Z}_2^n$. Clearly, for any finite set M, if $2^n < |M| \leq 2^{n+1}$, then M is a $\mathbb{Z}_2^k$-premanifold iff $n < k$. Thus while not every continuum can be given the structure of a manifold, every finite set can be made into a premanifold by representing it with binary vectors.

The upshot is that each premanifold modeled on discrete topological modules admits a global coordinate representation, obviating the complexity of the premanifold definition, and calling into question the utility of the concept. Of course, the discrete topology need not be the only topology of interest when one is considering discrete spaces, especially those involved in informational or computational systems. In such systems, the relevant topology might be the T_0 topologies of continuous Scott lattices, which lie between those of Euclidean metric spaces and discrete sets. Does the notion of a premanifold as defined provide a less trivial result when the representation topology is, for example, the T_0 Scott topology? Does some modified definition of premanifold provides a useful notion of local rerepresentation?

The algebraic structure provided by local charts lets us extend the tangent space notions of standard manifold theory to notions of tangent spaces for premanifolds. One path to extending traditional tangent space notions to the discrete case might be to regard translations over discrete factor spaces as representing "infinitesimal" tangents, and take the translation space as constituting the tangent space at each point. In this way we arrive at a notion of tangent spaces appropriate to hybrid mechanics. For each point $p \in \mathcal{S}$ in hybrid space, we take the hybrid tangent space to consist of the product of the factor tangent spaces; that is,

$$T_p\mathcal{S} = \prod_i T_{p_i}\mathcal{S}_i. \tag{5.46}$$

A more general theory might not assume that every point in $\mathcal{S}$ is a possible successor, or equivalently, that not all curves are "continuous." One natural isomorphism identifies a tangent (p, q) with q, making the tangent space $T\mathcal{S}$ isomorphic to $\mathcal{S} \times \mathcal{S}$, the set of all "transitions" between elements of $\mathcal{S}$.

5.4.5.3 State space

The notion of manifold was developed to formalize the state spaces of mechanical systems, spaces augmenting or replacing physical space with parameters appropriate to the system under study. For example, the parameters normally appropriate for describing the pendulum or double pendulum are not the usual Cartesian coordinates.

The conceptual danger of the state-space approach is that one loses sight of the underlying concept of space itself. Each parameter of the system description, be it mass, charge, or charm, becomes yet another dimension of state space, with no distinction in the formalism itself between dimensions related to space and those related to other physical concepts. This uniformity can offer mathematical and conceptual benefits, but at the cost of removing the underlying physical concepts from the formalism.

The worst cost of discarding the fundamental physical concepts is that one is left with mere variational mechanics. As I detail in Section 7.5, variational mechanics represents a formalism well suited to some mechanical systems but ill suited to the full range of physical systems, much less the psychological and economic systems of interest here. The variational formalism exploits the abstract state space, but requires one to encode both general physical laws and laws specific to the system of interest in a Lagrangian function. This obviously obscures the physical laws by making them seem *ad hoc* to each problem solved. It also implicitly requires the system laws to be unchanging over time and to be completely specified in advance. Neither of these assumptions fits the needs of psychology and economics well. It is worth noting that the underlying mechanical laws suffer no such problems.

5.4.5.4 Event worlds

With the preceding structures for hybrid space and time, we can describe a variety of event worlds from physics, computation, and other fields.

In the state spaces of hybrid system theory, and for some of the psychological systems considered here, the space S represents the product of discrete sets with differentiable manifolds, so that the event world looks like many copies (one per discrete spatial element) of the differentiable manifold. In many of these, the discrete factor itself bears the structure of a Euclidean space, such as the usual Euclidean structure on $\mathbb{Z}_2^n$ over the field $\mathbb{Z}_2$.

In plain computation, S and T are discrete, with $T = \mathbb{Z}$, and S taken to be the state space of the system, for example, the set of states of a finite automaton. The sets W, S, and T are given the discrete topology, so that homeomorphisms are just bijections.

In the case of computational models like perceptrons (Minsky & Papert 1969) or the Boltzmann machine (Hinton, Sejnowski, & Ackley 1984), and in econometrics, S is a Euclidean continuum and T is discrete.

For general parallel computers, including life machines, connection and grid machines, and cellular automata, S and T are discrete and Euclidean or possibly Minkowskian. Here space has the structure of the sum of the spaces of individual processors or cells. The spacelikeness restriction rules out instantaneous global states that do not also constitute proper instantaneous local states. In particular, this restriction narrows the global sum structure to a global product structure. In this setting, a metric on events that measures propagation or computation delays results in a more specific restriction, whose freedoms express the possible independent time rates of the individual processors or cells.

5.5 Bodies in space

Mechanics does not just concern bodies, space, and time, but also how bodies occupy portions of space and how these occupations change over time.

5.5.1 Placements

Axiom B8 requires that the set of body points possesses a topology, and Axiom S4 does the same for the set of locations. A *placement* of a body $\mathcal{B}$ in space $\mathcal{S}$ consists of a smooth mapping $\chi : \mathcal{B} \to \mathcal{S}$ of the body points of $\mathcal{B}$ into points of space, that is, a mapping χ that is continuous with respect to the topologies $(\mathcal{U}, \Theta_{\mathcal{U}})$ and $(\mathcal{S}, \Theta_{\mathcal{S}})$. Requiring continuity rules out placements that involve ripping or tearing of a body when placing it in space.

Most treatments of continuum mechanics in fact restrict attention to placements that constitute homeomorphisms of bodies and places, that is, continuous invertible (1-1) mappings that have continuous inverses. Requiring placements to be homeomorphisms means that placements cannot assign the same place to distinct body points, and so rules out placements that involve folding or penetration.

Because we regard each body as a subset of $\mathcal{U}$, we can express a placement of all bodies with a placement $\chi : \mathcal{U} \to \mathcal{S}$ of the universal body $\mathcal{U}$. The image $\chi(b)$ of a body point b is called its *location* or *position* in the placement χ.

We call the image $\chi(\mathcal{B}) = \{\chi(b) \mid b \in \mathcal{B}\}$ the *shape* of $\mathcal{B}$ in the placement χ. This association of shapes with bodies yields a function $\chi_{\mathcal{B}} : \overline{\mathcal{B}} \to \mathcal{P}(\mathcal{S})$ on bodies that assigns to each body the shape of the body. We call $\chi_{\mathcal{B}}$ a placement of the universe $\overline{\mathcal{B}}$.

We write $\mathcal{B}_{\mathsf{S}}$ to denote the *universe of shapes*, that is, the set of possible images across all placements $\chi_{\mathcal{B}}$. Placements need not fill all of space with bodies, so in general $\mathcal{B}_{\mathsf{S}}$ need not equal $\mathcal{P}(\mathcal{S})$. The assumption that $\overline{\mathcal{B}}$ forms a lattice of subsets of $\mathcal{U}$ means we can view each placement $\chi_{\mathcal{B}}$ as a lattice homomorphism $\chi_{\mathcal{B}} : \overline{\mathcal{B}} \mapsto \mathcal{B}_{\mathsf{S}}$. In fact, because $\overline{\mathcal{B}}$ forms a Boolean lattice of subsets of $\mathcal{U}$, the image of $\chi_{\mathcal{B}}$ forms a Boolean lattice with top element $\chi_{\mathcal{B}}(\mathcal{U})$.

5.5.2 Examples

In analytical dynamics, $\mathcal{U}$ is a finite set of body points with the discrete topology. Placements map these points into $\mathbb{R}^3$ or some other 3-manifold. The discrete topology means that every placement is continuous.

Continuum mechanics takes $\mathcal{U}$ to be the set of closed, regular, or fit regions in $\mathbb{R}^3$ or some other differentiable manifold, and takes $\mathcal{S}$ to be $\mathbb{R}^3$ or some other differentiable manifold. The more interesting topologies of these sets place significant restrictions on placements.

Computation takes bodies to be discrete sets and placements to be maps into state space. If $\mathcal{U}$ is a singleton (as is common), then each placement may be identified with a point, which in some cases can be thought of as the system's state.

5.5.3 Configurations

Although placements associate bodies and space, placements involve a global perspective on space in an essential way. This means that placements reflect the perspective of an observer. From the point of view of mechanics, we seek a more intrinsic notion of the relation between a body and space.

Noll characterizes the spatial organization of the body intrinsically in terms of spatial relations between the various body points rather than in terms of locations between places inhabited by body points and other places uninhabited by body points. He calls this intrinsic notion the *configuration* of the body, and defines a configuration κ of a body $\mathcal{B}$ as a metric $\kappa : \mathcal{B} \times \mathcal{B} \to \mathbb{R}^+$ defined on the points of $\mathcal{B}$ that gives the distances between points of the body. Each different metric constitutes a different configuration of the body. Metrics on $\mathcal{U}$ thus constitute configurations of the entire material universe.

Each placement $\chi : \mathcal{B} \to \mathcal{S}$ determines a configuration of $\mathcal{B}$. Pulling back the metric d on $\mathcal{S}$ through the placement χ induces a distance function d_χ such that $d_\chi(b, b') = d(\chi(b), \chi(b'))$. The metric d_χ thus constitutes a configuration of $\mathcal{B}$. The universe of shapes $\mathcal{B}_S$ thus gives rise to a universe of configurations we denote by $\mathcal{B}_C$. We write $\mathcal{B}_C(\mathcal{B})$ to indicate the set of all configurations of $\mathcal{B}$.

Going the other way, each configuration $\kappa \in \mathcal{B}_C$ corresponds to the set of placements $\mathcal{B}_S(d) = \{\chi \in \mathcal{B}_S \mid \kappa = d_\chi\}$ exhibiting that configuration.

5.5.4 Deformations

In addition to considering relations between placements and configurations, mechanics also considers relations between configurations. A *deformation* is a mapping of body points that carries one configuration into another. As with placements, continuum mechanics usually restricts attention to deformations that constitute homeomorphisms of bodies and places.

It is useful to consider deformations generated by homeomorphisms. If χ is a placement and $h_S : S \to S$ and $h_U : U \to U$ are homeomorphisms, then $\chi' = h_S \circ \chi \circ h_U$ is a placement as well, and constitutes a deformation of χ.

Standard practice in mechanics picks one particular placement χ_r to serve as a *reference placement*, thus also determining a *reference configuration* κ_r as the body metric d_{χ_r} obtained from the reference placement. Other placements and configurations are then regarded as deformations of these reference entities.

5.5.5 Extensions

It might prove useful to consider spaces of forms $\mathcal{B}_S$ that have distinctive structure apart from the topology of S. Continuous lattices, such as the domains characterized by Scott (1982) information systems, explicitly describe structural forms useful in characterizing computations. One issue here is whether the image $\chi_B(U)$ can still form a Boolean sublattice of $\mathcal{B}_S$. Scott domains can lack complements, but this might not matter, seeing as how placements need not fill all of space. Another issue concerns the interaction between the material topology on U and the topology of the continuous lattice. If one identifies a body B with the set of spatial points it occupies, can it be that one always has $\chi_B(B) = \overline{\chi_B(B)}$, so that the placement of the body is a proper element of the continuous lattice?

5.5.6 Special kinematic laws

The general kinematical laws place no particular restrictions on placements and configurations. Such restrictions are essential in characterizing common materials, however.

5.5.6.1 Deformation classes

Standard practice in mechanics identifies various classes of configurations that prove important in applications. Each of these classes corresponds to a different assumption about the constitution of the bodies or materials involved. Mechanics expresses the principal constitutive assumptions about configuration in terms of the classes of deformations allowed for the material in question. These characteristic classes are called *deformation classes*, and indicate the *deformation type* of the body or material at issue.

For example, one can characterize rigid materials as ones in which deformations must be isometries, that is, isomorphisms that preserve distances between body points. One can characterize continuous bodies as ones in which deformations must be bounded homeomorphisms.

In analytical dynamics, body points are allowed to collide, to occupy (temporarily at least) the same place. In ordinary continuum mechanics, bodies (continua) undergo only smooth deformations, with no interpenetration. This prescription accurately captures some continuum phenomena but not others, such as mixing of fluids, though continuum mechanics lacks effective means for treating general interpenetration and other nonsmooth phenomena.

We write $\mathcal{C}$ to indicate the set of all allowed configurations of $\overline{\mathcal{B}}$, and $\mathcal{C}(\mathcal{B})$ to indicate the set of all allowed configurations of $\mathcal{B}$.

5.5.6.2 Placement classes

The notion of deformation type of a material represents an intrinsic restriction on the ways in which the material appears in space. One can also consider a parallel notion of *placement type* based on *placement classes* that restricts where bodies can appear in space.

Traditional mechanics and physics do not involve the notion of placement classes directly, but instead typically assume bodies may be placed anywhere in space as long as the resulting configuration is consistent with the constitution of the body. The exception to this is in the curved space-times of general relativity. That theory says that black holes have an apparent location defined by the center of their event horizons, but that there really isn't any place there at all because space-time ends at the event horizon.

One finds perhaps stronger reasons for considering placement classes in psychology and economics. For example, legal configurations of a chess board require that same-color bishops must occupy squares of different colors, at least prior to any promotion of pieces, and legal configurations of a RMS require sets of conclusions that satisfy the reasons held by the system (see Doyle 1983e and Section 13.4).

5.6 Motion in space

Over time, bodies undergo changes of place, shape, and configuration. We call changes of configuration *deformation processes*, and changes of place *motion*. Motion thus decomposes into intrinsic motion characterized by the events related to the body, and extrinsic or framed motion relative to frames of reference.

The direct way of describing a motion is as a temporal curve $\chi : \mathcal{T} \to \mathcal{B}_S$ in the set $\mathcal{B}_S$ of placements, that is, as a function from $\mathcal{T}$ (or an open interval of $\mathcal{T}$) to $\mathcal{B}_S$. The motion thus yields a placement $\chi_t : \mathcal{U} \to \mathcal{S}$ for each time t. Accordingly, we can view a motion as a function $\chi(b, t)$ taking body points and times to places, or, holding the body point of interest fixed, as functions $\chi_b(t)$ taking times to places.

5.6.1 Deformation processes

Looking at bodies in intrinsic terms, we call a history $\kappa : I \to \mathcal{C}$ of configurations over a temporal interval I a deformation process. A deformation process does not indicate how a body moves through space, only how the parts of the body move relative to each other.

One obtains notions of material derivatives by considering rates of change within a deformation process.

5.6.2 Intrinsic motion

To characterize motion in space intrinsically, we need a description that does not depend explicitly on a framing of reference. Following the path of general relativity and Truesdell's (1991) exposition of continuum mechanics, we can characterize motions in more realistic terms as follows.

Consider the event world $\mathcal{W}$ and a framing $\phi : \mathcal{W} \to \mathcal{S} \times \mathcal{T}$, which we fix for the present discussion. A *world line* in $\mathcal{W}$ is a continuous curve in $\mathcal{W}$ whose image in the framing is functional in time, that is, a function from an interval of $\mathcal{T}$ into $\mathcal{W}$ such that no two points in the image have the same value in $\mathcal{T}$. A *world tube* is a set of world lines over the same interval. A *motion* of a body is a world tube over an interval of time consisting of a world line for each point in the body.

Formally, a motion of the universe over a temporal interval I consists of a function

$$\chi : \mathcal{U} \to \mathcal{PW} \tag{5.47}$$

such that each image $\chi(b) \subseteq \mathcal{W}$ is a world line over I. In what follows, let us write I_χ to denote the temporal interval over which a motion χ occurs, that is, the domain of definition of the motion. Using the assumed framing, we can thus view a motion as a family of placements

$$\chi_t : \mathcal{U} \to \mathcal{S} \tag{5.48}$$

such that χ_t assigns to each body point b its location $\chi_t(b)$ at the instant t.

Because each body forms a subset of the universal body, we can also regard a motion χ as assigning a placement or shape $\chi_t(\mathcal{B})$ to each $\mathcal{B}$ at each instant t in the interval of motion. Motions thus consist of curves in the set of shapes or placements, where we write

$$\chi_{\mathcal{B}} : \mathcal{B} \to (I \to \mathcal{B}_S) \tag{5.49}$$

to indicate the function assigning to each body $\mathcal{B}$ the placement curve $\chi_{\mathcal{B}}(\mathcal{B})$: $I \to \mathcal{B}_S$, so that $\chi_t = \chi_{\mathcal{B}}(\mathcal{U})(t)$. Noll calls such motions *kinematic processes*.

A motion is called *regular* or *invertible* if each instantaneous placement is invertible as a function of the body points. That is, χ is regular if for each t, the placement χ_t is an open, 1-1 (invertible) function. Intersections of world lines represent collisions or the creation or destruction of bodies or parts of bodies, so intuitively, a regular motion is one in which nothing "catastrophic" like ripping or interpenetration has occurred. Continuum mechanics usually rules out such occurrences, but I do not do so here.

More generally, I do not assume full continuity of motion as a central axiom of mechanics. I return to the question of continuity of motion and other mechanical quantities in Section 7.3, at which point I do assume a form of piecewise continuity.

5.6.3 Extrinsic motion

The notion of extrinsic motion comes about by combining the intrinsic motion with changes of frames of reference. A *frame of reference* or *reference process* consists of a family of Euclidean metrics on instants in some interval.

With a nonconstant reference process, one can view a body as exhibiting motion even though the body maintains a fixed configuration and a fixed shape in the reference placement.

One obtains rates of motion, velocities, and accelerations by considering spatial derivatives of placements relative to frames of reference in straightforward ways. Standard mechanics also assumes continuity of the first two derivatives of motions and frames of reference.

5.6.4 Hybrid motion

We write χ_i to denote the projection of a hybrid motion χ onto the event world $\mathcal{W}_i$.

The use of the product topology on hybrid space means that a motion through space is continuous iff each of its projections onto the different factor dimensions of space are continuous in those factor spaces. In particular, the motion of the body in ordinary physical space must be continuous, independent of its motion in other dimensions of space. In formalizing psychological systems of interest, use of a discrete topology on the mental dimensions of space makes every path through these mental dimensions continuous, independent of its motion in ordinary physical space. Of course, not all nonphysical spatial dimensions need use the discrete topology, as some might form continua with nondiscrete topologies.

5.6.5 Discrete motion

The notion of motion itself requires no weakening to cover discrete mechanics. The same definitions that work for traditional mechanics work as they stand for the discrete case.

The big difference comes in considering differential constructs from motion. Traditional mechanics and hybrids over traditional mechanics both support the standard concepts of differential calculus: limits, derivatives, integrals, and the like. These concepts either do not apply or provide less power in analyzing discrete trajectories and discrete spaces, though standard treatments of dynamics include notions of discrete derivatives and difference equations, and Lawvere (2002) develops abstract notions of microtransitions fulfilling the ideas of Galileo about the nature of smooth motion.

Substantial work has been done by Akers (1959) and others (Sellers, Hsaio, & Bearnson 1968; Thayse & Davio 1973; Yanushkevich *et al.* 2000) to develop various notions of a Boolean differential calculus that carry over a fair portion of standard calculus to the discrete setting, including discrete versions of partial and total differentials, Taylor series, and other familiar concepts. As the subsequent development makes clear, a *binary* differential calculus would have greater direct relevance to mechanics. In fact, treatments of some conceptions of Boolean differential calculus relate the Boolean calculus to a binary differential calculus. The lattice-ordered presentation of the Boolean calculus, however, obscures some of the ideas central to mechanical analysis, and a more direct development in binary form might aid analysis of discrete mechanics.

To develop a discrete mechanics as close to traditional mechanics as possible, later chapters examine a variety of additional partial replacements for the missing concepts of analysis, including conditional vectorial analogs of differentials and tangent vectors, and "continuity" notions based on conservatism of trajectories relative to comparative similarity relations, which one can view as taking seriously Truesdell's (1984d) discussion of the role of smoothest path principles in mechanics. I noted earlier that although one can choose to measure hybrid distances using a standard Euclidean distance, as in (5.39), this construct means little because the algebraic structure of the hybrid space comes directly from the structure of the factor spaces. The metrics in the factor spaces have mechanical meaning in defining the translation spaces; the seemingly arbitrary metric on the hybrid space has less direct mechanical meaning. In this setting, we may wish to avoid assuming the existence of a hybrid Euclidean distance metric and instead focus on a comparative similarity relation that tells when one translation dominates another, as in comparisons along individual dimensions, without providing an ordering of size over all possible translations. Such comparison relations then support minimum principles shaping discrete motions.

5.6.6 Motion from flows

In traditional mechanics, the behaviors of mechanical systems are specified in terms of differential equations or dynamical systems on manifolds.

A *dynamical system* on a differentiable manifold M is a *section* of the tangent space TM, that is, a *vector field*

$$\psi : M \to TM \tag{5.50}$$

assigning a tangent $(x, v) \in T_x M$ to every point $x \in M$. We define *integral curves* of the section ψ to be curves c in M such that $c \in \psi(x)$ for each $x \in c$, that is, curves whose tangent at each point x is given by the section value $\psi(x)$. If we think of the vector field ψ as the right-hand side of a differential equation on the manifold, then an integral curve is just a solution to the equation defined by the dynamical system.

Traditional mechanics focuses on dynamical systems over the tangent space $T\mathcal{S}$. Each point $(x, v) \in T\mathcal{S}$ represents both a position x and a velocity v. Such pairs are called *kinematical states*, and the tangent space $T\mathcal{S}$ is the state space. The behavioral laws of mechanical systems are expressed as a dynamical system on the state-space manifold, a section

$$\psi : T\mathcal{S} \to TT\mathcal{S} \tag{5.51}$$

specifying how positions and velocities change.

Many treatments of mechanics work with the *phase space* of the system rather than the state space. The phase space is the cotangent bundle $T^*\mathcal{S}$, where, in the traditional setting cotangents are linear functionals of tangents

$$g : T_x \mathcal{S} \to \mathbb{R}, \tag{5.52}$$

the idea being that cotangents carry information about "momentum" (mass and velocity) rather than simple velocity. The state-space and phase-space manifolds are homeomorphic, but the phase space carries a natural *symplectic* (or

Hamiltonian) structure, which simplifies analysis of some systems. In particular, dynamical systems obeying conservation laws (for instance, conservation of energy) have a particularly simple form, that of Hamilton's equations for a corresponding Hamiltonian function. Because of this, elements of phase space $(x, v^*) \in T^*\mathcal{S}$ are interpreted as positions x and *generalized momenta* v^*.

Discrete dynamical systems can be thought of as "movies" of continuous dynamical systems. That is, one follows the integral curves of a dynamical system, and notes where each ends up after one time unit. This defines a function (perhaps partial)

$$g : T\mathcal{S} \to T\mathcal{S}. \tag{5.53}$$

Iterating this function yields the values after successive time intervals. Thus if $\varphi(x, t)$ describes the solution curves for $x \in T\mathcal{S}$, we have

$$g(x) = \varphi(x, 1) \tag{5.54}$$
$$g^n(x) = \varphi(x, n). \tag{5.55}$$

More generally, each homeomorphism $g : \mathcal{S} \to \mathcal{S}$ of $\mathcal{S}$ with itself can be regarded as a discrete dynamical system, and as the unit time function of some continuous dynamical system. Still more generally, each continuous function $g : \mathcal{S} \to \mathcal{S}$ can be regarded as a discrete dynamical system, though not always as a movie of a continuous dynamical system.

Symbolic dynamical systems are discrete dynamical systems in which the manifold is replaced by a discrete topological space, especially finite sets with the discrete topology. That is, instead of unit time functions $g : \mathcal{S} \to \mathcal{S}$, we consider continuous functions $g : \mathcal{D} \to \mathcal{D}$. If $\mathcal{D}$ has the discrete topology, all functions are continuous, so we can consider the iterates g^n of any function g as giving successive elements of trajectories.

Given a section

$$\psi : \mathcal{S} \times \mathcal{S}' \to T\mathcal{S} \times T\mathcal{S}' \tag{5.56}$$

of a tangent bundle over the combination of a continuous manifold $\mathcal{S}$ and a discrete manifold $\mathcal{S}'$ as already defined, one defines the notion of integral curves in a straightforward way in terms of the projections of the section onto the different tangent spaces. A curve in $\mathcal{S} \times \mathcal{S}'$ is a function $c : \mathcal{T} \to \mathcal{S} \times \mathcal{S}'$, and c is an integral curve of ψ iff $\pi_\mathcal{S} \circ c$ is an integral curve of $\pi_\mathcal{S} \circ \psi$ and $\pi_{\mathcal{S}'} \circ c$ is a piecewise constant function with changes at points of change described by $\pi_{\mathcal{S}'}\psi$.

5.6.7 Nondeterministic motions

We say a set H of deterministic motions constitutes a *nondeterministic motion* just in case it is both *temporally uniform* in the sense that all of its deterministic motions share the same temporal interval of definition I_H, that is, $I_\chi = I_H$ for each $\chi \in H$, *referentially uniform* in the sense that each of the motions involves the same framing, and *materially uniform* in the sense that each of the motions is of the same body or set of body points $\mathcal{B}_H$.

The mathematical form of the description of nondeterministic systems can be brought close to that of deterministic ones by collecting together all possibilities into set-valued functions called *correspondences* (Klein & Thompson 1984). Economics makes heavy use of correspondences, which admit notions of continuity similar to the ordinary one. When used to express the vector fields defining nondeterministic dynamical systems, these correspondences are sometimes called *differential inclusions* (Aubin & Cellina 1984).

Each nondeterministic motion H over $\mathcal{B}_H$ and I_H induces, for each discrete sequence of instants $I_D \subseteq I_H$, a discrete correspondence function

$$\Delta_H : \mathcal{S} \times \mathcal{B}_H \times I_D \to \mathcal{P}(\mathcal{S}) \tag{5.57}$$

over states and instants defined so that at every point j in the sequence I_D, we have $x' \in \Delta_H(x, b, t_j)$ iff there exists some $\chi \in H$ in which $\chi(b, t_j) = x$ and $\chi(b, t_{j+1}) = x'$.

In turn, each correspondence $\Delta : \mathcal{S} \times \mathcal{B}_\Delta \times I_\Delta \to \mathcal{P}(\mathcal{S})$ over $\mathcal{B}_\Delta$ and a discrete sequence of successive instants $I_\Delta \subseteq \mathcal{T}$ induces a set H_Δ of discrete motions. Let $\mathcal{H}(\mathcal{B}, I)$ denote the set of all deterministic motions over the points of body $\mathcal{B}$ and the instants of a temporal interval I. We then define H_Δ by saying that a motion $\chi \in \mathcal{H}(\mathcal{B}_\Delta, I_\Delta)$ is in H_Δ iff $\chi(b, t_{j+1}) \in \Delta(\chi(b, t_j), t_j)$ at each point j in the sequence I_Δ. The induced correspondence clearly lacks information needed to reconstruct the original set of motions, since if two deterministic motions share the same state at some instant, the nondeterministic motion H_Δ generated by the correspondence representation includes all those deterministic motions obtained by splicing the past of one motion to the future of the other, even when the original set of motions lacks this composite motion.

6

Dynamics

The kinematics developed in the preceding chapter broadened traditional mechanical axioms to cover discrete and hybrid conceptions of bodies, space, time, and motion. The present chapter continues the development by similarly broadening traditional mechanical axioms for mass, force, and energy.

Just as in the case of kinematics, the broadening of dynamics to discrete and hybrid mechanics has precedent in traditional mechanics. The traditional kinematics of clocks and other discrete machines carries within it the notion of movement between discrete states, foreshadowing discrete mechanical systems. Traditional kinematics foreshadows hybrid mechanics in textbooks that first develop mechanics in the plane and then extend the treatment to mechanics in three-dimensional space. Traditional dynamics, in turn, foreshadows broader notions of mass and energy in its distinction between inertial and gravitational mass and between kinetic and internal energy.

6.1 Mass

Mass enters into informal characterizations in almost all realms of human activity, though mathematical usage is restricted largely to traditional physical mass (and some probability theories; see Shafer 1976). The notion of mass arises when one seeks to characterize the resistance of objects to changes in position. Newton pointed the way to Euler's characterization of the force of inertia generated by mass, and also characterized the role of mass in the force of gravitation.

Traditional mechanics posits a measure $m : \mathcal{B} \to \mathbb{R}^+$ that assigns to each body $\mathcal{B}$ a nonnegative quantity of mass $m(\mathcal{B})$. Mechanics assumes that each body's mass sums, in a continuous way, the masses of its separate parts. Noll and Truesdell axiomatize this notion by identifying the structure of bodies that have mass and by characterizing the relation between the mass of a body and the masses of its parts and other bodies as a measure function or integral over bodies. Other axioms, treated later in this book, concern the forces generated by masses.

In preview, the extensions to discrete and hybrid mechanics developed here extend the traditional scalar measures of mass to more complex vectorial measures of mass.

6.1.1 Massy bodies

The bodies of interest in dynamics have mass; let us call them *massy*. The massy bodies constitute a subclass $\mathcal{B}_m$ of the closed universe $\overline{\mathcal{B}}$. For the notion of mass to matter, let us first require that this subclass have members.

Axiom M1 *Some body has mass; that is,* $\mathcal{B}_m \neq \emptyset$.

Next, let us require the set of massy bodies to be closed under joins and takings of exteriors.

Axiom M2 *If* $\mathcal{B}_1, \mathcal{B}_2 \in \mathcal{B}_m$, *then* $\mathcal{B}_1 \sqcup \mathcal{B}_2 \in \mathcal{B}_m$.

Axiom M3 *If* $\mathcal{B} \in \mathcal{B}_m$, *then* $\mathcal{B}^e \in \mathcal{B}_m$.

It follows that meets of massy bodies are massy, and that $\mathcal{O}$ and $\mathcal{U}$ are massy. With these requirements, therefore, the massy bodies form a Boolean sublattice of $\overline{\mathcal{B}}$.

Mechanics normally assumes that the massy bodies exhaust the universe of bodies.

Assumption M4 *All bodies are massy; that is,* $\mathcal{B}_m = \overline{\mathcal{B}}$.

In light of this assumption, in the following I usually just write $\overline{\mathcal{B}}$ instead of $\mathcal{B}_m$.

6.1.2 Mass configurations

To say a body $\mathcal{B}$ is massy is to say that the body has a mass; but what mass, and when? Truesdell and Noll follow the custom in continuum mechanics of assuming a unique mass value for each body, independent of time, and so implicitly assuming conservation of mass through the implicit assumption of conservation of bodies. I capture the typical assumption of Truesdell and Noll in the following axiom, which requires nonnegative numerical mass values for each body.

Axiom M5 *For each $\mathcal{B} \in \mathcal{B}_m$, there exists a unique number $m(\mathcal{B})$ constituting the mass of $\mathcal{B}$, with $0 \leq m(\mathcal{B}) \leq \infty$.*

Let us write $\mathcal{M}$ to denote the set of all possible masses bodies can possess. Axiom M5 states that $\mathcal{M} \subseteq [0, \infty]$. This axiom also implies that the masses of bodies form what I call a *mass configuration*, that is, a function

$$m : \mathcal{B}_m \rightarrow \mathcal{M} \tag{6.1}$$

defined on $\mathcal{B}_m$ taking values in $\mathcal{M}$. We write $\mathcal{C}_m$ to denote the set of possible mass configurations.

Mechanics restricts mass configurations to ones that respect the role of mass in mechanics. Mechanics traditionally views mass as constituting a measure (integral) over bodies. This means, in the first place, that each mass configuration must be additive on separate bodies.

Axiom M6 *For each $m \in \mathcal{C}_m$, if $\mathcal{B}_1, \mathcal{B}_2 \in \mathcal{B}_m$ are separate, then*

$$m(\mathcal{B}_1 \sqcup \mathcal{B}_2) = m(\mathcal{B}_1) + m(\mathcal{B}_2). \tag{6.2}$$

Since $\mathcal{B}_1$ is the join of the separate bodies $\mathcal{B}_1 \sqcap \mathcal{B}_2$ and $\mathcal{B}_1 \sqcap \mathcal{B}_2^e$, Axiom M6 implies that massy bodies satisfy

$$m(\mathcal{B}_1 \sqcup \mathcal{B}_2) = m(\mathcal{B}_1) + m(\mathcal{B}_2) - m(\mathcal{B}_1 \sqcap \mathcal{B}_2). \tag{6.3}$$

Moreover, because each body is separate from the null body, Axiom M6 implies that the null body has zero mass, $m(\mathcal{O}) = 0$. A body assigned mass 0 is called *massless*. This is a different notion from *nonmassy*, which means not assigned any mass value at all. Thus $\mathcal{O}$, the null body, is massless, but there may be other massless bodies.

Mechanics *per se* does not generally specify the value $m(\mathcal{U})$ representing the total mass of all bodies, which Axiom M5 ensures exists.

Axiom M6, together with the axioms on bodies and the assumption that bodies are sets of points, implies that m is a finitely additive measure function. Continuum mechanics assumes further that the massy bodies are Borel sets of the space, so as to ensure the existence of measure functions over bodies. This assumption starts with a requirement about completeness of the lattice of massy bodies.

Assumption M7 *The universe of massy bodies forms a σ-complete lattice; that is, the join of a countable collection of bodies in $\mathcal{B}_m$ is also a body in $\mathcal{B}_m$.*

Because we assumed earlier that bodies consist of sets of body points, Assumption M7 implies that bodies form a σ-field or Borel field of sets. We then add the corresponding condition on mass configurations.

Assumption M8 *The mass configuration m constitutes a measure over $\mathcal{B}_m$.*

This assumption means bodies form a measure space. Continuum mechanics also assumes that on continuous bodies the mass measure possesses a continuous density function, so that we may write mass as an integral

$$m(\mathcal{B}) = \int_{\mathcal{B}} dm. \tag{6.4}$$

We do not formalize this assumption here, but include in the notion of integral summation over both continuous and discrete bodies, as in Stieltjes integration.

We also assume that the assignment of masses to bodies does not depend on the frame of reference used to describe the motion of the body.

Axiom M9 *Mass is frame indifferent; that is, $m(\mathcal{B})$ does not depend on the frame of reference.*

This axiom would require revision were we to attempt to treat relativistic mechanics, which regards the apparent mass of a body as changing with the velocity of the body relative to some observer. In Einstein's special relativity, mass is not a frame-indifferent quantity, but varies nonlinearly with the speed of the body in the frame of reference. Though mass varies, the mass of the body in a frame of reference in which the body is stationary constitutes a distinguished value called the *rest mass* of the body. Special relativity assumes that rest mass is frame indifferent with respect to changes of frame that leave the body at rest. Einstein's general relativity develops a theory of mass involving frame indifference with respect to much more general changes of frame.

6.1.3 Mass variation

Assignment of mass values directly to bodies implicitly requires that the mass of a body does not change with time or motion. Mechanics does not always make this assumption. Indeed, this principle proves false when one moves to the realm of quantum theory and quantum electrodynamics, in which split atoms and smaller particles emit energetic radiation that leaves the remainder with less mass than before the split. Broadening the perspective to that of general relativity, in which energy has a mass equivalent, recovers some of the conservation principle, but no strong reason is known to suppose the total mass of the universe remains constant, and no strong reason exists at this preliminary stage of investigation for assuming that conservation of mass applies uniformly in mental universes.

Accordingly, let us separate assumptions about conservation of mass from the basic formalism. The simplest way of doing this is to weaken Axiom M5 to require instead that each body has a mass value at each instant of time.

Axiom M5a *For each $t \in \mathcal{T}$ and $\mathcal{B} \in \mathcal{B}_m$, there exists a unique value $m_t(\mathcal{B})$, with $0 \leq m_t(\mathcal{B}) \leq \infty$, that constitutes the mass of $\mathcal{B}$.*

We retain the remaining axioms concerning the structure of mass configurations, and extend the notation to write $m_t(\mathcal{B})$ or $m(\mathcal{B}, t)$ to indicate the mass of body $\mathcal{B}$ at time t. We call a function

$$m : \mathcal{T} \to \mathcal{C}_m, \tag{6.5}$$

the variation of mass across time, a *mass variation*.

When mass varies over time, we call the change or rate of change at an instant the *mass flux* or *massing* at that instant.

6.1.4 Mass, place, and body

The question of mass conservation and variation involves complicated issues about the relation of mass to space and bodies. I pause briefly to summarize some of these issues.

Even without considering relativistic mass changes, nonrelativistic schoolbook mechanics considers bodies that change mass, such as a rocket expelling combusted fuel in its thrust, or a hot-air balloon leaking sand from one of its weights.

Traditional continuum mechanics does not view the rocket and balloon examples as true changes of mass because it takes a view of mass centered on the notion of matter rather than on human identifications of objects. Specifically, continuum mechanics identifies bodies with bits of matter, and maintains these identifications across motions of the parts of the bodies. Thus in continuum mechanics, if one starts with one body consisting of a bucket of blue sand and a second body consisting of a bucket of yellow sand, then, after one dumps one bucket into the other and stirs thoroughly, one still has the two bodies one had before, only with the placement of their parts intermingled. In this point of view, elements of matter constitute the underlying bodies, and apparent changes of mass consist of changing the body of interest, from the rocket full of fuel to the rocket less the fuel already expelled.

Indeed, from one point of view, continuum mechanics can dispense with the notion of mass altogether. To do this, one identifies the mass of a body as the measure or volume of the body in a reference configuration, and obtains the mass of any volume in a later configuration by inverting the motion mapping to obtain the original volume. If one tracks the motion of bodies, this representation naturally yields a conserved quantity, since the same body always maps back to the same reference configuration, at least in deterministic histories. Because of this possibility, Truesdell and Toupin remark that one may treat mass as a kinematical quantity, on a par with position, in fact, as one which may be defined in terms of positional quantities. They write this:

Kinematics is neither more nor less general after the introduction of mass. ... It would be possible, though less interesting and less fruitful, to develop all this material [on kinematical topics whose usefulness is connected with mass] without mentioning mass. (Truesdell & Toupin 1960, p. 465)

Truesdell and Toupin do not use spatial representation to render the notion of mass superfluous, however. Their discussion makes clear that the primary reasons for distinguishing mass from spatial quantities are not to be found in its kinematical structure, but in its dimensional independence from spatial quantities and in its different role in dynamical relationships.

Dimensional independence in traditional mechanics means that there is no natural way of converting mass values into position values. While one can compare meters along the horizontal with meters along the vertical, and thus say these two values are dimensionally similar, one cannot say how many meters equals a gram, except through entirely *ad hoc* means such as identifying mass with lengths by which a standard spring is extended by a depending body possessing that mass. This dimensional relation clearly does not serve for all possible mass values because of its specificity to the Earth's gravitational field. Relations between mass and position are, in contrast, almost routine fare in general relativity, in which mass distribution and the shape of space (the metric), and hence the possible positions, are mutually constraining in a manner expressed by Einstein's equations.

The difference in dynamical treatment of mass goes beyond the mere orthogonality of one dimension from another, which of course even multiple spatial dimensions exhibit. In traditional mechanics, differences in dynamical roles provide the reason why the purely spatial definition of mass derived from volume in a reference configuration is not a useful concept in relativity. The spatial definition applies to all mechanical systems, and requires that mass is always conserved. Relativistic dynamics offer no role for this kinematic conception of mass, but instead involves the usual notion of relativistic mass.

6.1.5 Discrete mass

Discrete mechanics broadens the traditional requirements on mass in ways parallel to the broadening of traditional requirements on space. In this setting, mass changes from a continuous measure to a discrete one, taking values in modules over rings rather than only in the nonnegative extended real numbers.

6.1.5.1 Mass values

As noted earlier, mechanics traditionally uses the set of mass values $\mathcal{M} = [0, \infty]$, apart from some esoteric theories that also employ negative or imaginary mass values. Real-valued mass measures fit well with the use of real vector spaces in modeling velocity, since then mass values may act as scalar multipliers in forming momentum values from velocities.

In the more general setting here, I avoid the standard prescription in favor of mass values that merely provide the algebraic properties necessary to serve in summing masses of bodies into masses of combined bodies. As with the treatment of discrete spatial dimensions in Chapter 5, admitting discrete masses results in mass values that have the structure of a free monoid over a ring. Indeed, mass values provide yet another motivation for regarding the translation space of places as a module. In this setting, one uses mass values as elements of the ring of scalars to form momentum values as products of mass and spatial-translation values.

To serve as measure values, the set of mass values must support a notion of combination or summation. Let us write such combinations additively, so that $m + m'$ means the combined value of the mass values m and m', and require mass addition to be commutative and associative, so that combined values do not depend on the order of combination.

Axiom M10 *Mass values admit a commutative and associative addition function* $+ : \mathcal{M} \times \mathcal{M} \to \mathcal{M}$, *so that for each* $m, m', m'' \in \mathcal{M}$, $m + m' = m' + m$ *and* $m + (m' + m'') = (m + m') + m''$.

We also require the existence of a zero mass value.

Axiom M11 *There exists a mass value* $\mathbf{0}_{\mathcal{M}} \in \mathcal{M}$ *such that* $m + \mathbf{0}_{\mathcal{M}} = m$ *for each* $m \in \mathcal{M}$.

Together, Axioms M10 and M11 require the zero mass value to be unique, and give $\mathcal{M}$ the structure of a commutative monoid under addition.

Although the traditional notions of mass measure mass in terms of nonnegative real numbers, discrete mass measures need not provide any corresponding and compelling notion of positivity of nonzero values. Accordingly, we follow the lead of traditional treatments and regard actual mass assignments (e.g., nonnegative real numbers) as occurring within a somewhat larger structure of potential values (e.g., all real numbers). Thus the next mass axiom requires that potential mass values have additive inverses.

Axiom M12 *For each* $m \in \mathcal{M}$ *there exists a mass value* $m' \in \mathcal{M}$ *such that* $m + m' = 0_{\mathcal{M}}$.

The preceding axioms require such inverses to be unique, so with this axiom, $\mathcal{M}$ forms a group. As usual, when $m + m' = 0_{\mathcal{M}}$ we write $m' = -m$.

In the case of traditional mass notions, Axiom M12 goes against the initial identification of $\mathcal{M}$ as the set of possible mass values and the methodology of realism, as it seems to posit quantities or entities that do not exist in the system being formalized. To avoid this, one might instead seek to axiomatize mass values in terms of semirings that only contain values that mass configurations might assign to bodies.

The traditional conception of mass also admits scaling of mass values, including scales chosen so as to make some particular value the *unit* mass value. This scaling implies that the space of potential mass values admits a scalar multiplication. Let us follow this lead in the next axiom, which posits a module structure for mass values based on the existence of a ring of mass scalars and a corresponding notion of scalar multiplication.

Axiom M13 *There exist both a commutative ring* $\mathcal{R}_{\mathcal{M}}$ *with multiplicative unity* $1_{\mathcal{M}}$ *of* mass scalars *and a corresponding scalar multiplication* $\cdot : \mathcal{R}_{\mathcal{M}} \times \mathcal{M} \rightarrow \mathcal{M}$ *that give* $\mathcal{M}$ *the structure of a free module over* $\mathcal{R}_{\mathcal{M}}$.

As was noted in the earlier discussion of translation spaces, every commutative group forms a module over the integers, but that module need not be free.

The traditional conception of mass inherits a notion of continuity of change from the ordinary topology of $\mathbb{R}$. We assume a corresponding notion of continuity exists for the more general conception of mass values in the following axiom.

Axiom M14 *There exists a topology* $(\mathcal{M}, \Theta_{\mathcal{M}})$ *on the set of mass values and a topology* $(\mathcal{R}_{\mathcal{M}}, \Theta_{\mathcal{R}_{\mathcal{M}}})$ *on the module scalars such that linear operations on the mass module are continuous.*

6.1.5.2 Examples

In the language of the broadened axioms for mass, traditional mechanics formalizes mass scalars $\mathcal{R}_{\mathcal{M}}$ and mass values $\mathcal{M}$ as the same space, $\mathbb{R}$.

In Chapter 10 I consider masses formalized as binary vector spaces, for example, the vector spaces $\mathbb{Z}_2^n$ over the field of scalars $\mathbb{Z}_2$. One may also consider such spaces as rings over themselves by defining multiplication componentwise, and thus also as modules over themselves.

Since Boolean lattices can be regarded as binary vector spaces over their atomic elements and hence as modules over $\mathbb{Z}_2$, we may trivially regard every massy universe as its own set of mass values, by taking $\mathcal{M}$ to be $\mathcal{B}_m$ and defining $m : \mathcal{B}_m \rightarrow \mathcal{B}_m$ to be the identity function. Addition then corresponds to Boolean exclusive-or.

6.1.5.3 Mass configurations

Discrete mechanics retains Axiom M9 requiring the frame indifference of mass, but the changes in the character of mass values requires some adjustment to the other requirements placed earlier on real-valued mass configurations. Naturally, the first step is to modify Axiom M5 a second time to remove the requirement of nonnegative numerical mass values.

Axiom M5b *For each $t \in \mathcal{T}$ and $\mathcal{B} \in \mathcal{B}_m$, there exists a unique value $m_t(\mathcal{B}) \in \mathcal{M}$ constituting the mass of $\mathcal{B}$.*

We still have mass configurations as possibly time-dependent functions from bodies to mass values. Our standing Assumption B7, that bodies consist of sets of body points, means that mass configurations constitute set functions on $\mathcal{B}_m$ taking values in $\mathcal{M}$ rather than (necessarily) the nonnegative extended real numbers.

We retain Axioms M6 concerning the structure of mass configurations, which in the discrete setting means that mass configurations form additive $\mathcal{M}$-valued set functions. The change of range does not change the familiar consequences noted earlier, such as the necessary assignment of the zero mass $\mathbf{0}_{\mathcal{M}}$ to the null body $\mathcal{O}$. We also retain Assumption M7, and restate Assumption M8 to require mass to constitute a countably additive set function.

Assumption M8a *Each mass configuration m constitutes a countably additive set function over $\mathcal{B}_m$.*

Possibly additional requirements might retain yet more of the measure-theoretic structure of traditional notions of mass.

In traditional mechanics, additivity of mass implies that the empty body has zero mass. Moreover, existence of relative complements implies that all parts of massless bodies are massless; that is, that if $\mathcal{B} \precsim C$ and $m(C) = \mathbf{0}_{\mathcal{M}}$, then $m(\mathcal{B}) = \mathbf{0}_{\mathcal{M}}$. Can one require the same of discrete mechanical mass? The converse of the massless part requirement is that if $\mathcal{B} \precsim C$ and $m(\mathcal{B}) \neq \mathbf{0}_{\mathcal{M}}$, then $m(C) \neq \mathbf{0}_{\mathcal{M}}$. This means that the join of two bodies of nonzero mass must also be of nonzero mass. Such a requirement would thus serve as a partial replacement for the notion of nonnegativity of traditional mass values. But if the discrete mass module has nonzero characteristic, the requirement that all parts of massless bodies be massless would imply that the total mass of the universe is less than the order of the mass module. This unexpected connection between the class of massless bodies and the set of possible mass values leads us to not impose such requirements on discrete mechanical systems.

More generally, should some order structure be required of discrete mass values? The axioms on mass values do not presume any sort of order or partial order on mass values. In the case of traditional mass, one knows that $\mathcal{B} \precsim \mathcal{C}$ implies $m(\mathcal{B}) \leq m(\mathcal{C})$. As with the requirement about massless bodies just considered, any formulation of an order requirement on discrete mass values must take into account the possibility that cyclic discrete values might add to smaller ones.

Questions about mass measures and mass orderings come together when we consider the regrets expressed by Truesdell (1991) concerning the dependence of the underlying mechanical theory of mass on the special assumption that bodies are sets. Truesdell observes that what one really wants is some purely algebraic method for constructing a measure over the Boolean lattice of bodies from the lattice structure alone, without any assumptions about decomposition of bodies into sets of body points. Such constructions might be possible by drawing on the work of McShane (1953), who develops a theory of integration on lattices, and the work of Schlechta (1995, 1997), who develops a notion of integration on logical spaces. It would be especially interesting to develop a notion of integration connected with the Scott (1982) construction of continuous lattices. Indeed, discrete mechanics could make use of such a theory not only for mass measures, but also for the theory of conservative motion discussed later.

6.1.5.4 Nonmassy bodies

Axiom M5b and, for that matter, Axiom M6, require that the universal body $\mathcal{U}$ has a mass value. These axioms do not specify what value this is, or even whether $m(\mathcal{U})$ is finite or infinite. One nevertheless might want to weaken the axioms.

Specifications of universal mass, when made, usually appear as part of cosmological theories. Theories have been proposed in which the total mass of the universe is finite, and others in which it is infinite. In some theories, however, the total mass of the universe is not a well-defined quantity. In such theories, it seems proper to omit the universal body from the set of massy bodies.

Are there other cases calling for treatment of nonmassy bodies within mechanics? Critics of Descartes' mental substances, of course, might have noted the lack of good suggestions from Descartes about how to regard the mass of such bodies, which he already viewed as lacking place. One might pursue that train of thought and declare all nonmassy bodies as outside the realm of mechanics.

Yet one should not be hasty in issuing such a declaration. Most of the general laws of force do not necessarily have anything to do with mass, and continue to place requirements on forces even without the involvement of mass-dependent forces like inertia and gravitation. Indeed, some natural phenomena, such as electromagnetism and rigid material structure, have no direct relation to the mass of a body. Noll gives the example of deformations of incompressible fluids (e.g., squeezing toothpaste from a tube) as a motion within mechanics in which the notion of mass plays essentially no role.

The example of infinite or undefined mass for the universal body might be taken more generally. Specifically, one might translate the difficulties attending the universal body to bounded bodies and question the usual assumption in mechanics that bounded bodies have bounded mass.

Traditional mechanics formalizes the standard notion of physical mass so that finite bodies have finite mass. Although no general mechanical principle forces discrete mechanics to make a similar assumption, we nevertheless seek to hew to the physical model in this regard. Doing so requires adding additional structure to what we have supposed for mass values, as modules used as spaces of mass values need not have any obvious notion of "infinite" values.

The assumption that bounded bodies must have finite mass bears further study. Computational theories of psychology typically assume finite information content for representations and states of mind, and certainly all of the computer programs written to date are characterized by finite information content. If we then regard information content as a cross-dimensional measure of total mental mass, this motivates translating the assumption of bounded mass for bounded bodies to mental bodies as well. If we instead consider idealized agents with infinite-dimensional mental spaces, or mental states employing continuous physical elements as representations, assumptions of finite information content become problematic.

6.1.6 Hybrid mass

Hybrid mechanics generalizes the traditional conception of mass directly by regarding hybrid mass as a product of mass values in component mechanical systems. Specifically, suppose that $\mathcal{B} = \bigoplus_{i \in \mathcal{I}} \mathcal{B}_i$ denotes the universe of hybrid bodies, and that for each $i \in \mathcal{I}$ the factor bodies, mass values, and configurations $\mathcal{B}_i$, $\mathcal{M}_i$, and $\mathcal{C}_{mi}$ satisfy the axioms given previously. We then form the set $\mathcal{M}$ of hybrid mass values as the product module $\mathcal{M} = \prod_{i \in \mathcal{I}} \mathcal{M}_i$ over the product scalar ring $\mathcal{R}_{\mathcal{M}} = \prod_{i \in \mathcal{I}} \mathcal{R}_{\mathcal{M} i}$ and the set $\mathcal{C}_m$ of hybrid mass configurations as $\prod_{i \in \mathcal{I}} \mathcal{C}_{mi}$. Then for each body $\mathcal{B} \in \mathcal{B}$, $m \in \mathcal{C}_m$, and $i \in \mathcal{I}$ we have

$$[m(\mathcal{B})]_i = m_i(\mathcal{B}_i). \tag{6.6}$$

These hybrid mass values and configurations clearly satisfy the mass axioms if the factor values and configurations do.

Although this construction provides a general definition of hybrid mass values, it seems reasonable to maintain the traditional mechanical constraint of nonnegative mass values as a constraint on mass configurations rather than as a constraint on potential mass values. We do this through the following axiom.

Axiom M15 *The mass values and scalars of traditional mechanics form a module isomorphic to the module of $\mathbb{R}$ over itself, and physical mass configurations only assign values corresponding to nonnegative extended real numbers.*

Consider, for example, the hybrid of a physical body characterized by the traditional sort of mass values and a mental body with mass values characterized by a binary (propositional) vector space. We take the traditional mass values to consist of the one-dimensional vector space of vectors $\mathbb{R}$ over scalars $\mathbb{R}$, and the mental mass values to consist of vectors in $\mathbb{Z}_2^n$ over scalars $\mathbb{Z}_2$. In this case, the set of hybrid mass values is just the module of elements $\mathbb{R} \times \mathbb{Z}_2^n$ over scalars $\mathbb{R} \times \mathbb{Z}_2$. If we take instead the mental mass values as elements in $\mathbb{Z}_2^n$ over scalar ring $\mathbb{Z}_2^n$, then the set of hybrid mass values is the module of elements $\mathbb{R} \times \mathbb{Z}_2^n$ over scalars $\mathbb{R} \times \mathbb{Z}_2^n$.

For a second example, consider a mental body $\mathcal{U}$ made up of several mental subbodies, such as a set of mental agents in Minsky's (1986) society of mind, or a set of interconnected computers. In this case, we might view each subbody $b \in \mathcal{U}$ as a distinct mechanical system with its own set of mass values $\mathcal{M}_b$. If so, the masses of the overall body would consist of products or disjoint sums of the subbody masses; that is,

$$\mathcal{M} = \bigoplus_{b \in \mathcal{U}} \mathcal{M}_b. \tag{6.7}$$

As this system illustrates, the mass values of the component bodies need not have anything in common.

The idea that mass might have different dimensions has a long history in traditional mechanics. Even Newtonian mechanics distinguishes, both conceptually and dynamically, between inertial mass and gravitational mass. Traditional mechanics makes their identity an explicit assumption adopted because all human experience showed inertial and gravitational mass to vary proportionately for all bodies at all times. This assumption received theoretical justification with the discovery of general relativistic mechanics, which enlarged the conception of mass so that both inertial and gravitational masses derive from the same fundamental conception of mass.

Hybrid mechanics enlarges the conception of mass once again, by considering multiple, possibly irreducible dimensions of mass. This enlargement serves to encompass distinctions between physical and mental mass at the outset, and further differentiation of mental mass into multiple dimensions of mental mass in more detailed investigations.

As in the case of inertial and gravitational mass, specific mechanical theories might propose ways of reducing all these dimensions to smaller sets of dimensions. For example, one might ask why ordinary three-dimensional space, which one might consider as a hybrid of three one-dimensional spaces, does not yield three dimensions of mass. One possible answer is that the first role of mass is in defining linear momentum. Ordinary physical mass would divide into three sorts only if one could readily distinguish linear motion along one dimension from linear motion along the other two. The assumed isotropy of physical space means that such is not the case, because a simple change of frame suffices to translate any linear motion into linear motion along a given axis. This interchangeability may be taken as the reason ordinary mechanics has the same conceptions of mass for the distinct spatial dimensions.

If superficially hybrid physical mass dimensions reduce to a single dimension of physical mass, can we not reduce more general hybrid masses to the usual physical conception of mass? One might seek to extend mechanics with measures of total mass that combine values in each dimension, but such measures would seem to suffer the same artificiality afflicting measures of distance that combine physical and mental positions. I do not pursue such reductions here, though I provide some speculations on relativistic notions. No one has exhibited any convincing practical means for verifying any putative theoretical reduction of psychological and economic matters to physical. Indeed, Jackson (1986) and Chapter 16 discuss reasons to think such a reduction might not exist. Unless and until we discover enough about the structure of the world to justify such theoretical assumptions, it seems unreasonable to impose such assumptions in the very fabric of mechanics itself.

6.2 Momentum

Mass and velocity combine to form momentum, so that momentum values exhibit the dimensionality of both mass and spatial tangents or velocities.

Traditional mechanics defines momentum in a reference process as the sum or integral of velocity with respect to mass. In the case of point bodies, this identifies the momentum as the usual product of the mass and velocity. Momentum values thus form a space isomorphic to the space of velocities $T\mathcal{S}$ due to the natural embedding of linear mass values $\mathbb{R}^+$ into the scalar field of the velocity vector space $\mathbb{R}^3$. The four pure momentum dimensions, one of mass and three of space, thus reduce to three mass-spatial mixed dimensions.

The nonlinear nature of mass in the present axiomatization requires that the formalization of momentum enlarge similarly on the traditional conception of spatial momentum. The differences shrink again when we compare our enlargement to the generalized momenta of traditional phase-space or Lagrangian mechanics.

6.2.1 Linear momentum

In traditional mechanics, the linear momentum of a body $\mathcal{B}$ is a functional $p(\mathcal{B}; \chi, m)$ of a body's spatial motion and mass variation. Here we overload the symbol p, using it to denote both a bilinear map $p : \mathcal{M} \times T\mathcal{S} \to T\mathcal{S}$ from mass and velocity values to momentum values and a corresponding mapping from bodies and motions to momentum histories. For a body point b possessed of a mass $m(b, t)$ and velocity $\dot{\chi}(b, t)$ at time t, the linear momentum is given by the familiar equation

$$p(b, m(b), \chi(b))(t) = m(b, t)\dot{\chi}(b, t). \tag{6.8}$$

The linear momentum of a general body $\mathcal{B}$ is the integral over the body of the velocity with respect to the mass density:

$$p(\mathcal{B}, \chi, m)(t) = \int_{\mathcal{B}} \dot{\chi}_t dm. \tag{6.9}$$

This expression is meant to indicate the usual formula for smooth spaces and traditional masses, and to indicate summing of momentum elements for each body point for discrete bodies.

6.2.2 Rotational momentum

In traditional mechanics, the notion of rotational or "angular" momentum with respect to some point of origin resembles the notion of linear momentum, but involves a dual of the velocity space instead of the velocity space's entering into linear momentum.

Specifically, the dual space $\mathcal{V}^*$ of a vector space $\mathcal{V}$ consists of the vector space of linear functions from $\mathcal{V}$ to $\mathbb{R}$. These linear functions are called *tensors* over $\mathcal{V}$. The *tensor product* $v \otimes w$ of vectors v and w in $\mathcal{V}$ consists of the linear map in $\mathcal{V}^*$ defined for all $u \in \mathcal{V}$ by

$$(v \otimes w)u = (w \cdot u)v. \tag{6.10}$$

The *alternating product* $v \wedge w$ of two tensors v and w consists of the tensor

$$v \wedge w = v \otimes w - w \otimes v. \tag{6.11}$$

Naturally, the alternating product has the property that $v \wedge v = 0$.

Each choice of an isomorphism $\diamond : \mathcal{V} \to \mathcal{V}^*$ induces a dual momentum functional $p^*(\mathcal{B}; \chi, m)$ such that

$$p^*(b, m, v^*) = p(b, m, \diamond^{-1}(v^*)). \tag{6.12}$$

To formalize rotational momentum, we choose some particular isomorphism $\diamond$, determine the corresponding dual momentum function p^*, and define the rotational momentum $L_{x_0}(b, x, m, v)$ of a body element b at location x of mass m and velocity v about a point x_0 by

$$L_{x_0}(b, x, m, v) = p^*(b, m, (x - x_0) \wedge v). \tag{6.13}$$

The linearity of the maps involved in this definition means we can rewrite rotational momentum as

$$L_{x_0}(b, x, m, v) = (x - x_0) \wedge p^*(b, m, v). \tag{6.14}$$

6.2.3 Discrete momentum

The traditional development of momentum just summarized simply defines momentum in terms of mass and motion. To understand the nature of momentum in this more general setting, we must reexamine assumptions implicit in the usual formalization.

The first axiom of momentum simply states that mass and velocity values uniquely determine momentum values.

Axiom P1 *For each mass value $m \in \mathcal{M}$ and velocity value $v \in T\mathcal{S}$, there exists a unique value of the momentum corresponding to m and v.*

We collect the momentum values corresponding to all mass and velocity values into a set $\mathcal{P}$. Axiom P1 implies the existence of a function

$$p : \mathcal{M} \times T\mathcal{S} \to \mathcal{P} \tag{6.15}$$

that constructs momentum values $p(m, v)$ from masses $m \in \mathcal{M}$ and velocities $v \in T\mathcal{S}$.

6.2.3.1 Momentum values

In the concepts of discrete mechanics just developed, both the set $\mathcal{M}$ of mass values and the set $T\mathcal{S}$ of local translations consist of free modules over commutative rings $\mathcal{R}_{\mathcal{M}}$ and $\mathcal{R}_{\mathcal{S}}$. We thus look to the set of momentum values to have a similar character.

Axiom P2 *The set $\mathcal{P}$ of possible momentum values forms a free module $\mathcal{P}$ over the ring of scalars $\mathcal{R}_{\mathcal{P}} = \mathcal{R}_{\mathcal{M}} \times \mathcal{R}_{\mathcal{S}}$ associated with the product module $\mathcal{M} \times T\mathcal{S}$.*

Alternatively, one might obtain the desired structure by rephrasing Axiom P2 to state that $\mathcal{P}$ forms a bimodule over the two rings $\mathcal{R}_{\mathcal{M}}$ and $\mathcal{R}_{\mathcal{S}}$. This might permit a simpler analysis that avoids introducing a ring of scalars when combining mass and velocity vector spaces over the same field.

6.2.3.2 Bilinearity

Mass and velocity values not only determine momentum values, they do so in a way such that separate sums and multiples of mass and velocity values yield sums and multiples of momentum values. The next axiom captures this algebraically.

Axiom P3 *The momentum mapping p constitutes a bilinear function from $\mathcal{M} \times T\mathcal{S}$ to $\mathcal{P}$.*

The bilinearity required by Axiom P3 permits us to view the momentum map as a tensor. The tensor definitions given in Section 6.2.2 apply more generally to bilinear maps from modules to rings, not just maps to $\mathbb{R}$, so that $\mathcal{M} \otimes_{\mathcal{R}} \mathcal{M}'$ denotes the tensor product of modules $\mathcal{M}$ and $\mathcal{M}'$ over a ring $\mathcal{R}$. This bilinearity has several implications.

The first implication of bilinearity comes about because the tensor product $\mathcal{M} \otimes_{\mathcal{R}_{\mathcal{P}}} T\mathcal{S}$ is universal among bilinear mappings from the product module $\mathcal{M} \times T\mathcal{S}$. This means simply that one can decompose the mapping p into the composition of the natural mapping that takes the pair $(m, v) \in \mathcal{M} \times T\mathcal{S}$ to the product tensor $m \otimes v \in \mathcal{M} \otimes_{\mathcal{R}_{\mathcal{P}}} T\mathcal{S}$ with the induced bilinear mapping $p^{\otimes} : \mathcal{M} \otimes T\mathcal{S} \to \mathcal{P}$ defined so that $p(m, v) = p^{\otimes}(m \otimes v)$ for each m and v.

By construction $\mathcal{P}$ forms the image of p, so by a standard theorem of algebra we know that $\mathcal{P}$ is isomorphic to a submodule of $\mathcal{M} \times T\mathcal{S}$. Each particular isomorphism lets us regard $\mathcal{P}$ as a submodule of $\mathcal{M} \times T\mathcal{S}$. We thus can regard the momentum construction function as reflecting an enlarged momentum mapping

$$p^\times : \mathcal{M} \times T\mathcal{S} \to \mathcal{M} \times T\mathcal{S}. \tag{6.16}$$

Composing the chosen isomorphism with the ordinary projection functions on $\mathcal{M} \times T\mathcal{S}$ thus induces mappings

$$p_{\mathcal{M}}^\times \quad : \quad \mathcal{P} \to \mathcal{M} \tag{6.17}$$

$$p_{\mathcal{V}}^\times \quad : \quad \mathcal{P} \to T\mathcal{S} \tag{6.18}$$

that project momentum values to mass and velocity values. The pair of functions $(p_{\mathcal{M}}^\times, p_{\mathcal{V}}^\times)$ thus represent the chosen isomorphism of $\mathcal{P}$ with $\mathcal{M} \times T\mathcal{S}$.

Traditional mechanics certainly has momentum values that form a submodule of $\mathcal{M} \times T\mathcal{S}$. Indeed, momentum values form a vector space identical to $T\mathcal{S}$ because mass values in $\mathbb{R}$ also represent scalars in the real vector space of translations $\mathcal{V}$. One can thus view traditional momenta as spatial vectors.

The second implication of bilinearity is that we can regard $p^\otimes$ as factoring through its arguments separately, so that each mass value $m \in \mathcal{M}$ determines a linear mapping $p_m^\otimes : T\mathcal{S} \to \mathcal{P}$ and each velocity value $v \in T\mathcal{S}$ determines a linear mapping $p_v^\otimes : \mathcal{M} \to \mathcal{P}$. The traditional conception of momentum certainly implies the existence of such mappings, but also requires more, namely that momentum be collinear with or proportional to the velocity. We thus restrict the momentum mapping to produce values collinear with the generating mass and velocity values. Formally, we deem two vectors v and v' in a module over a ring $\mathcal{R}$ collinear iff there is some $r \in \mathcal{R}$ such that $rv = v'$. Note that by choice of $r = 0$, the zero vector is collinear with every vector. We thus can capture the collinearity requirement in the following axiom.

Axiom P4 *For every $m \in \mathcal{M}$ there exists a scalar $a(m) \in \mathcal{R}_\mathcal{P}$ such that for every $v \in T\mathcal{S}$*

$$p_m^\times(v) = a(m)v, \tag{6.19}$$

and for every $v \in T\mathcal{S}$ there exists a scalar $b(v) \in \mathcal{R}_\mathcal{P}$ such that for every $m \in \mathcal{M}$

$$p_v^\times(m) = b(v)m. \tag{6.20}$$

The traditional conception of momentum satisfies this axiom easily: for mass m we have proportionality value $a(m) = m$, and for velocity v we have the proportionality value $b(v) = 1$. In my treatment of discrete memory in Chapter 10, we have the proportionality values $a(m) = 1$ and $b(v) = 1_{\mathcal{M}}$.

6.2.3.3 Dimensionality

Earlier we required that $\mathcal{M}$ and $T\mathcal{S}$ consist of free modules. The tensor product $\mathcal{M} \otimes T\mathcal{S}$ is therefore also a free module. Since $\mathcal{M} \otimes T\mathcal{S}$ is a module over a commutative ring $\mathcal{R}_{\mathcal{P}}$, it too has a well-defined dimension. By Axiom P2, the same holds true of $\mathcal{P}$.

In discrete mechanics, mass values need not admit an interpretation as spatial scalars, thus limiting the mixing of dimensions seen in traditional mechanics. In consequence, momentum values can form a space for which the number of dimensions lies between that of velocity space $T\mathcal{S}$ and the product $\mathcal{M} \times T\mathcal{S}$ of the mass space with the velocity space. The traditional physical momentum mapping illustrates a case in which $\dim(\mathcal{P}) < \dim(\mathcal{M}) + \dim(\mathcal{S})$ ($3 < 1 + 3$). The interpretation of discrete momentum presented in Chapter 10 illustrates a case in which $\dim(\mathcal{P}) = \dim(\mathcal{M}) + \dim(\mathcal{S})$.

Need mechanics place a nontrivial lower bound on the dimensionality of momentum values? All the examples we have considered resemble the ones herein, in which momenta have at least as many nontrivial dimensions as velocities. Extrapolating from these examples, we regard the spatial aspect of momentum as foremost, and assume that the dimensionality of momenta meets or exceeds that of velocities.

Assumption P5 *Momentum has at least as many dimensions as velocity; formally,* $\dim(\mathcal{S}) \leq \dim(\mathcal{P})$.

Of course, if Axiom P4 forbade collapsing maps and null constants of proportionality, it would imply that momenta have at least as many dimensions as mass or velocity. For example, if one assumes that there must always be some mass value m such that $p_m^{\times}(v) = \mathbf{1}v = v$ for every $v \in T\mathcal{S}$ (here $\mathbf{1}$ means $1_{\mathcal{R}_{\mathcal{P}}}$), then momentum must have at least as many dimensions as does velocity. The value $m = 1_{\mathcal{M}} = 1$ satisfies this requirement in traditional mechanics, and every mass value satisfies this requirement in the mechanization of memory considered in Chapter 10. Future investigation might uncover cases for which appropriate momenta resemble a proper subspace of velocities, or even resemble a subspace of masses with no spatial character.

When $\dim(\mathcal{P}) = \dim(\mathcal{S})$, I say that momenta are *spatial*, and when $\dim(\mathcal{P}) > \dim(\mathcal{S})$, I say that momenta are *superspatial*. We say the mechanical system as a whole is spatial or superspatial, respectively, as its momenta are spatial or superspatial. One cannot reduce the distinction between spatial and superspatial momenta to the distinction between linear and nonlinear masses. Even linear masses may yield superspatial momenta if the mass values do not fold into spatial scalars in the right way. In maximally superspatial momenta,

$\dim(\mathcal{P}) = \dim(\mathcal{M}) + \dim(T\mathcal{S})$, and one can decompose each momentum value into a unique mass and velocity value, while in spatial momenta, the same momentum value may not admit a unique decomposition. For this reason, one might alternatively label the spatial–superspatial distinction instead as the distinction between merged or separated momenta, or mass-indeterminate and mass-determinate momenta.

We do not yet understand how much of the special character of traditional mechanics stems from the special properties of three-dimensional space and how much stems from the spatial character of traditional momentum.

6.2.3.4 Geometry

Although the requirements stated earlier ensure that the set of momenta $\mathcal{P}$ forms a free module over a commutative ring, we have not yet required any sort of metric or inner product structure on this module. To extend the notion of rotational momentum to the discrete case in a comprehensive way, we now require that the space of momenta have a geometric structure akin to that required of the spatial translation space.

Axiom P6 *The module $\mathcal{P}$ of momentum values has a structure of a pseudo-Euclidean module of the same general structure as the spatial translation space, characterized by*

(i) *a Euclidean metric $d_{\mathcal{P}} : \mathcal{P} \times \mathcal{P} \to \mathbb{R}^+$,*

(ii) *a separation function $\sigma_{\mathcal{P}} : \mathcal{P} \times \mathcal{P} \to \mathcal{R}$ such that*

    (a) *$\sigma_{\mathcal{P}}(p, p') = 0$ (in $\mathcal{R}$) whenever $d_{\mathcal{P}}(p, p') = 0$, and*

    (b) *each bijection $\phi : \mathcal{P} \to \mathcal{P}$ preserves distance only if it also preserves separation, that is, if $d_{\mathcal{P}}(p, p') = d_{\mathcal{P}}(\phi(p), \phi(p'))$ for every $p, p' \in \mathcal{P}$, then $\sigma_{\mathcal{P}}(p, p') = \sigma_{\mathcal{P}}(\phi(p), \phi(p'))$ for every $p, p' \in \mathcal{P}$, and*

(iii) *a generalized inner product $\langle \cdot, \cdot \rangle : \mathcal{P} \times \mathcal{P} \to \mathcal{R}$ over $\mathcal{P}$ such that*

    (a) *$\sigma_{\mathcal{P}}(p, p') = \langle p - p', p - p' \rangle$ for every $p, p' \in \mathcal{P}$, and*

    (b) *for every every isometry $v \in \overline{V}_{d_{\mathcal{P}}}$, there exists a $p_0 \in \mathcal{P}$ and transformation Q orthogonal with respect to $\langle \cdot, \cdot \rangle$ on $\mathcal{P}$ such that $v(p) = v(p_0) + Q(p - p_0)$ for each $p \in \mathcal{P}$.*

This long axiom combines several axioms adopted earlier for space. We also obtain a topology on $\mathcal{P}$ from the metric $d_{\mathcal{P}}$.

6.2.3.5 Duality

We write $\mathcal{P}^{(*)}$ to denote a module that is semidual to $\mathcal{P}$ in the sense that

$$p_M^\times(p^*(b, m, v^*)) \;=\; p_M^\times(p(b, m, v)), \tag{6.21}$$

$$p_V^\times(p^*(b, m, v^*)) \;=\; \diamond(p_V^\times(p(b, m, v))). \tag{6.22}$$

Each isomorphism $\diamond$ of $\mathcal{V}$ with its dual $\mathcal{V}^*$ thus provides an isomorphism between $\mathcal{P}$ and $\mathcal{P}^{(*)}$.

We then define discrete rotational momenta much as before, but taking into account the semidual structure of $\mathcal{P}^{(*)}$, and recast (6.14) using a modified alternation product $\wedge^*$ defined so that

$$L_{x_0}(b, x, m, v) \;=\; (x - x_0) \wedge^* p^*(b, m, v) \tag{6.23}$$

$$=\; p^*(b, m, (x - x_0) \wedge v). \tag{6.24}$$

In the following discussion, let us streamline the notation by writing $\wedge$ even when $\wedge^*$ is meant.

6.2.4 Hybrid momentum

Hybrid momentum combines factor dimensions of mass and velocity into hybrid mass and velocity. Previous sections have described the structure of hybrid mass and velocity. We obtain hybrid momentum notions by direct products of those notions and the factor momentum mappings. These products retain all the desired structure, as the product of free modules over commutative scalar rings is again a free module over the product ring.

We briefly examine the special structure of momentum for traditional physical space. Section 5.4 required that hybrid spatial modules contain submodules representing different subspaces, sometimes including a real vector space $\mathcal{S}_p$ representing the ordinary conception of physical space and a module $\mathcal{S}_{\bar{p}}$ representing the nontraditional dimensions of space. We similarly can expect that mass contain at least the standard physical dimension. In this case, we of course use the standard definitions of linear and rotational momentum over the traditional dimensions $\mathcal{S}_p$. The standard definitions yield a hybrid rotational momentum consisting of the tensor product of the rotational momenta in physical and nonphysical component spaces.

6.3 Force

Mechanics extends geometry with the notion of forces acting on bodies, or more precisely, forces exerted by bodies on each other. We write $f(\mathcal{B}, \mathcal{C})$ to denote the force exerted on $\mathcal{B}$ by $\mathcal{C}$. This conception covers all pairs of bodies, including $f(\mathcal{B}, \mathcal{O})$ and $f(\mathcal{B}, \mathcal{U})$. Mechanics requires that the null body $\mathcal{O}$ exerts no force, but admits the possibility that the universal body $\mathcal{U}$ does exert forces on bodies it contains, forces one might think of as free-floating forces acting on a body but not associated with specific other separate bodies.

We characterize the fundamental properties of forces in terms of *systems of forces* or *force systems*, each of which describes the forces acting on all bodies at some instant. A force system consists of a mapping of pairs of separate bodies to force values in a set $\mathcal{F}$. Traditional mechanics identifies force values with spatial vectors in $\mathcal{V}$; discrete mechanics generalizes this to characterize $\mathcal{F}$ in terms of the space $\mathcal{P}$ of momentum values. Mechanics also concerns *systems of torques*, which consist of mappings, akin to systems of forces, of separate bodies and spatial locations to linear transformations of force values.

One may state mechanical axioms about forces in several equivalent ways, as does Noll (1958, 1963, 1972, 1973). The following employs a formulation of the axioms by Truesdell (1991) that separates the central structures from the specific assumptions of continuum mechanics somewhat more explicitly than do some of Noll's continuum-focused presentations.

To summarize, the first axiom of forces states that forces—exerted on or by separate subbodies of a body—combine additively. The second axiom states a balance of forces, expressed through the requirement that the exterior of a body exerts no force on the body, that the sum of all forces on each body vanishes. This last condition may seem strange, but really just amounts to treating all components of familiar force equations equally. In particular, this axiom leads to treating the inertial force $-ma$ as just one special sort of force canceling out the sum of all the other forces on the body, thus rewriting the familiar $f = ma$ as $f - ma = 0$. The third axiom states that a similar balance of torques holds for all bodies and all spatial reference points. These laws apply more generally than might appear, since they hold for all bodies and parts of bodies, not merely body points.

Each force system induces two subsidiary force systems, internal forces between separate parts of a body, and external forces exerted by the exterior of a body on its parts. The fourth axiom states that the internal forces are contact forces that vary continuously with the area of the contact boundary between the two parts, while the fifth axiom states that the external forces can be by contact and at a distance and vary continuously with the mass, volume, and contact boundary areas of the parts. Standard continuum mechanics shows that these axioms on body and contact forces imply the existence of Cauchy's stress tensor, which in turn summarizes both types of forces on the body through Cauchy's equation of motion $\dot{p} = B + \mathrm{div}(T)$, in which $p = mv$ is the inertia, $-\dot{p}$ is the inertial force, B is the body force, and $\mathrm{div}(T)$ is the divergence of the stress tensor T.

6.3.1 Systems of forces

A system of forces (or *force configuration*) on a universe $\mathcal{B}$ is an assignment f of elements of a set $\mathcal{F}$ of force values to all pairs of separate bodies of $\mathcal{B}$. Writing $(\mathcal{B} \times \mathcal{B})_0$ to mean the set of pairs of separate bodies of $\mathcal{B}$, we thus have

$$f : (\mathcal{B} \times \mathcal{B})_0 \to \mathcal{F}, \tag{6.25}$$

with $f(\mathcal{B}, \mathcal{C})$ denoting the force exerted on $\mathcal{B}$ by $\mathcal{C}$. Holding one or the other of these bodies fixed, we also write $f_{\Leftarrow \mathcal{C}} : \mathcal{B} \to \mathcal{F}$ to denote the forces exerted on bodies by $\mathcal{C}$ and $f_{\Rightarrow \mathcal{B}} : \mathcal{B} \to \mathcal{F}$ to denote the forces exerted on $\mathcal{B}$ by bodies, such that

$$f(\mathcal{B}, \mathcal{C}) \;=\; f_{\Leftarrow \mathcal{C}}(\mathcal{B}) \tag{6.26}$$
$$=\; f_{\Rightarrow \mathcal{B}}(\mathcal{C}) \tag{6.27}$$

for each separate $\mathcal{B}, \mathcal{C} \in \mathcal{B}$.

Since bodies are separate from their exteriors, we can consider $f(\mathcal{B}, \mathcal{B}^e)$, the *resultant force* on $\mathcal{B}$, or the force exerted on $\mathcal{B}$ by its exterior.

Each instant of a history may manifest a different collection of forces, each represented in the theory by an instantaneous force configuration. We write

$$\mathcal{C}_f = ((\mathcal{B} \times \mathcal{B})_0 \to \mathcal{F}) \tag{6.28}$$

to mean the set of all force configurations, and as with mass, extend the notation to write a *force variation* as a function

$$f : \mathcal{T} \to \mathcal{C}_f, \tag{6.29}$$

writing $f_t(\mathcal{B}, \mathcal{C})$ or $f(\mathcal{B}, \mathcal{C}, t)$ as convenient to mean the force exerted on $\mathcal{B}$ by $\mathcal{C}$ at time t.

6.3.1.1 Force values

We follow mechanical tradition in identifying $\mathcal{F}$ with the translation space of momenta $\mathcal{P}$, intending that forces can result in spatial motions, in mass changes, or both, and that changes in momenta cover all these cases.

Axiom F1 *The set $\mathcal{F}$ of force values forms a module isomorphic to the translation space of the momentum module $\mathcal{P}$.*

In traditional mechanics, this requirement identifies force values with spatial vectors because one can treat momentum values as spatial vectors. In the formalization of Chapter 10, this identifies force values with pairs of mass and velocity vectors.

Because traditional mechanics views $\mathcal{P}$ as a vector space, it admits an isomorphism with its translation space. We can do the same with our assumptions, and use the simplest such isomorphism by regarding $\mathcal{F}$ as the same space as $\mathcal{P}$, so that

$$\mathcal{F} = \mathcal{P} = T\mathcal{P}. \qquad (6.30)$$

The set of possible forces thus inherits the topology, metric, and inner product of the set of momenta.

The relation of force values to the space of translations and momenta raises the issue of how forces changes with changes of observer. We require that forces transform as vectors indifferent to the framing used to describe the motions of the bodies involved.

Axiom F2 *Forces are frame indifferent; that is,*

$$f^{\star} = Qf. \qquad (6.31)$$

6.3.1.2 Additive forces

We now turn to characterizing relationships holding within configurations of forces present at each some instant. The next two axioms on forces state that forces are additive on separate bodies.

Axiom F3 $f(\mathcal{C}_1 \sqcup \mathcal{C}_2, \mathcal{B}) = f(\mathcal{C}_1, \mathcal{B}) + f(\mathcal{C}_2, \mathcal{B})$ *for pairwise separate bodies* $\mathcal{B}$, $\mathcal{C}_1$, *and* $\mathcal{C}_2$.

Axiom F4 $f(\mathcal{B}, \mathcal{C}_1 \sqcup \mathcal{C}_2) = f(\mathcal{B}, \mathcal{C}_1) + f(\mathcal{B}, \mathcal{C}_2)$ *for pairwise separate bodies* $\mathcal{B}$, $\mathcal{C}_1$, *and* $\mathcal{C}_2$.

Writing $\mathbf{0}$ to denote the null or zero force, we easily extend any system of forces to $\mathcal{F} : (\overline{\mathcal{B}} \times \overline{\mathcal{B}})_0$ by defining

$$f(\mathcal{B}, \mathcal{O}) = f(\mathcal{O}, \mathcal{B}) = \mathbf{0} \qquad (6.32)$$

for all $\mathcal{B} \in \overline{\mathcal{B}}$ (including $\mathcal{B} = \mathcal{U}$ and $\mathcal{B} = \mathcal{O}$). In addition, we can extend these axioms slightly to avoid the assumption of separate bodies by taking as axioms instead the following, which reduce to the original ones in the case of separate bodies:

Axiom F3a $f(\mathcal{C}_1 \sqcup \mathcal{C}_2, \mathcal{B}) = f(\mathcal{C}_1, \mathcal{B}) + f(\mathcal{C}_2, \mathcal{B}) - f(\mathcal{C}_1 \sqcap \mathcal{C}_2, \mathcal{B})$.

Axiom F3b $f(\mathcal{O}, \mathcal{B}) = 0.$

Axiom F4a $f(\mathcal{B}, \mathcal{C}_1 \sqcup \mathcal{C}_2) = f(\mathcal{B}, \mathcal{C}_1) + f(\mathcal{B}, \mathcal{C}_2) - f(\mathcal{B}, \mathcal{C}_1 \sqcap \mathcal{C}_2).$

Axiom F4b $f(\mathcal{B}, \mathcal{O}) = 0.$

6.3.1.3 Measurable forces

Axiom F3 implies that the forces exerted on separate parts of a body $\mathcal{B}$ by its exterior $\mathcal{B}^e$ are additive; that is, if we have $\mathcal{A}_1 \precsim \mathcal{B}$, $\mathcal{A}_2 \precsim \mathcal{B}$, and $\mathcal{A}_1 \sqcap \mathcal{A}_2 = \mathcal{O}$, then we have

$$f(\mathcal{A}_1 \sqcup \mathcal{A}_2, \mathcal{B}^e) = f(\mathcal{A}_1, \mathcal{B}^e) + f(\mathcal{A}_2, \mathcal{B}^e). \tag{6.33}$$

The next axiom goes further and states that we may describe such exterior forces with a $\mathcal{F}$-valued measure on the body.

Axiom F5 *For each $\mathcal{B} \in \overline{\mathcal{B}}$, the function $f_{\Leftarrow \mathcal{B}^e}$ is a $\mathcal{F}$-valued measure over $\mathcal{B}$.*

Since we regard bodies as sets, this axiom means we can write

$$f(\mathcal{A}, \mathcal{B}^e) = \int_{\mathcal{A}} df_{\Leftarrow \mathcal{B}^e} \tag{6.34}$$

if $\mathcal{A} \precsim \mathcal{B}$. Another way of putting this is that if $\mathcal{A}$ and $\mathcal{B}$ are separate, $f_{\Leftarrow \mathcal{B}}$ is a measure over $\mathcal{A}$.

6.3.1.4 Pairwise equilibrated forces

The preceding axioms characterizing systems of forces provide a structure suitable for combining forces and apportioning them over subbodies, but otherwise say nothing about the relation of one force to another. The next axiom restricts forces more strongly.

If all mutual forces are equal and opposite, that is, if

$$f(\mathcal{B}, \mathcal{C}) = -f(\mathcal{C}, \mathcal{B}) \tag{6.35}$$

for all $(\mathcal{B}, \mathcal{C}) \in (\mathcal{B} \times \mathcal{B})_0$, we say the system of forces is *pairwise equilibrated*. The next axiom requires this property of mechanical forces.

Axiom F6 *Forces are pairwise equilibrated.*

This restriction recalls Newton's principle of action and reaction, but is not equivalent to it. Noll's early axioms for mechanics posit this axiom, but his later axioms instead derive this restriction on forces from an axiom requiring the frame indifference of a quantity called the *working* of the system of forces.

6.3.1.5 *Applied forces and self-forces*

In many practical situations we focus attention on a particular set of bodies and wish to understand the interactions and motions of these bodies, and we ignore the forces and motions outside the focus of attention except for their net effect on the parts of the subsystem of interest. This division of the universe is called *isolating the system*.

We express this restriction of attention in the notion of a *great system* or *locality*. A locality $\mathcal{G}$ is the subset of $\mathcal{B}$ of all the bodies of interest, so that its exterior $\mathcal{G}^e$ represents the parts of the universe we wish to leave unexamined. We consider $\mathcal{G}^e$ only through its resultant forces $f(\mathcal{B}, \mathcal{G}^e)$ on bodies $\mathcal{B} \in \mathcal{G}$, and ignore the internal dynamics of $\mathcal{G}^e$ itself. This restriction of attention yields a submotion of the full history, that of $\mathcal{G}$ alone.

The locality $\mathcal{G}$ induces a division of the exterior of $\mathcal{B}$ into two parts: $\mathcal{G}^e$, the exterior of the locality, and $\mathcal{B}_{\mathcal{G}}^e = \sqcup(\mathcal{G} \setminus \mathcal{B})$, the exterior of $\mathcal{B}$ within or relative to the locality. The resultant force $f(\mathcal{B}, \mathcal{B}^e)$ thus divides into two components: $f(\mathcal{B}, \mathcal{G}^e)$, and $f(\mathcal{B}, \mathcal{B}_{\mathcal{G}}^e)$, with

$$f(\mathcal{B}, \mathcal{B}^e) = f(\mathcal{B}, \mathcal{G}^e) + f(\mathcal{B}, \mathcal{B}_{\mathcal{G}}^e).$$

Mechanics uses the term *applied force* to refer to resultant forces within great systems, defining $f^a(\mathcal{B}) = f(\mathcal{B}, \mathcal{B}_{\mathcal{G}}^e)$. We call the force a body exerts on itself the *self-force* $f^s(\mathcal{B}) = f(\mathcal{B}, \mathcal{B})$.

The total force $f(\mathcal{B}, \mathcal{U})$ on a body $\mathcal{B}$ is thus the sum of the applied force, self-force, and nonlocal forces; that is,

$$f(\mathcal{B}, \mathcal{U}) = f^a(\mathcal{B}) + f^s(\mathcal{B}) + f(\mathcal{B}, \mathcal{G}^e). \tag{6.36}$$

Traditional mechanics considers many situations in which the nonlocal and self-forces vanish, so that the total force on a body consists of the applied force on the body.

6.3.1.6 *Balanced forces*

If all resultant forces are zero, that is, if

$$f(\mathcal{B}, \mathcal{B}^e) = 0 \tag{6.37}$$

for all $\mathcal{B} \in \overline{\mathcal{B}}$, then the system of forces is said to be *balanced*.

Because resultant forces satisfy the identity

$$f(\mathcal{B}, \mathcal{C}) + f(\mathcal{C}, \mathcal{B}) = f(\mathcal{B}, \mathcal{B}^e) + f(\mathcal{C}, \mathcal{C}^e) - f(\mathcal{B} \sqcup \mathcal{C}, (\mathcal{B} \sqcup \mathcal{C})^e), \tag{6.38}$$

it follows that a system of forces is pairwise equilibrated iff the resultant force $f(\mathcal{B}, \mathcal{B}^e)$, regarded as a function of $\mathcal{B}$, is additive on the separate bodies of $\overline{\mathcal{B}}$.

The constant function **0** is additive, so it follows that every balanced system of forces is pairwise equilibrated.

This does not mean that all forces between pairs of bodies are equilibrated. It can be shown (Truesdell 1991, pp. 20–21, 27–29) that universal forces equal self-forces in a balanced system of forces, that is,

$$f(\mathcal{B}, \mathcal{U}) = f(\mathcal{B}, \mathcal{B}), \tag{6.39}$$

so self-forces vanish only if the universal body is passive, that is, exerts no force. Thus a balanced system of forces is pairwise equilibrated for all bodies iff the universal body is passive.

6.3.1.7 Body and contact forces

Mechanics assumes that forces may be decomposed into two parts: *body forces* between arbitrary bodies, and *contact forces* between bodies sharing a boundary, that is, bodies sharing a nonnull subpart. Decomposability of forces in this way means that for each force $f(\mathcal{A}, \mathcal{C})$ we can identify a body force $f^{\mathrm{B}}(\mathcal{A}, \mathcal{C})$ and a contact force $f^{\mathrm{C}}(\mathcal{A}, \mathcal{C})$ such that

$$f(\mathcal{A}, \mathcal{C}) = f^{\mathrm{B}}(\mathcal{A}, \mathcal{C}) + f^{\mathrm{C}}(\mathcal{A}, \mathcal{C}). \tag{6.40}$$

Because bodies in contact may exert both contact and body forces on each other, just knowing the total force configuration does not tell one what body and contact forces exist. Instead, one must identify these forces separately, and regard the total forces as derived from these components. For this to make sense, we assume that body and contact forces form force systems on their own.

Assumption F7 *Body and contact forces constitute force systems that each satisfy Axioms F2, F3a, F3b, F4a, F4b, F5, and F6.*

It follows that the force system constructed as the sum of body and contact forces,

$$f = f^{\mathrm{B}} + f^{\mathrm{C}}, \tag{6.41}$$

also satisfies the axioms for force systems.

It is possible to derive both Axiom F5 and the content of Assumption F7 from a more fundamental axiom bounding the magnitude of forces by certain multiples of areas of contact and masses of bodies. I will not elaborate the details of this result, but instead summarize Truesdell's (1991, pp. 155–157) treatment. We write $\partial\chi(\mathcal{B})$ to denote the boundary of the shape of a body $\mathcal{B}$ in a placement χ, that is, the intersection of the topological closure of the shape $\chi(\mathcal{B})$ of the body and the closure of its complement. We write $\partial^{*}\chi(\mathcal{B})$ to denote the *reduced boundary*, by which we mean the set of all points in $\partial\chi(\mathcal{B})$ at which the boundary has an *outer normal*. Paraphrasing Truesdell slightly, the more fundamental axiom reads as follows.

Axiom F8 *Let $\mathcal{A}$ and $\mathcal{C}$ be separate bodies, the area of contact of whose shapes is sufficiently small, and let the mass of $\mathcal{A}$ be sufficiently small. Then*

$$|f(\mathcal{A},\mathcal{C})| \leq k_1 Area(\partial^*\chi(\mathcal{A}) \cap \partial^*\chi(\mathcal{C})) + k_2(\mathcal{C})m(\mathcal{A}), \qquad (6.42)$$

for some positive constant k_1 and some positive, bounded function $k_2 : \mathcal{B}_m \rightarrow \mathbb{R}$ such that

$$\lim_{m(\mathcal{C})\rightarrow 0} k_2(\mathcal{C}) = 0. \qquad (6.43)$$

One can then use this axiom to prove the existence of systems f^B and f^C of body and contact forces such that

$$\begin{aligned} |f^B(\mathcal{A},\mathcal{C})| &\leq k_2(\mathcal{C})m(\mathcal{A}) & (6.44) \\ |f^C(\mathcal{A},\mathcal{C})| &\leq k_1 Area(\partial^*\chi(\mathcal{A}) \cap \partial^*\chi(\mathcal{C})) & (6.45) \\ f(\mathcal{A},\mathcal{C}) &= f^B(\mathcal{A},\mathcal{C}) + f^C(\mathcal{A},\mathcal{C}). & (6.46) \end{aligned}$$

I will not develop the theory of body and contact forces other than to note one general result: if the system of forces f is balanced, then both the system of body forces and the system of contact forces are pairwise equilibrated. That is, if $f^B + f^C$ is balanced, then for all $(\mathcal{A},\mathcal{C}) \in (\overline{\mathcal{B}} \times \overline{\mathcal{B}})_0$, we have

$$f^B(\mathcal{A},\mathcal{C}) = -f^B(\mathcal{C},\mathcal{A}) \qquad (6.47)$$

and

$$f^C(\mathcal{A},\mathcal{C}) = -f^C(\mathcal{C},\mathcal{A}). \qquad (6.48)$$

As Truesdell (1991, p. 163) notes, one might call this the theorem of action and reaction.

6.3.2 Torques

The isomorphism between the spaces of force and momentum values lets us use the spatial inner product to form the inner product of forces and other vectors such as positions, velocities, and accelerations. We use this isomorphism and the momentum relations to define the *simple torque* F_{x_0} about the point x_0 generated by force f in the usual way, with

$$F_{x_0} = (x - x_0) \wedge f. \qquad (6.49)$$

Each force system f on a universe $\mathcal{B}$ and spatial point x_0 combine to produce a system of torques (or *torque configuration*), namely an assignment F of elements of a set $\mathcal{L}$ of torque values to all pairs of bodies of $\mathcal{B}$. We thus have

$$F : \mathcal{B} \times \mathcal{B} \times \mathcal{S} \to \mathcal{L}, \tag{6.50}$$

with $F(\mathcal{B}, \mathcal{C}, x)$ denoting the torque about x exerted on $\mathcal{B}$ by $\mathcal{C}$. In traditional mechanics, $\mathcal{L}$ is just $\mathcal{F}^*$, and in the discrete setting we assume $\mathcal{L} = \mathcal{F}^{(*)} = \mathcal{P}^{(*)}$.

Each torque configuration F must satisfy corresponding versions of Axioms F2, F3a, F3b, F4a, F4b, F5, and F6.

Axiom F9 $F(\mathcal{C}_1 \sqcup \mathcal{C}_2, \mathcal{B}, x_0) = F(\mathcal{C}_1, \mathcal{B}, x_0) + F(\mathcal{C}_2, \mathcal{B}, x_0) - F(\mathcal{C}_1 \sqcap \mathcal{C}_2, \mathcal{B}, x_0)$.

Axiom F10 $F(\mathcal{O}, \mathcal{B}, x_0) = 0$.

Axiom F11 $F(\mathcal{B}, \mathcal{C}_1 \sqcup \mathcal{C}_2, x_0) = F(\mathcal{B}, \mathcal{C}_1, x_0) + F(\mathcal{B}, \mathcal{C}_2, x_0) - F(\mathcal{B}, \mathcal{C}_1 \sqcap \mathcal{C}_2, x_0)$.

Axiom F12 $F(\mathcal{B}, \mathcal{O}, x_0) = 0$.

Axiom F13 *For each $\mathcal{B} \in \overline{\mathcal{B}}$, the function $F_{\Leftarrow \mathcal{B}^c}$ is an $\mathcal{L}$-valued measure over* $\mathcal{B}$.

Axiom F14 *Torques are frame indifferent; that is,*

$$F^* = QF. \tag{6.51}$$

Some traditional treatments of particle mechanics falsely suggest that torques represent a purely derivative concept of the concept of force, and that one needs only axioms on forces to capture mechanical law. In fact, mechanics involves laws on torques that stand independent of the laws on forces. The first of these, stated in the following axiom, requires that torques balance in addition to forces.

Axiom F15 *Torques are pairwise equilibrated; that is,*

$$F(\mathcal{B}, \mathcal{C}, x) = F(\mathcal{C}, \mathcal{B}, x) \tag{6.52}$$

for all bodies $\mathcal{B}, \mathcal{C}$ and locations x.

Like Axiom F6, Axiom F15 also recalls Newton's action–reaction principle.

6.3.3 Stress

As described in the preceding section, Noll's axiomatization starts with forces and motions, and then constructs the notion of torque from the notions of space and force. He then quickly proceeds to construct *stress* from force, torque, and body and contact forces. Stress serves as the primary analytical concept of continuum mechanics, and forms a symmetric tensor field, from which one can derive the body and contact forces existing at any point in or on a body.

Noll's construction of stress from body and contact forces proceeds by placing certain smoothness assumptions on the force and torque fields. Some of the smoothness assumptions only serve to make the mathematical constructions complete, and appear to lack strong physical motivation. Noll (1973) apologizes for the need to introduce the smoothness assumptions, and invites improvement of the axiomatization to render these technical assumptions superfluous. In light of the broader applications of mechanics considered in the preceding chapters, in which assumptions of continuity do not apply generally, the artificiality of Noll's continuity assumptions should not seem surprising.

Although the concept of stress provides the most natural mathematical formulation of continuum mechanics, and the most convenient means for many calculations in continuum mechanics, I do not develop the theory of hybrid and discrete stress here. The issue of smoothness assumptions just mentioned naturally gives one pause in seeking a notion of stress that provides analytical power in discrete mechanics. Indeed, the role of torque itself in discrete mechanics engenders some hesitations. I thus focus attention in what follows on the underlying notions of force and torque rather than on the theoretical construct of stress.

6.3.4 Discrete forces and torques

Discrete mechanics retains essentially all the structure given for forces in traditional and hybrid mechanics except for the traditional assumptions about the character of force values, which change to reflect the changed structures of space, mass, and momentum. Specifically, the structure of $\mathcal{F}$ constitutes the translation space of $\mathcal{P}$; $\mathcal{F}$ thus consists of a free module over a ring $\mathcal{R}_{\mathcal{F}}$. In the discrete case, the module and ring are discrete, while in continuum mechanics, $\mathcal{F}$ is a finite-dimensional real vector space.

As with mass, the principal deviation in the axioms from traditional axioms of force comes in Axiom F5, which changes from an axiom positing a measure function to one positing a countably additive set function.

Axiom F5a *For each* $\mathcal{B} \in \overline{\mathcal{B}}$, *the function* $f_{\Leftarrow \mathcal{B}^c}$ *is a countably additive $\mathcal{F}$-valued set function over $\mathcal{B}$.*

Axiom F13a *For each* $\mathcal{B} \in \overline{\mathcal{B}}$, *the function* $F_{\Leftarrow \mathcal{B}^\circ}$ *is a countably additive* $\mathcal{L}$-*valued set function over* $\mathcal{B}$.

I also assume one can carry over the bounds required by Axiom F8 to discrete mechanical systems by replacing the notion of area of reduced contact boundary with some other suitable function $A : \mathcal{P}(\mathcal{S}) \to \mathbb{R}$ in such a way as to obtain corresponding bounds on body and contact forces. I do not attempt to state an appropriate modification of Axiom F8 here, but instead state the desired conclusion as an assumption.

Assumption F16 *There exists a positive constant* k_1, *a positive, bounded function* $k_2 : \mathcal{B}_m \to \mathbb{R}$, *and a positive function* $A : \mathcal{P}(\mathcal{S}) \to \mathbb{R}$ *such that*

$$|f^C(\mathcal{A}, \mathcal{C})| \leq k_1 A(\partial^* \chi(\mathcal{A}) \cap \partial^* \chi(\mathcal{C})) \tag{6.53}$$

$$|f^B(\mathcal{A}, \mathcal{C})| \leq k_2(\mathcal{C})|m(\mathcal{A})| \tag{6.54}$$

for all pairs of separate bodies $\mathcal{A}$ *and* $\mathcal{C}$.

6.3.5 Hybrid forces

Force systems in hybrid mechanics take exactly the same form as the force systems in the component mechanics, namely a mapping $f : \mathcal{B} \times \mathcal{B} \to \mathcal{V}$ of pairs of bodies to spatial vectors. As in Noll's axioms, we require the hybrid force system to exhibit additivity on separate bodies, and in particular, on bodies from different components. We require the same balance of forces as in Noll's axioms, and the same continuity and boundedness constraints on body and contact forces within each factor mechanics. The differences between hybrid mechanics and traditional mechanics lie elsewhere.

The first difference comes in considering the balance of torques posited by Noll. The notion of torque makes sense in each of the component space-times, but in the hybrid space-time we must interpret torques as vectors of component torques, not as general linear transformations over the hybrid space. To retain the balance of torques, we insist that torques balance within each component system given the force value projections f_i.

If $\{\mathcal{F}_i \mid i \in \mathcal{I}\}$ comprises the set of factor force values, we form the set of hybrid force values as

$$\mathcal{F} = \prod_{i \in \mathcal{I}} \mathcal{F}_i. \tag{6.55}$$

Similarly, if $\{\mathcal{C}_{f_i} \mid i \in \mathcal{I}\}$ comprises the set of factor force configurations, we obtain the set of hybrid force configurations by

$$\mathcal{C}_f = \prod_{i \in \mathcal{I}} \mathcal{C}_{f_i}. \tag{6.56}$$

If $f \in \mathcal{C}_f$ and $\mathcal{B}, \mathcal{C} \in \mathcal{B}$, we have

$$[f(\mathcal{B}, \mathcal{C})]_i = f_i(\mathcal{B}_i, \mathcal{C}_i). \tag{6.57}$$

Hybrid force configurations clearly satisfy the axioms for force systems because the factor systems do. Note that (6.57) only connects the structure of factor and hybrid force assignments. It says nothing about how forces are generated.

6.4 Force and motion

Identifying force values as elements of the momentum module brings force and motion together into shouting distance, and I now turn to the relations between forces and motions that constitute the heart of mechanics.

6.4.1 Working

One general connection between force and motion comes through an axiom on rate of work that restates earlier axioms on balance of forces and torques.

We define the working of the system of forces on a body by

$$W(\mathcal{B}; \chi(\cdot, t); f_{\mathcal{B}^e}) = \int_{\mathcal{B}} \dot{\chi}(\cdot, t) \cdot df_{\mathcal{B}^e}. \tag{6.58}$$

Standard physics textbooks introduce the quantity *force* × *distance* as the work done in a motion. The definition of working captures the rate at which work is done on the body in a motion by forces external to the body.

Noll's initial axiomatizations of mechanics employed axioms corresponding to Axioms F6 and F15. His later axiomatizations replaced these two balance axioms with a single axiom stating the frame indifference of working.

Axiom F17 *Working is frame indifferent; that is,*

$$W^{\star} = W. \tag{6.59}$$

Truesdell (1991, pp. 62–63) provides a derivation of balance equations (6.35) and (6.52) from Axiom F17.

6.4.2 Inertia

None of the preceding axioms on forces state or imply Euler's famous law $f = \dot{p} = ma$, relating force to changes in linear momentum, because this law states a condition concerning inertial forces alone instead of a general condition concerning all forces. Indeed, Noll (1995) regards the axioms of inertia only as special laws, in part because they only concern one type of force, and in part because forces generated by masses play an important role in many, but not all, mechanical problems. He cites the motion of toothpaste out of a squeezed tube as an example showing the occasional effective irrelevance of mass to motion.

Noll's observation that motion can occur independent of mass, and that therefore one should regard laws of inertia as special rather than general laws, has broader implications than where to place axioms in a list. If physical mass need not always play a role in physical motion, it hardly seems strange to suppose it need not always play a role in mental motion. Conversely, it would hardly seem strange that mental mass need not always play a role in physical motion. Thus identifying laws of inertia as special rather than general laws fits well with viewing mechanics as a broad subject covering both the physical and the mental.

Labels aside, axioms relating force and inertia surely represent the most basic of the most general constitutive assumptions concerning fundamental physical forces. Here I follow Truesdell (1991), who formulates the mechanical laws of inertial forces in two axioms. The first axiom states the existence of *inertial* frames: frames of reference in which a body has constant momentum during some interval if and only if the resultant force on the body vanishes. The second axiom refines the first to say that in an inertial frame the resultant force on a body equals the negative derivative of the momentum of the body. Combining these axioms with the general balance laws of forces and torques yields Euler's fundamental laws $f = \dot{p}$ and $F = \dot{L}$ stating the respective balances of linear and rotational momentum.

Truesdell's axioms concerning force, inertia, and motion focus attention on a particular great system or locality $\mathcal{G}$. His first axiom states the existence of certain framings relative to the locality.

Axiom F18 *There is a framing $\phi \in \Phi$ such that $p(\mathcal{B}, \chi, m)$ is constant over an open interval of time in ϕ iff $f(\mathcal{B}, \mathcal{G}^e) = 0$ in that interval.*

A framing ϕ of the kind posited by Axiom F18 is an inertial framing, which we can think of as the point of view of an "unaccelerated" observer.

The second axiom of inertia forms the heart of many treatments of mechanics, whether classical or discrete, and states the relation known to all students as $f = ma$.

Axiom F19 *In an inertial frame,*

$$f(\mathcal{B}, \mathcal{G}^e) = -\dot{p}(\mathcal{B}; \chi). \tag{6.60}$$

Truesdell (1991, p. 68) motivates Axiom F19 as the simplest relation between force and motion consistent with Axiom F18 and exhibiting dependence only on motion of the body in question.

Mechanics complements this requirement on forces with a parallel requirement on torques.

Axiom F20 *In an inertial frame,*

$$F(\mathcal{B}, \mathcal{G}^e, x_0) = -\dot{L}_{x_0}(\mathcal{B}; \chi). \tag{6.61}$$

In traditional terminology, Axioms F19 and F20 state the balance of the *load* and the *reaction* for every body at every instant, where one regards the total force f and the total torque F as the two components of the load and the change $\dot{p}$ in linear momentum and the change $\dot{L}$ in rotational momentum as the two components of the reaction.

Axiom F20 joins Axiom F19 as a central element of continuum mechanics, but many people remain unaware of its independence of balance of linear momentum. Some traditional textbooks of physics communicate the false idea that balance of rotational momentum and torque follows from the balance of linear momentum and force. Such derivations hold true only in certain special and atypical mechanical systems, such as the motion of point bodies under the influence of mutual gravitation studied in celestial mechanics (Truesdell 1991, p. 72).

The fundamental laws of balance were first formulated by Euler: (6.60) as the "new principle of mechanics" in Euler (1750), and (6.61) in Euler (1775), long after Newton's (1687) *Principia*. These new laws rendered nearly every prior treatment of mechanical problems obsolete (Truesdell 1984c, p. 321).

Of course, natural philosophers recognized the existence of relationships between force and change of momentum long before the formulation of these laws, but they disagreed on the nature and role of these relationships. D'Alembert and others, for example, sought to define forces as changes of momentum, a relationship right in line with (6.60), but one that collapses utterly in the study of statics, in which opposing forces continue to exist even after the bodies involved reach equilibria that lack motion.

Discrete mechanics does not differ significantly from traditional mechanics as regards these axioms of inertia. However, a superspatial character of discrete momenta might make the identity mapping on $\mathcal{M} \times T\mathcal{S}$ the only momentum mapping consistent with Euler's law of linear momentum, as expressed in Axiom F19.

Hybrid mechanics also does not require modification of the axioms of inertia. Indeed, regarding mass as a vector concept means the familiar equation

$f = ma$ holds in each component system when we restrict attention to the projections f_i, m_i, and a_i of the values of a hybrid force system, masses, and accelerations into the values holding within each component mechanics.

The role of inertial frames in formulating Euler's laws means that the most useful changes of frames in mechanics change only position and velocity, but exhibit no acceleration. The class of such changes of frames is called the *Galilean* class of changes, those in which the rotation is constant (that is, the frame is not rotating in motion), and the displacement changes linearly in time, or formally

$$\phi_t(x) = Q_0(x - x_o) + (t - t_o)(\phi_1(x_o) - \phi_0(x_o)). \qquad (6.62)$$

Here we presume the change of frame places the body at the origin 0 at t_o, and that the quantity $\phi_1(x_o) - \phi_0(x_o)$ represents the constant translational velocity of the body.

6.5 Energy

The concept of energy plays an enormous role in modern physics and in many of the mathematical tools developed for analyzing physical systems, especially in the mathematical fiction of potential energy used to characterize motion in gravitational and electromagnetic fields. Apart from thermodynamics, in contrast, energy plays a much more limited role in the axiomatic foundations of mechanics. Potential energy plays no axiomatic role at all, as befits its nature as a convenient fiction.

Noll postulates a measure $E : \mathcal{B} \to \mathbb{R}^+$ assigning to each body its non-negative *internal energy*, together with a mapping $Q : \mathcal{B} \times \mathcal{B} \to \mathbb{R}$ called a *system of heatings*. The system of heatings satisfies axioms similar to those defining systems of forces and others that require that heatings correspond to transfers of energy between bodies. Noll defines work in terms of force and distance as usual, and, as noted in Section 6.4.1, proves the balance of forces and torques corresponds exactly to frame indifference of the working of the system of forces.

The treatment of energy in the broadened mechanics recapitulates changes seen earlier in the notions of mass and momentum. Discrete and hybrid conceptions of energy depart from the traditional conception mainly in moving away from a unidimensional conception to one in which energy takes multidimensional values.

6.5.1 Energetic bodies

In addition to having mass, the bodies of interest in dynamics have energy; we say they are *energetic*.

Energies have much in common with masses, and, as with massy bodies, the energetic bodies constitute a subclass $\mathcal{B}_e$ of the closed universe $\overline{\mathcal{B}}$, which we restrict to be closed under joins and takings of exteriors.

Axiom E1 *If $\mathcal{B}_1, \mathcal{B}_2 \in \mathcal{B}_e$, then $\mathcal{B}_1 \sqcup \mathcal{B}_2 \in \mathcal{B}_e$.*

Axiom E2 *If $\mathcal{B} \in \mathcal{B}_e$, then $\mathcal{B}^e \in \mathcal{B}_e$.*

It follows that $\mathcal{O}$, $\mathcal{U}$, and meets of energetic bodies are energetic. With these requirements, therefore, the energetic bodies form a Boolean sublattice of $\overline{\mathcal{B}}$. Moreover, we demand that energy always accompanies mass (but not necessarily the converse).

Axiom E3 $\mathcal{B}_m \subseteq \mathcal{B}_e$.

As we have already assumed that $\mathcal{B}_m = \overline{\mathcal{B}}$, this means we also assume that all bodies are energetic, that is, that $\mathcal{B}_e = \overline{\mathcal{B}}$, and hence $\mathcal{B}_e = \mathcal{B}_m$.

6.5.2 Energy values

We write $\mathcal{E}$ to denote the set of possible energy values. In traditional mechanics, momentum has dimensions of (mass)(distance)(time)$^{-1}$ and energy has dimensions of (mass)(distance)^2(time)$^{-2}$. These dimensional characterizations involve the same set of underlying dimensions, even though they differ in how these underlying dimensions combine. Let us follow this example by assuming that energy values have the same structure as momentum values.

Axiom E4 *The set of energy values forms a module $\mathcal{E}$ over a ring $\mathcal{R}_\mathcal{E}$ isomorphic to the momentum module $\mathcal{P}$.*

In the discrete and hybrid setting, these values need not take the traditional form of nonnegative numbers in $\mathbb{R}$. Because we allow multidimensional mass and superspatial momenta, this structure for energy values corresponds to allowing several sorts of energies, not all comparable. As with force values, we assume the simplest possible isomorphism, namely that $\mathcal{E} = \mathcal{P}$. We write $\mathbf{0}_\mathcal{E}$ to denote the zero energy value.

6.5.3 Energy configurations

An *energy configuration* consists of an energy function

$$E : \mathcal{B}_e \to \mathcal{E} \tag{6.63}$$

defined on $\mathcal{B}_e$ taking values in $\mathcal{E}$. We define the set

$$\mathcal{C}_E = (\mathcal{B}_e \to \mathcal{E}) \tag{6.64}$$

to be the set of all energy configurations. We write $E(\mathcal{B}, t)$ to indicate the energy of body $\mathcal{B}$ at time t, thus extending the notation E to also mean an *energy variation*

$$E : \mathcal{T} \to \mathcal{C}_E \tag{6.65}$$

giving the energy of each body point at each instant.

6.5.4 Additive energies

We require that the energy function E is additive on separate bodies.

Axiom E5 *If* $\mathcal{B}_1, \mathcal{B}_2 \in \mathcal{B}_e$ *and* $\mathcal{B}_1 \sqcap \mathcal{B}_2 = \mathcal{O}$, *then* $E(\mathcal{B}_1 \sqcup \mathcal{B}_2) = E(\mathcal{B}_1) + E(\mathcal{B}_2)$.

That is, for separate bodies, the energy of the join is the sum of the energies. We see $E(\mathcal{O}) = \mathbf{0}_\mathcal{E}$ by applying Axiom E5 to $\mathcal{O} = \mathcal{O} \sqcup \mathcal{O}$. The energy of the universal body, $E(\mathcal{U})$, need not be any special element of $\mathcal{E}$.

One might also wish to require that all bodies containing a body of nonnull energy also have nonnull energy. As in the case of mass, such an assumption has consequences for the set of possible energy values.

6.5.5 Heating

Let us use the term *heating* to describe changes (positive or negative) in internal energy. A system of heatings $Q : (\mathcal{B} \times \mathcal{B})_0 \to \mathcal{E}$ assigns an $\mathcal{E}$-valued amount $Q(\mathcal{B}, \mathcal{C})$ to each pair of separate bodies. Let us require each system of heatings to satisfy axioms E6–E8 like those F3–F5 satisfied by forces.

Axiom E6 $Q(\mathcal{C}_1 \sqcup \mathcal{C}_2, \mathcal{B}) = Q(\mathcal{C}_1, \mathcal{B}) + Q(\mathcal{C}_2, \mathcal{B})$ *for pairwise separate bodies* $\mathcal{B}, \mathcal{C}_1$ *and* $\mathcal{C}_2$.

Axiom E7 $Q(\mathcal{B}, \mathcal{C}_1 \sqcup \mathcal{C}_2) = Q(\mathcal{B}, \mathcal{C}_1) + Q(\mathcal{B}, \mathcal{C}_2)$ *for pairwise separate bodies* $\mathcal{B}, \mathcal{C}_1$ *and* $\mathcal{C}_2$.

Axiom E8 *For each* $\mathcal{B} \in \mathcal{B}_e$, *the function* $Q(\cdot, \mathcal{B}^e)$ *is an* $\mathcal{E}$-*valued measure over* $\mathcal{B}$.

In the discrete case, we interpret Axiom E8 as requiring a countably additive set function over body points. Again, since we assume that bodies are measurable subsets of $\mathcal{U}$, Axiom E8 means that when $\mathcal{A} \precsim \mathcal{B}$ we have

$$Q(\mathcal{A}, \mathcal{B}^e) = \int_\mathcal{A} dQ_{\mathcal{B}^e}. \tag{6.66}$$

The quantity $Q(\mathcal{B}, \mathcal{B}^e)$ is called the *resultant heating* of $\mathcal{B}$. In some special cases, the resultant heating exactly corresponds to the change in internal energy, that is,

$$\dot{E}(\mathcal{B}) = Q(\mathcal{B}, \mathcal{B}^e). \tag{6.67}$$

Such special circumstances are called *energetically perfect*.

We require that heatings be frame indifferent. Because we regard heatings and internal energies as vector-valued measures, frame indifference means that heatings transform as vectors indifferent to the framing used to describe the motions of the bodies involved.

Axiom E9 *Heatings are frame indifferent.*

6.5.6 Kinetic and total energy

The internal energy of a body reflects energy not connected with motion, such as heat or internal binding energy. In addition to internal energy, each body has a *kinetic energy* K that reflects its "energy of motion" within a frame of reference. Kinetic energy is defined for each body $\mathcal{B}$ and motion χ to be

$$K(\mathcal{B}; \chi(\cdot, t)) = \int_{\mathcal{B}} \dot{\chi}(\cdot, t) \cdot dp, \tag{6.68}$$

which in the traditional case reduces to

$$K(\mathcal{B}; \chi(\cdot, t)) = \tfrac{1}{2} \int_{\mathcal{B}} |\dot{\chi}(\cdot, t)|^2 dm. \tag{6.69}$$

Kinetic energy obviously varies with the frame of reference; a body in free inertial motion in an inertial frame of reference has zero velocity and zero kinetic energy, yet the same body has nonzero kinetic energy in any inertial frame in which it has nonzero velocity. We say the total energy of a body $\mathcal{B}$ in an inertial frame of reference is just the sum $E(\mathcal{B}) + K(\mathcal{B})$ of the internal and kinetic energy.

The first law of thermodynamics, also known as the balance of energy, states that the change in internal energy corresponds directly to the heating acting on the body and the rate of work done on the body, which we can express in the following axiom.

Axiom E10

$$\dot{E} = W + Q. \tag{6.70}$$

Axioms F17 and E9 stated the frame indifference of working and heating. Putting these together with Axiom E10, we see that $\dot{E}$ is frame indifferent, and hence E is as well.

In an inertial frame, the rate of work done on a body by the great system is called the *power P*. The axioms of mechanics imply that power, working, and kinetic energy are related by

$$W = P - \dot{K}. \tag{6.71}$$

This means that in an inertial frame, all work done on or by a body either changes the internal energy or changes the kinetic energy. In *mechanically perfect* systems, which include rigid bodies and point bodies, all work goes into kinetic energy, so that $W = 0$. Combining (6.71) with Axiom E10, we have

$$\dot{K} + \dot{E} = P + Q, \tag{6.72}$$

indicating that in an inertial frame each change in the total energy of a body derives directly from the heating and power acting on the body.

7

The character of mechanical law

The axioms on forces given in the previous chapter characterize the nature of inertial forces and the structure of systems of forces in isolation, but otherwise say nothing about how forces arise in the evolution of mechanical systems. Although the special laws of forces depend on the specific class of material involved, Noll states three additional general axioms concerning dynamogenesis that bear on the general character of mechanical forces.

The first of Noll's general axioms on dynamogenesis states the principle of determinism, that the history of body and contact forces (or equivalently, the stress) at preceding instants determines a unique value for these forces at a given instant. The second axiom states the principle of locality, that the forces at a point depend only on the configuration of bodies within arbitrarily small neighborhoods of the point. The third axiom states the principle of frame indifference, that forces depend only on the intrinsic properties of motions and deformation, not on properties that vary with the reference frame.

Although we follow the pattern set by Noll regarding frame indifference, the broader mechanics requires some adjustment in the conceptions of both determinism and locality. The discrete materials of psychology and economics provide different and somewhat weaker motivations for determinism and locality of dynamogenesis, even if one winds up making traditional determinism and locality assumptions in specific systems. In contrast, just stating correct axioms of determinism and locality for hybrid mechanical systems requires some technical restatement, as well as reconsideration of the motivations of the conditions. The following sections thus restate these dynamogenetic axioms for the extended mechanics.

The following examination of the character of mechanical law also goes beyond the three dynamogenetic axioms considered by Noll to address concepts of continuity, conservatism, reversibility, and optimality. Some of these characteristics appear implicitly as part of the traditional mechanical axiomatic setting. Some do not appear at all in the standard formalisms, but appear important in thinking about minds and economies as mechanical systems.

7.1 Mechanical processes

Stating axioms of determinism, locality, and frame indifference on dynamogenesis requires the ability to talk about possible behaviors that satisfy the preceding axioms of mechanics. As a first step in this direction, Noll (1973) defines a *mechanical process* to be a kinematical process or motion χ, a reference motion or observer frame χ^r, and time-varying force system f that satisfy Euler's axioms of mechanics at every instant of a temporal interval I, collected together into a triple (χ, χ^r, f).

The motion, reference frame, and force elements of Noll's conception of mechanical process form a minimal set sufficient for Noll's purposes, but not for the extended mechanics considered here. The simpler conception just stated presumes fixed masses for bodies, and ignores energetic and thermomechanical quantities. To support mechanical analysis in the broader setting, I extend the minimal notion of mechanical process to include mass variation, energy variation, and heating variation over the same interval, yielding an enlarged list $(\chi, \chi^r, f, m, E, Q)$.

Following common practice in the theory of computation and control theory, we abstract away from such unwieldy 6-tuples and write Σ to denote the set of instantaneous mechanical states. We write

$$h : I \to \Sigma \qquad\qquad (7.1)$$

to denote a deterministic history of states. We then regard mechanical processes as pairings (h, χ^r) that couple histories with reference processes over the same interval.

We regard the original process components χ, f, m, E, and Q as projections of mechanical histories (or states) onto the corresponding components. For most purposes, I omit explicit mention of the framing. In fact, I will assume each instantaneous state also includes values representing the low-order derivatives of the process quantities as well, so obtaining an even larger tuple representation $(x_t, \dot{x}_t, \ddot{x}_t, m_t, \dot{m}_t, p_t, \dot{p}_t, f_t, \dot{f}_t, E_t, \dot{E}_t, Q_t, \dot{Q}_t)$. Because we consider discrete mechanical systems that lack derivatives, some of these derivative quantities actually consist of difference or jump values, but distinguishing the correct nature will not be crucial in most of what follows. In fact, I will normally only mention the state quantities relevant to the discussion at hand rather than listing all the components of mechanical states.

I extend the notation presented earlier for nondeterministic histories to cover nondeterministic mechanical processes. A nondeterministic mechanical process H consists of a set of deterministic mechanical processes over the same temporal interval and employing the same reference frame, that is, such that the set $\{\chi(h) \mid (h, \chi^r) \in H\}$ forms a nondeterministic motion and such that $\chi_1^r = \chi_2^r$ whenever H contains both (h_1, χ_1^r) and (h_2, χ_2^r). Let us write $\mathcal{H}$ to denote the set of all histories, and $\mathcal{H}_I$ to mean the set of all histories over a common interval I.

7.1.1 Response functionals

Noll formulates his axioms of dynamogenesis in terms of *response functionals* of the materials in question. A response functional over histories gives the stress at each point of a body as a function of the history and present state of the materials.

Unfortunately, the very notion of a response functional builds in the notion of determinism in talk of the response "functional." To formulate the notion of mechanical response in a way amenable to the broader applications, the following sections view response as a set-valued function of the stress at a point and the history to that point, a function that represents the relation between the history and the stress at each point.

7.1.2 Frame indifference

Frame indifference distinguishes the underlying reality (motion) from particular ways of describing that motion (coordinates and speeds in reference frames). It may seem we have already assumed enough about the frame indifference of mechanical entities, but in fact we need to assume more.

We have already seen in the preceding chapters that Noll's axioms for mechanics require frame indifference in several ways. The first requirements, reflected in Axioms M9, F2, and F17, state the frame indifference of mass, force, and working. These axioms say only that the quantities we take as mass, force, and working must transform appropriately with a change of frame. Frame indifference of mass and force serves mainly to ensure we work with reliable concepts rather than accidents of the perspectives peculiar to particular observers. Frame indifference of working carries additional consequences, as it entails balance of forces and torques.

The frame-indifference conditions on mass, force, and working ensure the frame indifference of the general laws of mechanics, but the conditions impose no strong restrictions on special laws describing special materials. Noll's axiom of dynamical frame indifference concerns such special laws explicitly by requiring that the special laws should exhibit the same frame indifference as the general laws. Dynamical frame indifference requires that prescriptions for stresses transform appropriately under changes of reference frame, or formally, in terms of a stress-response functional θ,

$$\theta(h) = \theta^\star(h^\star). \tag{7.2}$$

We can express the same requirement without reference to stresses by retreating to Noll's (1958, 1963) more direct dynamical axioms that refer directly to frame indifference of the underlying forces and torques by means of force- and torque-response functionals θ_f and θ_F.

Axiom F21 *Force responses are frame indifferent; that is,*

$$\theta_f(h) = \theta_f^\star(h^\star). \tag{7.3}$$

Axiom F22 *Torque responses are frame indifferent; that is,*

$$\theta_F(h) = \theta_F^\star(h^\star). \tag{7.4}$$

Frame indifference retains its attractions even in discrete mechanics, although it is not clear that all forces of interest in psychology and economics exhibit this property. Frame indifference in the psychological context might entail some sort of semantic equivalence, which easily could be too strong for a realistic psychological theory in which one can hold different beliefs about the same thing (the planet Venus) under different descriptions (the morning and evening stars). However, it seems unlikely that frame indifference always requires semantic equivalence, since the invariant quantities can be mental structures and need not be sets of possible worlds. That is, a reasoning agent might represent some concept in many different ways, each of which has properties beyond those of the intended referent, but once the agent has settled on some particular structure with which to represent the concept, the properties of that particular representation do not depend on how one describes it in some external language. Later chapters return to these questions.

7.2 Determinism

Many people consider mechanics the paradigm example of a deterministic theory. High-school and college physics classes often instill a picture of mechanics deriving from Laplace's (1814) philosophical estimation of the import of Newtonian mechanics: to an unlimited intelligence capable of apprehending at one instant the positions of every particle and all forces acting on them "nothing would be uncertain and the future, as the past, would be present to its eyes."

He based this estimation on the success at explaining every then-known oddity of planetary motion purely in terms of Newton's gravitational theory. The focus on astronomy and inattention to the study of extended bodies misled him, however. Laplace's view of celestial mechanics, like Lagrange's portrait of analytical mechanics, of whirling particles and planets, evolving so precisely and delicately that one can continue their motion forever forward and backward in time to determine all of history, has little to recommend itself as a theory of our world, even considering only those aspects treated by classical mechanics, and less still when one broadens mechanics to include modern theories of quantum phenomena or the mental systems examined here. The Laplacian, or perhaps more deservedly Lagrangian, blinders focus attention on the smooth, easily intelligible portions of motion that occur between the nonsmooth, poorly visible, and less replicable events that produce the initial conditions for the smooth portions. Setting aside these blinders, one might view determinism as the exception, not the rule.

In the broadened mechanics developed here I abandon determinism as a universal requirement, but leave open adoption of determinism requirements suitable to restricted theories and systems. To help the reader understand the issues better, I further examine the role of assumptions of determinism in mechanics, psychology, and economics. Chapter 14 develops an analytical formalism for quantifying indeterminism and measuring characteristics of indeterminate states.

7.2.1 What is determinism?

Determinism represents a restriction on the set of possible histories of the system in question, a restriction that forbids distinct histories from sharing an initial segment. But another way, this restriction states that if h and h' take the same values for all instants preceding t, then $h = h'$. One can phrase determinism more incrementally as the restriction that identity of histories prior to instant t implies identity through instant t, and then prove this implies identity at all future instants, but the result is the same.

In mechanics, determinism reduces to the requirement that histories uniquely determine the forces or stresses at each instant. We can phrase Noll's axiom of determinism as follows.

Axiom F23 *The history of events to some instant uniquely determines the response at that instant; that is, if two histories h and h' involve exactly the same bodies and materials and agree at all times up to some instant t, then both assign the same response $\theta(h) = \theta(h')$ at each location in instant t.*

The basic dynamical axioms of mechanics require merely that the proper relationships hold between mass, velocity, force, and other mechanical quantities in any course of events. The axioms characterizing these notions fix many relations among mechanical quantities, but say nothing about the origin or uniqueness of forces, of materials or systems in which any of several force values might obtain at an instant. Without an axiom of determinism, these axioms still restrict motion within each possible history of the body so that the mass and the velocity in the history change so as to represent a momentum change equal to the force in the history. In symbols, if the material generates a set of possible forces $\{f_{t,i}\}$ on the same body, these would generate histories (or classes of histories) $\{h_i\}$ such that $f_{t,i} = m_{t,i}\ddot{x}_{t,i}$ in h_i. Noll's axiom of determinism on the response functionals that characterize materials specifically rules out a material generating multiple possible forces given its history, and the other mechanical axioms then produce a unique continuation of the history from this unique force. This uniqueness restriction then allows us to treat response as a function of history.

The broader mechanical axioms presented earlier offer the possibility of a less traditional role for mechanical determinism, in which a unique force value may be met with a set of possible responses. In traditional mechanics one might arrive at a set of histories for which $f_t = m_{t,i}\ddot{x}_{t,i}$ in each h_i. Each history distributes the change represented by the force differently across mass and motion. Superspatial momenta can leave less freedom, for if momenta keep mass and velocity as separate components, we have that $(m_i, \ddot{x}_i) = (m_j, \ddot{x}_j)$ iff $m_i = m_j$ and $\ddot{x}_i = \ddot{x}_j$, thus requiring different force values to obtain different reactions.

7.2.2 Why determinism?

Requirements of determinism stem from several sources, including the philosophical, the practical, and the mathematical.

Some philosophical motivations for assuming determinism stem from the mere existence of common repeatable phenomena. The quest for the most beautiful mechanical theory gravitates toward the deterministic idealization of this repeatability, requiring that everything be repeatable if only one can re-create the same past conditions. Other philosophical ideas include completely nonmechanical, somewhat therapeutic motivations, in which determinism offers reassurance that even though bad things happen to us and even though we do bad things, it could not have been otherwise.

The practical and mathematical motivations for determinism seem more central in mechanics. One expects to have an easier time making correct predictions in a deterministic world. With determinism, in each situation there is just one future to predict; with indeterminism, at best one can predict the possibilities but not know which one will occur. Similarly, one expects to have an easier time putting these predictions into mathematical calculations. With determinism, one looks for differential equations, especially ones with closed-form solutions; with indeterminism, one has search problems that often become harder rapidly as one looks to longer-term predictions.

Determinism, however, does not guarantee easier prediction and mathematical solution. As we will see in the following section, some deterministic systems can defy prediction and simple mathematical solution.

7.2.3 Is determinism true?

Although some assume that quantum mechanics has settled the issue in favor of an indeterministic world, the truth is somewhat more complicated, with pseudoindeterminism and pseudodeterminism adding twists to the already familiar complications concerning human behavior.

7.2.3.1 Pseudoindeterminism

In classical physics, theorists have long known that fairly simple deterministic equations of motion admit solutions of extreme complexity that resist reliable calculation beyond very short times. The phenomenon of turbulence in fluid mechanics provided the canonical example for many years, especially in its interference with weather prediction. In recent years, understanding of this possibility has grown more acute with the identification of properties of chaotic systems characterized by extreme sensitivity of solutions to initial conditions. Chaotic systems exhibit trajectories that diverge from each other at exponential rates even though starting from points as close as one chooses. Many aspects of the behaviors of these deterministic systems appear anything but deterministic.

If chaotic systems represented mathematical oddities, one might feel safe in ignoring them when seeking to predict behavior for realistic systems. In fact, chaotic systems pervade our world, and chaotic behavior arises through virtually all the standard equations of physical theory, providing at least one explanation for the appearance of indeterminism in physical observations. The same has been observed in standard models of economic behavior as well, showing the burden does not rest solely on physical theory. That is, even when one starts with equations developed by examining simple situations in which motion appears deterministic to the limits of the measuring apparatus, extrapolating from these same equations to laws covering more complicated systems saddles one with chaotic behaviors.

In some cases, we see seemingly chaotic and random behavior occurring by design. Modern cryptography, for example, develops the notion of pseudo-randomness, in which a sequence or set of data reflects a determinate rule too difficult to recognize in the sense that all procedures for identifying the rule require computational resources exponential in the length of the sequence or size of the data set. At present some numerical cryptographic methods rely on the fact that decoding appears to entail this level of computational effort, though we do not know this for a fact. Messages coded using these pseudorandom mechanisms provide obvious, if artificial, examples of seemingly random deterministic systems.

One might conclude that complicated deterministic behavior and the ordinary ambiguity of limited-resolution measurement together account for *all* apparent indeterminism. This conclusion, which one might view as a mathematical expression of some mysteries of religious faiths, undoubtedly provided some assurance to generations of natural philosophers, assurance akin to Hilbert's (1902, p. 412) completely conventional conviction of the decidability of all mathematical questions.

The discovery of quantum phenomena and the developments of early quantum theory began to undermine the hypothesis of physical determinism even before Gödel gave pause to Hilbert's conviction. The early quantum theorists, notably Bohr, explicitly denied the possibility that quantum indeterminism represents merely the indeterministic appearance of an underlying deterministic theory. Many adherents of determinism found it difficult to swallow this claim, and eventually it was proven false by Bohm (1952), who provided an entirely deterministic theory of quantum mechanics, complete with elementary particles bouncing off one another in a straightforward mechanical way. To do this, Bohm introduced a "vector potential" that provided the means by which behavior varied across repeated experiments. In principle, one could capture any complete history of the universe using deterministic physics and such a vector potential. In practice, one has no way of identifying the specific potential short of having such a complete history. The vector potential represents an initial condition dwarfing that of Laplace's all-seeing mind, and possesses a complexity unrivaled by those appearing in routine engineering situations. The deterministic equations of motion support all the chaotic behavior in this application that they do in more traditional models. This leaves one with ordinary indeterministic quantum mechanics as the best predictive tool. Somewhat later, Nelson (1966) derived some simple cases of the Schrödinger equation from classical mechanics, but later gave up the project because of difficulties in generalizing the solution to more complicated cases (Nelson 1985). The "many-worlds" interpretation of quantum mechanics described by Everett (de

Witt & Graham 1973) provided another framework for viewing quantum indeterminism in terms of classical histories, but this theory also proved difficult to
use in making predictions.

These deterministic quantum theories did little to abate the practical facts of
indeterminism, and left one with standard indeterministic quantum mechanics
as the best practical approach to prediction, much as even a devout determin-
ist uses a probabilistic model in calling the roll of the die. The hypothesis
of determinism suffered what many considered a more serious blow with the
appearance of Bell's (1966, 1987) theorems proving that any hidden variable
theories, such as those of Bohm, must exhibit nonlocal correlations. Since
the same physical intuition of microscopic behaviors provided both conviction
of determinism and locality, as seen in Noll's axioms, these theorems pit two
aspects of the same intuitions against each other. Many take the restrictions
posed by relativity theory on distant communication to weigh in on the side
of locality, and thus give up on determinism. This intellectual conversion does
not represent true repentance of deterministic doctrine, however. Bohr's principle that one cannot know more than statistical properties of quantum states
continues to grate against the methodological optimism of many scientists who
believe they can figure things out if they work hard enough.

7.2.3.2 Pseudodeterminism

We may turn the notion of pseudorandomness around to consider the notion
of pseudodeterminism. A pseudodeterministic system is an indeterministic
system that appears deterministic, but for which the cost in time or other resources of observing the indeterminism is impractically high. A simple but
artificial example is provided by a probabilistic finite automaton in which one
transition from each state has a probability extremely close 1, say $1 - 10^{-23}$.
Observing that this automaton is in fact indeterministic by observing its behavior can be expected to take a very long time, unless one is able to employ
molar-level parallelism, as in recent DNA and NMR computation techniques.
Indeed, if we assume quantum mechanics describes a true indeterminism of
the world, an isolated atom of uranium 238, an isotope with a half-life of 4.5
billion years, constitutes a fine pseudodeterministic system, with a decay probability around 3.5×10^{-18} per second. Even the far less stable U-234 atom, an
isotope with a half-life of 244,000 years, would serve well here. The fact is that
apart from radioactivity and the interference phenomena that gave rise to quantum mechanics in the first place, we have little basis for saying the apparently
deterministic parts of nature are deterministic rather than pseudodeterministic.

Of course, in psychology, pseudodeterministic behavior might reflect not
mere probability but actual intelligence and intentions to hide from observation.

The schoolteacher hears scuffling and whispers, but sees only properly seated students each time he or she turns from the blackboard to reprimand the class; Winston Smith makes sure he gives the expected answers, even though his heart has changed.

As a practical matter, however, the most familiar sorts of pseudodeterminism result from deliberate engineering design, in which levels of abstraction introduce forms of relative determinism that hide indeterminism at one level from observers of higher levels.

For example, good engineers develop a keen appreciation for the proper place of the notion of determinism. They ordinarily consider determinism a desirable but temporary and uncertain characteristic of designed mechanisms. They presume that most of the building blocks used in their design lack deterministic response, and regard doing otherwise as asking for trouble. For example, watchmakers design gear mechanisms to exhibit insensitivity to possible variations in the driving mechanisms, whether they arise through motions of pendulums, human arms, or crystals. Of course, this engineering wisdom merely improves on the common prudence most people gain as they grow up.

Strictly speaking, the engineers do not assume their building blocks possess true nondeterministic freedom of action. Except perhaps in moments of frustration, when they may bemoan Murphy's law or curse malevolent influences, they expect only a form of practical, epistemic indeterminism, resulting either from imperfect knowledge of the precise state of the components, from environmental noise or other unknown influences, from component failure, or from true nondeterminism on the part of the component. No one trusts mechanisms to work as designed without long experience, significant testing, and often, built-in self-testing mechanisms.

The practice of engineering does not support the false distinction between calculating the solution to a differential equation and verifying some logical property of a nondeterministic automaton, digital circuit, or distributed system. All engineering involves the verification of properties of indeterministic systems; the differences arise only in whether the proofs and experimental tests quantify or sample over continuous or discrete configurations and trajectories.

The original RMS, or indeed almost any computational system performing heuristic search, provides a good example of a system exhibiting determinism at one level but not at another. To the external observer, or in the external, summary theory captured in nonmonotonic logics, the RMS exhibits a freedom of choice or lack of determinism in many respects: first in the alternative sets of conclusions possible given sets of nonmonotonic base reasons, and second in the alternative revisions of conclusions possible given updates to the base reasons. This indeterminism serves the theory well, whether or not the

RMS actually operates deterministically. The original RMS, in fact, worked strictly deterministically. It recorded all reasons in lists with stable orderings, and employed regular ordered procedures for examining these lists, leading to identical results when rerunning the program from the same initial conditions. This implementation determinism, in turn, was relative to the underlying MACLISP/ITS/KA-10 system on which it ran, and these underlying levels were intended to operate reasonably deterministically relative to the quantum states of the KA-10 electronics, which in the conventional view operate indeterministically.

7.2.3.3 Human experience

Indeterminism and unpredictability abound in human experience, from the toddler's experience of apparent capriciousness of parents to the old-timer's experience of chance, bluff, and deception by opponents in card games. Essentially every regularity known from common sense and long experience suffers exceptions. If, following William of Ockham, we ask for the simplest explanation of this apparent indeterminism, we conclude that human behavior is indeterministic. One might interpret the standard economic theory of rational decisions in this way, as saying that rational people can choose freely among all alternatives of maximal expected utility, and groups of rational people acting together can join together in any of the equilibrium solutions to the games represented by their preferences.

Note that human indeterminism might happen even if all physical materials follow deterministic rules, for we have no evidence to suggest determinism holds for nonphysical materials. Indeed, all the evidence we have suggests indeterminism, not determinism. Of course, this indeterminism might reflect an underlying reality too complex to see as deterministic, but for practical purposes, we must view humans as either pseudoindeterministic or indeterministic. Experiments to determine any underlying determinism certainly seem infeasible. At the gross level available today, the experimenter lacks essentially all certain knowledge about the nature of the psychological material (how the subject behaves in different circumstances) and the state of mind of the subject. Worse still, the subject can remember what he or she experiences, and has the intelligence to exhibit deceptive behavior. All this serves to undermine the experimenter's ability to repeat experiments in the strictest sense, though it does not foreclose all possibility of an experimental psychology. It is remotely conceivable one could prepare two human beings to have the same state by cloning, isolation, and so on, in order to subject them to a series of tests to ascertain the identity of their responses, but the cost, not to say the immorality, of such an experiment is prohibitive.

More generally, a world fully deterministic at both physical and psychological levels would leave no room for free will, the ability to choose freely that forms part of the common human experience, no matter what one's beliefs on the reality of this appearance of freedom. This implication makes relevant some sources of nonobservational evidence, including the testimony or revelation available in numerous religions, and the near universal conviction that one can and should condemn some behavior as evil. A long theological, philosophical, and moral tradition argues that a world without choice is a world in which one cannot criticize choices, a world without good and evil. For many, the conviction one can and should condemn the person who hurts a loved one outweighs any aesthetic or engineering desire for a completely deterministic physical theory.

7.2.3.4 Free will

As noted, a deterministic world is a world without choice, at least as most understand the notion of choice. Yet acceptance of physical indeterminism does not require acceptance of free will, for psychology might be deterministic relative to some level above that of atoms and subatomic particles. Indeed, the controversy surrounding Penrose's (1989) suggestion that consciousness somehow depends on and reflects quantum indeterminacy stems in part from a belief held by many that psychological behavior should not depend on any particulars of motions at that level. But even if one believes mental behavior indeterminate, indeterminism does not in itself imply the sort of conscious freedom of choice bound up in the notion of free will. Few credit the uranium atom with free will, even if it exemplifies probabilistic indeterminacy.

Nothing in the technical development of mechanics given here requires taking a stand on the existence of free will. Decision making, though, forms a category of mental action fundamental to psychology, economics, artificial intelligence, and other fields, and one faces tough sledding to pursue the study of decision making and rationality without accepting free will at least as a sound theoretical viewpoint.

The simplest, and perhaps typical, response to this question was exhibited by William James, who overcame a severe depression by freely choosing to reject the idea that free will is an illusion and to instead believe he had the power to choose (1920, Vol. I, pp. 147–148). To use Festinger's (1957) language, one might speculate that the cognitive dissonance between the plain facts of human experience and the tenuous chain of hypothesis emboldening the psychological determinists eventually grew too great, at which point James surmounted the issue by deciding to believe in free will.

The point here is that the experience of free choice is as common and sure as the experience of the heat of fire and warmth of a mother's love; more sure, indeed, since some live without fire, and not all mothers love. Even the insane or addicted who regard some of their thoughts and impulses as beyond their control ascribe many of their decisions to their own choices, not to the tormenting afflictions. While in principle such apparent freedom to choose might prove an illusion, much of the modern push to view mind as deterministic stems from the deterministic illusion of Laplace and other interpreters who magnified the narrow and deterministic slice of mechanics formalized in the seventeenth and eighteenth centuries into a scientific justification for a deterministic metaphysics. The progress of modern science since that time has systematically eroded that deterministic illusion. The present work adds to the demonstrations that mere indeterminacy does not destroy science but enriches it. In this setting, it seems perfectly reasonable to interpret the human experience of choice as true choice.

7.2.4 Specializing determinism

The long-standing debates about determinism, from ancient disputes about free will to modern quantum mechanics and analyses of pseudodeterminism and pseudoindeterminism, suggest that universal axioms of determinism seem overly contentious components of a philosophically neutral mechanics intended to cover both mind and millstone.

The level-dependence of determinism means the theorist must choose carefully when deciding where to demand determinism. Noll's mechanics places the requirement at a general level above even assumptions about the presence and properties of mass, on the grounds that mass proves irrelevant to some mechanical systems and thus should not be considered as one of the fundamental concepts. Mass thus enters Noll's mechanics as a concept used in a broad but not exhaustive class of theories of special materials. With so much of the structure of mechanics standing independent of determinism assumptions, it seems reasonable to treat the axiom of determinism in the same way, demoting it from a universal principle governing all possible materials in all possible circumstances to one covering many but not all materials, and many but not all circumstances.

In hybrid mechanics, especially, the force on a body within some component system potentially depends on contributions exerted by bodies in other component systems as well as bodies within the same component system. This means that the axiom of determinism *cannot* hold within the component systems, unless the separate mechanical components evolve separately with no interaction. Accordingly, any general axiom of determinism must be stated at the hybrid level as a restriction on the system of hybrid forces, not as a restriction on the component force systems. I therefore omit dynamogenetic determinism as a general law of discrete mechanics, and relegate it to the status of a special law characteristic of specific types of materials or hybrid systems.

This demotion of determinism to a special and sometime property of mechanical systems need not make life more difficult for the student of mechanics. Axioms requiring determinism aid little if the remainder of the theory does nothing to shape behavior into deterministic paths. Although one can construct deterministic theories of special psychological materials, it seems more useful to construct theories in deterministic and indeterministic varieties. The indeterministic theories might exactly capture observational knowledge about people and their lack of deterministic responses to identical visible stimuli and aspects of mental states. The deterministic theories might augment the indeterministic theories with suppositions about underlying deterministic mechanisms.

For example, the standard theory of rational choice underlying psychology and economics explicitly permits multiple rational choices. One thus might doubt the utility of a deterministic theory obtained simply by adding an axiom of determinateness to such an otherwise indeterminate theory, for knowledge that only one of the possible paths occurs without some way of telling which one occurs leaves one unable to make many predictions beyond those available in the nondeterministic theory. One might instead achieve determinism by adding instead an axiom that states a specific rule for making all such choices, but there usually are many such rules possible, and most such assumptions introduce a level of detail more appropriate to specific materials or types of minds than to general mechanical analyses. The value of theories of special materials lies in their susceptibility to analysis and applicability to a reasonable class of actual materials. Exceedingly detailed constructions of deterministic behaviors greatly increase the risk that the resulting theory will not apply to some materials of interest. In such cases, the nondeterministic theory might prove useful for more purposes than would a special deterministic theory.

Indeed, even mathematical prediction need not be aided by determinism. For example, the concept of a finite automaton forms both a core idea in the theory of computation and a widely used computational tool. The theory of computation studies both deterministic and nondeterministic finite automata, which one can prove have equivalent computational power in terms of the formal languages they can recognize. This equivalence of power aside, both deterministic and nondeterministic concepts have advantages in different studies. For some purposes, such as implementing string pattern matching machines, deterministic finite automata are the tool of choice. Here one simply a constructs a finite automaton that recognizes the string or pattern in question and runs the data through it to find the matches. For other purposes, such as analyzing the existence of solutions, nondeterministic finite automata prove more useful. In particular, the full Kleene language of regular expressions involving sequence, negation, and union permits much simpler analyses of automata and languages than a deterministic sublanguage.

More generally, and for similar reasons, mathematics makes heavy use of nonconstructive existence proofs even when constructive proofs are possible. We thus regard the predictive benefits conferred by determinism on systems describable by differential equations as a special case of mathematical analysis, not as a limitation of predictive simplicity to deterministic systems.

7.3 Continuity

Many people believe that classical mechanics respects Leibniz's law of continuity: *Natura non facit saltum*, "Nature makes no jumps." Indeed, people have applied this dictum beyond the mechanical realm, to wit Darwin's rejection of genetic saltation and Marshall's (1949) use of it as the epigram of his famous economics textbook. Certainly everyone has keenly regretted this law when seeing someone one would rather not see coming down the hall from the other direction. What then should we make of continuity requirements in seeking a discrete mechanics?

Indeed, much of classical mathematical analysis relies on the notion of continuity. What fate awaits theories of discrete processes, such as computation, reasoning, decision making, and action, that involve mainly discontinuous motion? To help the reader understand this question, in the following section I examine the concept of continuity and the role it plays in mechanics and other systems. It turns out one can salvage important aspects of the classical framework even in the discrete setting.

7.3.1 What is continuity?

Although Leibniz's statement "nature makes no jumps" serves as a good first approximation to the notion of continuity, mathematics formalizes the notion in a variety of ways. The most familiar way says that small changes come from small changes; a function f is continuous at a point x if any value v suitably close to $f(x)$ can be obtained as the value $v = f(y)$ for some y suitably close to x.

To make this work as a general concept, mathematics defines a topology (X, O) on a set X to be a collection of sets O, called the *open sets* of the topology, closed under arbitrary unions and finite intersections. This definition admits a wide range of topologies and corresponding continuity notions. Mathematicians classify topologies according to various properties, especially according to how easy a topology makes it to separate one point from another by means of open sets that contain one point but not the other.

One should not confuse continuity with determinism or other notions. Intuitively, determinism means the motion admits no branches; continuity means the motion makes no jumps. To see the difference from determinism, one can consider the discrete state sequences of deterministic finite automata. These constitute deterministic functions from the nonnegative integers to automaton states, but utterly discrete functions. One can view these functions as continuous, but only by using trivial discrete topologies that make every function continuous. For a more subtle example, consider the pair of real functions consisting of the constant function 0 and the function that is 0 for all nonpositive numbers and is e^{-1/x^2} for every positive number x. Treating these functions as alternative paths of motion in a nondeterministic history, we see that the history presents a split at 0, even though both have everywhere continuous derivatives of every order, and all derivatives at 0 take the same value 0. Clearly continuity, whether of the path or of any of its derivatives, does not identify the split between these alternatives.

7.3.2 Why continuity?

Mathematical analysis thrives on continuity, which provides the foundation for limits, differentiation, and integration, and through these, equations of motion and their solution, which in turn provide the basis for predictive calculations throughout mechanical applications. As noted in the preceding examples, continuity is strictly speaking neither necessary nor sufficient for these elements of mechanical understanding and prediction, but these examples notwithstanding, traditional mechanics would look very different without routine continuity.

Continuity has other benefits as well. Continuity enables predictions of bounds and boundedness in many problems because the continuous image of a closed set is again a closed set. But the greatest benefit provided by continuity is the notion of successive or iterative approximation, the ability to quickly get an initial approximation and then work as long as desired to improve the approximation. Continuous functions offer the hope that additional work can improve the approximation, and perhaps bound the amount of improvement one can expect from further effort. Discontinuous functions need not support meaningful senses of further approximation, and can thus force reliance on other means in obtaining adequate answers.

7.3.3 Is continuity true?

The truth of claims about continuity of nature or mechanical systems depends on the sort of topology of interest in the system under analysis, for lacking a stipulated topology, the answer can be yes or no. One sees this dependence of continuity on topological assumptions in the previously noted example of the discrete topology. If one regards a space of points as having the discrete topology, in which every set is open, and every set is a neighborhood of every point it contains, then every function from that space to any other topological space is continuous. This trivial case provides little benefit other than to show the broadness of the mathematical concept. In terms of understanding, it provides only a meaningless notion of continuity that lacks any structure at all.

7.3.3.1 Physical continuity

Consider next some interesting answers that give lie to Leibniz's law of continuity. In fact, as Truesdell (1984d) points out, mechanics is full of examples of discontinuous behavior, examples known for hundreds of years. For this reason, modern mechanics formulates its dynamical laws as balance conditions that apply at both points of continuity and, as jump conditions, at points of discontinuity. Truesdell discusses some common occurrences in classical mechanics including the motion of vibrating strings and colliding bodies.

Mathematicians have made attempts to understand mechanical discontinuities in more detail through several programs of research.

Thom's (1975) catastrophe theory, which gained much prominence for a while, made an attempt to give singularities their due by using the tools of differential topology to study the possible bifurcation of classical systems. Thom hoped that understanding bifurcations in mechanics would help illuminate the nature of bifurcations in biological, social, and computational systems. While Thom investigated bifurcations in mechanics, he focused on the mere facts of discontinuity and nondeterminism, leaving open the question of whether all possible changes are equally likely to occur, and if not, their likelihood of occurrence. This weakness of the theory contributed to a decline in its influence.

More recently, the excitement once attending to catastrophe theory has been transferred to theories of chaos and deterministic but seemingly random behavior, theories that provide some means for estimating probabilities of different behaviors. Chaos theory highlights the importance of continuity in a dramatic manner, as it clearly distinguishes successive approximation of solutions to equations from successive approximations to initial conditions. Getting useful predictions requires both sorts of approximations. Chaos theory emphasizes how tiny variations in model or initial conditions can produce dramatic differences in behavior. This has big implications for successive approximation of solutions. Although it is easy to spend more and more effort to get further precision or accuracy in a solution to a system of equations, it normally is much more difficult to obtain more and more accuracy in measurements or prediction of initial conditions. Physical and informational limits on our knowledge of initial conditions thus lead to major limits on our ability to predict behavior, no matter how good our computational facilities.

Specifically, quantum mechanics provides the prime theoretical limitations on our ability to know initial conditions, for the uncertainty relations of quantum theory rule out simultaneous measurement of various pairs of quantities, such as position and momentum. In fact, Bohm's (1952) theory of the vector potential provides an excellent example of the power of knowledge of initial conditions, for it shows that one can describe every quantum history of the universe as the result of purely deterministic physical (mechanical, electromagnetic, or other) laws operating from a suitable deterministic initial condition. More famously, however, the foundation of quantum theory consists of continuous evolution of states punctuated by discontinuous jumps at measurement events, directly contradicting any uniform assumption of continuity.

7.3.3.2 Computational continuity

The theory of computation developed despite a lack of explicit notions of continuity, rendering the powerful tools of classical analysis either inapplicable or ineffective, and leading to laments like the following one by Smale.

> I would like to make it clear that I find merit in the Catastrophe theorists use of modern calculus and geometric techniques in models in science. In particular discontinuities can often be best understood via this kind of mathematics. For example, it would be important to find a calculus oriented model for the computer, a machine which is intrinsically discrete. Such a calculus model would not be exact, but it could give great insight to automata theory. (Smale 1978, p. 1366)

Of course, one can make the motions of discrete systems into continuous ones by employing the discrete topology, but that makes all possible paths continuous and so provides no conceptual or practical analytical help.

It might seem surprising, then, that even though computation seems inherently discrete and discontinuous, the attentions of some stellar mathematicians have begun to reconcile the theory of computation with traditional continuous analytic mathematics, to the point where the theory of computation actually showcases some of the main examples of continuity outside ordinary physical theory.

The fundamental insight comes by considering computation as a process of successive approximation. The most obvious perspective giving computation this character is that in which one views the computational process as constructing successive initial segments of a sequential trajectory of states. At each step of the process, the computation identifies the next state in the trajectory, and then moves to it.

This perspective bears clear resemblance to the standard situation in most numerical computations in the physical sciences, that of incrementally extending a solution of a system of differential equations over one interval to a solution over a slightly larger interval by using the equations to compute the value at the next grid point beyond the end of the current interval. The resemblance becomes stronger as one considers models of computation that formulate the state-transition determination as a set of equations, typically logical equations, as in a Prolog program (cf. Hermann 1990).

Of course, one usually does not meet the typical case of solutions that require numerical approximation in calculus textbooks, making the resemblance seem strained. Textbooks usually focus on the rather limited set of equations one can solve in closed form. Yet even in the computational realm, one finds a corresponding, if limited, set of equations one can solve in closed form. These include regular expressions, which provide closed-form descriptions or characterizations of the behavior of finite-state automata; context-free grammars for some unbounded automata; and a beautiful theory using formal power series to describe formal languages, which builds a bridge between a classical technique of continuous analysis and the discrete theory of languages and machines (Salomaa & Soittola 1978).

In traditional mechanical applications, one rarely encounters closed-form solutions outside of the classroom, but at least one has many rules of calculation for transforming the equations to forms that either reveal important structure directly or simplify the process of numerical solution or simulation (Truesdell 1958). Logical inference of properties of programs provides some corresponding help in the theory of computation, but generally leaves the automaton analyst little alternative to simulation, that is, running the automaton to see what behavior results. Such simulation or execution corresponds directly to numerical solution of differential equations.

Scott's theory of computable functions and data structures, based on nontrivial topology, limits, and continuous functions, represents the most direct attempt to exploit the notion of continuity in computation. This theory constructs data structures as sets of "atomic propositions" or points that satisfy specified abstract consistency and completeness conditions. Key to the construction is a T_0 topology based on set inclusion that lets one construct infinite functions on data structures as limits of finite partial approximations. This notion of approximation corresponds directly to normal computational notions like computing the next few digits of an answer, or the adjacent value of the function, yet satisfies all the formal requirements of the theory of continuous functions. The upshot is that although the set of all functions on these data structures contains many more functions than the computable ones, the set of continuous functions is closed under composition, product, and so on, and corresponds to the set of computable functions over the data structures. Scott describes the general character of his theory in the following terms.

Though the words 'calculus' and 'logic' do have general significance, I would propose calling the systems of Church and Curry λ-*algebra* (or if you like: *combinatory algebra*). This is in analogy to classical algebra. Their theories are *equational* theories of (type-free) functions in combination: the *algebra of functions*—whether formulated with λ-abstraction or with the so-called combinators. (True, it is a branch of logic like Boolean algebra; but we can usefully apply mathematical techniques.) What I have done is to introduce something new: limits and topology. Therefore, in analogy with classical mathematics, I would like to call the *extended* theory λ-*calculus*. Any system of rules can be called a calculus, if you like; but analysis (differential and integral calculus) only took wing from the starting point of algebra after the notion of limit was introduced.

  This sounds egotistical and is in a way, because I have not discovered anything quite as useful as the integral. But I am not quite mad, as I can show by example. We recall Church's troubles with normal forms and nonnormal forms. *These problems can all be completely analyzed in logical space with the aid of limits.* ...In other words: a certain infinite series can be written in closed form. Such a result seems to me to be very much in the spirit of classical analysis. There must be many other such results. We must develop the methods of proving them not only for logical space but for the many other analogous spaces that can be similarly constructed. (Scott 1973, pp. 186–187)

Other trains of work seek to exploit classical mathematical analysis in development of a theory of the complexity of computation over the real and complex numbers (Blum *et al.* 1998), to exploit functional analysis in a theory of machine learning (Cucker & Smale 2002), and to recast symbolic computation in the kinematical terms of differential geometry and dynamical systems (Hermann 1991).

7.3.3.3 Hybrid continuity

Recent hybrid system theories characterize state space as consisting of a set of disjoint manifolds, with a possibly different continuous flow (set of differential equations) governing motion within each component manifold, and with an automaton governing jumps of the motion between component manifolds. In the simplest and most tractable cases, the discontinuous jumps between the manifolds constitute the state transitions of a finite automaton, with each component manifold representing a single state of the automaton. One can thus view the system state space as the product of a manifold with the states of a finite automaton, and the dynamics as the combination of the finite automaton transitions together with possibly different continuous dynamics within each finite-state control region. The topology of the product space is the product of the manifold topology and a discrete topology on the automaton states. This topology makes trajectories continuous as long as their projections onto the manifold are continuous, with the discrete topology on the automaton states making the projection of trajectories onto automaton states automatically continuous.

Unfortunately, most hybrid system theories provide little structure for the discrete jumps beyond the simple notions of automata theory. A theory incorporating Scott topologies, for example, still awaits exploration.

7.3.4 Smoothness and relative continuity

No amount of attention to computational and hybrid systems can hide the appearance of discontinuities in traditional physical systems. In plain fact, some motions involve discontinuities of velocity or other quantities. Faced with these discontinuities, do we simply abandon Leibniz's law of continuity, or do we salvage something from it?

Truesdell (1984d) credits Euler with developing an approach to accommodating discontinuities into Leibniz's perspective that Truesdell calls the *principle of smoothest path*. This principle has two parts. One part says to expand domains of continuity as much as possible. Formally, we might think of this as introducing an ordering of paths according to "relative continuity" in which one path is more continuous than another if it has larger domains of continuity. The principle of smoothest path then requires that bodies follow motions maximal among the alternatives according to the ordering of relative continuity, so ensuring that domains of continuity are as large as possible. In contrast to Leibniz's doctrine, Euler's principle says that even if nature does make jumps, it makes as few jumps as possible, which we might render as *Natura non facit nimium saltum* ("Nature makes no unnecessary jumps").

To illustrate the principle of smoothest path, Truesdell recalls an example of Galileo's about motion of a point on a polygonal surface. Figure 7.1 depicts a traveling mass that meets an obstructing surface and continues in a motion along the surface. Although there are similar trajectories that have more than one discontinuity of velocity, the actual motion avoids those.

Although maximizing domains of continuity in this way certainly seems natural and desirable, it does not seem sufficient, and the second part of the principle of smoothest path requires that changes be as small as possible at the points of discontinuity. This part of the principle has a somewhat different

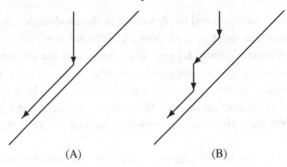

(A)   (B)

Fig. 7.1. A body in downward motion hits a slope. The downward motion follows path (A), not path (B), which, though it involves segments with the same character as in path (A), has unnecessary discontinuities in velocity.

character than the part about continuity. I continue the discussion of Eulerian smoothness in the subsequent discussion of conservatism.

7.3.5 The character of discontinuities

Mathematics includes examples of discontinuities of much worse character than those we expect to encounter in mechanics. For example, the function that takes the value 0 for all nonpositive numbers and for each $x > 0$ takes the value $\sin \frac{1}{x}$, takes all values between -1 and 1 in every positive neighborhood of 0.

In mechanics, we expect all quantities to be piecewise continuous with definite limits. To ensure this, I add the following axiom to the requirements on motion.

Axiom C1 *The mechanical state of each body point and its position, velocity, acceleration, mass, massing, momentum, momentum change, energy, and heating components form piecewise continuous functions of time in each mechanical history, and have temporal limits from both the past and the future at each instant.*

That is, all discontinuities take the form of a jump in values from one limiting value (limit from the past) to another (limit from the future). This rules out motions taking an intermediate value at points of discontinuity, such as placement at -1 for all earlier times, placement at 1 for all later times, and placement at 0 at the instant of discontinuity. Some theories of hybrid systems allow such intermediate values at discontinuities, but I do not pursue such possibilities here.

7.4 Conservation

As noted earlier, Truesdell (1984d) credits Euler with developing the principle of smoothest path, which says to expand domains of continuity as much
as possible, and to make motion as smooth as possible by making discontinuous changes as small as possible, so as to conserve as many properties of
the motion as possible at discontinuities. The first part of this principle concerns maximization of the intervals of continuity; the second, minimization of
the magnitude of change at discontinuities. In the following section, I examine ideas related to this sort of change minimization, including conservative
systems and invariants of motion.

7.4.1 What are conservative systems?

Using the size of jumps at the points of discontinuity to judge comparative
smoothness of paths has some similarity to the intuitive notion of continuity,
but a more accurate characterization of this notion of smoothness is as a principle of motion that conserves the values of mechanical quantities as much as
possible throughout the motion, as a conservation principle rather than an expression of continuity. Continuity means the motion makes no jumps; conservatism means that jumps are as small as possible. In these terms, the principle
of smoothest path says that motion is conservative and maximally continuous.

Now when physicists use the terms *conservation principles* and *conservative systems*, they mean principles according to which or systems in which
some quantity remains unchanged over time. Such principles and systems have
great importance, but outside physics the term *conservation* means economizing, minimizing change rather than complete changelessness. In this present
world, a conservator can only seek to slow the inevitable decline, not to prevent it entirely. Compared with this more ordinary meaning of the term, the
physicist's meaning reflects an especially crabbed conception of conservation.
To distinguish the two, I use the terms *invariance principles* and *systems with
invariants* to refer to principles or systems keeping things unchanged, and *conservative*, *conservation*, and *conservatism* to refer to principles or systems that
minimize how things change.

The principle of smoothest path expresses a temporally local restriction on
motion, the restriction that some quantity change as little as possible at each
instant. Truesdell (1984d) presents the illustrations reproduced in Figure 7.2 to
illustrate the principle. This illustration depicts a traveling mass that first meets
an obstructing surface and then continues in a motion that conserves as much
of its former momentum as possible—in these cases, with no change of energy,
as the motion is continuous, even if its derivatives are not. Truesdell notes that

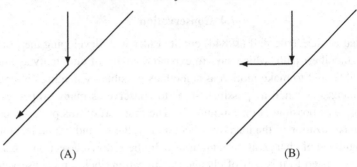

(A)   (B)

Fig. 7.2. A body in downward motion hits a slope. The downward motion follows path
(A), not path (B), which has the same point of discontinuity but changes the downward
momentum more than necessary.

the motion of the object preserves as much of its downward component as
possible.

As applied in mechanical settings, the principle of smoothest path may economize changes of position, mass, momentum, or energy. Schoolbook mechanics makes a point of how position and velocity change smoothly even though
acceleration may change discontinuously through impulse. Truesdell points
out that energy, which often depends on position and velocity, forms a more
general candidate, with maximal conservation of energy in some cases entail-
ing maximal conservation of position and velocity. For a still more general
conception, one can consider economizing of the quantity called *action*, which
provides the foundations of variational approaches to physics. I examine these
in Section 7.5.

7.4.2 Why conservative systems?

The utility of physical invariance principles, the strongest form of conservation principles, requires little explanation, as invariance principles allow one
to avoid calculation entirely in predicting the behavior of some systems.

Apart from least action principles, which I treat separately in the following
section, the utility of more general conservation principles is less well known.
Mechanics provides some examples of the utility of conservation principles;
psychology and other fields provide even more.

Truesdell and Toupin (1960) point out that although the standard principles
of mechanics do not suffice to determine the motion of a buckling column,
adding a principle of minimizing the elastic energy of the buckled column
does determines the motion. Similar energy-minimization principles appear in
statistical mechanics, and in real and simulated annealing.

The notion of conservation of belief or truth forms the basis of numerous theories in psychology and artificial intelligence, especially the theories of belief revision and counterfactuals. Prominent theories of belief revision (Doyle 1979, 1983e; Gärdenfors & Makinson 1988) provide formal versions of Quine's "maxim of minimal mutilation" (Quine & Ullian 1978), in which one accommodates new beliefs by making the minimal changes required in current beliefs. Corresponding theories of the meaning of counterfactual statements (Rescher 1964; Lewis 1973; Stalnaker 1984) rest on related ideas by saying a counterfactual is true just in case the consequent is true in those worlds making the antecedent true that are the most similar to, or are the least different from, the actual world.

7.4.3 Are conservation principles true?

We face two difficulties in assessing the truth of conservation principles.

The first difficulty concerns the nature of conservation principles. As stated herein, conservatism might apply to different mechanical attributes or qualities. One cannot say the general idea is true or false, only whether certain mechanical quantities are conserved or not. Experience in physics suggests that one varies what one thinks of as conserved to suit the system under analysis. In classical mechanics, one usually assumes that closed systems have invariant measures of total mass, but that assumption requires modification in cases of relativistic motion, atomic disintegration, and when one considers the mass of the entire known universe, which, according to general relativity, cannot be assigned a definite quantity. Similar ambiguity afflicts assumptions of invariant energy, which one assumes conserved in classical terrestrial settings of kinetic and "potential" energy, but must formulate more carefully in relativistic and quantum settings.

Rather than discuss the truth of conservatism in general, let us focus our attention in the following paragraphs on the nature and truth of conservatism in special cases.

The second difficulty in assessing the truth of conservation principles concerns metaphysics. The very statement of conservation principles refers to motion as smooth or as conservative *as possible*. The truth of such claims thus depends on how narrowly or broadly we conceive of the range of possible motions. Certainly *possible* must imply "possible according to the other laws of mechanics," but this implicit dependence means that the truth of conservation principles can change as we add, abandon, or emend other axioms of mechanics.

We return to the metaphysics of conservatism shortly.

Beyond these concerns, the truth of conservation principles might also interact with questions about determinism. In particular, conservation principles might be probabilistic, requiring that larger changes be less likely than smaller ones even when both are possible. Strict conservatism, which forbids nonminimal changes, then corresponds a probability distribution in which nonminimal changes have zero probability.

7.4.4 Formalizing conservation principles

Formalizing the conservative portion of the principle of smoothest path requires an order for comparing the magnitude of changes at discontinuities.

Although the term *smoothest path* implicitly indicates smoothness of spatial position and its derivatives, a general treatment of conservation principles requires treatment of histories of full states, not just histories of spatial motion. The relevant discontinuities are those of full histories, not just the spatial component, so that, as in Figure 7.2, we can treat the discontinuity of momentum even though position varies continuously.

By Axiom C1, one can represent changes of value or state transitions at each point of discontinuity by elements of $\mathbf{T}(\Sigma)$, the tangent space of the space of mechanical states Σ.

7.4.4.1 Ordering changes

We start by considering a binary relation $\preceq$ over $\mathbf{T}(\Sigma)$ for comparing state transitions, and read the comparison $(\sigma_1, \sigma_2) \preceq (\sigma_3, \sigma_4)$ as stating that the change from σ_3 to σ_4 is at least as large as the change from σ_1 to σ_2. We assume that the comparison relation constitutes a (partial) preorder over all possible transitions, that is, a reflexive and transitive relation.

Axiom C2 $(\sigma_1, \sigma_2) \preceq (\sigma_1, \sigma_2)$.

Axiom C3 *If* $(\sigma_1, \sigma_2) \preceq (\sigma_3, \sigma_4) \preceq (\sigma_5, \sigma_6)$, *then* $(\sigma_1, \sigma_2) \preceq (\sigma_5, \sigma_6)$.

We write $\prec$ to mean the strict portion of the relation $\preceq$.

We also require that null changes (points of continuity) rank as small as any other transition.

Axiom C4 $(\sigma, \sigma) \preceq (\sigma_1, \sigma_2)$.

These axioms do not restrict the choices of measures of the closeness of states in any substantive way, since the weakest comparison relation in which every state is equally close to every other is one possibility. Under this weakest comparison relation, every change is minimal and hence conservative.

In fact, we normally will want to compare only alternative transitions starting from the same state, that is, comparisons of the form

$$(\sigma, \sigma_1) \preceq (\sigma, \sigma_2). \tag{7.5}$$

This usage means that the transition-comparison relation induces a state-dependent ordering of states. We use the symbol $\preceq_\sigma$ to denote the order associated with state σ, and define this order by

$$\sigma_1 \preceq_\sigma \sigma_2 \text{ iff } (\sigma, \sigma_1) \preceq (\sigma, \sigma_2). \tag{7.6}$$

A formally similar comparison notion appears in logical treatments of counterfactuals, where the measure of size of change is called a *comparative similarity relation* (see Lewis 1973). The notion of comparative similarity relation has close connections with notions of metrics. Clearly, a metric on the transition space generates a comparative similarity relation, and one might think of such relations as deriving from metriclike functions that take values in partially ordered spaces instead of the reals. Schlechta and Makinson (1994) have shown that one can find a true metric generating the comparative similarity relation (or at least equivalent to it with regard to counterfactual conclusions) when one places certain conditions on the relation. One can also consider variations on the simple comparative similarity notion based on concepts akin to metrics, such as pseudometrics, or on concepts from topology, such as neighborhood systems and pseudotopologies.

7.4.4.2 Conservative histories

With a transition comparison relation as just described, we thus can introduce a nearest-state function $\nu : \Sigma \times \mathcal{P}(\Sigma) \to \mathcal{P}(\Sigma)$ defined so that for each state $\sigma \in \Sigma$ and finite set of states $S \subseteq \Sigma$, the set $\nu(\sigma, S)$ contains a state $\sigma' \in S$ just in case for each $\sigma'' \in S$ we have $(\sigma, \sigma') \prec (\sigma, \sigma'')$ whenever $(\sigma, \sigma'') \prec (\sigma, \sigma')$. This definition works for finite S, but can fail for infinite S without further assumptions about limits. We thus base the notion of conservative history on an explicitly topological construction.

We use the comparison relation to define conservative histories as follows. Consider a history h and a nondeterministic motion H, both over a temporal interval $I = I(h) = I(H)$. Axiom C1 guarantees that h and each history in H has forward and backward limits at each instant in I. We say that h is *conservative with respect to H* just in case for each path $h' \in H$ and instant $t_0 \in I(H)$, if $h(t) = h'(t)$ for each $t < t_0$, then

$$\lim_{t \downarrow t_0} h'(t) \not\prec_\sigma \lim_{t \downarrow t_0} h(t), \tag{7.7}$$

where

$$\sigma = \lim_{t\uparrow t_0} h(t) = \lim_{t\uparrow t_0} h'(t). \tag{7.8}$$

If $H \subseteq H'$, we say that the nondeterministic motion H is *conservative with respect to* H' just in case each history $h \in H$ is conservative with respect to H'. Clearly, if h is conservative with respect to H, then it is also conservative with respect to any $H' \subseteq H$. Finally, we say that H is *conservative* iff H is conservative with respect to itself.

The notion of conservative history just defined captures the obvious sense of forward conservatism. I do not treat here the corresponding notion of conservatism backward in time.

Note also that this definition of conservative motion subsumes the continuity-maximizing portion of the smoothest path principle, because if there is a continuous path, it will have the same forward and reverse limits at each point, and so its null transition at each point will make the continuous path be the only conservative one.

The notion of conservative history depends strongly on the reference class of histories. In particular, each history h is conservative with respect to the singleton history $\{h\}$. Thus if only one history is mechanically possible, the jumps it contains are the jumps that are necessary. To state the conservatism or smoothest path principle, we thus need to identify the reference class, which for us will be the mechanically possible motions.

Axiom C5 *In every fixed framing, the motion of a mechanical system, whether deterministic or nondeterministic, is conservative with respect to the set of all mechanical processes of the system.*

This axiom has a different character than the previous ones, in that it represents a "closure" axiom applying to the results of all the previous axioms, as captured in the notion of mechanical process defined earlier.

We do not need to assume frame indifference of the conservatism comparison relation because Axiom C5 only applies it within individual framings, not across framings.

7.4.4.3 Energetic conservatism

To move beyond purely formal conservation principles, we must consider conservation of different physical quantities. We begin by taking Truesdell's suggestion to apply the principle of smoothest path to the energy of a system.

The preceding section has stated no general laws about the total energy $K + E$ of the body other than equality (6.72) between the total change in energy

$\dot{K} + \dot{E}$ and the combined power and heating $P + Q$ in every inertial frame of reference. For the extreme body, $\mathcal{U}$, there is no external system and hence no power, and as a frame-indifferent quantity heating cannot contribute to kinetic energy, so the relation reduces to $\dot{E}(\mathcal{U}) = Q(\mathcal{U}, \mathcal{O})$; that is, the change of total energy is equal to the heating due to the null body. Applying Axiom E7 to the bodies $\mathcal{U}$ and $\mathcal{O} = \mathcal{O} \sqcup \mathcal{O}$ yields $Q(\mathcal{U}, \mathcal{O}) = \mathbf{0}_{\mathcal{E}}$, and hence $\dot{E}(\mathcal{U}) = \mathbf{0}_{\mathcal{E}}$; that is, total energy is constant.

The invariance of total energy forms the motivation for Hamiltonian formulations of mechanics, which express invariance of energy implicitly. In the Hamiltonian approach, one expresses the total energy of the system as an energy-valued function H of the instantaneous states of the atomic bodies, and takes as an axiom that the global motion must occur on a level set of H, that is, that the total energy is constant throughout the motion. Time-varying Hamiltonian functions are also employed when one considers nonisolated great systems instead of global motions. In the time-varying case, Hamiltonians are functionals of partial histories rather than functions of atomic states.

In the case of discontinuous and discrete systems, however, the simple assumption of invariant energy is inadequate. Applying the principle of smoothest path to energy, we assume that at discontinuities, the change of total energy is minimized. Phrased generally, this assumption subsumes the usual case, since at points of continuity the zero change of energy is as small as possible.

To make this notion precise, we need a preordering of the sizes of changes of energy that ranks the null changes (diagonal pairs) at bottom, that is, a relation $\preceq_{\mathrm{e}}$ on $\mathcal{E}^2 \times \mathcal{E}^2$ satisfying conditions on pairs of energy values like those stated for mechanical states in Axioms C2, C3, and C4. Pure energetic conservatism then consists of defining the relation $\preceq$ on mechanical states so that $\sigma \preceq \sigma'$ just in case $E(\sigma) \preceq_{\mathrm{e}} E(\sigma')$.

In traditional mechanics, the obvious preorder on energy pairs compares the absolute value of energy differences, that is, $(E_1, E_2) \preceq (E_3, E_4)$ iff $|E_1 - E_2| \le |E_3 - E_4|$. For energies taking values in $\mathbb{Z}_2^n$, we might define $(E_1, E_2) \preceq (E_3, E_4)$ to hold just in case $E_1 - E_2 \subseteq E_3 - E_4$, or just in case $d_{\mathcal{E}}(E_1 - E_2) \le d_{\mathcal{E}}(E_3 - E_4)$, or by using other measures of these difference sets.

Quantum mechanics suggests considering several generalizations of the notion of strict energy conservatism.

The first generalization is to probabilistic energetic conservatism, which makes the probabilities of a change a function of the size of the change in energy. In some systems, the probability of a transition in quantum mechanics declines with the increase in energy of the transition, so that the most probable transitions are the ones involving the least change of energy. Not all transition distributions have this character, however.

Probabilistic conservatism certainly plays a role in characterizing some notions of stochastic search, in which the probability of a transition is related to the negative exponential of an energy difference.

Another variation is that of level-bound restrictions, in which motions need not keep the same energy level, but must stay within a fixed range of energies. A related variation is a bounded-change restriction, in which the changes of energy at discontinuities are dominated by a fixed maximum value. And of course, one may consider a probabilistic version of each of these, in which the probability of transition is a function of the excessiveness of the energy change. These notions all relate to the stability of the system.

As in quantum mechanics, we say that the *spectrum* of a system is the set of possible changes of energy levels at discontinuities. Depending on the system, the spectrum may be continuous or discrete. The level-bound and bounded-change restrictions amount to restrictions on the size of the spectrum. In contrast, a purely conservative system may have an unbounded spectrum, for minimal changes may be large in absolute magnitude. As energy changes correspond to energy inputs or outputs of the system, it would be interesting to relate the spectrum of a computational system to its communication or input–output behavior. These inputs and outputs amount to the changes in the system observable by an outsider.

7.5 Economy

Although traditional physics has not made the principle of smoothest path a formal axiom, physical formalism makes heavy use of concepts connected with the principle of least action, a more familiar principle that specializes and strengthens the principle of smoothest path.

7.5.1 What is economy of action?

The principle of least action specializes the notion of smoothest path principle by focusing attention on a quantity, action, which standard treatments take to have dimensions

$$
\begin{aligned}
(\text{action}) &= (\text{energy})(\text{time}) \\
&= (\text{mass})(\text{length})^2(\text{time})^{-1} \\
&= (\text{force})(\text{length})(\text{time}) \\
&= (\text{length})(\text{momentum}) \\
&= (\text{mass})(\text{length})(\text{velocity}).
\end{aligned}
$$

The action quantity represents a path integral over the motion in question of a function of mechanical properties of the system. This function is typically called the *Lagrangian* (function) of the system. As the dimensional equations indicate, action normally melds notions of mass, position, velocity, momentum, and energy. One can thus view action as a proxy for all these quantities, and typically can choose action functions to reflect desired conditions on the smoothness of any of these other quantities.

The principle of least action strengthens the principle of smoothest path by moving from a local requirement to a global requirement. Instead of simply requiring that change be as smooth as possible at each instant, the strict principle of least action requires that the motion be such as to yield an action value representing a minimum value over all possible paths. Taking a minimum value means that the variation or derivative of the action with respect to variations in the path is zero. The normal principle of least action used in mathematical physics diverges from the strict principle by using vanishing variation of the action as the indicator of true paths, so dropping the requirement that the action take only a minimum value on that path. In the normal usage, therefore, on true paths the action might take a value representing maxima or inflection points as well as minima.

One easily sees that global least action implies both least action at discontinuities and a smoothest action principle at these points, for global least action amounts to requiring that the motion minimize the magnitude of change in action at the point of discontinuity relative to other possible motions. The converse implication, however, does not hold; local smoothest path does not imply global smoothest path, in that minimization of changes at each instant of discontinuity does not entail minimization of the net change over a multistep trajectory.

The principle of least action underlies the widely used Lagrangian and Hamiltonian formalisms. Lagrange derived the Euler–Lagrange equations as one consequence of setting the variation of the integral of the Lagrangian equal to zero; Euler derived them earlier from other assumptions. One then defines the Hamiltonian function from special cases of the Lagrangian function, typically assuming the Lagrangian function to have the form

$$L = K - U \tag{7.9}$$

for some potential function U, in which case the Hamiltonian function has the form

$$H = K + U \tag{7.10}$$

so that

$$H = 2K - L. \tag{7.11}$$

More generally, one obtains Hamiltonian functions from Lagrangian functions by means of Legendre transformations.

The least action principle, applied to such Lagrangian functions, implies the energy-minimizing principle of smoothest path. Since the minimization holds at discontinuities, the value of K is the same at the discontinuity, so minimizing L means minimizing ΔH.

7.5.2 Why economize action?

One can divide motivations for the principle of least action into three categories: the philosophical, the physical, and the mathematical. Let us examine these motivations in turn.

The oldest motivations for least action principles exhibit a philosophical character, stemming from notions of divine and scientific aesthetics. The oldest version, that of the economy or perfection of nature, traces back to Aristotle. This idea regards nature as exhibiting a form of economy or optimality on account of a divine abhorrence of waste, disorder, and superfluous motion in creating the world; surely an odd expectation from a culture organized around the chaotic Greek pantheon, but more in keeping with the monotheisms that replaced pagan pantheons around the Mediterranean. Leibniz made such notions an important portion of his philosophy, in which the actual world represents the best of all possible worlds, and in which economy represents one aspect of goodness and waste one aspect of badness.

Physical motivations for least action principles took strength from Fermat's discovery of the principle of least time in optics, namely that light takes a path that minimizes the time needed for travel between its source and destination. This experimentally demonstrable principle owed nothing to philosophy. Though it covers a very narrow range of phenomena compared with the more general philosophical notion, it bore within it the seeds of modern relativity theory, in which light paths explicitly constitute the shortest possible paths, namely those of zero length in the Lorentz metric on the four-dimensional space-time manifold. Maupertuis drew on Fermat's discovery and the philosophical tradition to propose that motions follow paths that minimize an integral of the motion, which Hamilton later formalized in his principle of least action. Related notions appear in D'Alembert's principle, which expresses the balance principles of mechanics in terms of the invariance of work under infinitesimal perturbations of the actual motion. Later still, the motivations for least action principles received additional strengthening by their utility in guiding the discovery of laws of quantum mechanics.

The mathematical motivations for regarding nature as exhibiting economy or optimality stem from the extreme fecundity and power of variational principles in computation. The first successes of these techniques, developed by the Bernoullis and Euler in solving the famous brachistochrone problem and others, antedated statements of least action principles. Variational methods received widespread application in later years with discovery of the Euler–Lagrange equations, and more application still with Hamilton's discovery of the Hamiltonian formulation of these principles.

The Lagrangian and Hamiltonian formalizations of mechanical systems offer four interrelated potential benefits. The first potential benefit of the Lagrangian and Hamiltonian formalism is simplifying the equations of motion by expressing these equations in terms of the most natural variables. Although one can try to simplify any equation by rerepresenting quantities, the form of the Euler–Lagrange equations offer a nice target for choosing such simplifications. Mathematical physics thus includes a repertoire of "canonical transformations" that constitute changes of variables that leave invariant the Euler–Lagrange and Hamiltonian equational forms.

The second potential benefit is that the Lagrangian and Hamiltonian formalisms simplify solutions by melding problem-specific constraints and laws into single expressions. This means that one need not first solve general equations and then throw out those violating specific constraints, but can find the target solutions directly. When combined with the first benefit, this second potential benefit means one can choose coordinate systems that simplify the combined requirements from general laws and problem-specific constraints.

The third potential benefit is that the Lagrangian and especially the Hamiltonian formalisms help identify invariant quantities, which themselves greatly aid the analysis of systems. Nöther proved a general result that the symmetry of a physical system under certain transformations implies the existence of a conserved quantity. In the Hamiltonian context, symmetries of the Hamiltonian function directly indicate conserved quantities.

A fourth potential benefit is that the Lagrangian and Hamiltonian formalisms allow one to economize on solution effort by using the same abstract form of equations for almost all physical systems. In the setting of automated computation, this permits one to immediately reapply numerical or analytical solution techniques developed for the solution of one system to the solution of others.

7.5.3 Is economy of action true?

In attempting to assess the truth of optimality claims, I distinguish between the philosophical senses of goodness and economy and the mathematical senses of vanishing variation, for these senses have very different answers.

I start with the mathematical sense. Assessing the truth of variational principles of physical law is easier than assessing the truth of philosophical claims of goodness or economy because the mathematical formalization represents a value-free formulation that dispenses with notions of goodness. Just as economists regard rational decisions as maximizing utility and statisticians regard exactly the same rational decisions as minimizing loss, the mathematics of variational or least action principles relies only on techniques that provide the same answers independent of moral interpretations involving goodness or badness. Once I address the truth of mathematical optimality, we stand better poised to tackle the more contentious philosophical claims.

7.5.3.1 Truth without consequences

Economy of action is true in a mathematical sense because all known physical theories indeed satisfy the principle of least action. This positive answer means less than one might think because *all* possible physical theories satisfy the principle of least action, even theories known to be false. This happens because, as noted earlier in Section 3.3.3, the variational framework of the Euler–Lagrange and Hamiltonian equations is physically vacuous. These formalisms say nothing at all about the physics of the system under consideration, even though they provide the important formal and computational advantages enumerated earlier. One gets just as much information about the world from the Lagrangian and Hamiltonian frameworks as one does from Rubel's (1981) universal differential equation.

To be specific, let us consider Lagrangian mechanics, perhaps the most widely used mathematical formulation of mechanical principles, one that leads directly to the formulation of Hamilton's equations. One misspeaks when one talks of the Euler–Lagrange equations, for these equations serve only as a schematic form for many different equations. The Euler–Lagrange equations themselves, in terms of an abstract Lagrangian function, involve no axioms of mechanical concepts, and indeed, involve no mechanical concepts at all. Feynman, for example, characterized the variational approach well by caricature, talking of a function U measuring the "unworldliness" of motions, chosen so that U is zero only on "worldly" motions that might actually happen according to the laws of mechanics, or according to whatever other theory one considers.

One sees the physical vacuity of the Euler–Lagrange equations clearly in the derivation of these equations. Sussman and Wisdom (2001) provide the clearest exposition of the classical approach. In summary, one starts by seeking a function U of paths that discriminates legal from illegal paths, as in Feynman's caricature. Reasoning about how the function must behave on subpaths, one seeks a function involving an integral. Simple considerations show that one cannot just look for this integral to vanish, for that entails that the integrand must vanish everywhere. One therefore follows established practice in looking to minimize (or maximize) this integral, using philosophical or aesthetic principles about the actual world's being the best possible; Sussman and Wisdom reason to much the same conclusion, looking for inflection points of the integral. One then derives the Euler–Lagrange equations relating the position and velocity on the path by requiring the derivative of the integral to be zero. Denoting the integrand function of paths by L, which one assumes to be a function of triples representing positions, velocities, and times, one obtains the equations

$$\frac{d}{dt}\frac{\partial L}{\partial \dot{x}} = \frac{\partial L}{\partial x} \tag{7.12}$$

in the traditional but confusing notation (Sussman and Wisdom employ a much clearer formulation). Nothing in this derivation expresses any known physical law; everything proceeds purely from the functional form of the quantities involved and the assumption of vanishing variation.

The equations of motion take an even simpler form when one moves from the Lagrangian function to the Hamiltonian function, which in mathematical abstraction becomes motion on symplectic manifolds. Using a Legendre transformation to transform generalized position and velocity coordinates to generalized position and momentum coordinates, one arrives at Hamilton's equations:

$$\frac{dq_i}{dt} = \frac{\partial H}{\partial p_i} \tag{7.13}$$

$$\frac{dp_i}{dt} = -\frac{\partial H}{\partial q_i}. \tag{7.14}$$

If the Euler–Lagrange equations say nothing about physics, why does physics find them so useful? To see why, I elaborate on the reasons given earlier.

One first sees that the Lagrangian approach makes the laws of physics into a parameter, in that to use the equations to analyze some system, one invents a Lagrangian function L that encapsulates the laws of that system. For example, the simple Lagrangian

$$L(x, \dot{x}, t) = \tfrac{1}{2}m\dot{x}^2 - V(t, x) \tag{7.15}$$

expresses the Eulerian laws governing the motion of a particle of mass m and position x moving in a potential field V. This parameterization of the system laws proves very useful in computing behaviors, since it lets one incorporate constraints specific to the system in question into the same formalism as expresses the general laws. The particular form given here violates the requirement of frame indifference, since it involves a Lagrangian defined in terms of a specific coordinate system, but Sussman and Wisdom show how to separate out the coordinatization of space and paths that demonstrates the frame indifference of the basic equations. In spite of this frame indifference, the variational equations still violate the principle of reality, however, because if one Lagrangian function characterizes a set of desired behaviors, an infinite number do. No one has managed to find the distinct equivalence classes of Lagrangian functions that might remedy this situation.

A formalism that applies to all physical theories has no physical content. The Euler–Lagrange and Hamiltonian equations say no more about physics than do English or Esperanto; all simply provide means for describing both physical and nonphysical systems.

The good side of this silence on physics is applicability to other systems of interest. Because the variational approach takes the laws of physics and of the system under consideration as a parameter, and so says nothing about mechanics or about any other part of physics, it therefore presumably applies to analyzing psychology and economics as much as it does to physics. Indeed, extant psychological applications include Lagrangian search techniques; extant economic applications including Lagrangian optimization techniques (see, for example, Cass & Shell 1976). Casting discrete systems of the form considered here poses additional challenges to the variational formulation, but Baez and Gilliam (Baez & Gilliam 1994; Gilliam 1996) have used techniques from commutative algebra and synthetic differential geometry to adapt standard Lagrangian mechanics to abstract discrete state spaces and so provide a discrete version of the Euler–Lagrange equations, complementing techniques for making discrete-time versions of Lagrangian and Hamiltonian techniques (Wendlandt & Marsden 1997; Guo & Wu 2003). They also analyze examples involving particles in potential fields, derive constructions for symplectic manifolds, and prove a discrete analog of Noether's theorem relating symmetries to conserved quantities.

Reconsider now the other potential benefit of the variational formalisms, that of helping to identify invariant quantities. These come out quite nicely in the Hamiltonian formalism, because the time rate of change of any function of states is given by its Lie bracket with the Hamiltonian,

$$\frac{df}{dt} = [f, H], \tag{7.16}$$

so that any invariant quantity or "constant of the motion" satisfies

$$[f, H] = 0. \tag{7.17}$$

In particular, since $[H, H] = 0$, the total energy H is constant during motions.

But pursuing the same reasoning just discussed about parameterizing the laws of mechanics, we see that this potential benefit is something of an illusion. The Hamiltonian function is a parameter of the system, and different Hamiltonians represent different sets of invariants. Use of the Hamiltonian formalism constitutes an admission that we do not know the invariants of the system. Picking the Hamiltonian means picking the full set of invariants, though perhaps not knowing all these invariants at the time of choosing.

7.5.3.2 The simple truth

Truth of the variational formulation of physical laws, even if physically vacuous, does nothing to decide the truth of Aristotelian and Leibnizian conceptions of the economy or optimality of nature, for the variational formulation makes no distinction between Leibnizian optimists who believe this is the best of all possible worlds and Voltairean pessimists who posit divine malevolence that ensures the worst possible outcomes. Mathematically, the mirroring relationships of these interpretations make it easy to switch between these interpretations, much as a bipolar psychology switches between depressive (pessimistic) and manic (optimistic) phases, or less dramatically but more commonly, as nonmonotonic reasoners may switch between complementary assumptions.

Some students of nature might say no evidence exists to decide the truth of physical economy. Others may take typical human tastes as evidence with which to distinguish optimism and pessimism in variational principles. On the basis of human tastes, the evidence clearly falls on the side of the optimality of nature. Indeed, conceptual beauty and simplicity constitute some of the fundamental guiding principles of the esthetics of scientific theorizing. One might adapt Dostoyevsky to express this aesthetic by saying that true theories are beautiful in the same way, while false theories are each ugly in their own way. The optimistic interpretation of nature provides the only metaphysical account of natural law consonant with the metaphysical principles of science itself. Others still may take human tastes in this regard to reflect divine characteristics of order and economy and call on supposed evidence of divine self-revelations to justify assuming the economy of nature. Finally, one can look to specific laws of economy, such as Fermat's law in optics, to justify the optimistic interpretation. Whichever body of evidence one takes, however, the evidence falls clearly on the side of optimism, of taking motion to be as simple as possible.

[T]here is no greatness where there is not simplicity, goodness, and truth.
  (L. Tolstoy 1869, Pt. 14, Ch. 18)

7.5.4 Economy of action as physical law

By bringing psychological notions of conservatism and rationality under the umbrella of mechanical formalism, the mechanics presented here provides additional motivation for regarding some variational principles as true physical laws on a par with Fermat's law of optics rather than mere mathematical devices. This motivation becomes stronger as one shifts attention from uniformly smooth and reversible Hamiltonian motion to discrete, discontinuous, and indeterministic motions of the sorts considered here. In the broader setting, least action principles provide needed constraints on motion as well as mathematical elegance in the formulation.

The Baez–Gilliam (1994) discrete formulation of Euler–Lagrange equations provides a starting point for seeking to apply traditional variational forms to discrete systems, but the overt discreteness of this formalism hides a more difficult problem for applying Lagrangian and Hamiltonian techniques to psychological systems. Such applications diverge from traditional ones both in their discreteness and in their openness.

Put another way, traditional Lagrangian and Hamiltonian formalisms apply to closed systems. Casting a discrete psychological force in Lagrangian terms requires formulating sensible laws by which psychological forces arise. The desired theory of psychology distinguishes internal from external forces, and seeks to take the external or exogenous forces as givens, rather than part of laws of the system. A Lagrangian formulation must somehow express interactions of the agent with its environment in terms of a Lagrangian function, so without some specific conception of the environment, one can only postulate the existence of a suitable Lagrangian function, not describe it. Since characterizing a realistic environment for the psychological systems of interest would seem to involve many complexities, I do not pursue that avenue here.

Despite the likely inapplicability of simple Hamiltonian models to psychological systems, in which conservatism is not the perfect energetic conservation of Hamiltonian motion, exploration of these models in the discrete settings considered here offers an interesting path for future work. For example, can one derive a result relating conserved quantities to smoothest path principles corresponding to the results relating invariant quantities to symmetries of the Hamiltonian? Since the smoothest path principle only seeks to approximate conservation of quantities, one cannot expect to find exactly conserved quantities in all cases. Trivially, one may say that the state is the approximately conserved quantity, but when can one determine that some quantity making up the state is in fact the object of approximate conservation?

The present formalization of conservative systems opens additional possibilities for exploration. What conditions on conservatism relations and action quantities make local smoothness consistent with global smoothness? Surely these conditions have more to do with the structure of the action quantity than with the conservatism relation, since even standard metrics on Euclidean space do nothing to require that the endpoints of curves are separated more than the intermediate points are.

7.6 Reversibility

Some people today view temporal reversibility as a fundamental characteristic of physical law. The following paragraphs examine the role of reversibility in mechanics.

7.6.1 What is reversibility?

Reversibility consists of a temporal symmetry in equations and their solutions that permits one to continue local solutions either forward or backward in time. This means it permits solution of the equations even when one reverses the direction of time and reverses all velocities. Reversibility is thus a much stronger notion than determinism, for it entails that the future determines the past, and the past determines the future.

7.6.2 Why reversibility?

Modern theories of reversibility stem from a reduction of the behavior of the world to the behavior of elementary particles of atomic and subatomic physics and from the theory of relativity. The local laws discovered so far governing such particles exhibit this temporal symmetry, and the theory of relativity explicitly considers observers moving backward in time relative to the ordinary sense of time to require the invariance of events with respect to such time-inverted observers.

Reversibility is also an essential characteristic of Hamiltonian dynamics, which forms the favored mathematical formulation of many physical theories, as it directly embodies conservation of energy in its simplest forms. Even when some particle acts irreversibly in some circumstances, the focus on Hamiltonian characterizations of behavior helps overlook these irreversible behaviors.

7.6.3 Is reversibility true?

The plausibility of reversibility varies as one looks at different aspects of mechanical theory and experience. In the remainder of this section I consider reversibility in both everyday experience and in the laws of physics.

7.6.3.1 Theoretical reversibility

The canonical reversible physical situations open in principle to everyday observation consist of planetary motions, since a system consisting of two rigid masses orbiting each other under the influence of mutual gravitation can be stable across all time and reversible as well. In fact, Truesdell points out that this system constitutes the primary example of a perpetual motion machine. Unlike idealized situations of perfectly elastic billiard balls on a pool table, this example could conceivably exist for a long time if suitably distanced from the rest of the matter in the universe.

Engineering attempts to harness reversibility have focused on the energy-conservation characteristic of reversible astronomical systems to use reversibility in the service of energy efficiency. Some have explored tangible versions of such reversible systems by designing computer logic gates that act reversibly at the computational level and come close to acting reversibly at the level of physical energy (Fredkin & Toffoli 1982; Toffoli & Margolus 1987, 1990; Frank 1999; Frank, Knight, & Margolus 1998).

7.6.3.2 Theoretical irreversibility

The truth of reversibility depends in part on the reducibility of all behavior to the behavior of particles that exhibit reversible behavior, since if the behavior of the entire world consists solely of motions of particles with behavior reversible at every instant of time, then clearly the world as a whole exhibits reversibility.

The macroscopic laws of thermomechanics impose a nonreversible condition on the evolution of systems, namely that the rate of entropy production be nonnegative. This condition is not reversible, because reversing the sense of time would yield histories in which the rate of entropy production is nonpositive. This means that the only reversible systems are those, like the planetary systems mentioned earlier, that have constant entropy across all time.

7.6.3.3 Phenomenological irreversibility

As everyone trying to clean badly stained garments knows, reversibility goes contrary to most everyday experience, in which one typically cannot run systems backward, even though they exhibit conservative motion. Even classical mechanics includes simple situations exhibiting such irreversibility. Figure 7.3, adapted from Truesdell (1984d), illustrates a body striking an inclined plane (A), where the reversed final motion (B) meets no obstruction and so differs from the forward motion. Reversibility in this case would require a passive plane to suddenly generate a subhorizontally directed force on the body at the point of departure.

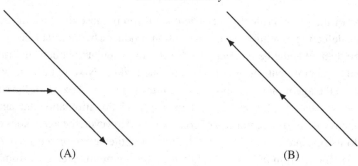

(A) (B)

Fig. 7.3. A body in sideways motion hits an incline. The sideways motion follows path (A), though reversing the motion subsequent to deflection by the incline yields path (B), which diverges from the forward motion.

Conservative psychological systems also exhibit such irreversibility. Consider, for example, the Nixon diamond, a famous example from the study of nonmonotonic logic (McDermott & Doyle 1980). This involves two plausible default rules and one or more awkward facts:

- Quakers are typically pacifists;
- Republicans are typically not pacifists;
- Nixon is Quaker and Republican.

Phrasing these rules as nonmonotonic reasons or default rules of the kind discussed in Section 2.1.3 yields the following.

$$Quaker(Nixon) \setminus\setminus \neg pacifist(Nixon) \quad \Vdash \quad pacifist(Nixon) \qquad (7.18)$$
$$Republican(Nixon) \setminus\setminus pacifist(Nixon) \quad \Vdash \quad \neg pacifist(Nixon). \qquad (7.19)$$

The first rule allows one to conclude that Nixon is a pacifist when one believes he is Quaker and does not believe he is not a pacifist. The second allows one to conclude he is not a pacifist if one believes he is a Republican and does not believe him to be a pacifist.

Suppose further that the agent starts with a set of beliefs containing the beliefs *Quaker(Nixon)* and *Republican(Nixon)*, and is told the two rules given here sequentially. Suppose the agent learns (7.18) first. With just one of the rules, there is no ambiguity about assumptions, and (7.18) produces the conclusion *pacifist(Nixon)* because the agent does not believe ¬*pacifist(Nixon)*.

When the agent next learns (7.19), the two rules and original beliefs now support two coherent sets of conclusions supported by these beliefs and rules, one making Nixon a pacifist, and one making him a nonpacifist. However, addition of the second rule produces no conclusion because the agent already holds its defeating condition as an assumption produced by the first rule.

If one then adds the belief ¬*pacifist(Nixon)*, the stipulated beliefs and rules have only one coherent set of conclusions, one making Nixon out to be non-pacifist, so the agent must abandon the assumption *pacifist(Nixon)* for the stipulated belief ¬*pacifist(Nixon)*. If one then takes back this stipulation, the agent is left again with two coherent sets of conclusions. However, the agent does not revert to its original assumption because retaining the belief ¬*pacifist(Nixon)* as an assumption from the second rule represents the minimal change from its preceding set of beliefs. Thus conservatism does not always produce reversible state changes.

7.6.3.4 Punctuated reversibility

The view that physical materials act reversibly stretches the scientific theories somewhat, since almost all reversible theories of particulate behavior focus on the intervals between collisions and other events of discontinuity. The reversibility of the laws applies to the intervals between these collisions, but not necessarily to the motions across these events. The physical theories typically make separate provision for characterizing motion across discontinuities.

Indeed, we see a different picture if we consider the axiomatic form of most physical theories. As seen earlier, the axioms of mechanics do not imply reversibility at all, though reversible systems can certainly satisfy them. The standard theory of thermodynamics does not provide for complete reversibility of motion except in special systems like the isolated planetary system mentioned previously. Quantum mechanics also possesses no axiom of reversibility. Indeed, standard theories of quantum mechanics involve the fundamentally irreversible notion of measurement, discontinuous events at which irreversible state changes take place. In between these events, quantum mechanics postulates Hamiltonian, and therefore reversible, motion, though no satisfactory account exists of when and where measurements occur. The special theory of relativity postulates temporal reversibility of behavior, but the general theory of relativity contains the notion of black holes that are not reversible. One reasonably wonders which theory involves the better approximation to the truth: special relativity with its temporal reversibility, or all the other major physical theories, with their patent irreversibility.

The focus on smooth intervals of motion is tied to the favored Hamiltonian formulations of laws. Hamiltonian motion is automatically reversible. The practice of theoretical computation in many areas of physical thought suppresses recognition of possible irreversibility by assuming a Hamiltonian formulation. Recall that our earlier discussion of Lagrangian and Hamiltonian formulations pointed out that these formulations essentially pack all laws of the system into the Lagrangian or Hamiltonian function, including both general laws and specific characteristics of the particular materials of the system in question. This approach to formalization of physical theories thus starts by assuming reversibility and prevents one from even expressing rules guiding irreversible behaviors. Much physical theorizing rests content with examining behavior between discontinuities; areas like continuum mechanics, for which the irreversibility of the phenomena of interest make Hamiltonian formulations either impossible or useless, form an exception.

Reversibility *per se* does not form a law of mechanics or of any of physical theory save relativity. There is no guarantee that any new laws discovered in the future will exhibit reversibility.

7.7 Locality

Noll's general axioms for mechanics include a requirement of locality stating that the forces or stresses on a body be determined by conditions obtaining in local neighborhood of the body. The following paragraphs examine the suitability of such axioms for both current physics and the broader mechanics developed here.

7.7.1 What is locality?

Noll's axiom of determinism requires the past to determine the future of a system. In making this stipulation, it permits all portions of the past to influence behavior at all portions of the future. In particular, it allows the immediate past of widely separated bodies to influence their behavior. This type of influence gained the name *action at a distance* in earlier years and became the subject of controversy for some time. The theory of relativity provided strong motivations for avoiding such distant influences, on the grounds that such influences would then represent transmission of something faster than the speed of light. Since relativity theory has proven so accurate in essentially every experimental test, the incompatibility of relativity theory with action at a distance provided strong motivation for requiring that all influences on behavior act locally. The requirement of locality thus extends the requirement of determinism by requiring that behaviors at some point of space be determined by each neighborhood (arbitrarily small) of the point. In effect, this makes local motions independent of motions at distant locations.

The usual approach to ensuring locality, now taken almost without comment, replaces supposed distant influences by fields extending across space, such that the field values at a point determine the force or stress at the point. Relativistic constraints then appear as restrictions on the speed at which changes in these fields may propagate across space.

Noll's axiom of locality phrases this requirement by saying that the local neighborhood determines the force or stress acting at the point.

Axiom F24 *The history of events to some instant locally determines the response at that instant; that is, if two histories h and h' involve exactly the same bodies and materials and agree at all times up to some instant t and in some neighborhood of an event e $\in$ t, then both assign the same response $\theta(h) = \theta(h')$ at that event.*

This phrasing represents a specialization of the general notion of locality in two ways.

First of all, Noll's axiom expresses determinism of behavior indirectly in terms of force or stress, rather than directly stating that the motion at the point is the same for all global behaviors that agree in a neighborhood of the point. This indirect specification does not matter too much, however, because continuum mechanics, through the presupposition of determinism and Euler's balance laws, provides an exact correspondence between local stress histories and local motions.

Second, Noll's axiom expresses locality only under the supposition of deterministic motion. Locality itself, however, represents a requirement applicable to indeterministic motion as well as deterministic motion. A more appropriate phrasing would require that the set of possible motions of a point be determined by neighborhoods of the point. Expressed indirectly in terms of force or stress, a indeterministic axiom of locality would require that the set of possible forces or stresses acting at the point be determined by neighborhoods of the point.

7.7.2 Why locality?

As mentioned earlier, the strong evidence for the theory of relativity motivates modern formulations of locality restrictions. Theorists sought locality long before the advent of Einsteinian relativity, however, since the notion of locality is central to the primary method of physical analysis, that of *isolating the system*. This isolation seeks to convert the experimental apparatus into its own closed universe of study in which no outside factors work in the phenomena under study. Such isolation is important in moving beyond the uncontrolled experience with which physical theory starts to obtain instead controllable experiments with which to manufacture structured variations on the initial observations, variations that provide information aimed at testing tentative theories about the behavior of the system. This scientific methodology has worked and continues to work well. Conceptual analysis of experience gained in this way has yielded many of the familiar laws of physics, and many less familiar bits of knowledge as well.

If locality aids in analyzing the properties of physical systems, it also aids in predicting their behavior. Locality means one can formulate behavioral laws in terms of differential equations or automata, as in the familiar equations of mathematical physics and in recent treatments of cellular automata (Toffoli & Margolus 1987). Instead of requiring knowledge about the global state to compute the next bit of behavior, one needs only the derivatives of the local motion.

More generally, human understanding ordinarily relies on analysis, on separating things into distinct objects of study. Nonlocality proves the bane of analysis, for it prevents the student of nature from understanding things by themselves.

7.7.3 Is locality true?

A totally local physics gladdens the heart of the student of nature, for it gives hope that in principle one might understand every bit of the universe by closer inspection, more careful isolation, and more effective calculation. To the delight of many, broad elements of physical theory take the form of local theories, including general relativity, electrodynamics, continuum mechanics, and many theories of special materials. For most practical purposes, the physics of interest is local, permitting exploitation of this locality in many branches of engineering.

7.7.3.1 Locality from local methodology

One should not take comfort from the prevalence of local physical laws, since the very methodology used to identify these laws, that of isolating the system, works best at identifying local laws, simply by the nature of the methodology itself. Isolating the system typically means making experiments that occur in small physical volumes over short periods of time. Such experiments, like numerical differentiation of a function at a point, tell us what happens locally in that region of space and time, but require separate verification that similar things happen at other places and in larger regions. Verification of behavior in other regions consists of repeating the experiment, perhaps varying the experimental parameters, perhaps varying the experimenter. Many of the accepted local laws have satisfied this test. Verification of the theory in larger volumes is more difficult, principally since we have no way of constructing experimental regions much larger than our planet or solar system, much less ways of isolating such experimental regions from other influences.

In consequence, most physical laws extrapolate local conditions near the surface of our planet to conclusions about the universe as a whole. Such parochial observations run a theoretical risk of missing out on characteristics of the universe in other regions. Consider the possibility of a law that forbade any particles or radiation from entering a sphere of space a meter in diameter located somewhere between our galaxy and M31 in Andromeda. Such a law would be peculiar to say the least, but it need not conflict with any known physical principles, even with frame indifference as long as the exclusionary region was determined by some topological or metric characteristic of the universe rather than by some coordinate-based definition. For that matter, consider the possibility of a great many such forbidden regions of space between the galaxies, or even between stars within galaxies. We have no reason to expect the existence of such regions or any law that would require them, but as long as their density was low, we also would be very unlikely to obtain evidence that they exist without actually running into them. As this concocted example suggests, from a logical point of view we have no evidence to suggest that there are not additional restrictions on the laws that apply to regions of space or time unobservable by us.

Most students of nature might scoff at the very idea of such nonuniformity of physical laws, for if we have no direct evidence to rule out forbidden regions or other nonuniformities, we also have no reason to expect them to exist in the form just described. On the other hand, we do expect black holes to exist on the basis of general relativity. Black holes constitute a different sort of nonuniformity, as we do not expect (and have no reasons to expect) standard physical laws to obtain inside black holes, whatever *inside* means for such objects. Even in everyday experience, we observe great nonuniformities in the world. It is perfectly reasonable to seek uniform underlying laws in spite of the nonuniformity of appearance, but the rational student of the universe must view postulates of uniformity more as fruitful and falsifiable hypotheses rather than as unquestionable dogma asserted as common sense.

7.7.3.2 Formal locality

Now I do not mean to suggest that the laws of mechanics, general relativity, and quantum mechanics (or laws very close to them) do not hold pretty universally throughout physical space. I only wish to point out that this assumption of universality is an extrapolation from limited and local evidence.

Of course, one can always take any any set of nonuniform laws and give them an artificial uniform appearance by explicitly making the context part of the law. Just as in logic the deduction theorem justifies concluding that A implies B from the provability of B given the assumption A, one transforms a law in region R stating that conditions C hold to a law holding everywhere that says that C holds if one is in R. Such "uniform" laws presumably violate frame indifference if they refer to specific locations in space.

In another form, however, laws relativized to surroundings play an important role in everyday mechanics, for laws of specific materials take such forms, laws stating the stresses, electromagnetic, or gravitational fields existing within materials of different sorts. Here the relativization refers to the environment of the location in question rather than to specific locations, and so avoids violating frame indifference. This sort of local law fits perfectly with our experience of the nonuniformity of the world, and provides a welcome theoretical reflection of the diversity we experience.

Laws of specific materials show we need not resort to concocted examples to acknowledge the existence of laws holding at intermediate scales. The question then is whether recognized "fundamental" laws fully determine all regularities at intermediate levels, or put another way, whether one can reduce all laws at intermediate levels to the fundamental laws operating in special circumstances. Intellectual honesty requires one to always ask if observed regularities admit reduction to other principles at other scales, but no principle of rationality or honesty requires one to accept without evidence the common scientific dogma of reductionism (discussed further in Chapter 16).

To ameliorate the risks posed by local observations, one can fall back on the wide variety of experience provided by the large and rich universe. In mechanics this means falling back on astronomical observations, and such observations have generally seemed to validate local mechanical laws on much larger scales. Seeming counterexamples have, over time, generally been found to offer some confirmation of the theoretical modifications represented by general relativity and quantum mechanics.

7.7.3.3 Intimations of nonlocality

Not all of physical law takes local form. Some mechanical properties fail to make sense, or may not be locally measurable. Examples extend from the whole universe, for which the notion of total energy does not make sense, to black holes, for which only mass and rotational momentum make sense, to elementary particles, which suffer the standard Heisenberg uncertainty relations in measuring position and momentum. Bell's theorem in quantum mechanics indicates the impossibility of making nonrelativistic quantum theory completely local. Partly in consequence, a completely satisfactory theory of general relativistic quantum mechanics still awaits discovery.

Even the very conditions of statements of locality offer some degree of uncertainty, since they refer to arbitrarily small neighborhoods. The theory of electrons traditionally suffered problems with infinite self-energies, due to the divergence of the field at small distances (Rohrlich 1965). Quantum electrodynamics swept some of these problems under the rug by means of renormalization methods. These methods seem to work, and produce theoretical predictions in remarkable agreement with the finest experimental measurements, but retain a degree of intellectual disreputability by their reliance on seemingly arbitrary mathematical manipulations. Various theorists have sought to avoid these difficulties by taking a different approach, in which one avoids the singularities that occur at extremely small scales by understanding physics in terms of elemental lengths, or, as in string theory, by ensuring that even the smallest particle has a nontrivial width. Some speculative theories raise the possibility that the observable physical universe represents the behavior of a vast cellular automaton with cells at the Planck length of 10^{-35} meters. These fundamental length theories thus offer their own sort of nonlocality by preventing inspection at smaller scales. Now it may be that locality at this scale suffices for all theoretical and practical purposes, but no one has demonstrated that yet, and in the context of mathematical limiting processes, even the Planck length looms large. Sussman (1996) has observed that if physics were local down to the Planck length, then one would have no way of telling what reality, if any, exists at smaller scales, because each of the cells of space at such lengths could be a universal computer, with all the flexibility that universal computation allows in exhibiting the desired behavior independent of the structure of the world below this length.

7.7.4 Localizing locality

The status of locality seems even more dubious when we extend the scope of mechanics beyond the traditional range of applications. For example, we might interpret the nonlocalities that so complicate economics in terms of the nonlocality of equilibria of global or extended markets, though in practice these markets rely on standard physical media in transmitting information, and so may be viewed as relativistically limited fields, akin to electrodynamic fields.

More serious doubts arise when we broaden the notion of space to include nonphysical dimensions. In such cases, the notion of spatial locality need not respect the topology of ordinary three-dimensional space. The axiomatization of these generalized spaces in Chapter 5 employs the product topology, which does not allow the nonphysical dimensions to disturb neighborhood relations in physical space, but it might well be that a better notion of space for psychology employs a different topology. Standard topologies on discrete sets provide only the discrete or indiscrete topologies, in which the notion of locality provides no useful restriction on dynamogenesis. The nontrivial discrete topologies of Scott's (1973) function theory might provide more useful alternatives here, as might putatively nontopological notions such as tolerance relations.

The preceding examples give reason to doubt the necessity of locality in a mechanics covering mental and physical systems. Accordingly, we also omit locality as a general restriction on dynamogenesis. As with the axiom of determinism, we instead look for specialized assumptions that require locality of specific materials, specific systems, or specific conditions. In fact, some internal constraints on the structure of reasoned mental states exhibit a natural sort of computational locality quite distinct from physical spatial locality (see also Doyle 1983e, 1994).

We do not yet know all the reasonable forms of locality that might play important roles in mechanical systems. We might find that locality constraints vary with types of forces, so that only some types of forces are determined by local states. The notion of reasoning locality just mentioned certainly has a very different character than the ordinary notion of spatial locality.

The investigation of types of locality also calls for investigation of non-Euclidean metric or locality relations on mental and physical space. While general relativity already employs non-Euclidean metrics, we might consider metrics that exploit additional mental dimensions to introduce "wormholes" in physical space, points much closer in the enlarged space than in purely physical space. The conservatism relations and metrics of Section 7.4, for example, offer conceptions of locality in which nearness is not symmetric.

Part III
Mechanical Minds

8

Mental varieties

Understanding psychology and economics in mechanical terms requires look-ing at specific concepts of psychology and economics from the mechanical point of view. If we look to the literature, however, we find that the cognitive sciences study a wide range of possible or hypothesized psychological orga-nizations as explanations of human thought. For example, the ideally rational agents of economics have one kind of mind, a kind very different from almost all known human minds. But even among humans, individual minds have very different characters, exhibiting different levels of intelligence at different tasks, different temperaments, different degrees of adaptability, and so on. The well-known Myers–Briggs test (Myers & Myers 1980), to give another example, sorts minds into sixteen well-populated classes. These classes correspond to recognizable and common types of personal character, types that give some insight and enable reasonable, though not perfect, predictions of individual behavior.

It does not take deep reflection to realize that if we are already on page 225 and just starting the mechanical examination of psychology and economics, we cannot hope to examine all the concepts of all hypothesized mental orga-nizations in this book, no matter how long, without exhausting all patience. I therefore undertake to examine the structure and mechanical nature of some special kinds of minds that serve to illustrate the mechanical nature of think-ing, in part to open the special classes to mechanical investigation, and in part to suggest ways of understanding other kinds of minds in mechanical terms.

In fact, mechanics provides additional motivations for examining specific types of psychologies that stand quite apart from questions of endurance on the part of the reader. We think of each of these kinds of minds as a different type of mental material, exhibiting constraints and responses characteristic of the specific mental material. As was also noted earlier, any physical mechanics broad enough to cover the great diversity of physical materials comes out so broad as to say little specific about the behavior of particular bodies. The same holds true in mental mechanics. To go beyond the generalities of discrete and hybrid mechanics presented earlier, we must focus attention on specific types of psychological organizations and behaviors. The specific types considered here still cover a wide assortment of human characters.

This narrowing of scope means that our discussion of some important topics in psychology and economics must remain informal, general, and speculative, reflecting the early stages of the mechanical investigation of psychology and economics.

8.1 What is plural discrete affective cognition?

The following chapters examine, in the main, a model of thinking in which minds exhibit core and peripheral sensorimotor organs or faculties, short- and long-term memories holding discrete mental attitudes and affects, and distinct episodes of rational deliberate and habitual rule-guided reasoning. For lack of a better term, I call this model *plural discrete affective cognition*, or PDAC. The term *affective cognition* refers to reasoning, reflection, and rational calculation that produces and takes into account both attitudes and affects. The term *discrete* refers both to discrete episodes or changes in mental state and to memory contents that identify discrete attitudes, affects, or representations. The term *plural* here refers to the division of the mind into parts, as opposed to indivisible individual agents.

In focusing on this type of psychology, I seek only to simplify the structure of the agent, not to simplify the content of mental states or behavioral patterns. For example, I discuss a wide range of types of reasoning and thought, including rationality, intentionality, volition, wanton and deliberate action, attention, automaticity, habit, and entrenchment. In discussing mental states, I consider belief, motivation, desire, intention, uncertainty, fears, loves, appetites, and enthusiasms. In considering agent substructure, I include physiological organs, mental faculties, types of memories, and mental subagencies.

8.2 Why plural discrete affective cognition?

The class of minds exhibiting PDAC encompasses a wide range of classical psychologies from philosophy and artificial intelligence, including the so-called BDI (belief, desire, intention) agents and the RMS. One might even regard it as capturing directly interpreted aspects of recently popular neurologically based theories, but I do not enforce such an interpretation. I focus on this model because it shares many features with more detailed and complex mental organizations studied in traditional approaches in artificial intelligence and numerous theories of cognitive psychology and philosophy, and so suggests ways in which one might extend a mechanical understanding of PDAC to understandings of more realistic psychologies. We have no reason to believe that human psychology decomposes in exactly the way PDAC suggests, but that does not diminish its utility any more than the inaccuracy of Hooke's law diminishes its utility in learning and applying physics to simple machines.

As in mechanics generally, my focus falls primarily on forces and the resultant motions of interrelated bodies. Most of my psychological simplifications thus concern the universe of bodies (the *plural* part of PDAC) and the geometry of spaces (the *discrete affective cognition* part of PDAC) of the agent.

8.3 Are such minds mechanical?

For present purposes, I say a mind or a kind of mind is mechanical just in case it satisfies the axioms of discrete and hybrid mechanics developed in the preceding chapters. I leave for future investigation whether minds are mechanical according to other axiom systems as well, such as those of modern rational mechanics, or different discrete and hybrid mechanics than the one we have formalized.

In the following chapters I examine a sequence of psychological concepts that illuminate the mechanical nature of some PDAC agents. I interpret short-term memory content as position, and long-term memory content as mass. I interpret desires as body forces and intentions as self-forces. I interpret communication with peripheral organs as contact forces. Volitional behavioral modes represent different material modes and types, with incoherent wanton behaviors resembling amorphous or stochastic gaseous bodies and different degrees of coherent deliberate behaviors as plastic, elastic, and rigid bodies. Attention involves generating self-forces to counterbalance all environmental forces save selected ones. Different volitional modes produce different stability and instability properties in agents subject to similar forces. Notions of rigidity, habit, entrenchment, conservatism, and uncertainty come out as constitutional properties in which internal forces are generated automatically (without conscious deliberation or action) by components of mental states, and by deliberate reasoning in which the agent shapes the forces acting upon itself.

I develop the sequence psychological concepts studied to exhibit increasing levels of detail and specificity. The first mental properties studied are fairly general, but later ones less so.

Even in the context of our hybrid and discrete mechanical axioms, two sorts of ambiguities cloud determinations of whether PDAC minds are mechanical: psychological ambiguities and interpretational ambiguities.

8.3.1 Psychological ambiguities

Although the PDAC framework focuses attention on one type of mental organization out of many possible ones, it does not restrict the class enough to say that all PDAC minds are mechanical. Instead, the PDAC psychology leaves many details of agent behavior unspecified, so that only some kinds of PDAC minds are mechanical.

Part of the problem here is one of uniformity. While traditional mechanics provides numerous theories of specific types of materials, the uniformity of physical materials that ensures that models of one sample of rubber or iron apply as well to the next batch does not hold in psychology at the level addressed by our simplified psychology. People come in batches of one, with each individual batch extremely different in details, if not in overall form, from the next. Gaining a better detailed understanding of prototype psychologies may benefit the search for abstract psychological materials or theories that make it easier to understand each person in turn, though everyone knows the way prototypes can mislead one in understanding individual people.

Part of the problem is theoretical. The PDAC framework accommodates a large variety of psychological theories of different degrees of formality. The structure exhibited by some of the fairly specific psychological organizations proposed in artificial intelligence constrains possible mechanical interpretations enough to say yes or no to the question of mechanical nature. No one, however, claims that the formal psychologies studied in artificial intelligence represent accurate accounts of any human psychology. Instead, the many theories of human psychology one finds in the literature offer much less precision and many fewer constraints on mechanical interpretation than do the artificial psychologies of artificial intelligence. We thus find a much wider range of possible mechanical interpretations for more familiar accounts of human psychology.

Mere observation does not promise a resolution to the ambiguities of psychological theory anytime soon. The only observables on which to base hypotheses are behavior and anatomical structure, but these observables offer few constraints on psychological organization due to the fungibility of information. As in the theory of computation, it is easy to produce the same behavior using very different programs executing on very different underlying machines; this production is, as they say, a "simple matter of programming." The underlying machine and observed behavior impose some limits, of course, but for stronger clues to psychological organization one must look instead at the available information, the motivations of the agent, and the structure of the environment.

To answer questions about mechanical nature, one needs to add further constitutive assumptions to the PDAC framework. Indeed, just as physical materials may exhibit different constitutions though composed of the same physical components, as in the case of ice, water, and steam, mental materials or psychological types may exhibit different constitutions involving what we think of as the same mental attitudes. The roles played by beliefs, desires, and intentions can differ in each of these constitutions in that the attitudes can generate forces in one constitution but no force or different forces in another. Just as theories of physical elasticity posit that elastic materials generate specific types of forces in response to deformation, theories of psychologies posit that agents generate specific types of forces from deformations or changes to the attitudes that represent the position of the agent.

8.3.2 Interpretational ambiguities

He who should hope, either in metaphysics or psychology, to see himself rewarded by perfect certainty of knowledge, nay even by a certainty generally communicable, on account of extreme carefulness bestowed upon the accuracy of definitions and correctness of conclusions, will certainly be sadly disappointed. (Herbart 1877, p. 263)

The following chapters show that some interpretations of PDAC psychologies are mechanical, but this judgment depends on an appropriate choice of interpretation. Lack of consensus regarding the nature of psychological notions means that one cannot expect consensus on the targets of formalization either. One may thus make different mechanical interpretations of a single psychological concept by shifting its meaning among those championed by different interpreters. Moreover, if one seeks a concept-by-concept mapping into mechanics, the very problem is underspecified because the specific behavioral features characteristic of that concept might be obtained by several mechanical means. To avoid this underspecification, one needs to construct mechanical interpretations of sets of related concepts all at once, so as to exploit the constraints these concepts place on each other.

In light of these ambiguities, one should take the interpretations and discussions presented here as speculations rather than reliable formalizations, as candidates for exploration or replacement rather than the last word.

It may be that the best approach is to follow the lead of physics, taken some centuries ago, to move away from viewing the problem as one of finding the forces and masses inherent in behavior, and instead to approach the problem as one of setting out or specifying forces and masses corresponding to a situation of interest and then calculating the resulting behavior. This doesn't banish the problem of understanding behavior, but it does transform it into a problem of matching predictions to measurements instead of one of matching abstract concepts against each other.

8.4 An example: reason maintenance

Although focusing on the PDAC class of psychological systems helps us to begin an examination of mechanical concepts of mind, the PDAC class still proves too general for us to illustrate some mechanical aspects of thinking. To obtain the needed level of specificity and concreteness, let us turn to a specific example.

Good examples serve to illustrate theories at many levels of abstraction, providing a set of target aspects or phenomena small enough to be comprehended and analyzed, yet complex enough to exercise the main dimensions of the theory. The best examples exhibit a depth to which the theorist may return again and again for new challenges and insight.

The first danger here lies in considering only very simple examples for which any approach will work. Such examples allow one to work out elements of an approach, but can lack the constraints needed to address other cases. For example, the generalization from classical to quantum mechanics began by examining one of the simplest mechanical systems, the simple oscillator. The simplicity of this example let theorists concentrate on identifying the desired changes from classical behavior. In later extensions of the theory, however, the simplicity of the oscillator hid the phenomena of interest, and so more complex examples were needed. Feynman puts it this way:

I hoped then to generalize to other than a harmonic oscillator, but I learned to my regret something, which many people have learned. The harmonic oscillator is too simple; very often you can work out what it should do in quantum theory without getting much of a clue as to how to generalize your results to other systems. (Feynman 1966, p. 703)

This same issue arises in psychology. Focusing on only the simplest systems, such as a finite-state automaton or even a universal Turing machine, can offer little purchase in making further progress if these systems do not exhibit some of the complexity that makes minds interesting. Even some form of universality, whether that of a universal Turing machine or that of the Euler–Lagrange equations, does not guarantee ready visibility of the important problems to be addressed. Indeed, one might worry that universality means the system hides rather than displays the characteristics of interest.

To better understand the mechanical interpretation of psychological organizations, we augment the PDAC conception with the more concrete example of the RMS (Doyle 1979). The RMS admits a full formal specification of its structure and behavior that refines that of PDAC, and one that clearly illustrates many issues concerning how mechanical notions work in psychological and economic systems.

8.4.1 What is reason maintenance?

A RMS provides limited central memory, reasoning, and introspective functions to higher-level mental operations.

In the original conception (Doyle 1977, 1979), a RMS serves as an automated subsystem of a reasoning or problem-solving system external to the RMS, receiving information about inferences made and actions taken by the external system, and providing information about the current conclusions or mental state resulting from these inferences. These operations go beyond mere database entries because the RMS revises conclusions on the basis of recorded inferences, not on the basis of simple instructions to add or remove conclusions.

To do this, the RMS stores changing sets of reasons, which constitute explicit records of inferences or changes of mental state that relate specific patterns of antecedents to specific patterns of consequences. The inferences recorded in reasons need not be deductive, and may concern any explicitly represented aspect of mental states: not just beliefs, but intentions, desires, preferences, and even emotions. The RMS uses these records as prescriptions and guidelines to construct the mental state, to update the state as new reasons are recorded, and to explain and introspectively analyze the composition of states. When all the antecedents of a reason fit the pattern indicated by the reason, the RMS acts to make its state fit the pattern indicated by the consequences of the reason.

Changes made to satisfy one reason may cascade, causing the RMS to add or remove other items to satisfy other reasons. When the higher-level mental operations determine the existence of an undesirable mental state, such as a set of contradictory beliefs or intentions, they may instruct the RMS to trace back through the reasons used to construct the state to identify assumptions or hypotheses that, if removed, might unravel the undesirable state by triggering consequential removals or additions. The defeasible reasons provided by the RMS permit accomplishing most updates by adding new reasons instead of removing old ones. The actual process of unraveling consequences requires special care, since mutually supporting consequences represent knots or tangles that, if undetected, would halt the desired unraveling prematurely.

External or higher-level reasoning systems can use the RMS operations of constructing and revising mental states in many ways, ranging from backtracking search in problem-solving, to switching of mental contexts or behavioral regimes, to generation of explanations. The structure of RMS also reflects central organizational aspects of many artificial intelligence systems, with elements related to short-term and long-term memory, propositional deduction rules, production rules, Bayesian probabilistic networks, artificial neural networks, noncognitive representations, and contextual linkages among representations.

The original RMS was developed in 1976 as an outgrowth of the dependency-based electronic circuit analysis systems developed by Sussman and Stallman (Sussman & Stallman 1975; Stallman & Sussman 1977) and as a key component of an approach to explicit declarative control of reasoning exemplified in the AMORD reasoning system (de Kleer *et al.* 1977). The original descriptions (Doyle 1976, 1977, 1979) used the name *Truth Maintenance System* or *TMS*, with the more apt name *RMS* adopted by Doyle in 1980 and used in later works. Later conceptions (Doyle & Wellman 1990; Doyle 1996) extended the original conception to provide a distributed, resource-limited service to external distributed problem-solving agents, one that maintained as coherent a picture of the information state as possible given its informational and computational resources.

As this telegraphic history of the RMS suggests, one may implement the abstract structure and behavior of the RMS in many ways. For example, some studies have examined numerous techniques for searching through reasons and their consequences. The ordering of this search may vary, as may the information employed and the amount of effort expended. Indeed, different versions of the original RMS employed simple depth-first search and more sophisticated searches based on identification of strongly connected topological components. The original RMS maintained a degree of determinism by basing order of search on the order with which reasons were constructed and identified as supporting conclusions, but other implementations might do better by randomizing the ordering. The original RMS incorporated mechanisms for backtracking through assumptions into its algorithms, but other implementations separate this higher-level activity from the underlying mechanisms for updating consequences. Different update methods also correspond to different conceptions of what constitutes conservative revision. In fact, different implementations might decouple groundedness and conservatism requirements to yield different behaviors (Doyle 1983e, 1992b). I view each of these possible varieties of a RMS as representing a different psychological material or type of mind (Doyle 1982a, 1990a).

I do not attempt to construct a mechanical interpretation for any actual RMS implemented in years past; though possible, doing so would prove somewhat tedious because of the complexity of those systems. Given the range of different types of implementations, and the range of types of possible implementations identified in work on reasoned assumptions (Doyle 1983e, 1994), I simplify our task by adjusting the target to suit the concepts at hand. I pick a behavior for a RMS compatible with identified implementations but modified to make mechanical analysis easier. Thus the examples presented here combine aspects of different RMS versions, including ones described by Doyle (Doyle 1979, 1983e, 1983b; Doyle & Wellman 1990; Doyle 1994, 1996). Not all of these have been implemented, and the composites employed here almost certainly have not been. The composites considered here extend the framework of Doyle (1983e) by permitting the enclosing system to stipulate changes in conclusions in addition to stipulating changes in reasons. I do not assume the enclosing system actually does or should stipulate conclusions, only that such stipulation be possible.

In the long run one should reverse this analytical approach and seek to identify a "most-mechanical" version of RMS as a target for implementation and use. I expect the patently mechanical behavior of such an implementation would display greater intelligibility and predictability by facilitating the application of familiar mechanisms for reasoning about the behavior of everyday mechanical situations to reasoning about reasoning systems as well.

8.4.2 Why reason maintenance?

Reason maintenance provides a good example for mechanical analysis in several ways.

First, as noted earlier, reason maintenance admits a concrete, precise, and detailed formalization. This specificity permits careful analysis of the mechanical nature (or nonmechanical nature) of RMS structure and behavior, including identifications of position and mass, kinematic constraints, and RMS dynamogenesis. In summary, the mechanical interpretation of the RMS views the RMS as a body interacting with its environment. The conclusions of the RMS constitute its position. The changes in these conclusions, which the RMS reports to its environment, constitute its velocity. The base reasons posited by the environment constitute its mass, which we view as a vector quantity rather than a scalar. The RMS obeys Euler's law of the balance of linear momentum, the familiar equation $f = \dot{p}$. Indeed, the changes wrought by the environment on the RMS mass and position are naturally interpreted as forces. More importantly, each reason used by the RMS in constructing its position determines a force, and so acts as a component of the stress suffered by the RMS body. The equilibrium states computed by the RMS, which satisfy the conditions expressed by the reasons they contain, in turn bear a natural interpretation as relaxed states of an elastic material. This interpretation extends to viewing the total force on the RMS as satisfying Cauchy's first law relating stress, body force, and momentum flux.

Second, although reason maintenance forms a somewhat simple system when compared with the full variety of computational, psychological, and economic systems, we can see in RMS structure and behavior limited forms of many of the central concepts of these broader fields, so that by formalizing the RMS in mechanical terms we also are formalizing a simple instance of a computational, psychological, and economic system.

Detailed explanation of the connections between the RMS and more general psychological and economic systems would enlarge the present work beyond endurance. Accordingly, the remainder of this section summarizes these broader interpretations of reason maintenance. The summarization is very brief in the case of psychological and economic notions, which subsequent chapters reexamine with more of the details most relevant to mechanical formalization. The summarization is less brief in the case of computation, so that before we proceed we may get a picture of how reason maintenance grew out of computational problems.

8.4.2.1 Computation

Formalizing the RMS in mechanical terms illustrates mechanical formalization of computational systems because RMS is itself a moderately complex computational system that involves several important aspects of computation.

In brief, the RMS presents a mutable state, external inputs, and effective state transitions, with these transitions determined by a set of instructions. The application of these instructions follows the characteristic scheme of recursive computation, with equilibrium states arrived at through cascading steps of similar form. The computational form of these states and policies resembles the axioms, rules, proof structures, and closure conditions that underlie Boolean circuit models of computation, logic programming systems, and logical semantics of data types. RMS computation combines these elements in forms seen in the higher levels of computational practice. First, it formulates explicit specifications of behavioral goals and invariants and then automatically searches for solutions. Second, it involves transaction and update operations on complex multipart objects, reversible updates that change parts of the complex objects in ways that preserve stipulated integrity conditions. The remainder of this section explains some of these in a bit more detail.

The RMS was developed with the idea, underlying most knowledge-based systems in artificial intelligence, that it is easier to specify what to do than to describe details about how to do it, and that one should design reasoning systems to concentrate on the hard problems while leaving the details to automatic mechanisms (cf. McCarthy 1958, Ginsberg 1996).

Computing did not start with this viewpoint. Many familiar computational systems exhibit a very simple method of operation in which an input signal and the current state directly determine the next state. This method characterizes finite automata as well as stored program and Turing machines. For example, a finite automaton observing an input symbol moves directly to the next state, while a Turing machine directly changes the tape contents, the head locations, and the controller state.

If one examines the range of computational systems studied in computation and artificial intelligence, however, one may also observe another approach to system operation. In this more complex method of operation, input signals and the current state directly determine only a portion of the the next state, which in turn constrains the choice of the remainder of the state. For example, a change of state of a RMS begins with direct specification of a new reason to be added to the set of base reasons, but ends with adjustment of the rest of the state as needed to reflect the conclusions supported by the stipulated reason.

Consider the following concrete example phrased in logical terms. We suppose the system state consists of a set of logical statements and their logical consequences, and that the system acts to ensure the closure of the consequences when the set of statements is modified. Suppose the current state is

$$Th(\{A \implies B, C \implies D\}), \tag{8.1}$$

where Th denotes the operation of taking all deductive consequences, and A, B, C, and D represent the sentences

$$A = \text{"Socrates is a man."}$$
$$B = \text{"Socrates is mortal."}$$
$$C = \text{"Socrates works for a living."}$$
$$D = \text{"Socrates owes taxes."}$$

If we now add A to the state, we get a new state

$$Th(\{A, A \implies B, C \implies D\}),$$

which also contains B, an additional element we did not specify directly when adding A. If we now add $B \implies C$, we get

$$Th(\{A, A \implies B, B \implies C, C \implies D\}),$$

which contains C and D as well.

In contrast to the implicit acquisition of beliefs seen in this example, a traditional computational approach would have no sentence carrying indirect consequences by itself, and thus would need to explicitly identify and add each consequence of statements already held in the state. One may view the direct state change method as a special case of the more complex one by supposing direct changes have no additional consequences.

There are a variety of motivations for considering indirect state changes. Perhaps the principal motivation is that the sheer complexity of minds and large software systems makes it easier to conceive of organizing them around the idea of self-specification than around the idea of modifications specific in every particular. That is, it is too difficult to completely comprehend the structure and state of a mind or complex system, so instead of spelling out how each aspect of the state should change, one only specifies what properties the new state should have, and lets the system figure out, perhaps by searching, how to change so as to satisfy these specifications (Doyle 1982a).

Early appearances of this motivation arose in logicist artificial intelligence planning systems, which sought to characterize the state of the world following some action. These planners used axioms that specified what changed as a result of taking the action. McCarthy and Hayes (1969) described the "frame problem" faced by these planners as the problem of avoiding the need to give additional (and innumerable) axioms specifying what did not change. The main approach taken by many planning systems in subsequent years was to describe actions in terms of STRIPS (Fikes and Nilsson 1971) add lists and delete lists stating properties of the world made true and made no longer true by the action, interpreted with the so-called STRIPS assumption that nothing changes as the result of an action except those properties appearing in the add or delete lists of the action description. The STRIPS assumption proved unsatisfying for realistically complicated situations, however, since the full set of changes engendered by an action includes both the primary effects of the action and a potential multitude of indirect effects. For example, the direct effect of Julius Caesar's crossing the Rubicon was to place him on the other side, while the indirect consequences of this action involved new, nonspatial relationships between Caesar and the Senate and people of Rome. Rather than force the action axioms to enumerate all of these possible ramifications of an action, it seemed preferable to simply list the primary or direct effects (whether these are considered to be intended or side effects), and then to deduce indirect effects from these via other axioms, not necessarily referring to the causing action, about the structure of the world. Organized in this way, a planner would update its beliefs about the current state of the world by augmenting the add and delete lists with the implications of these explicitly specified changes.

The RMS was developed to step back from the ordinary conception of programs in which programs directly modify their store of information. In ordinary programming one might assign a new value to a variable or to some component of a data structure or computational object, at which point the prior value becomes inaccessible. The RMS retreats from such direct changes by creating something like a transaction log for recording these actions, so as to permit undoing of changes, as in standard data management systems. In contrast to typical database transaction logs, however, RMS inference records explicitly indicate the dependence of one change on others, so that one may undo or redo only those changes that depend on a particular mental action. This indirect computational method makes it more appropriate to speak of the RMS as *constructing* the information state of the external system it supports, in the sense that the external system describes some base elements (axioms or boundary values) plus the interrelation of various possible elements of its state (inference rules, constraints, or equations) to the RMS, from which the RMS pieces together a picture (possibly partial) of the makeup of the state of the external system (see also Doyle 1980, 1982a, 1989). This lets the external system reason in terms of its natural hypotheses, with the RMS automatically changing derived information in response to changes in hypotheses.

8.4.2.2 Psychology

While the modest structure of the RMS offers only a pale reflection of the richness of the psychological systems found in human minds, the RMS exhibits some of the central characteristics and complications evident in those more complex systems.

The RMS structures of base rules and derived conclusions correspond to common divisions of memory into long-term and short-term memory. Sequential update of conclusions brings portions of memory into a bounded region of working memory that serves as a focus of inferential attention. Operation by adding reasons to the base set corresponds to memory growth and learning.

The rules and conclusions themselves can represent a variety of mental associations, attitudes, sentiments, and emotions. Individual reasons have a familiar associational character related to Minsky's (1980) K-line theory of memory and mental states, artificial neural networks, and Bayesian belief networks.

Reasons can be used to summarize or encapsulate larger sets of reasons in some forms of learning (Doyle 1979), and to produce conceptual clustering and inheritance structures into memory (Doyle 1980, 1983d).

The inferential structures represented by reasons lie at the base of numerous theories of nonmonotonic reasoning and logics (McDermott & Doyle 1980; Reiter 1980; Doyle 1983e, 1994; Marek & Truszczyński 1993), and have intimate connections with theories of belief revision and update (Doyle 1979; Harman 1986; Gärdenfors 1988; Doyle 1991, 1992b). Nonmonotonic reasons form a key method of specifying and indicating many of the plausible assumptions that pervade commonsense reasoning (Doyle 1979, 1983d; Touretzky 1986). The replay of reasons associated with RMS update induces a limited form of sequential thought.

From a more general or deeper point of view, the function of the RMS is closely related to limited notions of introspection and consciousness. Philosophical and mathematical analysis of RMS reasons and states brings out the fundamental role of reasons in the mind's self-specification, as noted earlier, and in the mind's self-construction, in how it distinguishes itself from its environment (Doyle 1982a, 1983e, 1990a, 1994). This sort of self-demarcation and self-construction lies at the heart of some theories of personhood (Frankfurt 1971).

The proximate motivation for developing the RMS was to provide means for exercising control in complicated reasoning tasks (Doyle 1976, 1979). This motivation encompassed the ability to make plausible assumptions before being forced to make implausible ones, and the ability to assign blame to faulty assumptions when things go wrong. RMS reasons can be used in straightforward ways to encode not just simple plausible assumptions, but also common patterns of sequential control (Doyle 1979, 1980). The reasons themselves can be marshaled in forms of preeconomic dialectical reasoning to choose among alternatives (Doyle 1980) effective in reflective decision-making methods.

8.4.2.3 Economics

Although the initial conception of reason maintenance focused on controlling reasoning and action through intelligent assumption making and update, the issue of control itself concerns effective decision making, and so the subject of economic rationality. It thus should not have been surprising to find the structure and behavior of the RMS reflecting economic notions of preference and choice, but in fact it took time for these connections to be realized, overshadowed as they were by the *prima facie* connections to logical reasoning.

Mathematical analysis of the content of RMS reasons and the structure of RMS states revealed that reasons and states could not be interpreted in purely logical terms, but instead involved notions of intention and preference in central ways (Doyle 1983e, 1994). Each reason carries a requirement that any acceptable set of conclusions exhibit a certain pattern, namely satisfying the reason consequent if satisfying the reason antecedent. Moreover, each reason also expresses a preference among the different ways sets of conclusions can satisfy the intended requirements, namely holding the preferred assumptions rather than not holding them. Indeed, by formalizing the notion of plausible reasoning in terms of expected reasoning utility, one can view reasons themselves as the outcomes of rational decisions, with each reason constituting a reasoning policy adopted on grounds that doing so increases the expected utility of the reasoner's abilities (Doyle 1983e).

The preferential content of reasons shows that the sets of conclusions in RMS states carry a natural interpretation as Pareto optimal economic equilibria. Each reason expresses a preference order over possible states, and it is not hard to prove that the standard nonmonotonic sets of conclusions satisfy maximal sets of the reason preferences (Doyle 1983e, 1985b). Indeed, the theoretical structure closely reflects the structure of group choice in political economy, and one can prove a version of Arrow's (1963) theorem that exposes limits on the rationality of nondictatorial nonmonotonic reasoning methods (Doyle 1985b, 1988b; Doyle & Wellman 1991).

The Arrow limits to rationality also are reflected in explicit decision-making procedures, such as the dialectical reasoned deliberation methods mentioned previously (Doyle 1980, 1981), in which the deliberator must periodically decide whether the arguments constructed so far present a clear case for one alternative or another.

More generally, recent decades have seen an increasing recognition of the role of economic rationality in shaping the structure of thinking as well as the structure of action (Doyle 1988a, 1992a; Russell & Norvig 2002).

8.4.2.4 Summary

The RMS makes a plausible proxy for illustrating the applicability of mechanics to psychology and economics. The RMS involves obvious elements of psychological reasoning, short- and long-term memory, learning, conceptual associations, commonsense reasoning, rationalization, explanation, intention, search, reflection, and self-consciousness. It involves obvious elements of economic preferences, constrained optimization, and individual and group decision making. These elements exhibit a fundamental and commonplace contextual dependence and ambiguity that highlights the commonplace forms of invention and conservatism seen in almost all thinking and decision making. This conceptual richness provides detail sufficient to guide the analysis to the desired end of providing insight into limited rationality and more elaborate forms of these aspects of mind and action, and comes close to providing something like a universal basis on which to construct a large variety of possible psychological and economic systems. At the same time, RMS structures are concrete and circumscribed enough to permit direct formalization and analysis.

If the RMS fails as a good example for guiding the reconstruction of mechanics, surely it fails by excessive complexity, not excessive simplicity. The complexity of the RMS noticeably exceeds that of the pendulum. One may legitimately question the necessity of this apparent extra complexity, but the combination of so many important aspects of psychology and economics in one small package at present seems an advantage rather than a disadvantage. Generalizing from Daniel Pearl's (1994) observation that "even a mediocre Stradivarius can be inspirational," I take heart that even a nonoptimal example of the right kind can serve present purposes adequately.

9

Mind and body

Traditional mechanics treats physical bodies, while psychology and economics concern persons and their minds. Let us begin our examination of mechanical minds by considering the structures of material universes appropriate to different arrangements of agents and their environments, as well as the force systems that describe the interactions of these mechanical bodies.

Almost all of the discussion in subsequent chapters concerns the case of a single person or agent interacting with his, her, or its environment. For the discussion in this chapter, let us regard the agent as a person and call the person René Maupertuis Schwartz, or René or R for short.

9.1 Bodies

Mechanically, we view the person of René as a body $\mathcal{B}_R$, and his environment as the body $\mathcal{B}_R^e$. For some purposes we could stop with this division and consider a material universe $\mathcal{B} = \{\mathcal{O}, \mathcal{B}_R, \mathcal{B}_R^e, \mathcal{U}\}$, with $\mathcal{U} = \{\mathcal{B}_R, \mathcal{B}_R^e\}$.

9.1.1 Simple dualism

Instead of viewing René as a unitary person, we instead assume that René has both a physical body and a nonphysical mind.

For the physical part of René we take the standard mechanical model, and identify the body of René as a body $\mathcal{B}_p$ existing within a universe $\mathcal{B}_p$ of physical bodies. We assume René has a physical environment, so the minimal structure needed in the physical universe consists of $\mathcal{B}_p = \{\mathcal{O}_p, \mathcal{B}_p, \mathcal{B}_p^e, \mathcal{U}_p\}$.

Similarly, for the mental part of René we identify the mind of René as a body $\mathcal{B}_m$ existing within a separate universe $\mathcal{B}_m$ of mental bodies. In a solipsistic world we might consider the mental universe to consist only of René's mind, with $\mathcal{U}_m = \mathcal{O}_m = \mathcal{B}_m$, but we instead assume that René's mind has a mental

241

environment too. This means the minimal structure for the mental universe consists of $\mathcal{B}_m = \{\mathcal{O}_m, \mathcal{B}_m, \mathcal{B}_m^e, \mathcal{U}_m\}$.

The person René then consists of the hybrid body $\mathcal{B}_R = \mathcal{B}_p + \mathcal{B}_m = \mathcal{B}_p \sqcup \mathcal{B}_m$ within the hybrid material universe $\mathcal{B} = \mathcal{B}_p \oplus \mathcal{B}_m$, in which the hybrid body $\mathcal{U} = \mathcal{U}_p + \mathcal{U}_m = \mathcal{U}_p \sqcup \mathcal{U}_m$ forms the universal body.

We presume René's physical body obeys all the usual physical laws. The only difference in our treatment consists of an admission of the theoretical possibility that physical forces on the body generated by the body and its environment may depend on René's state of mind as well as the physical state of his body, and may include forces exerted on the body by his mind. Let us concentrate our attention on the mechanical structure of the mind in the following section, and not discuss the physical body in much detail.

9.1.2 Mental sensorimotor substructure

Just as we need not assume René consists of a unitary, indivisible person, we need not assume René's mind lacks further subdivision. The next level of detail divides René's mind into portions on the boundary with its environment and an interior portion. As usual, the boundary portions include mental sensory or effector organs or faculties. Some of these naturally correspond to organs of the physical body. We make no identification between mind and brain, nor between mental interior and the brain. We may, if we choose, regard the mind and its parts as spread across different bodily organs in ways of no special relevance here.

For the mechanical analysis, we regard René, his mental organs, and his environment as mechanical bodies. The organs, of course, form subbodies of his mind. Some subbodies lie on the boundary with his environment; the join of these constitutes the boundary of René's mind. The relative complement of this boundary within his mind constitutes the mental interior body, and may itself exhibit further division into interior subbodies.

Specifically, we view the simple psychology as involving a universe of bodies, depicted in Figure 9.1, that further refines the mental universe just described. We might well further divide René's mental environment into parts, but that division will matter little in this initial mechanical interpretation compared with further division of his mind into parts.

The principal division of the mind distinguishes parts of the mind in contact with the mental environment from those parts not in such contact. We identify two parts of the mind in contact with the environment, or on the external boundary: the sensor part, and the effector part. We treat these parts as units in the present discussion, though each may admit subdivision into different types

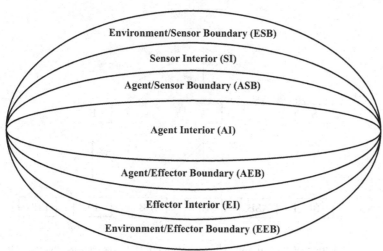

Fig. 9.1. The mechanical interpretation of the simplified psychology focuses on the bodies representing the agent, its sensors and effectors, its exterior environment, and the boundaries between these.

of sensors or effectors. We also simplify some of the discussion by treating the sensor and effector parts as separate, though in some psychologies these parts will overlap (consider human fingers, for example).

We divide the sensor body

$$\mathcal{B}_S = \mathcal{B}_{ESB} + \mathcal{B}_{SI} + \mathcal{B}_{ASB} \qquad (9.1)$$

into three possibly void parts. $\mathcal{B}_{ESB}$ is the boundary part of the sensor organs in contact with the environment. This boundary constitutes the communication medium between environment and sensor. The internal boundary part $\mathcal{B}_{ASB}$ of the sensor is shared with the cognitive interior part of the mind and constitutes the communication medium between sensor and this interior. For simplicity we assume that these two boundary portions are either separate ($\mathcal{B}_{ESB} \sqcap \mathcal{B}_{ASB} = \mathcal{O}$) or identical ($\mathcal{B}_{ESB} = \mathcal{B}_{ASB}$), conditions we can summarize by saying that the symmetric difference of the two sets of body points is null; that is, $(\mathcal{B}_{ESB} \setminus \mathcal{B}_{ASB}) \cup (\mathcal{B}_{ESB} \setminus \mathcal{B}_{ASB}) = \emptyset$. Finally, the sensor interior body $\mathcal{B}_{SI}$ consists of the (possibly null) remainder of the sensor body apart from the two boundary parts.

The effector body

$$\mathcal{B}_E = \mathcal{B}_{EEB} + \mathcal{B}_{EI} + \mathcal{B}_{AEB} \qquad (9.2)$$

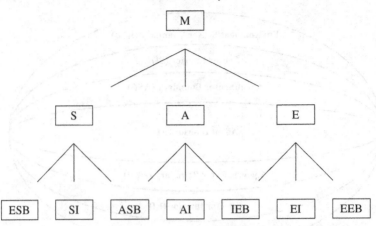

Fig. 9.2. The lattice of mental subbodies corresponding to the sensor, interior, and effector organs depicted in Figure 9.1.

has three similar parts: the boundary with the environment $\mathcal{B}_{EEB}$, the boundary with the agent interior $\mathcal{B}_{AEB}$, and the remainder of the effector $\mathcal{B}_{EI}$. The two boundary portions $\mathcal{B}_{EEB}$ and $\mathcal{B}_{AEB}$ are either separate or identical, and the interior part $\mathcal{B}_{EI}$ is separate from both of these.

The agent interior body

$$\mathcal{B}_A = \mathcal{B}_{ASB} + \mathcal{B}_{AI} + \mathcal{B}_{AEB} \qquad (9.3)$$

consists of the parts providing the internal boundaries with the sensor and effector bodies together with the remainder part of the agent interior $\mathcal{B}_{AI}$. As with the sensor and effector organs, we assume that the boundary bodies are either separate or identical, and that the interior is separate from both.

We can also depict the containment relations in the lattice diagram given in Figure 9.2.

The separation assumptions do not significantly restrict the number of point bodies within the agent. The sensor, for example, might consist of a single point body constituting both boundary portions, leaving a null sensor interior. In the same way, the agent itself might contain a single body point that constitutes both sensor and effector, with a null agent interior. Indeed, we can think of this last possibility as characterizing the single point body employed in most of the subsequent chapters.

If we assume that physical and mental bodies correlate exactly, then the overall universe of bodies consists of the product of universes of physical and mental bodies, each of which exhibits the structure depicted in Figure 9.1. This correlation breaks down if we decompose the mental states of the agent to reflect standard techniques of knowledge representation, for which the physical body provides no correlates. For simplicity, most of the following sections treat only correlated physical and mental body pairs at or above the level of Figure 9.1.

9.1.3 Mental substructure

Different psychological organizations for minds divide the interior portion of the mind into different structures.

One common interior organization postulates a long-term memory providing persistent storage of mental information and a short-term memory serving as the focus of attention or locus of consciousness. In such a division, one expects the long-term memory body to have an associated mass that persists across changes in long-term position. One also expects the short-term memory to have no associated mass and a position of reduced dimensionality, perhaps even a position that reverts to a distinguished origin or null vector periodically.

Faculty psychologies constitute another common organization for mind. A faculty psychology divides the mind into several mental faculties or cognitive organs, each of which forms a separate subbody of the mind. As with sensor and effector organs, each of the cognitive organs has its own mass and position embodying its own habits and local working memory, as in the distributed RMS described as Doyle (1996). One can regard Minsky's (1986) society of mind theory as a limiting case of faculty theories, dividing the mind into many small faculties and subfaculties called *mental subagencies*, each of which again has its own mass and position. In the larger setting of economics and social organizations, faculty psychologies correspond to corporate or bureaucratic organization. In these multiperson organizations, one regards departments, offices, and positions, or societies, groups, and agents, as bodies, hierarchically arranged. In addition, cognitive organizations need not have the sort of fixed organizational structures seen in organization charts, but instead can have more fluid teaming, political, or representational groupings, such as the association structures and reasoned conceptual societies of Doyle (1988a and 1983d, respectively).

More importantly, several such divisions might all represent the same mind. For example, faculty psychologies might spread short-term and long-term memories across different interior mental faculties, or even spread across all portions of the mind, whether on the boundary or in the interior. The formalism of the lattice of bodies permits one to slice and dice the mind in multiple ways.

Indeed, one can regard minds as having much finer decompositions into subbodies, especially in ways that do not correspond to any neurological substructure. The primary example here consists of conceptual organization, in which one regards the lattice-oriented taxonomic structure of concepts in terms of a lattice of bodies. In this setting, each concept is a body, as are the aspects, slots, or other defining elements of each concept. Subtype relationships between concepts then correspond to body–part relationships.

The conceptual universe idea applies beyond standard conceptual hierarchies to include libraries of conceptual designs. In this setting, lattices of bodies in the external world are mirrored in lattices of concepts representing them. For example, suppose we consider two offices with telephones that can reach each other. This set of things might be represented as three overlapping composite bodies and their parts: the two offices each having their telephone as a part, and the telephone network having the two telephones and the cable connecting them as parts. There may even be added levels of detail to consider: each telephone and the cable may have terminals as parts, and the cable may actually be many wires and a switching computer. The key idea, however, is that each object, concrete or abstract, is a body, atomic or composite, and some connections or relations between objects are bodies as well, shared parts of the things they connect. In this setting, one can have several distinct part-of relations, each of which projects the overall relation onto a subuniverse, with roles and subconcepts forming subuniverses and subrelations.

Artificial intelligence employs a variety of related representational ideas to characterize these mental structures, including constraints (Sussman & Steele 1980), ontologies, and description logics (Baader *et al.* 2003). In these applications, primitive or undecomposed concepts constitute atomic elements or point bodies, and the universe (or relevant subuniverse) consists of the powerset of the atomic elements. Most of the bodies in this powerset are of no interest and remain unnamed, but some one singles out to name and to reason about. Common computational systems for constructing such networks allow one to change the meaning of names, to create new atomic bodies, to add new parts to bodies, and to identify parts of different bodies, but in mechanics one thinks of the universe as fixed for each application—or at most, of infinite extent, with these computational operations merely changing the focus of interest by manipulations of names and references.

In most of what follows I simplify the discussion by regarding the agent memories as global configurations of the agent rather than by identifying distinct subbodies of the agent or agent interior that represent long-term and short-term memories. In fact, I take the simplified memories as properties of the mental interior, and regard the mind of the agent as consisting of a single body point, so folding sensorimotor organs into a unitary mind.

9.2 Forces

The forces operating in our simplified psychology include environmental forces acting on the agent and its parts, and internal forces exerted by the agent or its parts on the agent or its parts, including self-forces of agent parts on themselves.

The subsequent discussion of mental mechanics assumes that specified forces refer to an inertial frame of reference, so that we can express the body loads and reactions in the simple form of Euler's laws of the balance of linear momentum $f = \dot{p}$ (6.60) and rotational momentum $F = \dot{L}$ (6.61).

9.2.1 Hybrid forces

In accord with our simplifying assumption that the mind consists of a point body, we consider only a small set of the possible interactions we would see in minds with more substructure. The subsequent discussion mainly follows the decomposition of forces set out in Section 2.1.1, which took the decomposition $\mathcal{B}_R = \mathcal{B}_p + \mathcal{B}_m$ of the person René into mind and body and identified the forces exerted on René's mind and body by these parts of René and by René's environment, with the decomposition given in (2.6),

$$f_p(\mathcal{B}_p, \mathcal{U}) = f_p(\mathcal{B}_p, \mathcal{B}_p) + f_p(\mathcal{B}_p, \mathcal{B}_m) + f_p(\mathcal{B}_p, \mathcal{B}_p^{pe}) + f_p(\mathcal{B}_p, \mathcal{B}_m^{me}),$$

indicating the physical force acting on René's physical body and (2.7),

$$f_m(\mathcal{B}_m, \mathcal{U}) = $$
$$f_m(\mathcal{B}_m, \mathcal{B}_p) + f_m(\mathcal{B}_m, \mathcal{B}_m) + f_m(\mathcal{B}_m, \mathcal{B}_p^{pe}) + f_m(\mathcal{B}_m, \mathcal{B}_m^{me}),$$

indicating the mental force acting on René's mind.

As these decompositions indicate, although motion of the physical body stems from the physical force on the body, and motion of the mind stems from the mental force on the mind, each of these forces can depend on the other mechanical body. Hybrid mechanics thus offers a mathematically coherent framework for understanding systems inhabiting different spaces but coupled through dynamogenesis.

As noted earlier, the existence of this mathematical framework says nothing about whether our world provides instances of such coupled mechanical systems. In particular, apart from the apparent interaction of mind and body in individuals, we lack both demonstrable examples of physical forces produced by mental systems and proofs that such do not occur. Even suggestions like Truesdell's (1956) search for measurable physical forces generated by minds run into fundamental problems of will and cooperation, seen in the expectation that such forces will stem from choices of conscious or free agents, who, like ornery people everywhere, need not follow strict regulations ensuring uniform experimental response.

Nevertheless, even if finding evidence for some possible types of hybrid mechanical systems in nature proves difficult, one can look for such systems in artificial systems as well. In particular, artificial intelligence provides examples in which these hybrid forces play crucial roles within the nonphysical factor spaces. The subfield of control theory dealing with hybrid systems provides models and real examples of systems moving in multiple disparate spaces, though these models do not give mechanical form to the nonphysical factor systems.

9.2.2 Body, contact, and self-forces

Many physical theories assume that self-forces vanish, that $f(\mathcal{B}, \mathcal{B}) = 0$ holds for each body $\mathcal{B}$. As noted earlier, this assumption carries with it many pleasant consequences, such as the pairwise equilibration of both body and contact forces. Moreover, some theories in which bodies exert forces on themselves suffer conceptual difficulties, to wit, the infinite self-action evident in the classical theory of the electron (Rohrlich 1965), and the lightspeed temporal propagation limits that motivate the mass-space fields of general relativity.

The assumption of vanishing self-forces seems less desirable, however, if not outright unrealistic, in seeking mechanical formalization of conscious agents, for which it is natural to view communication between agent interior and sensors and effectors in terms of contact forces and some motivations as self-forces. Self-conscious or self-directed action seems to suggest a mind that exerts nonzero force on itself. For example, as I elaborate later, it is natural to view self-regarding desires and intentions of the agent as exerting forces on the agent. One might regard such self-forces as either body forces or contact forces, depending on whether one thinks of the agent as in contact with itself.

On the other hand, nonvanishing self-forces might prove unnecessary in formalizing some kinds of minds. In particular, one might formalize a mind organized into competing sets of mental subagents (as in Minsky 1986) as involving only forces between separate mental components, so avoiding the need for nonzero self-forces.

9.2.3 Intentionality

As stated earlier, I focus my examination on thinking that involves mental attitudes and sentiments including belief, desire, and intention. Such mental attitudes refer to objects or conditions existing outside or beyond the agent itself. Brentano (1874) called this referential relationship *intentionality*. Brentano characterized mental attitudes as "directed at" their objects, the property of intentionality, not to be confused with the specific mental attitudes called *intentions*, which also bear intentionality. Thus belief, desire, intention are all directed at things, as are hopes for, fears of, and so on. Other mental conditions do not bear intentionality as they are not directed at anything, such as pain, anxiety, happiness, depression, and the like, though perhaps some of these come in both directed and undirected forms (fear and anxiety might form such a pair).

The most notable mechanical concept that one thinks of in connection with a relation of "directed at" is that of force. It is natural then to ask whether intentionality reflects forces existing between agent and object of thought.

If intentionality reflects a force between agent and object, it would seem to be a force exerted by the object on the agent, not vice versa. It sounds a bit strange to say that my belief in something exerts a force on that thing, especially when the thing in question exists only in my imagination, though less strange to say that the thing exerts a force on me. This ability to have beliefs about imaginary objects suggests that perhaps any forces involved in intentionality connect different mental concepts to the agent, rather than external objects. One might regard Herbart's (1891) forces among concepts as an attempt to capture such notions.

Section 13.4 examines an important class of such self-forces, namely self-specifications or self-regarding intentions and preferences that constrain the mental positions of the agent to exhibit certain coherence properties.

The mechanical requirement that force systems be balanced constrains interpretations of intentionality in terms of forces. In the arrangement in which forces on the agent are directed by objects, we would view this force on the mind as conveyed by mental attitudes. For example, a dish of ice cream might exert a force on René, who desires ice cream. For a direct force of ice cream on René to be a balanced interaction, the direct force would require that René's desires exert a force on the ice cream as well. One usually doesn't observe such forces, except perhaps as the agent moves his hand to reach for the ice cream.

An easier way of obtaining balanced forces of intentionality involves changing perspective from objects to information. This perspective regards René's interactions with his environment as measurements, as exchanges of information. Information transmission is a balanced force, since information sent is just the information received at the boundary of the agent, though these two are not necessarily the same once transmitted to the interior of the agent.

With intentionality primarily concerned with transmission of information, we convert forces of intentionality into self-forces. Thus we view desire for ice cream as generating a force on René, leading him to seek out ice cream or to attend to ice cream in the immediate environment. In this way, the environmental ice cream gives rise to a force on the agent, but only indirectly, with the balanced force of information causing the force of desire.

In fact, as this example suggests, the role of the concept of force in understanding intentionality might have relations to the role of force in understanding deliberation. The ability to think in detail about acting without actually acting characterizes the human behavior of deliberation. In naive terms, deliberation seems to involve pretending to apply forces to find a resultant, but without actually applying the forces to the body until the point at which the decision is made to act. The end action in question may be either mental, such as a decision, or physical, such as a motor action.

It is not clear how one should view the stimulation of physical motion by deliberation. The direct way is to view deliberation as producing only mental forces until the end, at which time, if the end be a physical motion, the deliberation produces a physical force on the body. The physical force need not be large if we assume the body operates under the influence of signal amplifiers that convert small command signals from the mind into large-scale motions of the body.

10

Attitudes, outlook, and memory

Many theories of psychological organization posit both long-term and short-term memories. The long-term memories serve as persistent (but not necessarily perfect) repositories of knowledge, skills, and other elements of human capital; the short-term memories serve to store the fleeting facts of present experience, which then either are discarded or incorporated into long-term memory.

The notion of memory in these theories concerns the function of memory structures in thinking, but this function has mainly to do with issues of persistence, not with the content of memory. In common theories, memory content is assumed to contain elements of what we can call the outlook, point of view, or attitudes of the agent, as well as habits, skills, and other aspects of mind.

This chapter examines the notions of memory and outlook from the mechanical point of view, without adopting a position on the exact set of mental elements that define outlook. The fundamental identifications explored take mental outlook to constitute mental position, and memory to consist of both mental mass and persistent aspects of internal configuration reflected in the position. Thinking of memory as mass and configuration fits well with everyday usage. Mass persists across motion, and this also holds for long-term memory; some aspects of configuration, such as the support one belief has in others, also persist and can be used in explaining behavior. Thinking of mental attitudes as positions also finds a good home in everyday usage. The attitudes one holds are often spoken of as one's positions on the issues. Each change of belief or intention constitutes a change of position.

Mental mass and position do exhibit a somewhat more complex relation than do ordinary physical mass and position, in that many elements of memory are reflected in the outlook, meaning that some elements of the mass constrain some elements of position. Indeed, in learning or transfer into memory, some elements of position constrain some elements of mass.

251

10.1 Attitudinal structure and variety

There are many ways of thinking of what mental attitudes include. In so-called BDI agents, for example, the attitudes of the mind consist of beliefs, desires, and intentions. One can regard these as expressing simple statements of what is believed, desired, or intended. Alternatively, one can regard these attitudes as coming in different absolute and comparative forms, with the comparatives expressing that one thing is believed more, desired more, or intended more than another. In that conception, the set of attitudes contains at least six subtypes; absolute beliefs and relative likelihoods, absolute desires and preferences (relative desires), and absolute intentions and priorities (relative intentions). Even within these broad classes of attitudes, different theories consider different conceptions of what these attitudes mean, making for many different types of BDI agent attitudes.

We also consider mental outlook as involving reasons, rules, emotions, sentiments, and other elements in addition to attitudes of belief, desire, and intention. Some of these, such as reasons and rules, can also be thought of as mental habits or skills.

One can certainly find alternative conceptions of position to the extended BDI attitudes considered here. In the theory of ideal rationality, one constructs the space of positions from the sets of all preference orders over alternatives and all belief functions (probability distributions) over alternatives and outcomes. We might formalize the space of mental positions of an ideal rational agent in terms of an inhomogeneous module consisting of a product $U \times P$, in which a vector space U of all utility functions over outcomes uses $\mathbb{R}$ as the field of scalars and pointwise addition as the vector sum, and a vector space P of all probability distributions over actions and outcomes uses $\mathbb{Z}_2$ as the field of scalars and the normalized sum of distributions as the vector sum.

Many economic analyses use an even simpler conception of position, that of just the belief functions, and treat the preferences of the agent as fixed in its constitution, with all variation of decision obtained through variation in the agent's beliefs. While one can embed many desired ranges of agent behaviors into such belief-centered representations, in modeling ordinary human cognition one often finds it more natural to think of the agent's changing preferences as well as beliefs (Doyle 1992a; Doyle & Thomason 1999; Doyle 2004). Economists tend to avoid models involving change of preference mainly because they possess no empirical or prescriptive theory of how preferences change. One can formulate such changes in the standard framework of rational action by taking the self-management perspective exemplified by Pascal's (1962) wager and James' (1897) will to believe (Doyle 1980,

1989), in which the agent makes choices about adopting or abandoning discrete attitudes or sets of attitudes. The literature provides other patterns for preference revision as well (James 1890; Shand 1920; Russell 1930; Yates 1985; Doyle 1990b).

The self-management perspective of ordinary psychology imputes more structure to states of belief and preference than one can recover from utility functions and simple probability distributions. In consequence, the two-component space of positions seems unsuitable for a theory of bounded rationality. One needs instead a theory that encompasses discrete actions and bears close similarity to psychological theories based on discrete or semidiscrete conceptions of mental state, whether the conceptions involve beliefs, desires, intentions, and the like, or the structured representations used in computational decision theory (Boutilier, Dean, & Hanks 1999).

At a more fundamental level, when one characterizes mental positions directly in terms of utility functions and probability distributions, one builds the axioms of economic rationality into the very fabric of mental space. This makes weakening the notion of rationality fairly difficult, as one must work against the ideal nature of the points of space themselves.

To capture discrete psychological theories more directly, and to make weakening the rationality assumptions easier, I decompose mental positions into discrete elements of preference and belief information. Specifically, I replace the inhomogeneous two-component space of ideal rationality with homogeneous multidimensional binary vector spaces. To capture wider ranges of psychologies, I go further and employ inhomogeneous modules that augment the basic attitudes and representations of rational economic agents with other attitudes, feelings, emotions, sentiments, perceptions, and sensations.

In decomposing the space of positions into discrete attitudes, I move the consistency and completeness axioms of rationality out of the characterization of the structure of space, where they stand unmodifiable in particular mechanical systems, and into constitutive assumptions about dynamogenesis and the structure of admissible configurations. We may then modify these constitutive assumptions freely to characterize agents of different degrees of rationality. Constitutive assumptions of consistency and completeness in restricted cases exhibit a purely kinematic character akin to more familiar kinematic constitutive assumptions for rigid bodies and crystalline materials.

10.2 Discrete binary information space

The axioms for discrete mechanical systems do not require a specifically attitudinal structure for mental states. They can be satisfied by any space of mental positions that consists of a discrete free module S over a discrete commutative ring of scalars $\mathcal{R}_S$, by any space of masses that forms a discrete free module $\mathcal{M}$ over a discrete commutative ring $\mathcal{R}_\mathcal{M}$, and by a momentum module $\mathcal{P}$ formed as the product module $S \times \mathcal{M}$ over the product ring $\mathcal{R}_S \times \mathcal{R}_\mathcal{M}$. For discrete motion, the axioms are satisfied by instants that form a discrete interval $\mathcal{T}$, possibly improper, within $\mathbb{Z}$.

The discrete perspective on mental operation can make sense even when the underlying system also admits continuous characterizations, as evident in the ordinary practice of describing electronic computers in terms of discrete states and transitions rather than the underlying continuous electrical changes, as well as in the discussion of symbolic dynamics presented earlier. I thus do not assume that the discrete minds examined here have only discrete states or motions. My aim instead is to examine discrete characterizations of thought from the mechanical perspective and to understand them in mechanical terms.

I simplify the language used to discuss discrete mechanical systems by using the term *vector* to refer to elements of S, $\mathcal{M}$, and $\mathcal{P}$, even though these might only be elements of free modules over commutative rings and not elements of vector spaces. This mathematical inaccuracy will not matter in what follows, because I consider spatial and mass modules that form binary vector spaces, spaces that represent a conception quite familiar in artificial intelligence and the theory of computation.

To understand mental attitudes and representations in spatial terms, we start not with a vector-space conception, but with a simpler conception in which each mental position consists of a set of attitudes or other representations. Formally, we write $\mathcal{D}$ (think *dimensions* or *data*) to mean the set of all possible elements of spatial locations in the mind under consideration, so that each location consists of some subset $\lambda \subseteq \mathcal{D}$. Following RMS terminology, we use the terms *In* and *Out* to indicate indicate presence or absence of an element of $\mathcal{D}$ in a mental position. As in the RMS, *In* and *Out* do not stand for true and false, only for presence or absence. In particular, we view contrary mental attitudes as different attitudes, not as differing states of the same attitude. Thus a belief that "Bertrand is clever" would in the framework here constitute a different element of $\mathcal{D}$ than the belief that "Bertrand is not clever." By distinguishing propositions from their negations in attitudes, the formalism here naturally yields a four-valued logic of the sort described by Belnap (1976), which associates four possible information states with each statement: "told true," "told false," "told neither true nor false," and "told both true and false." The first two of these correspond to the familiar notions of true and false; the third to ignorance; and the fourth to a state of contradiction.

Note that this conception of mental space in terms of combinations of attitudes reflects only the internal structure of attitudes and does not depend directly on any external meanings we associate with the attitudes.

One should note that mental spaces that distinguish only *In* and *Out* represent only the simplest sort of space useful for analyzing mental states. In psychologies of realistic complexity, one can expect to look to conceptions of space that incorporate additional information about mental attitudes. For example, most RMS algorithms augment the primary *In* and *Out* labels with auxiliary or temporary labels representing information about the state of the labeling process. These algorithms start a revision episode by "unlabeling" each consequence of changed item, changing the labels of each of the items being reconsidered to *Nyl*, meaning "not yet labeled." The algorithms then replace each of these *Nyl* labels *In* or *Out* in the course of relabeling.

Consideration of other reasoning methods can motivate even more extensive conceptions of mental position. Looking again to the RMS for another example, we find that RMS also labels each *In* attitude with a "supporting reason" that identifies the reason on the basis of which the supported attitude has been labeled *In*. Such records of supporting reasons might form elements of the position, indicating temporary support, in contrast to their role in memory as permanent records of a possible inference.

10.2.1 Binary translation space

To obtain the translation space of attitude-set locations, we identify each set of attitudes with its characteristic function and represent each such subset-characteristic function as a binary vector. Formally, we represent each subset of $\mathcal{D}$ as a vector in the vector space $\mathbb{D} = (\mathbb{Z}_2)^{\mathcal{D}}$, in which vectors have coordinate values in the field $\mathbb{Z}_2$, interpreting *In* as 1 and *Out* as 0, and in which vectors add componentwise. We denote this vector space in tuple form by considering an enumeration $\{d_i : 1 \leq i < |\mathcal{D}|\}$ of $\mathcal{D}$ and adopting the convention that the set $x \subseteq \mathcal{D}$ corresponds to the vector in which coefficient $x_i = 1$ if $d_i \in x$ and $x_i = 0$ if $d_i \notin x$.

This space consists of a product of many dimensions, one for each mental attitude, with each distinct possible mental attitude giving rise to a separate dimension of position. We thus assume one spatial dimension for each belief, desire, and intention, and regard each dimension as a binary state space indicating presence or absence of the attitude in the state of mind or agent configuration. Accordingly, we can treat each element $d \in \mathcal{D}$ as a basis vector, and treat $x \subseteq \mathcal{D}$ as the vector

$$x = \sum_{d \in x} d. \tag{10.1}$$

Elements of $\mathbb{D}$ can thus represent changes to positions, with the element $x - y$ representing the change from position y to position x.

The following development takes $\mathbb{D}$ to represent the set of all positions $\mathcal{S}$, and switches back and forth among the interrelated set and vector representations as needed to simplify the analysis.

10.2.2 Binary algebra

We use $\mathbf{0}$ to denote the vector $(0, \ldots, 0)$ consisting of all zeros, which corresponds to $\emptyset$ in the set representation. We use $\mathbf{1}$ to denote the vector $(1, \ldots, 1)$ consisting of all ones corresponding to the set $\mathcal{D}$ in the set representation.

The algebra of vectors over $\mathbb{Z}_2$ exhibits the familiar properties $0x = \mathbf{0}$ and $1x = x$ for all vectors, as well as the special binary properties $x + x = \mathbf{0}$ and $x - y = x + y$ that obtain because the field $\mathbb{Z}_2$ is of characteristic 2.

The vector algebra $\mathbb{D}$ bears obvious connections with the Boolean algebra $\mathcal{P}(\mathcal{D})$ of subsets of $\mathcal{D}$, though the operations involved in these algebras differ. Where the vector space provides operations of vector addition and scalar multiplication, the Boolean algebra provides operations of union, intersection, set difference, and complement. Addition in this vector space corresponds to symmetric difference of sets; that is, $x + y = x \setminus y \cup y \setminus x$. We translate complement by $\overline{x} = \mathbf{1} - x$, and intersection as pointwise multiplication in $\mathbb{D}$; that is, $x \cap y = xy = (x_1 y_1, \ldots, x_n y_n)$. Intersection thus introduces a product operation in $\mathbb{D}$, a product satisfying $xx = x$, $x(y + z) = xy + xz$, $xy = yx$, $1x = x$, and $0x = \mathbf{0}$. We then translate set difference as $x \setminus y = x \cap \overline{y} = x\overline{y} = x(1 - y) = x - xy$, and union as $x \cup y = \overline{\overline{x} \cap \overline{y}} = 1 - (1 - x)(1 - y) = 1 - 11 - x1 - y1 + xy = xy - x - y$.

When $\mathcal{D}$ is a finite set, the space $\mathbb{D}$ is a free module over $\mathbb{Z}_2$, as called for in the mechanical axioms presented in Chapter 5. When $\mathcal{D}$ is infinite, however, the function module $\mathbb{D} = \mathbb{Z}_2^{\mathcal{D}}$ is not free, and to conform to the axioms we must restrict attention to a free submodule of $\mathbb{D}$. One standard free submodule, which we denote by $\mathbb{D}_f$, consists of all vectors in $\mathbb{D}$ with *finite support*, that is, with only finitely many nonzero coordinates. Each vector in $\mathbb{D}_f$ thus corresponds to a finite subset of $\mathcal{D}$. The vectors corresponding to single elements of $\mathcal{D}$ form a basis for $\mathbb{D}_f$.

The module $\mathbb{D}_f$ does not admit the desired correspondence with a Boolean algebra of sets, however, because it lacks the element $\mathbf{1}$. We thus extend $\mathbb{D}_f$

to a larger module by adding **1** as a new basis vector. We write $\mathbb{D}_b$ to denote the free module over $\mathbb{Z}_2$ generated by the elements of $\mathcal{D}$ and **1**. Each element of $\mathbb{D}_b$ represents either a finite set or the complement of a finite set, and so has either only finitely many nonzero coordinates or only finitely many zero coordinates.

In the following development, let us use the simpler notation $\mathbb{D}$ to mean $\mathbb{D}_b$ when appropriate to the dimensionality of $\mathcal{D}$.

10.2.3 Other algebras

Although the binary algebra of mental attitudes serves many purposes well, other discrete algebraic systems provide alternatives worth exploring. Chief among these are the free modules over $\mathcal{D}$, obtained by replacing the binary field $\mathbb{Z}_2$ by a commutative ring $\mathcal{R}$ that provides finer divisions or gradings of each positional element. This replacement yields a $\mathcal{R}$-module $\mathbb{D}_{\mathcal{R}}$ over $\mathcal{D}$, with $\mathbb{D}$ corresponding to $\mathcal{R} = \mathbb{Z}_2$. We write elements $x \in \mathbb{D}_{\mathcal{R}}$ in the form

$$m = x_1 d_1 \oplus x_2 d_2 \oplus \ldots. \tag{10.2}$$

The module addition $\oplus$ is performed componentwise, with

$$x \oplus y = (x_1 + y_1)d_1 \oplus (x_2 + y_2)d_2 \oplus \ldots. \tag{10.3}$$

Here the addition of coefficients (e.g., $x_1 + y_1$) takes place in $\mathcal{R}$. When $\mathcal{R} = \mathbb{Z}_2$, one removes an element simply by adding it in. If $\mathcal{R} = \mathbb{Z}$, one removes an element by subtracting it enough times, or with enough weight.

More complicated renditions might allow dimensions that provide a continuous grade or quantity for each attitude. Such representations exchange the attitude-set view of vectors in favor of vectors of coefficients or strengths, and replace the space $(\mathbb{Z}_2)^{\mathcal{D}}$ with $\mathbb{R}^{\mathcal{D}}$ or $[0,1]^{\mathcal{D}}$.

The polynomial rings $\mathbb{Z}_k(x)$ can also form alternative free modules for countable $\mathcal{D}$, with the enumeration indices of $\mathcal{D}$ corresponding to powers of the indeterminate x. Baez and Gilliam (1994) exploit these modules in their treatment of discrete mechanics. Indeed, the infinite-dimensional free module $\mathbb{D}_f$ is isomorphic to the additive module $\mathbb{Z}_2[x]$ over $\mathbb{Z}_2$, with each finite basis vector in $\mathbb{D}_f$ corresponding to a binary polynomial. The polynomial algebra of $\mathbb{Z}_2[x]$ is not the same as the binary algebra identified earlier for $\mathbb{D}_f$, however, as polynomial rings involve a multiplication operation different from the intersection product considered in the preceding, with products of powers of the indeterminate producing other powers of the indeterminate. Unless the attitudes in $\mathcal{D}$ have some corresponding composition property, polynomial multiplication seems a questionable addition to the underlying free module over $\mathbb{Z}_k$.

10.2.4 Inner products and metrics

To analyze the geometry of mental spaces, we make use of several generalized inner products, from which we derive two metrics.

The first generalized inner product $i_1 : \mathbb{D} \times \mathbb{D} \to \mathbb{D}$, defined by

$$i_1(x, y) = xy, \tag{10.4}$$

takes values in the ring $\mathbb{D}$, or equivalently, in the powerset of $\mathcal{D}$, and corresponds to the pointwise product or intersection of the two elements. This product produces a new vector by pointwise multiplication, so that for each component i of these vectors, $(xy)_i = x_i y_i$, taking the product of these values in $\mathbb{Z}_2$.

When $\mathcal{D}$ is finite, we define a second generalized inner product $i_2 : \mathbb{D} \times \mathbb{D} \to \mathbb{R}$ by

$$i_2(x, y) \;=\; \sum_i x_i y_i \tag{10.5}$$

$$\;=\; |i_1(x, y)|. \tag{10.6}$$

This product multiplies coordinates as in the ordinary Euclidean dot product, and thus counts the number of places in which the two vectors agree. This equals the cardinality of the intersection of the two positions viewed as sets. With this definition $x \cdot y = 0$ iff the vectors x and y have null intersection in $\mathcal{P}(\mathcal{D})$.

When $\mathcal{D}$ is infinite, sum (10.5) need not make sense. It is unproblematic when we consider only vectors in $\mathbb{D}_f$ that have finitely many nonzero entries, but not when we consider vectors in $\mathbb{D}_b$. To the extent that mechanics needs only concern distances between body points placed in vectors in $\mathbb{D}_f$, inner product (10.5) will do, but more generally one might instead vary (10.5) by introducing a convergent sequence $\{w_i \mid i \in \mathbb{N}\}$ of positive weights and define $i_3 : \mathbb{D} \times \mathbb{D} \to \mathbb{R}$ by

$$i_3(x, y) = \sum_i w_i x_i y_i, \tag{10.7}$$

where we assume $\sum_i w_i < \infty$. As a practical matter, such a weighted inner product need not differ much from starting out with a finite $\mathcal{D}$. Exceedingly complex complex beliefs simply do not appear in everyday cognition. If indices assigned to attitudes increase with complexity, we can expect that high-index attitudes receive vanishing weights and so really do not affect comparisons greatly. Unfortunately, the weighted approach generates problems concerning frame indifference.

The fourth generalized inner product $i_4 : \mathbb{D} \times \mathbb{D} \to \mathbb{Z}_2$, defined by

$$i_4(x, y) = |i_1(x, y)| \mod 2 \tag{10.8}$$

$$= \overset{(\mathbb{Z}_2)}{\underset{i}{\sum}} x_i y_i, \tag{10.9}$$

multiplies coordinates and sums these products in $\mathbb{Z}_2$. This inner product thus gives a 0 or 1 depending on whether the number of matching places in x and y is even or odd.

The generalized inner product i_2 induces two metrics on $\mathbb{D}$ in the usual way, by applying the quadratic forms associated with the products to differences of the vectors in question. The difference $x - y$ yields a vector z that has nonzero entries only at places in which x and y differ. Evaluating the quadratic form $i_2(z, z)$ thus yields a count of these places of difference. This count itself constitutes the Hamming or Manhattan distance between the two vectors, the Minkowski metric of exponent 1. The square root of this form, $\sqrt{i_2(x - y, x - y)}$, yields the standard Euclidean distance between x and y, the Minkowski metric of exponent 2.

Note also that the generalized inner product i_4, applied as a quadratic form to difference vectors, yields the parity of the Hamming distance of binary vectors.

10.2.5 Changes of frame

As stated in Axiom S1c, the free modules and vector spaces used in mechanics have the property that each isometry ϕ_t of the space at some instant t consists of the composition of a translation and orthogonal transformation, that is,

$$\phi_t(x) = \phi_t(x_\mathbf{o}) + Q_t(x - x_\mathbf{o}) \tag{10.10}$$

for some fixed point $x_\mathbf{o}$ representing the displacement of origin, or separation of the new observer from the old, and some orthogonal (distance preserving) tensor or rotation Q_t taking vectors into vectors.

In our binary vector space, orthogonal transformations consist of permutations of $\mathcal{D}$, that is, relabeling of state components with different elements of $\mathcal{D}$. We can represent these permutations with binary matrices that contain only zero entries except for exactly one 1 in each row and column, and show that every isometry of $\mathbb{Z}_2^n$ decomposes into a translation and permutation (Hartwig & Doyle 2002).

Constant linear motion and Galilean changes of frame in $\mathbb{D}$ consist of a type of cyclic motion. Recall from (6.62) the form of Galilean changes of frame is $\phi_t(x) = Q_0(x - x_\mathbf{o}) + (t - t_\mathbf{o})(\phi_1(x_\mathbf{o}) - \phi_0(x_\mathbf{o}))$. In $\mathbb{D}$ we interpret the product $(t - t_\phi)x$ as a $(t - t_\phi)$-fold sum of x with itself, that is,

$$
\begin{aligned}
1x &= x \\
2x &= x + x \\
3x &= x + x + x,
\end{aligned}
$$

and so on. As these repeated additions show, constant linear motion in the binary space consists of repeated flipping of position on some set of dimensions with a constant interval between flips.

10.3 Motion

Following Section 7.1, we think of each motion χ as part of a history $h : I_h \to$ $\mathcal{S}$ occurring over a temporal interval I_h. For simplicity, we restrict discussion to motion of body points. We treat discrete motions of body points as sequences of vectors in $\mathcal{S} = \mathbb{D}$. We write $x_{h,t} \in \mathcal{S}$ to denote the placement at instant t in the history h, or, more commonly, just x_t when the history is understood.

10.3.1 Velocity and acceleration

I define the instantaneous velocity as a difference vector, writing

$$
\dot{x}_t = x_t - x_{t-1} \tag{10.11}
$$

to denote the change in position at instant t. This change constitutes a trailing velocity. I treat velocity as a trailing quantity for two reasons.

First, most designs for automated reasoning agents have the agent choose its actions on the basis of its current state at some instant. This means that definitions of the state at some instant must be independent of or compatible with the different choices for successor states. In consequence, any velocity used as an input to or as grounds for these choices must be a trailing difference. Of course, the decision process will probably not restrict itself to considering only this input velocity, but might also consider alternative output or leading velocities. For example, a system attempting to choose its actions rationally will seek to compare alternative changes to its state, and these alternative changes correspond to or determine possible leading velocities.

Second, almost all artificial reasoning systems constructed in artificial intelligence rely on changes in beliefs, intentions, or other mental attitudes to trigger or initiate the application of some routine or habit or reasoning. The well-known production systems so common in psychological models provide a familiar example of such change-triggered behavior. This role for attitudinal changes in initiating behavior means that mental dynamogenesis involves velocity in crucial ways. Mental positions do not simply change in response to forces; trailing changes themselves help generate or shape forces at subsequent times. To do this, automated change-based reasoners use various means for tracking changes in position. The RMS, for example, keeps a record of the label of *In* or *Out* obtaining prior to the most recent update. The difference between these two labels across all information elements constitutes the velocity of the system. The RMS uses this velocity by informing its environment which of the state elements experienced a change of status.

Although we interpret velocity as a trailing difference, we view other other mechanical difference quantities as leading differences. In particular, we define $\ddot{x}_t$, the acceleration at t, to be a leading acceleration:

$$\ddot{x}_t = \dot{x}_{t+1} - \dot{x}_t \tag{10.12}$$
$$= x_{t+1} - x_t - \dot{x}_t \tag{10.13}$$
$$= (x_{t+1} - x_t) - (x_t - x_{t-1}) \tag{10.14}$$
$$= x_{t+1} - 2x_t + x_{t-1} \tag{10.15}$$
$$= x_{t+1} + x_{t-1}. \tag{10.16}$$

The last step, from (10.15) to (10.16), only holds in $\mathbb{D}$ and other modules over fields of characteristic 2, in which the middle term of (10.15) vanishes. The second equation, (10.13), expresses the acceleration in terms of the next position and the current position and velocity.

The mechanical development presented in the following focuses on reasoning that determines instantaneous forces on the basis of past motion. By (6.60), therefore, the results of decisions must determine leading accelerations if they are to represent forces that provide the next increment of motion. If a decision process needs to consider acceleration as input, the acceleration needs to be a trailing acceleration such as $\ddot{x}_{t-1} = \dot{x}_t - \dot{x}_{t-1}$.

We treat differential quantities in disparate ways for lack of an interpretation that measures all changing quantities in the same way. Although in the present development it makes sense to treat the main notions of velocity and acceleration differently because of the the different ways these concepts enter into the operation of computational agents, a more uniform interpretation might also be possible.

One more uniform interpretation, not adopted here because it does not address the preceding considerations concerning decision-making causality, is the definition of velocity employed by Toffoli and Margolus (1990), who use $x_{t+1} + x_{t-1}$ to characterize the velocity of a second-order cellular automaton

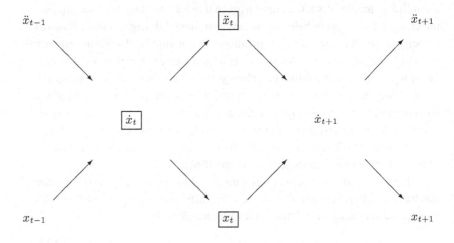

Fig. 10.1. The kinematical relationships among position variables in time. The boxed quantities denote conventional labels for the quantities of interest at instant t, with a reasoning agent observing x_t and $\dot{x}_t$ and choosing $\ddot{x}_t$.

at time t. One can view this quantity as related to the average of the trailing and leading velocity at time t,

$$x_{t+1} + x_{t-1} = (x_{t+1} - x_t) + (x_t - x_{t-1}). \tag{10.17}$$

Of course, in binary vector spaces velocity (10.17) is the same as the leading acceleration identified in (10.16). In the binary Toffoli–Margolus scheme, the average acceleration at t is the quantity $x_{t+2} + x_{t-2}$.

Velocity (10.17) represents twice the average velocity in ordinary real vector spaces, but we do not assume that the modules of interest in discrete mechanics have a normalizing scalar corresponding to $\frac{1}{2}$. In particular, $\mathbb{D}$ lacks such a scalar, so to accommodate the range of possible spatial modules, we treat this quantity as representing a kind of average. This average conception of velocity, however, does not correspond to a quantity readily available to a reasoning agent attempting to determine its position at the next instant.

In fact, the nonuniformity in treatment of discrete velocity and acceleration visible in (10.11) and (10.12) is reflected in a comparable nonuniformity in the treatment of cellular automata by Toffoli and Margolus, who employ a grid of integral and half-integral instants to depict these quantities. We adapt this device to depict the kinematical quantities as in Figure 10.1.

10.3.2 Configuration and deformation

Configuration and deformation in continuum mechanics concern the relative placement and change of relative placement of body points. Our focus here on the motion of reasoners considered as point bodies makes configuration and deformation into trivial matters, since a point body always has the same location as itself. This observation, however, does not suggest ignoring configuration as much as it suggests exploring richer, multibody models of mental structure, because the notion of configuration plays a clear role in some aspects of ordinary thought.

Despite some appearances, human minds do not change attitudes freely and randomly, but often preserve dependency relations among different attitudes. For example, I might maintain an intention to refuel the car at lunchtime, despite forming, carrying out, and discharging numerous other thoughts and plans throughout the morning, until my wife reports she filled it up while returning from an errand. Such thinking maintained the causal connection between a belief the car was low on fuel and the intention to refuel at lunchtime, and maintained the intention to refuel despite many changes to other intentions, perhaps changes that involved resolving conflicts between other intentions and the intention to refuel. We regard these persistent relations as aspects of the reasoner's configuration that form part of the memory of the agent. The idea of such persistent relations goes back at least to Hume, who regarded much thinking and intelligence as the product of associations between ideas. It also underlies the notion of RMS reason.

Although most of the following discussion of reasoning and learning treats the reasoner as a point body, for some purposes I view the multidimensional locations in $\mathbb{D}$ as representing placements of attitudes in $\mathcal{D}$ in a two-dimensional space of locations in order to treat the issue of mental configuration. I do not pursue here the elaboration of mental substructure needed to justify these complementary views of mental states.

I also do not draw a clear line between persistent relations represented in the mass of the agent and persistent relations represented in the position of the agent. I instead regard such relations as part of both configuration and mass, and regard formation and use of such relations as important aspects of learning and mental dynamogenesis.

10.4 Mass

The class of psychologies considered here distinguishes position from mass primarily by the dynamical role played by these aspects of agents. In psychological terms we speak of beliefs, desires, and intentions as stored in memory, but distinguish different types of memories, such as short-term and long-term memories, and cognitive and motor memories. In some cases distinctions between types of memories correspond merely to the type of contents held in the memory, but in other cases the distinctions follow differences in dynamical treatment.

Persistence over time constitutes one difference in treatment used to distinguish memory from outlook. For example, one usually distinguishes between short-term and long-term memory by saying that items in long-term memory persist across changes of attention, while items in short-term memory persist only through the current episode and are lost when attention shifts. In the mechanical setting, this suggests viewing long-term memories as connected with mass, and short-term memories as connected with position, because these identifications provide the normal persistence of mass across changes of position.

As the preceding remarks about configuration indicate, however, mere persistence does not provide a clear separation between outlook and memory. The differing roles of memory and outlook in generating forces on the mind provide more fundamental means for distinguishing the two.

10.4.1 Mass values

Because the primary distinction between mental position and mental mass lies in dynamical role rather than in psychological form, I simplify the discussion here by assuming that the same space of beliefs, desires, and other mental elements characterize the spaces of positions and masses. I therefore use the same space $\mathbb{D}$ to formalize mass values in $\mathcal{M}$ as we use to formalize locations. Particular psychologies might involve mental elements that can only appear in positions or in masses. When needed, we can recover such restrictions to subspaces by means of kinematic restrictions.

We write $m_t \in \mathcal{M} = \mathbb{D}$ to denote the mass of the agent at time t. Because we presume the agent determines a leading force and so leading acceleration and massing, our interest chiefly lies in the leading change of mass. We write $\dot{m}_t$ to mean this leading change; that is,

$$\dot{m}_t = m_{t+1} - m_t. \tag{10.18}$$

In identifying values in $\mathbb{D}$ as the mass of the body, we replace a scalar with a vector measure, a one-dimensional real Euclidean space with a multidimensional space. In traditional mechanics, it might be more natural to say that the mass elements in m, considered as a subset of $\mathcal{D}$, form the *material* of the body at instant t, and that $|m|$ or some other numerical measure over the elements represents the mass itself, which tradition conceives of as a measure of the quantity of matter. Instead of this traditional approach, we view m as the mass itself, and forego universal comparability of material quantities, giving up absolute mass along with absolute space and time. We can take each element of $\mathcal{D}$ to comprise a different type of matter, and view m as a vector of scalar mass values, one value for each type of matter. In this view, the vector m can be thought of as simultaneously representing both matter and mass.

10.4.2 Spatial representations

Using the same space $\mathbb{D}$ to represent both position and mass invites questions about the distinction between mass and position, in particular, whether mass values should just be considered additional spatial dimensions.

One might view the use of the same space to represent mental position and mass as a sort of spatial representation of material employing each spatial coordinate to distinguish a type of mass, and identifying the body with its placement in this space. This identification of mass with placement recalls the reference placement concept in continuum mechanics in which one identifies a body with its placement at some time, identifying points in space with points of the body, and deriving the measure of mass at other times from the measure of mass in the reference placement and from properties of the process by which the reference placement is changed into the placement in question.

This identification also may serve us better when we consider mental spaces corresponding to different agents. We can think of each body as having different types of matter, with no overlap on mass values. We thus avoid the need to find a single nonlinear space for all mass values, though of course we can construct one for any specific collection of bodies and types of materials by taking the direct sum of the separate spaces.

Why does ordinary three-dimensional space not yield three dimensions of mass in the same way? One possible answer is that the first role of mass is in defining linear momentum. Ordinary physical mass would divide into three sorts only if one could readily distinguish linear motion along one dimension from linear motion along the other two. Such is not the case, however, for a simple change of frame suffices to translate any linear motion into linear motion along a given axis, and the axioms of frame indifference require physical mass to remain unchanged through this transformation. This interchangeability may be taken as the reason ordinary mechanics has the same conception of mass for the distinct spatial dimensions.

A different situation obtains in the binary vector space $\mathbb{D}$ considered here, where no rotation suffices to change the linear motion into motion along a single dimension. Rotating the frame preserves the dimensionality of the motion, so the rotated representation of motion changes the same number of coordinates no matter what. One might consider other rerepresentations in which the direction of motion is mapped to a single nonbinary dimension, but I do not treat such here.

10.5 Momentum

In the discrete setting considered here, linear momentum takes values in the module $\mathcal{M} \times \mathcal{S} = \mathbb{D} \times \mathbb{D}$ with the two components representing the mass and velocity of the body. Because the factors in this product are homogeneous, we regard momenta as forming a module over $\mathbb{Z}_2$.

We write $p_t = (m_t, \dot{x}_t)$ to denote the linear momentum of the body at instant t. We write $\dot{p}_t$ to mean the leading change in momentum at instant t, that is,

$$
\begin{align}
\dot{p}_t &= p_{t+1} - p_t \tag{10.19} \\
&= (m_{t+1}, \dot{x}_{t+1}) - (m_t, \dot{x}_t) \tag{10.20} \\
&= (m_{t+1} - m_t, \dot{x}_{t+1} - \dot{x}_t) \tag{10.21} \\
&= (\dot{m}_t, \ddot{x}_t). \tag{10.22}
\end{align}
$$

We obtain the discrete rotational momentum $L_{y,t}$ with respect to some location y at time t as

$$
\begin{align}
L_{y,t} &= (x_t - y) \wedge p_t \tag{10.23} \\
&= (m_t, (x_t - y) \wedge \dot{x}_t). \tag{10.24}
\end{align}
$$

Change of rotational momentum follows the same pattern as change of linear momentum, namely

$$
\begin{align}
\dot{L}_{y,t} &= L_{y,t+1} - L_{y,t} \tag{10.25} \\
&= (\dot{m}_t, (x_t - y) \wedge \ddot{x}_t). \tag{10.26}
\end{align}
$$

To see this last equality, (10.26), we expand the definition of $\dot{L}_{y,t}$ to obtain

$$
\begin{align}
&L_{y,t+1} - L_{y,t} \\
&= (m_{t+1}, (x_{t+1} - y) \wedge \dot{x}_{t+1}) - (m_t, (x_t - y) \wedge \dot{x}_t) \tag{10.27} \\
&= (\dot{m}_t, (x_{t+1} - y) \wedge \dot{x}_{t+1} - (x_t - y) \wedge \dot{x}_t) \tag{10.28} \\
&= (\dot{m}_t, x_{t+1} \wedge \dot{x}_{t+1} - y \wedge \dot{x}_{t+1} - x_t \wedge \dot{x}_t + y \wedge \dot{x}_t). \tag{10.29}
\end{align}
$$

Consider now the spatial component $(\dot{L}_{y,t})_2$ of the value obtained in (10.29).

By rearranging terms and applying kinematical definitions, we obtain

$$(\dot{L}_{y,t})_2$$
$$= \quad x_{t+1} \wedge \dot{x}_{t+1} - y \wedge \dot{x}_{t+1} - x_t \wedge \dot{x}_t + y \wedge \dot{x}_t \qquad (10.30)$$
$$= \quad x_{t+1} \wedge \dot{x}_{t+1} - x_t \wedge \dot{x}_t - y \wedge \dot{x}_{t+1} + y \wedge \dot{x}_t \qquad (10.31)$$
$$= \quad x_{t+1} \wedge \dot{x}_{t+1} - x_t \wedge \dot{x}_t - y \wedge (\dot{x}_{t+1} - \dot{x}_t) \qquad (10.32)$$
$$= \quad x_{t+1} \wedge \dot{x}_{t+1} - x_t \wedge \dot{x}_t - y \wedge \ddot{x}_t. \qquad (10.33)$$

The portion of this quantity not involving the reference point y then reduces as follows.

$$(\dot{L}_{y,t})_2 + y \wedge \ddot{x}_t$$
$$= \quad x_{t+1} \wedge (x_{t+1} - x_t) - x_t \wedge (x_t - x_{t-1}) \qquad (10.34)$$
$$= \quad x_{t+1} \wedge x_{t+1} - x_{t+1} \wedge x_t - x_t \wedge x_t + x_t \wedge x_{t-1} \qquad (10.35)$$
$$= \quad -x_{t+1} \wedge x_t + x_t \wedge x_{t-1} \qquad (10.36)$$
$$= \quad x_t \wedge x_{t+1} - x_t \wedge x_t - x_t \wedge x_t + x_t \wedge x_{t-1} \qquad (10.37)$$
$$= \quad x_t \wedge (x_{t+1} - x_t - x_t + x_{t-1}) \qquad (10.38)$$
$$= \quad x_t \wedge (\dot{x}_{t+1} - \dot{x}_t) \qquad (10.39)$$
$$= \quad x_t \wedge \ddot{x}_t. \qquad (10.40)$$

Here the simplification from (10.35) to (10.36) uses the skew-symmetry of the alternation, which implies that $x_{t+1} \wedge x_{t+1} = x_t \wedge x_t = 0$. Putting (10.29) and (10.40) together gives

$$(\dot{L}_{y,t})_2 \quad = \quad x_t \wedge \ddot{x}_t - y \wedge \ddot{x}_t \qquad (10.41)$$
$$= \quad (x_t - y) \wedge \ddot{x}_t, \qquad (10.42)$$

so we again obtain result (10.26). Note that this result is also what we would find by taking change of rotational momentum to consist of the difference of moments formed using the current position with the successive velocities, namely

$$\dot{L}_{y,t} \quad = \quad (m_{t+1}, (x_t - y) \wedge \dot{x}_{t+1}) - (m_t, (x_t - y) \wedge \dot{x}_t) \qquad (10.43)$$
$$= \quad (\dot{m}_t, (x_t - y) \wedge \ddot{x}_t). \qquad (10.44)$$

These components are also what we would expect to obtain using the product rule for derivatives. The discrete change of m_t is just $\dot{m}_t$, and we obtain the discrete change of the spatial component $(x_t - y) \wedge \dot{x}_t$ by

$$
\begin{aligned}
\Delta[(x_t - y) \wedge \dot{x}_t] &= \Delta(x_t - y) \wedge \dot{x}_t + (x_t - y) \wedge \Delta\dot{x}_t &(10.45)\\
&= \dot{x}_t \wedge \dot{x}_t + (x_t - y) \wedge \ddot{x}_t &(10.46)\\
&= (x_t - y) \wedge \ddot{x}_t. &(10.47)
\end{aligned}
$$

Here (10.45) simply expresses the product rule. Note that to obtain (10.46) from (10.45) we must follow the earlier patterns and interpret the change in x_t as the trailing velocity $\dot{x}_t$ and the change in velocity $\dot{x}_t$ as the leading acceleration $\ddot{x}_t$. The result in (10.47) then matches that in (10.42).

10.6 Force

Forces take values in the momentum module $\mathcal{M} \times \mathcal{S} = \mathbb{D} \times \mathbb{D}$ over $\mathbb{Z}_2$, with the two components representing a massing and an acceleration of the body. We write f_t to denote a force acting at instant t.

In traditional mechanics, one can use Euler's first law either to determine motion given stipulated forces and initial conditions, or to determine the forces acting in a stipulated motion. One can do the same in the present case. We use Equation (6.60) as a prescription for identifying the forces corresponding to stipulated masses and motions by the rule that the force at instant t, f_t, equals the change in momentum at t, $\dot{p}_t$. That is, starting with a mechanical state $(x_t, \dot{x}_t, m_t)$ or (x_t, p_t), combining (6.60) with the preceding kinematic equations we obtain the successor state (x_{t+1}, p_{t+1}) as

$$
\begin{aligned}
(x_{t+1}, p_{t+1}) &= (x_{t+1}, (m_{t+1}, \dot{x}_{t+1})) &(10.48)\\
&= (x_t + \dot{x}_t + \ddot{x}_t, (m_t + \dot{m}_t, \dot{x}_t + \ddot{x}_t)). &(10.49)
\end{aligned}
$$

Put another way, taking initial values for position and momentum together with a sequence of momentum changes determines a sequence of successive positions and momenta. Conversely, a sequence of positions and momenta, together with an initial velocity value, determines a sequence of momentum changes.

The discrete torque $F_{y,t}$ with respect to some location y at time t takes the form

$$
\begin{aligned}
F_{y,t} &= (x_t - y) \wedge f_t &(10.50)\\
&= (\dot{m}_t, (x_t - y) \wedge \ddot{x}_t). &(10.51)
\end{aligned}
$$

As we require that the system of forces be balanced, torques do not depend on the reference point, so using the origin 0 for reference we have the simpler formula $F_t = (\dot{m}_t, x_t \wedge \ddot{x}_t)$.

Mental force systems over $\mathbb{D}^2$ satisfy the equilibration demands of Axiom F6 in a slightly different way than familiar physical force systems. Recall that the demand of equilibration is that for all bodies $\mathcal{B}$ and $\mathcal{C}$ the force system assigns values to $f(\mathcal{B},\mathcal{C})$ and $f(\mathcal{C},\mathcal{B})$ so that $f(\mathcal{B},\mathcal{C}) = -f(\mathcal{C},\mathcal{B})$. By taking forces to inhabit $\mathbb{D}^2$, a module of characteristic 2, we have $x = -x$ for all x, even when $x \neq 0$. Thus for mental forces in $\mathbb{D}^2$, force equilibration reduces to $f(\mathcal{B},\mathcal{C}) = f(\mathcal{C},\mathcal{B})$.

The divisions of mental states into mass and position permit us to look more closely at the forces producing mental motion, in particular, at the differences between forces in reasoning, learning, and other changes in mental state.

10.6.1 Environmental interactions

The mental interior enters into a sequence of interactions with its environment, in particular the agent's sensors and effectors. These interactions constitute the forces applied by the environment on the mind and by the mind on the environment. In the setting of minds and computational systems, it also seems natural to introduce an additional division of the resultant force $f(\mathcal{B}, \mathcal{B}^e)$ into input forces and output forces corresponding to input and output interactions with the environment.

The division between input and output forces or interactions cuts across the division of forces into body and contact forces. This division refers to the genesis of the forces, not to the medium of application. Because the system of forces is pairwise equilibrated, the force $f(\mathcal{B}, \mathcal{B}^e)$ exerted on the body by the environment is the opposite of the force $f(\mathcal{B}^e, \mathcal{B})$ exerted by the body on the environment. The notion of input and output interaction corresponds to a distinction between the quantity and origins of forces, making it sensible to refer to input forces as forces $f^i(\mathcal{B}, \mathcal{B}^e)$ generated by the environment on an agent, and to refer to output forces as forces $f^o(\mathcal{B}^e, \mathcal{B})$ generated by the agent on its environment. Using pairwise equilibration, we can thus write the resultant force as the combination

$$f(\mathcal{B}, \mathcal{B}^e) = f^i(\mathcal{B}, \mathcal{B}^e) - f^o(\mathcal{B}^e, \mathcal{B}) \qquad (10.52)$$

of input and output forces. When the environment of the great system in question is passive, the input and output forces also sum to yield the applied force f^a.

The input interactions fall into several categories, some simpler, some more complex. The simpler types of input interactions convey information or requests.

- The interaction may instruct the agent to change its position or mass in certain ways, typically by stipulating that certain sets of attitudes should be added to or removed from the attitudes *In* the position or mass.
- The interaction may query the agent about the status, *In* or *Out*, of a set of attitudes in the current position or mass.

Following standard terminology in artificial intelligence, we think of these as the input aspects of *Tell* and *Ask* interactions. We may take these transactions to occur singly or in combination without much difficulty, but the following chapters generally assume that at most one transaction occurs at each instant.

In addition to these fairly natural types of input interactions, common practice in artificial intelligence and psychology also considers a more complex type of input interactions that enlarges the set of attitudes, and so changes the mental space inhabited by the agent. Such an interaction instructs the agent to expand the set $\mathcal{D}$ of possible attitudes with one or more additional elements representing previously unimagined or unconsidered attitudes. Although this type of interaction seems natural in computational systems, one can formalize such interactions mathematically in ways that do not involve adding elements to $\mathcal{D}$. To do this, one thinks of $\mathcal{D}$ as an infinite set, and regards the agent as only using a finite portion of this set at any instant, as in $\mathbb{D}_f$ or $\mathbb{D}_b$. One then views the requests just described as indicating the agent should consider a somewhat larger finite subset of $\mathcal{D}$.

Although assuming all attitudes exist from the start obviates piecemeal construction of $\mathcal{D}$, it is not clear this is the best way of viewing human minds or artificial agents. The physical constitution of human brains can shape the mental constitution of human minds. It is possible that processes in which portions of the brain grow or die are best viewed as enlargement of or contraction in the dimensionality of mental space rather than mere enlargement or contraction of some active set of dimensions.

The output interactions fall into several categories, with the primary ones involving provision of answers and notification of changes.

- The interaction can convey answers to queries posed in *Ask* interactions. In some cases, these answers may form part of the same interaction as the query itself. Answers to some questions may provide extended sets of attitudes and other information, as when answering questions about why something attitude is held.

- The interaction can inform the environment about changes in specific dimensions of position or momentum.

Although these interactions can also take place in combination with others, we focus on the case in which only one output interaction occurs at a time.

The division of interactions between the mind and its environment into input and output interactions has little parallel in traditional mechanics. People do construct physical mechanical systems such as church bells in which interactions all take the form of external impulses, but nothing in ordinary mechanics enforces such a partition of motion. Such separations mainly serve to simplify system control and to enhance intelligibility of behavior. Future investigation of artificial psychologies might therefore seek to determine how much one loses by maintaining such divisions, and whether one can design control systems that carry out intended activities intermingling control actions with external impulses, as in fly-by-wire aircraft control systems or in distributed systems such as the rational distributed RMS (Doyle & Wellman 1990).

10.6.2 Spatial and mass forces

Forces change momentum, and hence can change both mass and velocity. However, not all forces need change both of these components of momentum. Some forces might take the form $(0, \ddot{x})$, indicating no change to the mass and some change to the velocity and hence to outlook. We call such a force a *spatial force* because it has a vanishing massing component. Indeed, traditional mechanics regards almost all forces as having a purely spatial character. Another force might take the form $(\dot{m}, 0)$, indicating a change only to mass, not to position. We call such a force a *mass force*, as it has a vanishing velocity component.

We thus can decompose forces applied to the agent into an applied mass force

$$f_t^{\mathbf{m}} = (\dot{m}_t, \mathbf{0}) \tag{10.53}$$

and an applied spatial force

$$f_t^{\mathbf{s}} = (\mathbf{0}, \ddot{x}_t), \tag{10.54}$$

yielding a total applied force

$$f_t^{\mathbf{a}} = f_t^{\mathbf{m}} + f_t^{\mathbf{s}} \tag{10.55}$$
$$= (\dot{m}_t, \ddot{x}_t). \tag{10.56}$$

Most automated agents studied in artificial intelligence, being built as sequential processes on sequential machines, obey a simplified pattern of action in which the agent suffers a single type of force at any instant. Such forces can come from the environment, as just summarized, or can constitute self-forces generated by the agent's own reasoning habits and volition. Sequential rule-based reasoning methods form a prime example of such sequential self-forces.

In the psychologies considered here, we think of simple reasoning as change in view or change in outlook, with no changes to long-term memory or habits except perhaps indirectly through the action of forces that embed attitudes into long-term memory when the attitudes persist over a long enough interval. Mechanically, therefore, we expect reasoning to stem from forces that change only the outlook or attitudes of the agent, and that do not directly change either long-term memories or the set of habits. In this case, spatial forces mediate simple reasoning.

Similarly, we think of learning as involving changes in long-term attitudes and habits. Such changes can involve changes in configuration or mass or both, with different types of learning involving different combinations of changes. Learning that acts only to embed long-held configurations into mass, for example, would consist of pure change of mass. Some sorts of learning might change mass directly, yet also cause consequential changes to outlook. Other types of learning might involve no change of mass, but instead consist of change of stable shape or configuration. In physical materials, plastic bending of an elastic metal band represents such spatial learning. In mental materials, plastic shift of shape or conservative update to accommodate stipulated changes represents a similar form of spatial learning.

10.7 Energy

Ordinary mechanics obtains the familiar formulas

$$K_t = \tfrac{1}{2} m_t \dot{x}_t^2 \qquad (10.57)$$
$$= \tfrac{1}{2} p_t \dot{x}_t \qquad (10.58)$$

for the kinetic energy of a body by assuming constant mass, rewriting the incremental contributions $\dot{p}_t \dot{x}_t$ as $m\ddot{x}\dot{x}$, and integrating over time. The factor of $\tfrac{1}{2}$ in this expression means we cannot use this formula in the binary vector space $\mathbb{D}$, in which the scalar ring $\mathbb{Z}_2$ lacks an element corresponding to $\tfrac{1}{2}$.

The discrete definition of kinetic energy builds on the definition of momentum, following the idea of the kinetic energy of a body as the "energy of motion." In this view, kinetic energy consists of the cumulative changes in momentum across distances, defined by

$$K_{t+1} \;=\; K_t + \dot{x}_t(\dot{m}_t, \ddot{x}_t) \tag{10.59}$$

$$\;=\; K_t + (\dot{m}_t, \dot{x}_t\ddot{x}_t), \tag{10.60}$$

where $\dot{x}_t$ represents the distance traversed in the time step t and the product $\dot{x}_t \dot{p}_t$ is the power P_t, that is, the work done by the force f_t across that distance. Integrating this across time we obtain

$$K_t = p_t \dot{x}_t \tag{10.61}$$

as the value for discrete kinetic energy. This value, which differs from the usual by a change of scale, represents the quantity called the *live force, vis viva*, used by Euler and Lagrange in the early days of rational mechanics.

We evaluate product (10.61) by preserving the natural separation of the components,

$$K_t \;=\; (m_t, \dot{x}_t\dot{x}_t) \tag{10.62}$$

$$\;=\; (m_t, \dot{x}_t) \tag{10.63}$$

$$\;=\; p_t. \tag{10.64}$$

We interpret the product $\dot{x}_t\dot{x}_t$ in (10.62) componentwise, and obtain (10.63) from (10.62) because componentwise squaring is the identity in the setting of binary vector spaces. In our discrete setting, therefore, kinetic energy turns out to be the same quantity as the momentum.

As in traditional mechanics, the kinetic energy depends on the frame of reference, since an observer moving with the body will see zero velocity or momentum and hence no kinetic energy, while an observer associated with a body in motion relative to the first will see a nonzero velocity and kinetic energy. The formalism makes this frame relativity clear by the explicit dependence of kinetic energy on the velocity, which is not indifferent to frame changes.

The equivalence of values of kinetic energy and momentum means that at least one form of energetic conservatism corresponds to a smoothest path principle for position and mass, that is, to conservation of position and mass in the face of alternative responses to force.

10.8 Illustration: simple computation

As a first illustration of the preceding framework for discrete mechanics, I recast briefly the familiar finite automaton model of computation.

Consider a finite automaton with n states, l symbols in its input alphabet, and m symbols in its output alphabet. The following interprets the automaton as a simple constant-mass mechanical system. We treat the n states as positions in the module $\mathbb{Z}_n$ over the ring $\mathbb{Z}$. Because the mass of the automaton does not change through any motion, it matters little what module we choose to represent the mass values. For simplicity we think of mass values as inhabiting the same module $\mathbb{Z}_n$ as positions. It also matters little which value we choose to represent the constant mass, and again for simplicity, we use the value 1.

We view the inputs and outputs of the automaton as portions of the position of the environment. We use the module $\mathbb{Z}_l$ over the ring $\mathbb{Z}$ to represent the inputs, and use the module $\mathbb{Z}_m$ over $\mathbb{Z}$ to represent the outputs. This means we can regard the environmental position, as seen by the automaton, as the module $\mathbb{Z}_l \times \mathbb{Z}_m$ over $\mathbb{Z}$, and can regard the entire space relevant to automaton motion as the module $\mathbb{Z}_n \times \mathbb{Z}_l \times \mathbb{Z}_m$ over $\mathbb{Z}$.

The conventional transition table of the automaton thus consists of a map

$$\Delta : \mathbb{Z}_l \times \mathbb{Z}_n \to \mathbb{Z}_m \times \mathbb{Z}_n \qquad (10.65)$$

representing a rule that says how to respond to receiving input symbols in automaton states by emitting output symbols and moving to new states. We can divide Δ into two projected maps that give the dynamics controlling the automaton for each input symbol. The first map

$$\Delta^{\mathbf{s}} : \mathbb{Z}_l \to (\mathbb{Z}_n \to \mathbb{Z}_n) \qquad (10.66)$$

tells how states map to states in the presence of a particular input symbol. The second map

$$\Delta^{\circ} : \mathbb{Z}_l \to (\mathbb{Z}_n \to \mathbb{Z}_m) \qquad (10.67)$$

tells how outputs vary with state in the presence of a particular input symbol. These projections are defined so that

$$\Delta(i, s) = (\Delta^{\circ}(i)(s), \Delta^{\mathbf{s}}(i)(s)). \qquad (10.68)$$

For each input symbol $i \in \mathbb{Z}_l$, we denote the resultant transition and output maps by $\Delta^{\mathbf{s}}(i)$ and $\Delta^{\circ}(i)$ respectively.

The most straightforward interpretation of automaton motion in terms of forces regards the mechanical state of the automaton as the automaton position. To do this, we characterize automaton motion with a sequence of quintuples $(x_t, \dot{x}_t, m_t, i_t, o_t)$. By hypothesis, we regard all mass components m_t as having the same constant value $m = 1$. We identify successive automaton states in accord with the transition table, so that

$$x_t = \Delta^s(i_{t-1})(x_{t-1}) \tag{10.69}$$

$$\dot{x}_t = x_t - \Delta^s(i_{t-2})(x_{t-2}). \tag{10.70}$$

We can thus regard the map $\Delta^s(i_t)$ as producing a vector field over the state space. We define acceleration as before and from (10.15) obtain

$$f_t = (0, \Delta^s(i_t)(x_t) + x_t - \dot{x}_t). \tag{10.71}$$

These definitions permit extension of the transition table to a map

$$\overline{\Delta} : \mathbb{Z}_l \rightarrow [(\mathbb{Z}_n^3 \times \mathbb{Z}_m) \rightarrow (\mathbb{Z}_n^3 \times \mathbb{Z}_m)] \tag{10.72}$$

that takes each input value to a map from partial states $(x_t, \dot{x}_t, m_t, o_t)$ to partial states $(x_{t+1}, \dot{x}_{t+1}, m_{t+1}, o_{t+1})$. We define $\overline{\Delta}$ so that we have, for each input $i \in \mathbb{Z}_l$,

$$\overline{\Delta}_i(x, \dot{x}, m, o) = (\Delta^s(i)(x), \Delta^i(i)(x) - x, m, \Delta^o(i)(x)) \tag{10.73}$$

The Markovian character of the finite automaton is as evident in this expanded transition map as in the original transition table, and in the values given by the mechanical translation.

One can enlarge this interpretation of finite automata to interpretation of other models of computation. For example, because one can regard a Turing machine as a writable tape controlled by a finite automaton, one can extend the mechanical description of a finite automaton to a mechanical description of a Turing machine. Such an extension would interpret the controller state as one dimension of the position of the body, with another dimension describing the infinitely many tape head positions, and with infinitely many mass values describing the tape contents as a variable mass. Other computational models offer similar mechanical formalizations. The random-access stored program, or RASP machine (Elgot & Robinson 1964), for example, would use its location pointer as the position, and its memory contents as mass. The projected maps described in the preceding paragraphs then resemble the RASP instruction-interpretation maps.

11

Reasoning

I distinguish reasoning from logical inference by identifying reasoning as change of view as opposed to mere relation between propositions (Harman 1986). This chapter recapitulates and expands on the mechanical analysis, sketched in Chapter 2, of motion and forces produced by simple types of rules called *reasons*. I first look at the simplest roles played by reasons in the RMS, and then present exploratory material in which the technical details have a more speculative nature. Examination of roles played by reasons in limited rationality, in learning, and in expressing kinematic constitutive constraints on mental configuration then continues in subsequent chapters.

11.1 Reasons

Earlier I presented reasons as four-part expressions

$$A \setminus\setminus B \Vdash C \setminus\setminus D,$$

and noted that reasons have connections to the propositional deduction rules, propositional default rules, propositional production rules, Bayesian probabilistic networks, and artificial neural networks that form the basis of various theories of reasoning and nonmonotonic knowledge representations in psychology and artificial intelligence. I will not pursue here the connections between such representations, but instead look in more detail at the origins, meaning, and variety of reasons.

11.1.1 Simple reasons

The original RMS employed two forms of reasons, the simplest of which was called a *support-list* reason (Doyle 1979). One can characterize each support-list reason r in terms of three components: the *inlist* A_r, the *outlist* B_r and the *consequent* c_r, where $A_r, B_r \subseteq \mathcal{D}$ and $c_r \in \mathcal{D}$. We denote such a reason with the notation

$$A_r \setminus\!\!\setminus B_r \Vdash c_r, \tag{11.1}$$

read as "A_r without B_r gives c_r." We interpret each support-list reason as requiring that the consequent element be *In* if all of the elements of the inlist are *In* and all of the elements of the outlist are *Out*. Formally, we say a position x *satisfies* the reason r just in case $c_r \in x$ whenever $A_r \subseteq x$ and $x \cap B_r = \emptyset$, or in vector terms, whenever $A_r \bar{x} + B_r x = \mathbf{0}$. We write $[\![r]\!]$ to mean the set of all positions that satisfy r, so we have

$$[\![r]\!] = \{x \in \mathcal{S} \mid A_r \subseteq x \subseteq \overline{B}_r \implies c_r \in x\}, \tag{11.2}$$

or in vector terms,

$$[\![r]\!] = \{x \in \mathcal{S} \mid A_r \bar{x} + B_r x = \mathbf{0} \implies \{c_r\}\,\bar{x}\}. \tag{11.3}$$

When the elements of the inlist are *In* some position and the elements of the outlist are *Out*, we say the reason is *valid* in the position. Thus a state must make the consequent of a valid support-list reason *In* in order to satisfy the reason; the state can satisfy an invalid support-list reason with an *Out* consequent.

We call the reason *monotonic* if the outlist is empty, and *nonmonotonic* otherwise. One can write monotonic reasons omitting the outlist altogether as

$$A_r \Vdash c_r. \tag{11.4}$$

One can view monotonic reasons as corresponding in some ways to logical inference rules. Nonmonotonic reasons can represent heuristic or plausible inferences by making assumptions absent information that would contradict or defeat the assumptions.

We earlier noted that the simplest sort of reasoning forces the agent into the position of holding a particular attitude. We can represent such a forced attitude with a monotonic reason r of the form

$$\emptyset \Vdash c_r. \tag{11.5}$$

The meaning is just what one expects, namely

$$[\![r]\!] = \{x \in \mathcal{S} \mid c_r \in x\}. \tag{11.6}$$

One naturally generalizes support-list reasons to encompassing multiple consequents, expressed as

$$A_r \setminus\!\!\setminus B_r \Vdash C_r \tag{11.7}$$

for a set $C_r \subseteq \mathcal{D}$. Such generalized support-list reasons were called *simple reasons* by Doyle (1983e). Simple reasons indicate that each of the consequents must be *In* if the hypothesis conditions hold, or formally,

$$[\![r]\!] = \{x \in \mathcal{S} \mid A_r \subseteq x \subseteq \overline{B}_r \implies C_r \subseteq x\}. \tag{11.8}$$

Support-list reason (11.1) thus corresponds to the simple reason

$$A_r \setminus\!\setminus B_r \Vdash \{c_r\}. \tag{11.9}$$

Simple reasons cannot forbid the presence of elements in mental states, but they do allow one to express reasons that remove other reasons from consideration. To accomplish this, one uses defeat of nonmonotonic reasons to remove the grounds for holding some attitude, and designs a system of uniformly defeasible reasons, in which one can defeat any previously stated reason simply by adding defeating information (Doyle 1983e).

11.1.2 Interval reasons

Although nonmonotonic reasons permit defeat of the grounds for holding an attitude, no amount of defeating information can force an agent clinging to some hopeless belief to abandon the belief. To accomplish this, one needs some way of expressing more than reasons that defeat reasons; one must express exclusion of attitudes.

We see exclusionary mechanisms motivating the backtracking procedures incorporated in the original RMS (Doyle 1979). In that scheme, based on the dependency-directed backtracking methods of Stallman and Sussman (1977), we represent the inconsistency of a set of beliefs by creating a "nogood" element stating the joint inconsistency of the beliefs, and by then using this nogood to provide a reason for a contradiction belief c. The backtracking system then would attempt to undo one of the assumptions directly underlying c. In effect, the backtracker would attempt to make the contradiction *Out*. If the backtracker could be guaranteed of success in its efforts, we could assign the interpretation $[\![c]\!] = \emptyset$ to the contradiction, meaning that c should not be held in any acceptable state of mind. In fact, however, the backtracker might fail to remove the contradiction, so the notions of nogood and contradiction elements do not represent pure exclusionary conditions on states.

Accordingly, we generalize simple reasons further still by introducing exclusionary conditions that produce a structural symmetry between hypothesis and consequent conditions. We write

$$A_r \setminus\!\setminus B_r \Vdash C_r \setminus\!\setminus D_r, \tag{11.10}$$

read "A_r without B_r gives C_r without D_r," to denote an *interval reason*. An interval reason bears the interpretation that each element of the consequences C_r must be *In* and each element of the exclusions D_r must be *Out* if each element of A_r is *In* and each element of B_r is *Out*. In set-theoretic terms, we write

$$[\![r]\!] = \{x \in \mathcal{S} \mid A_r \subseteq x \subseteq \overline{B}_r \implies C_r \subseteq x \subseteq \overline{D}_r\}. \tag{11.11}$$

In vector terms, we write instead

$$[\![r]\!] = \{x \in \mathcal{S} \mid A_r \overline{x} + B_r x = \mathbf{0} \implies C_r \overline{x} + D_r x = \mathbf{0}\}. \tag{11.12}$$

We may then view a simple reason of the form (11.7) shorthand for

$$A_r \setminus\!\setminus B_r \Vdash C_r \setminus\!\setminus \emptyset. \tag{11.13}$$

The interval reason satisfaction condition has a nice algebraic interpretation that suggests the interval reason terminology. When one views $\mathbb{D}$ as the lattice of sets $\mathcal{P}(\mathcal{D})$, one can interpret $A_r \setminus\!\setminus B_r$ and $C_r \setminus\!\setminus D_r$ as specifying intervals in this lattice, namely the intervals

$$[A_r, \overline{B}_r] \;=\; \{x \subseteq \mathcal{D} \mid A_r \subseteq x \subseteq \overline{B}_r\} \tag{11.14}$$

$$[C_r, \overline{D}_r] \;=\; \{x \subseteq \mathcal{D} \mid C_r \subseteq x \subseteq \overline{D}_r\}, \tag{11.15}$$

taking complements relative to $\mathcal{D}$, of course. The reason condition thus says that any set satisfying the reason must fall in the consequent interval if it falls in the interval specified in the antecedent of the reason.

11.1.3 Reasons as directional derivatives

The algebraic characterization of reason meanings apparent in (11.12) reflects an even more pleasing underlying mathematical nature, for we can also interpret reasons as representations of discrete directional derivatives in the sense of differential calculus. In this way, the development of RMS reasons to permit reuse of "rational" or "logical" derivations of conclusions in contexts different from those in which these conclusions were first derived makes use of what seems more than an amusing ambiguity in applying the English term *derivation*. Just as mathematics uses the notion of derivative to characterize change in traditional mechanics, psychology can use the notion of derivative, in the form of reasons, to characterize changes in position.

Consider first the appearance of derivatives and partial derivatives in the discrete setting. We start with a base point x and an incremental (direction) vector $y = \Delta x$. The direction vector represents a translation, as depicted in Figure 11.1.

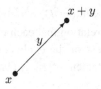

Fig. 11.1. A translation vector in the space $\mathbb{D}$. The vector x represents the origin of the translation, and y the translation vector itself.

Let $f : \mathbb{D} \to \mathbb{D}$ be a function on positions. A derivative at a point $x \in \mathbb{D}$ in the direction $y \in \mathbb{D}$ is given by the formula

$$\frac{f(y+x) - f(x)}{y} = \frac{f(x + \Delta x) - f(x)}{\Delta x}. \tag{11.16}$$

From this we obtain the quantities $f(x)$, $f(x + \Delta x)$, and

$$\Delta f(x) = f(x + \Delta x) - f(x). \tag{11.17}$$

The four quantities x, Δx, $f(x)$, and $\Delta f(x)$ give rise to a reason

$$r(x, f) = A_r \setminus\!\setminus B_r \parallel\!- C_r \setminus\!\setminus D_r \tag{11.18}$$

via the following identifications:

$$A_r = \Delta x\, \overline{x} \tag{11.19}$$

$$B_r = \Delta x\, x \tag{11.20}$$

$$C_r = \Delta f(x)\, \overline{f(x)} \tag{11.21}$$

$$D_r = \Delta f(x)\, f(x). \tag{11.22}$$

These identifications stem from viewing Δx and $\Delta f(x)$ as indicating the positive and negative changes from the reference values x and $f(x)$.

Though we derive the reason $r(x, f)$ from the directional derivative of f at x, the reason itself generalizes away from the point of derivation and yields an expression independent of the specific point. In particular, we cannot recover either the point x or the function f from the reason. It is easy to see that

$$\Delta x = A_r + B_r \tag{11.23}$$

$$\Delta f(x) = C_r + D_r, \tag{11.24}$$

but this gives no information about x itself. Moreover, even given the point x we know that

$$f(x) = C_r + D_r + f(x + A_r + B_r), \tag{11.25}$$

but this provides no way to recover the value $f(x)$.

The generality of the reason as compared with the specific change of conclusions from which it was derived was in fact one of the intentions of the RMS, to allow reuse of derivations (in the logical or rhetorical sense) in a context different from those in which the derivations were first applied or discovered.

11.2 Reasoned positions

Although we could employ the notion of reason only to analyze or express reasoning behavior, it is more natural to consider the possibility that some reasons appear as elements in $\mathcal{D}$. In fact, we assume that each element $d \in \mathcal{D}$ carries an interval reason interpretation $[\![d]\!] = A_d \setminus\!\setminus B_d \Vdash C_d \setminus\!\setminus D_d$.

This assumption is completely innocuous when we consider attitudes that carry no constitutive import. We note that every position satisfies the trivial reason condition

$$[\![d]\!] = \emptyset \setminus\!\setminus \emptyset \Vdash \emptyset \setminus\!\setminus \emptyset \tag{11.26}$$

with $A_d = B_d = C_d = D_d = \emptyset$. Thus extending reason interpretations to these elements changes nothing about the behavior of the reasoner.

This assumption does place a substantial restriction on meanings, namely that interval reasons represent the most complex meanings attributed to elements of $\mathcal{D}$. We will not worry about this restriction here, as interval reasons already allow significant complexity in psychological theories (Doyle 1983e, 1994).

We say that a position x *satisfies* its reasons (or is *satisfying*) just in case it satisfies the conditions expressed by each of its *In* reasons. Formally, x is satisfying iff $x \in [\![r]\!]$ for each reason r in x. Since we view every element in $\mathcal{D}$ as a (possibly trivial) reason, this means x is satisfying if $x \in [\![r]\!]$ for each r in x. We define

$$[\![x]\!] = \bigcap_{r \in x} [\![r]\!] \tag{11.27}$$

to be the set of all positions satisfying the *In* elements of x. With this definition, $x \in [\![x]\!]$ means that x is satisfying.

Section 13.5 examines a notion of equilibrium or relaxed states in which self-satisfying states represent a limiting case of temporal inference, the result of quiescence or closure with respect to sets of rules of reasoning. The following paragraphs examine the nonequilibrium case of simple reason-guided motion.

11.3 Reasoned motion

According to (10.49), an applied force $f_t^{\mathbf{a}} = (\dot{m}_t, \ddot{x}_t)$ and mechanical state $(x_t, m_t, \dot{x}_t)$ combine to produce a new state

$$(x_t + \dot{x}_t + \ddot{x}_t, (m_t + \dot{m}_t, \dot{x}_t + \ddot{x}_t)).$$

Although applied forces can change either mass or velocity or both, we here focus on spatial forces that do not involve learning of the sort that changes mass.

Typical conceptions of reasoning, like the theory of computation more generally, focus on reasoners that act in limited steps and do not proceed without further instruction. In rule-guided reasoning, the usual conception of rule application is that if the antecedent conditions of the rule are satisfied, then the rule produces the stipulated conclusions, and produces no further changes.

In the following sections, let us consider the motion resulting from application of a single reason, from application of several reasons, and from removal of reasons.

11.3.1 Single reason motion

Suppose the reasoner with position x_t and velocity $\dot{x}_t$ at instant t applies a reason

$$A_r \setminus\!\setminus B_r \mathrel{\|\mathord{-}} C_r \setminus\!\setminus D_r.$$

If the reason is valid, it stipulates the reasoner should hold the conclusions C_r and not hold the exclusions D_r. To determine the actual changes and so the velocity, one must translate these stipulated conclusions and exclusions into the corresponding sets of attitudes to be added to or removed from the position, so that one may then determine the velocity that carries the old position into the new.

Translating between stipulated conclusions and the corresponding conclusions and exclusions is straightforward. The stipulation $C_r \setminus\!\setminus D_r$ implies a set of additions

$$\dot{x}_{t+1}^{(+)} = C_r \setminus x_t = C_r \bar{x}_t \tag{11.28}$$

because the elements in $\dot{x}_t^{(+)}$, being not present in x_t, will appear in $x_{t+1} = x_t + \dot{x}_{t+1}$. The stipulation similarly implies a set of removals

$$\dot{x}_{t+1}^{(-)} = D_r \cap x_t = D_r x_t \tag{11.29}$$

because the elements in $\dot{x}_{t+1}^{(-)}$, already present in x_t, will not appear in x_{t+1}. By construction, $\dot{x}_{t+1}^{(+)}$ and $\dot{x}_{t+1}^{(-)}$ are disjoint even if C_r and D_r overlap, so we can obtain the changes as the single set

$$\dot{x}_{t+1} = \dot{x}_{t+1}^{(+)} \cup \dot{x}_{t+1}^{(-)} = \dot{x}_{t+1}^{(+)} + \dot{x}_{t+1}^{(-)}. \tag{11.30}$$

If the reason is invalid and so does not specify any changes to be made at the instant t, we view it as specifying empty sets of additions and deletions, which implies $\dot{x}_{t+1}^{(+)} = \dot{x}_{t+1}^{(-)} = \emptyset$, so that $\dot{x}_{t+1} = 0$ and $x_{t+1} = x_t$.

Putting these observations together, we see that the position resulting from applying a reason r should satisfy

$$x_{t+1} = \begin{cases} x_t + C_r \overline{x}_t + D_r x_t & \text{if } A_r \overline{x}_t + B_r x_t = 0 \\ x_t & \text{otherwise.} \end{cases} \tag{11.31}$$

This yields a velocity of

$$\dot{x}_{t+1} = \begin{cases} C_r \overline{x}_t + D_r x_t & \text{if } A_r \overline{x}_t + B_r x_t = 0 \\ 0 & \text{otherwise,} \end{cases} \tag{11.32}$$

and an acceleration of

$$\ddot{x}_t = \begin{cases} C_r \overline{x}_t + D_r x_t - \dot{x}_t & \text{if } A_r \overline{x}_t + B_r x_t = 0 \\ \dot{x}_t & \text{otherwise.} \end{cases} \tag{11.33}$$

We note that if A_r and B_r overlap, then r cannot be valid, and so indicates no motion.

Acceleration (11.33) implies that immediately applying the reason a second time leaves the position unchanged. Suppose r was applied at time t producing $\ddot{x}_t$, $\dot{x}_{t+1}$, and x_{t+1}, and is now to be applied again at $t+1$ to produce $\ddot{x}_{t+1}$, $\dot{x}_{t+2}$, and x_{t+2}. If the reason is no longer valid, then we have

$$\ddot{x}_{t+1} = \dot{x}_{t+1}, \tag{11.34}$$

while if the reason remains valid, we get the same result since

$$C_r \overline{x}_{t+1} = D_r x_{t+1} = 0. \tag{11.35}$$

The only change to the spatial state is that the velocity vanishes, since

$$\dot{x}_{t+2} = \dot{x}_{t+1} + \ddot{x}_{t+1} = \dot{x}_{t+1} + \dot{x}_{t+1} = 0. \tag{11.36}$$

11.3.2 Multireason motion

We obtain the motion due to applying a set of reasons R in a state $(x_t, m_t, \dot{x}_t)$ in a way similar to that used to obtain motion from single reasons. Multiple reasons only require modifying the desired changes to consist of the total changes indicated by all the reasons acting at the instant in question.

We first define $R^\sharp(x)$ to be the subset of reasons in R *valid* in x, that is,

$$R^\sharp(x) = \{r \in R \mid A_r \bar{x} + B_r x = \mathbf{0}\}. \tag{11.37}$$

We then introduce two functions

$$U, U^\flat : \mathcal{D} \to (\mathbb{D} \to \mathbb{D}) \tag{11.38}$$

to denote, respectively, the changes due to reasons taking into account the validity or invalidity of the reasons and the changes assuming validity. We define

$$U(r)(x) \quad = \quad \begin{cases} C_r \bar{x} + D_r x & \text{if } A_r \bar{x} + B_r x = \mathbf{0} \\ \mathbf{0} & \text{otherwise} \end{cases} \tag{11.39}$$

$$U^\flat(r)(x) \quad = \quad C_r \bar{x} + D_r x. \tag{11.40}$$

The function $U(r)$ provides the change value identified in (11.32), and vanishes when the reason is invalid in the state. The function $U^\flat(r)$, in contrast, simply applies the conclusions of the reason r to a state, and thus does not depend on whether the reason is valid or not.

We lift these functions to functions over sets of reasons

$$U, U^\flat : \mathcal{P}(\mathcal{D}) \to (\mathbb{D} \to \mathbb{D}) \tag{11.41}$$

by defining, for $R \subseteq \mathcal{D}$,

$$U(R)(x) \quad = \quad \sum_{r \in R} U(r)(x) \tag{11.42}$$

$$U^\flat(R)(x) \quad = \quad \sum_{r \in R} U^\flat(r)(x). \tag{11.43}$$

We follow the convention that an empty sum equals $\mathbf{0}$. The changes of interest, of course, do not depend on where in the formalism we take validity into account, in that

$$U(R)(x) = U^\flat(R^\sharp(x))(x). \tag{11.44}$$

We then identify the acceleration at time t produced by a set of reasons R_t as

$$\ddot{x}_t \quad = \quad U(R_t)(x_t) - \dot{x}_t \tag{11.45}$$

$$= \quad \left(\sum_{r \in R_t^\sharp(x_t)} C_r x_t + D_r \bar{x}_t \right) - \dot{x}_t. \tag{11.46}$$

Thus if there are no reasons to apply or all applied reasons are either invalid or satisfied, the resulting acceleration is zero, leaving the resulting velocity zero and the position unchanged.

Observe that acceleration (11.33) previously derived for a single reason r is just the value obtained in (11.45) for the singleton set $R_t = \{r\}$.

11.3.3 Removal of reasons

Note that (11.33) and (11.45) give the accelerations stemming from application of a reason or a set of reasons to a state. Taking back reasons R_t retains the requirement that the reason antecedents be satisfied, and reverses the sense of the state in applying the conclusions. This requirement obtains in a RMS that undoes portions of the state supported by the changed set of base reasons prior to constructing a new state corresponding to the changed reasons. It also holds during the search for global satisfying states when tentative constructions are undone to try different assumptions permitted by the reasons.

Accordingly, we define a function $\overline{U}$ to invert the production of conclusions compared with that in U, using the definition

$$
\overline{U}(r)(x) \;=\; \begin{cases} C_r x + D_r \overline{x} & \text{if } A_r \overline{x} + B_r x = 0 \\ 0 & \text{otherwise,} \end{cases} \tag{11.47}
$$

and lift this function to sets of reasons by

$$
\overline{U}(R)(x) = \sum_{r \in R} \overline{U}(r)(x). \tag{11.48}
$$

We then obtain the acceleration corresponding to removal of reason consequences for a set of reasons R_t as

$$
\ddot{x}_t \;=\; \overline{U}(R_t)(x_t) - \dot{x}_t \tag{11.49}
$$

$$
=\; \left(\sum_{r \in R_t^\sharp(x_t)} C_r x_t + D_r \overline{x}_t \right) - \dot{x}_t. \tag{11.50}
$$

11.4 Reason forces

Extending the preceding characterization of reasoned motion to a characterization of reason forces is straightforward, because we regard each reason as generating a spatial force. The interval reason $r = A_r \backslash\!\backslash B_r \Vdash C_r \backslash\!\backslash D_r$ generates the force

$$
f_r(x_t, m_t, \dot{x}_t) = (0, U(r)(x_t) - \dot{x}_t) \tag{11.51}
$$

in the mechanical state $(x_t, m_t, \dot{x}_t)$ at instant t, and a set R_t of reasons generates the force

$$f_{R_t}(x_t, m_t, \dot{x}_t) = (\mathbf{0}, U(R_t)(x_t) - \dot{x}_t). \tag{11.52}$$

The earlier remarks on accelerations imply concordance of these definitions, namely $f_{\{r\}}(x_t, m_t, \dot{x}_t) = f_r(x_t, m_t, \dot{x}_t)$.

11.4.1 Friction and inertial motion

The motion engendered by a rule application halts the instant after application. Motion from rule application thus resembles the familiar mechanical situation of pushing a heavy rough box across a carpet. This conception suggests a frictional character for the forces shaping reasoning. We see this mathematically as well because the reason force explicitly depends on the velocity of the body. Physics traditionally calls such velocity-dependent forces *frictional*. The coefficient of friction exhibited here suffices to damp the velocity to zero when applied forces cease.

Not all computational systems work this way. One might view operating systems as always doing something, even if just spinning endlessly in a wait loop, and recent theories of interactive computing might be viewed in similar ways. The existence of frictionless systems in traditional mechanics then raises the possibility of designing artificial reasoning agents in which reason forces lack or diminish this frictional component and exhibit something like free inertial motion.

Without the frictional component, a reason force applied at one instant and then withdrawn would engender free inertial motion that alternates between the preceding two positions. Specifically, a reason acceleration $\ddot{x}_t = A$ without the frictional term $-\dot{x}_t$ would still produce a change, but cessation of applied forces at some instant would then lead to linear cyclic behavior. For example, suppose that at time t we have $(x_t, \dot{x}_t, \ddot{x}_t) = (X, V, 0)$. We then would see a sequence of kinematic states of the form

$$
\begin{aligned}
(x_t, \dot{x}_t, \ddot{x}_t) &= (X, V, \mathbf{0}) \\
(x_{t+1}, \dot{x}_{t+1}, \ddot{x}_{t+1}) &= (X + V, V, \mathbf{0}) \\
(x_{t+2}, \dot{x}_{t+2}, \ddot{x}_{t+2}) &= (X, V, \mathbf{0}) \\
(x_{t+3}, \dot{x}_{t+3}, \ddot{x}_{t+3}) &= (X + V, V, \mathbf{0}) \\
&\vdots
\end{aligned}
$$

This behavior would fix conclusions in the state only after the reasoner made subsequent changes that did not affect the conclusions in question.

One might interpret such linear cyclic motion as introducing a small element of the distinction between long-term and short-term memory. The most recent changes would represent short-term memory, while older changes, now fixed in position, would represent long-term memory. Unlike standard conceptions of short-term memory, this type of frictionless reasoning induces a division of memory contents that depends on the actions of the reasoner rather than some architectural or structural aspect. As will be seen in Chapter 13, one direct interpretation of standard theories of long-term and short-term memory calls for explicit forces that generate changes in reasons or mass when certain conclusions remain sufficiently long in the conclusions or position. It would be interesting to know to what extent encoding or embodying memory dynamics in kinematical form can obviate the need for explicit memory-conversion forces.

One can also regard linear cyclic motion as inducing a degree of uncertainty about the mental position. The position of a body depends on the instant of observation in any free mechanical motion, but in the discrete space $\mathbb{D}$, the set of possible positions has just two members, rather than comprising an entire line or half-line, with a 50–50 probability distribution between the two possibilities. I examine some consequences of this and other mechanical uncertainties in Chapter 14.

11.4.2 Superposition and conflict resolution

The binary additive combination of reason conclusions embodied in (11.42) clearly represents only one of the simplest possibilities. The mechanical formalism presented herein presupposes that conflict resolution takes place in the course of determining the reasons on which to base changes. We view different means for resolving such conflicts as constitutive of different types of agents or psychological materials. Mechanics itself provides the notion of addition or superposition of forces; if this simple method of combining reason contributions does not provide the desired behavior, then conflict resolution must occur in determining the force due to the whole set of reasons.

One can view serial consideration of single reasons as the result of just such a conflict-resolution procedure, for example, one that uses an ordering of the reasons to find the first valid but unsatisfied reason and then produces the force due to that reason acting alone. A less serial conflict-resolution method might use a similar ordering on reasons to determine the force from all of the valid but unsatisfied reasons by summing the changes indicated by all the reasons, breaking conflicts by omitting the changes indicated by the higher numbered of the conflicting reasons. In such ways one might find reasonable means of shifting some of the burden to the combination function U that aggregates the individual reason contributions. The attractions of such an approach would have to outweigh the benefits offered by the superposition approach implicit in (11.42).

More generally, the mechanical interpretation says nothing specific about the genesis of reason forces or about how specific psychological materials or architectures resolve conflicts among reasons. Such specifics lie outside the bounds of mechanics proper, just as do electromagnetic, gravitational, nuclear forces, and the many specific material forces or response functionals of continuum physics. We may expect a wide range of types of forces in psychology and economics, especially in light of the artificial nature of these subjects (Simon 1981). At present we lack ways of even enumerating or envisioning all these possible forces, much less categorizing such forces into a small number of types.

11.4.3 Frame indifference

The way that reasons generate forces should not depend on the particular frame of reference from which we interpret the reasons. In the Truesdell notation, this means reason forces must satisfy

$$[f_r(x, m, \dot{x})]^\star = f_{r^\star}(x^\star, m^\star, \dot{x}^\star). \tag{11.53}$$

Mass plays no role in the reason interpretations under examination. Frame indifference of reasons means that the changes produced by reasons should transform as vectors with respect to orthogonal transformations of the reason quantities. We thus interpret (11.53) to mean

$$Qf_r(x, m, \dot{x}) = \tag{11.54}$$
$$\begin{cases} QC_r\overline{Qx} + QD_rQx - Q\dot{x} & \text{if } QA_r\overline{Qx} + QB_rQx = 0 \\ Q\dot{x} & \text{otherwise.} \end{cases}$$

To verify (11.54), we first consider the way reframing affects the set relations underlying reason interpretations. As noted earlier, orthogonal transformations represent permutations of the elements of $\mathcal{D}$ in the binary space $\mathbb{D}$, so frame indifference of reasons means invariance of effect under renaming of all state elements. Intuitively, therefore, frame indifference of reasons means that set intersections, complements, and symmetric differences transform with permutations of $\mathcal{D}$, and that permuting the reason identities as well preserves the structure of satisfying states. It is also clear that permutations of $\mathcal{D}$ do in fact preserve these things. We run through the formal verification as follows. Let Q be an orthogonal transformation (permutation) operator on $\mathbb{D}$, and let $x, y \in \mathbb{D}$. We know that such transformations preserve symmetric differences because the linearity of Q means $Q(x + y) = Qx + Qy$. We know that orthogonal transformations preserve complements because $Q\overline{x} = Q(1 + x) = Q1 + Qx = 1 + Qx = \overline{Qx}$. Finally, to see that orthogonal transformations preserve set intersections, we overload the notation and write $Q(e)$ to mean the element of $\mathcal{D}$ assigned to e in the permutation Q. Clearly $e \in Q(xy)$ iff $e = Q(e')$ for some $e' \in xy$. This holds iff $e \in x$ and $e \in y$, which holds iff $e \in Q(x)$ and $e \in Q(y)$, the two of which in turn hold iff $e \in Q(x)Q(y)$. Thus we have $Q(xy) = Q(x)Q(y)$.

Applying these algebraic results to (11.54), we have that

$$QA_r\overline{Qx} + QB_rQx \quad = \quad QA_rQ\overline{x} + QB_rQx \qquad (11.55)$$
$$= \quad Q(A_r\overline{x}) + Q(B_rx) \qquad (11.56)$$
$$= \quad Q(A_r\overline{x} + B_rx). \qquad (11.57)$$

Because $Q0 = 0$, (11.57) means that $QA_r\overline{Qx} + QB_rQx = 0$ iff $A_r\overline{x} + B_rx = 0$, so the reason condition changes appropriately with the frame. By similar reasoning we see that

$$QC_r\overline{Qx} + QD_rQx - Q\dot{x} = Q(C_r\overline{x} + D_rx - \dot{x}). \qquad (11.58)$$

Reason forces therefore transform as desired with the frame of reference.

The set-inclusion conditions underlying reason conditions and consequences do not appear indifferent to translations. In particular, even if we have $A \subseteq x$, the corresponding inclusion $A + z \subseteq x + z$ on the translates holds only if $z \setminus A \subseteq z \setminus x$, which combined with the inclusion $A \subseteq x$ implies $z \setminus A = z \setminus x$. This equality holds for all translation sets z only if $A = x$. Such sensitivity to choice of origin reflects a structure present in informational spaces such as $\mathbb{D}$ that is lacking in the physical spaces of ordinary mechanics. In this structure, the condition of holding some belief or reason has different consequences than the condition of lacking that belief or reason, introducing an asymmetry between *In* and *Out*. The relevant class of reference frames for assessing frame indifference thus appears to be the class of translation-free isometries, that is, the orthogonal transformations.

11.5 Reason stresses

The preceding identification of the forces induced by reasons suffices to complete the mechanical interpretation of reasoning at the level of Euler's law. The following section begins a more speculative development in which we consider additional interpretations aimed at uncovering additional and possibly deeper mechanical structures exhibited by forces of reasoning.

Toward this end, we first consider the possibility of interpreting reasons as generating or embodying stresses, as tensors that take vectors into vectors. The notion of stress arises in continuum mechanics when we consider the representation of forces acting across surfaces within or without a body. Mechanics conceives of stress as a tensor that, when applied to a vector normal to a surface element of a body, yields the contact force acting across the surface.

Stress plays a central role in the analysis of many systems and in many equations of continuum mechanics. First among these equations is Cauchy's first law of motion,

$$\dot{p} = B + \mathrm{div}(T), \tag{11.59}$$

which relates the inertial force $-\dot{p}$ to the body force B, and the stress tensor T. The following sections show that reason forces admit an interpretation satisfying (11.59) under suitable identifications of the stress tensor, body force, and body surfaces. Our point of departure in developing a theory of reason stresses is to interpret the change operator U as a stress "tensor" that depends on a set of reasons R acting in a mechanical state $(x, m, \dot{x})$.

11.5.1 Reasons as tensors

A tensor is a linear function from a vector space into itself, and a tensor of order n maps n copies of the space into itself. The tensors of primary interest in mechanics are tensors of order 2 that map a pair of vectors into a third vector. As befits most linear algebra, the tensors of order n over a vector space form a vector space themselves.

We can regard the function $U^{\flat}(r)$ as a tensor, because it is a linear function exhibiting the tensorial additive structure identified in (11.43), according to which $U^{\flat}(R)(x)$ is the superposition or sum of the component values $U^{\flat}(r)(x)$.

The function U also exhibits the additive structure identified in (11.42), with $U(R)(x)$ being the superposition or sum of the component values $U(r)(x)$. We cannot, however, properly call $U(r)$ a tensor because it is a nonlinear function of conclusion states. The nonlinearity comes about through the conditionality expressed by the antecedent of the reason, which makes $U(r)$ piecewise linear over two regions of $\mathbb{D}$, and which can make the superposition $U(R)(x)$ piecewise linear over more complicated parts of $\mathbb{D}$. We call a superposition of such piecewise linear functions a *piecewise-linear (PL) tensor*. Let us summarize linear analysis in each of the linear regions by treating the piecewise-linear operator $U(R)$ as a tensor, dropping the piecewise linear qualification when possible but distinguishing the two concepts as necessary.

Another path for investigation might regard reason tensors as proper linear operators over a transformed space by moving to a larger space in which each vector in the original space represents a dimension of the enlarged space. Invertible or reversible operators on the original space then become permutation matrices over the enlarged space, and that, as linear operators, constitute proper tensors.

11.5.2 Reasoner surfaces

Stress represents the forces acting across body surfaces. Applying the stress at a point to the normal to the surface of the body at that point yields the traction force on the body across that surface. The total contact force on the body is thus the sum of the traction forces for each point on its surface.

The preceding treatment of reasoning has primarily considered the reasoner as a point body, to which placements assign a point location in space. To regard reasons as stresses acting on the body, we must find a way of treating the reasoner as a body with surfaces.

One way to approach this difficulty is to regard the reasoner's position as a degenerate surface. In this approach, we regard multiple reasons as multiple stresses all acting on the same degenerate surface, from which we find the total stress by superposition.

Another approach is to regard the set of conclusions previously treated as a point location in a multidimensional space as instead representing a set of points, a form or shape or "volume" occupied, so to speak, in the space of mental attitudes. In this approach, we regard different reasons as referring to different surface elements of the reasoner. Recall that our earlier discussion of reasons as directional derivatives showed how to construct a reason that represents a directional derivative based at a specific point. As was pointed out, the use of these reasons to shape motion at other points involves a generalization step, abstracting the derivative at the original point of discovery to a derivative holding at other positions as well. As was also pointed out, we can interpret the antecedent condition $A \setminus\!\setminus B$ of an interval reason $A \setminus\!\setminus B \Vdash C \setminus\!\setminus D$ as referring to a subspace in the lattice $\mathcal{P}(\mathcal{D})$, which corresponds to a region or subspace in $\mathbb{D}$. The volumetric perspective on reason stresses regards each of these antecedent conditions as specifying a surface in $\mathbb{D}$. If we can interpret the antecedents $A \setminus\!\setminus B$ as specifying a surface in $\mathbb{D}$, we can also interpret the consequent $C \setminus\!\setminus D$ as specifying a vector associated with the surface. The volumetric perspective on reason stresses regards this associated vector as a normal vector for the surface. Distinct reasons with the same antecedent superpose to yield the total stress acting across that surface. We get the total traction by summing these contributions over all the surfaces, that is, over all the reasons.

The analysis that follows appears to fit either of these approaches. It develops a stress corresponding to a set of reasons acting either on a degenerate surface encompassing the body or on multiple surfaces of the body, treating individual reasons as stresses acting simultaneously on these surfaces and obtaining the overall stress by summing the stresses derived from the individual reasons. In the following discussion we assume $\mathcal{D}$ is finite with $|\mathcal{D}| = n$ and that elements $d_i \in \mathcal{D}$ for $1 \leq i \leq n$ enumerate $\mathcal{D}$.

11.5.3 Cauchy's first law of motion

Consider first the gradient of U. The gradient of a function over a vector space is, when expressed in a coordinate system, a vector of partial derivatives over the coordinates of the space. We then have

$$\nabla U(R)(x) \;=\; \left(\frac{\partial U(R)}{\partial d_1}(x), \ldots, \frac{\partial U(R)}{\partial d_n}(x) \right) \qquad (11.60)$$

$$=\; \sum_{i=1}^{|\mathcal{D}|} \frac{\partial U(R)}{\partial d_i}(x)\, d_i. \qquad (11.61)$$

In (11.61) we regard each d_i as a basis vector, and the partial derivatives as coefficients. We interpret a partial derivative $\frac{\partial U(R)}{\partial d_i}(x)$ here to be the set of conclusion changes we get if the set of reasons changes from $R \setminus \{d_i\}$ to $R \cup \{d_i\}$; that is,

$$\frac{\partial U(R)}{\partial d_i}(x) = U(R)(x) - U(R \setminus \{d_i\})(x). \qquad (11.62)$$

In the binary algebra of $\mathbb{D}$, this difference also represents the change in conclusions seen in moving from R to $R + d_i$, regarding d_i as a basis vector in $\mathbb{D}$, or

$$\frac{\partial U(R)}{\partial d_i}(x) = U(R)(x) - U(R + d_i)(x). \qquad (11.63)$$

From the definition of U, we see that this difference reduces to

$$\frac{\partial U(R)}{\partial d_i}(x) = \begin{cases} U(d_i)(x) & \text{if } d_i \in R \\ 0 & \text{otherwise.} \end{cases} \qquad (11.64)$$

Next we consider the divergence of U. The divergence is the trace of the gradient, that is, the sum of the coefficients of the gradient vector. In the present case, this means

$$\text{div}(U)(R)(x) = \text{tr}(\nabla U(R)(x)) \qquad (11.65)$$

$$= \sum_{i=1}^{|\mathcal{D}|} \frac{\partial U(R)}{\partial d_i}(x). \qquad (11.66)$$

Combining this definition with the values of these partial derivatives as given in (11.64), we have

$$\text{div}(U)(R)(x) = \sum_{r \in R} U(r)(x) = U(R)(x). \qquad (11.67)$$

We can now recognize formula (11.52) for reason forces as an instance of Cauchy's first law (11.59). To see this, we identify the inertial force $\dot{p}$ with $(0, \ddot{x})$, the body force B with the frictional force component $(0, \dot{x})$, and the stress tensor T with $(0, U(R)(x))$. In this interpretation, $(0, U(R)(x))$ also represents the traction due to R exerted at x, and $(0, U(r)(x))$ represents the traction due to r exerted at x.

One might also view the production of forces by reasons in other terms as well. For example, one might view the function U as additively superposing potentials produced by each reason, in which case the preceding obtains the total reason force as the gradient of the total potential. Reasons appear in this picture as carriers of charges that produce fields that produce forces. Such reason potentials might also be used in a discrete Lagrangian formalism (Baez & Gilliam 1994). Another possibility is to interpret reasons tensors as expressing or generating torques acting on the reasoner.

11.5.4 Serial composition

The interpretation of reason tensors as indicating stresses on the reasoner makes use of the superposition of tensors, the operation of adding tensors together to get another tensor. These tensors are of order 1 and, as functions from a vector space to itself, may also be composed to obtain other tensors. We may use serial composition of reason tensors to view some state transitions as resulting from the serial composition of a series of reason tensors, each of which applies or undoes the application of an individual reason.

We write such serial tensors as tensor products

$$r_1 \otimes r_2 \otimes \cdots \otimes r_n. \qquad (11.68)$$

Assuming all the elements of such a product represent application of reasons without any removals, we may obtain the interpretation of such a product by the formula

$$U(r_1 \otimes r_2 \otimes \cdots \otimes r_n)(x) = U(r_1)[U(r_2)[\ldots [U(r_n)(x)]\ldots]]. \quad (11.69)$$

Here each reason adds its bit to the conclusions, so each is interpreted as an operator, not as a difference. As we would expect, taking tensor products in different orders produces different resultant positions or sets of conclusions.

12

Rationality

The preceding treatment of reasoning indicates how we can interpret psychological rationality in terms of mechanical processes. Let us now look at the ways in which mechanical concepts enter into characterizing forms of economic rationality.

12.1 Limits on rationality

The difficulty and slowness with which real agents change their mental state constitutes one of the most evident limitations on rationality. As noted earlier, we can see reflections of the mechanical connection between momentum and force in "the more you need to change, the more you have to force yourself," "the more you know, the harder it is to change your mind," and other truisms of popular psychology. We can read the first of these truisms as stating a monotonicity relation between the size of changes and the size of the required forces and work done, and the second as stating a monotonicity relation between the mass and the force required for given changes. Notions of monotonicity and proportionality among the numerical magnitudes of momentum and force are familiar in traditional mechanics, but how do these apply in the discrete mechanical setting?

A mechanical interpretation of thinking also naturally relates slowness of change to inertia. From the same perspective, the unreality of ideal rationality appears because when we determine actions by finding the maxima of an expected utility function generated by instantaneous beliefs and desires, large changes can come from small impulses. This lack of proportionality between the new information causing changes and the resulting changes suggests we view these systems as operating without inertia.

To fully understand limits to change, however, one must consider concepts beyond that of mere inertia. Simon (1955) pointed out long ago that the ideal rationality of economics lacks measures of the effort required to make decisions. The modern theory of computational complexity studies a number of specific and abstract measures of procedural difficulty, some of which were inspired by the concepts of physical science (Hartmanis 1994). Computational time is patterned after physical time, even though computational time measures generally have no fixed relation to physical time, only the compatibility requirements seen in the treatment of hybrid time presented earlier. The theory of computation patterns its measures of computational space after notions of length and area in physics; in this case with even less connection to the physical notions. Information theory, in turn, patterns measures of information content after measures of physical mass, with strong formal connections to physical concepts of entropy. Recent theories of rational allocation of inferential resources exploit these measures in addressing questions about mental effort (Horvitz, Cooper, & Heckerman 1989).

The great generality of abstract measures of computational effort need not prevent one from looking for more specific measures of computational effort relative to specific mental organizations and bodily structures. The prime candidate for investigation here is, of course, the human mind. On some tasks people will differ greatly in the effort they require, but on other tasks one can find more uniformity. Mental rotation of mental images forms an interesting example, in that the time people need to perform mental rotation of objects they have been asked to visualize seems to exhibit the dependence on angle of rotation one would expect of fixed-speed physical rotation (Freyd 1987). Rotation-dependent timings might arise through a variety of mechanisms, not necessarily mechanical ones, but the connections might bear investigation, especially in light of evidence that the mind uses portions of the brain for both perceiving physical motion and for reasoning about such motion.

12.1.1 Work and effort

The mechanical perspective brings yet another way of thinking about these issues by interpreting effort not just as assignments of resources to tasks but as mechanical work, the exercise of force across distance. Devoting resources to tasks produces changes of resources (mass) accompanied by changes of position (task achievement), which forms a quantity of work.

Section 2.2.3.2 identified the mechanical work performed in a special case of reasoning. Let us revisit this calculation in light of the subsequent formal development. We focus on the power exerted by the environment on the reasoner as a gauge of the work done on the agent, because we treat a reasoner as a point body, for which every motion is rigid, and the working of any balanced system of forces vanishes in a rigid motion. The power exerted or work performed a force $f_t = (\dot{m}, \ddot{x}_t)$ at time t producing a velocity $\dot{x}_{t+1}$ over the same temporal interval is given by

$$
\begin{aligned}
P_t &= \dot{x}_{t+1}(\dot{m}_t, \ddot{x}_t) & (12.1) \\
&= (\dot{m}_t, \dot{x}_{t+1}\ddot{x}_t) & (12.2) \\
&= (\dot{m}_t, \dot{x}_{t+1}(\dot{x}_{t+1} - \dot{x}_t)) & (12.3) \\
&= (\dot{m}_t, \dot{x}_{t+1} - \dot{x}_{t+1}\dot{x}_t), & (12.4)
\end{aligned}
$$

using the idempotence of multiplication in $\mathbb{D}$ in obtaining (12.4). As noted in the earlier discussion, the cross-time term $\dot{x}_{t+1}\dot{x}_t$ vanishes if the reasoning under consideration does not immediately reverse any changes made at the preceding instant. The term also vanishes if we follow the pattern of common computation and assume motion halts after every step of reasoning. In that setting, the velocity vanishes going into every step of reasoning, and vanishes again the instant after completing the reasoning. The cross-time terms always vanish in this form of motion, and the work done in every step of reasoning counts twice, once instigating the movement, and once halting the movement, a uniform doubling that simply changes the scale of measurement. We thus simplify calculations of work done by assuming the cross-time term always vanishes, leaving us with

$$
P_t = (\dot{m}_t, \dot{x}_{t+1}) \tag{12.5}
$$

as the expression for power.

To use (12.5) in a measure of the quantity of work done at an instant, we consider the magnitude of this expression, calculated by extending the ordinary inner product i_2 defined in (10.5) to the product space $\mathbb{D}^2$. We then obtain

$$
\begin{aligned}
|P_t| &= |(\dot{m}_t, \dot{x}_{t+1})| & (12.6) \\
&= |\dot{m}_t| + |\dot{x}_{t+1}|, & (12.7)
\end{aligned}
$$

which identifies the quantity of work as the total number of changes made to mass and position elements. We obtain the total work performed over some extended motion by summing the contributions at each instant, thus obtaining a measure that counts the total number times mass or position elements are changed during the motion.

By way of application, we note that this relation between external work and the applied force lets us use the notions of power and work to reexpress familiar measures of computational effort in Turing machines. If we interpret Turing machines mechanically by regarding the finite controller state as position and the tape contents as mass, we see that the instantaneous change in position is bounded by the size of the finite controller and the instantaneous change in mass is bounded by the width of the tape window in which the tape head can move in a single step. For each particular Turing machine these bounds are constants, so the amount of work performed in a computation is bounded by an amount proportional to the number of steps performed.

To use this measure of work performed to understand limits on change, we begin by looking at the way the character of mental forces limits the changes undergone by the mind, especially in the way force magnitude and direction limit change. We can interpret limitations on the magnitude of forces as limiting the rate at which the environment stimulates change in the agent's mental state, and limitations on the direction of forces as influencing the coherence and focus of the agent's actions. In fact, because reasoning and learning consist of changes in mass and position, Euler's law means that force and inertia both limit the scope and speed of reasoning and learning. Combining forces with the changes they produce yields notions of work related to familiar economic measures that combine measures of costs and benefits into measures of work.

12.1.1.1 Magnitude of force

Continuum mechanics divides forces into contact and body forces, with contact forces acting across a shared boundary and body forces acting directly on a body without need for contact. Continuum mechanics also ordinarily assumes that body and contact forces vary smoothly as we vary the size of the contact area and body mass. More precisely, it assumes that contact forces vary continuously with the area of the contact boundary and that body forces vary continuously with both the surface area and mass of the body. We formalized these smoothness conditions in terms of inequalities that, as in Axiom F8, bound contact forces by some multiple of the area of the contact surface and bound body forces by multiples of the mass of the body. We carried over such assumptions to discrete mechanics in Assumption F16.

In psychology, one naturally views communications between agent and environment and between agent interior and periphery in terms of contact forces. Indeed, communication of information through shared boundary bodies between agent environment, sensors, cognition, and effectors provides a natural connection between mechanical and psychological concepts in which the inequalities expressed in Assumption F16 highlight certain natural limits on force and change.

12.1.1.2 Channel capacity

In continuum mechanics, boundaries between bodies typically have zero mass. These boundary bodies nevertheless impose limitations on the forces acting on bodies as a result of Axioms F7, F5, and F8.

We see similar limitations on the magnitude of forces in the psychological realm, this time as bounds reflecting information content. In the psychological setting, as in continuum mechanics, boundary bodies serve only to communicate forces. Forces do not change the mass of these bodies, only their position and velocity.

In mental mechanics, however, simple boundary bodies correspond to communication channels; more complex ones to sensors. We may view the communication boundary bodies as fixed-area contact regions. The dimensionality (number of orthogonal components) of the binary state spaces of these communications boundaries is proportional to the dimensionality of the boundary body. We can use this dimensionality measure as a substitute area measure for use in Assumption F16 to obtain limits on the magnitude of contact forces. The dimensionality of nonbinary state spaces provides related bounds flowing from the limits on channel capacity identified in Shannon's (1948) theory of communication across a noisy channel.

12.1.1.3 Rate of change

We might regard the Shannon theorems as providing a theoretical basis for the traditional mechanical conception of limited forces. In continuum mechanics, the assumption of bounds is motivated both by natural experience, as we observe such bounds in everyday physics, and by mathematics, where the bounds ensure the integrability of the forces over boundaries and bodies. The Shannon limits concern only transmission of discrete symbols through noisy media. Traditional forces need not come in discrete quantities, except in the setting of quantum mechanics, and we normally do not regard boundaries as noisy, though Shannon's concept applies as well to zero noise levels. We might thus seek a communication-theoretic analysis of traditional mechanical forces. In this direction, Margolus and Levitin (1997) have calculated bounds on the rate of computation possible within traditional physical law.

We can apply the same same kind of reasoning to body forces as applied to contact forces and see that the dimensionality of the mental momentum space limits the magnitude of body forces on the mind. In this case, the dimensionality of momentum corresponds to both the mass and the area. Because forces are limited to changing mass or position elements along these dimensions, the dimensionality of forces limit the magnitudes of body forces as well. This implies that the rate of change decreases with increasing momentum when the magnitude of the force is held constant. It seems natural to ask if such decreasing rates of change help explain some cases of diminishing returns in psychology and economics, in which the motivational effects of specific quantities of money, food, and other goods decrease with increasing levels of wealth on satisfaction.

12.1.1.4 Continuity

In addition to limits on forces imposed by the dimensionality of the spaces mediating forces, it appears that other limits on forces stem from the continuity of the functionals that characterize mental dynamogenesis.

Continuity means that distance plays a role in restricting forces. Continuing the earlier discussion of Turing machine computation, one can say the bounded changes implicit in the finite controller and explicit in the head-motion window clearly limit the magnitude of forces, and thus the rapidity of motion.

One might ask, however, if such limits merely reflect inessential aspects of Turing machines or constitute essential elements of the notion of computation by machines. Common wisdom in the theory of computation says that all "reasonable" models of computing machines are such that switching from one reasonable model to another increases the time and space needed to compute functions by at most a polynomial. That is, if one reasonable machine M computes a function in time bounded by $T(n)$ and space bounded by $S(n)$, then for any other reasonable machine M' that computes the same function there is a polynomial p such that M' computes the function in time and space bounded respectively by $p(T(n))$ and $p(S(n))$.

This common definition of reasonability of models of computation is important in classifying problems by computational complexity. The famous expectation $P \neq NP$ depends on some restriction of this kind. For example, the vector machine model of computation, like the RASP model of Elgot and Robinson (1964), involves changes in position of magnitude varying with the values stored in memory. Vector machines, in contrast, allow operations that shift a value in memory by an amount obtained by interpreting the vector as a number; Pratt, Rabin, and Stockmeyer (1974, 1976) showed that such rapid changes of value permit vector machines to compute results in polynomial time that require polynomial time on nondeterministic Turing machines and random access machines, thus speeding up these computations beyond what is permissible according to standard expectations that $P \neq NP$. The conventional conclusion drawn is that vector machines of this sort do not constitute a reasonable model of computation.

The mechanical point of view suggests one might seek to reinterpret the received notion of reasonability of models of computation in terms of the continuity and boundedness of forces one expects in mechanics. This might involve looking for natural bounds and computational topologies that distinguish P from NP, treating the change of position seen in Turing machines as continuous but treating the changes made by self-shifting vector machines as discontinuous. Notions of computational continuity already play an important role in distinguishing functions computable by Turing machines from functions uncomputable by Turing machines. The model here comes from Scott (1973, 1976), who showed how to use continuity notions to characterize Church–Turing computability itself.

A specific question of interest is whether the mere existence of bounds on the rate of work suffices to entail the reasonability criterion that demands that effort in different machine models be related by polynomial transformations. Another mechanical question for investigation is the relation of continuity and locality conditions. Scott's computational topologies explicitly capture a notion of continuity of computation, but this notion seems quite different from the bounds one sees placed on the motion of the tape heads in Turing machines. Are the head-motion bounds best formalized in terms of continuity conditions or as locality principles that rule out action at sufficiently great distances?

12.1.2 *Attention and volition*

The preceding limits on rationality all stem from bounds on the magnitude of forces and effort available. To these we now add limits relating to the direction of forces, which matter just as much in psychology as in physics. In particular, persistence or stability in direction of force enters into the concepts of attention and volition.

In traditional mechanics, all forces values inhabit the same three-dimensional space, so all forces combine by superposition in a simple way. The forces applied to a body combine by vector addition to produce a resultant or total force that, in general, represents both forces applied by the environment on the body, and forces applied to the body by the body itself or by its parts. The algebraic combination means that sometimes different applied forces can cancel each other out, leaving unopposed forces untouched in the resultant.

In the hybrid mechanics considered here, different forces can inhabit separate subspaces of $\mathcal{F}$, and though they still combine by additive superposition, the response of the material to force-generating components in one subspace can exhibit a degree of nonlinearity due to the presence of force-generating components in another subspace.

In human terms, superposition of forces from disparate motivations leaves one confused, pulled in different directions. The agent's volition reflects its response to observations of these competing forces and the mental elements that generate them. Most decision making involves a nonlinear response in which competing desires yield distinct actions corresponding to the strongest desire rather than mixtures of actions in proportion to the several desires.

As in standard physical materials, one expects different agents, exemplifying different psychological materials, to follow different rules in generating forces from their history and environment. Such differences correspond to the different psychological types observed in people. Some individuals are deliberate and consider every change carefully; others are wanton or impulsive and follow strong desires irrespective of prior actions or plans. For example, a highly wanton individual might act on some desire or intention picked at random at each point of action. Little differentiates desires and intentions in the psychology of such an agent. A somewhat less wanton individual might simply act on the strongest desire at any instant, and on the highest-priority intention if no desires remain unsatisfied. The agent presented in Doyle (1980) lies at the other end of the spectrum, as it first carefully deliberates about what intentions, if any, to form on the basis of beliefs and desires, and then systematically carries out intentions according to their priorities. That pattern of volition strongly differentiates between desires and intentions, letting desires conflict all one wants, requiring consistency of intentions, and only acting directly on intentions, not on desires.

We thus may interpret volitional differences in terms of the way agents generate the forces they exert on themselves. In wanton agents, forces tend to produce action immediately in the direction of some desire, while in deliberate agents, the agent itself shapes the forces leading up to action by summarizing them in a considered intention. In particular, intentional agents decouple construction of self-forces from application of these forces. Intentional agents shape forces they expect to apply to themselves prior to applying them.

12.1.2.1 Attention and stable deliberate response

An agent seeking to act coherently in a complex world must deal with many types of distractions. Some distracting forces might come from outside the agent, as the environment produces forces or force stimuli that would push the agent from the chosen path. Other distracting forces might come from conflicting desires or motivating forces operating within the agent. In wanton volition, which lacks much sense of consciousness, the agent merely acts in whatever way these combined influences point. The normal disunity of internal and external forces then produces the normal incoherence of wanton action. To act coherently, the agent must deliberate about its actions. Deliberation generally forms a conscious process, which in mechanical terms involves the agent's identifying and applying forces to itself to shape the direction of the resultant of these self-generated forces with other environmental and internal forces. Deliberate dynamogenesis thus involves intentional forces that seek to maintain attention or focus in the agent's actions and state.

Attention as such does not appear explicitly in the ideal theory of rational action. The fickle economic agent can jump from one activity to another to track minute shifts in the levels of expected utility of alternative activities. Although such behavior might serve the agent's purposes well, shifting activities can consume significant cognitive and external resources. Such task-shifting costs normally slow progress on intended activities and thus represent costs worth avoiding. Realistic rationality requires that the agent account for these costs in assessing expected utility. Attention thus appears only implicitly, as an epiphenomenon of the structure of expected utility assessments, rather than as a quality directly visible in the formalization.

In the extreme of concentrated attention, the agent views one force as the focus of attention and all other forces as distractions. It then tries to channel its actions to address the focus of attention by blocking the distractions. That blocking involves generating self-forces that by superposition cancel the unwanted distracting forces, leaving only the desired focus force in the resultant. For example, reasoned deliberation as described in Doyle (1980) makes decisions by constructing defeasible arguments for and against alternatives. A deliberator dead set on some course of action will seek to multiply arguments for the chosen course and to defeat any proposed counterarguments, and similarly, will seek to make arguments against other alternatives and to defeat arguments favoring the other alternatives. Ordinary human experience also has something of this character, though not always consciously. Sometimes noticing a distraction causes one to spend a brief period thinking explicitly about how not to pay attention to the distraction. Although the intent to suppress the distraction is conscious, the suppression itself, if successful, is not.

Maintaining attention involves work, a truism known to everyone who learns discipline. When distractions exert forces that move attention away from the intended direction, the agent does mental work in exerting either a force that restores the desired position from the perturbed one, or a force to reintroduce or maintain the countervailing force itself, or both, in order to restore the integrity of the desired force. Such self-restorative forces serve to producing deliberate entrenchment or commitment of mental attitudes. These forces seek to ensure a behavioral coherence in the agent's mental motion by ensuring a structural coherence within the agent's mental state.

The work required to maintain attention motivates the use of additional attention-focusing mechanisms when one must concentrate attention over long periods of time. In some cases, agents that seek to maintain a prolonged focus of attention might find it easier to move to avoid circumstances that would produce distracting forces than to continually generate restorative forces to counteract or defeat the forces of distraction.

Unfortunately, distractions never cease, and limits on the time and effort available to the agent limit the rationality of the agent's actions. As the agent's countervailing efforts fall short of the distractions, the agent's actions become more wanton, and when the agent becomes attentionally exhausted, purely wanton behavior can result.

At the same time, even a capable deliberative agent can fail to meet the ideal of economic rationality because it acts on the basis of its intentions even when changes in its preferences make some other action more desirable. However, agents that deliberate little will presumably exhibit lesser degrees of rationality than agents that deliberate longer, though one must take some care in the formal definition of rationality comparisons for this to hold.

12.1.2.2 Couples and unstable wanton response

In the psychological setting, pure wanton volition represents perhaps the simplest but most unstable response to superpositions of disparate motivational forces, acting whichever way the wind blows. Purely wanton psychologies exhibit little if any rationality, since their actions will prove rational only by accident.

As hinted earlier, one might regard even the perfectly rational economic agent as a wanton agent. If the agent has preferences that reflect a set of goals (Wellman & Doyle 1991) and is in a state of ignorance, the agent always acts on the strongest desire. More generally, if we view the forces as graded by a utility or desirability function that assigns qualitatively different magnitudes to different types of motivations, then addition of forces will select out the biggest of the forces. One might view some behavior-based robot architectures as exemplifying such wantonness, though of course such architectures are normally designed to exploit the grading of magnitudes to achieve some sort of coherence in action.

In many common human situations, conflicting desires have comparable magnitudes and the force superposition rule produces moderately unpredictable results. When conflicting forces largely counterbalance each other, leaving a small or vanishing resultant, we might say the agent experiences confusion, with the mutually defeating forces yielding no clear direction for motion. Unlike the stable equilibrium obtained when acting on all reason forces produces a self-satisfying state, the near-equilibrium of confusion represents an unstable equilibrium, one in which variations in the strengths of the conflicting forces produce net forces in varying directions. One can expect such variations as a result of uncertainty of inferred attitudes in some agents. In human terms, one can feel pulled in many directions, with momentary strengthenings in one direction soon changing to strengthening in other directions or returns to equilibrium.

Now a rational response to conflicting desires might consist of compromise, as when conflicting desires for a family sedan and workhorse pickup truck stimulate purchase of a minivan. The minivan might not be directly related to either of the conflicting motivations, but it nevertheless might lie closest to their resultant.

Rational response to conflict is hardly the norm, however. In some cases, balanced conflicting desires can lead to paralysis, to the inaction of Buridan's ass, with the agent unable to decide what to do. Mechanically, this situation recalls static equilibrium of forces. In other cases, seemingly random behavior can result, with the person liable to do something else entirely as an escape from or response to the conflicting pressures. From a logical point of view, we might view conflicting motivations as contradictions from which the agent can draw any conclusion. Indeed, folklore says people are liable to do anything when pressured enough by conflicting demands. From a mechanical point of view, however, one might interpret this type of response in terms of the notion of *couples*. Couples form when balanced forces operate on a body in parallel but opposite directions and combine to exert rotational torques on the body.

From the mechanical perspective one can group human response to conflicting demands into several categories. In one group of responses, the person suffering conflict acts in some way unrelated to either of the conflicting forces, moving orthogonally to escape the conflict. In a second group, the person chooses which demand to follow and generates a force in line with that competing demand, in effect ignoring the opposing force. In a third group, the person seeks to act in ways that give something to each conflicting force, to switch or spin in attempts to satisfy each of the demands in turn. The first group of responses recalls the response of a squeezed toothpaste tube. The second recalls material collapse. The third group of motions, translated into the physical realm, exemplify material response to couples.

In plural minds, couples appear through the action of conflicting mental subagencies on the mind. It requires little effort to extend this observation to theories of group behavior, in which the individuals consist of persons rather than submental agencies. Many of the oft-noted limitations of committee decision making might reflect compromises orthogonal to the principal interests of the committee members.

It might be possible, or even desirable, to regard the interplay between deliberation and action, especially between deliberation and physical action, as formation of and response to a couple. The deliberation builds up a complex of

mental forces that either constitutes a couple and eventually produces motion
in some orthogonal external direction, or that the agent eventually counters
with a force to terminate the deliberation, with the opposition between the deliberation result and the terminating force producing the motion.

12.1.3 Rigidity

Rigid motion constitutes the simplest type of spatial deformation, in which the
shape and distances between body parts remain constant as the body changes
position. As in traditional mechanics, we can think of rigid bodies as expe-
riencing internal or constitutive forces that carry body parts along with their
neighbors and so preserve the configuration throughout changes of placement.
In rigid motion, these constitutive forces maintain perfect coordination. In traditional mechanics, rigid motion consists of translation and rotation, and every
motion of a point body is rigid. The same holds true in the broadened mechanics because of the requirement that space enjoy pseudo-Euclidean properties.

The mere possibility of rigid motion in both traditional and broadened mechanics does not in itself mean one can expect to find rigid materials in psychology or economics. Indeed, if rationality involves flexibility and adaptation
to circumstances, one might view rigidity as the most extreme sort of limitation
on rationality, even the antithesis of rationality. This need not be true, however,
for as the saying goes, even a stopped clock is right twice a day. A completely
rigid system might be just the tool for certain purposes.

Consider, for example, an agent with distinct sensor bodies and mental interior. Rigid motion means that movements of sensors and mental interior track
exactly, which would seem to be a good thing. But what does rigidity really
mean in psychological terms? One might regard mind-sensor rigidity as saying that thinking immediately keeps up with perception, that just as the sensors
observe something the mind notes it too. Does that mean that thinking adds
nothing to perception, that the mind cannot move beyond what the sensors
observe? Not necessarily. Although there are useful reflex agents in which
pure sensor-bounded tracking might be desirable, one ordinarily expects the
mind to do more with the senses. In fact, rigidity need not limit thinking to
replicating the sensor reports if thinking changes mental state in dimensions
separate from those characterizing sensor reports. Suppose that the position
of the interior mental body decomposes into a pair (X, Y) in which X represents only the sensor reports and Y represents only the results of thinking,
that is, the sensor body occupies only the first subspace of this interior space.
Thinking upon some fixed sensor report thus changes location from (X, Y) to
some (X, Y'). Let $|Y' - Y|$ denote the distance between these two locations.

In this case, rigid motion would mean that $|Y' - Y|$ stays constant throughout thinking. Algebraically this means thinking serves to rotate the mind to different locations in a hypersphere centered at (X, Y). Psychologically, this might mean that thinking only changes the contents of a working memory of fixed size, always removing one element in order to insert another.

Although it is unclear that any interesting reasoning fits the sort of psychological rigidity just described, one might find better applications for other forms of rigid motion. The next chapter examines a very useful class of partial rigidities, namely preserved configurational conditions that represent some of the memory of a reasoner. Another form of rigidity consists of uniform change of representation across a computational system. This can change the location of each point in the same way, but leave the distances intact. Address translation systems, such as dynamic software module linkers and network address translation schemes, might be viewed in these terms.

12.2 Inherent rationality

Traditional mechanics uses constitutive kinematic assumptions to characterize special types of materials or systems. Rigid materials, for example, reflect a restriction of configurations to ones in which all body parts retain a fixed set of mutual distances. Crystalline materials enforce a particular rigid lattice geometry on the body parts. Isotropic materials are locally the same in every direction, but in polarized materials, some directions offer behavior others do not. Finally, incompressible materials, especially fluids, are characterized by rigid volume constraints instead of rigid distance constraints.

Some traditional kinematical assumptions might apply to some mental materials. Point bodies, of course, are trivially rigid; mental organs might exhibit fixed contact boundaries; and we typically think of cellular automata as inhabiting crystalline lattices. We expect, however, that the kinematic constraints of importance in psychology and economics will differ from those in traditional physics because of the different character of space in mental mechanics.

The first and most natural kinematic constraints in mental mechanics take the form of restrictions on possible locations or configurations. The preceding chapters have developed mental space as the product $\mathbb{D}$ of all the individual attitudinal positions. Although this space provides a good algebraic setting for examining mental motion, it does not reflect natural constraints on sets of attitudes realistic agents exhibit. For example, the constitution of an agent might keep it from ever exhibiting attitude d_1 at the same time as d_2, or might require exhibiting d_2 whenever it exhibits d_1. Database theory calls these sorts of restrictions "integrity constraints" (Reiter 1988), but similar restrictions appear in many other guises in computing, including "information systems" (Scott 1982), "system laws" (Minsky 1988), and "admissible state semantics" (Doyle 1983a). Such nonmetric rigidity restrictions mean that the agent can inhabit only a subspace of $\mathbb{D}$ rather than the full product of individual attitudinal positions.

Restrictions on location appear in traditional mechanics mainly in the context of restrictions that forbid two bodies from inhabiting the same locations at the same time. The exact analog in mental mechanics would require us to view individual attitudes as body points, 0 and 1 as the only two locations, and vectors in $\mathbb{D}$ as representing placements of all individual attitudes in the two available locations. We instead treat vectors in $\mathbb{D}$ as representing complex locations of individual bodies with restrictions on locations shaping the allowed subset of positions rather than respective positions of different bodies.

12.2.1 Constitutive logics

One of the principal advantages of using materials exhibiting kinematic constraints in traditional engineering is that the constitution of the materials does some of the work for you. To throw a javelin, you need only toss the handhold of the spear the right way and the rest of the javelin follows. To elevate a car, you need only push the hydraulic fluid on one end of the jack and the incompressible fluid inside lifts the car mounted on the other end.

Kinematic constraints serve as a similar aid in approaching psychological engineering, enforcing certain properties of the agent without requiring ongoing attention or effort on the part of the designer. In particular, they permit one to divide reasoning into a portion performed automatically, always without need for conscious attention, and a portion performed deliberately, only through conscious effort.

We expect that automatic reasoning forms an important part of what we think of as the native intelligence exhibited by an agent. The native intelligence places a lower bound on the degree of intelligence exhibited by the agent (Doyle 1988a).

Kinematically imposed lower bounds on reasoning abilities have a large influence on the average or peak intelligence exhibited by the agent as well. Geniuses and dullards alike sometimes err in allocating effort and sometimes take stupid actions, but the less able suffer from abnormally low lower bounds on their constitutional abilities. Most can perform the same reasoning as the more able in principle, but must perform much more of their reasoning consciously, at enormous cost in attention and resources. Because they must attend to the bookkeeping needed to keep attention focused as well as to the external focus of reasoning, the half-witted find things not uniformly twice as hard, but exponentially (in the complexity of the problem) harder than their full-witted cousins. Even extreme diligence finds this handicap hard to conquer.

The difference between novices and experts constitutes an important special case of this difference personally familiar to most people. Novices, even when possessed of adequate instructions, must perform every step consciously, and expend much effort in keeping track of their progress and of their understanding of the instructions. The expert performs almost all of this reasoning automatically and seemingly effortlessly. Normal novices have adequate automatic reasoning powers, but have not yet committed their instructions to these powers. Their intelligence in other arenas helps but little in their new subject.

Inherent reasoning also affects the degree of rationality exhibited by the agent through the levels of consistency, completeness, and inferential competence they provide in the agent's beliefs and preferences (Doyle 1988a, 1992a, 2004). For example, we interpret limitations on the rationality possible in humans and other nonideal agents as requiring us to drop the completeness assumptions underlying the ideal theory of rational choice and consider agents with partial, not total, weak preference orders. With plural minds composed of interacting and conflicting subagencies, it becomes sensible to treat the construction of the mental state of the agent as a group decision problem, subject to an appropriate adaptation of the axioms of group rationality (Doyle & Wellman 1991). This treatment provides added incentive to weaken completeness assumptions. We similarly give up consistency of the preferential order and allow the agent to possess conflicting pieces of preference information. We need not, however, abandon all consistency and completeness constraints. We instead consider agents in which inherent structure ensures at least some degree of consistency and completeness.

Thus the most natural kind of kinematical constraint in psychology consists of constraints on the logic of attitudes. For example, a logically idealized agent might occupy only consistent closed positions in which its beliefs contain all their deductive consequences and do not contradict each other. Other types of agents might inhabit positions that contain some consequences and avoid some contradictions, but miss some consequences and contradictions. Some agents might inhabit subspaces in which they always hold or avoid some attitudes, no matter what.

12.2.2 Information systems

One can capture restricted forms of completeness and consistency using the formalization of information systems developed by Scott (1982) as a way of formalizing incremental computation over general data types or computational domains.

As we apply them here, each information system captures a constitutive logic of consistency and closure on mental attitudes and states. Information systems view each element of $\mathcal{D}$ as an "atomic proposition" about states in an abstract logical system, and each set of elements as a partial description of some state, with bigger sets representing better descriptions.

Although information systems capture a natural and flexible notion of inherent intelligence, they cannot express all forms of constitutional intelligence. In particular, they enjoy the key logical property of monotonicity, meaning that more axioms produce more consequences. Information systems thus cannot directly express nonmonotonic or defeasible inferences of the kind common in human reasoning and artificial intelligence systems, which must be expressed by other means, such as reasons and other configurational intentions.

The fundamental concepts of information systems begin by considering finite amounts of information about states, represented by the finite subsets of $\mathcal{D}$. We write $\mathcal{P}_f(\mathcal{D})$ to denote the class of all such finite subsets. This is much the same starting point as was taken in defining the space $\mathbb{D}$ of positions, which, in the case of infinite $\mathcal{D}$, was defined to include the free module $\mathbb{D}_f$ of positions of finite support. Clearly, the vectors in $\mathbb{D}_f$ are just the characteristic functions of the sets in $\mathcal{P}_f(\mathcal{D})$. As we shall see, the difference in treatment is that the preceding development of mechanics rested content to consider just such positions of finite support (in the form of $\mathbb{D}_b$ of positions of finite or cofinite support), while the theory of information systems uses convergent sequences of such finite descriptions to identify ideal states of possibly infinite support.

12.2.2.1 Limited consistency

Let us define abstract consistency relations on $\mathcal{D}$ as follows. We define a *finite consistency relation* to be a set $Con \subseteq \mathcal{P}_f(\mathcal{D})$ of finite subsets of $\mathcal{D}$, interpreted as setting out the "consistent" finite subsets. We require that Con satisfy the following two conditions.

The first condition on consistency relations states that subsets of consistent sets are consistent. Formally, we require that for each $X, Y \subseteq \mathcal{D}$, if $X \subseteq Y \in Con$, then $X \in Con$.

The second condition states that each individual attitude is consistent, or formally, that for each $e \in \mathcal{D}$, if $e \in \mathcal{D}$, then $\{e\} \in Con$. This stipulation means that each individual element of a state of mind is possible in isolation. The intent of a consistency relation is only to rule out combinations of different elements deemed inconsistent with each other, not to rule out isolated elements.

We then call an arbitrary set $X \subseteq \mathcal{D}$ *consistent* just in case each finite subset $Y \subseteq X$ is consistent according to *Con*.

12.2.2.2 Limited entailment

We define abstract entailment relations relative to a consistency relation *Con* as relations between finite consistent sets of $\mathcal{D}$ and individual elements of $\mathcal{D}$. We require an entailment relation $\vdash$ on *Con* $\times \mathcal{D}$ to satisfy three conditions.

The first condition states that addition of entailed consequences preserves consistency. Formally, for each $e \in \mathcal{D}$ and $X \subseteq \mathcal{D}$, if $X \vdash e$, then $X \cup \{e\} \in$ *Con*.

The second condition requires that consistent sets entail their own elements. Formally, this means that if $e \in X$, then $X \vdash e$, for each $e \in \mathcal{D}$ and $X \subseteq \mathcal{D}$.

The third condition states that entailments of entailments are also entailments. Formally, for each $e, e' \in \mathcal{D}$ and $X, Y \subseteq \mathcal{D}$, if $Y \vdash e$ for all $e \in X$, and $X \vdash e'$, then $Y \vdash e'$.

We extend the notation of entailment in the natural way to say that $X \vdash Y$ iff $X \vdash e$ for each $e \in Y$. With this extension, we can rephrase the second condition as stating that entailment is reflexive, that is, $X \vdash X$, and can rephrase the third condition as stating that entailment is transitive, that is, that $X \vdash Z$ whenever $X \vdash Y$ and $Y \vdash Z$.

We say that a set $X \subseteq \mathcal{D}$ is *(deductively) closed* just in case $e \in X$ whenever $Y \subseteq X$ and $Y \vdash e$. Clearly $\mathcal{D}$ is closed, as are intersections of closed sets.

If X is consistent we define the *closure* $Th(X)$ of X to be the least closed superset of X. The operator Th exhibits properties similar to those of the usual deductive closure operator in ordinary logic. One easily checks that Th is monotonic: $Th(X) \subseteq Th(Y)$ whenever $X \subseteq Y \subseteq \mathcal{D}$; idempotent: $Th(Th(X)) = Th(X)$; and identifies the closed sets as its fixed points: X is closed iff $X = Th(X)$. Computational domain theory usually restricts attention to closures of consistent sets, but we find it useful to employ the unrestricted notion as well.

The least closed set is $Th(\emptyset)$, which also consists of the intersection of all closed sets. If $\emptyset \vdash e$, we say e is a *tautology*.

12.2.2.3 Information elements and approximation

An information system $\mathbf{I} = (\mathcal{D}, Con, \vdash)$ over a set $\mathcal{D}$ consists of $\mathcal{D}$ together with a consistency relation *Con* and entailment relation $\vdash$.

We say that a set $X \subseteq \mathcal{D}$ is an *element* of the information system (not to be confused with an element of $\mathcal{D}$) just in case X is both closed and consistent. We write $Elt(\mathbf{I})$ to denote the set of elements of $\mathbf{I}$.

The primary relation between elements of information system is *approximation*, which gives rise to a lattice structure on the elements of the information system. We say that X *approximates* Y, written $X \sqsubseteq_\mathbf{I} Y$ or simply $X \sqsubseteq Y$, whenever both are elements of the information system and $X \subseteq Y$. Every element in a domain is the limit of its finite approximations, and there is a rich theory of approximation that forms the basis of the theory of computation over domains (see Scott 1982). In terms of approximations, the closure $Th(X)$ of a set is the least element of $Elt(\mathbf{I})$ approximated by X.

We naturally view some elements of the information system as the partial (or incomplete) elements of the domain. The most incomplete, and hence minimal, element in the information system consists of $\bot = Th(\emptyset)$, the consequences of the empty set.

The *total* (or complete) elements are those elements maximal under set inclusion, that is, elements $X \in Elt(\mathbf{I})$ such that $Y = X$ if $Y \in Elt(\mathbf{I})$ and $X \sqsubseteq Y$. We write $Elt^+(\mathbf{I})$ to mean the set of total elements of $\mathbf{I}$.

12.2.2.4 Frame indifference

Information systems and their constitutive relations exhibit frame indifference in a manner akin to forces, that is, as relations that transform with the frame rather than as relations invariant under changes of frame.

Specifically, we say that an information system is frame indifferent just in case its constituent notions of consistency and entailment transform as frame-indifferent relations over $\mathbb{D}$. We earlier noted that the orthogonal transformations Q of $\mathbb{D}$ correspond to permutations of $\mathcal{D}$. As before, we write $Q(e)$ to denote the permuted element corresponding to $e \in \mathcal{D}$. We also write $Q(X)$ to denote the set of permuted elements corresponding to $X \subseteq \mathcal{D}$.

Given an information system $\mathbf{I} = (\mathcal{D}, Con, \vdash)$, we define the orthogonal transform $Q\mathbf{I} = (\mathcal{D}, QCon, \vdash_Q)$ of $\mathbf{I}$ by

$$QCon = \{Q(X) \mid X \in Con\} \tag{12.8}$$

and

$$\vdash_Q = \{(Q(X), Qe) \mid X \vdash e\}. \tag{12.9}$$

We say that the information system $\mathbf{I} = (\mathcal{D}, Con, \vdash)$ is frame indifferent just in case the information system elements and order transform accordingly in the sense that

$$Elt(Q\mathbf{I}) = QElt(\mathbf{I}) \tag{12.10}$$

and

$$\sqsubseteq_{QI} = \sqsubseteq_I. \tag{12.11}$$

It is not hard to verify information systems are frame indifferent in this sense.

Requiring invariance of information system consistency and entailment relations, in the sense of $QCon = Con$ and $\vdash_Q = \vdash$, proves much too strong a requirement on logical kinematic structure. One can easily see that not all information systems exhibit such invariance. For example, if one has $\{e\} \vdash e'$ and $\{e'\} \not\vdash e$, an isometry that simply swaps e and e' would have the result that $\{\phi(e')\} \vdash \phi(e)$.

Invariance of consistency under changes of frame means that all sets are consistent. Invariance of entailment under changes of frame means that any nontrivial entailment must mean universal entailment, in the sense that if $X \vdash e$ for some $e \notin X$, then frame invariance requires that $X \vdash e'$ for every $e' \in \mathcal{D}$. This means there are just two frame-invariant information systems. In one, sets entail only their own members, and the elements of the information system consist of all subsets of $\mathcal{D}$. In the other, each set entails all of $\mathcal{D}$, so the only element of the information system is $\mathcal{D}$ itself.

These observations highlight the representational nature of logical structure. Information systems and traditional logics directly characterize the structure of representations. Indeed, a prime application of information structures is in characterizing data structures, computational representations *par excellence*.

Information systems do not, however, characterize directly the information represented by their elements. Such information content instead appears as the subject of information theory. Indeed, information measures in information theory take the same form as theories of mass, exhibiting the same sort of frame invariance as that seen in the mass measures of traditional nonrelativistic mechanics. Information content in discrete mechanics differs from this traditional setting in having different, noncomparable dimensions of mass. In the discrete setting, frame indifference requires that mass transforms as a vector instead of as a scalar. With these distinctions, one can regard information theory as a theory of computation based on frame-invariant algorithms specified in terms of information and information-determined operations on information rather than on data structures.

One can use information systems to study structures independent of representational details by identifying information systems with isomorphic sets of elements. That is, one regards $\mathbf{I}$ over $\mathcal{D}$ equivalent to $\mathbf{I}'$ over $\mathcal{D}'$ just in case the ordered sets $(Elt(\mathbf{I}), \sqsubseteq_{\mathbf{I}})$ and $(Elt(\mathbf{I}'), \sqsubseteq_{\mathbf{I}'})$ are isomorphic. Each equivalence class of information systems then characterizes a certain type of data or structure independent of the representational details inherent in the underlying sets of atomic propositions.

12.2.3 Admissible positions

One can use information systems to state useful constitutive kinematic assumptions about the positions a body can occupy. The idea here is that instead of taking S to be isomorphic to $\mathbb{D}$, one instead requires that positions be elements or total elements of an information system; that is, $S \subseteq Elt(\mathbf{I})$ or $S \subseteq Elt^+(\mathbf{I})$.

When using such assumptions to characterize the constitutive intelligence of a type of agent, one varies the assumed level of inherent intelligence by varying the strength of the constitutive consistency and closure relations. If one takes trivial consistency and closure relations, the information system places no general restriction on positions, and every set of elements is acceptable. If one takes full logical consistency and implication, the information system places strong conditions on positions. Suitable intermediate relations can express restrictions to subspaces that contain or avoid certain combinations of attitudes, or that always recognize certain obvious or easy inferences and inconsistencies.

12.3 Rational motives

Rational behavior optimizes one's pursuit of one's desires, or put in the formalism of mathematical economics, maximization of one's expected utility. Understanding rationality in mechanical terms thus means understanding how the underlying motivations and character of the agent shape the generation of forces, understanding how the generated forces shape optimization of expectations, and understanding how limitations on these forces shape limitations on the degree of rationality exhibited by an agent.

12.3.1 Motivational forces

In psychology, motivation consists of those forces an agent exerts on itself. Although we sometimes speak of external things as exerting attractions—a person, a bottle, an unopened letter, a possible promotion—outside of fiction such locutions usually mean that a mental event, such as sight of the object or thought about the condition, generates a force that shapes the agent's subsequent actions. In seeking to understand these forces, psychology studies a variety of motivations as grounds for or impetus to action, including forms of desire, likes, dislikes, will, and intention. We regard all these different concepts as playing special roles in mental dynamogenesis.

Motivational self-forces take exactly the same form as external forces. The main difference comes in the classification of self-forces as body or contact

forces. Classifying external forces as body or contact usually poses few difficulties, but to classify self-forces in this way requires knowledge of the structure of the agent. If one part of the mind battles with another for control of the
agent's attention, we might consider these forces to be contact forces joined in
a working memory that serves as the boundary of the two parts, but such an interpretation seems less well suited to the attractions generated by true love. Although the distinction between body and contact force might prove significant
in understanding some aspects of attention and volition, let us focus instead on
the origins and roles of motivational forces.

12.3.2 Motivational character

Many aspects of personal character in psychology and legal, organizational,
or economic character in economics relate as much to dynamogenesis as to
structural properties. Personal character, whether the character of a specific
individual or the character of a personality type, provides the structure of underlying motivations and behavior, as distinguished from the instantaneous impulses and thoughts of the person. In particular, personal character shapes the
response of the person to different forces or burdens. Variation of response to
the same mechanical loads provides a clear separation between material types
in traditional mechanics. Consider, for example, placing an anvil on the surface of a flagstone, on the surface of a trampoline, and on the surface of a lake.
Even in economics, where attention lies more on structural aspects of multi-
agent systems, we can distinguish different types of economic character that
reflect organizational goals, such as missions or profit maximization, and behavioral rules, such as negotiation and communication protocols, social norms,
or legal constitutions.

Although mechanics distinguishes laws that relate forces existing at an instant to motion at that instant from dynamogenetic characteristics of materials
that give rise to the instantaneous forces, psychology does less well at making
this distinction clear in language. For example, terms like *desire* and *moti-*
vation can refer to specific temporal attitudes and sentiments that act at some
instant as well as to underlying desires and motivations that persist and on oc-
casion give rise to specific temporal manifestations. In the mechanical view,
we interpret desires both as forces and as generators of forces. We interpret
individual desires active at particular instants as particular forces acting on or
within the agent, and desires more generally as mental elements participating
in the genesis of particular forces. The more general type of desire or motivation represents a part of the mass of the agent, an aspect of the agent's character
or constitution, or both.

12.3.3 Utility gradient forces

Psychology and economics have made some attempts to regard decision making and motivation in terms of the field viewpoint that has proven so useful in physics. The force fields of physics include attractive and repulsive forces in which the variation of force with position is expressible in terms of the gradient of a scalar potential field. For example, the electromagnetic potential field is formed by summing the contributions of positively and negatively charged bodies distributed in space, and the gravitational field is obtained by summing the fields generated by masses distributed in space.

The primary use of field theory in psychology and economics has been to regard preference, supply, and demand information as generating a utility field over decision outcomes. The optimization characteristic of rational agents then corresponds to the generation of gradient forces from this utility field or from its expectation transform. These gradients of the utility surface indicate directions of attractions to local maxima and repulsions from local minima. Numerous "hill-climbing" economic optimization methods follow these local gradients to find local maxima or minima. Stochastic variations on these methods seek to find global maxima or minima. Prominent market-equilibration mechanisms, such as Walrasian iteration, also use these local gradients to guide market participants toward prices that balance supply and demand for all goods (Wellman 1993; Cheng & Wellman 1998).

Field methods are used in these economic applications not because people believe the fields are describing some natural phenomena, but because of the wealth of mathematical and computational techniques developed by mathematicians for using them. These techniques support numerous methods of economic analysis that borrows concepts and tools from mathematical physics (Arrow & Hahn 1971; Cass & Shell 1976; Samuelson 1971; Smale 1980). However, as noted in Chapter 3, when one looks at the scientific content of the applications of field ideas, one can find them lacking (Mirowski 1989). In particular, applications of field theories in economics suffer from both superficiality and complexity compared with physical fields.

The field-theoretic treatment of utility exhibits a certain simplicity compared with physics because it reduces all psychological motivations to the preferences they entail concerning possible choices made by the agent, in contrast to the multiplicity of physical forces and constraints. The utility function thus acts as a sort of "unified field" description for agent behavior. But the utility function does not constitute what physics would call a "unified field theory," namely a theory that explains a range of formerly disassociated phenomena. Instead, the utility function superficially combines the underlying motivations in such a way that although one can determine overall behavior, one cannot easily recover the underlying motivations from this overall behavior. Rather than explaining numerous phenomena, utility fields obscure them. A true understanding of psychology and mental action thus cannot rest content with the simplified framework adopted by economics. It instead must probe deeper to find the underlying motivations that shape the utility surface, or that perhaps even deny the applicability of the economic assumptions.

In addition, the utility fields corresponding to familiar human or ideal behavior exhibit structures that do not fit well with generation of utility from simple charges. For example, economic preferences often exhibit complementarity, in which the decision maker values some combination of items highly but attaches no value to proper subsets. The soldier has no use for bullets without guns; the skydiver has no use for the parachute without the aircraft; the teenager has no use for fashionable clothes without somewhere to go in them. One thus cannot represent desires for the component elements of a set with utility-generating charges, for complementarity denies the superposition principle for such component desires. If one is to represent such common preferences as charges, the fields these charges generate have to vary nonlinearly with the presence or absence of other charges, as in the forces produced by reasons treated in Chapter 11. For another example, consider the ordered rules of logic programs and the ordered hierarchy of behaviors in robotic subsumption architectures. Regarded as charges, one of these rules or behaviors generates a nonzero force only if all higher-ranked rules or behaviors generate null forces. One can expect combinations of motivations and preferences to exhibit all the structures seen in other forms of knowledge, with conditionality, nonmonotonicity, abstraction hierarchies, and exception hierarchies (Russell & Norvig 2002). Each of these structural characteristics goes against the simple additivity of physical charge theories.

On the other hand, decision analysts commonly seek to construct utility functions out of linearly weighted combinations of single-attribute subutility functions. Such linear-additive utility functions admit a simple interpretation as the result of charges, with the linear subutility functions corresponding to functions that give the variation of the strength of the field resulting from a charge with "distances" of the decision point to the charge. In the simplest models, the component fields vary linearly with the distance. Despite the convenience of such models, one cannot expect that one can always find dimensions that give any realistic utility function with this linear structure, or that the linearizing dimensions remain fixed as preferences change. The nonlinear models of artificial intelligence make one dubious that linear models always exist, and the experience of artificial intelligence with constructing such models automatically makes one hesitant to think one can always construct the models with reasonable effort.

These doubts about the linearity of utility fields notwithstanding, one can consider reasonable interpretations of charge-generated utility fields as long as one is willing to admit nonlinear interactions between charges. To do this, one looks to goal-based representations of preference information studied in artificial intelligence (Wellman & Doyle 1991; Doyle, Shoham, & Wellman 1991; Doyle & Thomason 1999; Doyle 2004). In this framework, one interprets qualitative goals as positive or negative charges, and one interprets trade-off preferences as expressing interactions among these charges.

Problem-solving goals constitute the most familiar class of sources of attractive and repulsive forces. The representation of a goal usually identifies a list of one or more conditions or attributes required to satisfy the goal, and one identifies solutions by a successful match of the goal characteristics with the solution characteristics. If we use points in $\mathbb{D}$ to represent both goal conditions and current circumstances, we can then get different match conceptions by means of different inner products on $\mathbb{D}$. A perfect match produces the norm of the goal vector as the result of the inner product of the goal vector with the situational vector. The inner product decreases in magnitude with each unsatisfied goal, and so indicates the need for further work to solve the problem. One can interpret numerical inner products as distances of the current situation from the desired one. One can interpret set-valued inner products that produce the set of satisfied or unsatisfied goals as the sort of goal-matching measures introduced in GPS (Newell, Shaw, & Simon 1960). A wide variety of problem-solving techniques use the unmatched difference itself to guide the problem solution.

Without trade-off preferences, one can form a utility function by means of the inner product of goals with situation. In any realistic application, however, one must add preferences expressing trade-offs among partial satisfactions. Tradeoff preferences of the sort seen in logics of preference *ceteris paribus* (Wellman & Doyle 1991; Doyle, Shoham, & Wellman 1991) modify the simple distance measures by taking complex configuration conditions into account.

12.3.4 Cognitive forces

Some applications of field concepts in psychology have started with more substantive notions than the generic utility conception of economics. As noted earlier, Shand (1920) characterizes many types of emotions and sentiments in terms of particular patterns of forces acting to increase certain types of order in mental states. From his perspective, one might think of each distinct type of attitude, emotion, or sentiment—desires, likes, dislikes, fears, hates, unease, and so on—as representing a different type of charge, each generating a different characteristic field of position-dependent attractive and repulsive forces. These forces might still be used to construct a utility function, but the utility function then represents the strength of desires or motivation traceable to the specific attitudes generating it.

This perspective has something in common with the goal-preference utility decomposition just discussed, and recognizes the existence of noncognitive motivations underlying human behavior. The main departure from simple goal-based utility is that each desire or other motive might itself involve a multidimensional evaluation of the situation or of specific objects. As with the goal-preference decomposition, one expects to see numerous nonlinear interactions between these different types of forces.

The slower-changing intentions and plans that humans and artificial agents use to mediate action represent the most visible departure from linear force generation. Beliefs and desires guide decisions to adopt or abandon intentions, and these intentions persist until the agent acts on them or makes further decisions that change them. Will or intention exhibits similarities to motivation or desire in that we also naturally view intentions as having direction in exactly the same way that we understand the directionality of desire.

Intention and desire differ, however, in that the notion of strength of desire has no natural correspondent in intention. The relative strengths of conflicting desires constrain which one produces action. Intentions, in principle, should not exhibit explicit conflicts with each other, and so do not carry a notion of relative strength in the same sense as desires. Instead, one must address conflicts among intentions by giving up at least one of the intentions in order to achieve consistency. Seriality conflicts, conflicts about what to do first, are resolved by temporarily releasing the claim of one intention on immediate action. Strength of intention in this sense thus corresponds to priority of intention. Logical conflicts, conflicts about whether to achieve some end or not, are resolved by abandoning one of the conflicting intentions. Strength of intention in this sense thus corresponds to firmness or entrenchment of the intention, to the order in which one abandons intentions when forced to by circumstances. Many things might enter into determining the firmness of some intention. Firm intentions are ones held in spite of changes of desires or external circumstances that now make other actions more desirable. The firmest intentions are those that persist despite failures experienced in trying to carrying them out in the face of active opposition. Weakness of will manifests in abandoning intentions when desires change, or in hesitation that postpones attempts to carry out intentions when uncertainty grows.

Firmness and entrenchment correspond to a notion of persistence not associated with desires. No one judges an agent badly for strongly desiring something at one instant and then having no desire for it at the next instant. The notion of intention, in contrast, brings with it a notion of commitment that requires progressive changes to intentions rather than arbitrary fluctuations.

12.3.5 Habit

Like intentions, habits constitute persistent generators of forces. Where intentions form considered constraints that generate persistent forces maintaining or achieving some condition, habits generate instantaneous forces that shape mental motion along well-worn pathways. As Hobbes (1656) put it, "Habit is motion made more easy and ready by custom." Indeed, common expressions refer to the "force of habit" and "force of will."

The simplest sort of habit of reasoning consists of persistent attitudes. Because we take the outlook or point of view of the agent to include its mental attitudes, we regard persistent attitudes as habits that continually reproduce their own content in the agent's outlook. Put another way, a habitual belief in memory causes a belief of the same content to appear in the outlook, either at all instants or whenever needed. In the mechanical setting, this means that a persistent belief occurring in the mass produces the same belief in the position.

Slightly more complex but still simple habits of reasoning consist of reasoning rules that produce new conclusions from antecedents, as were examined in Chapter 11. In this case, though, we can still regard the habit as reproducing its content in the outlook, but the more interesting product consists of the conclusions, if any, generated by applying the rule. In this sense, habits of reasoning constitute automatically operating rules that produce changes of outlook.

We can distinguish rules in memory that produce conclusions automatically from those that produce conclusions only when consciously applied. The former constitute habits of reasoning; the latter conscious rules of reasoning. Of course, we do not distinguish these two types of rules by their "logical" content. Habitual and consciously applied rules might have exactly the same productive content, the same antecedents producing the same consequents. We instead distinguish them by their role in mental operations. The habitual rules produce new or changed conclusions whenever their antecedent or triggering conditions are satisfied, while conscious rules produce no new conclusions on their own, but only after conscious decisions on the part of the reasoner to perform the reasoning indicated by the rules. Indeed, one way of learning a habitual rule of some form is to practice a conscious inference rule of the same form.

Habits operate unconsciously and without volition even when the agent consciously recognizes their existence and action. Such unconscious and automatic action contrasts with volition, in which some amount of conscious deliberation usually occurs in choosing actions. Indeed, the effective agent will need to acknowledge and expect habitual behavior, because habitual behavior, operating unthinkingly and independently of current beliefs and desires, can result in the agent's taking certain actions contrary to conscious desires and intentions, actions the agent judges irrational immediately afterward. Going against habit requires force, to counteract the forces exerted by habit.

Lack of desire as well as lack of consciousness can distinguish habit from volition. Many habits form through repeated action in line with the agent's desires and intentions. We can thus consider some habitual action as action motivated by past desires, although habits can produce action even when the present desires provide no motivation for the action.

Habit and volition also differ in the degree of persistence they exhibit. We regard habits as part of long-term memory that persist across episodic actions and changes of situation, so that changing habits requires force. Volition, in contrast, produces intentions and actions that typically remain operational only through present or near-term episodes of actions. Indeed, as every parent knows or quickly learns, a standard means of defeating someone's intention is to distract the person in hopes that during pursuit of the distraction the person will forget his or her intention before committing it to memory.

These typical differences do not constitute necessary differences, however, and the distinction between habit and volition is not sharp. As considered here, anything a habit can do can also be done by volition. More to the point, many of the steps occurring within the operation of ordinary volition can occur through the action of habit. Indeed, some efforts in artificial intelligence seek to reduce volition to combinations of mental habits that characterize particular patterns of thought and action.

12.3.6 Refraction and elastic forces

In an elastic material, deformation from a relaxed configuration generates a restorative force. Hooke's law, for example, says that a spring exhibits a linear elastic response under small deformations, with the restorative force proportional in magnitude to the size of the deformation, to the distance the spring is compressed or stretched. Most realistic elastic materials exhibit forces that vary nonlinearly with the deformation, and exhibit an elastic response that varies from material to material.

Characterizing some force as elastic does not say how it arises, only that it varies with the deformation from a "relaxed" configuration. Because elasticity depends only on material behavior, not on material identity, we can interpret some forms of both intentional and unintentional psychological behavior as exhibiting an elastic character. In particular, we might think refractory forces arising both through the action of habits and through deliberate thought as elastic forces. Human refraction involves habitual or active resistance to imposed change that seeks to nullify the imposition and, in willful behavior, maintain or even strengthen current attitudes and activities.

Refraction can also represent the obverse of conscious efforts to focus reasoning on a goal. As was discussed earlier in the context of focus of attention, this deliberate form of elasticity arises when the agent generates and applies forces to maintain focus by counterbalancing the forces of distraction, leaving only forces in the intended direction. In such cases, the intended properties or direction of motion constitutes the zero-point of the elastic response.

In planning, for example, an agent might expend significant effort to enforce the consistency and completeness of the intentions that make up its plans, or to enforce some other relation of mutual coherence or compatibility among its attitudes. In such a setting, removal of some intention might only remove the plan step temporarily, until the agent reconstructs the step to restore the expected degree of coherence in its plan. Similarly, if new information undermines the motivations for some intentions or portions of plans, the agent might choose to reconsider these. This character of a responsible planner is similar to the restoration of RMS conclusions, and quite reasonably in light of the underlying interpretation of RMS reasons as intentions to draw specific conclusions in specific circumstances. With intentions generating forces, these intentions to restore coherence represent forces the agent generates on itself to counteract certain types of external forces. Finally, if new stimuli motivate new plans that threaten to draw attention from primary concerns, the agent might choose to temporarily defeat or postpone the new plans to keep action focused on the primary concerns.

More generally, one might interpret many forms of negative feedback in terms of elastic response. Many simple control systems employ negative linear feedback modeled directly on Hookean elasticity.

Refraction also can include habits that act to maintain habitual positions or behaviors. Some habits, for example, might undercut or repress discomforting thoughts, or might act to infer or reintroduce desired or obsessive thoughts. One can see action of this character in the RMS, in which an attempt to change position by defeating a reason for some attitude can fail if some other reason represents an uncountered habit that offers alternative support.

"Good" habits can further the progress of intentional actions; "bad" habits can impede such progress. As everyone knows who has fought bad habits, these habits tend to generate fixed desires seemingly independent of intentional consideration, desires that can undermine resultant forces in a way that creates weakness of will or backsliding. But application of course-correcting forces to counteract these habitual forces does real work, accounting for the effort so familiar in maintaining resolve, and for some of the difficulty in continuing the expenditure of this effort. Because habits tend to restore distractions over and over, seeking to maintain a course of action in spite of recurring habitual distractions involves a great deal of work. When strong desires or fears threaten to undermine the ability to act on intentions, the agent might choose to set up additional intentions as backups or to take preliminary actions to shape the circumstances in ways that prevent backsliding or weakness of will (Elster 1979).

Perhaps understandably, the philosophical tradition of studying rationality in thought and action has devoted little attention to the nature of active stubbornness or refraction. Examples include Shand's (1920) discussion of reactions generated by various circumstances in agents of different mental character, and Minsky's (1986) discussion of active conflicts among mental subagencies. One cannot avoid refraction in seeking to understand rational behavior, however. Efficiency in action demands that much behavior be habitual rather than deliberate. The problem of refraction arises because good habits can easily turn bad when the circumstances of action change.

The notion of elastic response depends on a notion of baseline state from which one measures elastic deformations. Mechanics calls these states *relaxed states*, and assumes that simple materials placed in a certain shape move toward and eventually reach a relaxed state.

Computational theories of mind involve a variety of equilibrium notions we can regard as relaxed states of the agent, most notably the states representing closure of mental attitudes with respect to sets of inference rules, a topic I return to in the next chapter. In forward chaining inference systems, for example, the reasoner applies every applicable inference rule each time one adds new axioms, and continues this process as inference rules add new conclusions, stopping only when all applicable rules have been applied, at which point we say the reasoner has reached a state of closure or quiescence. From the mechanical perspective, we regard new information obtained by the reasoner as a new boundary condition that triggers motion to a new relaxed state. We can think of such boundary conditions as expanding or stretching the shape of the mental body, necessitating a period of reequilibration.

Plastic deformation occurs when the deformation moves the "set-point" state to a different relaxed state than existed prior to the deformation. One might regard adoption of new intentions in action as effecting such deformations.

12.3.7 Conceptual forces

For the first half of the journey, from Krementchug to Kiev, all Rostov's thoughts—as is apt to be the case with travellers—turned to what he had left behind—to his squadron. But after being jolted over the first half of the journey, he had begun to forget his three roans and his quartermaster, Dozhoyveyky, and was beginning to wonder uneasily what he should find on reaching Otradnoe. The nearer he got, the more intense, far more intense, were his thoughts of home (as though moral feeling were subject to the law of acceleration in inverse ratio with the square of the distance). At the station nearest to Otradnoe he gave the sledge-driver a tip of three roubles, and ran breathless up the steps of his home, like a boy. (L. Tolstoy 1869, Pt. 7, Ch. 1)

One also finds several psychological subjects concerned with what one might regard as mutual attractive forces. As noted earlier, Herbart (1891) regarded mental concepts as exerting "forces" on each other. Some of the similarity-based and density-based clustering methods of machine learning represent modern ideas related to such conceptual forces.

For example, one class of density-based clustering methods pretends that each item in a set of numeric-attribute data generates a symmetric single-peaked potential field, for example, in Gaussian shape. One then sums the fields from all data items, applies a threshold, and interprets the regions of the attribute space exceeding the threshold value as clusters of data points. One might regard this as having these data density fields acting on one's notion of the cluster centers.

Another important class of clustering methods relies on similarity measures. Some similarity-based learning methods compute inner products of the attribute vector of a data item with the attribute vector of prototypes to classify the data item according to its "cosine" similarity with different prototypes. When classifying new data items with respect to a known set of clusters, one uses the inner product in a one-sided manner by finding the prototype most similar to the data item and assigning the data item to that prototype's cluster. When analyzing a new data set to choose a set of prototypes representing clusters, one instead uses the inner product in a two-sided manner by clumping together similar data items in a symmetric fashion.

One can treat desires for objects in a way related to the similarity-based clustering methods by thinking of a desire as specified by some vector of binary attributes characterizing the objects of desire and so specifying the direction of the force of desire, so that each different object of desire corresponds to a different direction in attribute space, and the direction corresponding to compound objects represents the sum or combination of the directions corresponding to its elements. We then obtain a degree of desire for some object by considering the match between the vector of desired attributes with the vector of attributes characterizing the object.

The attribute-vector formulation of desire does not easily capture the full range of underlying attitudes and sentiments. It does not even capture all the expressions of preference and relative desire, which in more general cases require interpreting desires in terms of regions in attribute space rather than as mere directions or hyperplanes. We have already seen such nonlinearity in the reason forces detailed earlier, which generate zero force in one range of positions and generate a nonzero force elsewhere.

One might also regard some forms of decision making as involving mutual attraction expressible in related forms. Consider Festinger's (1957) notion of cognitive dissonance, in which the holder of clearly conflicting points of view on some matter experiences pressure to resolve the conflict. Although the simplest means for conflict resolution is to abandon one of the points of view in favor of the other, one might also consider consensus formation as a process of mutual attraction by the different sides, in which the similarity measures indicate the strength and direction of force pulling each point of view toward the other.

13

Learning

While reasoning can produce temporary changes of location, learning produces persistent changes of mass or configuration. When someone temporarily responds to instruction or threat but then reverts to an old behavior when the teacher or threat departs, we say that person did not learn anything. Mechanically, we would identify such response with an elastic material that rebounds on relief from compression, but such elastic behavior does not produce the permanent changes we associate with thought. True learning, involving change of mass or deformation of spatial configuration, constitutes plastic changes in the character of the material, including dynamogenetic changes that affect material response. In this chapter, let us consider learning involving changes of habits represented in the mass and changes of configuration represented in position. We distinguish types of reasoning and learning both by the types of changes involved and by the types of forces producing the change.

13.1 Accretion

The simplest sort of changes to memory just add new elements to the long-term memory represented by the mass of the agent. Such accretion also represents the effects of the most common sort of inference and learning mechanisms.

Many psychological theories view learning as transfer of information from short-term memory to long-term memory. Different theories of learning posit different means for effecting this transfer. Some theories require transfer to long-term memory of some beliefs in short-term memory simply because they persist long enough in short-term memory. We might regard each of these forms of learning as occurring through the generation of forces in which some event, such presence of a belief in certain circumstances, or presence after passing a certain length of time, generates a force adding that element of position to the mass.

326

The chunking mechanism of Soar (Laird, Newell, & Rosenbloom 1987), for example, creates a new rule or habit every time the reasoner solves a problem or subproblem. This new rule encapsulates the essential elements of the solution in a form independent of the context of the solution, in a manner patterned after the fundamental deduction theorem of logic. The solution justifications typical of problem solving in AMORD (de Kleer *et al.* 1977) constitute propositional instances of the sorts of rules created by Soar's chunking mechanism. The conditional-proof justifications of the RMS (Doyle 1979) instruct it to learn new simple justifications in much the same way, adding new simple justifications as the RMS passes through different positions that reveal them to exemplify the conditional-proof justifications. All of these are instances of learning mechanisms that take short-term beliefs or other attitudes involved in certain forms of reasoning and transfer them to long-term memory.

Once transferred to memory, rules or beliefs represent new habits of reasoning. We note that creating such habits requires effort, namely the effort needed to rehearse or maintain the habitual behavior long enough to trigger or enable the transfer process. Breaking habits also requires effort, of the sort needed to counteract or disrupt the forces produced by the habits being undermined.

13.2 Stretching

Accretive learning operating in isolation can take the agent through a nonrigid motion. Traditional designs for automated agents have the agent thinking for some period of time in between the instants at which percepts provide new information. During this interval, deduction or other inferential processes derive new or additional conclusions from existing beliefs or other attitudes. In such a process, the perceptual organs stay in a fixed position, while the mental interior first acquires the new percept from the perceptual bodies, then performs reasoning, and so shifts position accordingly. One can thus think of this sort of reasoning as producing a stretching of the mental configuration, with the reasoning conducted between perceptual events modifying the distances between perceptual organs and the mental interior.

Simple accumulation of conclusions represents an atypical form of learning, especially because reasoning is commonly nonmonotonic, not merely deductive. Other forms of learning involve nonadditive changes that exemplify more interesting kinds of stretching of mental configuration.

We see the deformation character of learning in a more specific way by considering kernel learning methods, such as support-vector machines (SVMs) (Burges 1998; Müller *et al.* 2001).

Recall that Noll (1973) identifies spatial configurations with body metrics that specify the sets of distances between each pair of body points in the configuration. One can represent a body metric κ by a symmetric matrix with zero diagonals, in which the $\kappa_{i,j}$ entry gives the distance between body points b_i and b_j.

The same sorts of distance metrics appear in SVM theory as the Gram matrices of the data set. These learning methods implicitly develop nonlinear separation boundaries between classes of data, and encapsulate the emerging geometry of the data examined so far by matrices that give the distances separating each pair of data points. As sketched in Section 2.2.3.1, from the mechanical point of view kernel machines deform the initial geometry of the data so that distinct classes admit separating hyperplanes or approximately separating hyperplanes.

One finds a common manifestation of deliberate plasticity in familiar learning and exercise stratagems, in which the learner pushes beyond current abilities in order to expand those abilities and come to rest at some new equilibrium point beyond the current frontier. Some negotiation protocols exploit a similar form of plasticity, making knowingly unacceptable demands or bids intended to reset the expectations and appetites of other participants. Each of these forms of learning work against a natural elasticity or refractory nature by seeking to bend the material until it breaks, or undergoes a plastic transformation to a new relaxed state different than was possible before.

13.3 Shearing

The stretching induced by SVM learning methods to reflect separation between distinct concepts or behaviors represents just one of the sorts of division induced by learning and reasoning. The more familiar division reflects the distinction between the intended and unintended effects of actions, which we might interpret in terms of shear forces that move one part of the body relative to the rest.

13.3.1 Intentions and differential effects

Much reasoning and some learning happen as the result of deliberate action, action that aims to effect specific changes in mental state. For example, deliberate reasoning seeks to obtain specific conclusions; deliberate external action seeks to achieve specific effects in the environment; and deliberate learning seeks to discover specific new information or inculcate specific new habits.

Intentions thus divide the changes involved in reasoning and learning into the intentional changes and the unintentional changes or side effects. To a first approximation, we think of the intentional changes as the aims of the action and the unintentional changes as the additional adaptation needed to effect the intentional changes. Action thus seeks to achieve specific aims independent of other changes.

An agent typically only knows a portion of the direction of its intended motion, namely the intended effects. The actual motion will involve some combination of intended and unintended effects due to environmental or configurational constraints. In mechanical terms, we regard intentional self-change as shearing the body, moving a portion to a new configuration in the intended direction while leaving the rest of the configuration intact. The intentionality of action thus corresponds not to a full force, but to a partial force that indicates changes along only some of the dimensions of $\mathbb{D}$. The total force is determined from the partial shearing forces together with the constitutive forces shaping adaptation, such as conservative update or relaxation. In contrast to the intentionality of the intended aims, this adaptation lacks specific aims and instead works to minimize changes or discrepancies independent of the action causing them. This distinction blurs a bit if we consider actions intended to adapt the body to specific conditions.

13.3.2 Conservative response

The most common property exhibited by mental deformation appears in the typical and habitual conservatism of human thought when the agent adopts or abandons elements of mental states. Accommodating a new conclusion can require abandoning a prior assumption; adding a new habit can demand replacing or modifying another. The typical change of memory or outlook therefore involves several separate changes rather than a single change. We regard these secondary or consequential changes as adaptation of the state of the agent to the required changes.

One sees adaptation vividly in theories of belief revision. Most theoretical prescriptions in philosophy (see especially Quine & Ullian 1978, Harman 1986, Gärdenfors 1988) and actual practice in artificial intelligence restrict the admissible changes of state to ones that keep as much of the previous state of belief as possible. For example, in addition to the STRIPS assumption, each of the backtracking procedures used in artificial intelligence represents some notion of minimal revisions. In "chronological" backtracking, the agent keeps all beliefs except the ones most recently added. "Nonchronological" or "dependency-directed" backtracking is even more conservative, abandoning as small a set of beliefs as possible regardless of the order in which they were adopted. For instance, the DDB procedure (Doyle 1979) for dependency-directed backtracking minimizes the changes by abandoning only "maximal assumptions." Indeed, conservatism appears in the action of the RMS even without backtracking, for when new information defeats prior conclusions, the RMS seeks a new state satisfying constitutional consistency, completeness, and grounding requirements but standing as close as possible to the previous state. Conservatism figures similarly in studies of updates in databases (Fagin, Ullman, & Vardi 1983).

Conservatism also plays a role in some forms of deliberate learning. For example, analogies and metaphors are often very useful in problem solving and learning. While all forms of learning call for the reasoner to adapt explanations, hypotheses, and theories to new information, in using analogies and metaphors the reasoner deforms one explanation or concept into another and judges the aptness of different deformations according to how mildly or greatly they torture the original (Carbonell 1986). Finding the mildest deformation is just another version of conservatism in reasoning.

Conservative update also plays a central role in some economic theories of adaptation. Schumpeter's (1934) theories make destruction of outmoded hand-me-down habits and practices a key to economic progress. One finds similar concerns in Nelson and Winter's (1982) evolutionary theory of economic processes, in Elster's (1979) theories of rational change, and in Leibenstein's (1980) theory of X-efficiency, in which updates retain outdated habits after the reasons motivating their adoption disappear.

Section 7.4 characterized conservative revision in terms of a distance notion for mental states, or more generally a comparative similarity relation that embodies a preorder on state transitions. Even a weak comparison suffices to identify the minimal changes that include the intended changes while satisfying constitutional requirements. Indeed, several theories of belief revision employ a notion of "epistemic entrenchment" (Gärdenfors & Makinson 1988) to formalize the sorts of minimum-change revision principles just discussed. The idea is to order beliefs by degree of entrenchment, so that when the agent removes beliefs to retain consistency, it removes the least entrenched beliefs first. Similar notions apply to changes to preferences and other mental qualities as well (Doyle 1990b).

13.4 Configurational intentions

In contrast to physical materials, which exhibit behavior but do not choose their own behavior, minds exhibit both inherent and chosen behavior. A physical material exhibits the same behavior as long as it exists, with a set pattern of variation across temperature, pressure, and other physical conditions. A mind can bind itself to new patterns by means of its intentions. Although an agent adopts many intentions concerning actions it will perform, some intentions it adopts concern properties of the agent itself. Indeed, one can view a large portion of thinking as a process of *self-specification* and *self-construction* by means of such self-regarding intentions (Doyle 1980, 1982a, 1990a).

The following section treats such self-regarding intentions as intentions that express restrictions on the configuration of the reasoner. Thus, we can regard such intentions as expressing learnable and revisable constitutive assumptions (Doyle 1983e, 1983a, 1988a). The following treatment paraphrases that of Doyle (1994).

13.4.1 Self-specifications

We regard self-specifications as mental attitudes in $\mathcal{D}$, as we do with other kinds of intentions. We interpret these intentions as identifying a set of acceptable positions or mass values represented by admissible subsets of $\mathcal{D}$. Formally, we assume a *meaning function* $[\![\ ]\!] : \mathcal{D} \to \mathcal{P}(\mathcal{P}(\mathcal{D}))$, or in positional language, $[\![\ ]\!] : \mathcal{D} \to \mathcal{P}(\mathbb{D})$, interpreted so that the meaning $[\![e]\!]$ of an element e consists of the set of possible states that satisfy the constitutive intent, if any, of the element. We assume the meaning function applies to all elements of $\mathcal{D}$, by taking $[\![e]\!] = \mathcal{P}(\mathcal{D}) = \mathbb{D}$ when e has no constitutive import. This meaning places no restrictions on possible states.

Chapter 11 ascribed such meaning to reasons, and noted that they can express nonmonotonic kinematic restrictions not expressible using the consistency and closure notions of ordinary monotonic logic or information systems.

Although we interpret elements of $\mathcal{D}$ as representing (possibly vacuous) self-specifications, the only self-specifications that actually matter in a particular case are the ones the agent actually holds. For an agent to satisfy its own self-specifications, its position need not satisfy all intentions in $\mathcal{D}$, only those self-regarding intentions its current position contains. This was the basis for the notion of satisfying position introduced earlier.

As a formal method, one might apply the idea of self-specification to physical systems as well as to mental systems, for example, regarding bits of rubber as specifying that they themselves obey the laws governing rubber, or regarding each bit of mass as specifying something about the local geometry governing motion in the vicinity of the mass as in general relativity.

13.4.2 Satisfaction systems

I develop the notion of *satisfaction system* as a way of formalizing the notion of configurational self-specification. Satisfaction systems broaden the notion of satisfying position introduced earlier to encompass a wider range of self-specifications not tied to reasons.

Satisfaction of self-specifications means that the configurations inhabited by the agent must satisfy the self-specifications held by the agent. In this way, mental positions themselves set out part of their own constitution. We thus might regard configurational intentions, as well as more the fixed constitutional logics treated in Section 12.2, as fitting Boole's notion of "laws of thought," with state-inspecific restrictions capturing fixed legal constitutions of the agent, and state-specific restrictions capturing variable laws and amendments to the fixed constitution.

Formally, a satisfaction system $\mathbf{S} = (\mathcal{D}, [\![\,]\!])$ over $\mathcal{D}$ consists of $\mathcal{D}$ together with a meaning function $[\![\,]\!] : \mathcal{D} \to \mathcal{P}(\mathcal{P}(\mathcal{D}))$. The *elements* or *satisfying sets* $Sat(\mathbf{S})$ of the satisfaction system consist of those subsets of $\mathcal{D}$ that satisfy the constitutive import of each of the elements they contain. Formally, $X \subseteq \mathcal{D}$ is satisfying just in case $X \in [\![e]\!]$ for each $e \in X$, a condition we can also write as

$$X \in \bigcap_{e \in X} [\![e]\!]. \tag{13.1}$$

We extend the meaning function over elements of $\mathcal{D}$ to a function over subsets of $\mathcal{D}$ by defining $[\![\emptyset]\!] = \mathcal{P}(\mathcal{D})$ and $[\![X]\!] = \bigcap_{e \in X}[\![e]\!]$ for each nonempty $X \subseteq \mathcal{D}$. With this extension, X is satisfying just in case $X \in [\![X]\!]$.

The empty set always satisfies all its elements, meaning that $\emptyset \in Sat(\mathbf{S})$ for every satisfaction system $\mathbf{S}$. Indeed, inadmissibility of $\emptyset$ is essentially the only condition inexpressible by satisfaction systems.

13.4.3 Locality

Practical satisfaction systems do not involve arbitrarily complicated relations between elements of $\mathcal{D}$, but instead concern only local conditions on finite portions of states, even when the states themselves might be infinite, corresponding to the compactness properties exhibited by many traditional logical systems. We define an analogous notion of compactness for satisfaction systems as follows.

If $G \subseteq \mathcal{D}$, we write $\pi_G : \mathcal{P}(\mathcal{D}) \to \mathcal{P}(G)$ to denote both the natural projection function of subsets of $\mathcal{D}$ onto subsets of G and its lifting to sets of subsets, so that $\pi_G(X) = X \cap G$. We say that $[\![e]\!]$ has *basis* $G \subseteq \mathcal{D}$ just in case $S \in [\![e]\!]$

iff $\pi_G(S) \in \pi_G(\llbracket e \rrbracket)$ for every $S \subseteq \mathcal{D}$. For example, the meaning given in (11.8) has basis $A \cup B \cup C$. We say that $\llbracket \ \rrbracket$ has basis G iff $\llbracket e \rrbracket$ has basis G for each $e \in \mathcal{D}$, and that a satisfaction system is *compact* iff for each $e \in \mathcal{D}$, whenever $\llbracket e \rrbracket$ has basis G there exists a finite $G' \subseteq G$ such that $\llbracket e \rrbracket$ has basis G'.

Clearly, every meaning has basis $\mathcal{D}$, so every component meaning of a compact satisfaction system has a finite basis. Not all interesting meanings have finite basis; in particular, the meaning $\mathcal{P}(\mathcal{D}) \setminus \{\emptyset\}$ expressing only nonemptiness of states does not have finite basis if $\mathcal{D}$ is infinite. However, the trivial meaning $\mathcal{P}(\mathcal{D})$ has finite (indeed, empty) basis, so the trivial satisfaction system assigning this meaning to each element is compact.

Locality also enters into other computational notions. In artificial neural networks, for example, each artificial neuron has connections to a fixed set of other neurons. One can characterize the equilibrium states of these networks with requirements that the activation level of each neuron matches the appropriate function of the activation levels of its children. We also see locality in cellular automata, which base changes in a cell on the inhabitants of the cells in some diameter-bounded neighborhood. Cellular automata do not typically involve any kinematic constraints, however, so that the locality notion only restricts changes and not the resultant states.

13.4.4 Frame indifference

We say that a satisfaction system is frame indifferent just in case its constituent meanings transform as frame-indifferent relations over $\mathbb{D}$. Formally, for each satisfaction system $\mathbf{S} = (\mathcal{D}, \llbracket \ \rrbracket)$ we define the orthogonally transformed system $\mathbf{QS} = (\mathcal{D}, \llbracket \ \rrbracket_Q)$ so that

$$\llbracket Q(e) \rrbracket_Q = Q(\llbracket e \rrbracket) \tag{13.2}$$

for each $e \in \mathcal{D}$. We say that $\mathbf{S}$ is frame indifferent just in case

$$Sat(\mathbf{S}_Q) = QSat(\mathbf{S}). \tag{13.3}$$

It is not hard to verify that satisfaction systems are frame indifferent in this sense.

Asking that satisfaction relations remain invariant under changes of frame asks too much. Invariance under change of frame would mean that $\llbracket Q(e) \rrbracket = Q(\llbracket e \rrbracket)$ for each $e \in \mathcal{D}$. This can happen only if $\llbracket \ \rrbracket$ is constant, and further, contains only sets invariant under framings. Since the only sets of that kind are $\emptyset$ and $\mathcal{D}$, a meaning function can be invariant under frame changes only if there is some subset X of $\{\emptyset, \mathcal{D}\}$ such that $\llbracket e \rrbracket = X$ for every $e \in \mathcal{D}$.

13.4.5 Constitutive self-specification

Just as we can think of the same logical inference as occurring automatically by virtue of a constitutive logic or deliberately through a process of intentional reasoning, we divide self-specifications into ones fulfilled by virtue of the agent's constitution and ones fulfilled by virtue of the agent's deliberate actions. The self-specifications forming part of the fixed constitution of the agent then define a satisfaction system imposing constraints on mental states at the same level as the constraints imposed by constitutive logics.

In fact, one can use the notion of constitutive self-specification to capture almost every constitutive logic. Given any information system $\mathbf{I}$, one can embed the restriction to elements of the information system within a satisfaction system by replacing each meaning $[\![e]\!]$ by the refined meaning $[\![e]\!] \cap Elt(\mathbf{I})$. For a finite information system, one can achieve the same effect by recasting the finite entailment and minimal inconsistent sets in terms of monotonic reasons and denials. More generally, recalling that satisfaction systems cannot express nonemptiness, one can recover any set $E \subseteq \mathcal{P}(\mathcal{D})$ such that $\emptyset \in E$ by defining $[\![e]\!] = E$ for every $e \in \mathcal{D}$. Simple nonemptiness is not expressible in constitutive logics either, but these can easily require that every state contain some particular element.

13.4.6 Constructive configurations

The kinematic integrity constraints formalized in satisfaction systems can apply to position alone, to mass alone, or to the combination of the two, expressing relationships that must hold between position and mass.

It might seem odd to have configurational connections between mass and position, but these do appear in traditional mechanics. For example, one expects a proper theory of soap bubbles to restrict the configuration of the soapy water to sizes that maintain a minimum density of soapy water. One drop of soapy water cannot form a bubble the size of Texas.

One expects relationships between position and mass to play a larger role in psychology, because of the obvious connections between memory and outlook in familiar psychological organizations.

One can regard some learning mechanisms in terms of constraints that position places on mass. Soar's mechanism of chunking (Laird, Newell, & Rosenbloom 1987), for example, adds element to memory whenever the reasoner adds problem solutions to position. These new memory elements summarize the dependence of the solution on other attitudes. One might try to view learning mechanisms that add long-lived attitudes to memory in the same way, but as discussed earlier, one ordinarily thinks of such transfer mechanisms as relying on persistence in outlook over time rather than involving configurational constraints.

Let us focus here on constructive constraints that require that elements of mental position be grounded in elements of mental mass. This type of constructive relationship is exemplified in the RMS, which requires that conclusions be grounded in the reasons stored in memory.

13.4.6.1 Grounded construction

The constitution of the RMS requires that the state it presents to its environment satisfy its configurational self-specifications. The main RMS conception of satisfaction requires that the position satisfies the meaning of each reason it contains. This amounts to the stability condition that each positive conclusion of every valid reason is *In*. The RMS groundedness configuration condition strengthens this pure satisfaction condition (Doyle 1983e, 1994).

The RMS views groundedness in terms of reasons, and more specifically, in terms of positive conclusions of reasons. This means RMS groundedness does not involve the denial component of interval reasons. Formally, x is a *grounded* position with respect to mass m just in case for each $e \in \mathcal{D}$ we have $e \in x$ iff there is a finite sequence $\langle e_0, \ldots, e_m \rangle$ of *In* elements of x such that $e = e_m$ and for each $i \leq m$, either $e_i \in m$, or there is some $j < i$ such that

(i) $e_j = A \setminus\!\setminus B \mathrel{\|\!\!-} C \setminus\!\setminus D$,
(ii) for each $e' \in A$, $e' = e_k$ for some $k < j$,
(iii) for each $e' \in B$, $e' \notin x$, and
(iv) $e_i \in C$.

The base condition means that every element *In* m is also *In* x.

Putting all these conditions together, we say a position x is a *legal* or *admissible position* of the RMS just in case x consists exactly of the grounded consequences of the reasons m and satisfies the reasons in x. In other words, x is a legal position if the set of *In* items satisfies every reason in x and if every item in x is supported by a noncircular argument from the valid reasons in m. We say the *In* conclusions of a legal position form an *admissible extension* of the mass reasons m, and write $\alpha(m)$ to denote the set of all consistent, closed, and satisfying positions x grounded with respect to m.

The nonmonotonicity of reasons introduces an ambiguity of interpretation familiar from the study of nonmonotonic logics (McDermott & Doyle 1980; Reiter 1980; Marek & Truszczyński 1993), an ambiguity that lets some sets of reasons possess more than one stable grounded labeling, some sets possess exactly one, and some sets none at all. For example, the single nonmonotonic reason

$$\{\emptyset \setminus \{e\} \Vdash \{e\}\} \tag{13.4}$$

supports no admissible extensions, the single nonmonotonic reason

$$\{\emptyset \setminus \emptyset \Vdash \{e\}\} \tag{13.5}$$

supports one, and if $e \neq e'$, the two nonmonotonic reasons

$$\{\ \emptyset \setminus \{e\} \Vdash \{e'\},\ \emptyset \setminus \{e'\} \Vdash \{e\}\ \} \tag{13.6}$$

supports two admissible extensions.

13.4.6.2 Rational construction

The grounded constructions characterizing RMS states also reflect economic structures. As stated earlier, each reason expresses an intention of the reasoner about the structure or degree of coherence of its state, namely that the labeling should satisfy the condition on labelings expressed by the reason. Each reason in addition expresses preferences over possible labelings. For monotonic reasons, these preferences rank all labelings equally. For nonmonotonic reasons, the preferences rank labelings yielding the conclusions over labelings in which defeaters prevent the reason from yielding the conclusions.

Stable grounded labelings exhibit Pareto optimality with respect to these preferences (Doyle 1983e, 1985b, 1988a, 1994). Such labelings satisfy maximal sets of nonmonotonic reasons, so that making some defeated reason undefeated requires defeating some other reason. This means one cannot increase preferability with respect to one reason without decreasing preferability with respect to some other reason, rendering the labeling an equilibrium point of an optimizing process. Indeed, this preferential import of reasons means that a version of Arrow's theorem on the impossibility of rational social choice methods applies to RMS labeling methods as well (Doyle & Wellman 1991).

13.4.6.3 Personal construction

Frankfurt's (1971) theory of personhood takes possession of attitudes toward one's own attitudes as the criterion of personhood. In a sense, self-regarding attitudes delineate the boundary between the person and his or her environment, so that the person determines his or her own identity. One sees evidence for something like this view in reports by survivors of terrible torture or injury, some of whom report separating themselves from the suffering body parts, saying something like "Look at that crushed arm over there. Isn't that curious?"

Constitutive self-specifications serve exactly this purpose, although perhaps on a limited scale. They determine which attitudes are *In* and which are *Out*, terminology that itself suggests a boundary between self and other. More compellingly, self-construction based on nonmonotonic reasons involves a choice of position, with the mind choosing its own contents in accord with its intentions and preferences about its own makeup. This sort of self-construction, and the self-interpretation enabling it, certainly seem to meet the requirements of Frankfurt's personhood criterion.

One therefore might also regard self-construction as involving consciousness or self-consciousness to some extent. The satisfactive and constructive integrity notions represented by self-intentions and self-preferences carry intentionality, with the mind and its constitution as the intentional objects. In ordinary intentions and desires, intentionality involves only pure direction, and no necessary element of consciousness. Self-specifications and constructive attitudes, in addition, involve a notion of self that provides some awareness of self together with awareness of the distinction between self and other. This might legitimate ascription of a type of self-consciousness to agents exhibiting such integrity.

13.5 Relaxation and adaptation

The standard notion of kinematic constraint in mechanics interprets such constraints as properties of the body holding at each instant. Thus a rigid body always has the same form, and an incompressible fluid always has the same volume. Psychology also has need of such invariant constraints, especially in understanding underlying character and architectural features of agents.

The sequential reasoning forces generated by reasons or sets of reasons examined earlier produced direct changes that might not preserve the integrity of the mental state with respect to configurational intentions. What do configurational intentions mean if reasoning need not respect them? To answer this question, we look to the notion of relaxed states from continuum mechanics.

13.5.1 Integral motion

Mechanics uses the notion of relaxed states to characterize a response of adaptation to maintained stresses. Exerting stresses on the surface of a body leads to internal stresses. If one holds the superficial stresses constant, the internal stresses change over time to a stable pattern, that is, a relaxed state of the material.

It seems natural to regard some psychological and economic systems in terms of relaxed states as well, identifying relaxed states with those states that

satisfy all the configurational intentions. We thus view the mind as occupying some relaxed state until some impulse or perception forces transition to a
different relaxed state, with the mind remaining in that new relaxed state until
suffering some further impetus. We think of such transitions among relaxed
states as occurring over time, and involving motion through one or more nonintegral states in the course of the transition.

We call movement from one relaxed state to another *integral motion*. Integral motion of the RMS and other psychological systems represents the point
of view of an observer who only sees the macroscopic integral states and transitions between them, but not any of the microscopic substructure involved in
motion between the integral states.

For example, we view the RMS as computing integral positions that satisfy
satisfaction and grounding conditions. Interactions that add or remove new
reasons to the RMS memory represent impulses that can trigger movement to
a new integral state. When such change is necessary, the RMS computes a
new integral state, but traverses various nonintegral states in the course of unlabeling and relabeling elements. Different implementations involve different
sequences of intermediate states, but all follow this same basic pattern.

The remainder of this section examines the mechanical character of movement between integral states. It focuses on the example of the RMS for concreteness, even though this involves some simplifications one would not expect
in more complicated mechanical systems.

13.5.2 Subintegral motion

Mechanics does not restrict the duration of the relaxation process taking some
perturbed state to a new relaxed state. In some special materials it may reach a
limiting state rapidly, while in others, no finite time suffices to reach a limiting
relaxed state. This variability fits the computational operation of the RMS
well, because the RMS requires a process of indefinite length to find a new
equilibrium state given a change of reasons. Because the integral transitions
can take differing lengths of time to complete, we abstract away the underlying
notion of time to a discrete conception of "integral time" that labels successive
integral states with successive integers, taking each integral transition to last
just one unit of integral time. This corresponds to regarding the RMS as a
hybrid system itself, in which one factor moves directly from integral state to
integral state at succeeding instants, while the other moves from integral state
to integral state through a sequence of nonintegral states, without a fixed ratio
relating the flow of time in the two factor systems.

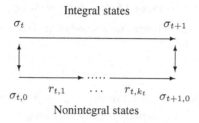

Fig. 13.1. Decomposition of an integral transition between two integral states into a sequence of nonintegral transitions representing application or unwinding of individual reasoning steps.

I depict the relation of integral and nonintegral motion in Figure 13.1, taking a view that admits arbitrary but finite numbers of nonintegral intermediate positions. Let us decompose each transition

$$\sigma_t, \sigma_{t+1}$$

through integral states into a series of k_t transitions through nonintegral states

$$\sigma_t, \sigma_{t,1}, \ldots, \sigma_{t,k_t}, \sigma_{t+1}.$$

In the simplest case, each of the intermediate nonintegral states results from the action of one or more reasons, along the lines presented earlier. For simplicity, let us consider here only single-reason trajectories. We denote the reason applied or removed at microstep i of instant t by $r_{t,i}$, and view each such reason as an operator that produces a new state from an old one.

$$\sigma_{t,1} = r_{t,0}(\sigma_t) \tag{13.7}$$

$$\sigma_{t,i+1} = r_{t,i}(\sigma_{t,i}) \tag{13.8}$$

$$\sigma_{t+1} = \sigma_{t,k}. \tag{13.9}$$

If we extend the topologies already assumed on times, places, and body points to a topology on the set of states, we can extend the notion of integral transition to allow an infinite number of microtransitions between integral states and to regard relaxation as an infinite equilibration process by taking

$$\sigma_{t+1} = \sigma_{t,\infty} = \lim_{i \to \infty} \sigma_{t,i}, \tag{13.10}$$

assuming this limit exists. For the finite sequences of microtransitions, of course, we take the limit value to be the final state.

13.5.3 *Applied forces and self-forces*

Each integral state transition begins with some impulse or perturbation, namely an applied force of the form

$$f_t = (\dot{m}_t, \ddot{x}_t). \tag{13.11}$$

For simplicity we follow the model of the original RMS and consider perturbations that only change the mental mass by adding new reasons. These take the form of an applied mass force

$$f_t^{\mathrm{m}} = (\dot{m}_t, \mathbf{0}). \tag{13.12}$$

The subintegral transitions then result from a series of self-forces corresponding to the reasoning steps

$$f_{t,1} = (\mathbf{0}, \ddot{x}_{t,1}) \tag{13.13}$$

$$\vdots$$

$$f_{t,n} = (\mathbf{0}, \ddot{x}_{t,n}), \tag{13.14}$$

changing only the conclusions, that is, the velocity and position. Upon reaching quiescence in a new integral state, the integral transition comprises a spatial self-force

$$f_t^{\mathrm{s}} = (\mathbf{0}, \ddot{x}_t) \tag{13.15}$$

that we can regard as transmitting velocity or change signals to the environment.

Of course, this decomposition of applied and self-forces across time and across mass and space represents just one possible means for organizing reasoning. No mechanical principle forbids applied or self-forces from mixing mass and velocity changes. Indeed, the distributed RMS described by Doyle (1996, 1997) permits external forces to stipulate changes to conclusions as well as to base reasons. Such stipulations appear necessary to allow each part of a distributed system to reason without undue dependence on other parts. Similar mixed forces might also be applied by reasons in subintegral transitions, or better still, by schematic reasoning rules applied during the course of updates.

Although we can describe the forces involved in integral motion in mechanical terms, the preceding description does not provide a reasonable train of causality, in that it requires computing the complete successor state in order to determine the force acting at an integral instant. The ordinary sense of causality familiar in traditional mechanical prediction and calculation determines the force at an instant as a function of the current state or past history, or as an external given, and then computes the next state directly from the force. Of

course, no notion of causality inheres in these mathematical equations themselves, and in fact this apparent reversal of causality is somewhat misleading.
The causal discomfort in this description of behavior does not result from any
acausality of the reasoner itself. The discomfort results from splitting the determination of force across both the mind and its environment. Rather than taking
the force as an input to the reasoner and using this force to determine a new
velocity and mass, this interpretation implies that the environment determines
the mass velocity component of the force, while the mind itself determines the
spatial acceleration component of the force. Thus if we seek to view the environment as specifying the force on the mind, this interpretation requires the
environment to predict the acceleration component determined by the mind
from the mass change component. Such prediction seems problematic because
of the indeterminacy of conclusions with respect to base reasons.

13.5.4 Conservatism

As noted earlier, constructive integrity sometimes involves a degree of indeterminism in constructing admissible extensions of states. Such indeterminism of
admissible extensions leads directly to indeterminism of integral motion. The
notion of conservatism plays an important role in shaping integral motion by
acting to minimize the unnecessary changes and keep the new state as close as
possible to the prior one.

Define the function $\alpha^{\sharp} : \mathcal{M} \to \mathcal{P}(\Sigma)$ to pick out those states having positions that are admissible extensions of specified masses, that is,

$$\alpha^{\sharp}(m) = \{\sigma \in \Sigma \mid m(\sigma) = m \wedge x(\sigma) \in \alpha(m)\}. \tag{13.16}$$

Using the nearest-state operator ν of Section 7.4.4, we can express the requirement of conservative update as the condition

$$\sigma_{t+1} \in \nu(\sigma_t, \alpha^{\sharp}(m(\sigma_{t+1}))), \tag{13.17}$$

which requires successor states to have positions that are admissible extensions
as close as possible to the preceding state.

The original RMS was constructed to produce conservative position updates
given changes to the reasons represented by the mass. In this conception,
the conservatism order on state changes stems from a conservatism order on
changes of position. Given a change of mass from m_t to m_{t+1}, the position would change from x_t to a new position $x_{t+1} \in \alpha(m_{t+1})$ minimizing
the velocity $\dot{x}_{t+1} = x_{t+1} - x_t$ in the sense of a nearest-position operator
$\nu^{\flat} : \mathcal{S} \times \mathcal{P}(\mathcal{S}) \to \mathcal{P}(\mathcal{S})$, so that

$$x_{t+1} \in \nu^{\flat}(x_t, \alpha(m_{t+1})). \tag{13.18}$$

The original RMS also was designed to embody a notion of conservatism based on topological locality notions. In the RMS, the natural notion of locality concerns the topology of the network of dependencies induced by the reasons among nodes representing components of mental positions. Topological notions such as partial ordering of nodes and strongly connected components of the dependency graph induce a natural notion of neighborhood, in which each node has a set of nearest neighbors as seen from the connections given by the reasons. Indeed, one can reasonably view the RMS reason-following process as propagating contact forces through the body, with each reason in contact with others through its meaning. The original RMS revision methods exploited these topological relations by seeking to remove contradictions by changing assumptions holding maximal positions in the topological order underneath the contradiction. The original formalization of reasoned assumptions (Doyle 1983e) explicitly treated the notion of local groundedness, both as a way of formalizing a weak notion of groundedness in which all reasons employed in reasoning only relate nodes that are close to each other. That original formalization also provided means for considering that some sets of nodes are close to each other a priori, as was later exploited in the notion of RMS "locales" employed in the distributed RMS of Doyle and Wellman (1990; 1996), and as had been exploited earlier in the notion of local theories (Doyle 1980).

Rather than address the complications of this topological order, the formalization in Doyle (1983e) reformulated the intent of RMS conservatism as minimizing set differences; that is

$$\sigma_1 \prec_\sigma \sigma_2 \text{ iff } x(\sigma) + x(\sigma_1) \subseteq x(\sigma) + x(\sigma_2). \tag{13.19}$$

This means that no change is acceptable if its additions and deletions strictly include those of some other change. We can regard it as minimizing a norm based on the inner product i_1 introduced earlier. If the current set of conclusions included A and B, and a new reason ruled out any state in which both of these conclusions appear, then the RMS would give up either A or B to obtain a legal state, but would not seek to give up both of these, nor any unrelated conclusions. The design of the original RMS addressed the difficulty of computing such set minimizations by employing methods that approximate the desired behavior. As explained in Doyle (1983e), the heuristic method used by the original RMS to minimize changes provided no assurance that the changes made were actually minimal.

One also could consider instead RMS variants in which the transition rule embodies some other comparison between states. For example, the comparison relation

$$\sigma_1 \prec_\sigma \sigma_2 \text{ iff } |x(\sigma) + x(\sigma_1)| \le |x(\sigma) + x(\sigma_2)| \tag{13.20}$$

compares the number of changed items, and so represents a norm based on the inner product i_2 given earlier. Harman (1986) calls this the simple measure. One might generalize this by employing a measure function μ over $\mathcal{S}$ to compare measures of sets of changes instead of cardinality of these sets, as in

$$\sigma_1 \prec_\sigma \sigma_2 \text{ iff } \mu(x(\sigma) + x(\sigma_1)) \le \mu(x(\sigma) + x(\sigma_2)). \tag{13.21}$$

One might choose such measure functions to represent probability, utility, or other properties of the sets of conclusions. The theoretical freedom to choose conservation relations in these theories represents different possible conserved quantities. Both these theories may be extended to cover additional aspects of mental states, permitting expression of conservation of yet more quantities. The approach taken in Doyle (1983e), in one sense, already covered many possible quantities since it made no presuppositions about the nature of the mental state components entering into the conservation restrictions.

13.6 Evolution of geometry

The RMS exhibits a form of conservatism in which the nature of conservative updates changes as the RMS mass changes. Because the conservation relations reflect locality relations derived from the set of reasons, the apparent local structure of space changes as the RMS changes the set of base reasons that constitute the mass of the system. Changes of spatial locality relations thus follow changes of mass distribution. This interaction of matter and space in RMS conservatism recalls the interaction of matter and geometry in general relativity, in which the structure of locality changes over time in response to changing distributions of matter. The following section provides some highly speculative reflections on this observation.

The preceding section has interpreted reasons as constraints on the geometry and shape of states, constraints that give rise to the pseudometrical structure of the space of equilibrium states. The reasons determine the admissible positions or configurations of the body. Putting these determinations together for all mass values, we obtain the set of all equilibrium configurations as a subset of the set of all positions, so that the reasons taken together with mass values determine a reduced space of positions.

The equilibrium of reasons and positions present in such states resembles the equilibrium of matter and space in general relativity, expressed in the slogan "Space acts on matter, telling it how to move. In turn, matter reacts on space, telling it how to curve" (Misner, Thorne, & Wheeler 1973, p. 5). The reasons in the mass of the RMS determine much of the structure of the comparative similarity relations employed in formulating conservation principles that shape RMS motion.

Comparative similarity relations do not yield proper metrics formally; a pre-order over the space of state transitions need not correspond to a numerical measure of distance satisfying the triangle inequality. Comparative similarity relations may also fail to represent metrics on conceptual grounds as well, as the smoothness of paths may depend on full states rather than just position. That is, to view them as metrics, one must take them as metrics over phase space, not over the position space. It would be interesting to know if one can relate conservation relations to something like symplectic structure on phase space.

Another question is whether we can regard comparative similarity relations themselves as constituting a weakened concept of configuration. We earlier followed Noll (1995) in defining the configuration of a body as the set of all body-centric metrics, that is, as the set of functions, one for each subbody B, such that the function for B indicates the distance from B to all parts of the enclosing body. Can we interpret comparative similarity relations as playing a similar formal role, that of a characterization of the configuration independent of any particular frame of reference? Comparative similarity relations certainly can capture the underlying ordering relations expressed by a metric configuration, and provided the basis for the initial explorations of RMS conservatism. The question is whether this ordering information itself suffices to distinguish different mechanical configurations, or whether the additional metric information is needed to characterize the intrinsic structure of a body.

Attempting to connect mass-dependent conservatism to the geometric dynamics of general relativity also suggests reconsidering conservative motion as a form of geodesic motion. *Geodesics* represent "straight" lines in manifolds. It is tempting to identify at least some types of conservative motion as approximations to geodesic motion, specifically, geodesic motion on a discrete manifold constrained so that not all tangents represent possible motions within the manifold. In this setting, one might define *pseudogeodesics* to be curves that are as straight as possible, given the geometry of the manifold.

In its simplest form, the RMS change-minimization principle amounts to minimizing velocity, an interpretation that naturally suggests relations to geodesic motion as employed in general relativity, in which motion proceeds by the straightest and longest or locally slowest possible route. Macroscopic changes begin, in the most common way, by changing the mass of the RMS and then undergoing additional accelerations that minimize the state change.

If one simplifies this to choosing a minimal macroscopic acceleration, the resulting motion can then be viewed as pseudogeodesic, as the path is as straight as possible given the influence of mass on position.

One can view RMS conservatism geometrically as something like straight-line motion by observing that the velocity being minimized consists of the symmetric difference between current position and the successor position. Minimizing this velocity means in part maximizing the conserved elements or overlap between current and successor states. One can obtain this overlap as the inner product of the current and successor states, as the projection of new on old. This projection is maximized when the motion keeps the same direction, when the new is the same as the old, so conservative RMS motion approximates geodesic motion in a quite natural way.

Of course, the notion of geodesic motion applies to vector fields generally, not just to dynamical geometries. Thus one might also return to the interpretation of reasons as generating potential fields that determine state-dependent forces on the body. Instead of simply viewing the reason potential as generating reason forces as gradients, one might view the reason potential as giving the geometry of the space in which the reasoner moves, with reason-following motion consisting of geodesic motion in this geometry.

14

Uncertainty

The preceding development of mental mechanics does not require determinism of mechanical systems. It instead requires only that motion satisfy mechanical relationships independent of determinism requirements.

The preceding chapters also illustrated several sources of possible indeterminacy. Reasoning, whether habitual or deliberate, can produce indeterminism when several reasons apply at the same instant, requiring serialization or conflict resolution. In addition, rational deliberation can result in several possible self-constructions from reasoning rules; conservative update in response to reasoned changes can follow multiple resolutions; and volition can encompass multiple choices of action on the basis of the same desires and intentions. These sources of mechanical indeterminism complement the forms of indeterminism acknowledged in traditional mechanics, including situations of indeterministic collapse and bifurcation considered in continuum mechanics and the pervasive indeterminacy of quantum physics. All of these forms of indeterminacy represent theoretical allowances of multiple possibilities that stand separate from uncertainties arising from the practicalities of measurement connected with repeatability and resolution of measuring apparati.

From the viewpoint of psychology, mechanical indeterminism generates what one can call a "kinematical" notion of uncertainty, in which one seeks to measure the amount of indeterminism, or degree of uncertainty about predictions introduced by indeterminism. In the simplest terms, qualities of motion shared by all possible histories represent certain predictions about motion, while qualities exhibited by some histories but not by others represent uncertain predictions about motion. The kinematic conception of uncertainty provides means for comparing these degrees of certainty and uncertainty in quantitative terms. This chapter develops formal concepts for measuring and describing uncertainty over indeterministic histories. Apart from a speculative formalization of measurement algebras at the end of the chapter, the concepts presented here all represent straightforward adaptations of well-known techniques.

The kinematic conception of uncertainty measures the degree of certainty irrespective of the sources of the uncertainty, whether these sources lie in volitional choices, indeterministic discrete laws of motion, or elsewhere. The kinematic conception also constitutes an external conception of uncertainty, capturing the uncertainty in motion as seen by an omniscient observer who sees all possible motions.

The kinematic conception of uncertainty is distinct from any subjective uncertainty experienced by the agent, which includes subjective probabilities and degrees of belief, weakness of will, and preference and strength of desire. These phenomena do not merely involve measurements of uncertainty by an external observer; they involve the agent itself gauging its own level of uncertainty.

14.1 Measurement uncertainty

Practical measurements of mechanical quantities involve uncertainties due to the repeatability of measurement events and uncertainties due to the resolution of the measuring apparatus. Even if one assumes a deterministic world, one may be uncertain about exactly which state one measured (perhaps just before or after the state one intended to measure), about the actual functioning of the measuring apparatus, or about the interpretation of the measuring apparatus' state. These uncertainties mean the agent suffers partial observability of its world.

Traditional approaches to measurement view measuring apparati as noisy channels. If the function of the apparatus is stable enough to permit repeatable behavior, one can model the uncertainty of the measurement as a distribution giving the probability $pr(v_m|v)$ of the measurement of some quantity V yielding a value v_m in a set V_m of possible measurement outcomes given an actual value $v \in V$. If one also has *a priori* estimates $pr(v)$ of the probabilities of the distinct possible values $v \in V$, one may use Bayes rule to obtain the probabilities $pr(v|v_m)$ of actual values given measured values by the formula

$$pr(v \mid v_m) = \frac{pr(v)pr(v_m \mid v)}{pr(v_m)} \qquad (14.1)$$

where

$$pr(v_m) = \sum_{v' \in V} pr(v')pr(v_m \mid v'). \qquad (14.2)$$

One then obtains a revised probability distribution pr' for actual values v from a measured value v_m by using the formula

$$pr'(v) = pr(v|v_m). \tag{14.3}$$

Of course, not all mechanical quantities need suffer from measurement uncertainties. Digital circuits, clockworks, and other kinematic systems with a discrete character are designed specifically to provide certain sorts of measurements with no uncertainty.

14.2 Probabilistic indeterminism

Indeterminism introduces additional uncertainty into measurement beyond that already present as a result of the practicalities of measurement. To quantify uncertainties due to indeterminism, we employ probability measures over histories in the same way as done by Feynman (1949), Everett (1957), and others (Beltrametti & Cassinelli 1981; Nelson 1985; van Fraassen 1991) in quantum theory.

Let $\mathcal{H}$ be the set of all linear histories of the universe in question, with $\mathcal{H}(\mathcal{B}, I)$ denoting the restriction of $\mathcal{H}$ to motions of the body $\mathcal{B}$ over the temporal interval I. The history-measure approach assumes one has a probability measure $\mu^{\mathcal{H}} : \mathcal{P}(\mathcal{H}) \to [0, 1]$ on some measure space of sets over $\mathcal{H}$. In the finite case, each such measure assigns a number to each possible world representing how likely it is to be the actual world. We then determine the probabilities of a value of a quantity by Feynman's rule, by summing the probabilities of all the different ways the value might occur. That is, we measure the set of all possible histories in which that value or event occurs. This results in a probability distribution on the possible values of the quantity.

The mathematical concept of measure space underlies this approach to measurement. A measure space consists of a base set, a set of its subsets comprising the measurable subsets, and a function mapping the measurable subsets to $\mathbb{R}$ (ordinarily). When the base set is finite, one may deem all subsets measurable, though nothing requires this. When the base set is infinite, one ordinarily cannot consider all subsets measurable, so measure spaces require only that the set of measurable subsets satisfy some simple properties, namely additivity on disjoint subsets and across countable subcollections. Measurable sets contained in a nonmeasurable subset provide lower bounds on its measure, and measurable sets containing the nonmeasurable one provide upper bounds on its measure. For measurable sets, these lower and upper bounds coincide.

Since the set of all deterministic histories contained in a nondeterministic history does not depend on any framings, we see that this source for probabilities is attractively frame independent. Because the objects assigned probabilities (the linear histories) are so primitive, it is hard to conceive of a metaphysically more modest approach.

A measure on the set of all histories permits calculation of many other frame-independent quantities. For example, the degree with which one frame-independent condition entails another is just the relative measure or conditional probability of the two corresponding sets of linear histories.

14.2.1 Probabilities of states

We call a function assigning probabilities to sets of instantaneous mechanical states a *density function*. Such a function is simply a measure function μ^{Σ} : $\mathcal{P}(\Sigma) \rightarrow [0,1]$ such that $\mu^{\Sigma}(\Sigma) = 1$, that is, a function that says that the system must be in *some* state. Every nontrivial measure function $\mu : \mathcal{P}(\Sigma) \rightarrow [0,\infty)$ such that $\mu(\Sigma) > 0$ induces a density function by normalization, defining for $S \subseteq \Sigma$

$$\mu^{\Sigma}(S) = \frac{\mu(S)}{\mu(\Sigma)}. \tag{14.4}$$

The set of all density functions on Σ forms a convex set. That is, $w_1\mu_1^{\Sigma} + w_2\mu_2^{\Sigma}$ is a density function whenever μ_1^{Σ} and μ_2^{Σ} are density functions and $w_1 + w_2 = 1$.

Each measure on histories induces a probability distribution on instantaneous states. The induced probability measure on states is frame dependent because instants are. The state probability distribution at instant t is given by

$$pr(\sigma, t) = \mu^{\mathcal{H}}(\{h \in H \mid h(t) = \sigma\}), \tag{14.5}$$

where $h(t)$ is the configuration at time t in the history in the chosen framing.

14.2.2 Probabilities of state transitions

We use the measure on histories to derive probabilities on the unit time transitions at each instant in a similar way. The distribution over successor states σ_2 given that state σ_1 obtains at instant t is given by

$$pr(\sigma_1, \sigma_2, t) = \mu^{\mathcal{H}}(\{h \in \mathcal{H} \mid h(t) = \sigma_1 \ \wedge \ h(t+1) = \sigma_2\}). \tag{14.6}$$

The probability $pr^+(\sigma_1, \sigma_2, t)$ that σ_2 will occur at some instant later than t is given by

$$pr^+(\sigma_1, \sigma_2, t) = \mu^{\mathcal{H}}(\{h \in \mathcal{H} \mid h(t) = \sigma_1 \ \wedge \ \exists t' > t. \ h(t') = \sigma_2\}). \tag{14.7}$$

Similarly, we may obtain the probability $pr^{\rightarrow}(\sigma_1, \sigma_2)$ that one state directly transforms into another at any time during the histories by the formula

$$pr^{\rightarrow}(\sigma_1, \sigma_2) = \begin{aligned}\mu^{\mathcal{H}}(\{h \in \mathcal{H} \mid \exists t, t+1 \in I_{\mathcal{H}}. \\ h(t) = \sigma_1 \wedge h(t+1) = \sigma_2\})\end{aligned} \tag{14.8}$$

$$= \int_{I_{\mathcal{H}}} pr(\sigma_1, \sigma_2, t). \tag{14.9}$$

14.2.2.1 Markovian probabilities

We follow tradition in calling systems *Markovian* just in case successor states depend only on the immediately preceding states and not on any more distant portions of the past history. Transition probabilities relate very simply to probabilities of histories in Markovian systems. The Markov property means that the transition probabilities $pr(\sigma, \sigma', t)$ giving the probability of a state σ directly transforming into the successor state σ' do not depend on time, so that we may write $pr(\sigma, \sigma', t) = pr^{\rightarrow}(\sigma, \sigma')$. From such probabilities, we then construct the probability of an individual history h as

$$pr(h) = \prod_{I_h} pr(h(t), h(t+1)) \tag{14.10}$$

and the probability of a nondeterministic histories by

$$pr(H) = \int_H pr(h). \tag{14.11}$$

With Markovian transition probabilities, we can describe the temporal evolution of probability distributions over states in terms of instantaneous density functions. We assume an initial density function μ_0^{Σ} for $t = 0$, for example,

$$\mu_0^{\Sigma}(\sigma) = \begin{cases} 0 & \sigma \neq \sigma_0 \\ 1 & \sigma = \sigma_0 \end{cases}. \tag{14.12}$$

We then apply the transition probabilities to determine the probabilities through the sequence of successive times

$$\langle \mu_0^{\Sigma}, \mu_1^{\Sigma}, \mu_2^{\Sigma}, \dots \rangle. \tag{14.13}$$

We compute these successive density functions by combining the probability that the system is in a particular state with the probability of moving from that state to specific other states. We add up the probabilities of reaching a state, and we have the new density function. Formally, we define μ_{t+1}^{Σ} for each $\sigma \in \Sigma$ by

$$\mu_{t+1}^{\Sigma}(\sigma) = \sum_{\sigma' \in \Sigma} \mu_t^{\Sigma}(\sigma') pr(\sigma', \sigma). \tag{14.14}$$

The resulting function μ_{t+1}^{Σ} is a density function since by induction

$$\sum_{\sigma' \in \Sigma} pr(\sigma', \sigma) = 1 \qquad (14.15)$$

and μ_{t+1}^{Σ} is the convex combination of density functions.

Mechanical systems generally do not exhibit the Markov property, at least kinematically, as the applied force may depend on the nonkinematic history of the system and on the environment of the body in question. The usual way around this difficulty is to define the "total" state to contain all information required to decouple future behavior from past behavior, in the sense that the probability of a transition given the current state is the same as the probability of the transition given the full history to that point; that is,

$$pr(\sigma_{t+1} \mid \sigma_t) = pr(\sigma_{t+1} \mid \sigma_t, \sigma_{t-1}, \ldots). \qquad (14.16)$$

Identifying such total states may be possible for specific materials, but enforcing such a requirement in general has important implications for the construction of physical theory, in that discovery of new behaviors can require revision of the conception of what information characterizes total states. Such revision has occurred often in the past, first adding thermal and electromagnetic properties to mechanical properties, and then, in the atomic realm, adding spin, charm, color, and other influences on behavior.

14.2.2.2 Constructive probabilities

We may seek to avoid imposing inappropriate assumptions of Markovian behavior by going deeper still and constructing transition probabilities from nondeterministic mechanical trajectories together with probabilities derived from structural aspects of the transitions themselves.

Each set H of histories induces a possibly nondeterministic transition function $\Delta_H : \Sigma \times \mathcal{T} \to \mathcal{P}(\Sigma)$ giving the set of possible successor states at each instant, defined by $\Delta_H(\sigma, t) = \{h(t+1) \mid h(t) = \sigma\}$. Each measure function μ on Σ such that $\mu(\Delta_H(\sigma, t)) > 0$ gives rise to a probabilistic interpretation of the transition table Δ_H by defining the probability of moving from σ to σ' at t to be

$$pr(\sigma, \sigma', t) = \frac{\mu(\{\sigma'\})}{\mu(\Delta_H(\sigma, t))}. \qquad (14.17)$$

This interpretation recalls the relation between the standard and many-worlds interpretations of quantum mechanics (de Witt & Graham 1973; Van Fraassen 1980).

For instance, one may make a Laplacian assumption saying that each possible nondeterministic transition from a state is equally likely. This assumption corresponds to the natural *counting* measure $\mu^\dagger$ that gives every state equal weight, that is,

$$\mu^\dagger(\{\sigma\}) = 1. \qquad (14.18)$$

With this measure, the degree of certainty of a state component in a set of successor states is just the fraction of them in which it appears.

Alternatively, one might assume that transitions to simple states are more likely than transitions to more complex states. Vacuum fluctuations provide a relevant physical model here. Quantum theory implies that something is always happening even when nothing is happening, in the sense that empty regions of space are subject to fluctuations in quantum fields that one may interpret as momentary creation and destruction of particles and fields. The probability of such events depends largely on the characteristics of the events themselves. Instantaneous creation and destruction of a simple structure, such as an electron–positron pair, has a much greater probability than instantaneous creation and destruction of more complicated structure, such as copies of *l'Arc de Triomphe de l'Étoile* or *das Brandenburger Tor*.

For psychological uncertainty to follow this model, possible constructions would make temporary appearances occur with probabilities determined by structural simplicity measures. The *specificity* measure μ^* provides a natural example of such a structure-dependent measure function. This measure weights states by how "specific" they are. Let $N(\sigma) = |x(\sigma)| + |m(\sigma)|$ denote the function that counts the numbers of attitudes occurring in the position and mass in the state σ. We can think of N as assessing the specificity of a state. We then use N to construct a specificity measure μ^* that takes values given by

$$\mu^*(\{\sigma\}) = 2^{-|N(\sigma)|}. \qquad (14.19)$$

One way of looking at this measure is to think of states as partial descriptions of all the sets of components extending them, and to weight states proportionally to the number of possible supersets. To obtain such weights, one would instead define μ^* by

$$\mu^*(\{\sigma\}) = 2^{2|\mathcal{D}|-|N(\sigma)|}. \qquad (14.20)$$

Definition (14.20), of course, simply multiplies each of the specificity weights given in (14.20) by the constant $2^{2|\mathcal{D}|}$, and so changes none of the relative weights of states. Constructions similar to the Laplacian and specificity measures were proposed by Carnap in his theory of probability as "degrees of entailment" (Carnap 1950; Kyburg 1970).

Transition probability rules from physics suggest other possibilities as well. One might have that the probability of state transitions vary with some characteristic of the state change, such as the change of energy or the distance traversed. Yet another structural probabilistic measure derives from information content (Kolmogorov 1969; Chaitin 1975). The probabilities for this measure require that states with more information content have lower probabilities. The information-theoretic origin for probabilities has many conceptual attractions, but it poses problems as a target for computational implementation because the information content of a state is generally uncomputable.

Specific psychological organizations might engender their own structural probabilities. For example, the construction of conclusions from reasons in the RMS suggest choosing probabilities that reflect how frequently some attitude occurs in randomly selected admissible extensions, or how many valid reasons support the attitude, or how many nonmonotonic assumptions it depends on. Each of these choices captures different intuitions about the meaning of "degree of certainty," and might be preferable in different circumstances (Doyle 1983e, 1983c). In a similar way, one might derive probabilities not from frequency in admissible extensions but instead from frequency in the results of the conservative revision performed by the RMS. These frequencies reflect the resilience of mental attitudes or the relative ease with which they may be obtained or avoided in successor states. If a frequency is large, most successors will contain the attitude in question, so it is difficult to avoid. These frequencies measure not only of degrees of belief but of strength of desire and firmness of intent, and might serve as degrees of epistemic entrenchment (Gärdenfors & Makinson 1988). Pursuit of this interpretation leads to an interesting non-Bayesian decision theory. One may view all of these as probabilities tied to the comparative similarity relations that Section 7.3 used to formalize conservatism. Constructions of this form also seem related to probabilistic logics (Bacchus *et al.* 1996; Nilsson 1986).

We can motivate psychostructural measures in terms of either incomplete information or probabilistic algorithms. In the first view, we interpret probabilities as reflecting how likely the actual behavior is to occur among the behaviors compatible with incomplete knowledge. Alternatively, we can treat these measures as specifications for probabilistic algorithms (Rabin 1976) in which the agent makes a series of random choices (of legal transitions or constructions) and then decides what to do by exact means based on the the results of the choices. At present, we lack efficient algorithms for computing admissible extensions according to specified measure functions. RMS implementations make arbitrary choices in constructing admissible extensions, and while several authors have suggested designs that make these choices depend on properties of the foreseen resulting extensions, there is no known way of deriving the resulting measure on states from these intra-algorithmic choices, nor any known recipe for finding an appropriate algorithm when the final measure is specified.

14.2.2.3 Inertial indeterminacy

We might also interpret constructive probability in physical terms. Section 11.4.1 observed that we might interpret constant linear motion through positions in the binary space $\mathbb{D}$ as generating a limited form of uncertainty, as a position x and constant velocity $\dot{x}$ generate a sequence of positions $x, x + \dot{x}, x, x + \dot{x}, x, x + \dot{x}, \ldots$ that repeatedly "flips the bits" represented by the velocity $\dot{x}$. Considering these two alternating states as possible outcomes of measurement, we see that constant linear motion engenders a probability distribution on $\mathcal{D}$ that assigns the values 1 to each element of $\mathcal{D}$ in x but absent from $\dot{x}$, 0 to each element absent from both x and $\dot{x}$, and $\frac{1}{2}$ to each element present in $\dot{x}$. We obtain a similar but shifting distribution from inertial motion that superposes constant rotation on constant linear translation.

More speculatively, we might also regard uncertainty as reflecting rotation on alternation through constructive extensions. In this interpretation, we regard extensions as arranged around the circumference of a circle. We divide the circumference into regions, with the length of each region representing the probability (e.g., Laplacian or specificity) of one associated extension. If we imagine the mechanical state as a radial vector spinning with some frequency around the center of this circle, we can then expect to observe extensions with the proper probability by repeated observations of the region in which the radial vector lies, as long as the frequency of spin exceeds and is incommensurate with the frequency of sampling.

It seems unlikely that one can regard this sort of spin as some form of rotation through space, but one can continue the speculation in different ways. One might replace nonuniform weighting of circumferential portions by regarding the circumference as tilted with respect to the axis of spin and let measurement report which circle segment lies closest to the radial vector. The orientation of the circle with respect to the axis of rotation then affects the probability of observation of different extensions. One might also replace nonspatial spin through extensions with a more spatial conception of rotation through sets of assumptions underlying the extensions. For example, some RMS implementations analyze the dependency graph of reasons into a directed graph of strongly connected components. Each strongly connected component represents a set of assumptions that could be varied independently of downstream portions of the dependency network. One might consider each clique of reasons as sets spinning independently, perhaps with differing rates of spin or differing orientations, and so obtain differing probabilities for the resulting overall extensions.

14.2.3 Probability of belief

One may easily extend the preceding constructions to measuring the probability of inhabiting a state that exhibits particular properties. If $S \subseteq \Sigma$ consists of the states satisfying some property, we obtain

$$pr(S, t) = \mu^{\mathcal{H}}(\{h \in H \mid h(t) \in S\}) \qquad (14.21)$$

as the probability that the state at t exhibits the property S. One may use this same idea to assess the expected value of functions of states. If $f(\sigma)$ gives the numerical value of the quantity of interest in state σ, then the expected value $\langle f_t \rangle$ at time t is just

$$\langle f_t \rangle = \int_{\Sigma} f d\mu^{\mathcal{H}}. \qquad (14.22)$$

Some of the most interesting probabilistic questions about states concern whether the state exhibits certain beliefs, desires, or intentions. Probabilities of beliefs, desires, and intentions all arise in the same way. For example, the probability that a belief b appears in the position x is given by a transform of the property-probability formula picking out those states having the property of exhibiting that belief, namely

$$pr(b, t) = \mu^{\mathcal{H}}(\{h \in H \mid b \in x(h(t))\}), \qquad (14.23)$$

Viewing the belief b as a 0-1-valued characteristic function of states, we can rewrite this as

$$pr(b, t) = \langle b_t \rangle = \int_{\Sigma} b(\sigma) d\mu^{\mathcal{H}}. \qquad (14.24)$$

A probability measure on a nondeterministic history induces a measure quantifying probability of belief at each instant of the history. How might these probabilities of belief relate to the degrees of belief assumed by decision theory? Mechanics, of course, imposes no necessary connection between probability of belief and belief probability, as it states no properties of belief at all. In the following paragraphs, let us explore ways of relating probability of belief to subjective probability and other notions.

It is clear that probability of belief and subjective probability have some apparent differences.

First, the influential Bayesian view of belief as subjective probability holds that the beliefs of an agent form a probability distribution over states of affairs.

Believing that snow is white with subjective probability .999 means that one thinks that of states of affairs compatible with one's beliefs all but one one-thousandth make snow white. In contrast, having the belief "snow is white" hold with probability .999 means that of the possible states of belief, all but one one-thousandth contain the belief that snow is white.

Second, the probability of belief derived from measures on histories applies not just to absolute statements of belief, such as "snow is white," but also to direct representations of probability in mental position, as in a probability entry in a Bayesian network stating that "the probability of 'snow is white' is .999." One might be ready to interpret a .999 probability of belief in "snow is white" as a .999 degree of belief, but how should one interpret a .999 probability of belief in "the probability of 'snow is white' is .75"?

Third, probabilities of belief induced by measures on histories need not satisfy all the laws of subjective Bayesian probability. For example, unless all states are complete, that is, contain at least one of each belief or its contrary, the degrees of belief will be non-unitary. Formally, suppose that $e, \neg e \in \mathcal{D}$ represent some belief and its negation. If the agent can inhabit incomplete positions in which neither of these beliefs is *In*, then it can happen that

$$pr(e) + pr(\neg e) < 1. \tag{14.25}$$

If the agent can inhabit inconsistent positions in which both of these beliefs are *In*, then it can happen that

$$pr(e) + pr(\neg e) > 1. \tag{14.26}$$

Thus even though a measure on histories induces a probability distribution on instantaneous states, these instantaneous state distributions need not induce probability distributions on beliefs.

14.3 Self-measurement

We can reduce the difference between psychological and subjective probability if we take the "subjective" in subjective probability seriously and regard subjective probability as the result of the agent's assessing or measuring its own degree of belief. If the agent can perform such measurements, the lack of direct representation of psychological uncertainty forms less of an impediment to rational behavior.

To give a personal example, I observe that I determine my degree of certainty about difficult decisions or questions by repeated self-polling, going through the decision several times to see what answers I get. If one answer comes up every time, or most of the time, I interpret that answer as the one with the greatest certainty. When I have no reason to expect psychological uncertainty, I can simply poll or query myself once and use the resulting answer.

Self-measurement by collecting statistics about one's self corresponds naturally to the notion of probabilistic algorithms. Probabilistic primality testing, for example, repeatedly picks a random value for a certain parameter and then performs some arithmetic operations on the target number, operations that depend on the randomly chosen number. If the operations say the number is composite, the number truly is composite, but if the random operations say the number is prime, all one knows is that the number is prime with some low probability. Repeating this test a number of times, using different random parameters each time, enables one to rapidly determine either that the target is composite or is prime with exceedingly high probability. The degree of certainty appears nowhere in these measurement processes, at least as an explicit parameter somewhere that one can simply observe. The degree of certainty instead comes from the statistics of the measurement process.

Self-measurement need not rely on deliberate variation of construction by the agent. Classical and quantum measurement provide ample expectation of a changing world in which the distribution of answers to repeated measurements follows from the dynamical evolution of the system under measurement.

Of course, self-measurement lacks the explicitness and amenability to direct manipulation, update, and measurement that make direct uncertainty representations like Bayesian networks the approach of choice in artificial intelligence. In indeterministic reasoners, however, it seems there is no way of avoiding psychological uncertainty, even if mental states employ explicit representations of subjective uncertainty. One thus looks for ways of using measurements to recalibrate explicit representations.

14.3.1 Subjective probability

Because realistic states of belief need be neither complete nor consistent, subjective self-measurement probabilities of Bayesian decision theory appear to overidealize by confusing properties of minds with properties of the world inhabited by the minds. The aforementioned constructions indicate the naturalness and importance of the idea of strength of beliefs on which Bayesianism is based, but also cast doubt upon the identification of degree of belief with subjective probability. The measure of degree of belief via psychological or historical probability is a perfectly good probability measure, but the projection of this measure onto the logical structure of states is not in general a probability measure without a sometimes specious axiom of completeness and a sometimes unachievable axiom of consistency. As in quantum theory, the projected measure represents a lattice of possible events, and only represents a Boolean lattice in the special case of complete states (Birkhoff 1967; Beltrametti & Cassinelli 1981).

The Bayesian might respond that the preceding constructions do not capture subjective probabilities, but only *lower bounds* on subjective probabilities, as in the Dempster–Shafer theory of evidence (Shafer 1976). This reply may offer a way of reconciling the views, but it faces difficulties posed by paradoxical sentences, and I do not pursue it here (see Lewis 1980). We only observe that whatever the attractions of the stronger Bayesian theory for more competent agents, in computationally realized agents, the lower bounds offered by our construction may be the only reasonable choices for "degrees of belief."

If consideration of historical probabilities provides motivations for some of the concerns of subjective Bayesian probability theory, it also helps us understand Zadeh's (1975) notions of fuzzy sets and concepts. Statements like "Sue is tall" are considered vague because "tall" is not a well-defined concept; there are many heights Sue could reach and be thought tall. Zadeh formalizes this notion by introducing a spectrum of truth values for the sentence, a spectrum derived from a spectrum of tallness values. We might instead develop a theory of fuzzy concepts in terms of state probabilities. Rather than simply *assuming* tallness spectra, we could formulate exact theories of tallness and simply look to see what distribution these entail for particular statements. For example, we might require exact theories of tallness to specify exact intervals of height, and given this restriction, look to the admissible extensions of the statement "Sue is tall." If there are many intervals saying one height is tall and fewer intervals saying another height is tall, then the first height will be "more tall" than the second.

14.3.2 Weakness of will

The concept of degree of belief is very different from the concept of degree of conviction, or as it is also called, *epistemic entrenchment*. Degree of belief corresponds to frequency of answering a certain way under repeated questioning, while degree of entrenchment reflects the order in which one gives up beliefs when forced to change one's beliefs. For example, lacking any information to the contrary, Alice might believe that Bob's pet bird can fly, even if Alice exhibits psychological uncertainty regarding other conditions. Alice also might readily give up the belief that Bob's bird can fly upon learning it is a penguin. At the same time, Alice might believe that Bob never jokes or lies, and be quite unwilling to give up this belief. If Bob tells Alice his pet bird cannot fly, she must either give up her belief that the bird flies or her belief in Bob's reliability, so she abandons her belief about Bob's bird because it is less entrenched than her belief about Bob's reliability. Thus one can view the degrees of belief resulting from historical indeterminism as involving unforced changes of belief. Entrenchment, in contrast, concerns forced changes of belief. One might measure the expected degree of entrenchment by assessing entrenchment in different extensions.

Although the conviction or entrenchment of belief is important to understanding behavior, this notion appears even more important for understanding weakness of will, the inability to carry through on one's intentions. We can think of weakness of will as occurring through several means, including psychological uncertainty of intention, entrenchment of intention, and susceptibility to distractions and fears.

Psychological uncertainty engenders weakness of will when each of the agent's self-measurements of intent prior to the point of action show an intention to act, but the agent's self-measurement at the point of action lacks the intent in question. As in measuring degree of belief by repeated queries, degree of intention follows the fraction of alternative states exhibiting the intention. The main difference between the case of belief and intention comes from volition, which takes actions based on intentions but not on belief. Volition can fail to produce action even when strength of will is high, if action comes through a measurement yielding an atypical answer.

Entrenchment of intention, or properly speaking, lack of entrenchment, also can play a role in weakness of will. The issue here is how easily is the intention displaced as a result of forces of reasoning, distraction, or fear. As in considering the elastic character of entrenchment, ease of displacement involves how many reasons or other mental forces stand ready to restore the intention upon attempted removals, and on how ready the agent stands to maintain or generate the forces of concentration needed to cancel forces that distract from the intended actions.

Susceptibility to fear is similar to susceptibility to distraction, but in fear the forces diverting attention stem not from the environment but from within the agent itself. Everyone experiences fears that start small when the action in question lies in the distant future but that grow larger and larger as the time for action nears. In such cases, the countervailing forces must increase along with the fears if the agent is to carry through. This continual increase and counterbalancing requires the additional work on the part of the agent, since it involves continued replacement, augmentation, or refreshing of the forces generated to block the fear.

The problem in many situations of action is that the resultant grounds of action represent an unstable equilibrium of forces and countervailing forces, so small fluctuations can produce large changes in probabilities. Ease of deflection in distractable agents can result either from unstable equilibria, in which slight changes to forces can tip the outcome from the desired one, or from low mass agents, in which even slight forces can yield a significant motion. The larger the mass of the agent, the less slight discrepancies between distracting and blocking forces matter. Highly deliberate agents provide a good example here, as complete arguments buttressing the chosen path and defeating the alternatives will not be changed by slight perturbations in conclusions. The arguments for the action and against the alternatives will provide redundancy adequate to withstand random changes, or perhaps only certain types of variations.

14.3.3 Consequential measurement

Physics recognizes that measuring a system can change the system. Consequential measurement occurs in classical mechanics when the measuring apparatus touches or otherwise perturbs the system being measured, but careful design of the apparatus can minimize or eliminate such effects. In contrast, consequential measurement forms a key aspect of quantum mechanics. Quantum mechanics posits that the act of measurement forces the measured system from a state reflecting a superposition of pure states into a state reflecting a pure value of the measured quantity.

We see a similar variation in psychological systems. Many traditional artificial reasoners answer queries without changing the state of the reasoner in any way that affects its attitudes or future actions. In other artificial reasoners, queries do change the state of the reasoner. For example, SOAR's chunking mechanism produces new rules in the course of answering a query, and reasoners employing reason maintenance learn new reasons. Rule and reason learning, however, typically constitute deterministic effects of measurement.

Reasoners exhibiting constructive indeterminacy of the sorts discussed earlier offer the possibility of consequential measurements more like those seen in quantum mechanics. In particular, answering queries in the presence of both constructive indeterminacy and conservative motion might produce a determinate state with respect to the object of the query in distinct ways, either by fixing the extension or by introducing new reasons or conclusions that constrain the extension to one determinative of the answer to the query.

The reasoner considered in Section 7.6 has reasons for concluding that either that Nixon is a pacifist because he is Quaker or that Nixon is not a pacifist because he is Republican. If the reasoner has not yet considered these possibilities, we might regard it as inhabiting an indeterminate state with respect to Nixon's pacifism, a state combining the two definite states. Asking the reasoner whether Nixon is pacifist or not would then lead to it making one assumption or the other, and conservatism would have it keep that assumption in place. In this way, the operation of querying the indeterminate state produces a determinate state corresponding to one of the pure states contributing to the former indeterminism.

More generally, an agent conducting the sort of self-polling described earlier might use the result not just to assess a degree of belief but to adopt a position on the question. In such cases, we find an intimate connection between self-measurement and self-construction, and a connection between self-measurement and a form of self-awareness or self-consciousness.

These observations suggest we take a second look at the relation of self-measurement and the self-action involved in reasoning. Chapter 11 treated reasons in terms of forces and stresses. Stresses are tensors or, in the previous examination, piecewise-linear tensors that act on mechanical states to produce reason forces. The following discussion presents some speculative ideas for formalisms that attempt to follow the pattern set by quantum-mechanical notions of measurement in the context of discrete mental systems. To do this, I introduce a formalism using the familiar Dirac notation to characterize reason forces and stresses as state operators akin to those used in the operator calculus of quantum mechanics.

I present these speculations mainly to indicate something of the range of explorations possible within the mechanical framework. Quantum measurement perspectives have been studied previously in the theory of computation. The most prominent usage today occurs in connection with quantum computation, in which quantum states encode a multiplicity of deterministic computations, and the ideas examined here have direct connections with the idea of observing sets of possible histories. When used to treat theories of thinking, finding roles for quantum measurement in the formalization of reasoning methods might also yield connections with Penrose's (1989) ideas relating quantum gravity to consciousness.

Note that Manthey and Moret (1983) sketched a quantum-mechanical analogy for computation not intended to be limited only to actual quantum computation. Their work consisted largely of an abstract analogy, with no specific interpretation or axiomatic basis underlying the informal suggestions. It does provide a useful direction for extending the present developments, however. It employs a mass measure consisting of the number of bits in a word (or perhaps the information content), and measures speed of change as number of bits changed. This approach represents a compromise between the vector-mass approach developed here and the scalar theories of traditional mechanics.

14.3.3.1 Dyadic states

Let us begin by recasting reason forces using the familiar Dirac notation from quantum mechanics to express algebraic reasoning operators. We move from thinking of mental states as positions in the vector space $\mathbb{D}$ to thinking of them as "state vectors" in $\mathbb{D} \times \mathbb{D}$. We regard $\mathbb{D} \times \mathbb{D}$ as a vector space by means of the obvious extension of the scalar multiplication and addition in $\mathbb{D}$ to the product space. We denote vectors in this space with the Dirac ket notation; that is, we write an element of $\mathbb{D} \times \mathbb{D}$ in the form $|X, Y\rangle$.

Although we can view $\mathbb{D}^2$ as the translation space over $\mathbb{D}$, we now take a different approach, and regard vectors in the space as representing "present" and "absent" subsets of $\mathcal{D}$. In particular, we reinterpret each position x as the state vector

$$\psi = |x, \overline{x}\rangle. \tag{14.27}$$

Clearly $|x, \overline{x}\rangle$ contains the same information as does x; we only change the form of the representation for the new analysis. If one has in mind the stress interpretation of reasons presented earlier, it might be useful to think of $|x, \overline{x}\rangle$ as a vector based at the point x and normal or orthogonal to the degenerate surface x.

We earlier introduced both a product operation and an inner product on $\mathbb{D}$. We now introduce a symmetric bilinear form

$$\langle \ | \ \rangle : \mathbb{D}^2 \times \mathbb{D}^2 \to \mathbb{D} \tag{14.28}$$

over $\mathbb{D}^2$ defined so that

$$\langle W, X \mid Y, Z \rangle = (WZ) + (XY). \tag{14.29}$$

This operation is clearly linear, and also symmetric, in that

$$\langle W, X \mid Y, Z \rangle = \langle X, W \mid Z, Y \rangle. \tag{14.30}$$

We define the conjugate of the vector $|X, Y\rangle$ to be the bra $\langle Y, X|$, and so regard the "bracket" product $\langle W, X \mid Y, Z \rangle$ as denoting the product of the state vectors $|X, W\rangle$ and $|Y, Z\rangle$.

We can easily extend these definitions to larger state vectors by defining the conjugate of $|X_1, \ldots, X_n\rangle$ to be $\langle X_n, \ldots, X_1|$, and by defining the product $\langle X_n, \ldots, X_1 \mid Y_1, \ldots, Y_n \rangle$ by

$$\langle X_n, \ldots, X_1 \mid Y_1, \ldots, Y_n \rangle = (X_1 Y_1) + \ldots + (X_n Y_n). \tag{14.31}$$

This form rephrases linear form (10.5) used in defining inner products.

14.3.3.2 Dyadic reasons

We next seek to interpret each reason

$$r = A_r \;\backslash\backslash\; B_r \;\Vdash\; C_r \;\backslash\backslash\; D_r$$

in a way fitting the dyadic state conception, namely as a dyadic tensor

$$r = |D_r, C_r\rangle\langle A_r, B_r|. \tag{14.32}$$

As noted earlier, the condition stating the validity of the reason r is

$$A_r\overline{x} + B_r x = \mathbf{0}. \tag{14.33}$$

In the dyadic representations we can reexpress (14.33) in the condition

$$\langle A_r, B_r \mid x, \overline{x}\rangle = \mathbf{0}. \tag{14.34}$$

Similarly, we can reexpress the changes produced by r when valid, namely

$$C_r\overline{x} + D_r x, \tag{14.35}$$

as the product

$$\langle C_r, D_r \mid x, \overline{x}\rangle \tag{14.36}$$

since adding in this result to x will add the necessary elements of C_r and remove the necessary elements of D_r.

Were it not for the nonlinearity of the conditional evident in (11.32), we could seek to use these algebraic identities to write the result of applying the reason tensor to a state $|x, \overline{x}\rangle$. We now consider two paths in this direction. Neither one admits as simple a characterization as one might want because of the nonlinearity of reasons, but I entertain the hope that future investigations will find better possibilities.

In the first approach, we attempt to regard the reason an operator something like

$$f_r = |D_r, C_r\rangle\langle A_r, B_r|, \tag{14.37}$$

so as to obtain the changes resulting from reason application as the "expectation value"

$$f_r = \langle \overline{x}, x \mid D_r, C_r\rangle\langle A_r, B_r \mid x, \overline{x}\rangle. \tag{14.38}$$

To do this, we recast the reason interpretation in a nonlinear function

$$Z : (\mathbb{D}^2 \times \mathbb{D}^2) \to (\mathbb{D}^2 \to \mathbb{D}) \tag{14.39}$$

defined so that

$$Z(|A_r, B_r\rangle, |C_r, D_r\rangle)(|x, y\rangle)$$
$$= \begin{cases} \langle C_r, D_r \mid x, y\rangle & \text{if } \langle A_r, B_r \mid x, y\rangle = 0 \\ 0 & \text{otherwise.} \end{cases} \quad (14.40)$$

From the earlier remarks, we see that $Z(|B_r, A_r\rangle, |D_r, C_r\rangle)(|x, \overline{x}\rangle)$ provides the conclusion changes called for by the reason r in state x. Thus

$$Z(|B_r, A_r\rangle, |D_r, C_r\rangle)(|x, \overline{x}\rangle) = U(r)(x). \quad (14.41)$$

We see that Z has a structure suitable for additive superposition of operators corresponding to different reasons. If we define

$$Z_r = Z(|B_r, A_r\rangle, |D_r, C_r\rangle) \quad (14.42)$$

and

$$Z_R = \sum_{r \in R} Z_r, \quad (14.43)$$

we then have

$$U(R)(x) = \sum_{r \in R} U(r)(x) \quad (14.44)$$

$$= \sum_{r \in R} Z_r(|x, \overline{x}\rangle) \quad (14.45)$$

$$= Z_R(|x, \overline{x}\rangle). \quad (14.46)$$

In the second approach, we seek to regard the reason as something like an operator of the form

$$f_r = \langle C_r, D_r|\langle A_r, B_r|, \quad (14.47)$$

which, when applied to the state $|x, \overline{x}\rangle$, yields the operator

$$f_r|x, \overline{x}\rangle = \langle B_r, A_r \mid x, \overline{x}\rangle\langle C_r, D_r|, \quad (14.48)$$

that we can apply in turn to the state to obtain the reason-induced changes. To do this, we recast reason interpretation as a function

$$Z^\sharp : (\mathbb{D}^2 \times \mathbb{D}^2) \to (\mathbb{D}^2 \to \mathbb{D}^2) \quad (14.49)$$

such that

$$Z^\sharp(|B_r, A_r\rangle, |D_r, C_r\rangle)(|x, y\rangle)$$
$$= \begin{cases} \langle C_r, D_r| & \text{if } \langle B_r, A_r \mid x, y\rangle = 0 \\ \langle 0, 0| & \text{otherwise.} \end{cases} \quad (14.50)$$

Thus

$$Z^\sharp(|B_r, A_r\rangle, |D_r, C_r\rangle)(|x, \overline{x}\rangle)|x, \overline{x}\rangle$$
$$= Z(|B_r, A_r\rangle, |D_r, C_r\rangle)(|x, \overline{x}\rangle). \quad (14.51)$$

We also define

$$Z_r^\sharp = Z^\sharp(|B_r, A_r\rangle, |D_r, C_r\rangle) \quad (14.52)$$

and

$$Z_R^\sharp = \sum_{r \in R} Z_r^\sharp, \quad (14.53)$$

so that

$$Z_R^\sharp |x, \overline{x}\rangle = \left(\sum_{r \in R^\sharp(x)} \langle C_r, D_r| \right) |x, \overline{x}\rangle \quad (14.54)$$

$$= \left(\left\langle \sum_{r \in R^\sharp(x)} C_r, \sum_{r \in R^\sharp(x)} D_r \middle| \right) |x, \overline{x}\rangle > \quad (14.55)$$

$$= \sum_{r \in R^\sharp(x)} C_r x + \sum_{r \in R^\sharp(x)} D_r \overline{x} \quad (14.56)$$

$$= \sum_{r \in R^\sharp(x)} C_r x + D_r \overline{x} \quad (14.57)$$

$$= \sum_{r \in R} Z_r(|x, \overline{x}\rangle) \quad (14.58)$$

$$= Z_R(|x, \overline{x}\rangle). \quad (14.59)$$

14.3.4 Measurement operators

The use here of the Dirac notation differs from the operator formalism of quantum mechanics in two respects: the discrete states do not inhabit the complex vector space usually employed in quantum theory, and nothing ensures the normalization of these vectors needed to obtain probabilistic measurements. Let us examine these issues in turn.

14.3.4.1 Hermitian operators

Quantum theory identifies measurable quantities or measurement actions with Hermitian (complex linear self-adjoint) operators on quantum states. The eigenvalues of each operator correspond to the possible values of the measurable quantity.

Along these lines, one might view the "two-dimensional" structure of the algebraic form of reasons as reflecting the structure of complex numbers, viewing the vector $|A, B\rangle$ as denoting the quantity $1A + iB$. This translation into complex numbers has some attractions, such as taking orthogonally interpreted vectors $|1, 0\rangle$ and $|0, 1\rangle$ into orthogonal dimensions with units 1 and i. However, this algebra retains the quality of real vector spaces. In particular, since $B = -B$ in the binary vector space, we have $A + iB = A - iB$. Thus every such quantity is its own complex conjugate, a property normally associated with real numbers. Now in quantum theory, the conjugate of the vector $|A, B\rangle$ is the complex conjugate of its transpose,

$$|A, B\rangle^* = \langle B^*, A^*|. \tag{14.60}$$

Because complex conjugation degenerates to the identity in the binary setting, vector conjugation degenerates to transposition; that is,

$$|A, B\rangle^* = \langle B, A|. \tag{14.61}$$

Quantum mechanics requires all operators representing physical observables to be Hermitian operators, defined to be linear operators H such that

$$H = H^*. \tag{14.62}$$

The degeneracy of complex conjugation in the binary setting means that Hermitian operators reduce, in the present case, to symmetric operators

$$H = H^{\mathrm{T}}. \tag{14.63}$$

These considerations highlight a substantial divergence of the theory of reason materials from both standard quantum mechanics and continuum mechanics, which for very different reasons, ordinarily requires symmetry of the stress tensor, though it does consider asymmetric stresses in analyzing polar media and other special materials. Let us define the transpose of a reason tensor by

$$(|D, C\rangle\langle A, B|)^{\mathrm{T}} = |B, A\rangle\langle C, D|. \tag{14.64}$$

For such an operator to be Hermitian, the reason would need to have the symmetric form

$$|B, A\rangle\langle A, B|,$$

corresponding to the action of adding the elements B and removing the elements A if the elements A are present and B are absent. But we see very little motivation for requiring reasons, when viewed as either state operators or stress tensors, to exhibit any kind of symmetry. The only case in which such symmetric reasons have been used is in the special case of so-called free defaults, in which $A = \emptyset$, so that the symmetric reason could be written in the form

$$\emptyset \setminus\setminus B \Vvdash B \setminus\setminus \emptyset. \tag{14.65}$$

Such reasoning draws conclusions based only on the absence of those same conclusions, and forms the basis for assumption making in McAllester's (1980) TMS. It would be interesting to find cases in which the more general form of symmetric reasons play a significant role.

14.3.4.2 Probability amplitudes and graded states

In addition to regarding measurement operations as Hermitian operators on states, and measurable quantities as eigenvalues of Hermitian operators, quantum mechanics also considers states as vectors scaled with phase factors ϕ of the form e^{ix}, roots of unity. Quantum mechanics regards vectors differing only by a factor of e^{ix} as representing the same physical state because such factors cancel out in measurements, that is,

$$\langle (e^{ix})^* \psi^* | H | e^{ix} \psi \rangle = e^{-ix} e^{ix} \langle \psi^* | H | \psi \rangle = \langle \psi^* | H | \psi \rangle. \tag{14.66}$$

The phase factor is nonetheless crucial in considering how multiple histories add together, as it provides the means for quantum interference.

The simplest way of carrying over the notion of phase factors to binary state spaces is to note that there is only one root of unity, namely 1, equal to its own negative. Binary spaces thus exhibit only trivial phase factors. Less trivial notions of phase factors might offer some attractions, however, in reflecting notions ranging from degrees of belief to frictionless motion in mechanical states.

Consider first an expansion of the notion of mechanical states that moves from binary vector spaces to states graded by an infinite ring $\mathcal{R}$, thus moving from positions inhabiting $\mathbb{D} = (\mathbb{Z}_2)^D$ to positions inhabiting $\mathcal{R}^D$. In such a theory, positions would consist of weighted combinations of elemental state-components. One might grade states with integers ($\mathbb{Z}^D$), rationals ($\mathbb{Q}^D$), or real numbers ($\mathbb{R}^D$), so that positions allow each element of D to carry a numeric weight. We continue to interpret mental positions in terms of the nonzero attitudes they contain rather than the associated weights, and obtain theories related to quantum mechanics and probabilistic networks through different means of reading out these attitudes from the weighted states.

Measurements of such graded states might either normalize the states to unit vectors, such as probability distributions, or leave states unnormalized. Such schemes would use normalization of states to identify position information within states. Just as varying the complex phase of a state vector in quantum mechanics does not change the physical reality of the state represented by the vector, one might consider the set of conclusions represented by a graded position vector to be independent of the weights on the conclusions in the vector, with conclusions being those dimensions with nonzero weight.

Such graded states offer interesting possibilities for constructing more detailed analyses of RMS behavior. Forces would add or remove reasons as before, but velocities would adds conclusion weights as integers. Abstractly, one thinks of the conclusion weights as either degrees of strength (perhaps probabilities when normalized), or multiplicities indicating inertia values for each dimension in $\mathcal{D}$, so that to remove some conclusion one has to remove it once for each of its supporters. More concretely, one might use the weights to indicate how many reasons support each conclusion. Such measures of support might be superficial, counting either the number of reasons or number of valid reasons supporting the conclusion, or they might measure the number of independent arguments supporting the conclusion. Each of these interpretations suggests viewing the weights as mass or momentum values of a sort, as indicating how many reasons must be disposed of in order to change a conclusion. With no normalization, one may think of the weights as representing mass values for each dimension, thus providing a return to the traditional distinction between scalar mass and vectorial material.

One might use weights in $\mathbb{R}$ to indicate magnitude of forces and certainty factors or perhaps probability increments that change the weights representing probability distributions over the conclusions. The weights corresponding to a given reason might depend on the complexity of the reason itself. For example, if each reason represents a specific force, then multiple conclusions might be interpreted as splitting this force, so that a single-conclusion reason offers a more effective charge for its conclusion than a multiple-conclusion reason. The force associated with the reason might also vary with the antecedents as well, especially if one views reasons with many hypotheses as less compelling than reasons with only one or two hypotheses.

Extending the interpretation of reasons to include real-valued weights might yield a mechanical theory that comes closer to the traditional mechanics distinction between massive materials and mass values.

14.3.4.3 States versus actions

Traditional quantum mechanics considers temporal evolution operators as well as measurement operators, with a Hamiltonian operator specifying the temporal evolution of a quantum system. As in classical Hamiltonian mechanics, the quantum Hamiltonian incorporates all relevant physical laws in a single package. Quantum Hamiltonian systems thus share the problem noted earlier in connection with classical Hamiltonian systems, namely that such characterizations fit poorly with minds and other open, self-acting systems that change the rules of their behavior as they go along.

This uncomfortable fit shows up in the preceding treatment of reasoning operators as well. One ordinarily regards reasoning operations as forms of mental action undertaken by the reasoner, not as measurements. The measurements occurring in reasoning instead take the form of the assessments of attitudes needed to evaluate the applicability of reasons and to determine the effects of reason application on states of mind. Rather than thinking of reasons as measurement operators, it is more natural to think of them as evolution operators that produce later states from earlier ones.

The order dependence of the results of reasoning noted in our earlier discussions of conservatism and reversibility suggest that for some purposes the reasoning steps leading up to some instantaneous state represent more fundamental information about the agent than does the instantaneous state that results from these reasoning steps (Doyle 1992b). The reasons contained in the state are ambiguous and support multiple admissible extensions. The sequence of reasoning steps leading up to an instantaneous state does not admit the same ambiguity.

This observation about reasoning recalls David Finkelstein's (1996) argument that quantum states provide only impoverished ways of talking about quantum behavior, so that one should treat sequences of acts as the primary units of analysis in quantum mechanics. One can take the same point of view in the preceding analysis of reasoning by considering serialized application of reasons or sets of reasons in the tensor composition (11.68).

14.3.5 Simultaneous measurability

The most interesting aspects of quantum-theoretical uncertainty do not concern the measurement issues raised in the preceding section, but instead relate to questions of observability and simultaneous observability, since these questions can bear on what one thinks of existing. Standard quantum theory finds position and momentum to be complementary quantities; that is, one can measure position and momentum precisely or simultaneously, but not both precisely and simultaneously.

Some complementarity relations might arise from fairly general considerations applicable in the discussion of state statistics earlier in this chapter.

For example, the Cramer–Rao inequality

$$J \cdot \delta f \geq 1 \tag{14.67}$$

of statistics reveals such uncertainty relations by examination of the properties of the Fisher information content measure

$$J = \int_{-\infty}^{\infty} pr(x) \left[\frac{d}{dx} (\ln pr(x)) \right]^2 dx \tag{14.68}$$

and variance of statistics f, such as the mean

$$f = \overline{x} = \int_{-\infty}^{\infty} x pr(x) dx. \tag{14.69}$$

It is tempting to view some standard quantities from the theory of computation in such terms, interpreting time–space trade-offs as indications of complementarities between these quantities, especially since at least one of the founders of the theory explicitly sought to follow the model of physics in finding quantitative measures for computational effort (Hartmanis 1973, 1994). Such speculations call for some restraint, however, since some computational trade-offs exist only presupposing special circumstances, and do not represent general measurement incompatibilities of the sort expected of position and momentum.

We may seek similar sets of complementary quantities in psychology and economics. If we look at the RMS, we see indeterminism of momentum with respect to position and vice versa, since a set of base reasons may support several possible extensions, and two different sets of base reasons may give rise to the same extension. These indeterminacies, however, do not prevent simultaneous measurement in all cases.

Numerous other questions about measurement in psychological systems deserve attention if the preceding links from reasoned states to quantum theory prove to be more than mere coincidence. In the RMS, for example, one might ask about which states are observable by measurement. The original RMS only made relaxed (integral) states observable to the environment. These relaxed states thus constituted eigenstates of the observation operators, giving a probability distribution over relaxed states. In contrast, the rational distributed reason maintenance service, RDRMS (Doyle & Wellman 1990; Doyle 1996), made nonrelaxed states observable to the environment, so that tentative answers might be available for use before the RDRMS finished constructing a new relaxed labeling (if ever). For such a system, could one prove that the distribution of answers centers around the equilibrium answer, and that sequential measurements converge to the equilibrium answer?

Part IV
The Metaphysics of Mechanics

15

Materialism

Science and natural philosophy largely abandoned ideas about parallel worlds of mind and matter in the years following Descartes and his dualistic philosophy. By the twentieth century, most of science exhibited an unhesitant materialistic metaphysics. The present investigation occasions an opportunity to reexamine ideas about materialism.

15.1 What is materialism?

The standard conception of materialism is the thesis that all events in the world consist of ordinary physical matter, energy, and other physical properties, denying the existence or causal influence of other things. It does not deny the possibility of using nonphysical properties to characterize physical things; civilization's use of numbers to quantify physical dimensions would suffer greatly were this so. But it does deny that these nonphysical characterizations play any physical role.

One should note that materialism exhibits an open-ended character. When philosophers first bruited materialism, it referred to everything being the tangible, visible stuff of the world. Eventually this conception required enlargement to include the invisible, intangible stuff—energy, electromagnetic fields, spin, neutrinos—that later physics developed as physical entities or properties, even though some of these are far removed from the direct experience characteristic of the original conceptions of physical materials.

In the current sense of this standard conception, many psychological and economic entities, such as beliefs, preferences, and strategies, do not count as material objects, or at best count as alternative ways of referring to conventional physical objects, as in Minsky's statement that the mind is what the brain does, or Searle's statement that brains cause minds, that is, the term *mind* is

373

an alternative term for the activity of the brain, or for some abstraction of the brain's activity.

This received sense of materialism clashes with the terminology used in the present development, in which we speak of classes organizations for minds as psychological materials. It might be more appropriate to use the term *physicalism* for the doctrine of materialism to dissociate the thesis about physical properties from the term *material*. I say more about this clash of terminology in the following sections.

15.2 Why materialism?

There is no direct scientific evidence for materialism. Indeed, since it denies the existence of a broad class of things defined only by their difference from physical things, it has more the character of a thesis that can be falsified but never proven.

Lack of direct evidence for materialism, and even the impossibility of direct evidence, does not mean no evidence exists. The primary evidence for materialism is indirect, consisting of the gradual advance of science in finding physical explanations for many aspects of the world. These many successes, some coming through an expansion of the conception of the physical, now appear to explain many of the mechanisms of astronomy, weather, geology, engineering machines and materials, the biological mechanisms of the body, and the neuronal mechanisms of the brain. There are still plenty of things not yet reduced to physical theory at all, such as literature, art, sociology, and politics. Reductions of other things have been proposed that remain controversial among society as a whole, such as the origins of species and the operation of conscious human intelligence. The prevalence of materialist convictions among scientists makes these reductions much less controversial in scientific circles.

Compared with prescientific days, in which every ill wind blew by the action of a capricious, inexplicable, and invisible spirit, the success of materialist explanations have been immense. Moreover, though science includes many competing and clearly imperfect theories, the intellectual coherence and predictive power of science as a whole forms a stark contrast with the much deeper disagreements among most theories of everything else, from psychology and political economy to philosophy and theology. Many materialist convictions no doubt arise by combining these successes, using repeated successes to justify expectations of continued and eventual complete success, with a sort of Ockham's razor of intelligibility instructing one to adopt the simplest and most coherent theory.

15.3 Is materialism true?

The materialist thesis has engendered controversy for thousands of years. The reality of greed, envy, and intense hatred is obvious to even the dullest observer, and claims that these obvious realities do not exist or represent only chemical arrangements strike many as absurd. The courage of heroes, the honor of leaders, and the love of mothers cannot be directly observed, but appear to many as no less real than particles for which the observations consist of tracks left in a cloud chamber. Ideas inspire, desires drive, and ferocity frightens in declamatory epic and written novel, but physics explains at best how sound travels and ink adheres, not how these represent human existence. For many, these appearances lie beyond physical materials but not beyond human knowledge, understanding, and science (see, e.g., Jackson's 1986 refutation of physicalism). Taking overt appearances as a guide, humans live in a world populated by both physical materials and nonphysical objects. No one knows the boundary between these types of entities, but the nearly universal recognition given to both makes a dualist view of the world seem more plausible than either strict physical materialism or strict physical immaterialism. In this view, the indisputable advance of science helps illuminate the extent of the physicalist realm, and comes closer and closer to its boundaries, but has no more chance of extending the physical realm at will than Knut had of driving the sea from Danish shores.

Faced with the unverifiable character of the materialist thesis and the obvious and seemingly ineradicable nonmaterial appearances of human existence, some have backed away from claiming materialism as a thesis to taking materialism as the methodology of looking for explanations of phenomena supposing that the materialist thesis is true. Methodological materialism offers some respectable attractions, but in itself no greater attractions than a corresponding methodological immaterialism that looks for explanations as if immaterialism were true. Methodological materialism shares most of its attractions with materialism itself, namely the success of materialist explanations in physics, successes generally less forthcoming from methodological immaterialism.

The difficulties with methodological materialism are two. First, it offers no inbuilt failure criterion. The point of science is to find coherent ways of understanding experience. Methodological materialism, as usually phrased, does not say to seek materialist explanations first, and then look for immaterial explanations when materialist explanations are not forthcoming, or remain less enlightening or become far more complex than dualist explanations. Methodological materialism just says to keep seeking materialist explanations, independent of the quality of either the resulting physical explanations or of alternative explanations. Without some stopping criterion that recognizes the ordinary intellectual norms of scientific explanation, methodological materialism is hard to distinguish from overt materialism itself. The second difficulty with methodological materialism relates closely to the first. Scientists are people, and people are notoriously (but not necessarily universally) incapable of living as if something were true without eventually coming to believe it true, more or less independently of evidence they gain for the truth or falsity of the belief. Thus methodological materialism is not just methodologically hard to distinguish from the materialist thesis itself, but pursuing it strongly inclines one to become a materialist.

15.4 New materials for materialism

The present broadening of mechanics provides a way out of materialist controversies, or at least of converting them to more focused technical questions, and does this in a fairly traditional way.

One cannot see, taste, feel, hear, or touch broadcast radio waves, but this insubstantiality did not cause scientists to scrap materialism. Discovering some intelligible phenomenon outside of the then-current scope of materialism led physicists to expand the notion of physical events and properties to include electromagnetic fields as part of the physical universe. This expansion seemed reasonable because the effects of radio waves were visible (and audible) given the right physical detecting apparatus, and because these fields had measurable effects on indisputably physical materials, these days represented by loudspeaker cones and the soup in the microwave oven.

Bringing the stuff of psychology and economics into the realm of mechanical description constitutes a similar expansion of the notion of material, one that offers some possibility of making the positive content of materialism true. The idea of radio waves was plausible and even accepted long before one had mathematical equations characterizing their relation to motion and charges because people were already very familiar with waves in water, and mathematical characterizations of these familiar waves made the idea of waves in some invisible ether seemed just as respectable and ultimately intelligible as their proven analogs on pond and sea. In the same way, showing that psychological and economic entities share structural and behavioral axioms with planets and electrons provides reasonable justification for regarding these additional inhabitants of the material realm. The lack of proven theories of the behavior of these new materials does not make this expansion unreasonable. It is true that our theories of psychological and economic behavior are weaker, more diverse, and more riddled with yet-unexplained exceptions than is celestial mechanics, but natural philosophers considered ethereal waves reasonable objects of investigation long before Maxwell developed his equations and long before anyone could explain why some waves passed through a body and why others were stopped cold (or more correctly, stopped hot).

The nature of interactions between the mental and the physical forms a key topic relevant to the reasonability of this expansion of materialism. In the broadened mechanics, one can view people as consisting of both physical and mental materials. Now it might be that all forces are either ones generated by and affecting only physical materials or generated by and affecting only mental materials. This strict independence seems unlikely, as mental events clearly have physical consequences, as anyone punched in the face by an enraged playground bully can attest.

It might also be that physical and mental materials move in exact correspondence. When such exact correlations exist, one may suppose that one type of entity determines the other. Traditionally this has been viewed as the supervenience of the mental over the physical; immaterialists might take it just as well as cases of supervenience of the physical over the mental.

More exciting questions arise as one seeks to identify interactions lacking both strict independence and exact correspondence. Now while we have clear evidence of physical changes that leave mental state invariant, as when someone lost in thought rides an elevator, and examples of mental changes that leave physical situations untouched, as when wishing does not make something come true, we have no clear and repeatable evidence of how physical matter might exert forces on mental states, perhaps leaving the bodily state unchanged, or how mental materials might exert forces on physical bodies, as in psychokinesis. Truesdell's (1956) *Isis* query mentioned earlier sought evidence regarding such some types of such forces. Presumably Truesdell would have said more about it if anyone answered him affirmatively and convincingly. Yet not all such investigations have failed. Recent experiments conducted using standard double-blind experimental methodologies have shown improved medical outcomes for patients when people pray for them over those not receiving such attentions. Even if one denies all deities and interprets prayer only as directed mental activity, these results, if true, may identify prayer as involving nontrivial mental–physical interactions. Experiments studying the effects of placebos may also shed light here.

It is clear that investigating the properties of mental materials poses great challenges. Detecting neutrinos is hard, but this difficulty is not enlarged by attempts of the neutrino to hide from the detector. However, if one asks a group of teenagers and their parents to raise their hands if they have engaged in premarital sex, one faces a different type of observational difficulty, in past times if not still today.

Even if the broadened mechanics developed here offers a means for enlarging the scope of materialism so as to convert some points of controversy into subjects of theoretical and experimental investigation, it may not prove acceptable to everyone. For some, the negative content of traditional materialism—the nonexistence of spirits, souls, gods, and the like—might be as important as the positive content asserting the universal involvement of physical entities. For some, strict physical materialism might be an essentially religious conviction, not a hypothesis subject to scientific disconfirmation. For others, the expectations of successfully demonstrating mental forces producing physical effects may seem so remote that any expenditure of effort on attempting such demonstrations would constitute a waste of effort better spent on more certain needs.

Such possible rejections of an expanded conception of materialism do not undercut the central hypothesis of the current investigation. However one approaches the question of materialism, even a theory in which nonphysical masses and forces were completely determined by physical ones would still be of intellectual value in understanding and investigating the nature of mental processes their limits. These limits might always be traceable back to physical limitations, but the particular details of how the mental processes are realized in physical systems may obscure the interesting details. Such considerations are familiar in the philosophy of language and logic; while the shape and strength of a dinner table might derive from its molecular and atomic structure, those details are essentially irrelevant to the properties of interest to one contemplating ordinary uses of the table.

16

Reductionism

The preceding discussion of materialism raised the issue of the reducibility of all natural law to the behavior of materials, especially to ordinary physical materials, concluding that mechanical laws of mental and economic entities can prove useful whether or not one can reduce such laws to the behavior of physical materials. This chapter examines the question of reducibility among natural laws in more detail.

16.1 What is reducibility?

The notion of reducibility of theories in logic means nothing more than the entailment of one theory by another upon the addition of suitable definitions to the reduced theory. That is, we say that theory T_1 is reducible to theory T_2 just in case there exist definitions $D(T_1, T_2)$ such that

$$T_2 \models T_1 \cup D(T_1, T_2). \tag{16.1}$$

For this to make sense, we must assume that the two theories and the definitions have been expressed in terms of the same language, possibly by extending the languages of each of the original theories to include both of these and all the terms introduced in the definitions.

We contrast the logical notion of theoretical reducibility with the thesis of physical reductionism, which we normally just call reductionism. This thesis, which has often accompanied materialism, states that one can reduce all behavior of our world and its parts to the pure theory of physical entities. To many physicists and others, this has driven the search for fundamental particles and their behavioral laws, on the assumption that knowledge of the laws governing these fundamental particles and the arrangement of particles at some instant would determine the behavior of the entire universe, or at least provide all possible knowledge about it. Most people assume this reduction to fundamental

379

particle behaviors proceeds by stages; economics reduces to psychology, psychology reduces to biology, biology reduces to chemistry, chemistry reduces to nuclear physics, nuclear physics reduces to quarks, and quarks reduce to string theory.

16.2 Why reducibility?

To the logically minded, the second question for any scientific or mathematical theory, following the question of truth, is whether the theory already follows from something else one understands. Nonlogicians, in contrast, often find questions of the consequences of the theory more interesting than possible reductions to other things. One must distinguish this common logical and scientific interest in whether one theory reduces to another from the theory of physical reducibility, for the standard interest comes to the question looking for an answer, while the theory of physical reducibility comes to the question maintaining an answer.

The reasons for physical reducibility have much in common with the reasons for materialism. The aesthetics of science provide some motivation to hope for reducibility. Scientists look for parsimony in their theories, and many view a thoroughly reductionist theory as simpler and less presumptuous than a theory based on different theories for each level, no matter how complicated the reduction definitions bridging the levels. The main reason, however, stems from the materialist assumption itself. If everything is composed of pieces of matter and nothing else, the simplest behavioral expectation takes the behavior of the complex to consist of the behavior of the pieces and nothing else.

16.3 Is physical reducibility true?

To assess the truth of the hypothesis of physical reducibility, let us examine some of the successes of reducibility, some of the failures, and considerations regarding whether we can extrapolate with justification from these successes and failures to embrace or reject the hypothesis.

16.3.1 Successes of reducibility

The progress of science has provided many reductions, some spectacular, of phenomena at one level to smaller-scale laws and structural assumptions to bolster belief in reducibility.

The derivation of the everyday uniform gravity of the Earth from the original Newtonian theory and the Newtonian theory from the deep geometric theory of general relativity provide simple examples. Newtonian gravitation implies the force of gravity differs between the elevation of one's feet and one's head. Rational mechanics shows this force to vary not with distance from the surface of the Earth but with distance from the center of mass of the Earth, and a simple calculation of the difference, given the great distance at which we stand from the center, shows that the difference in this force lies beyond that which can be measured without extremely sophisticated apparatus. Similar calculations show how Newtonian gravitation approximates the more exact calculations of general relativity, in which variations in the mass composition of nearby portions of the Earth's interior modulate the primary dependence on distance from center of mass. Indeed, scientists used this theory to construct intricate devices for mapping subterranean features by measuring and interpreting these minute variations in gravitational field.

The example of gravitation illustrates a satisfying and common but mundane example of successful reduction of one theory to another. The explanation of the periodic table of the elements in terms of the quantum-mechanical atomic theory provides a more spectacular example, explaining the primary chemical properties of pure elements of matter, with decomposition into neutrons, protons, and electrons explaining relative weights of elements, and the orbital shell structure of the electrons explaining the chemical valences. This reduction too involves approximation, but in this case the approximations make no practical or theoretical difference to the essentially discrete observable features of the different elements.

Other examples populate many areas of science up to and including the human level, such as the role of the helical structure of DNA and RNA in mediating production of biological materials.

16.3.2 False successes

These truly successful reductions deserve attention and praise, but not all putative reductions actually serve as claimed. Indeed, standard scientific education enshrines prominent cases of false and unproven reductions involving mechanics. In the first case, many textbooks claim that continuum mechanics follows as the limiting case of the particle mechanics of many particles. This assertion has been known false since the time of Euler, who discovered the independence of the law of rotational momentum from the law of linear momentum, but a continuing stream of textbooks propagate the clear falsehood that this law of rotational momentum follows from the law of linear momentum. This independence does not rear its head in the realm of (nonrelativistic) celestial mechanics, because balance of linear momentum does imply balance of rotational momentum in the special case of particles that move under mutual forces. The independence of linear and rotational balance laws appears unavoidably in the mechanics of continuous materials, in which this independence underlies the fundamental concept of the stress field.

The second case consists of the claim that classical mechanics follows from quantum mechanics as the limit of the quantum theory as we assign smaller and smaller values to Planck's constant. We do not yet know whether this limiting process does yield classical mechanics, only that the putative "proofs" are either flawed or concern only simple examples that provide little basis for extrapolation to more complicated systems. Instead of providing convincing arguments, the extant proofs rely on approximation assumptions of such substantial character as to call the reasonability of the derivation into question as instances of assuming the hypothesis rather than true reducibility. One might hope that future theoretical progress will provide the claimed limit results, but such results lie far beyond current computational abilities.

16.3.3 Failures of reducibility

As indicated by these examples, while some theoretical reductions are exact, many involve approximations. What these examples do not illustrate as well is that almost all these reductions deduce only some of the qualities of the larger entity from its components and their arrangement. A thoroughly successful reduction of scientific laws to laws involving the structure of small bits of matter and energy must answer many questions left unaddressed by the examples of reductions we currently possess.

Of the many things left unreduced, we may classify some as cases in which reductions seem hopeless from a theoretical or computational point of view, and others as cases in which reductions seem obviously preposterous.

16.3.3.1 Hopeless reductions

Hilary Putnam (1975, pp. 275–276) presents an example involving a small cube and a board pierced by a round hole and a square hole. Because of the dimensions of the cube and holes, the cube passes through the square hole but not through the round hole. Putnam points out this explanation has no connection with the underlying physical laws; at best one can compute all possible trajectories of the cube and observe that none pass through the round hole, a metaphysical explanation rather than a physical one.

Just as with the lack of connection between physical law and the geometric properties of the board and cube, the general problem plaguing claims of reducibility is that the definitions on which reductions depend, definitions some philosophers call *bridge laws*, offer no easy way of coping with the wide variety of materials or means of realizing common physical arrangements. Bridge laws for the holes and cube would seem to require complexity rivaling that of the universe, which hardly makes them candidates for reasonable physical laws satisfying the usual criteria of simplicity and intelligibility.

Truesdell (1984c, p. 29) offers additional examples in which we can actually comprehend something of the complexity and essential irrelevance of the reduction. Mathematically, we can construct the rational numbers from the integers, the real numbers from the rationals, and the complex numbers from the reals. Whitehead and Russell (1910) spend three volumes seeking to develop arithmetic from logic. No one looks for explanations of the Cauchy–Riemann equations or other central aspects of the theory of complex functions in terms of natural numbers. Truesdell likens hypothesized reductions of properties of fluids to nuclear physics to using only logical concepts to analyze functions of complex variables. This comparison seems too generous to reductionist claims, for we actually have the tower of fairly complete mathematical constructions of number systems mentioned earlier, but have no comparably complete construction of the viscosity of honey from quantum mechanics.

Gargantuan bridge laws may make some reductions theoretical or computational intractable, but other reductions go beyond mere theoretical or computational intractability and involve proof-theoretic or computational undecidability. The familiar differential equations of physics generally admit numerical integration, but Pour-El and Richards (1989) and others have shown that some solutions to these equations are recursively uncomputable (see also Blum *et al.* 1998). More generally, Branicky (1994, 1995) and others have demonstrated simple physical models for which the equations exhibit arbitrary behaviors. The complexity of these behaviors goes beyond the merely chaotic. Merely chaotic systems alone call reductionistic computations into question even in principle, for solving them to a given level of accuracy may require computational precision expanding at an exponential rate with the size of the temporal interval involved. The arbitrarily complex solutions permit encoding of arbitrary binary sequences in solutions, such as the solution to the halting problem for Turing machines, which is computationally uncomputable. One example consists of a three-body mechanical problem, in which a minute planetesimal orbits between two very massive bodies. We say that the altitude of the planetesimal has a zero crossing whenever the planetesimal passes through the axis connecting the massive bodies. Given any sequence of positive numbers, one can find an orbit of the system such that the durations between zero crossings of the planetesimal correspond to the stipulated sequence of numbers.

These examples of recursively uncomputable reductions shade off into the realm of the preposterous because the difficulties generally involve initial conditions of infinite precision, or at least physically infeasible amounts of information. Chapter 18 discusses hopes for avoiding these difficulties by positing a finite universe, in which every initial condition involves only a finite amount of information.

16.3.3.2 Preposterous reductions

If reduction seems hopeless in these examples, claims of reducibility seem preposterous in other cases. The obvious cases involve meaning, significance, and perhaps consciousness. No one expects the physical characteristics of ink on paper to determine properties of the novel, symphony, or portrait formed by these elements. One might talk through a causal process by which these elements have the appropriate effects on persons, but such a process would exhibit a complexity and specificity to make Putnam's cube and holes example seem utterly straightforward.

Even relevance of physical considerations to some aspects of a problem does not mean that the problem can be reduced to lower levels of physical detail. As Truesdell (1984c, p. 47) puts it, physicists know better than to tell a psychologist to solve quantum-mechanical equations to predict the behavior of rats, or to chastise a traffic engineer for constructing a stochastic model of traffic flow that ignores the physics and chemistry of individual vehicles.

The impossibility of these reductions is especially clear if one holds to some traditional nonmaterialist views, according to which some psychological behavior proceeds independently of physical laws. But even if one assumes that such behavior operates in terms of physical materials alone, no plausible story exists at present in which supposed psychological or economic laws would appear as consequences of physical laws. On the evidence, psychological and economic laws could very well represent additional constraints on the universe beyond those posed by standard physical laws.

In the impoverished subset of psychology addressed by the theory of computation we find a realm of behavior explicitly separated from any means of realization in matter or persons. Universal machines constitute a somewhat less problematic case in which reductions simply don't make sense. As Gandy (1980) has shown, the notion of universal computation admits a wide range of variations in the physics of the world. Indeed, the notion of universal machines is intended to decouple the behavior of the machine from the behavior of the materials from which it is constructed. One constructs universal machines to deliberately foil any reduction of the machine behavior to the underlying physics; the behavior of the machine reduces entirely to abstract properties of the initial conditions of the physical realization. This sort of reduction to initial conditions might be called a reduction, but it certainly is not a very compelling one.

We think of computation, however, as an essentially mathematical and artificial subject, not as something existing in nature and exhibiting natural regularities. The case is much less clear regarding psychology, which represents entities occurring naturally and presumably exhibiting regularities of their own. Suppose that economic rationality, or some restricted version of such, characterizes the behavior of the portions of the universe we call humans. If this behavioral law does derive from fundamental physical principles, it cannot be through the received meanings of these principles, which involve utterly different concepts. At best, the limits in laws of limited rationality might owe some of their shape to physical laws. Even if one expands the conception of physical laws along lines suggested in the present investigation, laws of rationality might, as noted earlier, represent additional constraints on behavior beyond those found in traditional physical laws.

16.3.4 Extrapolation from experience

What can we say about the truth of physical reducibility upon consideration of these successes and failures? Many people maintain a strong belief in the continued advance of the reductionist program and in its ultimate success in what some physicists call a "theory of everything," a theory of the laws of the ultimately small particles or physical components, currently thought to be superstrings. Many take belief in such reducibility as a fundamental tenet obvious to everyone, not as a hope based on evidence or other knowledge. The many successful reductions of complex system behaviors to behavior of subsystems, which underlie a wide range of engineering successes, certainly helps maintain such belief. We nevertheless cannot view reductionism as guaranteed of success, for as the preceding discussion has indicated, the success of reductionism would imply progress beyond all that is currently conceivable.

This is not to say that belief in physical reducibility lacks all justification. Extrapolation from experience certainly justifies many human expectations, and the reductionist may well cite the history of successful reductions to extrapolate continuation of such successes. The problem with this argument is that the progress of scientific reductions is a logical process, not a continuous process. Indeed, most examples of reductions bridge significant differences of levels, as in the case of the quantum-theoretic explanation of the periodic table. While continuous processes naturally admit extrapolation, at least over short intervals of time, and continuation of past experience forms a staple of scientific expectations, the logical structures of science offer no notion of continuity to incur the expectation that reducibility of one theory indicates reducibility of the next. If physical reducibility were itself some continuous physical process, it might be reasonable to judge physical reducibility proven by the past history of examples reductions. Because reducibility is a logical conception, no principle exists to justify concluding general physical reducibility on the basis of some examples.

The plain fact is that one expects laws at one level to have *some* consequences at higher levels, even many consequences at those levels, so the mere existence of such reductions and their applications should not surprise anyone or lead to suppositions that all important facts at the higher levels follow from those at the lower levels. Indeed, consequences at the higher levels, even if extremely numerous or infinite, provide little evidence for any assumption of universal reducibility to laws at any level.

Peano arithmetic, a standard and fairly simple logical theory, illustrates this point. Peano arithmetic axiomatizes the basic arithmetic operations on natural numbers in terms of the constant 0 and a successor function. This successor function can be considered as existing at a lower level than familiar arithmetic facts. Indeed, it resembles nothing so much as the finger counting of the very young student. In spite of this low level of expression, one can prove infinitely many consequences from the axioms of Peano arithmetic, ranging from many arithmetic facts used every day in commerce and engineering to important number-theoretic generalities, including the principles of provability in Peano arithmetic captured in Boolos' (1979) System G. Peano arithmetic thus exemplifies the low-level theory with a perhaps infinite number of higher-level consequences. In spite of this plenitude of consequences, Peano arithmetic does not suffice to demonstrate all important higher-level arithmetic consequences. The first example of such was identified in a landmark paper by Paris and Harrington (1977) showing that a reasonably natural true assertion about Ramsey functions is expressible but unprovable in Peano arithmetic. Other logicians have subsequently identified even more natural arithmetic propositions unprovable in Peano arithmetic. One thus cannot extrapolate the reducibility of many interesting truths of arithmetic to Peano's axioms to conclude the reducibility of all interesting truths of arithmetic to this theory.

The speedup theorem of the theory of automata provides an example of a somewhat different character. This theorem indicates that computation of any function can be sped up arbitrarily much, essentially by reducing computation of any finite portion of the function to computation by a finite automaton or lookup table, which reduces the effort in computing values on that finite portion to negligible amounts. Such speedups hold for any recursively computable function, even though the entire function may lie far beyond the computational capabilities of finite automata. The speedup does not affect the overall difficulty of computing the function, of course, for no improvement to a finite number of input values outweighs the costs incurred on the infinite number of remaining values.

For another example, consider a thermonuclear bomb. On disassembly, one can understand a nearly complete succession of its parts in terms of familiar kinematic or electronic behaviors: switches, wires, levers, and the like. Yet no matter how numerous these parts, the central functions of nuclear fission and fusion lie quite outside kinematics and electronics, rendering the extrapolation to electromechanical reducibility false.

Indeed, if one seeks to extrapolate prospects for reducibility from past experience, one seems equally justified in expecting failure of reducibility. If one looks at the history of physics for evidence, relativity and quantum mechanics show how irrelevant past successful reductions were to expecting the utterly unexpected phenomena of quantum mechanics and general relativity. Newton and his contemporaries could look at the world and see what we now call electromagnetic forces at work in light, magnets, lightning, and static sparks and know that they had yet to find a complete theory of such forces. Even the phenomena suggesting the need for relativistic and quantum laws were unseen apart from explaining the solidity of matter. The classical theory of the electron eventually revealed difficulties seemingly insurmountable within the framework of this theory; the mass of the electron in motion from cathode ray tubes revealed problems with the reigning conceptions of conservation of mass.

Just as uncontroversial axioms of set theory may require augmentation by special principles, such as the relatively acceptable axiom of choice or more esoteric axioms found necessary in some specialized studies, the evidential situation in physics offers no good reason for assuming that the consequences of the recognized laws explain all experience. When it comes to understanding scientific structure, not to mention ordinary designs, we enjoy no general principle ensuring the existence of reductions or explanations for the entire system from the existence of partial reductions or explanations.

16.4 Science without reductionism

The preceding discussion casts strong doubts on the truth of the reductionist thesis, though not on continued success at finding reductions among theories. Most of these doubts have existed for some time, however, so it seems unlikely that reductionists will change their minds soon. The doubts, perhaps strengthened by the mechanics presented here, do raise the question of how the outlook of science changes if it abandons the currently conventional reductionism.

Abandonment of reductionism changes little about the practice of science in its local details. Scientists still look to understand experience, to generate new experience (experiments) relevant to theoretical questions or areas of interest, to detect regularities in this experience, to identify structures, to decompose and aggregate behaviors. These activities give rise to new laws, and ordinary scientific prudence seeks to check the logical and mathematical interrelations of these laws with others. We can expect to see reductions obtained in some cases, but not in others. Indeed, sometimes conceptual analysis of the new laws reveals not reductions to laws known earlier, but discovery of better or deeper conceptualizations of the new laws in isolation, perhaps by separating the force of the new laws into several aspects that support generalization more easily. Such reductions represent descents in new directions rather than descents to lower levels of existing laws.

In contrast, abandonment of reductionism promises to change the global shape of science. Rather than having a single tree of theories that bottom out in a fundamental theory of everything, the picture changes to a forest of intertwined trees and vines sharing some roots and leaves but enjoying substantially independent existence. This forest of theories restores science to an open, potentially endless activity as new laws are discovered in each of the trees, and even as new trees are discovered. In this view, each of the fields of computation, biology, psychology, and economics represents a significant scientific discipline, but in each case one must view the laws of the subject, such as they are, as additional laws constraining the world, not as regularities derivable from more fundamental physical theories.

This pluralistic view of science turns the conceit of ordinary reductionism on its head. Conventional reductionism hopes for a fundamental theory of everything, ordinarily viewed as a theory of the smallest particles or elements of the universe, so that the local laws of these elements capture all of physical law and determine all behaviors of constructs from these fundamental elements. Recent debates about the "end of science" refer to such a reductionist viewpoint, since if one determines laws for string theory, then science has done its job and can retire to let the engineers and computers do the rest. Engineering remains because, to paraphrase Dostoyevsky's character in *The Brothers Karamazov*, if there are no other laws, everything else is permissible, and the question is how to use this freedom to achieve what one wants. Science without reductionism makes the laws of these tiny elements just one source of constraint among many, and perhaps not even the most constraining when compared with laws at higher levels that rule out vast areas of the freedoms given by the microscopic laws. Rather than falling on fundamental laws that provide the sole source of constraints, the burdens of cutting down possibilities to actualities may fall on higher-level laws that themselves answer almost all questions about behavior at the higher levels independent of the fundamental laws. Laws of rational or bounded rational decisions might determine all we need to know about some aspects of human behavior, and might still determine these answers even if some aspect of superstring theory were different.

Abandoning reductionism changes expectations about the content of physical laws as well. For example, the main reason for the conventional suppositions that physics is local and reversible is that the laws of some fundamental particles are local and reversible. If these laws exhaust the constraints on our world, then physics itself and all that lies above are local and reversible as well. If laws of biology, psychology, and economics stand independent of laws of fundamental particles, we find no reason to suppose natural law local and reversible unless each of these independent sets of laws exhibit the same characteristics. More likely, the larger scale constraints imposed by these higher-level laws represent nonlocalities and irreversibilities that filter out many of the natures possible given only the local and reversible microscopic laws.

Abandoning reductionism also changes the value system of science. The conventional value system of science values deeper and more fundamental principles more highly than superficial manifestations or phenomena explained by these principles. The aim of science is understanding, and the deeper principles explain more. This is not the only reasonable value structure; engineering often turns this around and values the superficial conclusions more highly than the underlying explanations when these conclusions provide the immediate direction or application in practice. The standard consequence of the conventional value system has been to value physics more highly than, say, materials science. If physics provides the fundamental laws, then it provides the greatest scientific benefit. Abandoning reductionism changes this value system by spreading scientific value across independent fields. In each of these fields, scientists may accord more value to more fundamental areas, but across fields comparisons would more likely involve opportunities for immediate progress and impact on technological opportunities.

16.5 The end(s) of science

Many scientists evince the prejudice that the laws of physics are almost completely known and that these laws determine all characteristics of the universe save the initial conditions; and some harbor hopes that these laws also determine most of the characteristics of the initial conditions as well. Smart and articulate scientists of this stripe do a good job of convincing many laypeople and other scientists that we therefore stand close to the end of scientific inquiry. This view is as false today as it was a century ago, when scientists made the same claims and exerted similar persuasion just prior to the discovery of relativity and quantum theories.

The false view of the end of science starts with a misconception going back to Leibniz: if everything is constructed out of particles, and the laws governing the particles are known, then all physical behavior is deducible in principle from the laws and the initial conditions. This is wrong, in both practical terms and in principle.

In practice, most ordinary properties of ordinary objects (such as tables and chairs) are largely independent of the behavior of the particulate materials from which the tables are constructed, just as properties of computations are mainly independent of the type of machine conducting the computations.

In principle, initial conditions are unknowable, and important properties of systems remain uncomputable even if known. We possess no evidence for the freedom of physical laws from exceptional cases or from higher-level constraints that introduce nonlocalities or irreversibilities. As far as we have observational or experimental evidence, physical laws at one level are generally independent of laws at lower levels. The higher levels need not be deducible from the lower. If one can embed Turing machines in physics, as seems likely, some higher-level questions will be uncomputable from the lower levels. Even supposing we do complete the so-called theories of everything, we haven't a clue as to the initial conditions, especially cosmologically.

Most areas of direct human interest—psychology, biology, sociology, politics, economics—are utterly independent of familiar physical law, much less more subtle theories of everything. The same behavior could be realized in many different ways. Proposed theories of everything do not provide the concepts needed to answer (or even pose) these questions. How can something be a theory of everything when it cannot even state most interesting questions? Much of science, even reductionistic science, is trying to find formulations defining phenomena or concepts in terms of other, perhaps more fundamental, concepts. Are these scientific problems not scientific problems? As we stand nowhere near the point at which all scientific questions have been answered in principle, formulating and answering questions about the world are problems that will be with us as far as we can see.

Proposed theories of everything hardly spell the end of science. Virtually all subjects of scientific or human interest are independent of these theories, which rather than providing final answers, simply form the theoretical materials from which we construct objects of interest. Theories of everything end science just as much as a theory of ink and paper ends literature, music, and art. These theories remain irrelevant to most of science, and vast vistas of unknown answers fill the foreseeable future. The end of science is to answer these questions and understand the world around us; we may rejoice that this occupation may never end.

17

Effectiveness

As was noted earlier, the traditional conception of what we call mechanical computation or computation by machine relies on a purely kinematical conception of mechanics. It entirely omits any notion of force and focuses attention only on abstract states and motion between them. In this it follows a trend in mechanical formalism that moved away from considering forces and spatial motions to considering mainly Hamiltonian motion through abstract spaces, with no mention of either the central notion of force or the key notion of mass (cf. Hermann 1990, Sussman & Wisdom 2001).

This disconnect between mechanical computation and mechanics comes closest to being bridged in the related field of information theory, in which some authors have viewed information content as a type of mass measure (Manthey & Moret 1983) and have produced formal relations between information content and thermostatic theories of entropy (Chaitin 1975). These ropes tossed across the gap lack tether to the notion of force and still leave the crossing perilous.

Let us now reconsider the notion of computation from the mechanical point of view, to treat "mechanizability"—viewed in terms of machines—as *mechanizability*—viewed in terms of mechanics. We seek to understand the notion of effectiveness as involving not just abstract kinematics but also those fundamental concepts that distinguish mechanics from geometry, especially the concepts of rate of motion limited by limits on force and bounds on the rate of work.

Discussions in previous chapters have touched on these ideas already. We examined elements of these ideas related to information-theoretic bounds on communication rates. We also have examined the notion of memory as mass, and most computational models, especially Turing machines and random access machines, involve notions of memory.

392

17.1 What is effective computation?

We can formulate the common notion of effective computation in several equivalent ways, but all reduce to computation using a fixed set of simple operations that we can perform without error.

The theory of computation as we know it today was initiated by Church and Turing in the mid-1930s. Church's (1941) theory grew from purely logical sources, and was phrased in terms of symbolic operations that reflected elementary logical operations. Though Church himself knew mechanics well, his theory of computation was not a mechanical one, but a procedural one. Indeed, Church's thesis had nothing to do with machines, but with the reducibility of all "effective" procedures to procedures expressed in terms of his elementary logical operations of naming, abstraction, application, substitution, and simplification. Today Church's thesis seems utterly unexceptional, and teachers may be hard pressed to convey to the student how strong this thesis seemed at the time, so deeply has the culture absorbed the concept of "a simple matter of programming" implicit in programs millions of lines long.

Turing (1936), in contrast, viewed mechanical computation in terms of physical mechanism from the start by focusing attention on the properties and abilities of the computer. At the time, of course, the word *computer* meant a person who performed computations. For example, the 1946 resume of one of Truesdell's wartime co-workers at the MIT radiation laboratory listed *computer* as her occupation. Only later did the meaning change to refer to the mechanical or electrical devices called computers today. Turing's analysis looked to the visual, cognitive, and manual capabilities of computers to formalize computation in terms of writing clearly distinguishable marks on regions of paper and moving of attention to adjacent or nearby regions on the basis of simple rules. Turing's analysis argued for finite alphabets on the grounds that infinite alphabets of necessity must have symbols resembling each other arbitrarily closely, thus violating the requirement of clear distinguishability, and for simple motion of hand and eye to nearby parts of the paper as representative of clearly feasible physical motions. He argued for simple rules determining the markings and motions appropriate to the locally visible markings as the only sort a person can follow without confusion.

Most regard Turing's initial arguments as perfectly adequate to demonstrating that effective computability encompasses at least the operations he formalized in what have since become known as Turing machines, namely machines with a finite set of tapes, a finite set of heads for reading or writing symbols from a finite alphabet on the tapes, and a finite-state machine for guiding the actions of the heads based on the contents of the tape squares underlying them.

The importance of the class of things computable by Turing machines became clearer with Turing's proof of the equivalence of his notion of mechanical computability with Church's notion of recursive computability. Because these two very different conceptions of computability produced the same class of functions, many people at the time and in later years have regarded this class as capturing the correct or natural notion of effective computability.

Recent years have seen other characterizations of the notion of effective computation, notably Scott's (1982) topological characterization in terms of limits in spaces of finite approximations.

17.2 Why effectiveness?

The initial reason for formulating the notion of effective computation was to answer a question posed by Hilbert's (1902, p. 414) second problem, which asked for direct methods of determining the consistency, consequences, and truths of logic. It seemed somewhat scandalous that mathematicians had worked for two millennia trying to prove Euclid's fifth or parallel postulate of geometry before Lobachevsky described a non-Euclidean geometry that demonstrated the independence of the fifth postulate.

Gödel (1931) proved that Hilbert's request cannot be satisfied in general, as logical systems expressive enough to include the natural numbers must exhibit either semantic incompleteness or inconsistency. Incomplete theories lack answers to some questions, and thus preclude mechanical means for answering all questions. One could still hope to find mechanical means for determining those answers actually provided by the theory. Church's notion of effectiveness and Turing's notion of mechanical computation both sought to formalize the notion of mechanical inference precisely enough to respond to Hilbert's challenge.

17.3 Is computation effective?

Even though most people accepted computation by Turing machines as a definition of effective computability, Turing clearly did not agree. He knew that not all functions could be computed by using only these operations; indeed, the main point of his original paper was to demonstrate that these machines could not compute all answers to Hilbert's decision problem. His original analysis argued that many unproblematic physical operations performable by a (human) computer could be reduced to the simple set employed by his machines. He then observed that because of this reducibility, augmenting his machines with operations reducible to machine procedures did not expand the range of functions computable by the machines. We now know that additional operations can change the difficulty of computations even if they do not change what can be computed. The vector machines of Pratt, Rabin, and Stockmeyer (1974, 1976), for example, reduce nondeterministic polynomial time computability to polynomial time computability.

Turing knew he had no proof that all physical operations reduce to his machine operations. Indeed, Turing matched his matchless achievements in the theory of computation with theories of physical computation in biology and chemistry, discovering the theory of cell morphogenesis that bears his name today. He soon promulgated his theory of O-machines, now called *oracle machines*, to formalize the notion of mechanical computation over richer sets of operations, as well as to formalize mechanical computation over arbitrary, possibly uncomputable starting points (Turing 1939). Oracle machines differed from his original machines through access to "oracles," which one can think of as devices for answering a range of questions. His original reducibility argument showed that use of oracles answering only questions already computable by Turing machines did not expand the range of computable functions, but that oracles answering questions uncomputable by unadorned Turing machines, such as the halting problem for Turing machines, would expand the range of computable functions.

17.3.1 Physical computability

Turing left open the question of whether any further physical operations available to humans satisfy the determinateness and definiteness requirements of his original analysis. This question of physical computability lay dormant for some time until it was taken up by a variety of people (see Copeland 2002 for more on the history of this idea).

Pour-El's and Richards (1981, 1989) concern was to determine if Turing computation was capable in principle of computing all solutions to the equations of physics. They showed it was not, in that the wave equation and other standard physical equations have uncomputable solutions. This uncomputability occurs in two different ways. The way Pour-El and Richards discovered is that while many solutions of the wave equation are computable, one can choose initial conditions to obtain solutions not Turing computable. Their analysis has been improved in later years by Blum, Shub, and Smale (1998), and augmented by discoveries in mechanics. I have already mentioned an example of the latter, in which one can choose the sequence of times at which a planetesimal of infinitesimal mass passes between two very massive bodies to encode the answers to the halting problem, so providing a very traditional and simple physical system with solutions not computable by Turing machines.

Feynman's concern was to determine if answers to quantum-mechanical questions could be computed quickly. The issue here is that indeterminate quantum-mechanical evolution can be viewed as pursuing many possible determinate paths concurrently. Feynman proposed to use this indeterminism to effect many determinate computations concurrently, and in particular, to perform quantum-mechanical computations directly. This suggestion has been exploited in subsequent theories of quantum computation. To date, however, these techniques have only been used to propose means for faster computation of things already computable by Turing machines.

Although Pour-El, Richards, and Feynman were mainly concerned with understanding how computation could be used to answer physical questions, Gandy's (1980) concern was to reexamine Turing's original arguments to see how the nature of physics itself shaped them and to assess the dependence of the arguments on physical law, ignoring, as usual, questions about the finiteness of the physical universe in considering questions about infinite computations. Gandy attempted to describe ways in which slight variations in the physics of our world permit the functions computable by Turing's operations to include nonrecursive functions, simply by allowing the "same" physical operations to involve more information or information paths than usual. He also sketched other variations in physical law that would render fewer functions computable. For example, if physics allowed only light and no matter, or only gases but no solids, then Turing's operations would not be physically realizable and hence nothing could be computed using them in such a world. From such considerations, the coincidence of recursive computability and mechanical computability seems entirely fortuitous. The further coincidence of these notions matching in extent the things one can compute using determinate physical operations seems entirely too dubious for ready acceptance.

17.3.2 *Effective operations*

According to Copeland's (2002) brief history, people have proposed several possible physical operations as extensions to Turing's initial analysis. My own contribution to the discussion (Doyle 2002b), developed in what now appears to be ignorance of most of the history, stemmed from applying my studies in physics to understanding the structure of the RMS, which, as described earlier, occupies states one can view as equilibria with respect to conditions required by self-specifications. In numerous physical systems the primary behavior is motion toward and occupation of equilibria. The precise equilibria reached depend on the boundary conditions, and in some cases, such as molecular states, the possible equilibria form discrete spectra. With this wealth of common equilibrating systems at hand, it seemed reasonable to ask if one could compute more in an unproblematic way by augmenting Turing's operations with tests based on equilibration. In particular, one might look at setting up charge distributions and asking if a test particle stayed put or not, or constructing molecules and asking if they folded to a certain shape, or constructing a molecule and seeing if it has an energy state in a certain interval. Building devices to perform such operations might require some care and ingenuity in the engineering, but if possible offers the potential of providing operations not computable with plain old Turing machines.

Current ideas about hypercomputation, to use Copeland's term, certainly provide serious doubts about the traditional interpretations of the Church–Turing doctrine, even if these doubts eventually prove false. The lesson they teach remains, however, even if none of the physical approaches pan out, for broadening of mechanics to cover new mental materials opens the possibility that one can bring new materials and forces and operations into the service of computation. In particular, infinite-dimensional discrete spaces offer the possibility of equilibration tests that answer super-Turing questions. Mechanics also provides detailed theories of static balance and stress that might be pressed into computational service even without considering nonphysical mechanical systems.

17.3.3 Physics of computation

Recent years have seen the growth of a lively study of the physics of computation. This name covers a good bit of ground, but the core refers to the attempt to understand the physical realization of and limits on computation. Physics of computation clearly has points of contact with the mechanical investigations conducted in the present work, but the aims of the two are largely orthogonal. Physics of computation seeks to understand and exploit physics in computational terms. The present investigation seeks to broaden the theories of physics to cover more of experience than the strictly physical.

In the most straightforward developments, physics of computation includes work on quantum computing, which holds some promise for speeding certain sorts of computations by exploiting quantum superposition and probability laws. It also includes exploiting molar-scale parallelism through chemical computing, using nuclear magnetic resonance devices for readouts, and shading off into computing techniques that use nucleic acids.

In more speculative developments, the physics of computation includes work that seeks to develop information-theoretic or computational accounts of physical law. This ranges from deriving limits on computational abilities through thermodynamic and energetic laws (Kolmogorov 1969; Chaitin 1975) to constructing discrete generators of physical laws by viewing the universe as a vast cellular automaton (Fredkin & Toffoli 1982; Toffoli & Margolus 1987; Noyes 1996; Frank & Knight 1998). The area also includes studies of reversible computing mechanisms, which now are entering practical applications.

18

Finitism

Many should find familiar the notions of materialism and reductionism, and should recognize that these doctrines enjoy large numbers of adherents. Fewer need have heard of finitism because of its presently smaller number of adherents, though many should recognize some of its aspects in current scientific and technological trends. This chapter tries to collect and address some of these issues as they relate to a broadened mechanics.

18.1 What is finitism?

I use the term *finitism* to refer to the thesis that the spatial and material world and its behavior are finite, not just finitely axiomatizable (as are the infinity of natural and real numbers) but actually finite in the sense of being composed of a finite number of bits of stuff that may undergo finite numbers of possible changes at each of a set of discrete temporal instants. The finitistic picture of the world in some locality thus resembles an enormous, possibly nondeterministic or probabilistic finite automaton, or more naturally, as a cellular automaton.

One can consider strengthenings of this local notion of finiteness to finiteness of space and time as well. Finiteness of space means that at each instant there are only finitely many places at which events may occur, so that the entire universe looks instantaneously like a cellular automaton. Finiteness of time means that the event world contains only finitely many temporal instants. Thus the strongest notion of finitism, involving both spatial and temporal finiteness, views the entire universe as a gigantic finite automaton.

18.2 Why finitism?

Finitism arises naturally out of several converging trends in the past century, trends that one may characterize in terms of presumptions of finitude of the universe and its behavior. Central to this development are the ideas that humans and their grasp are finite.

The first trend started early in the twentieth century with the Dutch mathematician L. E. J. Brouwer, who grew disenchanted with exotic examples from the topology he helped create and sought to refound mathematical rigor and logic on a finitary basis, a project he called *intuitionism*. The specific focus of intuitionism was a rejection of the law of the excluded middle as a rigorous principle of reasoning, in part on the grounds that its most egregious consequences all stem from using it to avoid considering an indefinite and possibly infinite number of cases. The ideas of intuitionism have not conquered mathematics, much less the rest of science, but they have had great impact on development of new branches of investigation. One result of this effort has been to show that most mathematics lies within the bounds of what Brouwer would have considered indubitable, constructible by definite finite means from finite bases, with no appeals to arbitrary infinities or even unenumerated sets of alternatives.

The second trend started not much later with the English mathematician Alan Turing, who analyzed the notion of computation and developed the notion of mechanical computation that we today know as Turing machines. Turing's concerns in this model shared much with those of Brouwer, in that all mental perceptions and operations of the computer were required to be definite and finite in nature, with no appeals to infinite powers of perception or infinite capabilities for action. This model of computation, reformulated by engineers and by the mathematicians Calvin Elgot and Abraham Robinson (1964), eventually became the basis for the artificial computers in common use today.

The third trend started later still with physicists seeking to avoid the infinities of classical and quantum electromagnetism by postulating a finite structure for the universe, one characterized by a fundamental length at the Planck level (about 10^{-35} meters). Not long after, cosmologists found reasons for considering the universe to have finite extent and contents. While the finite extent of the universe has become the standard view, the fundamental length theories remain speculative, though actively pursued by various communities (Margolus 1984; Toffoli & Margolus 1987; Kauffman & Noyes 1996; Noyes 1996).

These trends remain in force and appear to be increasing at present, especially with the growing influence of ideas related to machine computation. The mindset of computer scientists and even mere computer users has encouraged views in which the universe is finite, perhaps even a gigantic cellular automaton, and appears continuous only because the finite numbers involved are so large or small they fall below the resolution of our senses and present measuring apparati. Everyone who has watched television or motion pictures (or even a computer monitor) has direct experience of the false continuity of experience. The claims of finitism merely extrapolate this experience to our experience of the world as a whole.

18.3 Is finitism true?

However true it is that analysis and topology of continua force one to consider mathematical results that are fairly surprising and possibly implausible or repugnant to normal sensibilities, proving the truth of finitism involves many difficult conceptual problems. The first of these is that the limited observational and mental powers of human scientists and mathematicians are ill equipped to perform the experiments necessary to determine the truth of finitism. Modern computer technology has accentuated this difficulty, controlling motors and displays discretely but with swift enough progressions between minute enough steps that the results appear continuous to humans even after significant magnifications and accelerations of observation frequency. The theory of recursive functions and of computational complexity has opened eyes to the truly huge magnitudes of even fairly small finite numbers, with some simply described numbers, such as Knuth's (1976) example of $10 \uparrow\uparrow\uparrow\uparrow 4$, beggaring comprehension. These "finite" numbers can induce longing for the radical finiteness of arithmetic explored by Yessinin-Volpin (1970). Even model theory has contributed to the confusion by proving the existence of countable models of continuum theories, such as the theory of real numbers. It is thus difficult to see how observations could prove finiteness false.

One can imagine, however, that theoretical considerations might lead one toward adopting finitism. If quantum mechanics and general relativity both appear true and can only find reconciliation in a theory positing discreteness of space, as some think today, that seems to bolster the case for finiteness. Mere spatial discreteness, however, does not imply temporal discreteness; but if the Planck length provides a measure for discreteness of space, then the Planck time of about 10^{-43} seconds, the time light takes to traverse the Planck length, may provide a lower bound on the resolution of transition speeds.

18.3.1 Probabilities

To my mind, the big physical difficulty for finitism concerns probabilities. Quantum theory makes plausible the idea that each of the Planck-level bits of the universe may inhabit only one of finitely many states, though arguing that requires much more knowledge of physical behavior than we presently possess. Even if we suppose these fundamental bits to possess only finitely many states, nothing we know suggests that the transition probabilities must be restricted to only finitely many values, and if our theories permit arbitrary probability distributions, then physics maintains its continuous character.

Truesdell and Toupin (1960) point to the work of Noll (1955) extending earlier results (Irving & Kirkwood 1950). Noll proves that classical systems of discrete particles can exhibit statistical average properties that obey the laws of continuous mechanical fields, so that even discrete materials will look continuous at normal levels of inspection.

18.3.2 Initial conditions

We can augment these considerations with Sussman's (1996) argument that the universality of computation means we cannot rule out the possibility that Planck-level cellular automata may consists of minute universal machines with infinite state spaces and transition tables since universal machines can simulate the behavior of finite ones. Universal machines might also simulate probabilistic automata to arbitrary levels of precision. All told, even if we assume the cells to act discretely, nothing constrains them to even appear finite, much less actually be finite.

If each elementary cell has infinitely many states, then we remain in a situation in which physical motions depend on initial conditions of infinite precision. With infinite state spaces for the cells, the numbers of initial conditions become uncountable, so probability distributions over these may well be continuous.

18.3.3 Mental materials

Even if quantum mechanics and general relativity imply some measure of local discreteness or even finiteness in ordinary matter, broadening the scope to include mental materials renders arguments for finiteness meaningless unless augmented with further arguments for the finiteness of these additional materials and spatial dimensions. We possess no grounds for expecting such finiteness at present, except by supposing a strict physical materialism that denies the existence of such additional dimensions of space and substance.

18.4 Summary

Physics may well imply some granularity in space and time, in addition to known quantizations of state. Such implications, if true, do not suffice to ensure a finite universe, for they include nothing restricting transition probability to finitely many values. The physical evidence remains equivocal because of the limits on human powers to discriminate between the continuous and the exceedingly fine but discrete. Decisions about finitism thus would seem to depend on additional sources of evidence not considered herein.

The beauty of continuous mathematics aligns with the aesthetic of scientific beauty to suggest to some that even though finite structures can approximate the continuous, lack of reasonably strong evidence for a thoroughgoing finiteness covering space, time, state, and probability makes it unreasonable to strive very hard to make things that look continuous into something discrete. Even continuous structures provide plenty of roles for discrete properties and qualities. The gardens of continuous analysis may contain some strange creatures, but, as with Hilbert (1926), these do not repel enough to push one out. Every life is full of things one cannot expect to understand or fully appreciate, even after a lifetime of study. Mathematical puzzles provide just one species among many.

Part V
Conclusion of the Matter

19

Reflections

Space and Time! now I see it is true, what I guess'd at,
What I guess'd when I loafed on the grass,
What I guess'd while I lay alone on my bed,
And again as I walk'd alone the beach under the paling stars of the morning.
  (Walt Whitman, *Song of Myself*)

The preceding chapters presented the beginnings of a mathematical and mechanical theory of mind.

We began by examining the curious divorce between mechanical understandings of mind and nature that occurred when natural philosophy developed mathematical techniques useful in characterizing physical mechanics but inapplicable to mental mechanics. The mathematical study of mental materials developed separately, but with the key mathematical theories of logical and economic rationality lacking any connection to mechanics. The mechanical reconciliation of mind and nature began to take shape only when the development of artificial computers enabled construction of artificial minds precise and concrete enough to relate to a new rational mechanics broad enough to encompass mental as well as physical materials. The reconciliation promises not only to open traditional philosophical questions to new forms of technical analysis, but also to provide a new formal vocabulary for describing agents of limited rationality and for engineering computational and social systems based on such agents.

We then examined two sides of the reconciliation of physical and mental mechanics. On the physical side, we recast the axioms of modern rational mechanics so as to cover discrete mechanical systems and their hybrids with physical mechanical systems. These axioms share almost all important structure with traditional formulations, differing primarily in the separation of continuum assumptions from other structural assumptions. Mathematically, the principal difference comes down to working with algebraic spaces that are

407

almost but not quite vector spaces, namely free modules over commutative rings, formed by taking products of vector spaces over different scalar fields and regarding these as product modules over the ring product of the scalar fields. The recasting also provides a different perspective on traditional variational formulations of mechanics by elevating concepts of conserved quantities and least action principles into notions of conservative motion.

Turning to the mental side, we sketched the mechanical description of an important and broad class of mental materials, namely psychologies characterized by sets of mental attitudes distributed among mental organs or faculties, including both short-term and long-term forms of memory. We paid special attention to the RMS as an important exemplar of numerous mechanical concepts, including kinematic constitutive assumptions and elastic and frictional behavior. We showed how to interpret inference rules as generators of mental forces, and characterized sets of such rules in terms of stress tensors that satisfy key mechanical equations. We also showed how to relate the uncertainty exhibited by sets of nonmonotonic reasoning rules to the subjective uncertainty of Bayesian decision theory and, in certain ways, to the measurement concepts of quantum mechanics.

We then reflected on some implications of this reconciliation, especially on questions of materialism, reductionism, and computability. The broadening of mechanics explored here would appear to deflate many of the usual claims of materialism, but adds little to the reasons already present in traditional mechanics for rejecting reductionism and computationalism.

Mechanics remains a living subject, not a lifeless tradition. A mechanics exemplified by minds does not lessen the wonders of the mind or trivialize mechanics but increases awareness of the awesome magnificence visible in the world around us, in which such disparate appearances exemplify a common order.

19.1 Assessment

I wish you would reserve judgment on that.

J. S. Mac Nerney to a critic of the Moore method (Schatz 2003)

Tolstoy apparently believed the application of mechanical concepts to psychology reasonable because the same concepts prove useful in explaining both psychological behavior and the motion of inanimate bodies. The existence of mathematical formalizations of these concepts specifically addressing the inanimate motions did not make the notion of inertia in psychology entirely different or incomparable with the notion of inertia in ballistics, nor did such axiomatizations disqualify the original broad concepts from their original broad applications in continuum mechanics. I believe the further broadening of the formal mechanical concepts to cover psychology and economics is reasonable for much the same reason.

19.1.1 Importance

The present formalization of the mechanical axioms and its application to psychological and economic systems is clearly incomplete, and we can be reasonably confident that some of the present details and speculations will prove mistaken or misguided. Yet we can also be reasonably confident that many of these flaws can be remedied, with many of these remediable through improved treatments bearing much similarity to the present one, even if such remedies might take a long time to effect. The major question of assessment, however, is whether the theory makes any difference.

I believe the broadening of mechanical applications to include psychology and economics has important consequences even if the applications yield no "new" theoretical conclusions beyond those already known in psychology and economics. Providing a unified theoretical framework for psychological and physical theories demonstrates the consistency of these theories and improves our understanding of the coherence and order of the world.

Even without new results, this unification brings new analytical concepts to each of the fields involved, and helps different fields share mathematical tools more easily. If Freud thought that informal hydrodynamic analogies provided some insight into mental functioning, could detailed formal concepts and theorems from fluid dynamics offer more? If quantum theorists find themselves wanting to talk about uranium atoms "deciding" to decay or electrons "trying" to move across gaps, can models of these as rational agents add to our understanding? The answers for these specific questions might all be "no," but formal connections between the theories allow us to explore such possibilities at a technical level, rather than only at the level of cocktail-party speculation.

At a philosophical level, formal unification of the theories offers means for justifying things "everyone knows," and helps dispense with some long-standing arguments against some psychological and physical theories. I do not expect the discussions given here concerning determinism, materialism, and the like will settle any issues. I do expect that the formal connections may enable new progress in understanding these ancient issues.

19.1.2 Interpretation

The specific mechanical interpretations of psychological concepts discussed in the preceding chapters support enough of the usual mechanical structure to indicate the reasonability of these interpretations. Advances in mathematics in some areas might well make other identifications even more reasonable.

As with all scientific theories, the issue of identification of theoretical terms is more one of reasonability and comparative reasonability than truth, since some physical theories admit different interpretations, all simultaneously true. The Truesdell–Toupin discussion of concepts of mass examined in Section 6.1.4 illustrates this point, identifying different quantities as mass, with different identifications true and useful for different purposes.

I have striven to illustrate these interpretations with positive examples of systems that exhibit a mechanical character and negative examples of systems that do not exhibit a mechanical character in order to minimize the dangers of developing what Truesdell (1984d) has called *floating* theories. Truesdell used that adjective to describe a lack of solid connection between theory and reality that requires different theorists to apply the theory idiosyncratically, in effect, if not in intent, to reach the conclusions they happen to seek. The catastrophe theory of Thom (1975) and Zeeman (1977) triggered Truesdell's denunciation of such theories, but such theories pervade the social sciences, and had been denounced earlier by others (Post 1974; Andreski 1972). Incautious floating theories clearly deserve wariness. We should certainly avoid floating theories when solid theoretical interpretations exist, and try to anchor attractive floating theories as rapidly as possible.

That said, one cannot always escape floating theories, at least at the early stages of formalization. One needs some way of thinking about subjects of interest, and prior to discovering some obviously reasonable and solidly productive theory and interpretation. Students of the area of necessity flounder around trying out different theories and interpretations. Indeed, the present effort stands in good company, in that traditional mechanics itself suffered just such a period of floating theories prior to Newton's work, which in part gave the productive theoretical interpretations needed to solidly ground mechanics in experience. The universal character of mathematics, however, means that escape from floating theories at one time does not hold them at bay forever, since newly observed or studied aspects of nature may engender new periods of theoretical floundering.

Present-day theoretical psychology continues to explore new theoretical possibilities. We have much knowledge about the structure and function of the brain and nervous system at the physiological, electrical, and chemical levels, but even disregarding the ambiguities and uncertainties in that knowledge, the gulf between function at these levels and mental life and behavior remains nearly as great as during Descartes's lifetime, or for that matter, when Homer sang the wars of Greeks and Trojans. This gulf renders most psychological theories floating theories. We might thus seek to base a mechanical interpretation on more realistic psychologies than the simple one employed here. We cannot yet expect such an improvement to remove many of the theoretical ambiguities unless we seek to use naturalness of the mechanical interpretation as a criterion for judging candidate psychological theories. Such a criterion may be justified one day after we better understand the nature of mechanics in this new setting, but seems premature at present.

19.1.3 Inspiration

I have taken an axiomatic, mathematical approach in the hope that such an approach offers the best path to identifying a sound theoretical grounding that avoids the dangers of floating theories.

Newton's axiomatic mechanics changed the terms of discussion in natural philosophy from seeking to intuit forces hidden in behavior to stipulating forces and then solving to see what the behavior would be. Axiomatic characterization of theoretical concepts does not remove all ambiguities of interpretation, but at least it ties theoretical concepts to each other in ways that reduce the purely theoretical ambiguities. As he does so often, Truesdell puts it well. Truesdell starts by quoting an observation of André Weil.

Rigor is to the mathematician what morality is to man. It does not consist in proving everything, but in maintaining a sharp distinction between what is assumed and what is proved, and in endeavoring to assume as little as possible at every stage. (Weil 1954, p. 35)

Truesdell then paraphrases Weil's statement about rigor:

Mathematical discipline is to science what civilization is to man. It does not consist in replacing all experiment by reasoning, but in making a sharp distinction between what is measured and what is derived by reason, and in endeavoring to reduce as much as possible the need for measurement at every stage. (Truesdell 1984e, p. 113)

In a related way, Noll's axiomatization of mechanics changed the subject from something like a cult in which the members "got" the notion of force, energy, and other mechanical concepts. Prior to Noll's work, one could argue endlessly about what forces are, for mechanical theories provided only ways of computing from forces, not any delineation of their nature or properties. Noll's axiomatization transformed the discussion by identifying forces as those things that satisfy his axioms. As in most other areas of mathematics, this move frees one from continual decisions about whether this entity or the next is a force; one verifies that the axioms provide a suitable characterization of the notion of force, and then checks to see what things satisfy them. The axioms enjoy no magical properties in this process. Even seemingly suitable axioms may someday seem inadequate as one considers more and more examples of things that satisfy or fail to satisfy them. When this happens, one then revises the axioms or extends them to introduce more restricted notions, but at each point of time one may answer the question "Is this a force?" by comparing the properties of the object of the question with the properties required by the axioms.

19.2 Prospects

Developing the mechanics of psychological materials to levels matching the mechanics of common physical materials requires substantial advances in mathematics, psychology, and economics.

The keenest need for further investigation lies in mathematics. Current mathematics lacks many of the tools one might want in seeking to understand the novel structures formalizable in discrete and hybrid mechanical systems. Although exceedingly rich and deep, the mathematics of today provides the most leverage on the oldest problems of continuous geometry and motion. I hope that having mechanical formulations of new psychological and economic materials will spur mathematical investigation today as much as mechanical ideas motivated the development of classical mathematics.

In psychology, I look for further progress in artificial intelligence to elaborate precise formal models for thinking. Here the keenest need lies in exploring psychologies explicitly designed around mechanical notions and principles, as these offer at least some hope of new means for obtaining intelligible behavior.

I regard the needs in economics as consisting mainly of reworking existing theories to exploit the structural concepts of both artificial intelligence and mechanics.

In pursuing completions of the present theory, one should keep in mind that the principal aim of this effort has not been to provide definitive formulations or formalizations, much less to rework all standard mechanical theorems in the new setting and for new materials, but only to provide preliminary formalizations and identifications suitable for technical investigation and correction. It might happen, though I doubt it, that a proper development of mechanical theories of psychology and economics will omit almost every formal suggestion made here. Even though the heavy reliance on sound axioms for traditional mechanics makes this seem unlikely, debugging a flawed theory usually proves much easier than debugging a blank sheet of paper. As Minsky (1974) says, "thinking begins first with suggestive but defective plans and images that are slowly (if ever) refined and replaced by better ones." The theory presented here undoubtedly has its share of defects, but I hope it suggests and motivates fruitful corrections to these defects.

19.2.1 *Axiomatic psychology*

The axiomatic approach may eventually help change the field of psychology in ways similar to the way it changed mechanics at the times of Newton and Noll. To date, however, axiomatic approaches have enjoyed primarily theoretical use in methods of direct formalization that attempt to understand the mind by taking mental phenomena at face value, to use the terms people ordinarily use to describe themselves, and to seek formalized theories directly on the basis of observations interpreted in these formal terms.

The direct analysis of mental phenomena can be viewed as an axiomatic enterprise in the tradition of Hilbert's call for mathematical axiomatization of physics. In this approach, one seeks to axiomatize psychological concepts directly. One can view much of philosophical logic, some of theoretical artificial intelligence, and some parts of mathematical economics as embodying just this approach, and perhaps also the sort of modeling in differential equations exemplified by Rashevsky's (1938) work. Here one starts with naive or linguistic expressions of commonsense psychology and seeks to use the terms of these expressions in developing logics of various attitudes and mental qualities, such as logics of belief, preferences, and rational choices.

Such direct analyses are based on observations, whether these be the informal observations that inform commonsense theories of behavior, or formal psychological or economic experiments undertaken to determine the properties of the attitudes held by people and the way people make choices.

A correct theory of belief, desire, and intention in their own terms is not to be scorned, and such may be the product of direct analysis and observation. Nevertheless, direct analysis can leave psychological theories somewhat disconnected from rest of the sciences. Indeed, it seems necessary to relate the overtly psychological level to at least certain aspects of physiology and physics to obtain a theory of adequate accuracy, for direct analysis produces psychological theories that, like all theories, have a restricted domain of accuracy. Classical continuum mechanics, after all, is one of the most successful and accurate scientific theories known, even though some phenomena lie outside its fairly broad domain of applicability. In the same way, we can expect direct formalizations of psychological theories to offer some success, but to leave some matters requiring other types of formalizations.

Most uses of axiomatics in psychology have sought mainly to better understand or identify theoretical notions rather than to understand particular systems. The more telling role for axiomatics comes through using the axiomatic constructs to stipulate the structure of a particular system and then use the theoretical concepts to analyze that particular system or its behavior. To date, this role for axiomatics has been fairly neglected apart from axiomatic presentations and analyses of simple examples used to motivate or explicate axiomatic theories. More significant treatments employ the axiomatic theory to present formal specifications for a system of interest and then use this formal specification either as the basis for analysis, for checking of the specification itself, or to guide implementation or realization. Formal specification checking plays an increasingly large role in many engineering disciplines, notably those using computer-aided design techniques, but it has not yet played a large role in psychological engineering, in which all artificial psychologies designed to date have been designed manually by people.

Application of the mechanics presented here to psychology may permit a similar change of focus from seeking to make sense of the insensibly complex to understanding the behavior of stipulated psychological systems. For example, debates about consciousness have gone on at least as long as debates about force. Given the possible relations between mental intentionality and force and the intimate connections between intentionality and consciousness, such longevity should surprise no one. Psychology might progress beyond these debates by identifying axiomatic characterizations of the properties of consciousness and then using these axioms to judge things conscious or not. Mere definitions cannot answer the problems of consciousness, any more than they can answer the question "What is life?" Axiomatic theories, nonetheless, might permit delineation of specific classes on which all sides can agree. The situation regarding consciousness differs from that regarding forces, however, because few people felt they had some stake riding on the decision about whether something constituted a force or not, while many people might think they have some stake in decisions about whether their persons, pets, plants, particles, and planet satisfy the conditions of consciousness. In spite of disagreements on these questions, a more explicit pursuit of direct axiomatization and formalization of psychological concepts seems worthwhile.

19.2.2 Psychological engineering

Psychology and economics currently lack consensus on any detailed models of economic agents of limited rationality. Advances in the formal basis of the mental and social sciences open the possibility of rigorous engineering disciplines in mental and social domains.

Although newspapers today readily discuss social engineering and economic fine-tuning as if they were secure human capabilities, these activities differ little from the usual floundering people do in circumstances beyond their understanding, for there is no way known to precisely describe situations or the effects of actions, and so no way known to calculate and compare with any confidence the consequences of alternative actions. To aim for psychological, economic, social, or political engineering, one must first aim for the tools of the engineer—sound theories, good data, and effective methods of calculation.

For example, philosophers have long debated the merits of various political, social, and economic organizations, comparing different organizations in best and worst cases, and arguing about how different theories about human nature (as individuals and in groups) support different social, political, or economic ideals, and vice versa. While opinions and intuitions abound, few sound results have been secured because most such claims lack mathematical substantiation or refinement. One long-range hope motivating this book is that with proper formalizations, various organizations for political economies may be mathematically analyzed and compared, to determine not just their best case and worst case, but also their expected case performance; their best-, expected-, and worst-case evolution over time; and the sensitivity of their performance and evolution to the qualities of their members. Of course, the theories of welfare economics and public choice treat some of these issues, but under the assumption that people are ideally rational. In some cases this "locally false" assumption correctly yields "globally true" conclusions, and so is a useful tool of analysis. But current economics has no principled way to vary this assumption formally to consider more realistic agents and to ask if any conclusions must then be changed. To overcome this limitation, theories like that developed in this book should offer more realistic formal assumptions about the people making up the world. How to live is perhaps the most important choice a people may make. It is desirable that the natures of the alternatives be clearly understood.

19.2.3 Is intelligence intelligible?

We view intelligence as involving rationality, knowledge, habits, and skills. Although people fancy their intelligence as what sets them apart from mere beasts, much of intelligence consists of good habits, both mental and physical, rather than rational calculation. Rationality plays a large role in guiding our habitual behavior base into productive paths. At the same time we rely on habits of thought to efficiently determine rational actions. In this way rationality shapes the bounds on rationality, and bounds on rationality shape the character of rationality.

The preceding chapters have raised but not answered the question of whether intelligence is intelligible. The application of mechanics to psychology aims to aid the intelligibility of the subject by providing a language for describing and analyzing psychologies that offers compact descriptions and intuitive understandings of the limitations of psychological systems. I hope that at least some of the progress made in the rational mechanics of physical systems will carry over to offer simpler understandings of the more complicated systems studied in psychology and economics. Nevertheless, all these considerations only represent hopes, not demonstrated results.

The fundamental hurdle in understanding the mind is the limited capacity of the mind itself. The sheer complexity of the mind poses its own barrier no matter what kind of finite mind seeks the understanding. The problem at hand is whether the human mind, even the spectacular examples represented by Newton, Euler, and others, has the capacity to understand nontrivial fractions of its own complexity.

We see this question clearly in the experience of artificial intelligence in attempting to formalize the large body of knowledge humanity possesses about the world in which we live. This knowledge includes innumerable facts, and many generalities. It varies, at least in some respects, from person to person, culture to culture, discipline to discipline, task to task, and time to time. Artificial intelligence has sought many different ways of representing this knowledge, trying to simplify the process in many ways, but so far has kept running up against the sheer magnitude of the body of knowledge, an enormity quite at odds with the subjective perspective reflective people have on how little we know.

All efforts to simplify the task of understanding intelligence founder on the question of how complex the subject really is. Can one reduce all knowledge to some very simple basis? As Chapter 16 has suggested, this seems unlikely, though perhaps many subjects that seem large today might seem small with full knowledge. Until then, however, psychology and artificial intelligence might be doomed to proceed as a sort of Ptolemaic science, with a practical theory dominated by specification of initial conditions, rather than reduction to small set of simple principles. For example, in standard approaches to representing commonsense knowledge, almost all "facts" admit exceptions, which one formalizes in terms of defeasible properties and exceptionalizable categorizations. As one learns of new exceptions, one adds the corresponding rule. Exception rules constitute a wonderful device for making simple corrections simply, and might be the best possible approach to the task, but it certainly reeks of post-Ptolemaic compounding of epicycles. The question is whether these corrections to corrections serve to approximate some simpler structure.

Can we do better? Maybe, but almost all experience to date suggests that true progress in simplifying bodies of knowledge comes about only when one individual manages to comprehend the body of knowledge to be simplified.

This is difficult, and ordinarily must proceed in a cascade of partial simplifications as different people each spend a lifetime understanding one portion or another until these partial simplifications shrink the overall theory to a size that will fit in the mind of a single person.

One can hope that automation of reasoning might eventually yield machines with greater capacities for comprehension than humans. To the extent that one has to know a lot to be able to comprehend more, this hope promises a long wait as mere people understand enough using the old, slow processes to construct such comprehension. In such a setting, acceleration follows numbers; as Whitman says, "Produce great people, the rest follows."

19.2.4 Additional applications

The extension of mechanics need not stop with minds and economies.

In particular, recent years have seen numerous projects applying economic ideas to understanding the nature of cultural change in anthropology (Boyd & Richerson 1985). Popular language might apply mechanical concepts to cultural statements less often than in discussing psychology and economics, but mechanical formalization might naturally carry over from understanding economic change to shed light on anthropological questions as well. We might also expect such carry-over from the psychological perspective, as we characterize cultures in terms of cultural norms, habits, and values, much as we characterize individuals with these concepts. Of course, we typically do not think of a culture as a person in the same way we think of people as persons. Like people, cultures exhibit a degree of self-awareness in the sense of holding norms and values that indicate what practices and things stand outside the culture, and what stand within. Unlike people, cultures might lack the sort of second-order desires that Frankfurt (1971) uses to identify persons. But a difference with respect to personhood need not matter to understanding the genesis and difficulty of cultural change.

One might also examine biology for unappreciated mechanical structure. Molecular genetics, whether of the individual or of a population, provides one obvious starting point, with the genotype of an individual constituting its biological mass and the phenotype constituting its biological position.

Genetic algorithms interpret simple types of computational memories as genetic information that determines constructed states. The preceding mechanical interpretation of constructive reasoners might thus prove readily adaptable to constructing mechanical interpretations of artificial genetic reproduction and variation, and so extend to interpreting actual genetic processes. In this view, biological mutation, recombination, and reproduction possibly constitute mechanical actions in biological space. Admissible chemical processes of molecular constitution might then provide limits on the magnitudes of forces exerted in natural genetic processes.

At the individual level, one would look to formulate environmental and organic forces related to reproduction, nutrition, and defense. At the population level, one would look to formulate environmental forces related to survival and selection.

At the level of evolutionary history, one might distinguish changes occurring through mutation and selection as small steps moving between equilibrium states, obtaining a theory of punctuated equilibria corresponding to integral motion.

19.3 Perspective

One can expect that working out the mathematical, computational, and psychological advances needed to realize the promise of the extended mechanics and its application to psychology and economics will require decades, if not centuries. Why pay attention to ideas when their coming to fruition, if it occurs at all, lies so far in the future? No author can demand patience of his readers, but a bit of history might put this task in perspective.

Abraham Robinson (1974, p. x) once remarked on the surprising delay between the invention of infinitesimal analysis and its establishment as a proper part of mathematics. In fact, this delay forms just one part of three similar and related delayed developments.

About three and a half centuries ago, Descartes formulated a dualistic theory of mind, Newton and Leibniz invented the infinitesimal calculus, and Newton propounded axioms for mechanics and gravitation. These ideas suffered a similar fate: natural philosophy abandoned the initial form of each of these contributions, made much progress for 300 years, and then returned to the ideas in curiously related ways a half century ago.

19.3.1 Mathematics

Consider first the mathematical idea of the infinitesimal calculus. Although this idea solved problems plaguing mathematicians from Zeno to Galileo, mathematicians abandoned infinitesimals because they seemed to obey no set rules, and introduced errors into mathematics and applications when people used infinitesimals in ways chosen to obtain the results desired. Cauchy and Weierstrass brought great relief by showing how to develop analysis without infinitesimals, using notions of limits and convergence to obtain reliable definitions of mathematical objects. Mathematicians quickly abandoned infinitesimals to the realm of mythology, an idea useful once but now seen as merely misguided intuition.

The late nineteenth century saw the discovery of non-Euclidean geometries in mathematics, and Hilbert's shocking methods in algebra that introduced the idea that axiomatic consistency sufficed to define a subject and result, independent of computation from familiar numbers or worldly objects. On this basis he recast geometry in modern axiomatic form. He challenged mathematicians to pursue the axiomatic approach in other areas, claiming this would provide the basis for solving all mathematical problems. This challenge helped stimulate research in mathematical logic, including Gödel's proof of the incompleteness of Peano arithmetic, Turing's proof of the undecidability of number theory, and Tarski's proof of the decidability of real arithmetic. These results represented fruits of much work in model and proof theory.

Attitudes toward infinitesimals began to change about half a century ago when Abraham Robinson, simultaneously a leading mathematical aerodynamicist and logician, realized that algebraic model theory provided means to make a proper mathematical theory of infinitesimals, and showed how to redevelop much of classical mathematics within nonstandard analysis, a result that then led to proofs of some new results that had seemed too difficult to obtain in standard models of the real numbers.

19.3.2 Mechanics

Newton transformed mechanics from a descriptive, philosophical subject to a mathematical subject based on an axiomatic perspective. It was not long, however, before mathematicians and physicists abandoned Newton's axioms as vague and informal, especially after Euler invented what we now call Newton's equations to use in practical computations, and Cauchy discovered the concept of stress that forms the basis of most of continuum mechanics. The achievements of Euler and Cauchy represented merely the most visible elements of the thoroughgoing mathematization of mechanics in subsequent years.

Seeds of change began to stir with David Hilbert's (1902) call to action in 1900. Hilbert's Sixth Problem asked for an axiomatic basis for physics. The call was first answered by Georg Hamel (1908), who made good progress but did not find a suitable way of axiomatizing the key mechanical notion of force.

Relativity and quantum mechanics intervened, which further lessened the interest in and attention available to pursue mechanics as a subject in its own right. Physicists took these new theories to mean that mechanics was both wrong and useless as a subject of investigation, quickly abandoning mechanics as a subject of scientific study in favor of a reductionistic focus on field theories of smaller and smaller particles. "Classical mechanics" became a background course with no research potential to the physics student, and physicists left mechanics to the mechanical engineers.

Although these new mechanics engaged the imaginations of many physicists, they also returned physics to a state of confusion not seen since the early troubles with infinitesimals (cf. Streater & Wightman 1964, p. 31 and Jost 1965, pp. xii-xiii). Indeed, to try to restore some order to the subject, von Neumann (1932) sought to set quantum mechanics on a firm mathematical basis, but it remained until the axiomatic work of Wightman (1956), Glimm and Jaffe (1981), and others to provide a respectable basis.

At about the same time as the beginnings of axiomatic quantum mechanics, Clifford Truesdell recruited Walter Noll to undertake to axiomatize mechanics. Noll (1958) succeeded in producing the first true axiomatization of mechanics, and improved his initial axiomatization over the following decade or two into an axiomatic theory of great beauty and generality that revolutionized the theory and practice of mechanics.

It seems somewhat remarkable that mathematics required about the same length of time to establish both infinitesimals and mechanics on proper mathematical bases. In fact, Noll's accomplishment was much greater than that of filling out some list of axioms. Noll transcended centuries of specious rigor in physical theorizing to construct a systematic mathematical axiomatization of mechanical concepts that point the way to ranges of future research well beyond what he may have imagined. Truesdell made the following remarks about Cauchy, but one might say similar things about Noll's contributions to mechanics.

From the above account, it is clear that every conceptual element in CAUCHY'S theory was to be found in one or another of the special theories constructed in the previous century. Moreover, in researches of FRESNEL done in 1821–1822, with which CAUCHY must certainly have been familiar, many of CAUCHY'S results are more or less implied, although in FRESNEL'S work the concepts of stress and strain are always connected through a presumed linearly elastic response.

Thus it might seem that CAUCHY'S achievement in formulating and developing the general theory of stress was an easy one. It was not. CAUCHY'S concept has the simplicity of genius. Its deep and thorough originality is fully outlined only against the background of the century of achievement by the brilliant geometers who preceded, treating the special kinds and cases of deformable bodies by complicated and sometimes incorrect ways without ever hitting upon this basic idea, which immediately became and has remained the foundation of the mechanics of gross bodies.

Nothing is harder to surmount than a corpus of true but too special knowledge; to reforge the tradition of his forebears is the greatest originality a man can have. (Truesdell 1968a, pp. 236–238)

Perhaps Noll would disavow comparison with Cauchy's achievement, and perhaps it remains to some future peer of Cauchy to provide correct mathematical concepts, whether of stress or of some other concept, appropriate to the broadened mechanics that will provide similar insight and power. Even if so, one cannot help but appreciate how far Noll's achievements have brought us in preparing the ground for these future achievements.

19.3.3 Mind

Although Descartes' skepticism provoked much controversy and imitation as the burgeoning Enlightenment sought to distance itself from Christianity, his dualism fared less well as philosophers discarded dualism for materialism and idealism. Descartes' successors thought mind–body interactions nonsensical, or at best inconsistent with Newtonian physics and the rapidly advancing sciences. With physicists seeming to find more and more of nature falling under materialist characterizations, idealism eventually gave way to materialist psychology and neurophysiological reductionism.

Discordant notes entered the materialist picture after Gödel's results on the incompleteness of Peano arithmetic. Developed in response to Hilbert's call to action, Gödel's results stimulated Alonzo Church (1941) and Alan Turing (1936) to look more closely at the nature of mechanism and so lay the foundations for the modern theory of computation.

Though many regard the theories of Church and Turing as representing the same result because they yield the same set of computable functions, this assessment misrepresents the situation. Church's purely symbolic, formal, and mathematical theory involves a very different set of concepts than does Turing's theory based on mechanistic, physical operations. In Church's framework, recursive functions arise as naturally and as (non)uniquely as do the natural numbers in set theory. They suggest no obvious way of varying the construction to obtain other sets of functions. Turing's framework, in contrast, makes it obvious that different classes of functions might arise through similar constructions, as it bases these functions on a notion of physical computability. Turing argues convincingly (and correctly, given subsequent engineering achievements) that the simple operations embodied in his notional computing machines represent mechanizable physical operations. He does not demonstrate that the identified operations suffice to represent all possible mechanizable operations. On the contrary, his later theory of oracle machines seems clearly aimed at making the available physical operations a parameter of his machines in anticipation of later physical or engineering discoveries.

Turing's work on computation inspired his psychological speculations on intelligent machines, which in turn helped inspire the modern field of artificial intelligence. Indeed, Turing was not alone in turning his attentions in this direction; von Neumann, one of the architects of economic game theory and developer of electronic computing machinery, also began thinking about the structure of the brain and its relation to thinking. These represented serious investigations of computational embodiments of thought, embodiments that at least superficially exhibited the Cartesian dissimilarity from physical materials.

Church's influence on the convergence of physics and psychology was less direct, though perhaps no less important. Church's lambda calculus, widely used in modern artificial intelligence through its reflection in Lisp, the programming language invented by Church's student John McCarthy (1965), constitutes the most obvious but perhaps not the most important influence. Church, far more than Turing, was a logician, with a logician's interest in formulating and studying systems of axioms. This concern with axiomatics also characterizes McCarthy's artificial intelligence work, in which he proposed an axiom-accepting "advice taker" that eventually inspired much work, including reasoning systems like the RMS.

19.3.4 Merging

These histories of mathematics, mechanics, and mind have connections more amazing than the coincidence of starting in the mid-seventeenth century and flowering in the mid-twentieth century.

The principal upshot of work in artificial intelligence was the production of precise, concrete models of rational thought and their embodiment in physical mechanisms of the sort envisaged by Turing. These models exploited logic directly in models of thinking, in the language of thought, and in identification of mental spaces of a kind denied to Descartes. These models of thought not only furthered the automation of human knowledge and activity, but also provided the first analyses of thinking detailed and precise enough to enable the present analysis in terms of mechanics. Indeed, these precise models of thought also came to involve Newton's infinitesimal analysis, first in formal psychological theories of belief, in which infinitesimal probabilities of all orders characterize comparative strength of conclusions and enter into rules of plausible reasoning (Pearl 1990), and then reintroduced into theories of mechanical systems to analyze hybrid systems, in which one can view some transitions of the discrete component of the system as occurring in infinitesimal time steps between real instants of continuous motion of the continuous system component.

This dovetailing of ideas is not the only convergence represented in this history; von Neumann himself represented a convergence of mathematics, quantum mechanics, and the mind of economics not seen since, and provided inspiration and support to Marvin Minsky, who along with McCarthy counts as a founder of artificial intelligence and the theory of computation. But the most surprising convergence concerns Alonzo Church. We already noted his relations with Turing and his influence on his student McCarthy. Yet if we look at the first edition of Church's (1944) textbook, we find it constitutes the notes taken by another student who Church infected with a concern for axiomatics and conceptual beauty: Clifford Truesdell, who in later years championed the axiomatic and mathematical renewal of rational mechanics that provided the axiomatic basis for mechanics from which the present work derives both conceptual and technical inspiration.

Should it seem curious that Turing, who openly considered physical problems also directly addressed psychological issues, while Church, who confined his attention to logical matters, indirectly stimulated work on both psychology and physics?

19.3.5 Moral

If reconnecting infinitesimals to mathematics alone took three centuries, perhaps one should thus not find it too surprising that three centuries were needed to rejoin mechanics proper, and not just its mathematical tools, to the study of mind. And if this is the time scale along which important ideas develop, it may well take time to see how to apply mechanical concepts to obtain improvements in scientific understanding and engineering power in psychology and economics. The centuries separating the original invention and recent formalization of ideas in mathematics, mechanics, and mind should give us motivation to continue these investigations even if we do not yet see clearly how or whether the present ideas will bear fruit. Hilbert said it well, regardless of subsequent discoveries that showed his conviction requires minor modification unrelated to the present application:

This conviction of the solvability of every mathematical problem is a powerful incentive to the worker. We hear within us the perpetual call: There is the problem. Seek its solution. You can find it by pure reason, for in mathematics there is no *ignorabimus*. (Hilbert 1902, p. 412)

System of Notation

I write "iff" as shorthand for "if and only if."

I use an overline or superposed bar both to denote closures of sets and systems, and to denote negations or complements of propositions. The context of usage generally indicates which interpretation is intended, and I indicate the intended interpretation when any potential for confusion exists.

Some symbols appear more than once in the table that follows to avoid confusion about ambiguities of classification.

Mathematics

$\mathbb{N}$	the natural numbers
$\mathbb{Z}$	the integers
$\mathbb{Z}_2$	the binary field of integers modulo 2
$\mathbb{Z}_k$	the ring of integers modulo k
$\mathbb{Q}$	the rational numbers
$\mathbb{R}$	the real numbers
$\mathbb{R}^+$	the nonnegative real numbers
$^*\mathbb{R}$	the nonstandard real numbers
$\mathcal{R}$	a commutative ring
$\emptyset$	the empty set
$\subseteq$	subset
$\cap$	intersection
$\cup$	union
$\overline{X}$	complement of the set X
$\setminus$ or $-$	set difference (asymmetric)
$\mathcal{P}$	powerset function
$\upharpoonright$	restriction of a relation or function
$\circ$	composition of relations or functions
$\times$ or $\prod$	Direct (Cartesian) product

$\oplus$	Direct (disjoint) sum, coproduct
$\mathcal{I}$	an index set
i	an index in $\mathcal{I}$
$[\,]_i$	ith component of a product element
$\wedge$	logical conjunction of two propositions
$\vee$	logical disjunction of two propositions
Th	deductive closure
$\sqcup$ or $+$	lattice join (least upper bound)
$\sqcap$	lattice meet (greatest lower bound)
$\top$	top element of a lattice
$\bot$	bottom element of a lattice
$[A, B]$	interval between A and B in an ordered set
Θ	a topology (set of open sets)
$\overline{X}$	closure of a set X in a topology
int X	interior of the set X
X^e	exterior of the set X
$+$	vector and set addition
d	a distance or metric function
$|\,|$	absolute value

Bodies

$\mathcal{B}$	the material universe
$\overline{\mathcal{B}}$	the closed material universe including $\mathcal{O}$ and $\mathcal{U}$
$\mathcal{G}$	a great system or locality
$\mathcal{O}$	the null body
$\mathcal{U}$	the universal body
$\mathcal{U}_{\mathcal{B}}$	the universal body in universe $\mathcal{B}$
$\mathfrak{U}$	set of all atomic bodies, identified with $\mathcal{U}$
b, X	atomic body points

$\mathcal{A}, \mathcal{B}, \mathcal{C}, \mathcal{D}$	various bodies
$\mathcal{B}^e$	exterior or environment of the body $\mathcal{B}$
int $\mathcal{B}$	interior of the body $\mathcal{B}$
$\underset{\sim}{\overset{\mathcal{B}}{}}$	subbody or part relation
$\overset{\mathcal{B}}{\prec}$	proper part relation
$(\mathcal{B} \times \mathcal{B})_0$	pairs of separate bodies

---

Events

$\mathcal{W}$	the event world
e	an event in $\mathcal{W}$
ϕ	a framing or section
Φ	the set of all framings

Time

$\mathcal{T}$	the set of times or temporal indices
t	a time in $\mathcal{T}$, a function representing instants with temporal indices
Γ	the set of instants
τ	an instant in Γ
$\vec{\tau}$	a hybrid vector of instants
$\hat{t}$	a time-lapse function on events
$\bar{t}$	a time-lapse function on instants
$\overset{\mathcal{T}}{\approx}$ or $\approx$	the simultaneity relation on events
$\overset{\mathcal{T}}{\lessapprox}$ or $\lessapprox$	the temporal order
$\overset{\mathcal{T}}{<}$ or $<$	the strict temporal order
I	an interval of time
$[t, t']$	interval of time starting at t and ending at t'

Space

$\mathcal{S}$	the set of spatial locations
$\mathcal{S}_p$	the set of physical locations
$\mathcal{S}_{\bar{p}}$	the set of nonphysical locations
Λ	the set of spatial locations
λ	a location in Λ
$\hat{d}$	distance function on events
$\hat{d}_\tau$	distance function on instant τ
σ	a separation function on locations

$\mathcal{V}$	the translation space of locations
$\mathcal{V}^*$	the dual of the translation space
v	a translation vector
v_ϕ	value of vector v in framing ϕ
$v^\star$	value of vector v in framing $\phi^\star$
s	a scalar multiplier in a vector space
s_ϕ	value of s in framing ϕ
$0_\mathcal{V}$	null or identity translation
x, v, w	vectors, module elements, or points on a manifold
ϕ	an isometry of places or locations
$\overline{\mathcal{V}}$	isometries of $\mathcal{V}$
$\overline{\mathcal{V}}_d$	isometries of $\mathcal{V}$ with respect to metric d
$\overline{\mathcal{V}}_\sigma$	isometries of $\mathcal{V}$ with respect to separation σ
Q	orthogonal transformation (rotation)
$\otimes$	tensor product of vectors or module elements
$\wedge$	wedge (alternating, symplectic) product
$\langle , \rangle$ or $\bullet$	inner product
q	a quadratic form
$\times$	cross product
div	divergence of a tensor
M	a manifold or premanifold
ϕ	a local chart on a manifold
U	the domain of local chart
$\mathcal{A}$	an atlas of charts on a manifold
$\mathcal{A}^*$	an atlas structure on a manifold
$T_x M$	tangent space to M at x
TM	tangent bundle of M
$T^* M$	cotangent bundle of M
ψ	section of tangent space
$\mathcal{M}_\phi$	module for premanifold chart ϕ
$\mathcal{R}_{\mathcal{M}_\phi}$	scalar ring of chart module $\mathcal{M}_\phi$
χ	placement of a body
$\chi(b)$	placement of a body point b
$\chi(\mathcal{B})$	shape of body $\mathcal{B}$ in placement χ
$\chi_\mathcal{B}$	placement of the material universe
$\mathcal{B}_S$	universe of shapes
d_χ	distance in a placement χ
κ	the configuration mapping
$\mathcal{B}_C$	the universe of configurations
$\mathcal{C}$	the set of all configurations
$\mathcal{C}(\mathcal{B})$	the set of allowed configuration of body $\mathcal{B}$

Motion

χ_t	placement at time t
$\chi(b, t)$	or placement of b at time t
$\chi_b(t)$	
$\dot{\chi}$	the spatial velocity
$\ddot{\chi}$	the spatial acceleration
χ^r	a reference motion or observer frame
h	a history
H	a set of histories over the same interval
Δ_H	correspondence for histories H
H_Δ	histories with respect to correspondence Δ
g	discrete dynamical map
π_{S_i}	projection onto S_i component of hybrid space
x	the position vector
$\dot{x}$	the velocity vector
$\ddot{x}$	the acceleration vector

Force

$\mathcal{F}$	space of force values
f	force system, force value, force variation, force configuration
$f(\mathcal{B}, \mathcal{C})$	force of $\mathcal{C}$ on $\mathcal{B}$
$f_\Rightarrow$	force exerted on
$f_\Leftarrow$	force exerted by
$\mathcal{C}_f$	set of force configurations
f^{B}	body force
f^{C}	contact force
$\mathbf{b}$	body force density
$\mathbf{t}$	traction (contact force density)
$\mathbf{T}$	the stress tensor
F	a torque, torque system, or torque configuration
$\mathcal{L}$	set of all torque values
$F_{\Leftarrow \mathcal{B}}$	torque resulting from $\mathcal{B}$
F_{x_0}	torque about location x_0
$\theta(h)$	response functional giving stress from h

Mass

m	a mass function, mass variation, or mass configuration
m_t	mass at time t
$\mathbf{m}$	a mass vector
$\dot{m}$	massing or mass flux
ρ	the spatial mass density
$\mathcal{B}_{\mathrm{m}}$	the massy universe
$\mathcal{M}$	the space of mass values
$\mathcal{R}_\mathcal{M}$	the ring of module scalars
$\mathbf{0}_\mathcal{M}$	the null mass
$\mathbf{1}_\mathcal{M}$	the unit mass
$\mathcal{C}_{\mathrm{m}}$	the set of mass configurations

Energy

W	working
$\mathcal{B}_{\mathrm{e}}$	the energetic universe
$\mathcal{E}$	the space of energy values
E	internal energy function; energy value; energy configuration
$\mathcal{R}_\mathcal{E}$	the ring of energy scalars
$\prec$	the energy order
$\mathcal{C}_{\mathrm{E}}$	the set of energy configurations
E	internal energy
$\dot{E}$	change in internal energy
K	kinetic energy
$\dot{K}$	change in kinetic energy
Q	a heating function

Momentum

$\mathcal{P}$	space of momentum vectors
p	linear momentum map or momentum value
$\dot{p}$	momentum flux
p^*	dual momentum map
$p^\times$	enlarged momentum map
$p^\otimes$	bilinear momentum map
L	rotational momentum
L_{x_0}	rotational momentum about x_0
$\dot{L}$	rotational momentum flux

Variational formalism

H	Hamiltonian function
L	Lagrangian function
U	potential function

Mechanical processes

Σ	the set of all mechanical states
σ	a mechanical state

Conservatism

$\prec$	conservatism comparison relation
$\prec_\sigma$	state-based comparison relation
ν	nearest-state function

Psychology and RMS

$\mathcal{D}$	set of mental attitudes or elements
d, e	individual state components or dimensions
$\mathbb{D}$	binary vector space $\mathbb{Z}_2^{\mathcal{D}}$ over $\mathbb{Z}_2$
$\mathbf{0}$	binary all-zeros vector in $\mathbb{D}$
$\mathbf{1}$	binary all-ones vector in $\mathbb{D}$
In	Label of elements in a mental state
Out	Label of elements not in a mental state
Nyl	Indicator of elements not yet labeled
r	a reason
R	a set of reasons
$A \setminus\!\setminus B$	sets with A but without items B
$X \Vdash Y$	Y holds if X holds
α	Admissible extension relation

Uncertainty

pr	a probability distribution
$\mu^{\mathcal{H}}$	probability measure on histories
μ^{Σ}	probability density measure
μ	a measure function
$\mu^{\dagger}$	counting measure
μ^{*}	specificity measure
$\langle f \rangle$	expected value of function f
$\langle x \mid y \rangle$	Dirac bracket of vectors
$\langle x |$	bra covector
$| y \rangle$	ket vector

Decision theory

$\sim$	Indifference relation
$\prec$	Strict preference relation
$\precsim$	Weak preference relation
$\mathcal{A}$	Set of decision alternatives
Ω	Set of decision outcomes
ω	Individual decision outcome
u	Utility function
$\hat{u}$	Expected utility function

Information systems

$\mathbf{I}$	information system $(\mathcal{D}, Con, \vdash)$
$\mathcal{D}$	domain of propositions
e	an atomic proposition in $\mathcal{D}$
$\mathcal{PD}$	domain powerset
Con	set of consistent finite sets
$\vdash$	entailment relation
Th	entailment closure operator
$Elt(\mathbf{I})$	closed and consistent elements
$Elt^{+}(\mathbf{I})$	total elements

Satisfaction systems

$\mathbf{S}$	satisfaction system $(\mathcal{D}, [\![\,]\!])$
$[\![\,]\!]$	meaning function
$Sat(\mathbf{S})$	satisfying sets

Bibliography

Abelson, H., and Sussman, G. J. 1985. *Structure and Interpretation of Computer Programs*. Cambridge, MA: MIT Press.

Abraham, R., and Marsden, J. E. 1978. *Foundations of Mechanics*. Reading, MA: Benjamin, second edition.

Ackley, D., Hinton, G., and Sejnowski, T. 1985. A learning algorithm for Boltzmann machines. *Cognitive Science* 9:147–169.

Aczel, P. 1988. *Non-Well-Founded Sets*. Stanford, CA: Center for the Study of Language and Information.

Akers, S. B. 1959. On a theory of Boolean functions. *Journal of the Society for Industrial and Applied Mathematics* 7:487–498.

Alur, R., Courcoubetis, C., Henzinger, T. A., and Ho, P.-H. 1993. Hybrid automata: An algorithmic approach to the specification and verification of hybrid systems. In Grossman, R., Nerode, A., Ravn, A., and Rischel, H., eds., *Hybrid Systems*, Volume 736 of *Lecture Notes in Computer Science*, 209–229. Berlin: Springer-Verlag.

Andreski, S. 1972. *Social Sciences as Sorcery*. New York: St. Martin's Press.

Aristotle. 1962. *Nichomachian Ethics*. Indianapolis: Bobbs-Merrill. Translated by M. Ostwald.

Arrow, K. J., and Hahn, F. H. 1971. *General Competitive Analysis*. Amsterdam: North-Holland.

Arrow, K. J. 1963. *Social Choice and Individual Values*. New Haven, CT: Yale University Press, second edition.

Aubin, J. P., and Cellina, A. 1984. *Differential Inclusions: Set-Valued Maps and Viability Theory*. Berlin: Springer-Verlag.

Aumann, R. J. 1964. Markets with a continuum of traders. *Econometrica* 32:39–50.

Baader, F., Calvanese, D., McGuinness, D., Nardi, D., and Patel-Schneider, P., eds. 2003. *The Description Logic Handbook: Theory, Implementation and Applications*. Cambridge, UK: Cambridge University Press.

Bacchus, F., Grove, A. J., Halpern, J. Y., and Koller, D. 1996. From statistical knowledge bases to degrees of belief. *Artificial Intelligence* 87(1–2):75–143.

Baez, J. C., and Gilliam, J. W. 1994. An algebraic approach to discrete mechanics. *Letters in Mathematical Physics* 31:205–212.

Bell, J. S. 1966. On the problem of hidden variables in quantum mechanics. *Review of Modern Physics* 38:447–452.

Bell, J. S. 1987. *Speakable and Unspeakable in Quantum Mechanics*. Cambridge, UK: Cambridge University Press.

429

Belnap, N. D. 1976. How a computer should think. In Ryle, G., ed., *Contemporary Aspects of Philosophy*. Stocksfield: Oriel Press. 30–56.

Beltrametti, E. G., and Cassinelli, G. 1981. *The Logic of Quantum Mechanics*. Reading, MA: Addison-Wesley.

Benvenuto, E. 1991. *An Introduction to the History of Structural Mechanics*. New York: Springer-Verlag. In two volumes.

Birkhoff, G. 1967. *Lattice Theory*. Providence, RI: American Mathematical Society.

Blum, L., Cucker, F., Shub, M., and Smale, S. 1998. *Complexity and Real Computation*. New York: Springer-Verlag.

Bohm, D. 1952. A suggested interpretation of the quantum theory in terms of "hidden variables," Parts I and II. *Physical Review* 85:166–179,180–193.

Bolles, R. C. 1975. *Theory of motivation*. New York: Harper & Row, second edition.

Boolos, G. 1979. *The Unprovability of Consistency: An Essay in Modal Logic*. Cambridge, UK: Cambridge University Press.

Boutilier, C., Dean, T., and Hanks, S. 1999. Decision theoretic planning: Structural assumptions and computational leverage. *Journal of Artificial Intelligence Research* 11:1–94.

Boyd, R., and Richerson, P. J. 1985. *Culture and the Evolutionary Process*. Chicago: University of Chicago Press.

Brams, S. J. 1980. *Biblical Games: A Strategic Analysis of Stories in the Old Testament*. Cambridge, MA: MIT Press.

Brams, S. J. 1983. *Superior Beings: If They Exist, How Would We Know? Game-Theoretic Implications of Omniscience, Omnipotence, Immortality, and Incomprehensibility*. New York: Springer-Verlag.

Branicky, M. S. 1994. Analog computation with continuous ODEs. In *Proceedings of the IEEE Workshop Physics and Computation*, 265–274. New York: IEEE.

Branicky, M. S. 1995. Universal computation and other capabilities of hybrid and continuous dynamical systems. *Theoretical Computer Science* 138(1):67–100. Special issue on hybrid systems.

Brentano, F. C. 1874. *Psychologie vom empirischen Standpunkte*. Leipzig: Duncker and Humblot.

Bressan, A. 1978. *Relativistic Theories of Materials*, Volume 29 of *Springer Tracts in Natural Philosophy*. Berlin: Springer-Verlag.

Brooks, R. A. 1991. Intelligence without representation. *Artificial Intelligence* 47:139–159.

Burges, C. J. C., and Schölkopf, B. 1997. Improving the accuracy and speed of support vector learning machines. In Mozer, M., Jordan, M., and Petsche, T., eds., *Advances in Neural Information Processing Systems 9*. Cambridge, MA: MIT Press. 375–381.

Burges, C. J. C. 1998. A tutorial on support vector machines for pattern recognition. *Knowledge Discovery and Data Mining* 2(2): 121–167.

Burgess, J. P. 1984. Synthetic mechanics. *Journal of Philosophical Logic* 13:379–396.

Carbonell, J. G. 1986. Derivational analogy: A theory of reconstructive problem solving and expertise acquisition. In Michalski, R. S., Carbonell, J. G., and Mitchell, T. M., eds., *Machine Learning: An Artificial Intelligence Approach*, Volume 2. San Francisco, CA: Morgan Kaufmann. 371–392.

Carnap, R. 1950. *Logical Foundations of Probability*. Chicago: University of Chicago Press.

Cass, D., and Shell, K. 1976. *The Hamiltonian Approach to Dynamic Economics*. New York: Academic Press.

Chaitin, G. J. 1975. A theory of program size formally identical to information theory. *Journal of the ACM* 22:329–340.

Cheng, J., and Wellman, M. 1998. The WALRAS algorithm: A convergent distributed implementation of general-equilibrium outcomes. *Computational Economics* 12:1–24.

Church, A. 1941. *The Calculi of Lambda-Conversion*. Number 6 in *Annals of Mathematics Studies*. Princeton, NJ: Princeton University Press.

Church, A. 1944. *Introduction to Mathematical Logic, I*. Number 13 in *Annals of Mathematics Studies*. Princeton, NJ: Princeton University Press. Based on notes taken by C. Truesdell.

Churchill, W. 1941. Radio broadcast of the 1941 University of Rochester Commencement Address. Rochester, NY: University of Rochester. http://hdl.handle.net/1802/2139.

Cobham, A. 1966. The recognition problem for the set of perfect squares. In *Conference Record of the Seventh Annual Symposium on Switching and Automata Theory*, 78–87. New York: IEEE.

Coolidge, J. L. 1909. The gambler's ruin. *The Annals of Mathematics, 2nd Series* 10(4):181–192.

Coolidge, J. L. 1940. *A History of Geometrical Methods*. Oxford, UK: The Clarendon Press.

Copeland, B. J. 2002. Hypercomputation. *Minds and Machines* 12(4):461–502.

Cucker, F., and Smale, S. 2002. On the mathematical foundations of learning. *Bulletin of the American Mathematical Society* 39:1–49.

Davis, M. 1981. Obvious logical inferences. In *Proceedings of the Seventh International Joint Conference on Artificial Intelligence*, 530–531. San Francisco, CA: Morgan Kaufmann.

Davoren, J. M. 1998. *Modal Logics for Continuous Dynamics*. Ph.D. Dissertation, Cornell University.

de Kleer, J., Doyle, J., Steele Jr., G. L., and Sussman, G. J. 1977. AMORD: Explicit control of reasoning. In *Proceedings of the ACM Symposium on Artificial Intelligence and Programming Languages*, 116–125. New York: ACM.

de Witt, B. S., and Graham, N. 1973. *The Many-Worlds Interpretation of Quantum Mechanics*. Princeton, NJ: Princeton University Press.

Dieudonné, J. 1963. *La Géométrie des Groupes Classiques*, Volume 5 of *Ergebnisse der Mathematik und ihrer Grenzgebiete*. Berlin: Springer-Verlag, second edition.

Doyle, J., and Thomason, R. H. 1999. Background to qualitative decision theory. *AI Magazine* 20(2):55–68.

Doyle, J., and Wellman, M. P. 1990. Rational distributed reason maintenance for planning and replanning of large-scale activities. In Sycara, K., ed., *Proceedings of the DARPA Workshop on Planning and Scheduling*, 28–36. San Francisco, CA: Morgan Kaufmann.

Doyle, J., and Wellman, M. P. 1991. Impediments to universal preference-based default theories. *Artificial Intelligence* 49(1–3):97–128.

Doyle, J., Shoham, Y., and Wellman, M. P. 1991. A logic of relative desire (preliminary report). In Ras, Z. W., and Zemankova, M., eds., *Methodologies for Intelligent Systems, 6*, Volume 542 of *Lecture Notes in Artificial Intelligence*, 16–31. Berlin: Springer-Verlag.

Doyle, J. 1976. The use of dependency relationships in the control of reasoning. Working Paper 133, MIT AI Laboratory.

Doyle, J. 1977. Truth maintenance systems for problem solving. In *Proceedings of the Fifth International Joint Conference on Artificial Intelligence*, 247. San Francisco, CA: Morgan Kaufmann.

Doyle, J. 1979. A truth maintenance system. *Artificial Intelligence* 12(2):231–272.

Doyle, J. 1980. A model for deliberation, action, and introspection. Technical Report AI-TR 581, MIT AI Laboratory.

Doyle, J. 1981. Three short essays on decisions, reasons, and logics. Technical Report 81-864, Computer Science Department, Stanford University.

Doyle, J. 1982a. The foundations of psychology. Technical Report 82-149, Department of Computer Science, Carnegie Mellon University.

Doyle, J. 1982b. What is Church's Thesis? An outline. Written at Carnegie Mellon University and privately circulated thereafter (eventually published as Doyle 2002b).

Doyle, J. 1983a. Admissible state semantics for representational systems. *IEEE Computer* 16(10):119–123.

Doyle, J. 1983b. The ins and outs of reason maintenance. In *Proceedings of the Eighth International Joint Conference on Artificial Intelligence*, 349–351. San Francisco, CA: Morgan Kaufmann.

Doyle, J. 1983c. Methodological simplicity in expert system construction: The case of judgments and reasoned assumptions. *AI Magazine* 3(2):39–43.

Doyle, J. 1983d. A society of mind: Multiple perspectives, reasoned assumptions, and virtual copies. In *Proceedings of the Eighth International Joint Conference on Artificial Intelligence*, 309–314. San Francisco, CA: Morgan Kaufmann.

Doyle, J. 1983e. Some theories of reasoned assumptions: An essay in rational psychology. Technical Report 83-125, Department of Computer Science, Carnegie Mellon University.

Doyle, J. 1983f. What is rational psychology? Toward a modern mental philosophy. *AI Magazine* 4(3):50–53.

Doyle, J. 1985a. Expert systems and the "myth" of symbolic reasoning. *IEEE Transactions on Software Engineering* SE-11(11):1386–1390.

Doyle, J. 1985b. Reasoned assumptions and Pareto optimality. In *Proceedings of the Ninth International Joint Conference on Artificial Intelligence*, 87–90.

Doyle, J. 1988a. Artificial intelligence and rational self-government. Technical Report CS-88-124, Department of Computer Science, Carnegie-Mellon University.

Doyle, J. 1988b. On universal theories of defaults. Technical Report CS-88-111, Department of Computer Science, Carnegie-Mellon University.

Doyle, J. 1989. Constructive belief and rational representation. *Computational Intelligence* 5(1):1–11.

Doyle, J. 1990a. The foundations of psychology: A logico-computational inquiry into the concept of mind. In Cummins, R., and Pollock, J., eds., *Philosophy and AI: Essays at the Interface*, A Bradford Book. Cambridge, MA: MIT Press. Chapter 3, 39–77.

Doyle, J. 1990b. Rational belief revision. Presented at the Third International Workshop on Nonmonotonic Reasoning, Stanford Sierra Camp, CA.

Doyle, J. 1991. Rational belief revision (preliminary report). In Fikes, R. E., and Sandewall, E., eds., *Proceedings of the Second Conference on Principles of Knowledge Representation and Reasoning*, 163–174. San Francisco, CA: Morgan Kaufmann.

Doyle, J. 1992a. Rationality and its roles in reasoning. *Computational Intelligence* 8(2):376–409.

Doyle, J. 1992b. Reason maintenance and belief revision: Foundations vs. coherence theories. In Gärdenfors, P., ed., *Belief Revision*. Cambridge, UK: Cambridge University Press. 29–51.

Doyle, J. 1994. Reasoned assumptions and rational psychology. *Fundamenta Informaticae* 20(1–3):35–73.

Doyle, J. 1996. Toward rational planning and replanning: Rational reason maintenance, reasoning economies, and qualitative preferences. In Tate, A., ed., *Advanced Planning Technology: Technological Achievements of the ARPA/Rome Laboratory Planning Initiative*. Menlo Park, CA: AAAI Press. 130–135.

Doyle, J. 1997. Final report on rational distributed reason maintenance for planning and replanning of large-scale activities (1991-1994). Technical Report TR-97-40, ADA328535, U.S. Air Force Research Laboratory.

Doyle, J. 2001. Matter, mind and mechanics: New models for dynamogenesis and rationality. Available via http://www.csc.ncsu.edu/faculty/doyle/.

Doyle, J. 2002a. A rational mechanics of reasoning (extended abstract of Doyle 2001).

Doyle, J. 2002b. What is Church's thesis? An outline. *Minds and Machines* 12(4):519–520.

Doyle, J. 2004. Prospects for preferences. *Computational Intelligence* 20(2):111–136.

Einstein, A. 1916. Die grundlage der allgemeinen relativitätstheorie. *Annalen der Physik* 49(4):769–822.

Elgot, C. C., and Robinson, A. 1964. Random access stored program machines, an approach to programming languages. *Journal of the ACM* 11(4):365–399.

Elster, J. 1979. *Ulysses and the Sirens: Studies in Rationality and Irrationality*. Cambridge, UK: Cambridge University Press.

Euler, L. 1750. Découverte d'un nouveau principe de méchanique (Discovery of a new principle of mechanics). *Mémoires de l'Académie des Sciences, Berlin* 6:185–217.

Euler, L. 1775. Nova methodus motum corporum rigidorum determinandi (A new method for determining the motion of a rigid body). *Novi Commentarii Academiae Scientiarum Petropolitanae* 20:208–238.

Everett III, H. 1957. "Relative state" formulation of quantum mechanics. *Reviews of Modern Physics* 29(3):454–462. Reprinted in de Witt & Graham (1973).

Fagin, R., Ullman, J. D., and Vardi, M. Y. 1983. On the semantics of updates in databases. In *Proceedings of the Second ACM SIGACT-SIGMOD Conference on Principles of Database Systems*, 352–365. New York: ACM.

Festinger, L. 1957. *A Theory of Cognitive Dissonance*. Stanford, CA: Stanford University Press.

Feynman, R. P. 1949. The theory of positrons. *Physical Review* 76:749–759.

Feynman, R. P. 1966. The development of the space-time view of quantum electrodynamics. *Science* 153(3737):699–708.

Fikes, R. E., and Nilsson, N. J. 1971. STRIPS: A new approach to the application of theorem proving to problem solving. *Artificial Intelligence* 2:189–208.

Finkelstein, D. 1996. *Quantum Relativity*. Heidelberg: Springer-Verlag.

Frank, M. P., and Knight, T. F. 1998. Ultimate theoretical models of nanocomputers. *Nanotechnology* 9(3):162–176.

Frank, M., Knight, T., and Margolus, N. 1998. Reversibility in optimally scalable computer architectures. In *Unconventional Models of Computation (Auckland, 1998)*. Singapore: Springer. 165–182.

Frank, M. P. 1999. *Reversibility for Efficient Computing*. Ph.D. Dissertation, Massachusetts Institute of Technology.

Frankfurt, H. 1971. Freedom of the will and the concept of a person. *Journal of Philosophy* 68:5–20.

Fredkin, E., and Toffoli, T. 1982. Conservative logic. *International Journal of Theoretical Physics* 21:219–253.

Freud, S. 1895. Project for a scientific psychology. In Strachey, J., ed., *Standard Edition of the Complete Psychological Works of Sigmund Freud*, Volume I. London: Hogarth Press. Reprinted in 1966.

Freyd, J. J. 1987. Dynamic mental representations. *Psychological Review* 94(4):427–438.

Gandy, R. 1980. Church's thesis and principles for mechanisms. In Barwise, J., Keisler, H. J., and Kunen, K., eds., *The Kleene Symposium*. Amsterdam: North-Holland. 123–148.

Gärdenfors, P., and Makinson, D. 1988. Revisions of knowledge systems using epistemic entrenchment. In Vardi, M. Y., ed., *Proceedings of the Second Conference on Theoretical Aspects of Reasoning About Knowledge*, 83–95. San Francisco, CA: Morgan Kaufmann.

Gärdenfors, P. 1988. *Knowledge in Flux: Modeling the Dynamics of Epistemic States.* Cambridge, MA: MIT Press.

Geertz, C. 1983. Common sense as a cultural system. In *Local Knowledge*. New York: Basic Books. 73–93.

Gilliam, J. W. 1996. *Lagrangian and Symplectic Techniques in Discrete Mechanics.* Ph.D. Dissertation, University of California, Riverside.

Ginsberg, M. L. 1996. Do computers need common sense? In Carlucci Aiello, L., Doyle, J., and Shapiro, S., eds., *Proceedings of the Fifth International Conference on Principles of Knowledge Representation and Reasoning*, 620–626. San Francisco, CA: Morgan Kaufmann.

Glimm, J., and Jaffe, A. 1981. *Quantum Physics*. New York: Springer.

Gödel, K. 1931. Über formal unentscheidbar sätze der Principia Mathematica und verwandter system I. *Monatshefte für Mathematik und Physik* 38:173–198.

Greenspan, D. 1972. A new explicit discrete mechanics with applications. *Journal of the Franklin Institute* 294:231–240.

Guo, H.-Y., and Wu, K. 2003. On variations in discrete mechanics and field theory. *Journal of Mathemathical Physics* 44(12):5978–6004.

Gurtin, M. E. 1981. *An Introduction to Continuum Mechanics*. New York: Academic Press.

Hamel, G. 1908. Über die grundlagen der mechanik. *Mathematische Annalen* 66:350–397.

Hamming, R. W. 1962. *Numerical Methods for Scientists and Engineers*. New York: McGraw-Hill.

Harman, G. 1986. *Change in View: Principles of Reasoning*. Cambridge, MA: MIT Press.

Hartmanis, J. 1973. On the problem of finding natural computational complexity measures. Technical Report TR 73-175, Department of Computer Science, Cornell University.

Hartmanis, J. 1994. Turing award lecture on computational complexity and the nature of computer science. *Communications of the ACM* 37(10):37–43.

Hartwig, R. E., and Doyle, J. 2002. Solid motion of binary vectors. Unpublished manuscript.

Herbart, J. F. 1877. Possibility and necessity of applying mathematics in psychology. *Journal of Speculative Philosophy* 11:251–264.

Herbart, J. F. 1891. *A Text-Book in Psychology: An Attempt to Found the Science of Psychology on Experience, Metaphysics, and Mathematics*. New York: Appleton. Translation of the second revised edition of 1834 (Hamburg: Hartenstein, 1886). First edition 1816.

Hermann, R. 1990. A 'geometric' view of the dynamics of trajectories of computer programs. *Acta Applicandae Mathematicae* 18:145–182.

Hermann, R. 1991. *Geometric Computing Science: First Steps*, Volume 25 of *Interdisciplinary Mathematics*. Brookline, MA: Math Sci Press.

Hilbert, D. 1902. Mathematical problems. *Bulletin of the American Mathematical Society* 8:437–479. Lecture delivered before the 1900 International Congress of Mathematicians at Paris.

Hilbert, D. 1926. Über das unendliche. *Mathematische Annalen* 95:161–190.

Hinton, G. E., Sejnowski, T. J., and Ackley, D. H. 1984. Boltzmann machines: Constraint satisfaction networks that learn. Technical Report CMU-CS-84-119, Department of Computer Science, Carnegie-Mellon University.

Hobbes, T. 1656. *Elements of Philosophy*. London, UK: Leybourn.

Horvitz, E. J., Cooper, G. F., and Heckerman, D. E. 1989. Reflection and action under scarce resources: Theoretical principles and empirical study. In Sridharan, N. S., ed., *Proceedings of the Eleventh International Joint Conference on Artificial Intelligence*, Volume 2. San Francisco, CA: Morgan Kaufmann 1121–1127.

Horvitz, E. J. 1987. Reasoning about beliefs and actions under computational resource constraints. In *Proceedings of the Third AAAI Workshop on Uncertainty in Artificial Intelligence*, 429–444. Menlo Park, CA: AAAI.

Irving, J., and Kirkwood, J. 1950. The statistical mechanical theory of transport processes. IV. The equations of hydrodynamics. *Journal of Chemical Physics* 18:817–829.

Iwasaki, Y., Farquhar, A., Saraswat, V., Bobrow, D., and Gupta, V. 1995. Modeling time in hybrid systems: How fast is 'instantaneous'? In *Proceedings of the Fourteenth International Joint Conference on Artificial Intelligence*, 1773–1780. San Francisco, CA: Morgan Kaufmann.

Jackson, F. 1986. What Mary didn't know. *The Journal of Philosophy* 83(5):291–295.

Jaffe, A. M. 1984. Ordering the universe. *SIAM Review* 26(4):473–500.

James, W. 1890. *The Principles of Psychology*. New York: Henry Holt. In two volumes.

James, W. 1897. *The Will to Believe and Other Essays in Popular Philosophy*. New York: Longmans, Green.

James, W. 1920. *The Letters of William James*. Boston: Atlantic Monthly Press. Edited by Henry James, in two volumes.

Jost, R. 1965. *The General Theory of Quantized Fields*. Providence, RI: American Mathematical Society.

Kalman, R. E., Falb, P. L., and Arbib, M. A. 1969. *Topics in Mathematical System Theory*. New York: McGraw-Hill.

Kauffman, L. H., and Noyes, H. P. 1996. Discrete physics and the derivation of electromagnetism from the formalism of quantum mechanics. *Proceedings of the Royal Society of London, Series A* 452(1944):81–95.

Klein, E., and Thompson, A. C. 1984. *Theory of Correspondences: Including Applications to Mathematical Economics*. New York: Wiley.

Knight, F. H. 1956. Statics and dynamics: Some queries regarding the mechanical analogy in economics. In *On the History and Method of Economics*. Chicago: University of Chicago Press. 179–201.

Knuth, D. E. 1976. Mathematics and computer science: Coping with finiteness. *Science* 194:1235–1242.

Kock, A. 1981. *Synthetic Differential Geometry*. Cambridge, UK: Cambridge University Press.

Kolmogorov, A. N. 1969. On the logical foundations of information theory and probability theory. *Problems of Information Transmission* 5(3):1–4.

Krantz, D. H., Luce, R. D., Suppes, P., and Tversky, A. 1971. *Foundations of Measurement*. New York: Academic Press.

Kyburg, Jr., H. E. 1970. *Probability and Inductive Logic*. New York: Macmillan.

LaBudde, R. A., and Greenspan, D. 1974. Discrete mechanics—a general treatment. *Journal of Computational Physics* 15:134–167.

Laird, J. E., Newell, A., and Rosenbloom, P. S. 1987. SOAR: An architecture for general intelligence. *Artificial Intelligence* 33:1–64.

Lakoff, G., and Núñez, R. E. 2000. *Where Mathematics Comes From: How the Embodied Mind Brings Mathematics into Being.* New York: Basic Books.

Lamport, L. 1978. Time, clocks and the ordering of events in a distributed system. *Communications of the ACM* 21(7):558–565.

Laplace, P.-S. 1814. *Essais Philosophique sur les probabilités.* Paris: Courcier.

Lawvere, F. W. 2002. Categorical algebra for continuum micro physics. *Journal of Pure and Applied Algebra* 175 (2002):267–287.

Le Bon, G. 1895. *La Psychologie des Foules.* Paris: F. Alcan.

Leibenstein, H. 1980. *Beyond Economic Man: A New Foundation for Microeconomics.* Cambridge, MA: Harvard University Press, second edition.

Lewin, K. 1951. *Field Theory in Social Science.* New York: Harper.

Lewis, D. 1973. *Counterfactuals.* Oxford, UK: Blackwell.

Lewis, D. 1980. A subjectivist's guide to objective chance. In Harper, W. L., Stalnaker, R., and Pearce, G., eds., *Ifs.* Dordrecht: Reidel. 267–297.

Loui, R. P. 1998. Process and policy: Resource-bounded nondemonstrative reasoning. *Computational Intelligence* 14(1):1–38.

Mac Lane, S. 1986. *Mathematics: Form and Function.* New York: Springer-Verlag.

Manthey, M. J., and Moret, B. M. E. 1983. The computational metaphor and quantum physics. *Communications of the ACM* 26(2):137–145.

Marek, V. W., and Truszczyński, M. 1993. *Nonmonotonic Logic: Context-Dependent Reasoning.* Berlin: Springer-Verlag.

Margolus, N., and Levitin, L. B. 1997. The maximum speed of dynamical evolution. *Physica D* 120:188–195.

Margolus, N. 1984. Physics-like models of computation. *Physica D* 10(1–2): 81–95.

Marsden, J. E., and Hughes, T. J. R. 1983. *Mathematical Foundations of Elasticity.* Englewood Cliffs, NJ: Prentice-Hall.

Marshall, A. 1949. *Principles of Economics.* New York: Macmillan, eighth edition.

McAllester, D. A. 1980. An outlook on truth maintenance. Report AIM 551, MIT AI Laboratory.

McCarthy, J., and Hayes, P. J. 1969. Some philosophical problems from the standpoint of artificial intelligence. In Meltzer, B., and Michie, D., eds., *Machine Intelligence 4.* Edinburgh, UK: Edinburgh University Press. 463–502.

McCarthy, J., et al. 1965. *Lisp 1.5 Programmer's Manual.* Cambridge, MA: MIT Press, second edition.

McCarthy, J. 1958. Programs with common sense. In *Proceedings of the Symposium on Mechanisation of Thought Processes,* Volume 1. London: Her Majesty's Stationery Office. 77–84.

McDermott, D., and Doyle, J. 1980. Non-monotonic logic—I. *Artificial Intelligence* 13(1–2):41–72.

McKinsey, J. C. C., Sugar, A. C., and Suppes, P. 1953a. Axiomatic foundations of classical particle mechanics. *Journal of Rational Mechanics and Analysis* 2: 253–272.

McKinsey, J. C. C., Sugar, A. C., and Suppes, P. 1953b. Transformations of systems of classical particle mechanics. *Journal of Rational Mechanics and Analysis* 2: 273–289.

McShane, E. J. 1953. *Order-Preserving Maps and Integration Processes.* Number 31 in *Annals of Mathematics Studies.* Princeton, NJ: Princeton University Press. Reprinted by Kraus Reprint Corporation (1965).

Miller, G. A. 1986. Dismembering cognition. In Hulse, S. H., and Green, Jr., B. F., eds., *One Hundred Years of Psychological Research in America.* Baltimore: Johns Hopkins University Press. 277–298.

Milnor, J., and Husemoller, D. 1973. *Symmetric Bilinear Forms.* New York: Springer-Verlag.

Minsky, M., and Papert, S. 1969. *Perceptrons: An Introduction to Computational Geometry.* Cambridge, MA: MIT Press.

Minsky, M. 1963. Steps toward artificial intelligence. In Feigenbaum, E. A., and Feldman, J., eds., *Computers and Thought.* New York: McGraw-Hill. 406–450.

Minsky, M. 1965. Matter, mind, and models. In *Information Processing: Proceedings of the IFIP Congress,* 45–49. Amsterdam: North-Holland.

Minsky, M. 1967. *Computation: Finite and Infinite Machines.* Englewood Cliffs, NJ: Prentice-Hall.

Minsky, M. 1974. A framework for representing knowledge. AI Memo 306, MIT AI Laboratory. Reprinted in abbreviated form in *Mind Design,* J. Haugeland, ed., Cambridge, MA: MIT Press (1981). 95–128.

Minsky, M. 1980. K-lines: A theory of memory. *Cognitive Science* 4:117–133.

Minsky, M. 1986. *The Society of Mind.* New York: Simon & Schuster.

Minsky, N. H. 1988. Law-governed systems. Technical report, Computer Science Department, Rutgers University.

Mirowski, P. 1989. *More Heat Than Light: Economics as Social Physics: Physics as Nature's Economics.* Cambridge, UK: Cambridge University Press.

Misner, C. W., Thorne, K. S., and Wheeler, J. A. 1973. *Gravitation.* San Francisco: Freeman.

Mitchell, T. M., Keller, R. M., and Kedar-Cabelli, S. T. 1986. Explanation-based generalization: A unifying view. *Machine Learning* 1(1):47–80.

Müller, K.-R., Mika, S., Rätsch, G., Tsuda, K., and Schölkopf, B. 2001. An introduction to kernel-based learning algorithms. *IEEE Neural Networks* 12(2):181–201.

Myers, I. B., and Myers, P. B. 1980. *Gifts differing.* Palo Alto, CA: Consulting Psychologists Press.

Nelson, R. R., and Winter, S. G. 1982. *An Evolutionary Theory of Economic Change.* Cambridge, MA: Harvard University Press.

Nelson, E. 1966. Derivation of the Schrödinger equation from Newtonian mechanics. *Physical Review* 150(4):1079–1085.

Nelson, E. 1985. *Quantum Fluctuations.* Princeton, NJ: Princeton University Press.

Newell, A., Shaw, J. C., and Simon, H. A. 1960. Report on a general problem-solving program. In *Proceedings of the International Conference on Information Processing,* 256–264. Paris: UNESCO.

Newell, A. 1982. The knowledge level. *Artificial Intelligence* 18(1):87–127.

Newton, I. 1687. *Philosophiæ Naturalis Principia Mathematica.* London: Royal Society.

Nilsson, N. J. 1986. Probabilistic logic. *Artificial Intelligence* 28:71–87.

Noll, W., and Virga, E. G. 1988. Fit regions and functions of bounded variation. *Archive for Rational Mechanics and Analysis* 102:1–21.

Noll, W. 1955. Die herleitung der grundgleichungen der thermomechanik der kontinua aus der statischen mechanik. *Journal of Rational Mechanics and Analysis* 4: 627–646.

Noll, W. 1958. The foundations of classical mechanics in the light of recent advances in continuum mechanics. In L. Henkin, P. Suppes, and A. Tarski, eds., *The Axiomatic Method, With Special Reference to Geometry and Physics. Proceedings of an International Symposium Held at the University of California, Berkeley, December 26, 1957–January 4, 1958.* Studies in Logic and the Foundations of Mathematics, 266–281. Amsterdam: North-Holland. Reprinted in Noll (1974).

Noll, W. 1963. La mécanique classique, basée sur un axiome d'objectivité. In *La Méthode Axiomatique dans les Mécaniques Classiques et Nouvelles (Actes Quatrieme Colloque International de Logique et Philosophie des Sciences, Paris, 1959),* 47–56. Paris: Gauthier-Villars. Reprinted in Noll (1974).

Noll, W. 1964. Euclidean geometry and Minkowskian chronometry. *American Mathematical Monthly* 71:129–144. Reprinted in Noll (1974).

Noll, W. 1972. A new mathematical theory of simple materials. *Archive for Rational Mechanics and Analysis* 48:1–50. Reprinted in Noll (1974).

Noll, W. 1973. Lectures on the foundations of continuum mechanics and thermodynamics. *Archive for Rational Mechanics and Analysis* 52:62–92. Reprinted in Noll (1974).

Noll, W. 1974. *The Foundations of Mechanics and Thermodynamics: Selected Papers.* Berlin: Springer-Verlag.

Noll, W. 1995. On material frame-indifference. Technical Report 95-NA-022, Department of Mathematics, Carnegie Mellon University.

Noyes, H. P. 1996. Some thoughts on discrete physics and the reconstruction of quantum mechanics. Technical Report SLAC-PUB-7145, Stanford Linear Accelerator.

Paris, J., and Harrington, L. 1977. A mathematical incompleteness in Peano arithmetic. In Barwise, J., ed., *Handbook of Mathematical Logic*, Volume 90 of *Studies in Logic and the Foundations of Mathematics*, Chapter D.8, 1133–1142. Amsterdam: North-Holland.

Pascal, B. 1962. *Pensées sur la religion et sur quelques autres sujets.* London: Harvill. Translated by M. Turnell, originally published 1662.

Pearl, J. 1988. *Probabilistic Reasoning in Intelligent Systems: Networks of Plausible Inference.* San Francisco, CA: Morgan Kaufmann.

Pearl, J. 1990. System Z: A natural ordering of defaults with tractable applications to default reasoning. In *Proceedings of TARK-90*, 121–135. San Francisco, CA: Morgan Kaufmann.

Pearl, D. 1994. Stradivarius violin, lost years ago, resurfaces but new owner plays coy. *The Wall Street Journal.* October 17.

Penrose, R. 1989. *The Emperor's New Mind: Concerning Computers, Minds, and The Laws of Physics.* New York: Oxford University Press.

Post, H. R. 1974. *Against Ideologies.* Inaugural Lectures. London: Chelsea College.

Pour-El, M. B., and Richards, I. 1981. The wave equation with computable initial data such that its unique solution is not computable. *Advances in Mathematics* 39(3):215–239.

Pour-El, M. B., and Richards, J. I. 1989. *Computability in Analysis and Physics.* Berlin: Springer-Verlag.

Pratt, V. R., and Stockmeyer, L. J. 1976. A characterization of the power of vector machines. *Journal of Computer and System Sciences* 12(2):198–221.

Pratt, V. R., Rabin, M. O., and Stockmeyer, L. J. 1974. A characterization of the power of vector machines. In *STOC, Proceedings of the Sixth Annual ACM Symposium on Theory of Computing* 122–134. New York: ACM.

Putnam, H. 1975. Philosophy and our mental life. In *Mind, Language, and Reality.* Cambridge, UK: Cambridge University Press. 291–303.

Quine, W. V., and Ullian, J. S. 1978. *The Web of Belief*. New York: Random House, second edition.

Rabin, M. O., and Scott, D. 1959. Finite automata and their decision problems. *IBM Journal of Research and Development* 3:114–125.

Rabin, M. O. 1976. Probabilistic algorithms. In Traub, J. F., ed., *Algorithms and Complexity: New Directions and Recent Trends*. New York: Academic Press. 22–39.

Ramadge, P. J., and Wonham, W. M. 1982. Supervisory Control of Discrete Event Processes. In *Feedback Control of Linear and Nonlinear Systems (Bielefeld/Rome, 1981)*. Berlin: Springer. 202–214.

Ramadge, P. J., and Wonham, W. M. 1987. Supervisory control of a class of discrete event processes. *SIAM Journal on Control and Optimization* 25(1):206–230.

Rashevsky, N. 1938. *Mathematical Biophysics: Physico-Mathematical Foundations of Biology*. Chicago: University of Chicago Press.

Reiter, R. 1980. A logic for default reasoning. *Artificial Intelligence* 13:81–132.

Reiter, R. 1988. On integrity constraints. In *Proceedings of the Second Conference on Theoretical Aspects of Reasoning About Knowledge*, 97–111. San Francisco, CA: Morgan Kaufmann.

Rescher, N. 1964. *Hypothetical Reasoning*. Amsterdam: North-Holland.

Roberts, F. S. 1979. *Measurement Theory, With Applications to Decisionmaking, Utility, and the Social Sciences*, Volume 7 of *Encyclopedia of Mathematics and its Applications*. Reading, MA: Addison-Wesley.

Robinson, A. 1974. *Non-Standard Analysis*. Amsterdam: North-Holland, revised edition.

Rohrlich, F. 1965. *Classical Charged Particles: Foundations of Their Theory*. Reading, MA: Addison-Wesley.

Rosenschein, S. J., and Kaelbling, L. P. 1986. The synthesis of machines with provable epistemic properties. In Halpern, J., ed., *Proceedings of the Conference on Theoretical Aspects of Reasoning About Knowledge*, 83–98. San Francisco, CA: Morgan Kaufmann.

Rubel, L. A. 1981. A universal differential equation. *Bulletin of the American Mathematical Society (New Series)* 4(3):345–349.

Russell, S. J., and Norvig, P. 2002. *Artificial Intelligence: A Modern Approach*. Englewood Cliffs, NJ: Prentice-Hall, second edition.

Russell, B. 1930. *The Conquest of Happiness*. New York: Liveright.

Salomaa, A., and Soittola, M. 1978. *Automata-Theoretic Aspects of Formal Power Series*. New York: Springer-Verlag.

Samuelson, P. A. 1971. Maximum principles in analytical economics. *Science* 173(4001):991–997.

Savage, L. J. 1972. *The Foundations of Statistics*. New York: Dover, second edition.

Schank, R. C. 1982. *Dynamic Memory: A Theory of Learning in People and Computers*. Cambridge, UK: Cambridge University Press.

Schatz, J. A. 2003. Personal communication.

Schlechta, K., and Makinson, D. 1994. Local and global metrics for the semantics of counterfactual conditionals. *Journal of Applied Non-Classical Logics* 4(2): 129–140.

Schlechta, K. 1995. Logic, topology, and integration. *Journal of Automated Reasoning* 14(3):353–381.

Schlechta, K. 1997. *Nonmonotonic Logics. Basic Concepts, Results, and Techniques*, Lecture Notes in Artificial Intelligence. Berlin: Springer-Verlag.

Schölkopf, B. 2000. Statistical learning and kernel methods. Technical Report MSR-TR 2000-23, Microsoft Research.

Schumpeter, J. A. 1934. *The Theory of Economic Development: An Inquiry Into Profits, Capital, Credit, Interest, and the Business Cycle.* Cambridge, MA: Harvard University Press. Translated by R. Opie.

Scott, D. 1973. Models for various type-free calculi. In Suppes, P., Henkin, L., Joja, A., and Moisil, G. C., eds., *Logic, Methodology and Philosophy of Science IV.* Amsterdam: North-Holland. 157–187.

Scott, D. 1976. Data types as lattices. *SIAM Journal of Computing* 5:522–587.

Scott, D. S. 1982. Domains for denotational semantics. In Nielsen, M., and Schmidt, E. M., eds., *Automata, Languages, and Programming: Ninth Colloquium*, Volume 140 of *Lecture Notes in Computer Science*, 577–613. Berlin: Springer-Verlag.

Scott, D. S. 1989. Domains and logics (extended abstract). In *Proceedings of the Fourth Annual Symposium on Logic in Computer Science (LICS '89)*, 4–5. Washington, DC: IEEE.

Sellers, Jr., F., Hsaio, M. Y., and Bearnson, L. W. 1968. Analyzing errors with the Boolean difference. *IEEE Transactions on Computers* C-17:676–683.

Shafer, G. 1976. *A Mathematical Theory of Evidence.* Princeton, NJ: Princeton University Press.

Shand, A. F. 1920. *The Foundations of Character: Being a Study of the Tendencies of the Emotions and Sentiments.* London: Macmillan, second edition.

Shannon, C. E. 1948. A mathematical theory of communication. *Bell System Technical Journal* 27:379–423, 623–656.

Simon, H. A. 1955. A behavioral model of rational choice. *Quarterly Journal of Economics* 69:99–118.

Simon, H. A. 1956. Rational choice and the structure of the environment. *Psychological Review* 63:129–138.

Simon, H. A. 1981. *The Sciences of the Artificial.* Cambridge, MA: MIT Press, second edition.

Simon, H. A. 1982. *Models of Bounded Rationality: Behavioral Economics and Business Organization*, Volume 2. Cambridge, MA: MIT Press.

Skinner, B. F. 1969. *Contingencies of Reinforcement: A Theoretical Analysis.* New York: Appleton-Century-Crofts.

Smale, S. 1978. Review of E. C. Zeeman's "Catastrophe Theory: Selected Papers 1972–1977." *Bulletin of the American Mathematical Society* 84:1360–1368. Reprinted in Smale (1980).

Smale, S. 1980. *The Mathematics of Time: Essays on Dynamical Systems, Economic Processes, and Related Topics.* New York: Springer-Verlag.

Stallman, R. M., and Sussman, G. J. 1977. Forward reasoning and dependency-directed backtracking in a system for computer-aided circuit analysis. *Artificial Intelligence* 9(2):135–196.

Stalnaker, R. C. 1984. *Inquiry.* Cambridge, MA: MIT Press.

Streater, R. F., and Wightman, A. S. 1964. *PCT, Spin and Statistics, and All That.* New York: Benjamin.

Sussman, G. J., and Stallman, R. M. 1975. Heuristic techniques in computer-aided circuit analysis. *IEEE Transactions on Circuits and Systems* CAS-22(11): 857–865.

Sussman, G. J., and Steele Jr., G. L. 1980. CONSTRAINTS—A language for expressing almost-hierarchical descriptions. *Artificial Intelligence* 14:1–39.

Sussman, G. J., and Wisdom, J. 2001. *Structure and Interpretation of Classical Mechanics.* Cambridge, MA: MIT Press. With Meinhard E. Mayer.

Sussman, G. J. 1996. The universality barrier. Talk presented at the Santa Fe Institute, March 29, 1996.

Thayse, A., and Davio, M. 1973. Boolean differential calculus and its application to switching theory. *IEEE Transactions on Computers* C-22(4):409–420.

Thom, R. 1975. *Structural Stability and Morphogenesis: An Outline of a General Theory of Models*. Reading, MA: Benjamin.

Toffoli, T., and Margolus, N. 1987. *Cellular Automata Machines: A New Environment for Modeling*. Cambridge, MA: MIT Press.

Toffoli, T., and Margolus, N. H. 1990. Invertible cellular automata: A review. *Physca D* 45(1–3):229–253.

Tolstoy, L. 1869. *War and Peace*. New York: Modern Library. English translation of 1904 by Constance Garnett.

Touretzky, D. S. 1986. *The Mathematics of Inheritance Systems*. San Francisco, CA: Morgan Kaufmann.

Truesdell, C., and Noll, W. 1992. *The Non-Linear Field Theories of Mechanics*. Berlin: Springer-Verlag, second edition.

Truesdell, C., and Toupin, R. 1960. *The Classical Field Theories*, In Volume III/1 of *Encyclopedia of Physics*, S. Flügge, ed. Berlin: Springer-Verlag.

Truesdell, C. 1956. Bounded magic. *Isis* 47:59. Query No. 150.

Truesdell, C. 1958. Recent advances in rational mechanics. *Science* 127:729–739.

Truesdell, C. 1966. *Six Lectures on Modern Natural Philosophy*. Berlin: Springer-Verlag.

Truesdell, C. 1968a. The creation and unfolding of the concept of stress. In *Essays in the History of Mechanics*. Berlin: Springer-Verlag. 184–238.

Truesdell, C. 1968b. *Essays in the History of Mechanics*. Berlin: Springer-Verlag.

Truesdell, C. 1984a. The computer: Ruin of science and threat to mankind. In *An Idiot's Fugitive Essays on Science: Methods, Criticism, Training, Circumstances*. New York: Springer-Verlag. 594–631.

Truesdell, C. 1984b. Experience, theory, and experiment. In *An Idiot's Fugitive Essays on Science: Methods, Criticism, Training, Circumstances*. New York: Springer-Verlag. 3–20.

Truesdell, C. 1984c. *An Idiot's Fugitive Essays on Science: Methods, Criticism, Training, Circumstances*. New York: Springer-Verlag.

Truesdell, C. 1984d. Our debt to the French tradition: "Catastrophes" and our search for structure today. In *An Idiot's Fugitive Essays on Science: Methods, Criticism, Training, Circumstances*. New York: Springer-Verlag. 80–94.

Truesdell, C. 1984e. The role of mathematics in science as exemplified by the work of the Bernoullis and Euler. In *An Idiot's Fugitive Essays on Science: Methods, Criticism, Training, Circumstances*. New York: Springer-Verlag.

Truesdell, C. 1984f. Suppesian stews. In *An Idiot's Fugitive Essays on Science: Methods, Criticism, Training, Circumstances*. New York: Springer-Verlag.

Truesdell, III, C. A. 1991. *A First Course in Rational Continuum Mechanics, Volume 1: General Concepts*. New York: Academic Press, second edition.

Turing, A. M. 1936. On computable numbers with an application to the entscheidungs-problem. *Proceedings of the London Mathematical Society Series 2* 42: 230–265.

Turing, A. 1939. Systems of logic based on ordinals. *Proceedings of the London Mathematical Society* 45:161–228.

Turing, A. M. 1950. Computing machinery and intelligence. *Mind* 49:433–460.

Turing, A. M. 1952. The chemical basis of morphogenesis. *Philosophical Transactions of the Royal Society of London* 237:37–72.

Van Fraassen, B. C. 1980. A temporal framework for conditionals and chance. In Harper, W. L., Stalnaker, R., and Pearce, G., eds., *Ifs*. Dordrecht: Reidel. 323–340.

van Fraassen, B. C. 1991. *Quantum Mechanics: An Empiricist View.* Oxford, UK: Oxford University Press.

van Gelder, T. 1998. The dynamical hypothesis in cognitive science. *Behavioral and Brain Sciences* 21(5):615–665.

von Neumann, J., and Morgenstern, O. 1953. *Theory of Games and Economic Behavior.* Princeton, NJ: Princeton University Press, third edition.

von Neumann, J. 1932. *Mathematische Grundlagen der Quantenmechanik.* Berlin: Springer.

Weil, A. 1954. Mathematical teaching in universities. *American Mathematical Monthly* 61(1):34–36.

Wellman, M. P., and Doyle, J. 1991. Preferential semantics for goals. In *Proceedings of the National Conference on Artificial Intelligence*, 698–703. Menlo Park, CA: AAAI Press.

Wellman, M. P. 1993. A market-oriented programming environment and its application to distributed multicommodity flow problems. *Journal of Artificial Intelligence Research* 1:1–23.

Wendlandt, J. M., and Marsden, J. E. 1997. Mechanical integrators derived from a discrete variational principle. *Physica D* 106(3-4):223–246.

Whitehead, A. N., and Russell, B. 1910. *Principia Mathematica.* Cambridge, UK: Cambridge University Press.

Wightman, A. S. 1956. Quantum field theory in terms of vacuum expectation values. *Physical Review (2)* 101:860–866.

Willems, J. C. 1972a. Dissipative dynamical systems. I. General theory. *Archive for Rational Mechanics and Analysis* 45:321–351.

Willems, J. C. 1972b. Dissipative dynamical systems. II. Linear systems with quadratic supply rates. *Archive for Rational Mechanics and Analysis* 45:352–393.

Yanushkevich, S., Bochmann, D., Stankovic, R., Tosic, Z., and Shmerko, V. 2000. Logic differential calculus: Progress, tendencies and applications. *Automation and Remote Control* 61(6 part 2):1033–1047.

Yates, B. T. 1985. *Self-Management: The Science and Art of Helping Yourself.* Belmont, CA: Wadsworth.

Yessinin-Volpin, A. S. 1970. The ultra-intuitionistic criticism and the antitraditional program for foundations of mathematics. In *Intuitionism and Proof Theory*. Amsterdam: North-Holland. 3–45.

Zadeh, L. 1975. Fuzzy logic and approximate reasoning. *Synthese* 30:407–428.

Zeeman, E. C. 1977. *Catastrophe Theory: Selected Papers 1972–1977.* London: Addison-Wesley.

Zipf, G. K. 1949. *Human Behavior and the Principle of Least Effort: An Introduction to Human Ecology.* Cambridge, MA: Addison-Wesley.

Index

Maxwell, James, 72, 377
McAllester, David, 367
McCarthy, John, xvii, 236, 422, 423
McCulloch, Warren, 63
McKinsey, John, 80
McShane, Edward, 144
measurement, 50
  psychophysical, 58
mechanically perfect, 172
mechanics, 71
  analytical, 177
  arithmetic, 44
  axiomatic, 7
  axioms of, xii, 72
  celestial, 382
  classical, 420
  continuum, 88, 89, 94, 96, 98, 125, 127,
    128, 130, 299
  discrete, 65
  factor, 88
  nature of, 71
  prediction, 43
  quantum, 190, 361, 362
  rational, xiii, 5
  relativistic, 97, 98, 105, 119, 140, 147, 211,
    214, 215
  synthetic, 81, 115
  variational, 124
mechanizability, 392
memory
  long-term, 245, 251, 264, 287
  short-term, 245, 251, 264, 287
mental interior, 244
metric, 259
  Euclidean, 100, 106, 107, 114
  Hamming, 114, 259
  Manhattan, 259
  Minkowski, 98, 259
  temporal, 99
Miller, George, xiii
mind, kind of, 225
Minkowski, Hermann, 98
Minsky, Marvin, xii, xv, xvii, 54, 55, 90, 146,
  237, 245, 323, 373, 412, 423
MIT
  Artificial Intelligence Laboratory, xvii
  Laboratory for Computer Science, xvii
module, 110
  dimensional, 110
  free, 110, 115
momentum, 147
  dimensionality, 152
  discrete, 149
  force and, 165
  generalized, 133
  hybrid, 154
  inner product, 153

linear, 148
mental, 34
metric, 153
physical, 154
rotational, 148
  independence of, 381
spatial, 152
superspatial, 152, 167
topology, 153
Moore, Robert, 408
Moret, Bernard, 361
Moses, Joel, xvii
motion, 128, 129
  cyclic, 287
  discrete, 131, 260
  extrinsic, 130
  hybrid, 130
  inertial, 286
  integral, 337
  intrinsic, 129
  nondeterministic, 134
  perpetual, 212
  regular, 130
  subintegral, 338
Myers–Briggs typology, 225

nearest-state function, 199
negative feedback, 322
Nelson, Edward, 180
Nelson, Richard, 54, 330
Newell, Allen, xvii, 65
Newton, Isaac, 5, 7, 33, 49, 72, 79, 85, 158,
  167, 177, 387, 410, 411, 413, 418, 419,
  422
Nixon diamond, 213
nogood, 278
Noll, Walter, xii, xvii, 32, 43, 74, 79, 81–83,
  86, 87, 89, 95, 96, 99, 101, 105, 107, 108,
  111, 112, 115, 121, 126, 135, 136, 145,
  155, 158, 163–165, 168, 173–176, 178,
  181, 185, 215, 328, 344, 402, 411, 413,
  420, 421
nonlinear response, 301
normal, outer, 161
Norvig, Peter, xiv
Nöther, Emmy, 205
Nyl, 255

observer, 98, 108, 126
operator calculus, 361
optimist, 209
oracle, 395
organizational structure, 245
orthogonal transformation, 108, 111
Out, 254
outlist, 276
outlook, 251

Printed in the United States
by Baker & Taylor Publisher Services